PERSONALITY

NELSON-HALL SERIES IN PSYCHOLOGY

Series Editor: Stephen Worchel
Texas A & M University

Valerian J. Derlega
OLD DOMINION UNIVERSITY

Barbara A. Winstead
OLD DOMINION UNIVERSITY

Warren H. Jones
UNIVERSITY OF TENNESSEE

PERSONALITY

Contemporary Theory and Research

NELSON-HALL PUBLISHERS/CHICAGO

Project Editor: Dorothy Anderson
Copy Editor: Jean Scott Berry
Designer: Tamra Campbell-Phelps
Illustrator: Corasue Nicholas
Cover Painting: Warren Brown Prindle

Library of Congress Cataloging-in-Publication Data

Personality: contemporary theory and research/[edited by] Valerian
   J. Derlega, Barbara A. Winstead, Warren H. Jones.
        p.   cm.—(Nelson-Hall series in psychology)
   Includes bibliographical references and index.
   ISBN 0-8304-1182-8
   ISBN 0-8304-1383-9 pbk.
   1. Personality.   2. Personality—Research.   I. Derlega, Valerian
J.   II. Winstead, Barbara A.   III. Jones, Warren H.   IV. Series.
BF698.P359   1991
   155.2—dc20   90-40627
                                                                        CIP

Manufactured in the United States of America

10   9   8   7   6   5   4   3   2   1

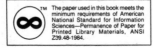

CONTENTS

Preface   xi

Chapter 1

Personality: An Introduction   1

VALERIAN J. DERLEGA, BARBARA A. WINSTEAD,
AND WARREN H. JONES

Personality: A Definition   2
An Overview of Personality Theories   4
Personality in the 1990s   9
Summary   10
SUGGESTED READINGS   11
REFERENCES   12

PART ONE

Basic Issues in Personality

Chapter 2

Personality Measurement   15

STEPHEN R. BRIGGS

Introduction to the OSS Assessment
    Project   16

What to Measure?   17
    Measuring Variables
    Measuring a Concept
ACTIVITY BOX: Measuring
    Conscientiousness   20
    The Concept of Personality
    Measuring Personality
How to Measure It?   24
    The OSS Assessment Procedures
    Putting the Pieces Together
    Classifying Methods for Measuring
      Personality
How Good Is the Measure?   39
    Reliability
    Validity
Which Variables Are Important?   43
Why Measure Personality Variables?   48
Summary   50
SUGGESTED READINGS   51
REFERENCES   52

Chapter 3

Heredity   55

DAVID C. ROWE

History   57
    Francis Galton: Founder of Behavioral
      Genetics

Modern Behavioral Genetics:
    Foundations   60
    Single Gene Versus Polygenic Traits
    Apportioning Trait Variation
    Shared Versus Nonshared Heredity
    Shared (or Common) and Nonshared
        Environment
    Discovering the Sizes of Genetic and
        Environmental Effects
Modern Behavioral Genetics: Findings and
    Implications   68
    Normal (Nonintellectual) Personality Traits
    Intellectual Traits
ACTIVITY BOX: Family Correlations for
    Authoritarianism   72
    Abnormal Traits
How Heredity Can Be Disguised in
    Environmental Concepts   80
Postscript   82
Summary   83
SUGGESTED READINGS   83
REFERENCES   84

Chapter 4

Biological Approaches to the Study of Personality   87

RICHARD J. DAVIDSON

Introduction   88
Conceptual Issues in the Study of Biological
    Bases of Personality   89
    Three Approaches to the Use of Biological
        Measures in the Study of Personality
    Correlate or Substrate?
    Does Substrate Imply Cause?
Methodological Considerations in the Study
    of the Biological Bases of
    Personality   93
    Psychometric Considerations
    Resting or Task-Related Measures?
    Some Commonly Used Physiological
        Measures in the Study of Personality
An Empirical Example of the Biological
    Approach to Personality: Cerebral
    Asymmetry and Affective Style   98

Introduction
Individual Differences in Anterior
    Asymmetry and Affective Reactivity
ACTIVITY BOX: Measuring Your
    Hemisphericity   108
Summary   108
SUGGESTED READINGS   110
REFERENCES   110

Chapter 5

Personality Development   113

PATRICIA L. WATERS AND JONATHAN M. CHEEK

Overview of Major Theories   115
Freud and the Psychoanalytic
    Tradition   116
    The Tripartite Structure of the Mind
    The Psychosexual Stages
    Defense Mechanisms
Attachment Research—A Neoanalytic
    Perspective   121
    Internal Working Models
    The Continuity of Internal Working Models
ACTIVITY BOX: Measuring Adult Attachment
    Patterns   126
    Attachment and Intimacy
Behaviorism and Social Learning
    Theory   129
Rogers and Humanistic Psychology   131
    The Fully Functioning Person
    Contemporary Research Applications
The Biosocial and Sociocultural
    Tradition   136
    Adlerian Individual Psychology
    Sullivan's Interpersonal Approach—Peer
        Influences
    The Sociocultural Approach of Horney
Future Directions: Toward a Transactional
    Theory of Personality
    Development   143
Summary   143
SUGGESTED READINGS   145
REFERENCES   145

Chapter 6

The Person–Situation Debate: Do Personality Traits Really Exist? 149

DOUGLAS T. KENRICK AND DAVID C. FUNDER

Introduction   150
Hypothesis I: Personality Is in the Eye of the Beholder   154
    Errors of Judgment
    Lack of Agreement Between Judges
Hypothesis II: Agreement Is Due to Baserate Accuracy   158
ACTIVITY BOX: Comparing Personality Self-Ratings with Friends' Ratings   158
Hypothesis III: Agreement Is Due to Stereotypes Based on Obvious (but Erroneous) Cues   160
Hypothesis IV: Agreement Is Due to Discussion Between Observers   161
Hypothesis V: Agreement Is Due to Seeing Others in the Same Setting   163
Hypothesis VI: Compared with Situational Pressures, Cross-Situational Consistencies in Behavior Are Too Weak to Be Important   164
What Have We Learned?   166
    Person-Situation Interactions
    Combining Personality and Social Psychology
    Gene-Environment Interactions
Summary   171
SUGGESTED READINGS   171
REFERENCES   171

Chapter 7

Motives   175

DAN P. MCADAMS

Four Traditions in the Study of Human Motivation   176
    Optimism: People Are (Basically) "Good"
    Pessimism: People Are "Bad" (and Usually Miserable)
    Neutrality: People Are "Blank"
    Diversity: People Are "Many Things"

Biology Versus Cognition in Human Motivation   180
    Drive, Reward, Instinct
    Expectancies, Schemas, Attributions
Individual Differences in Three Social Motives   187
ACTIVITY BOX: Scoring Stories for Power and Intimacy   201
    Wanting to Do Better: The Achievement Motive
    Wanting to Have Impact: The Power Motive
    Wanting to Be Close: The Intimacy Motive
Summary   200
SUGGESTED READINGS   201
REFERENCES   201

PART TWO

Topics in Personality Research

Chapter 8

The Unconscious   207

THOMAS HILL AND PAWEL LEWICKI

Personality and the Unconscious   208
ACTIVITY BOX: Nonconscious Perception   209
    The Psychoanalytic Tradition
    The Information Processing Model
Nonconscious Information Processing   214
Nonconscious Information Processing in Social Situations   215
Some Properties of Nonconscious Information Processing Algorithms   218
Applications to Personality Psychology   219
    Mere Exposure Effects
    The Self-Image Bias
The Acquisition of Dispositions via Self-Perpetuation of Encoding Biases   222
    Studying the Self-Perpetuation Mechanism
Concluding Remarks   226

Summary   227
SUGGESTED READINGS   227
REFERENCES   228

Chapter 9

Personal Efficacy   231

JAMES E. MADDUX

Introduction   233
Basic Principles of Self-Efficacy
    Theory   233
  Basic Cognitive Processes
  Sources of Self-Efficacy
Personal Efficacy and Psychological
    Adjustment   237
ACTIVITY BOX: Increasing Self-Efficacy   238
Other Models of Personal Efficacy   243
  Effectance Motivation
  Level of Aspiration
  Expectancy-Value Theory
  Locus of Control
  Self-Concept and Self-Esteem
  Achievement Motivation
Research on Self-Efficacy Theory   247
  Relationships Between the Basic Components
  Linking Self-Efficacy Theory to Other
    Theories
Summary   258
SUGGESTED READINGS   259
REFERENCES   260

Chapter 10

Sex and Gender   263

BARBARA A. WINSTEAD, VALERIAN J.
DERLEGA, AND RHODA K. UNGER

Introduction   264
Differentiating Sex and Gender   265
Sex as a Subject Variable   266
  Antecedents of Sex Differences
  Limitations to the Use of Sex as a Subject
    Variable
Psychological Dimensions of Masculinity and
    Femininity   271
  Early Research Attempts

  Androgyny
  Gender Schema Theory
ACTIVITY BOX: Avoidance of Gender-
    Inappropriate Behavior   278
Sex as a Social Category   279
Summary   283
SUGGESTED READINGS   278
REFERENCES   284

Chapter 11

Control   287

JERRY M. BURGER

The Impact of Perceived Control   290
  Positive Aspects of Perceived Control
  Negative Aspects of Perceived Control
Individual Differences in Perceived Control:
    Locus of Control   293
  Some Differences Between Internals and
    Externals
  Issues in Locus of Control Research
Individual Differences in Motivation for
    Control: Desire for Control   299
ACTIVITY BOX: The Desirability of Control
    Scale   300
  Cognitive Responses
  Motivational Responses
  Affective Responses
Summary   308
SUGGESTED READINGS   309
REFERENCES   309

Chapter 12

Self-Awareness and Self-Consciousness   313

MARK H. DAVIS AND STEPHEN L. FRANZOI

Past and Present Concepts Related to Private
    Self-Awareness   316
Past and Present Concepts Related to Public
    Self-Awareness   317
Current Self-Awareness and
    Self-Consciousness Theories   319
  Self-Awareness Versus Self-Consciousness
  The Self-Consciousness Scale

ACTIVITY BOX: The Self-Consciousness
   Scale   322
   The Texas Connection
   Wicklund's Approach: Objective
   Self-Awareness
   Buss's Approach: Self-Consciousness Theory
   Carver and Scheier's Approach: A
   Control-Theory Model
Concluding Remarks   341
Summary   343
SUGGESTED READINGS   344
REFERENCES   344

Chapter 13

Self-Concept and Identity   349

ROY F. BAUMEISTER

Introduction   350
Self-Concept   352
   Formation of the Self-Concept
   Self-Esteem: Evaluating the Self
ACTIVITY BOX: Measuring Your
   Self-Esteem   356
   Research on Self-Esteem
   Other Aspects of Self-Concept
   Maintaining Self-Concept and Self-Esteem
Identity   370
   Structure and Functions of Identity
   Identity Crises
Summary   376
SUGGESTED READINGS   377
REFERENCES   378

Chapter 14

Moral Character   381

NICHOLAS EMLER

Moral Character: The Fall and Rise of a
   Concept   382
   The Psychology of Moral Character—An
   Historical Introduction
   Rule-Breaking: The Reality of Individual
   Differences
Discovering and Accounting for
   Character   391

   The Consistency of Conduct
   Individual Differences in Character: How
   Well Do Existing Theories Do?
ACTIVITY BOX: Deviance and Attitudes to
   Authority   394
   The Visibility of Conduct and the
   Anonymity of Society
Moral Character: Some Final Thoughts on
   Pinning Down Explanations   401
Summary   404
SUGGESTED READINGS   405
REFERENCES   405

Chapter 15

Emotion   407

RANDY J. LARSEN

Introduction and Issues   408
Emotional States Versus Emotional
   Traits   408
Emotional Content Versus Emotional
   Style   409
   Emotional Content
   Emotional Style
ACTIVITY BOX: Affect Intensity
   Measure   424
Concluding Remarks   429
Summary   430
SUGGESTED READINGS   431
REFERENCES   431

Chapter 16

Human Sexuality   433

SUSAN S. HENDRICK AND CLYDE HENDRICK

Overview   434
   Sex Researchers
Research on Personality and Sexuality   436
   Sociocultural Influences
   Interpersonal Influences
   Personality Variables and Sexuality
   Gender and Sexuality
   Sexual Preference
   Sexual Variants

Sexual Dysfunction
The Study of Sexual Attitudes   445
    Measurement of Sexual Attitudes
    Sexual Attitudes and Related Constructs
ACTIVITY BOX: Sexual Attitudes Scale   448
    Gender Differences Revisited
    Integrating Sex with Love
Summary   452
SUGGESTED READINGS   453
REFERENCES   453

Chapter 17

Aggression   457
HAL S. BERTILSON

Introduction   458
Definitional Issues   459
    Personality
    Aggression
Longitudinal Stability of Aggression   462
ACTIVITY BOX: Defining Aggression   462
Heritability of Aggressiveness   465
    Behavioral Genetics
    Temperament
**A Coercion Model: The Development of
    Antisocial Behavior   467**
Anger and Aggression   468
Catharsis   471
    Emotional Catharsis
    Behavioral Catharsis
Aggressive Habits   474
Rational Aggression   476
Summary   477
SUGGESTED READINGS   478
REFERENCES   479

Chapter 18

Stress and Illness   481
CHARLES K. PROKOP

Introduction   482
Historical Overview   483

Definitions of Stress and Illness   485
Personality, Stress, and Illness   489
    Type A Behavior Pattern and Hostility
    Approach and Avoidance
**ACTIVITY BOX: Scale of College
    Stresses   494**
    Optimism and Pessimism
Hardiness   497
Summary   504
SUGGESTED READINGS   505
REFERENCES   505

Chapter 19

Personality and Relationships   509
WARREN H. JONES

The Psychology of Relationships   510
    Definition
    Importance of Studying Relationships
    Methodological Issues in Studying
        Relationships
    Relationship Development and Processes
    Some Conceptual Issues
Personality and Relationships   521
    Relationship Influence in the Development of
        Personality
    Personality Influences on the Development of
        Relationships
**ACTIVITY BOX: Experience of Loneliness in
    Various Situations   526**
Concluding Remarks   530
Summary   532
SUGGESTED READINGS   532
REFERENCES   533

Contributors   537

Name Index   539

Subject Index   547

PREFACE

Having spent several years studying, reading, writing, and conducting research in order to receive a Ph.D. from a program in personality psychology, one of the editors of this text was surprised to discover when she was assigned to teach an undergraduate course in personality that she was teaching material that bore little relation to what she had learned in graduate school. Why, she wondered, must undergraduates learn about Freud, Rogers, Maslow, and Skinner and not about the research in which personality psychologists are currently engaged? It reminded her of a story she had heard about a school that taught the regular students that America was discovered by Christopher Columbus and the "fast track" students that it was really Leif Erikson who arrived first. Other recently graduated students of personality as well as the editors of this text have experienced the frustration of trying to teach the ideas that they are most excited about to students who are reading a text that does not cover contemporary research in personality. The idea for this book was born then. We believe this text is unique in presenting many areas of current personality research written at a level that can be understood by undergraduates by psychologists actually doing some of that research.

In preparing this book, we invited psychologists who are experts in particular areas of personality to contribute chapters. The goal in each chapter is to present an overview of a particular area (including introductions, a history of constructs, definitions, methodological issues, and a review of a variety of avenues in research within the area). In most chapters, authors give a detailed description of a specific research program (of their own work, whenever possible) to illustrate how research in personality is conducted.

The book is divided into two major sections. Part 1 deals with Basic Issues in Personality, including methodology, personality measurement, heredity, biological approaches, personality development, traits, and motives. The chapters on basic issues summarize major traditions of research in personality and present an up-to-date account of current work in these areas. Part 2 deals with Topics in Personality Research that are influential, including the unconscious (especially from a cognitive approach), personal efficacy, sex and gender, self-awareness and self-consciousness, self-concept and identity, moral character, emotions, human sexuality, aggression, stress and illness, and relationships.

Besides providing coverage of important issues and topics in personality research, the chapters indicate the relevance of personality processes in understanding human behavior. The chapters include Activity Boxes that illustrate how the material discussed in the chapter can be applied.

This text is an introduction to personality that focuses on current theory and research; and it makes a distinctive contribution by adopting this approach. *Personality: Contemporary Theory and Research* is suitable for an undergraduate course in personality in which the goal is to introduce students to major concepts and research. The book is also suitable as a graduate-level text focusing on empirical research in personality. The level of writing is directed at undergraduate students in junior and senior level courses in personality.

Many individuals helped in planning and organizing this volume. In particular, we extend our thanks to the authors of the individual chapters, who enthusiastically took on the responsibility of writing for students. We are also grateful to the editorial staff of Nelson-Hall, who encouraged us to develop this text. Steve Ferrara and Ron Warncke were especially supportive.

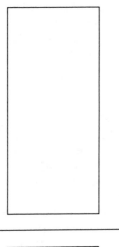

CHAPTER 1

Personality: An Introduction

VALERIAN J. DERLEGA, BARBARA A. WINSTEAD, AND
WARREN H. JONES

Personality: A Definition
An Overview of Personality
    Theories
Personality in the 1990s

Summary
SUGGESTED READINGS
REFERENCES

Who are you? Most people would answer this question by describing their *personality*. Personality is, simply put, who you *are*. But, consider these questions: How does one go about *accurately* describing someone's personality? Is personality learned or inborn? What difference do circumstances or situations make? Are people aware of how their personalities affect others? How does personality influence behavior? Is personality too elusive and mysterious a topic even to study? There are no simple answers to these questions. But psychologists have learned that the study of personality is not so mysterious as people may have once thought and that some answers to the questions we have asked are available based on the work of modern-day personality researchers.

This book is about recent theories and research in personality. Major issues and research topics are described. In this chapter we will provide a brief introduction by defining what we mean by personality, summarizing major historical influences on personality theory and research, and providing an overview to the topics to be covered in subsequent chapters.

Personality: A Definition

According to Shontz (1969), "the study of personality is identified by its concern for inferred mediating processes that account for organization in the behavior of the individual person" (p. 7). Personality refers to the enduring, inner characteristics of individuals that organize their behavior. Writers have speculated for thousands of years about what people are like, but only in this century have psychologists systematically studied the inner characteristics that influence behavior.

In considering how to define personality, it is worthwhile noting what is excluded from the definition. Social psychology, for instance, studies how other people influence how we think, feel, and act. The emphasis in social psychology is on studying the social stimuli that influence an individual's behavior. Sensory–perceptual psychology studies how people integrate sensory data (including vision, hearing, and other sensory systems) to interpret and understand the world around them. Developmental psychology studies changes in behavior as a function of age. Clinical psychology studies psychopathological processes in individuals and interventions (psychotherapies) designed to restore mental health.

An essential feature of personality psychology (as opposed to other fields in psychology) is an examination of the inner characteristics of individuals that modify their behavior and of how other people's behavior influences personality. Personality researchers are also interested in how individuals' personal characteristics influence how they perceive and make sense of events and how personality characteristics may develop and change over the life span. Although for some individuals personality characteristics will be indicative of psychopathology, personality psychologists focus primarily on normal, healthy personality.

Some popular definitions of "personality" do not reflect how psychologists define the term (see Hall & Lindzey, 1978). People may use the term personality to refer to "social skill or adroitness" in interacting with others (p. 7). For instance, we hear that someone has a "lot of personality." Personality as a social skill emphasizes being successful or socially competent when meeting people. In this view personality is tantamount to having personal characteristics that can produce positive reactions from others (e.g., being skillful at putting people at ease or making them laugh). On the other hand, someone who we say "has no personality" may be perceived to lack skills associated with getting along and winning the friendship and respect of others (e.g., making people uncomfortable or upset while looking to them for approval). The term personality may also be used to represent "the most outstanding or salient impression" (Hall & Lindzey, 1978, p. 7) that an individual conveys in interacting with others. An individual may be considered "a go-getter" (someone who works hard and is goal oriented), "aggressive" (belligerent and easily irritated), "domineering" (taking charge in situations and needing to have things done her or his way) or "shy" (socially withdrawn, introverted, and anxious with people). A salient characteristic, which appears to describe much of someone's behavior, may thus be pinned on individuals and then used, correctly or incorrectly, to "explain" why they behave the way they do.

Personality characteristics influence how we come across in social interactions as well as how big or small an impression we make on others, but these features do not define what the personality researcher means by the term. The study of personality focuses on the inner characteristics of individuals that influence their behavior. These inner characteristics are assumed to have causal properties (which means that personality mediates the behavior of individuals with the world around them); and these personality characteristics are systematically organized and do not operate in a random manner. Also personality influences how individuals behave in various situations and behavior is not simply due to the particular situation in which individuals find themselves.

Personality endures across time and situations. Psychologists acknowledge that human behavior may change over time and that an individual's behavior is often influenced by situational factors. But it is still possible to speak about a set of characteristics (an individual's personality) that organizes behavior and that as Maddi (1980) notes *"may not be easily understood as the sole result of the social and biological pressures of the moment"* (p. 10).

An Overview of Personality Theories

In this section we will introduce theories that have been historically important in the field of personality, including the psychoanalytic, humanistic, learning, and trait approaches. Let's first describe a hypothetical person and then show how the theories might explain his behavior.

Michael is a first-term senior majoring in finance. He is quiet, shy, and hardworking. When he graduates in June, he plans to join his father's firm and be an investment broker. Michael's father is eager for Michael to follow in his footsteps as a successful businessman.

Michael has maintained a B+ average throughout college by being planful and studying hard. This fall, for the first time, it is difficult for him to organize his time effectively. In the first weeks of school he failed a test in a business course, which he had never done before.

Most students at Michael's college who do homework on personal computers spend some of their time on computer games. Michael has always been able to avoid the games and do his work. Lately he has been putting the work off and playing the computer games. Sometimes Michael finds himself playing games he does not even enjoy.

Michael's courses are harder this semester and he's also supposed to be doing an honor's project that requires independent work. Every morning Michael promises himself that he will stick to his schoolwork. But when he sits down at the computer he starts playing some game and pretty soon hours have passed. He realizes that even if he manages to catch up with his course work he will soon be unable to complete the honor's project.

Michael's father has always been a very hard worker. When Michael was growing up his father constantly reminded him that he would never get ahead if he didn't "keep his nose to the grindstone." Good grades earned monetary rewards until Michael went to college. His father was also very competitive and enjoyed beating Michael and his siblings at games and contests. On the other hand, Michael's mother encouraged her children to enjoy themselves. She seemed to have given up on getting her husband to relax, but she loved taking her children on outings or to the park. If they said they needed to study or do homework, she always replied, "Don't worry there will always be another test. You can pass that one."

How would you go about explaining Michael's behavior and problems based on a theory of personality? Remember that the focus of personality is on the inner characteristics that influence an individual's behavior. We might say Michael is under a lot of pressure, that is, harder courses and an honor's project, and that explains his poor work habits. These are *situational* factors, not personality characteristics. They may, in fact, play a role in explaining Michael's behavior, but not every senior responds to these pressures by playing more computer games and avoiding schoolwork. There must be something about Michael himself that contributes to his behaviors.

Major theories of personality differ in how they explain Michael's problems (see chapter 5, Personality Development). Particularly in the early history of the psychological study of personality, scientists offered "grand theories" to explain behavior. For instance, Sigmund Freud, who was probably the most influential personality theorist, developed the psychoanalytic approach to explain individual behavior (see Brenner, 1974, for an excellent introduction to Freud's ideas). Freud emphasized the role of the unconscious and early childhood experiences in the development of adult personality. The psychoanalytic approach stresses unconscious psychological conflicts that a person might not even be aware of as an explanation of behavior. Michael, for instance, might be avoiding his schoolwork because he is conflicted about his pursuit of a career in business.

Freud hypothesized that all children (from three to six years of age) experience an oedipal complex during which they are "in love with" the parent of the opposite sex and "in competition with" the parent of the same sex. In normal development children resolve this complex by repressing their sexual feelings for the opposite-sex parent and identifying with the same-sex parent. Freud argued that many individuals do not successfully resolve the oedipal complex and that unconscious feelings of attraction to one parent and hostility toward the other continue to shape their behavior.

In Michael's case, his impending graduation from college and job in his father's firm will bring him into direct competition with his father. This may arouse unconscious hostile feelings toward his father that he wishes to avoid. Trouble with courses now may reflect his anxiety about pursuing this occupation, which is so much like his father's. His willingness to divert himself with computer games may also be indicative of an unconscious wish to please his mother, who was always in favor of taking time off for fun.

The humanistic approach to personality, associated with the ideas of psychologists such as Carl Rogers (1959, 1961), Abraham Maslow (1962, 1971), and Rollo May (1967), highlights the innate motivation that people have for personal growth and self-actualization. People will strive under optimal conditions to fulfill their potential. According to Rogers, if people have a relationship with others based on unconditional positive regard (i.e., one person extends unqualified acceptance to another), then they will develop in a manner that fulfills their potential. If people experience conditional positive regard (i.e., one person extends acceptance only if the other behaves in certain ways), then they might be discouraged from pursuing their natural tendencies or experience anxiety when they seek to do so. For instance, Michael, in his desire to earn the approval and love of his father, may have put aside other interests. Michael's choice of a business career may not be an expression of his natural inclinations. This choice may reflect instead a desire to win his father's approval. The game playing may also emerge from a wish to please his mother. Perhaps neither represents Michael's true needs or talents.

Although personality theories usually emphasize the role of internal, psychological factors influencing behavior, the learning approach originally emphasized the role of external factors. At the simplest level, according to the learning approach, behaviors are acquired by some form of learning (e.g., classical conditioning, operant conditioning, or observational learning). Some learning theorists, who were called radical behaviorists (e.g., Skinner, 1953), suggested that all behavior could be explained on the basis of learning principles (e.g., if you could know or influence someone's reinforcement history, it was argued, you could predict current behavior). Inner personality concepts, such as the unconscious, the self-concept, or self-actualization, would not be considered because behavior could be explained by observable events (e.g., the stimulus that preceded the behavior or the reinforcing event that followed it), according to the radical behaviorist position. In Michael's case, according to the behaviorist position, rewards for good grades should lead to behaviors (e.g., studying) that result in those rewards. If the rewards stop, the behavior will stop. His mother's rewards (e.g., praise) for playing would predict that behavior as well.

Looking back in the history of personality, the radical behaviorist approach was important because it highlighted how learning has a role in the development of personality. It also provided the foundations for other personality theorists who were interested in integrating the ideas of psychoanalytic theory with laboratory research conducted on learning. Dollard and Miller (1950) agreed with psychoanalytic theory that emotional problems may be due to unconscious conflicts that developed in childhood, but they did not rely on the Freudian concepts to describe the components of personality that might be in conflict with one another.

Based on the results of laboratory research, Dollard and Miller viewed conflicts in terms of the goals that individuals wanted to approach and/or avoid. Dollard and Miller described three basic types of conflict. For instance, approach and avoidance tendencies to the same situation or object is an approach-avoidance conflict. Michael may be attracted to a career in business (approach tendency), but he may find this career choice upsetting because of the possibility of being unsuccessful (avoidance tendency). The avoidance tendency increases more sharply than the approach tendency, according to Dollard and Miller (1950). Thus, as the time gets closer for Michael to make a decision about a business career (he is now a senior in college), the avoidance tendency associated with the career choice is intersecting the approach tendency. The two are balanced, and that creates a high degree of conflict. In previous years, when the actual commitment to work in business was still a distant goal, the approach tendency was stronger than the avoidance tendency. It was easier in the past for Michael to be enthusiastic about a business career.

Michael's problems may also represent an avoidance–avoidance conflict in which he is faced with two competing avoidance tendencies. Michael may be afraid of failing at a career in business and he also may want to avoid his father's disapproval if he does not pursue a business career. An approach-approach conflict (based on two competing approach tendencies) might also be the source of Michael's problems if he is divided between two goals that are equally desirable, that is, between doing his homework and playing games on the computer.

Dollard and Miller's ideas have not been widely adopted in personality research, but they have been influential. Most important,

Dollard and Miller showed how theory and research derived from laboratory research on learning and conflict could be applied to understand how inner, psychological activities operate.

There was a significant shift in theory and research about learning with the development of cognitive social learning theory (e.g., Bandura, 1977; Mischel, 1973, 1977; Rotter, 1966). This approach focuses on the role of perceptions, thoughts, and beliefs (i.e., cognitions) as mediators of behavior. Cognitive social learning theory describes how people learn to think about, interpret, and make plans about the world based on their social experiences, including learning by observing the behavior of others (see chapter 9, Personal Efficacy, for a review of this approach). As one example, Bandura (1977) showed (in what is called observational learning) how individuals can learn actions by observing the behavior of another individual, storing this information in memory, and then performing the behavior if positive consequences are expected to occur. Based on observational learning, Michael may have been imitating his father when he expressed a desire for a career in business and studied hard. On the other hand, Michael may be imitating his mother (who enjoyed games) when he spends his time playing on the computer.

Trait theories of personality (e.g., Allport, 1931, 1966; Cattell, 1950; Eysenck, 1970, 1975) are another important approach. These theories emphasize the role of personal characteristics, called traits, in accounting for the behavior of individuals. Learning approaches to personality explain similarities and differences in the behavior of individuals based on the similarities and differences in the learning histories or circumstances under which individuals were reared. But trait theories explain sameness or difference in behavior based on whether or not individuals share certain personality characteristics. People who are similar in their personality traits are expected to behave similarly to one another across a variety of situations, and people should behave differently from one another if they are different on a particular trait. Traits represent a predisposition or tendency to act in a certain way. They can be very general (influencing most of the individual's behavior) or they can be very specific (influencing behavior only in certain types of situations). A major goal of the trait approach to personality has been to find out which independent personality dimensions are useful in identifying differences between individuals. Eysenck (1970) argues that individuals can be described by three personality dimensions: introversion–extroversion, neuroticism, and . According to Eysenck, the typical introvert is quiet, ..., and unsociable. As an introvert, Michael has chosen an aspect of business, finance, that can be a solitary pursuit; and when avoiding doing his schoolwork, he plays computer games rather than going out with friends.

Criticism has been directed at the trait approach by psychologists who favored a "situational" approach to personality (e.g., Gergen, 1968; Mischel, 1968, 1973). An extreme situational position would hold that personality is a set of learned responses and that behavior is determined by the environment. "Situationists" argue that "internal traits" cannot predict behavior of individuals across a variety of situations. For instance, a "moral" person (i.e., one who has a tendency to respect rules) should behave morally across a variety of situations, including school, work, home and not just, say, at work. A situationist would argue that there is no morality trait, but that an individual acts morally when she or he interprets a situation as one in which moral behavior will be reinforced. For example, a man who never cheats at sports, because he wants to be regarded as a fair player, may engage in petty theft at work because the company owes him more than he makes. Research (see chapter 6, The Person-Situation Debate: Do Personality Traits Really Exist?, and chapter 14, Moral Character) indicates that personality traits do exist and that they can predict behavior in a variety of situations. However, an important lesson from the trait–situation debate is that the best way to predict behavior is to use information about an individual's personality as well as the situation. Personality doesn't operate in a vacuum; situational factors are also influential.

Personality in the 1990s

Despite a rich history of theory and research, personality is still a young and vigorous field of study. Personality has moved away from the all-encompassing theories associated with the psychoanalytic, humanistic, learning, and trait approaches. Contemporary research focuses on specific and perhaps better defined topics than was the case in the past. Personality researchers are highly trained in research and their studies display a high level of empirical rigor.

Our textbook summarizes major developments that are going on right now in the field of personality. The ideas of outstanding (and often brilliant) psychologists such as Sigmund Freud, Carl Rogers, Gordon Allport, and B. F. Skinner provided the foundations for the development of personality. They identified along with other prominent theorists major issues that continue to be studied. However, the level of current work in the field tends to be more precise. As many chapters in this book will illustrate, contemporary personality researchers usually focus on one construct or set of constructs and investigate their value for explaining behavior.

Researchers are expanding knowledge in personality and developing new ways of testing and validating personality concepts. The chapters in this book (which are written by experts on particular topics) describe major issues and research topics in personality. The chapters also provide an insider's look (based on the authors' experiences) at how research is conducted in personality. It is our hope that readers will find the book useful in beginning an exploration of contemporary theory and research in personality.

Summary

Personality refers to the enduring, inner characteristics of individuals that organize their behavior. On the other hand, popular definitions of personality have used the term to refer either to a social skill or to salient personal characteristics that seem to explain someone's behavior.

Theories that have been historically important in the field of personality include the psychoanalytic, humanistic, learning, and trait approaches. The psychoanalytic approach focuses on the unconscious and early childhood experiences to explain the development of adult personality. The humanistic approach emphasizes the innate motivation that people have for personal growth and self-actualization, which can be impeded if individuals experience conditional positive regard (i.e., one person extends acceptance based on the other's meeting certain conditions). The learning approach originally emphasized the role of external factors influencing personality. But some learning theorists (Dollard and Miller) showed how laboratory research on learning and conflict could be used to integrate psychoanalytic ideas. More recently, cognitive social learning theories indicate how perceptions, thoughts, and beliefs (termed cognitions) mediate personality functioning. People may learn to think about, interpret, and make plans about the world based on their social experiences, including learning by observing others' behavior. Trait theories focus on how individuals may have distinctive tendencies or predispositions to act in a certain way in various situations. A major goal of the trait approach has been to find out which independent personality dimensions are useful in identifying differences and similarities between individuals.

Personality psychology has moved away from the broad theories originally associated with the field. Contemporary research focuses on specific and relatively well-defined topics. Our textbook describes these developments in contemporary research and theory in personality.

The book is divided into two parts: (1) basic issues and (2) topics in personality research. The six chapters in the first part cover personality measurement, heredity, biological approaches to personality, personality development, the person–situation debate, and motives. These topics are covered in most personality texts, although the focus on current research in several of these chapters would probably not be found in other texts. The second part of the text is composed of twelve chapters, each one covering an area of research that personality psychologists are continuing to pursue. These chapters present ideas and research on the unconscious, personal efficacy, sex and gender, control, self-awareness and self-consciousness, self-concept and identity, moral character, emotion, human sexuality, aggression, stress and illness, and personality and relationships.

Each chapter includes an introduction that provides basic definitions and concepts needed to understand the topic and relevant research, an Activity Box that gives readers an opportunity to see for themselves how certain personality measures or research stimuli work, a summary, and suggested readings. Each chapter is written by a different author or set of authors. This has advantages and disadvantages. The disadvantage is that not all authors have the same writing style or the same way of organizing material, and so reading a new chapter will mean adjusting to the author's manner of presentation. The advantage is that the authors are all experts writing about what they know best. No one psychologist or set of authors could be aware of current developments in all of the areas covered in this text. Because psychologists who are doing research in the areas have written the chapters, each chapter represents an expert opinion. For covering contemporary research in personality, we believe the advantages of an edited text outweigh the disadvantages. We hope you agree.

SUGGESTED READINGS

Hall, C. S., & Lindzey, G. (1978). *Theories of personality* (3rd ed.). New York: Wiley. A "classic" summary of historically important theories of personality.

Pervin, L. A. (1984). *Current controversies and issues in personality* (2nd ed.). New York: Wiley. An excellent review of controversial issues in personality research, including the importance of personality versus situations in affecting behavior, the contribution of genetic factors in personality, and the ethics and methodology of personality research.

Shontz, F. C. (1965). *Research methods in personality*. New York: Meredith. A thoughtful introduction to research and methodological issues in the field of personality.

Scientific Journals

Journal of Personality. Published by Duke University Press.

Journal of Personality and Social Psychology: Personality Processes and Individual Differences. Published by the American Psychological Association.

Journal of Research in Personality. Published by Academic Press.

Personality and Social Psychology Bulletin. Published by the Society for Personality and Social Psychology—Division 8 of the American Psychological Association—by Sage Publications.

REFERENCES

Allport, G. W. (1931). What is a trait of personality. *Journal of Abnormal and Social Psychology, 25,* 368–372.

Allport, G. W. (1966). Traits revisited. *American Psychologist, 21,* 1–10.

Bandura, A. (1977). *Social learning theory.* Englewood Cliffs, NJ: Prentice-Hall.

Brenner, C. (1974). *An elementary textbook of psychoanalysis.* Garden City, NY: Anchor.

Cattell, R. B. (1950). *Personality: A systematic, theoretical, and factual study.* New York: McGraw-Hill.

Dollard, J., & Miller, N. E. (1950). *Personality and psychotherapy: An analysis in terms of learning, thinking, and culture.* New York: McGraw-Hill.

Eysenck, H. J. (1970). *The structure of human personality* (3rd ed.). London: Methuen.

Eysenck, H. J. (1975). *The inequality of man.* San Diego: Edits Publishers.

Gergen, K. J. (1968). Personal consistency and the presentation of self. In C. Gordon & K. J. Gergen (Eds.), *The self in social interaction* (pp. 299–308). New York: Wiley.

Hall, C. S., & Lindzey, G. (1978). *Theories of personality* (3rd ed.). New York: Wiley.

Maddi, S. R. (1980). *Personality theories: A comparative analysis.* Homewood, IL: Dorsey Press.

Maslow, A. H. (1962). *Toward a psychology of being.* New York: Van Nostrand.

Maslow, A. H. (1971). *The farther reaches of human nature.* New York: Viking Press.

May, R. (1967). *Psychology and the human dilemma.* Princeton, NJ: Van Nostrand.

Mischel, W. (1968). *Personality and assessment.* New York: Wiley.

Mischel, W. (1973). Toward a cognitive social learning reconceptualization of personality. *Psychological Review, 80,* 252–283.

Mischel, W. (1977). On the future of personality measurement. *American Psychologist, 32,* 246–254.

Rogers, C. R. (1959). A theory of therapy, personality, and interpersonal relationships, as developed in the client-centered framework. In S. Koch (Ed.), *Psychology: A study of a science* (Vol. 3, pp. 184–256). New York: McGraw-Hill.

Rogers, C. R. (1961). *On becoming a person.* Boston: Houghton Mifflin.

Rotter, J. B. (1966). Generalized expectancies for internal versus external control of reinforcement. *Psychological Monographs, 80,* (Whole No. 609).

Shontz, F. C. (1969). *Research methods in personality.* New York: Appleton-Century-Crofts.

Skinner, B. F. (1953). *Science and human behavior.* New York: Macmillan.

PART ONE

BASIC ISSUES IN PERSONALITY

CHAPTER 2

Personality Measurement

STEPHEN R. BRIGGS

Introduction to the OSS
  Assessment Project
What to Measure?
  Measuring Variables
  Measuring a Concept
ACTIVITY BOX: Measuring
  Conscientiousness
  The Concept
    of Personality
  Measuring Personality
How to Measure It?
  The OSS Assessment
    Procedures
  Putting the Pieces Together
  Classifying Methods for
    Measuring Personality

How Good Is the Measure?
  Reliability
  Validity
Which Variables
    Are Important?
Why Measure Personality
    Variables?
Summary
SUGGESTED READINGS
REFERENCES

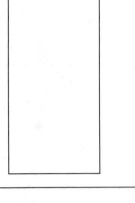

Introduction to the OSS Assessment Project

As the United States lurched headlong into World War II following the surprise bombing of Pearl Harbor, the President and Congress created a special wartime agency to conduct a variety of tactical and covert operations. The Office of Strategic Services (OSS) was the forerunner of today's Central Intelligence Agency (CIA). Its functions included gathering information about the enemy's activities and strengths, analyzing this information to identify areas of vulnerability, aiding and training resistance movements, and conducting guerrilla operations behind enemy lines.

Soon after its inception, the OSS was busily and somewhat haphazardly recruiting hundreds of men and women. As these recruits were trained and deployed, the need for a more rigorous screening process became apparent. To meet this need, an assessment staff of psychologists and psychiatrists was established in late 1943. The task assigned to the OSS assessment staff was to eliminate the unfit and to predict which recruits would be useful to OSS by developing a set of procedures that would reveal the personalities of OSS recruits. Although this task derived from the specific needs of the war effort, the type of problem that confronted the assessment staff has considerable generality: What is the best way to assess an individual's personality, and can such an assessment be used to make accurate predictions? Contemporary examples abound. Can we predict what sort of person will be able to endure the stress of being an air traffic controller? What kind of person is likely to steal from his employer? Which applicant has the best potential as a teacher or a salesperson? Who is likely to sustain an early heart attack? Which incoming freshmen should be paired as roommates? Each of these questions focuses in part on the personal qualities or characteristics of an individual that enhance or diminish the likelihood of certain outcomes. To answer such questions, a researcher must work through several steps:

1. Define the outcome (e.g., the task or the event) that the researcher is attempting to predict.
2. Identify the personality characteristics that are likely to influence the outcome.
3. Develop assessment procedures that will reveal those personality characteristics.
4. Communicate the information that is acquired about an individual to decision makers in a useful manner.

The assessment staff at OSS incorporated these guidelines into their selection process. Their work was complicated by a number of factors including the lack of adequate job descriptions (what would be this recruit's assignment?), the great variety of assignments (from clerks and secretaries to historians and linguists to undercover agents and saboteurs), and the diverse ethnic backgrounds of the recruits (e.g., Greeks, Romanians, Germans, Poles, Chinese, and Koreans, as well as Americans). Despite these problems and the hurried development of the testing procedures, the assessment staff was able to process 5,391 individuals in less than two years. Their work was vital to the wartime effort, and their approach to the study of personality had a significant impact on postwar research conducted at laboratories around the country. Throughout the chapter we will use the OSS assessment project to illustrate various issues and methods that are relevant to personality measurement. This material is drawn from a book that describes (including pictures) the wartime effort of the OSS assessment staff (U.S. Office of Strategic Services, 1948).

What to Measure?

Measuring Variables

Measurement is the process by which numbers are used to acquire and express information about an object, event, or organism. We can measure the length of a room, the weight of an infant, or the duration of a temper tantrum. Notice that we cannot measure an object or event in its entirety, but rather only its various attributes. In the science of psychology, these attributes are typically called *variables*. For example, age, race, eye color, height and weight, intelligence quotient (IQ), cheerfulness, marital status, and income are all attributes that can be used to describe people. For each of these variables, an individual can be assigned a *value*. In many cases values are based on a particular *unit of measurement*. For age, the unit of measurement might be years, and one value (thirty years) can be compared with other values (twenty or sixty years) using various mathematical operations (i.e., addition, subtraction, multiplication, and division). But units of measurement are generally arbitrary. Why choose years instead of months or minutes? Why is a yard thirty-six inches long, and exactly how long is an inch? What matters most is that different observers agree about the unit of measurement. Thus, an inch, an ounce, and a second are all defined with some exactness, the accuracy being ensured by national and international regulatory standards (e.g., seconds are calibrated precisely by an atomic clock at the Naval Observatory).

Not all variables, however, can be defined in terms of a unit of measurement. In the case of eye color, for example, we can distinguish blue from brown, and we can arbitrarily assign blue the number 1 and brown the number 2. But what is the unit of measurement? Is brown twice as big, or twice as long, or twice as important as blue? In this case we are using numbers like words to classify objects with respect to some variable. However, the numbers are not values that can be compared mathematically. Thus, there are several classes of variables that differ in terms of what a specific value represents. Table 2.1 describes four kinds of variables.

The fact that we can measure variables and quantify the world

TABLE 2.1

Four Types of Scales

Type of Scale	Nominal	Ordinal	Interval	Ratio
Defining characteristic	attributes are assigned to mutually exclusive categories	attributes are logically ordered	attributes are spaced at equal intervals defined by the unit of measurement	a value of zero indicates absence of the attribute
Function of the scale	to compare group membership; to classify	to compare rank order; to assign position	to compare amount; to count	to compare ratios or proportions
Mathematical properties	no mathematical functions; numbers used as names	greater than or less than	add and subtract	multiply and divide
Familiar examples	Zip Codes; Dewey Decimal System	class rank; ratings of top 20 teams in college basketball	SAT scores; temperature in centigrade degrees	miles per hour; temperature in kelvin degrees

around us does not necessarily mean that this is a wise use of our time. In fact, some psychologists argue that the qualities of mind, character, and personality that describe an individual in the fullest and deepest sense may by their very nature preclude rigorous definition or measurement. From this perspective, knowledge about people that is truly significant always transcends numbers: "If you can measure it, that ain't it." Other psychologists counter that anything that exists can be measured and that psychology will advance as a science only if variables are defined and measured with precision. This point of view is captured in a famous quote by Lord Kelvin, the British physicist who established the Kelvin scale for temperature:

> When you can measure what you are speaking about, and express it in numbers, you know something about it; but when you cannot measure it, when you cannot express it in numbers, your knowledge is of a meager and unsatisfactory kind: it may be the beginning of knowledge, but you have scarcely, in your thoughts, advanced to the stage of science, whatever the matter may be." (cited in Kaplan, 1964, 172)

This chapter is about measurement, and it would not make sense to assume from the outset that whatever is interesting about personality is unmeasurable. Nevertheless, we should not recklessly adopt the opposite point of view either. Numbers and statistics do not have magical properties. Advances in measurement are important as means to an end. Assigning increasingly precise numbers to objects or events is not, however, valuable in and of itself. Measurement is useful in proportion to what it allows us to achieve.

Measuring a Concept

Measurement is useful in part because it proceeds hand-in-hand with defining a concept. Everyday communication is possible because people agree more or less about the meaning of words. But the extent of agreement is far from perfect. For example, when I call Anne assertive, the positive characteristics that I have in mind may be different from the negative image that word creates for you. Words and concepts are colored by an individual's own experiences and biases. The connotative meaning of a word occasionally results in misunderstandings and conflict, but the cost exacted by such problems is offset by the richness and diversity of the words with which we communicate. Scientific progress, however, requires greater precision and agreement about words and concepts than everyday discourse. *Conceptualization* is the process by which we define exactly how we are going to use a specific term. Thus, if we want to know whether hostile people have more health problems, before we can even study the question, much less agree on an answer, we need to agree on what we mean by the two concepts—hostility and health problems.

Agreeing on what a concept means usually boils down to specifying a set of representative *indicators*. In the case of health problems, we might specify the presence of any of the following as a sign of ill health: cardiovascular disease, essential hypertension, peptic ulcers, cancer, disorders of the immune system, or elevated cholesterol and triglyceride levels. Notice, however, that this list of indicators includes

---

ACTIVITY BOX

Measuring Conscientiousness

As we observe ourselves and others in the course of everyday life, we often notice that people differ in terms of what they do and how they do it. Some people respond to criticism with anger and sarcasm, others are earnest and concerned, whereas still others are distraught. As we recognize certain tendencies, we tend to label the response: that person reacted spitefully, or candidly, or calmly. The adverb describes the specific reaction rather than the person generally. However, if we notice that a particular individual often reacts in a certain way, we may also want to label the person using a comparable adjective: we say that the person is generally spiteful, candid, or calm. Once we have noticed a tendency in some people, we can examine others to assess whether they also have this tendency. We begin to think of the tendency as a characteristic that is possessed to a greater or lesser extent. Does this person have the trait of spitefulness, candidness, or calmness? This progression from adverb to adjective to noun involves an increasing level of abstraction; we move from describing behavior to describing people to describing an idea.

Personality psychologists are often interested in a familiar concept. For example, a researcher may decide to study the concept of conscientiousness. Each of us has a general understanding of this term, and we can point to those around us who are more or less conscientious. But can we be precise in our definition? The task of the researcher is to specify behaviors that adequately define the idea or concept: What list of behaviors would indicate the presence or absence of this trait?

To test your ingenuity as a researcher, try drawing up a list of specific, observable behaviors that could be used to measure the trait of conscientiousness in the average college student. What behaviors in class, in the dorm, in the library, in the cafeteria, etc., would serve as legitimate and convincing measures of conscientiousness?

both diseases and risk factors and that it is far from exhaustive. Should we include colds, toothaches, allergies, or broken limbs on the list? In the same way, we can specify various indicators that signify what we mean by hostile: reacting aggressively to frustration, verbally insulting and picking on people, and flying off the handle when provoked. Again, these indicators are far from complete and less than perfect, but they begin to flesh out what we mean by a particular concept. The process of conceptualization involves specifying a variety of indicators that are reasonably clear and representative of the idea we are attempting to convey. This process is often more difficult than it sounds (see Activity Box), but it is the meat-and-potatoes work of the research psychologist.

Measurement is the logical end product of conceptualization. As we move from a vague concept first to a working definition and then to a set of specific indicators, the appropriate means by which to measure the concept becomes clearer. To return to a point made earlier, measurement is more than just assigning numbers to some aspect of an object or event. Measurement implies that we have an end in mind other than just quantification. Measurement provides a way to describe an object or an event in a systematic and standardized manner; it enhances our knowledge of that object or event. Advances in measurement result in increasingly subtle discriminations and correspondingly more precise descriptions that in turn allow for a more complete understanding of how one variable (e.g., physical health) relates to and changes as a function of some other variable (e.g., hostility). Thus, in an important way, measurement is the foundation on which an empirical science is built, but it in turn arises from the bedrock of conceptualization and theory.

The Concept of Personality

From the preceding discussion, it should be clear that in order to measure personality, we must first reach some agreement about what the concept means. What exactly is it that we are wanting to quantify? Personality has been defined in many different ways. In the definitive treatment of this issue, Gordon Allport (1937) recorded fifty different definitions of the concept of personality as it has been used in various academic disciplines (e.g., theology, philosophy, sociology, and law). Fortunately, most uses of the term can be summarized in terms of two major themes (MacKinnon, 1944).

One meaning of the term originates from the perspective of an observer, and it involves an individual's public presence and social reputation. The term personality derives from the Latin word *persona* for the mask worn by actors during ancient theatrical performances. Persona was used to describe the role or part assumed by an actor in a drama, as well as the distinctive personal qualities attributed to an individual. In this sense, then, personality refers to how an individual appears to others.

Personality in the second sense refers to the inner self or being of an individual—one's private, vital, and essential nature. This meaning of the term can be traced back to the efforts by early Christian theologians to expound the distinct personalities of the Trinity. With time, personality in this sense has come to mean the deep and enduring structures of an individual that form the central core of the self.

The measurement of personality is complicated by the fact that these two perspectives are not easily integrated and require quite different measurement strategies; one emphasizes the outer visible aspects, the other focuses on the inner, dynamic whole. For the outer perspective on personality, the characteristics to be studied, classified, and measured are reasonably observable, but for the inner perspective, the important characteristics are often hidden below the surface, emerging only in subtle and indirect ways. In the course of this chapter, we will encounter methods of measurement that have developed in line with each of these perspectives.

Measuring Personality

As the OSS assessment staff set to work in 1943, they were confronted with several immediate problems. First, what aspects of personality should they attempt to measure? At the outset, the staff had only vague descriptions of the functions that men would be expected to perform overseas, and many of the operations were still in the planning stages or were being performed behind enemy lines where even the officers in charge had only limited knowledge about the requirements of the job. Thus, it was impossible to assess men in relation to a specific, well-defined job or task. Instead, the assessment staff decided to assess men in relation to a cluster of general qualifications that were thought to be necessary for effective functioning in a wide variety of OSS activities.

Over a period of time, the assessment staff identified seven major personality variables that branch chiefs and administrative officers judged essential for completing assignments in their units:

1. *Motivation:* war morale and interest in OSS activities
2. *Energy and initiative:* level of effort and activity
3. *Effective intelligence:* ability to select strategic goals and *attain them efficiently:* practical, resourceful, original, and discerning
4. *Emotional stability:* steady, able to endure stress

5. *Social relations:* ability to get along with others, team player
6. *Leadership:* social initiative, ability to elicit cooperation, accepts responsibility, organizational ability
7. *Security:* discrete, cautious, able to keep secrets, can bluff and mislead

In addition to these personality dispositions, potential recruits were also judged on several dimensions of ability (athletic skills, observational and analytic skills, and propaganda skills), and in terms of suitability for different levels of involvement (front lines versus support staff) and different levels of authority and responsibility.

Two points are worth noticing with regard to the selection of these particular variables. First, in the decades following World War II, researchers have used increasingly sophisticated statistical methods to identify the primary dimensions of personality by which individuals describe others or themselves. As we shall see later in the chapter, the variables that were identified intuitively by the assessment staff bear a remarkable resemblance to the factors identified empirically in subsequent research.

The other point concerns an assumption that is implicit in the staff's decision to measure these particular variables. By choosing to evaluate all candidates on the same seven dimensions, the staff assumed that these particular dimensions could appropriately and fairly describe all candidates. In the terminology of Gordon Allport (1966), the staff decided that it was more practical and advantageous to describe candidates in terms of seven *common traits* than in terms of *personal dispositions*. Common traits are characteristics on which everyone can be judged (e.g., talkativeness or aggressiveness), presumably because the normal demands of living in a particular culture require people to respond in certain ways; personal dispositions are characteristics that apply especially well to particular individuals (e.g., meticulousness), but not necessarily to everyone, because they are not intrinsically related to functioning successfully in that environment. Allport endorsed the use of common traits as a way of gathering information about large numbers of people, but he also pointed out the costs associated with forcing a unique individual into a mold that was designed with the philosophy of "one size fits all." Sometimes the fit is not good; in some cases only one of the variables may be especially salient or central, and this variable may be expressed in a way that is slightly askew from the way that the common trait is defined. Thus, the assessment staff's decision to focus on seven common traits was to some extent a calculated risk. Given the constraints of the moment, they had little choice and their selection of variables was fortuitous. Nevertheless, when it comes to describing a particular individual, some researchers would argue that it is important to study the regularities and patterns that characterize the individual specifically, instead of relying on broadly defined common traits that might have little relevance for any single individual (Lamiell, 1987; Runyan, 1983).

How to Measure It?

Whereas personality variables seem more complex and abstract than some other individual characteristics (e.g., body size, physical health, or musical ability), the general measurement strategy is not all that different. Probably the single overarching principle is that of triangulation—gathering evidence from multiple vantage points and looking for convergence. The idea is to gather information from different perspectives (a friend, a supervisor or teacher, a parent, oneself) using different kinds of methods (subjective impressions versus objective measurements) in order to examine whether these different perspectives and methods give similar answers. Consider, for example, how to go about describing a woman's physique.

One strategy might be to ask a woman to describe herself or to provide relevant information. Of course, although people have a considerable store of knowledge about their bodies, they also have a vested interest in how such information is evaluated. We would not necessarily want to assume the accuracy of the self-reported description. Another strategy might be to ask other people to describe the target person. Presumably others would provide a more objective description of her body although they would have access to less information (e.g., the observers may be fooled by clever tailoring). Some close friends may have more information than a first-time observer, but then they will also be somewhat more likely to describe their friend kindly.

An alternative strategy would be to acquire more standardized measures of height and weight. But these figures alone provide a limited picture; they do not readily distinguish muscle from fat. We could add, therefore, measures of circumference, somatotype ratings, and perhaps even a displaced-water test to flesh out the description of the woman's body type, but incorporating these additional measures underscores the original point. No one source of data can provide a complete picture. The woman may describe herself as overweight, her coworkers may say she looks great, her weight may be average for her height, and her percentage of body fat may be above normal. Together these different pieces of information, although not entirely consistent, present us with a well-balanced description. Our confidence in a description increases as the perspectives and methods of measurement become more varied and as the various lines of evidence converge. Any single source of data is susceptible to a variety of problems, but by adopting multiple modes of measurement, biases and errors can often be canceled out or minimized.

In the same way, adequately measuring a personality variable requires several different sources and methods. In the OSS assessment project, the staff went to great lengths to gather information about a person in a variety of contexts or situations and from the vantage point of multiple observers. In fact, they developed an elaborate procedure for acquiring an enormous amount of information about each candidate in a limited period of time. The basic strategy is worth exploring in greater depth, in part because similar strategies have been adopted subsequently by a number of major corporations (for the selection and promotion of executives) as well as by university research institutes.

The OSS Assessment Procedures

Station S (for Secret) was the primary OSS assessment school. Located in Fairfax County, Virginia, eighteen winding miles from Washington, DC, Station S was a fine country estate with a large main house and a number of other smaller structures that were situated on several acres of varied terrain. Every few days a canvas-covered Army truck carrying a group of eighteen OSS candidates arrived at Station S for a three-day stopover. Candidates were recruited in a variety of ways; some were military personnel, others were civilians. Most had only a vague understanding of the nature of the OSS or the specific assignment for which they were being considered.

Students at Station S were required to hide their true identity for security reasons. The assessment staff capitalized on this requirement by instructing each student to create and maintain a cover story during his stay at Station S. He was to hide from the staff and other students his real birthplace, educational history, occupation, and current residence. All of the candidates wore Army fatigues that provided no clues as to their personal identity or rank. Only at special times during their stay (which were called X conditions) were they allowed to break their cover story. The rest of the time the students were to guard painstakingly their true identity because the assessment staff would attempt to catch them off guard.

For three or four days, the candidates were subjected to an intense and exhausting series of missions, tests, problems, interviews, and games. The staff worked hard to create an atmosphere of friendly competition and camaraderie. From the moment a group disembarked, however, the assessment staff was collecting data that would become grist for the assessment mill.

Consider, for example, how the assessment staff gathered information about a candidate's capacity for leadership. Recall that leadership was one of the seven common traits identified for study. The staff defined it as "a man's ability to take the initiative in social situations, to plan and organize action, and in so doing to evoke cooperation" (U.S. Office of Strategic Services, 1948, p. 301). The staff also distinguished, at least in their thinking and observations, between leadership assertion and leadership efficiency: assertion described the drive to assume the position of leader, and efficiency referred to how well a leader functioned when placed in that role by his colleagues or circumstances.

In the final stages of the assessment project, the leadership variable was assessed using seven procedures. Three of these involved situational tests in which a team of candidates was confronted with a standard problem or task and the staff observed how the team performed and who exerted leadership. Two other tests were designed to reveal leadership in the context of verbal interaction. A candidate's leadership ability was also rated by his peers (the other candidates) and by a staff member who had interviewed the candidate and who had access to the results of a variety of personality inventories. This multimethod approach to measurement was essential to the logic of the assessment school. At some point, of course, the diverse and independent sources of data had to be reconciled and interpreted to provide a summary report and recommendation. We will look at how this integration was achieved in a subsequent section. First, however, we will look more closely at how leadership was measured using specific procedures.

Recall from our earlier discussion that measurement is the logical end product of conceptualization. To measure leadership, we move first from a vague concept to a working definition and then to a set of specific indicators. These indicators become our *operational definition* of leadership; the operational definition spells out in concrete terms exactly how this particular concept or variable is going to be measured. Adopting a set of procedures provides a standardized and systematic way of measuring leadership. Nevertheless, these indicators are almost surely incomplete and less than perfect, which means that from the outset we have invested in a conception of leadership that we know is in some ways flawed and inaccurate.

The Brook Situation

One of the situations a team of candidates would be confronted with on the first day of testing involved moving several large objects and members of the team across a shallow, quiet stream with banks about eight feet apart. On one bank was a log, on the other bank a heavy rock. Both sides of the brook had trees. Scattered on the ground along the bank where the candidates stood were several boards, none long enough to reach the other bank, three lengths of rope, a pulley, and a barrel with both ends knocked out. The candidates were given the following instructions:

> Use your imagination. Before you, you see a raging torrent so deep and so fast that it is quite impossible to rest anything upon the bottom of the stream. The banks are sheer, so it will be impossible for you to work except from the top of them.
>
> You are on a mission in the field, and having come to this brook you are faced with the task of transporting this delicate range finder, skillfully camouflaged as a log, to the far bank, and of bringing that box of percussion caps, camouflaged as a rock, to this side. In carrying out this assignment, you may make use of any materials you find around here. When the job is done, all of you, as well as any material you have used, are to be back on this side.
>
> This is a group problem. We would suggest that you first discuss your method of procedure. When you have decided upon your plan and are ready to go to work, let us know so that we may time you, for in the actual execution of this problem you will be working against time. (U.S. Office of Strategic Services, 1948, pp. 95–96)

All solutions to this problem involved getting one or more team members to the other side of the brook by building a bridge with the boards and rope (the rope could be used to bind several boards together) or by roping a branch on the far side of the bank and rigging an overhead cable, or by swinging across to the opposite bank on a rope tied to a high branch of a tree on the near bank. The objects could then be transferred in a similar manner. Groups were allocated one hour to solve this problem. Some groups were unable to accomplish the mission in this time period whereas at least one team completed the task in only four minutes.

Leadership in this context emerged in a variety of ways. Specific indicators included a candidate's ability to propose and implement a successful strategy, to organize the group into an effective working team, to combine judiciously ideas from several sources, and to minimize friction and maximize cooperative effort. A man who took the lead initially was not necessarily the same man who directed things at the end. Sometimes the candidate who guided the discussion would lose his leadership to someone who was more gifted athletically. Or perhaps the role would be reassigned when an idea failed or a better plan was proposed. The leader was not always the most assertive individual; sometimes a group might reject a member who attempted to dominate the decision making in favor of a less forceful member whose ideas were more practical.

The actions and interactions that occurred at the brook were recorded by a staff member and observed by several others. Each candidate was rated independently by the staff members and these ratings were always discussed subsequently prior to arriving at a final rating for leadership.

The Construction Task

Also on the first day, each candidate had an individual appointment behind the barn. The candidate's task was to direct two helpers in constructing a wooden frame structure. But the problem was not as innocent as it seemed. The two assistants—Kippy and Buster—were actually members of the assessment staff posing as hired farmhands. Their assignment was to annoy and obstruct the candidate to the best of their ability but without disobeying any direct orders. Kippy generally acted in a passive, sluggish manner and would do little to help unless specifically instructed, whereas Buster was surly and cantankerous, full of impractical suggestions and quick to criticize. For instance, the following excerpt occurred toward the end of a typical encounter:

> *Buster:* We don't seem to be getting much done here, do we?
>
> *Candidate:* Well, if you guys would get to work we would.
>
> *Buster:* Well, it seems to me it's sorta late now. Why don't you be a man and admit that you can't do this job? After all, it's only a toy and sort of foolish for a grown man. It's nothing to be ashamed of that you can't build it. It's just not in your line.
>
> *Candidate:* Well, I'd like to do as much of this as possible. Will you help me?
>
> *Buster:* Sure, sure, we'll help you, but it doesn't seem to be much use. What do you want us to do now?
>
> *Candidate:* Well, one of you build a square over there just like this one while the other one puts in the uprights and diagonals on this one.
>
> *Kippy:* May I ask a question?
>
> *Candidate:* Sure, go ahead.
>
> *Kippy:* Why build one over there? What are you going to do with it then?
>
> *Candidate:* Well, we'll put it on top—the top of this cube is like the bottom.
>
> *Kippy:* Well, if that isn't the most stupid thing I ever heard of. Since when do you build it right on the top? Listen, when you build a house you build the foundation, then the walls, and then the roof. Isn't that right?
>
> *Candidate:* Well, that is usually the way it's done, but I think we can do this job this way. In fact, I don't think it matters much which way we do it. Either way is O.K., I guess.
>
> *Buster:* You guess, you guess. What kind of a man are you anyway? Why in hell don't you make up your mind and stick to it? Be decisive—didn't

they tell you that in OCS?—be decisive—even if you are wrong, be decisive, give an order. What are you—man or mouse?

Kippy: Oh, it's no use talking, Buster, when he doesn't have a bar on his shoulder he doesn't know what to do. Listen, Mac, you're not on Company Street now. You haven't a sergeant to do your work for you. You're all alone and you look pretty silly. Why, you can't even put together a child's toy.

Candidate: Now listen to me, you guys, are you going to work for me or aren't you?

Buster: Sure, we want to work for you. We really don't care. We'd as soon work for you as for anyone else. We get paid all the same. The trouble is we can't find out what you want done. What exactly do you want? (U.S. Office of Strategic Services, 1948, p. 109)

Originally conceived of as a test of leadership, the construction task allowed each candidate to be scored in terms of whether he controlled the situation, outlined the task and explained his reasoning adequately, earned the respect of his helpers, listened to their suggestions, motivated them to work, and minimized friction and hostility. Again, the leadership variable was rated by several independent observers and later combined into a summary evaluation. Although evidence of leadership was certainly revealed by the candidates in this context, Kippy and Buster performed their roles so effectively that no candidate ever completed the construction task and most never got very far. Their behavior was designed to frustrate the candidates, perhaps provoking an impulsive act, and thus the task came to be seen more as a test of emotional stability than a measure of leadership.

Discussion

Each team met to discuss the question, What are the major postwar problems facing the United States, and (if you have time) along what lines do you think they should be solved? The team was to arrive at a consensus and then have one member present its conclusions. Leadership was rated in terms of whether a candidate was able to keep the discussion on track, command the respect of the others by virtue of his contributions, facilitate the participation of all group members, and guide the discussion toward a conclusion by summarizing points and positions and detecting agreement.

Debate

Late in the evening on the second day, all of the candidates were divided into two teams for a debate. The topic of the debate varied over time in order to keep it current: "What are we fighting for?", "What shall we do with Germany after the war?" and "Can we trust Russia in the postwar world?" The groups had twenty minutes to prepare their positions, and the staff observed the preparations as well as the debate itself. Although similar to the group discussion, the debate differed in that the audience was larger, the issue more competitive, and the participants better acquainted. Perhaps most important of all, however, was that prior to the debate a free bar was opened for the remainder of the evening. The abundance of liquor undoubtedly accentuated the emotional intensity of the issue being discussed, and the debate often revealed a different view of a candidate's leadership abilities.

Assigned Leadership Tasks

Many of the tasks at Station S began without a leader, and the staff watched to see who emerged on top. In these contexts, however, it was not always apparent whether other men might also have acted effectively as the leader if they had been assigned the task. Thus, a series of situations was designed such that members of the group would alternate as leader. Typically, a candidate was assigned a problem that seemed particularly relevant to him. A variety of situations was used:

1. *Mined road:* Move the team safely across a mined road.
2. *Sentry:* Move the team, including a wounded member, across a road without being detected and in less than ten minutes.
3. *Agent's room:* Search a room for important papers. (Shortly after the search was begun, the room was approached by a German soldier.)
4. *Blown bridge:* Repair a damaged bridge using the materials available before an enemy patrol returns. (After seven minutes, the enemy patrol opened fire with cap guns from behind a nearby wall.)
5. *Killing the mayor:* Plan a mission that involves moving the squad several miles across town to assassinate the mayor. (Several problems cropped up along the way, including a confrontation with a German patrol.)

In this way, the staff was able to assess each candidate's ability to organize his team, develop strategy, respond to emergencies, and maintain his role.

Sociometric Ratings

Each candidate at Station S during a given session was asked to rate the other candidates in his class. Candidates responded to 11 questions about the other men. Two of the questions were directly relevant to leadership ability: "Whom would you recommend as supervisor of a group dealing with problems of planning and organization" and "If you were a member of a group on a dangerous mission, whom would you prefer to have as your leader?" Candidates answered these questions by nominating classmates. They could nominate as few or as many other classmates as they wanted. The sociometric ratings were introduced to the class as a way of helping the staff assess the other candidates, but also as a way of evaluating each candidate's ability to judge others accurately. This introduction was thought to enhance the quality of the ratings.

The Interview

The single most important component of the OSS assessment strategy was the clinical interview, because the interviewer would eventually write the first draft of the personality profile that would accompany the final evaluation of the candidate. Using insights gleaned from the interview session, the interviewer integrated the various bits of information derived from the situational tasks, the batteries of self-report tests and personality inventories, and the ratings by peers.

Each candidate met alone for an hour and a half with a senior member of the staff under X conditions (i.e., the candidate was free to reveal his true identity and history and could set aside for the moment his cover story). The interview session was used to explore the candidate's life history including relationships with family members and friends, school and athletic achievements, medical illnesses, romances, wishes and fears, hopes and aspirations, and opinions and beliefs. The interviewers were generally not as interested in the exact truthfulness of a candidate's account as they were in how he interpreted and presented his past. For example, it would have been difficult for the staff to assess the veracity of a candidate's description of how he and his father got along, but regardless of accuracy, how a candidate spoke of this relationship was revealing. Did he describe his father affectionately, or was he bitter and hostile? Was he distant and reserved in his description or glowing and unrealistic? Similarly, interviewers were as attentive to how a candidate reacted to the interview situation as they were to the content of what was said. Was the candidate withdrawn or at ease, evasive or frank, flexible or rigid? What did he want to talk about, and what made him edgy? The interviews followed no standard protocol; they varied considerably depending on the particular mix of interviewer and interviewee.

In this context, perceptions about a candidate's leadership potential were deduced from his previous accomplishments (had he been a leader in high school, had he been a leader in the military or in business?), his reactions to probing questions and an authority figure, his hobbies and interests, his motivation, and the general strength and resiliency of his character as interpreted by an experienced psychologist or psychiatrist. Although the picture of the candidate that developed during the interview generally formed the basis for the personality profile included in the final report to the candidate's recruiting officer, this picture was not independent of the other information gathered at the assessment school because the interviewer had already observed the candidate in a variety of test situations and also had access to his scores on a variety of personality tests. Thus, this session enabled the interviewer to test, refine, and consolidate an impression that was already partially formed.

Putting the Pieces Together

On the final day of each assessment session, the staff met as a whole to decide about the fitness of each of the candidates. This process involved integrating a wealth of material into a single description or personality profile. The method for doing this revolved around the primary dimensions of evaluation: the seven personality variables and the three ability variables.

Using the case of leadership as an example, each of several observers would have rated a candidate on a particular task (e.g., the Brook Situation) using a 6-point scale:

0	1	2	3	4	5
Very Inferior 7%	Inferior 18%	Low Average 25%	High Average 25%	Superior 18%	Very Superior 7%

(The percentages refer to the number of candidates who would ideally fall into each category over the full term of the project. Raters were encouraged to use all points on this scale, but in the correct proportion.) Immediately after the task, the raters met together to compare notes. Whenever discrepancies occurred, the raters worked to understand the nature of the disagreement and to resolve it. In this way, a single rating was recorded for a candidate for each task, and this rating reflected the consensus of the observers who were present for that situation.

Ratings on each task and each personality variable were posted on a large board using color-coded thumbtacks. By the final staff conference, complete information about a candidate was displayed using separate columns for the primary rating variables and subcolumns for the separate situations. At a glance, a staff member could ascertain a candidate's average rating across the seven leadership tasks and could also check for any obvious inconsistencies.

During the staff conference, the interviewer would read the candidate's personality profile and one of the other observers would characterize the situational ratings of the candidate. The rest of the staff would then comment on and critique these findings and would offer their own insights, observations, and anecdotes. The group would confer about that candidate until all issues and discrepancies had been resolved and a final recommendation had been reached. In many cases, this consensus was achieved quickly and easily. Sometimes, however, a consensus was reached only after heated discussion and freely expressed disagreement. Nevertheless, agreement was almost always attained without resorting to a mechanical tallying of votes.

The OSS assessment project is an important landmark in the history of personality assessment. This massive undertaking exceeded any previous attempts to study a large group of individuals in depth; many distinguished psychologists contributed to its success. Although we could profitably examine many aspects of this project in greater detail, for now three points warrant emphasis:

1. The OSS staff began the assessment enterprise by identifying the relevant personality variables and devising ways to assess these variables. Conceptualization led to a working definition that in turn suggested specific indicators or measures.
2. The OSS staff measured each personality variable in several different situations and incorporated several different methods. Using different indicators to triangulate on a specific personality variable provided evidence about the coherence of these indicators and helped to ensure that no one indicator was overinterpreted or overemphasized.
3. The OSS staff worked as a group to observe and describe a candidate's personality. Multiple observers provided another form of triangulation that helped to ensure the accuracy of the ratings and acted to minimize biases associated with any one viewpoint or observer.

These three points are inherent in the logic of measurement, and they must be attended to in doing research of any type including personality measurement. The first of these points we covered earlier in this chapter. The other two points we will look at more thoroughly in the remaining pages.

Classifying Methods for Measuring Personality

Over the years, investigators have concocted many ingenious ways of assessing personality constructs. Nevertheless, the term "personality measure" is sometimes confused with one particular method: the self-report inventory. Questionnaires of this sort are used so extensively that it is easy to understand how this approach has become virtually synonymous (even in professional journals!) with personality measurement. But there are multiple strategies for assessing personality, and it would be unfortunate and self-defeating for researchers to limit themselves to a single method. The purpose of this section is to review some of the various ways in which personality can be assessed and to organize these approaches within a conceptual framework.

Several schemes for categorizing personality measures have been proposed. Our discussion will follow loosely a system developed by Donald Fiske (1971). (It is worth noting that Fiske—then a lieutenant in the U.S. Navy—was part of the OSS Assessment Staff and was one of the principal authors of the book that chronicles the work at Station S.)

TABLE 2.2

Classifying the Methods for Measuring Personality

	Mode 1	Mode 2	Mode 3	Mode 4	Mode 5	Mode 6	Mode 7
Description	trait inventories	state experiences	ability tests	subjective ratings	objective ratings	behaviorial measures	physiological measures
Source of the data	self	self	self	other	other	instrument	instrument
Time frame	past	current	current	past	current	current	current
How the source functions	interprets	perceives	executes	interprets	interprets or transcribes	records mechanically	records mechanically
Nature of the task	describe yourself	describe your experience	answer correctly	describe this person	describe this person	record behavioral response	record physiological activity
Type of variable	ordinal	ordinal	ordinal, interval, or ratio	ordinal	ordinal	interval or ratio	interval or ratio
Typical variables	traits, attitudes, beliefs	preferences, judgments, feelings	knowledge, skills, abilities	traits, complex behaviors	traits, behaviors	simple behavioral responses	cortical or autonomic arousal
Typical examples	MMPI, CPI	mood surveys, perceptual judgments	rod & frame, ability tests	ratings by peers or supervisors	clinical interviews or ratings	reaction time	EEGs, heart rate, blood pressure

The system we will examine differs in several respects from the one presented by Fiske, but it defines the basic modes (or categories) using the same primary factors: the source of the data (who or what produces it) and the role the source plays in producing the data.

The classification system is described in table 2.2. The rows of the table list the defining factors, and the columns identify seven different modes (one more than was used by Fiske). Distinctions among the modes will become apparent as we look briefly at each.

Mode 1 is the familiar self-report questionnaire in which respondents are asked to endorse the accuracy of self-descriptive items. Respondents presumably select responses after considering thoughtfully their past behavior and store of self-memories. Because no other observer can access these private vaults or amass knowledge that is comparable, the self-report of an individual provides an essential perspective. However, one cannot assume that the information obtained from a self-report inventory is entirely accurate or highly perceptive. Consider some of the limitations of the self-report method. Respondents might:

1. Misconstrue some of the items on a questionnaire
2. Hurry to finish and become careless
3. Not cooperate and choose deliberately to distort answers
4. Lack insight into their own motives, feelings, and actions
5. Wish to present themselves in a favorable light

These last two problems in particular have troubled researchers who use self-report instruments (Paulhus, 1986). The one problem involves *self-deception:* some people do not accurately comprehend their own personalities. The other issue concerns *impression management:* people often offer only an idealized view of themselves. This mode of measurement provides an important resource for personality researchers but one that can be deciphered correctly only in concert with other sources of information.

The second mode of measurement also relies on an individual's self-description, but the focus is on current experiences rather than previous history. For example, a cola taste test ("Do you prefer cola A or cola B?") asks a respondent to report an immediate preference and does not require an interpretation of how the respondent acts or feels typically. There is less need for inference and less opportunity for the report to be influenced by the constructive process of memory. Thus, the report of a *state* experience is more straightforward than the report of a *trait* tendency.

The distinction between trait and state is an important one and was recognized even by ancient thinkers.

> It is one thing to be irascible, quite another to be angry, just as an *anxious temper* is different from *feeling anxiety*. Not all men who are sometimes anxious are of an anxious temperament, nor are those who have an anxious temperament always feeling anxious. In the same way there is a difference between intoxication and habitual drunkenness. (Cicero, 45 BC; quoted in Eysenck, 1983)

Traits refer to personal characteristics that are stable, long-lasting, and internally caused; states describe features that are temporary, brief, and linked to external circumstances. Whereas trait concepts enable people to predict how individuals will act now or in the future based on how they have acted before, state concepts describe actions that are influenced by and may be predicted from a particular context (Chaplin, John, & Goldberg, 1988). Trait tendencies are more central to the study of personality than are state experiences, although trait tendencies often involve an increased likelihood of certain state experiences: people who have the trait of anxiety are more likely than most to experience anxious moods, just as alcoholics are more likely than most to experience the state of intoxication.

Although the report of a state experience requires less interpretation and self-knowledge than the report of a trait tendency, it is still susceptible to some of the same problems. Respondents may attempt to portray themselves in a favorable light (by choosing an answer or reporting a mood that seems more socially acceptable) or they may be uncooperative and deliberately sabotage the research.

The third mode of measurement again relies on a respondent's self-report. In this case, however, the task is to answer an item correctly rather than to rate its typicality or applicability. Items of this sort are analagous to questions on a school exam or in a trivia game. Although most psychologists distinguish between items that measure personality and those that measure ability (e.g., IQ tests), there are measures that combine elements of both. For example, tests of social intelligence—such as having to discern a person's viewpoint or having to identify correctly the meaning of social cues and facial expressions—are relevant to the measurement of certain personality variables (e.g., empathy and dominance). Tests of this sort are more objective than the self-report measures that are located in Modes 1 and 2 in that they require little in the way of interpretation or self-knowledge and the test taker cannot fake good answers (although occasionally a respondent will attempt to look bad in order to avoid the draft, jail, etc.). Because of this greater objectivity, some researchers have attempted to construct personality measures using an ability approach (e.g., Willerman, Turner, & Peterson, 1976), although this strategy has not been widely adopted.

Modes 4 and 5 both originate from the perspective of an observer.

They differ primarily in the extent to which the observer is knowledgeable and objective. Mode 4 is the counterpart to Mode 1; the observer's task is to decide whether an item accurately describes the target person. This interpretation is presumably grounded in the many observations of the target that the rater has accumulated over time and in a variety of contexts. Thus, this approach assumes that the observer is a knowledgeable informant. Friends, one's spouse, a roommate, or a coworker could all serve appropriately in this capacity. The closer the relationship, the richer the observational base. However, as the degree of intimacy increases, so does the likelihood that the rater will feel compelled to describe the target favorably. One's companions and chums generally fill that role by choice; by definition they are not impartial bystanders. Because this mode of measurement relies on the same type of interpretive judgments as self-reports, it is subject to many of the same constraints and biases.

To minimize biases of this sort, researchers often recruit impartial observers—individuals who have had no contact with the target person prior to the period of observation. Ratings of this sort (Mode 5) are based solely on information derived from the observational setting or other available records. Much of the data collected during the OSS assessment project involved this strategy of measurement: ratings by observers during the various tasks and situations, ratings from the clinical interview, and sociometric (peer) ratings. Unlike ratings by knowledgeable informants (Mode 4), impartial observers offer a reasonable degree of objectivity. They should be less reluctant to assign unfavorable marks. For example, most employers interview job applicants rather than rely solely on personal references. The interviewer's evaluation is presumably more objective than the ratings provided by a self-selected reference. Nevertheless, this approach also has its limitations. Most important, the observers' knowledge is necessarily restricted by the context and time frame of the observations. An interviewer must form an impression based on a short, highly constrained conversation. Even the intense, three-day schedule of testing at Station S provided only a narrow range of observational opportunities. Objective raters usually derive inferences from information that is insufficient and superficial. In addition, objective observers are subject to many of the same rating biases as observers who are well acquainted with the targets.

Two common forms of rater bias are *leniency* and *halo*. Leniency is the tendency to give generally positive ratings. For instance, students often rate all of their professors as above average in teaching effectiveness although it should be obvious that at least some instructors must be below par. That friends might be lenient in their ratings should not be overly surprising. The leniency from impartial strangers probably derives from a general tendency to think kindly about others and to avoid being seen as negative or critical.

Halo involves a blurring of conceptual distinctions. When an individual has a particularly salient personal trait, this characteristic may bias an observer's ratings more generally. For example, if a woman is invariably hostile toward others and bitter about life, the negative feelings elicited by her antagonism may influence ratings of other aspects of her personality that are presumably independent (e.g., her work habits or intellectual ability). Halo refers, therefore, to a generally favorable or unfavorable rating of an individual that is rooted in a single prominent aspect of his or her personality.

One way to avoid rating biases such as leniency and halo is to employ the observer as a transcriber rather than as an interpreter. For example, the observer might count the number of questions an individual asks during a conversation or record the length of the conversation. The researcher seeks to minimize the role of interpretation generally by providing explicit instructions about how to measure a specific and simple behavior. In this approach, the observer performs a machine-like function; in fact, in most instances of this sort, given the opportunity, researchers would replace the human observer with an automated device.

Modes 6 and 7 involve this transition from human observer to mechanical instrument. In both cases, the premium is on precise measurement and a standardized mechanism. Responses are measured in terms of frequency (how often?), latency (how soon?), duration (how long?), rapidity (how often per unit of time?), and intensity (how strong?). Interpretation and subjective ratings are eliminated as much as possible. Barring equipment failure or miscalibration, the researcher is justifiably confident about the accuracy and objectivity of the data record. But this sense of precision can be somewhat misleading. After all, the researcher still must link these automated recordings to a personality construct and this requires a fair amount of interpretation. Is reaction time the same as impulsivity? Is increased muscle tension for certain facial muscles equivalent to anger or sadness? Are increased heart rate and blood pressure a measure of anxiety? Claims of this sort may be conceptually reasonable, but they are hardly straightforward. Thus, no method of measurement can avoid the need for interpretation, although *who* provides the interpretation (an observer or the researcher) and at what point (when the rating is made or when the research is designed) varies across the seven modes.

The chief distinction between Mode 6 and Mode 7 involves the content being measured. In Mode 6, the participant in a research study responds to some event in a relatively observable and controlled way—by pushing a button or flipping a switch. A machine records this response. In Mode 7, the instrument records ongoing physiological activity (e.g., heart rate, muscular tension, or brain activity) that is relatively private and that may be apprehended only vaguely by the person himself or herself.

Taken together, the seven modes of measurement provide researchers with a diverse and adaptable set of tools. Different instruments are applicable to different types of problems and choosing the appropriate instrument is always crucial to the success of a research project. There is no perfect tool or method. Instead there are always trade-offs: the ease of data collection versus the richness of the data set, an observer who is knowledgeable versus one who is objective, an observer's interpretation as to the meaning of a complex behavior versus a researcher's interpretation about the psychological meaning of a simple response. Given these trade-offs, many researchers hedge their bets by selecting more than one measure of a personality variable. In order to balance the trade-offs, conventional wisdom also advocates selecting measures from more than one mode. The advantages of a multipronged approach were discussed earlier in the chapter, and one statement is worth repeating: Our confidence in a description increases as the perspectives and methods of measurement become more varied and as the various lines of evidence converge; any single source of data is susceptible to a variety of problems, but by adopting multiple modes of measurement, biases and errors can often be canceled out or minimized.

How Good Is the Measure?

Researchers routinely construct new measures of personality. Of course, some of these measures are better than others. The adequacy of a psychological measure is defined primarily in terms of two fundamental principles of measurement: *reliability* and *validity*.

Reliability

To be useful, a measure must be accurate and dependable. The degree of precision necessary, however, depends on the task at hand. If the purpose is to know the temperature outside (is it cold enough for a coat?), a reading that is accurate to within a few degrees will surely suffice. But when measuring a person's temperature (does the child have a fever?), the acceptable range of error is far smaller.

For temperature, weight, length, speed, and a host of other variables, the accuracy of a measure can be evaluated in relation to a standard. Thus, in the early 1900s meters were calibrated against a rod of platinum-iridium kept in a vault at the International Bureau of Weights and Measures in Sevres, France. Today the meter is defined as 1,650,763.73 vacuum wavelengths of monochromatic orange light emitted by a krypton atom of mass 86. This definition is accepted in specialized fields of science requiring exact precision and standardization of length; it provides values that are designated as true or perfectly accurate.

Assessing the reliability of psychological constructs, however, is complicated considerably by the fact that the constructs are more abstract and less rigorously defined. There are no formally defined standards against which to compare constructs such as intelligence, leadership, extraversion, or conscientiousness. Nevertheless, this same measurement model is applied so that personality measures are said to be reliable to the extent that they produce values that reflect a hypothetical *true score;* the more they miss this fictional mark, the greater is their *error.*

Because there is no tangible standard with which to compare measures of personality variables, their reliability is estimated by comparing various measures or measurements with one another. This approach is analogous to several people trying to decide which of several watches is accurate. In the absence of an external standard, two watches that agree provide some degree of confidence as to the actual time. If the watches do not agree, it is impossible to know which of them is inaccurate. The solution to this dilemma, of course, is to consult additional watches. The more watches that agree, the greater the likelihood that each of the individual watches is reliable. Five watches all in close agreement provide a reasonable degree of certainty. Even if the watches do not agree exactly, calculating an average across the five of them should provide a good working estimate of the time assuming that they are not all inaccurate in the same way (too slow or too fast). Averaging a number of imprecise measurements to obtain a more accurate estimate is a common practice in personality research and is called the principle of *aggregation* (Epstein, 1983). This is the rationale for including many items on a personality questionnaire rather than just one, but the principle is equally true for other modes of measurement as well; thus, aggregating observers' ratings (Mode 4 or Mode 5) or behavioral responses (Mode 6) will increase the reliability of these measures.

In the realm of personality measurement, reliability is estimated by collecting information at more than one time point, from more than one observer, using more than one version of the instrument, or collecting more than one sample of behavior. These various approaches lead to several different types of reliability:

1. *Test–retest reliability:* Does a measure yield the same value from one moment to the next; is it stable over time?
2. *Interobserver agreement:* Does a measure yield the same value from one observer to the next; do observers use the instrument in the same way?
3. *Parallel forms:* Does a measure yield the same value as a comparably constructed instrument; is it interchangeable with an alternate form of the instrument?
4. *Internal consistency:* Do the parts of a measure function similarly; are different items or behaviors interrelated?

Each of these approaches assumes a working definition of reliability and each provides a way to measure it. In other words, reliability itself is a construct that can be defined and measured in multiple ways. Although conceptually related, these various measures of reliability do not necessarily yield the same results.

Validity

In addition to being accurate, a good measure ought to be useful. Validity has to do with whether it is appropriate to use a measure in a particular way to meet a particular need. Because there are different kinds of uses for personality measures, it is possible to specify different kinds of validity. Thus, it is technically improper to ask whether a personality measure is valid or not because a measure is valid only with respect to some specific use. It is more correct to ask whether there is any evidence to support using a measure in a specific way (to predict success as a spy or a business executive) or to make a specific kind of inference (that this person is smart or shy). In this sense, validity is analogous to a kind of "truth in advertising." In the context of personality measurement, three kinds of validity are usually distinguished (Cronbach & Meehl, 1955).

Criterion Validity

Does a measure predict performance or success on some relevant criterion? Do students who score high on the SATs or ACTs do better in college than those who score low? Did the candidates who were rated highly at the OSS school make better agents and operatives than those who were rated poorly? In both cases the measures are used to screen candidates on the assumption that they can predict future (or even current) behavior. Is this a valid inference?

Content Validity

Does a measure adequately represent all aspects of the variable being studied? Does the final examination in a course systematically sample from all of the material contained in the lectures and the text? Did the seven factors of personality measured in the OSS Assessment Project adequately represent the dimensions that would be important in the war theater? In both cases the assessment procedure is designed to cover the domain of interest in a comprehensive and methodical fashion. Is this a valid inference?

Construct Validity

Does a measure assess the construct that it purports to measure? Does an intelligence test really measure the construct of intelligence? Did the Brook Situation really provide information about an individual's leadership abilities? Recall that the Construction Task, which was originally designed as a test of leadership ability, was later judged to be more of a measure of emotional stability. But is this a valid inference? How do we know for sure that this task actually measures either construct?

Construct validity is a difficult concept to grasp as well as a difficult concept to measure for reasons that are not unlike the problem we encountered with reliability. Constructs are abstractions; leadership, intelligence, anxiety, and other psychological constructs are theoretical ideas rather than concrete objects. We can point to examples of these constructs but we cannot grab hold of the construct itself. Thus, we can establish a working definition (of what leadership is), and we can proceed to measure the construct using specific indicators (taking charge in the Brook Situation or being rated as a leader by one's peers), but how can we be certain that these indicators (or measures) actually assess the theoretical construct of leadership? Any one measure of leadership might be flawed. However, if several different measures all yield the same answer, then we can be more confident about our measures and about our decision.

In the OSS Assessment Project, the construct of leadership was assessed in seven different ways. Did these seven different measures provide similar answers? Table 2.3 shows the correlations among the various measures. A *correlation coefficient* is a statistical index of the relationship between two variables that can be interpreted in terms of direction and size. A positive correlation means that the two variables are directly related (e.g., height and weight); higher scores on one measure are associated with higher scores on the other as well. A negative correlation means that the variables are inversely related; higher scores on one measure are associated with lower scores on the

TABLE 2.3

Intercorrelations Among the Measures of Leadership

	Brook situation	Construction task	Discussion	Debate	Assigned leadership tasks	Sociometric ratings	Clinical interview
Brook situation	—	.37	.47	.41	.42	.41	.57
Construction task	.37	—	.30	.33	.33	.24	.44
Discussion	.47	.30	—	.56	.37	.41	.48
Debate	.41	.33	.56	—	.39	.52	.47
Assigned leadership tasks	.42	.33	.37	.39	—	.37	.53
Sociometric ratings	.41	.24	.41	.52	.37	—	.54
Clinical interview	.57	.44	.48	.47	.53	.54	—

Adapted from Table 63, U.S. Office of Strategic Services (1948).

other. The size of a correlation ranges from 0 to 1.0. As the size approaches 1.0, the relationship becomes stronger—changes in one variable are closely linked to changes in the other. As the size approaches 0, the two variables become increasingly unrelated or independent.

The correlations in table 2.3 are all positive and mostly in the .3 to .5 range. This indicates that the various measures are at least moderately related, and it increases our confidence that something like leadership is being measured. Of course, many of these ratings were made by the same team of observers on the OSS Assessment Staff, so perhaps the moderate agreement is partly due to a desire of the raters to be consistent with themselves. When various measures are related to one another and they all derive from the same method of measurement, the positive correlation may be due to the method and not the construct. This artifact is called *method variance*. One way to avoid this confound is to use other modes of measurement; in this case, peer ratings would be an example. Disentangling constructs from methods is an important part of establishing a measure's construct validity (Campbell & Fiske, 1959).

Which Variables Are Important?

Researchers in the field of personality have studied hundreds of variables using literally thousands of self-report inventories, observational rating forms, and behavioral indices. A researcher who initiates a new study is faced with the daunting prospect of having to choose from this jumble of variables and measures the ones that are best suited for his or her specific project. Of course, these many variables and measures are not equally important nor is each unique. Many overlap in substantial ways. It would be advantageous to know how these various constructs and measures are related to one another; in other words, it would be helpful to have a *taxonomy* of personality variables.

A taxonomy is a systematic and orderly classification of variables according to their presumed natural relationships. In biology, Linné studied the morphological features of animals and plants and classified them into groups or categories (e.g., phylum, genus, and species). In chemistry, Mendeleyev observed regularities in the properties of various elements as a function of their atomic numbers and charted the Periodic Table. In the field of personality, researchers have studied attributes of people in an attempt to identify a set of primary or fundamental dimensions of personality.

The most methodical and extensive efforts to develop categories of personality variables have been based on the study of words that people use to describe others and themselves; this is called the psycholexical approach to the study of personality taxonomy (Goldberg, 1981; John, Angleitner, & Ostendorf, 1988). The English language contains thousands of trait descriptors. Allport and Odbert (1936) identified nearly eighteen thousand terms in their analysis of Webster's New International Dictionary, but most of these terms are obscure (e.g., atrabilious) or refer to physical characteristics (redhead, roly-poly) or abilities (dexterous) instead of personality traits. Therefore, investigators have asked individuals to rate peers (Mode 4 in table 2.2) using a shorter lists of adjectives that vary in length from 60 to 1,600 adjectives. These sets of adjectives are selected for familiarity, relevance, and breadth.

In the psycholexical approach to taxonomy, each observer rates the extent to which each of the trait adjectives is similar or dissimilar to one or more "target" individuals. For example, a study might involve 100 men, each of whom is rated on 60 adjectives by his wife. This *matrix of observations* is then analyzed in terms of whether certain adjectives are used similarly and could therefore be grouped or clustered together. Intuitively, we might expect people who are described as quiet also to be described as shy and thoughtful as well as not outgoing and not assertive. These intuitions can be evaluated empirically by calculating correlation coefficients. Terms that are used similarly by most raters will show large positive correlations, whereas antonyms will be negatively correlated. Two terms that have little in common will have a correlation of near zero.

Each adjective can be correlated with every other adjective to form a *matrix of correlations*. In the example of 100 men rated by their wives on 60 adjectives, each of the adjectives can be correlated with each of the other adjectives to form a 60 × 60 matrix of correlations: Term 1 would be correlated with Terms 2, 3, 4, and so on out to Term 60, then Term 2 would be correlated with Terms 3, 4, 5, and so on out to Term 60, and so it would go for all 60 terms. This matrix would contain 1,770 nonredundant correlation coefficients. Perhaps it would be possible to make sense out of this massive matrix of correlations if one studied it long enough, but fortunately there are also ways to mathematically evaluate and simplify this set of data through a procedure called *factor analysis*. Although this procedure involves rather elaborate statistical algorithms, the logic of it is reasonably straightforward. Factor analysis attempts to identify a small number of hypothetical factors or dimensions that will account for the relationships among a larger number of items (in this case adjectives). Each factor will be defined by its relationship with a subset of adjectives. Some adjectives will be highly related to a factor and some will not. The strength of the relationship between an item and a hypothetical factor is described by a factor loading that is similar to a correlation coefficient.

Consider, for example, the *matrix of factor loadings* presented in table 2.4. These findings are derived from peer ratings of a large group of men and women who have participated in a research project that began in the late 1950s (McCrae & Costa, 1987). The column on the left lists pairs of adjectives that raters used to describe their friends who are participants in the Baltimore Longitudinal Study of Aging. In this case, the factor analytic results suggested that this list of adjectives could be described more simply in terms of five basic factors. Factor 1 is defined primarily by the first four adjective pairs: sociable–retiring, affectionate–reserved, talkative–quiet, and warm–cold. These adjective pairs all have large loadings on the first factor (greater than .55), whereas most of the other adjective pairs have loadings of less than .20 on this factor. In the same way, each of the other factors is defined by a set of four pairs of adjectives. Although each factor represents a hypothetical entity, that entity can be defined in part by the items that are highly related to it. These high factor loadings share something in common that is not shared with the near-zero loadings. It is up to each investigator to decide how to interpret what it is that the high loading items share in common. Notice that in a few cases (e.g., warm-cold and good natured-irritable) the adjective pairs load above .3 on two different factors. These dual loadings suggest that the adjective pairs are related to and help to define both Factor 1 and Factor 2.

The five basic factors represented in table 2.4 have emerged repeatedly from analyses of peer ratings in a variety of samples: air force officers and cadets, fraternity brothers, Peace Corps trainees, and spouses. Recent work has shown that these five factors can also be

TABLE 2.4

Factor Loadings of Adjective Pairs in a Sample of Peer Ratings by Friends
(N = 738)

Adjective Pairs	Factors				
	I	II	III	IV	V
Sociable–retiring	.71	.08	.08	−.14	.08
Affectionate–reserved	.65	.25	−.15	−.08	.12
Talkative–quiet	.64	−.19	.00	.01	.06
Warm–cold	.57	.54	.06	−.05	.09
Softhearted–ruthless	.27	.70	.11	.12	−.01
Forgiving–vengeful	.11	.70	.16	−.15	.07
Selfless–selfish	−.02	.65	.22	−.07	.04
Good-natured–irritable	.34	.61	.16	−.17	.09
Careful–careless	−.07	.11	.72	−.08	−.01
Reliable–undependable	.04	.23	.68	.14	.05
Well-organized–disorganized	−.02	−.05	.68	.14	.05
Hardworking–lazy	.17	.03	.66	−.07	.14
Calm–worrying	−.05	.20	−.05	−.79	.01
At ease–nervous	.08	.21	.05	−.77	.06
Relaxed–high-strung	−.04	.34	.02	−.66	.01
Secure–insecure	.16	−.07	.39	−.63	.08
Original–conventional	.12	.08	−.04	−.06	.67
Creative–uncreative	.09	.11	.25	−.08	.56
Imaginative–down-to-earth	.03	−.10	−.12	.16	.54
Broad interest–narrow interests	.20	.18	.27	−.15	.52

Adapted from table 3, McCrae & Costa (1987). Used with permission.

Loadings above .4 are printed in italics. Positive loadings signify a positive relationship with the adjective on the left; negative loadings indicate a relationship with the adjective on the right.

replicated in adjective self-ratings and personality questionnaires (McCrae & Costa, 1987). These five factors (sometimes called the Big Five) are generally assigned the following labels:

    I. Extraverted or Surgent versus Introverted
    II. Agreeable or Likeable versus Antagonistic
    III. Conscientious versus Negligent
    IV. Emotionally Stable versus Emotionally Unstable or Neurotic
    V. Inquiring Intellect or Open to Experience versus Closed to Experience

Reducing the enormous number of trait descriptors in the English language to a small number of useful dimensions is an important achievement in the search for a taxonomy of personality variables. These five factors provide us with a basic framework for describing how people think about others and themselves. This framework qualifies as a significant advance for several reasons (Briggs, 1989). First, it provides a structure for researchers to use when constructing rating scales and self-report measures of personality; it helps to ensure that the domain of personality trait terms will be sampled broadly and systematically, and thereby serves to enhance the content validity of these measures. Second, it allows us to locate the seemingly endless supply of new constructs and measures in relation to what is already known; it clarifies the relations between what is new and what is established, and it exposes areas of needless redundancy. Third, it enables us to generate more precise hypotheses when attempting to relate personality variables to other constructs and measures. And finally, it suggests that these five dimensions deserve special attention in the continuing search for the mechanisms underlying individual differences in personality.

Although this five-factor model of the structure of personality ratings has emerged reliably across a number of studies, it is also important to examine how these dimensions stand up when compared across different modes of measurement. For example, Costa and McCrae (1985) have developed the NEO Personality Inventory, which measures the five basic factors along with a number of more narrowly defined constructs. To evaluate the validity of their measure and the five-factor model more generally, they have collected a variety of kinds of information on the individuals participating in the Baltimore Longitudinal Study of Aging mentioned earlier. The correlations presented in table 2.5 compare self-reports on the NEO Personality Inventory with ratings by spouses and with the average rating of several peers on a parallel version of the inventory.

The correlations in this table represent two important kinds of validity coefficients. The ones in italics that run diagonally through the table are called *convergent validity coefficients;* the rest of the correlations are *discriminant validity coefficients.* Convergent validity means that the correlation coefficient is assessing the relationship between two variables that are conceptually the same (e.g., both scales measure Extraversion) even though one is a self-report and the other a peer or spouse rating. In contrast, the discriminant validity coefficients reported in this table measure different constructs (e.g., the correlation between Extraversion and Agreeableness) using different observers. Ideally, the convergent validity coefficients should be large relative to the discriminant validity coefficients. This holds true for each type of comparison. Self-reported Extraversion correlates .53 with the spouse's rating and .44 with the average rating across several peers, but is relatively uncorrelated with the spouse's ratings of the other four

TABLE 2.5

Correlations of Self-Reports with Spouse and Peer Ratings Using the Five-Factor Model

	Self-reported factors				
Spouse Ratings	I	II	III	IV	V
I Extraversion	.53	.18	−.01	.09	.07
II Agreeableness	.14	.60	.03	.03	.09
III Conscientiousness	−.23	.15	.57	−.05	−.06
IV Neuroticism	.03	.18	−.01	.53	−.10
V Openness	−.11	.00	−.06	−.07	.59
Average of Peer Ratings					
I Extraversion	.47	.02	.02	−.04	−.25
II Agreeableness	−.25	.30	−.12	−.12	.03
III Conscientiousness	−.02	.08	.43	−.14	.08
IV Neuroticism	−.02	.11	.14	.42	−.02
V Openness	.13	.02	−.13	.03	.57

Adapted from Table 2, McCrae & Costa (in press) and Table 6, McCrae & Costa (1987). Used with permission.

Convergent validity coefficients are printed in italics. Correlations in upper half of table are based on $N = 144$; for the lower half, $N = 255$ to 267.

dimensions (the next highest correlation is −.23 with Conscientiousness) or with the average ratings of several peers for the other four dimensions (the highest correlation is −.25 with Agreeableness). This same pattern holds across the various scales and observers and suggests that individuals and informed observers agree about what is meant by these five personality dimensions as measured by the NEO Personality Inventory.

Why Measure Personality Variables?

One of the points made at the beginning of the chapter was that measurement is a means to an end, useful only in proportion to what it allows us to achieve. Psychology as a science is characterized by two, broad strategies of research: *experimental* and *correlational* (Cronbach, 1957). The experimental approach emphasizes manipulation and control. The experimenter is interested primarily in changes that he or she has produced. The experimenter studies how manipulating a particular variable or treatment condition (the *independent* variable) changes behavior, attitudes, feelings, etc. (the *dependent* variable or outcome measure). In its most straightforward form, the experiment contrasts participants in a treatment condition with those in a control condition. Ideally the members of the two groups would be exactly the same before the treatment. Any individual variation that exists naturally prior to the manipulation is a problem (called *error variance*) that needs to be avoided or minimized.

Ironically, it is this natural individual variation (this "error variance") that is of primary interest to the correlational researcher. The correlationist emphasizes the variation that occurs naturally among individuals, between groups, between the genders, and across species. The correlational approach does not necessarily involve the correlation coefficient as its statistical index, and another common name for this approach is differential psychology.

Personality research by and large is located in the correlational tradition. Personality variables involve naturally occurring differences among people and there is no way to manipulate or control experimentally characteristics of this sort. Furthermore, it would be unethical to study personality as a dependent variable (that is, to manipulate other variables in order to determine their impact on an individual's personality) except perhaps in the case of psychotherapy in which an individual wishes for certain changes to occur. Thus, in the science of personality, the emphasis is more on careful measurement than on rigorous manipulation. Researchers study individual differences in relation to three important kinds of questions.

1. *The study of ontogeny:* What are the origins of an individual's personality and how do these characteristics emerge over time?
2. *The study of structure:* What are basic dimensions of an individual's personality and how do the parts fit together to form a whole?
3. *The study of prediction:* What can we infer about an individual's future behavior given what we know now?

The subsequent chapters in this book will focus on these issues from a variety of perspectives. The information presented is grounded on the principles of conceptualization and measurement that have been introduced in this chapter. At times, it may be easy to overlook the fact that the various concepts and ideas are always tied to specific measures or indicators that may or may not be adequate. In evaluating the various ideas and arguments, it is always important to examine the measures with a critical eye. Have researchers established the reliability and validity of the measure? Have they used multiple modes of measurement?

Within the field of personality, researchers often disagree with regard to such fundamental issues as the appropriate mode of measurement (e.g., self-report or behavioral indices), the unit of analysis (e.g., traits or motives), and the level of analysis (e.g., broad or narrow constructs). Some researchers even argue that our present approach is completely wrongheaded because it focuses on how individuals differ from one another rather than on the individuals as individuals (Lamiell, 1987). As you learn more about these competing ideas and approaches, you will have to decide for yourself which of them make the most sense and which offer the most compelling evidence.

Summary

Formal methods for assessing personality arose out of practical concerns such as identifying individuals who would be productive, who would handle stress well, or who would get along with others in a group. The goal of personality assessment is to identify a relevant variable or personal characteristic, to define it unambiguously, and to devise a way to measure it that is consistent with the definition. The process of defining a characteristic is called conceptualization, and the process of choosing appropriate measures is called operationalization. Both processes push researchers toward clarity and precision as they define their concepts in terms of tangible indicators. Typically, the researcher assigns a number or value to represent an individual's standing on a particular variable in terms of a standard unit of measurement.

Although the number of potential personality variables is enormous, researchers have studied the words people use to describe others and themselves in order to develop a systematic way to classify personality traits. The most widely accepted taxonomy of personality descriptors is the five-factor model that was derived from factor analyses of peer ratings. A matrix of observations by peers is summarized in terms of a matrix of correlations among the observations, which in turn is reduced to a matrix of factor loadings wherein each hypothetical factor is defined by its relationship with the originally observed variables. Although this model is empirically derived, it has emerged consistently in a variety of samples. Thus, these five factors provide a basic set of dimensions that seem important for the description of personality.

Personality characteristics are generally complex, and no one indicator or measure can represent adequately the richness and diversity of a concept. Any particular indicator will be subject to specific flaws, biases, and shortcomings. The best way around these limitations is to use multiple indicators involving different methods and perspectives. The more varied the methods and perspectives, the more likely that the problems and weaknesses will balance out and that the concept will be measured in a full and fair manner. Common modes of measurement include self-report trait inventories, subjective or objective ratings by peers, behavioral measures, and physiological measures. A multi-method, multiperspective approach to measurement enables the researcher to examine whether the concept looks the same from different angles. If diverse measures agree, the researcher has more confidence in the results. Convergence among measures is one way of demonstrating that the various indicators are in fact measuring the correct concept.

The adequacy of a measure is evaluated in several ways. Reliability indexes estimate how much error has occurred when an individual is assigned a particular value on a measure. The higher the reliability, the more accurate are the assigned values. A measure is said to be valid to the extent that there is evidence to support a particular claim or inference. Convergent validity involves showing empirical relationships among measures that should be related conceptually. Discriminant validity involves showing the absence of a relationship between measures that are conceptually distinct. Construct validity requires evidence that an indicator (or set of indicators) actually measures a specific concept or construct. Criterion validity requires evidence that an indicator will predict scores on a particular criterion or outcome measure.

Being able to measure aspects of an individual's personality enables researchers to test their ideas. Hypothesis testing is central to the process of scientific inquiry, and thus personality measurement provides the basis for the scientific study of personality.

SUGGESTED READINGS

Angleitner, A., & Wiggins, J. S. (Eds.). (1985). *Personality assessment via questionnaires: Current issues in theory and measurement.* Berlin: Springer-Verlag, 1985. A recent review of important issues in the construction and use of personality questionnaires. Some of the chapters will be too technical for those outside the field, but the volume provides a good starting point for individuals interested in exploring specific topics.

Fiske, D. W. (1971). *Measuring the concepts of personality.* Chicago: Aldine. An excellent introduction to the study of personality by one of the key participants in the OSS Assessment Project. Fiske provides a broad-minded look at personality measurement, posing questions and discussing issues in a down-to-earth manner. Nevertheless, his book focuses on how to define and measure personality attributes for the purpose of doing basic research in the field of personality.

Lanyon, R. I., & Goodstein, L. D. *Personality assessment* (2nd ed.). New York: Wiley, 1982. A useful introduction to personality assessment in applied settings. It reviews various approaches to clinical assessment and presents well-known examples of each. It also covers basic psychometric principles.

West, S. G. (Ed.). (1983, September). Personality

and prediction: Nomothetic and idiographic approaches. *Journal of Personality, 51.* During the 1970s and early 1980s, the field of personality went through a period of rigorous self-examination regarding the utility of personality traits in the prediction of behavior. This special issue contains contributions by major researchers in the field, who summarize and present evidence in support of various positions.

West, S. G. (Ed.). (1986, March). Methodological developments in personality research. *Journal of Personality* (special issue), *54.* Personality assessment is a necessary part of personality research. This collection of

articles examines recent developments in the scientific study of personality and locates assessment issues within this larger context.

Wiggins, J. S. (1973). *Personality and prediction: Principles of personality measurement.* Reading, MA: Addison-Wesley, 1973. An in-depth study of personality assessment with an emphasis on the prediction of socially relevant criteria. This book examines a number of technical issues in the practice of personality assessment, and it is an important resource book for anyone considering graduate study in personality or clinical psychology.

REFERENCES

Allport, G. W. (1937). *Personality: A psychological interpretation.* New York: Holt.

Allport, G. W. (1966). *Pattern and growth in personality.* New York: Holt, Rinehart, & Winston.

Allport, G. W., & Odbert, H. S. (1936). Trait names: A psycho-lexical study. *Psychological Monographs, 47,* No. 211.

Briggs, S. R. (1989). The optimal level of measurement for personality constructs. In D. Buss & N. Cantor (Eds.), *Personality research for the 1990s* (pp. 246-260). New York: Springer-Verlag.

Campbell, D. T., & Fiske, D. W. (1959). Convergent and discriminant validity by the multitrait-multimethod matrix. *Psychological Bulletin, 56,* 81–105.

Chaplin, W. F., John, O. P., & Goldberg, L. R. (1988). Conceptions of states and traits: Dimensional attributes with ideals as prototypes. *Journal of Personality and Social Psychology, 54,* 541–557.

Costa, P. T., Jr., & McCrae, R. R. (1985). *The NEO Personality Inventory manual.* Odessa, FL: Psychological Assessment Resources.

Cronbach, L. J. (1957). The two disciplines of

scientific psychology. *American Psychologist, 12,* 671–684.

Cronbach, L. J., & Meehl, P. E. (1955). Construct validity in psychological tests. *Psychological Bulletin, 52,* 281–302.

Epstein, S. (1983). Aggregation and beyond: Some basic issues in the prediction of behavior. *Journal of Personality, 51,* 360–392.

Eysenck, H. J. (1983). Cicero and the state–trait theory of anxiety: Another case of delayed recognition. *American Psychologist, 38,* 114–115.

Fiske, D. W. (1971), *Measuring the concepts of personality.* Chicago: Aldine.

Goldberg, L. (1981). Language and individual differences: The search for universals in personality lexicons. In L. Wheeler (Ed.), *Review of personality and social psychology* (Vol. 2, pp. 141–165). Beverly Hills, CA: Sage.

John, O. P., Angleitner, A., & Ostendorf, F. (1988). The lexical approach to personality: A historical review of trait taxonomic research. *European Journal of Personality, 2,* 171–203.

Kaplan, A. (1964). *The conduct of inquiry:*

Methodology for behavioral science. San Francisco: Chandler.

Lamiell, J. T. (1987). *The psychology of personality: An epistemological inquiry.* New York: Columbia.

MacKinnon, D. W. (1944). The structure of personality. In J. McV. Hunt (Ed.), *Personality and the behavior disorders.* New York: Ronald Press.

McCrae, R. R., & Costa, P. T., Jr. (1987). Validation of the five-factor model of personality across instruments and observers. *Journal of Personality and Social Psychology, 52,* 81–90.

Paulhus, D. L. (1986). Self-deception and impression management in test responses. In A. Angleitner & J. S. Wiggins (Eds.), *Personality assessment via questionnaire: Current issues in theory and measurement* (pp. 143–165). Berlin: Springer-Verlag.

Runyan, W. M. (1983). Idiographic goals and methods in the study of lives. *Journal of Personality, 51,* 413–437.

U.S. Office of Strategic Services (1948). *Assessment of men: Selection of personnel for the office of strategic services.* New York: Rinehart.

Willerman, L., Turner, R. G., & Peterson, M. (1976). A comparison of the predictive validity of typical and maximal personality measures. *Journal of Research in Personality, 10,* 482–492.

CHAPTER 3

Heredity

DAVID C. ROWE

History
 Francis Galton: Founder of
  Behavioral Genetics
Modern Behavioral Genetics:
  Foundations
 Single Gene Versus
  Polygenic Traits
 Apportioning Trait Variation
 Shared Versus Nonshared
  Heredity
 Shared (or Common) and
  Nonshared Environment
 Discovering the Sizes of
  Genetic and Environmental
  Effects
Modern Behavioral Genetics:
  Findings and Implications

 Normal (Nonintellectual)
  Personality Traits
 Intellectual Traits
 Abnormal Traits
ACTIVITY BOX: **Family**
  Correlations for
  Authoritarianism
How Heredity Can Be Disguised
  in Environmental Concepts
Postscript
Summary
SUGGESTED READINGS
REFERENCES

When they were reunited at age thirty-nine years, the famous "Jim twins"—Jim Lewis and Jim Springer, identical twins separated at birth and raised by different families—discovered a trail of amazing coincidences. Comparing their lives, they learned of their common interest in woodworking; of their common experiences in school, such as liking math and disliking spelling; of their similar jobs as part-time security guards; and of a common medical problem, migraine headaches. A string of name coincidences also connected the pair: they had married first wives named Linda and second wives named Betty; they named their sons James Alan and James Allen; and their dogs, Toy. They had vacationed on the same three-block-long beach in Florida. A search by one of the twins led to their reunion. At the very least, these coincidences are uncanny; at most, they are an indication of how heredity (and coincidence) can make people born with identical genetic constitutions alike, despite rearing in different families, unknown to one another. These twins are among 44 pairs currently enrolled in Thomas Bouchard's new study of twins raised apart (Tellegen, Lykken, Bouchard, Wilcox, Segal, & Rich, in press). They join several hundred adult Swedish twins raised in different families, but with various degrees of separation (Pedersen, McClearn, Plomin, & Friberg, 1985), in a modern investigation of the lives of twins who were reared apart. The purpose of this chapter is to explore the evidence surrounding the idea that personality traits have partly genetic origins. Later in the chapter, we will return to a study of twins raised apart to learn what it can teach us about hereditary influences on personality traits and to place the results in the broader context of the field of *behavioral genetics*.

History

Behavioral genetics is a scientific discipline, with roots in psychology, genetics, biology, and related fields, that explores the empirical evidence on the *nurture* (meaning environment) versus *nature* (meaning heredity) debate. The term nature-nurture debate refers to an argument that is older than the discipline of psychology itself—a debate over whether personality traits result from genetic constitution or from environmental influence, or, if from some combination of them, how they combine and in what amounts. Even in antiquity people had some evidence for the "nature" side, namely, the regularity with which dogs could be bred for a variety of temperamental traits. Nothing particular in handling or conditions of rearing seemed to distinguish a retriever from a sheepdog, but it was clear that these behavioral tendencies ran in the dogs' blood lines and that they could be further modified by mating the right sets of parents. Nevertheless, human personality traits might be environmental in origin: the importance of child rearing as a molder of personality appears in scholarly writings from the Renaissance to the present.

Francis Galton: Founder of Behavioral Genetics

Behavioral genetics did not arise as a distinguishable scientific discipline until the mid-1800s. Francis Galton was directly responsible for founding behavioral genetics; an inventive man with diverse interests, he identified and labeled pressure bars in meteorology and created the correlation coefficient statistic to quantify familial resemblances for physical and behavioral traits. He invented the questionnaire-method of collecting data, and he anticipated that it might become something of an annoyance if overused. He traveled through Africa during the time of European exploration and wrote a best-seller entitled *The Art of Travel,* giving practical advice to people who might want to venture into the then mysterious continent of Africa.

His contribution to behavioral genetics was first to frame the question about genetic influences in terms of individual differences and, second, to propose practical methods by which the nature-nurture question could be studied scientifically. Galton's interest was, foremost, in human differences in intellectual ability. Fancher (1985) has speculated that Galton's fascination with this question may have had a source in a personal frustration. Despite being something of a child prodigy, as an undergraduate at the prestigious Cambridge University Galton was unable to attain the top score on a rigorous examination in mathematics on which all students were ranked. Although probably disappointed, Galton did not lose the opportunity to observe that an enormous range of individual differences existed in mathematical performance: the gap between the top-place finishers and the remainder of students was often huge. Galton—possibly from his personal efforts—thought that mathematical ability, like physical strength, could be improved only to a limit even with the most grueling training. Beyond that, the remaining individual differences would reflect inborn differences in intellectual capacity and talent.

Galton made several clever proposals for demonstrating the suspected hereditary influence on intellectual abilities. His first design was a *family study* of "eminence"—great accomplishment in a field of human endeavor. The family study method involves tracing personality traits through blood relatives. Because relatives are genetically alike, they should show some resemblance for biologically inherited traits. In his book *Hereditary Genius,* Galton listed the names of people in the *pedigrees*—the family trees—of chosen individuals who were eminent as judges, statesmen, commanders, literary men, men of science, poets, artists, and clergy (his own younger half-cousin, Charles Darwin, was included). Galton noted the percentage of these immediate relatives of eminent people who themselves had eminent accomplishments. Figure 3.1 presents one such family pedigree from Galton's book. He then compared this percentage with the percentage of all Englishmen (men only because nineteenth century biographies and newspaper accounts of famous individuals were most often about men) who were eminent. The latter figure was quite low; Galton estimated that no more than 250 in each million Englishmen had made such an outstanding accomplishment as to be "eminent," a standing perhaps equal to that of people featured in *Time* cover stories today. Among fathers, brothers, and sons of eminent men, however, as many as 31 percent to 48 percent of these relatives were themselves eminent. Eminence was passed on in families, Galton decided, and he regarded this as the solid proof he needed of biological inheritance of intellectual and temperamental traits.

Galton was, however, aware of a problem with the family method—namely, the confounding of heredity and family environmental treatments. Biological relatives usually shared greater wealth and social advantage than other Englishmen. Therefore, they may have acquired the traits to make their outstanding intellectual and social accomplishments from these favorable family environments. Galton replied with the invention of yet another method to study the nature–nurture question: the adoption study method. He proposed looking at the eminence of the adopted sons of Italian Roman Catholic clergy. They had social advantages, but none of the biological advantages of his English comparison group. In accord with his belief, the adoptees were not eminent; environmental advantage did not appear to be the key to eminence. Galton admitted, however, that his Italian kinships had not been done with the same thoroughness as the English ones.

The last method Galton invented was the twin study method. He

FIGURE 3.1

Pedigree of a Family from Francis Galton's *Hereditary Genius*

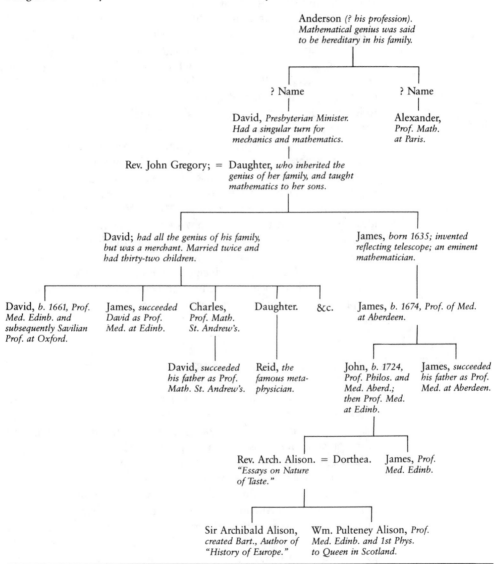

Anderson *(? his profession)*. *Mathematical genius was said to be hereditary in his family.*

? Name

? Name

David, *Presbyterian Minister. Had a singular turn for mechanics and mathematics.*

Alexander, *Prof. Math. at Paris.*

Rev. John Gregory; = Daughter, *who inherited the genius of her family, and taught mathematics to her sons.*

David; *had all the genius of his family, but was a merchant. Married twice and had thirty-two children.*

James, *born 1635; invented reflecting telescope; an eminent mathematician.*

David, *b. 1661, Prof. Med. Edinb. and subsequently Savilian Prof. at Oxford.*

James, *succeeded David as Prof. Med. at Edinb.*

Charles, *Prof. Math. St. Andrew's.*

Daughter.

&c.

James, *b. 1674, Prof. of Med. at Aberdeen.*

David, *succeeded his father as Prof. Math. St. Andrew's.*

Reid, *the famous meta-physician.*

John, *b. 1724, Prof. Philos. and Med. Aberd.; then Prof. Med. at Edinb.*

James, *succeeded his father as Prof. Med. at Aberdeen.*

Rev. Arch. Alison. = Dorthea.
"Essays on Nature of Taste."

James, *Prof. Med. Edinb.*

Sir Archibald Alison, *created Bart., Author of "History of Europe."*

Wm. Pulteney Alison, *Prof. Med. Edinb. and 1st Phys. to Queen in Scotland.*

noted that there were two kinds of twins—twins who appeared physically alike at birth and twins who were physically different. Based on questionnaires and biographical materials, he discovered that the twins who were unalike at birth had remained unalike both in personality and appearance in adulthood; in other words, rearing environments were unable to overcome their initial differences. In contrast, he found enduring personality similarity for the physically alike twins. This was the first twin study to consider twins' life-time similarity in behavioral traits.

In his will, Galton made his final contribution to behavioral genetics. He left moneys to the University of London to establish a chair in eugenics. A succession of distinguished scientists have occupied this chair, including Karl Pearson, who perfected Galton's correlation coefficient (hence, "Pearson correlation"), and Ronald A. Fisher, the outstanding statistician and geneticist. The word *eugenics* (meaning well-born) describes another of Galton's intellectual legacies. Galton argued that the human race could be improved by encouraging intellectually bright people to marry and have large families. Although Galton thought of eugenics as a matter of social policy encouraging large families, some social activists proposed a more negative form of eugenics in which some people would be prevented from having children. In Europe's darkest hours of World War II, the Nazis put this idea into action in their philosophy of racial superiority and in their program of extermination carried out against the Jewish people and against other groups in German society. This history of the abuse of genetics—in which genetic principles were distorted to serve political aims—is a sadly tragic one. Scientists and citizens have a responsibility to oppose inaccurate or oversimplified renderings of genetic principles and to oppose their abuse in the political arena.

Modern Behavioral Genetics: Foundations

Modern behavioral genetics has gone far beyond Galton's beginnings. Workers in the field today, like Galton, are interested in the genetic bases of personality traits. As he did, they use the family, twin, and adoption study methods to separate genetic and family-environmental influences on behavior. At the same time, some new aims are apparent. Using the revolutionary techniques of molecular genetics and new advances in statistics, some researchers are probing for single genes that influence behavior. Already, one dominant gene has been isolated that may contribute to an inherited form of manic depressive psychosis in the Pennsylvania Old Order Amish (Kolata, 1986). The search for single genes influencing behavior will often fail, however, because behavioral traits are usually influenced by many genes, each one with a small and barely measurable effect. Such traits are referred to as *polygenic* traits (from poly, meaning "many").

Another direction taken by human behavioral geneticists is analyzing environmental influences. One theme of this chapter is that, without making provision for genetic influences, one cannot properly gauge environmental ones. Theories in psychology can be seriously flawed if genetic influences are misinterpreted as environmental. An example is that many researchers have attributed children's authoritarianism, a personality trait characterized by a belief that authority and tradition are always right, to the social influence of parental role models. We will see later that this is an unfounded attribution.

The balance of this section will present some fundamental concepts in the study of the nature-nurture question. We can then explore the contribution of heredity to normal traits and abnormal traits, and also to trait variation often interpreted as environmental.

Single Gene Versus Polygenic Traits

Although many discoveries in genetics were made in the first half of the twentieth century, we must move our story ahead to the discoveries with the greatest bearing on behavioral genetics. In 1953, James Watson and Francis Crick made this century's greatest biological discovery. In a two-page paper published in *Nature,* they announced the structure of the DNA (deoxyribose nucleic acid) molecule, the bearer of heredity. Although we cannot review the details of molecular genetics here, we do note that molecular genetics can explain the structure of the gene as consisting of a segment of DNA. In these segments, biochemically active molecules are arranged in a sequence analogous to letters in a word. These "letters" (e.g., the four biochemical bases, Tymine, Adenine, Cytosine, and Guanine) comprise the genetic code, with different combinations of three letters in sequence coding for each of the twenty amino acid building blocks of proteins. A string of these biochemical "words" form a gene, the unit of genetic information. Although it was once thought that one gene coded for only one protein product, we know now that the situation is much more complex. Nevertheless, this way of thinking about the gene is generally correct, and it is useful for understanding behavioral genetics.

Genes always occur in pairs: one gene is always inherited from one's mother, the other from one's father. For a behavioral geneticist, the less interesting genes are those that are the same in all individuals. The more interesting ones are those that come in slightly different forms so that genetic constitutions can vary among people and within a person. The genes involved in eye pigmentation vary in this way. If B produces brown pigment and b blue pigment, the genetic constitution of a person for a single gene pair allows three possibilities: BB, Bb, and bb. In other words, the person may have brown eyes (BB, Bb), where the brown pigment produced by a single gene is enough to color the whole eye; or blue pigmentation (bb). The possibilities for a child will naturally depend on the genetic constitution of the parents. For example, the marriage of two brown-eyed individuals (BB × BB) can produce only brown-eyed children, whereas the marriage of two brown-eyed individuals with mixed genetic constitutions (Bb × Bb) can produce children with brown or blue eyes. In genetics, the term *genotype* refers to the genetic constitution of an individual; the term *phenotype* refers to the trait that is actually observed and measured in some way. From this example, we note that different genotypes (BB, Bb) can give rise to the same phenotype (brown color).

Single, defective genes typically produce extreme behavioral abnormality. For example, Tay-Sachs syndrome is caused by a single gene and produces severe mental retardation and aberrant behaviors such as self-mutilation. Medical scientists have classified over five-hundred biochemical disorders that have single-gene origins. These single gene traits, however, are not usually of interest to psychologists, who deal with trait variation in a "normal" range or who deal with psychopathology lying at one extreme of a bell-shaped distribution.

Apportioning Trait Variation

We must therefore understand genetic and environmental influences on these polygenic personality traits. As an illustration, though, let us first consider a physical trait—height—that is known to be a polygenic trait. Height is affected by many genes that probably determine the level of growth hormone, the number of cell receptors for this hormone, and many other, related biochemical events. Variation among individuals in *phenotype* (height in this case) is the result of variation in the *genotype* (e.g., aabbcc to AABBCC and all possible combinations in between) plus variation in *environmental* factors that influence height (e.g., diet). If genetic variation (the different genotypes) is small relative to the environmental variation, then we say that the trait has a low *heritability*. If this variation is large, then we say that the trait has a high heritability. Heritability is a statistic defined as V_g/V_p, where V_g is the genetic variance and V_p is the phenotypic variance.

Figure 3.2 illustrates this idea. The height of children was imagined to be manipulated in two ways: either by varying diets to include primarily "junk" foods or healthful foods or by picking parents who differ greatly in height—NBA basketball players versus jockeys. As this example illustrates, the parent–child resemblance produced by heredi-

FIGURE 3.2

Family Dietary Versus Parental Heights "Manipulations" of Children's Heights

FAMILY DIET

"Junk Foods"

Potato chips

Milkshake

"Healthy Foods"

Steak

Grapes

Orange

Height of Children

5'7"

5'7"

PARENTAL HEIGHTS

Height of Children

Saddle

Jockey

5'4"

Basketball

11

NBA Basketball Players

6'

ty would have a great effect, whereas little height difference would be found among children with different diets. This example, although exaggerated to make a point, is not far from the truth. The heritability of height in America is about 90 percent, so that most height differences result from the effects of different parental heights and genetic recombination (that is, the particular set of genes a child has received from each parent). Little variation is explained by family differences in nutrition or by other nonfamily environmental factors.

Some cautions apply to interpreting the heritability statistic (Plomin, DeFries, & McClearn, 1980). They are that heritability depends on the composition of the population; it is an imprecise number; and it does not apply to a single individual:

1. Heritability will depend on the population of people included in a particular study. When the range of genetic differences among people (relative to the total variation) is greater, the heritability tends to be high, because people drawn from above and below the population mean will have different genotypes. On the other hand, when the range of environmental variation is large, then the heritability tends to be low. Hence, a study including a range from poverty-stricken families to rich ones would tend to find a lower heritability for IQ than one including just middle-class families. Conversely, the more American social policies successfully equalize environmental opportunities for children's education, the more their remaining IQ differences will be genetic in etiology. Ironically, a more egalitarian American society probably would mean a higher heritability for IQ.

2. Heritability is an inexact number. Studies involve samples, not everyone. So the numbers deduced from them are usually imprecise. For instance, one opinion poll will show that 57 percent of the voters favor John Doe; another one, that 55 percent of the voters favor him. We may presume that Mr. Doe will win the election, although we do not know exactly what percentage of all people favor him. The same kind of sampling imprecision is found in the heritability statistic when sampling variation is the major source of difference among studies.

3. Heritability does not apply to a single person. A heritability of 70 does not mean that 70 percent of a single person's height was due to heredity. Heritability, however, can be used to estimate a person's *genotypic value* (his or her genetic potential for a trait) from information on how both the mother and the father scored on a trait (see behavioral genetic texts; Hay, 1985; Plomin, DeFries, & McClearn, 1980). Many of these same limitations, such as

dependence on population composition and imprecision, also apply to estimates of environmental influence.

Shared Versus Nonshared Heredity

Biological relatives share more or less of their heredity. Parent and children and siblings share about half their heredity. Parent and grandchild share about one-quarter. Cousins share about one-eighth. Therefore, for genetically influenced traits, brothers and sisters or parents and children will be more alike than "kissing cousins" and other, more distant relatives. The laws (in a scientific, not legal, sense) of genetics also state that neither parents-children nor siblings will be perfectly alike. For example, the sibling of a schizophrenic child has about a 10 percent risk of schizophrenia himself. That is a greater risk than to people in general because only about 1 percent of people in the American population would be diagnosed as schizophrenic. On the other hand, 90 percent of siblings of a schizophrenic child are themselves nonschizophrenic. In part, this reflects the process of inheritance, because one sibling may have inherited the genes disposing toward schizophrenia from a parent, whereas the luckier child may not have inherited them. It is important to recognize that genetic laws predict certain values of the parent-child or sibling phenotypic correlation; but not exactly the same phenotypes for family members (except for identical twins for a completely congenital trait such as eye color).

Shared (or Common) and Nonshared Environment

Behavioral genetics also makes a partitioning of environmental influences into those that operate to make family members alike (the shared influences) and those that operate to make family members unalike (the nonshared influences). Literally thousands of scientific studies have been devoted to shared influences such as social class and intact versus divorced households (see table 3.1). These influences can be regarded as shared because siblings' exposure to them would be about equal. Their effect is to produce a correlation between siblings or between parent and child.

Unlike shared ones, nonshared influences involve factors making siblings (or parent-child pairs) different. An exemplar of a nonshared influence is birth order. Because siblings have different birth orders, environmental effects associated with the order of birth will operate to make siblings different from one another. Rowe and Plomin (1981) have categorized nonshared influences as accidental events, perinatal traumas, family constellation (e.g., birth order, birth spacing), sibling

TABLE 3.1

Common-Family and Within-Family Environmental Variables

Variable	Common family	Within family
Social class	P	
Parental religion	P	
Parental values	P	
Child-rearing styles	P	S
Father absence	P	
Maternal employment	P	
Neighborhood	P	
Family size		P
Birth order		P
Perinatal trauma		P
Peer groups	S	P
Teachers	S	P

Adapted from Rowe (1987), p. 220. Published with permission of the American Psychological Association.

Note: P = predominate emphasis; S = secondary emphasis.

mutual interaction, unequal parental treatments, and influences outside the family (for example, when siblings have different teachers). Such nonshared influences will usually reduce the sibling or parent-child trait correlation. As we will see later, nonshared environmental influences appear to play a role about equal with that of heredity in the determination of nonintellectual personality traits.

Discovering the Sizes of Genetic and Environmental Effects

In modern behavioral genetics, the procedures for discovering the sizes of genetic and environmental effects are complex. Instead of carrying out a study with a single type of family—such as adoptive siblings—it is now standard in behavioral genetics to combine data from several different family types in a single study. So, for instance, a study might include both adoptive children and twins. A procedure for estimating genetic and environmental effects is called *structural equation modeling*. It involves "fitting" equations that include genetic and environmental parameters to data from different family types. A parameter is simply an unknown number, like *x* or *y* in an algebraic equation. In a basic genetic model, the unknowns are heritability and the shared environmental effect. The process of "fitting" is one of picking the best values of the unknowns to reproduce the data correlations.

An example should help to clarify these ideas. The resemblance of adoptive siblings is due entirely to the shared environment of their adoptive homes. We find adoptive siblings when adoptive parents successively adopt two children. Each adoptive child, then, has a different set of biological parents. Because they have different parents, their hereditary constitution is dissimilar; a more exact way of saying this is that their hereditary constitution is uncorrelated. If we know their IQ correlation, we can write the following equation:

$$r_{IQ} = C$$

where r_{IQ} is the adoptive siblings' IQ correlation (their resemblance for intelligence) and C a common environment parameter. In other words, the equation means that their IQ resemblance is entirely due to sharing a family environment.

Monozygotic (MZ) twins, so-called "identical" twins, are the result of the division of a single fertilized egg cell and thus possess identical genetic heredity. Dizygotic (DZ) twins, so-called "fraternal twins," are each the product of different fertilized egg cells and so bear the same genetic resemblance to one another as ordinary siblings. MZ twins, when raised in the same family, have an IQ resemblance resulting from two influences: shared family environment, like the adoptive siblings' IQs, and heredity. Because MZ twins possess exactly the same genetic constitution, we can write another equation:

$$r_{IQ} = h^2 + C$$

where h^2 is the hereditary parameter and C is, as before, common family environment.

Using these two equations, we can solve for h^2 and C. For example, if the MZ twin correlation were .81 and the adoptive sibling correlation were .26, we arrive at an estimate of $C = .26$ and $h^2 = .55$. In other words, 55 percent of the variation in IQ scores in this hypothetical study was due to genetic variation; 26 percent was due to the effects of family environment. Other values of the correlations, however, could give nonsensical results. For example, if the MZ twins correlated .41 and the adoptive siblings correlated .47, then the estimate of heritability would be $-.06$. Because the heritability cannot be less than zero, one would have to conclude either that the heritability was zero or that the model was wrong for some reason (e.g., contrast effects in MZ twins such that they competed with one another and became dissimilar as a result).

Genetic models, of course, can be more complex than this example and involve more types of family relationships at once. They also can include more parameters, which permits the testing of more subtle and realistic assumptions about the influences on behavioral traits. For example, structural equation models can test for the consequences of *selective placement*. This term refers to adoptive agencies' trying to match the adoptive children's *biological* parents' traits with the *adoptive* parents' traits (e.g., placing higher social class children into high social class adoptive homes). Nevertheless, this example does show the essential elements of behavioral genetic work: having a genetic model that is expressible in a mathematical form and fitting that model to data correlations. These models, of course, state many ideas that we can understand intuitively, as we saw that heredity can contribute to the resemblance of one kind of relative (MZ twins) but not another kind of relative (adoptive siblings).

Modern Behavioral Genetics: Findings and Implications

In the century since Galton's *Hereditary Genius,* there has been a gradual accumulation of studies of normal personality traits, intellectual traits, and psychopathology. A remarkable feature of these data are their consistency and replicability; adoptive studies completed in the 1920s have found essentially the same results as those completed in the past decade, except that IQ heritability from recent studies is lower. Moreover, these studies together are beginning to point to some fairly general conclusions. This chapter will now turn to highlighting behavioral genetic knowledge about these categories of personality traits. It will identify some of the major generalizations—the mountains if you will—but not delve into every study or every controversial issue—the foothills around particular topics.

Normal (Nonintellectual) Personality Traits

The domain of normal personality traits is a broad one. A number of different classification schemes have been put forward in this domain, but we lack a single, unified scheme endorsed by most psychologists. Some agreement has been reached, however, that at least five dimensions of personality exist in personality rating data where knowledgeable raters describe the traits of friends and acquaintances (i.e., neuroticism, extraversion, openness, agreeableness, and conscientiousness; McCrae & Costa, 1986). Self-report studies can make do with no fewer than 3 broad dimensions of personality, such as Hans Eysenck's system of Neuroticism (i.e., anxiety, depression); Extraversion (i.e., sociability, impulsiveness); and Psychoticism (i.e., lack of empathy, cruelty; Eysenck, 1953; Eysenck & Eysenck, 1968). These broader dimensions, like Eysenck's "big three" dimensions just listed, are formed of some combination of more specific and narrow traits. The number of such specific trait dimensions may be large; for instance, Cattell identified sixteen subordinate dimensions of personality (Cattell, 1982). At this level, the best form of trait description may depend on one's purpose, as well as on the structure of personality itself.

One unifying feature of normal traits is that being near the average on the trait, rather than at either trait extreme, is probably most adaptive. For example, neither extreme shyness nor unbridled gregariousness is an adaptive trait—the former because one fails to make friends, the latter because one has many superficial acquaintances without forming close and enduring social ties. Assuming that these traits have been genetically selected, the average person would have a genotype balancing shy and sociable behavioral tendencies. Persons at an extreme would have one kind of genotype or the other and would be at a distinct social and possibly at a reproductive—meaning the chances of marrying and having children—disadvantage. According to evolutionary theory, traits such as these are likely to show a considerable heritability, and the behavioral genetic evidence supports this conclusion.

Although we could survey many kinds of evidence, one of the most easily interpreted studies is the comparison of identical twins raised apart and together. At the start of this chapter, we considered the case of the "Jim twins," whose life histories were so similar. From a single pair of MZ twins, however, one cannot separate chance similarities from real ones. With a group of MZ twins, on the other hand, one can compute the twins' correlation coefficient for a personality trait, and the statistical significance of this correlation would show that the pairs' resemblance is more than just a chance matching. MZ twins raised apart, because they were adopted into different families, lack the shared environmental experiences of siblings or twins raised in the same family. Even if the families were occasionally somewhat alike, they were surely more unalike than an upbringing under one roof with the same mother and father. For MZ twins raised apart, we can expect that their trait correlation is mostly due to their shared heredity. Hence, we can write the equation:

$$r_{\text{trait}} = h^2$$

where h^2 is heritability. For MZ twins raised together, common family environment is potentially an additional source of twins' trait resemblance. The equation for twins raised together is:

$$r_{\text{trait}} = h^2 + C$$

where C is the family environmental effect.

In the past ten years, a new sample of MZ twins raised apart has been collected at the University of Minnesota (Tellegen, Lykken, Bouchard, Wilcox, Segal, & Rich, in press). The sample currently numbers 44 twin pairs. These pairs come from both the United States and England. Half had been separated before one year of age; most of the remainder, in the preschool years. The separation time (number of years from separation to first contact) averaged thirty-four years. These twins were compared with a sample of 217 twins reared together in Minnesota. Both members of each twin pair completed the Multidimensional Personality Questionnaire independently.

Both the MZ twins reared apart and those reared together showed remarkable similarity in their personality test scores for eleven different personality traits (see table 3.2). An estimate of the effect of sharing a family environment on personality resemblance can be made by solving for C. Table 3.2 reveals that the values of C—simply the MZ-apart correlation subtracted from the MZ-together correlation—were about half negative and half positive. The average value of C across the eleven trait scales was only .03. In a more extensive analysis combining these data with data from two more samples, DZ twins raised apart and together, Tellegen et al. (in press) found that the common family environment effect was statistically significant for the Social Closeness trait (see the .28 environmental effect in table 3.2). Although we have emphasized the data from this one study of twins raised apart and together, the lack of substantial family effects is supported by many other studies and by other techniques of data analysis (see Rowe, 1987). The Activity Box presents another example of a personality trait—authoritarianism—showing a surprising level of genetic influence.

These results reveal a rather puzzling truth about personality. The average heritability of personality traits is substantial—about 50 percent based on the average of the correlations for MZ twins raised apart—but the effect of family environments on most traits is a very weak one. The real environmental effect resides in nonshared environmental influences. These influences account for the differences among identical twins (the fact that the MZ twin correlation is about .50 less than a perfect 1.0). Such nonshared influences may involve parenting in that parents can treat children (siblings) in the same family differently, but more probably they involve many kinds of environmental influenc-

TABLE 3.2

Twin Correlations for Monozygotic Twins Reared Apart and Together and Their Genetic and Environmental Interpretations

	Twin group and interpretation		
	MZ twins together: Environment plus heredity	MZ twins apart: Heredity only	Difference: Environment only
Multidimensional Personality Questionnaire scales	*r*-Together	*r*-Apart	(*r*-T − *r*-A)
Well-being	.58	.48	.10
Social potency	.65	.56	.09
Achievement	.51	.36	.15
Social closeness	.57	.29	.28
Stress reaction	.52	.61	−.09
Alienation	.55	.48	.07
Aggression	.43	.46	−.03
Control	.41	.50	−.09
Harm avoidance	.55	.49	.06
Traditionalism	.50	.53	−.03
Absorption	.49	.61	−.12
Number of twin pairs	217	44	
Mean correlation	.52	.49	.03

Data from Tellegen, Lykken, & Bouchard Jr. (1988), p. 1035. Used by permission.

es that are external to the family. Research on nonshared environmental factors is just beginning.

There are a couple of ways of thinking about the inheritance of personality. One is that if you were raised in a different family, with parents who used different child-rearing methods, who had different values, and who modeled different kinds of behaviors, you would be remarkably like the person you are now. Another is that children raised in the same family (exposed to one family environment) tend to be very different if their heredity is dissimilar. We know this because personality correlations for adoptive (i.e., biologically unrelated) siblings are very low.

This result is so counter to everyday intuitions that it is hard to understand or accept. One reason is that we notice familial similarities in personality and tend to attribute them to the family environment. However, this attribution neglects the heredity that parent and child (or siblings) share. The second is that we have strong emotional reactions

Family Correlations for Authoritarianism

Many people believe that social attitudes originate in a child's imitating or adopting parental attitudes. We consider here one social attitude, authoritarianism, an attitude characterized by a rigid acceptance of authority and tradition and by a lack of acceptance of any form of nonconformity or difference. This social attitude could be learned at one's parents' knees. Is it?

The first step of this activity box is to complete the authoritarian personality questionnaire. If you can, ask a brother, sister, or parent to complete it also. Follow the scoring instructions under the questionnaire.

Average scores range from 100 to 120; scores below 100 are more nonauthoritarian; and scores over 120 are more authoritarian. If you have tested other family members, determine whether you and they scored alike—within 10 points of one another.

The second issue is what influence produces this social attitude. We suggest that you first try to list all the family environmental reasons that family members score alike on this questionnaire. Next, list all the *genetic* reasons you think family members might score alike.

Sandra Scarr (1981) found results suggesting that family environment may not be so important in shaping this social attitude. She compared familial correlations in nonadoptive families (in other words, ordinary families) and adoptive families (in which members were not related by blood). The table that follows summarizes her results.

	Nonadoptive: Environment plus heredity	Adoptive: Environment only	Difference: Heredity
Father Child	.37	.14	.23
Mother Child	.41	.00	.41
Sibling	.36	.14	.22

You can see that most of the family resemblance is located in the nonadoptive families. Discuss what this implies about the inheritance of authoritarianism.

Scarr also discovered that a high IQ was negatively correlated with authoritarianism (a person with a higher IQ score tended to score lower on an authoritarianism scale). She interpreted this result to mean that people tend to reason to their own beliefs about authoritarianism—so that family environments are less important in creating acceptance of this social attitude than a person's own thinking processes. What do you think?

QUESTIONNAIRE

Answer each question, entering the number value of your response in the space provided. For items marked (8−), subtract the number value of your response from 8 before entering it. For example, if you answered question 2 this way: agree a little (5) you would enter 3. Your score is the sum of your entries.

1 = I disagree very much
2 = I disagree pretty much
3 = I disagree a little
4 = No Opinion
5 = I agree a little
6 = I agree pretty much
7 = I agree very much

_____ 1. It is essential for learning or effective work that our teachers or bosses outline in detail what is to be done and how to do it.

(8−) 2. One of the most important things children should learn is when to disobey authorities.

(8−) 3. People ought to pay more attention to new ideas, even if they seem to go against the grain of American life.

_____ 4. Most people don't realize how much our lives are controlled by plots hatched in secret places.

_____ 5. Most of our social problems could be solved if we could somehow get rid of the immoral, crooked, and feebleminded people.

_____ 6. Human nature being what it is, there will always be war and conflict.

(8−) 7. It is highly unlikely that astrology will ever be able to explain anything.

_____ 8. What youth needs most is strict discipline, rugged determination, and the will to work and fight for family and country.

ACTIVITY BOX (Continued)

Family Correlations for Authoritarianism

——— 9. No weakness or difficulty can hold us back if we have enough will power.

(8–) 10. If it weren't for the rebellious ideas of youth, there would be less progress in the world.

(8–) 11. Most honest people admit to themselves that they have sometimes hated their parents.

(8–) 12. Books and movies ought to give a more realistic picture of life, even if they show that evil sometimes triumphs over good.

——— 13. Every person should have complete faith in a supernatural power whose decision he obeys without question.

(8–) 14. The artist and the professor are probably more important to society than the businessman and the manufacturer.

(8–) 15. The findings of science may some day show that many of our most cherished beliefs are wrong.

(8–) 16. An urge to jump from high places is probably the result of unhappy personal experiences rather than anything inborn.

——— 17. Nowadays more and more people are prying into matters that should remain personal and private.

(8–) 18. In spite of what we read about the wild sex life of people in important places, the real story is about the same in any group of people.

——— 19. No sane, normal, decent person could ever think of hurting a close friend or relative.

——— 20. Sex crimes, such as rape and attacks on children, deserve more than mere imprisonment; such criminals ought to be publicly whipped or worse.

---

to events in our families, and it is hard not to believe that they affect us. These data do not disprove an impact; but they do show that the impact is not one to make parents and children alike. We can perhaps accept the result more readily if we realize that personality traits depend in part on how the brain is structured and how it operates. The unprecedented discoveries of neuroscience show that moods and emotions depend on neurotransmitters and on other brain biochemicals. It is probably through influencing brain function that heredity makes MZ twins who were raised apart alike, despite their different life histories. And such genetically regulated brain function is probably equally important for our own personality development.

Intellectual Traits

More than any other trait, the inheritance of IQ (i.e., general problem-solving ability and knowledge) has sparked bitter controversy and endless debate. In the early 1970s, this debate flared over the inheritance of racial differences in mean IQ scores—an issue that has subsided in the 1980s. The practical use of IQ and IQ-correlated aptitude tests in the placement of children into classes for the educationally handicapped or gifted, in the selection of students into prestigious universities, and in the assignment of employees to particular jobs gives them a practical importance that is greater than most other personality tests. When dollars and real-world decisions are at stake, a debate over IQ testing takes on some urgency. In this chapter, we will not discuss the research literature on the fairness of IQ tests to minorities and poor children (see Jensen, 1980). Instead, we will focus on the inheritance of IQ scores and, complementarily, on family environmental influences on them.

Table 3.3 shows the IQ correlations for different pairs of biological and nonbiological relatives based on a summary of 111 studies (Bouchard & McGue, 1981). The pattern of correlation is clear: the more closely two people are biologically related, the greater is their IQ correlation. Some comparisons can be challenged. For example, some

TABLE 3.3

Kinship Correlations for IQ

Kinship	Correlation	Number of Pairings
MZ twins reared together	.86	4,672
MZ twins reared apart	.72	65
DZ twins reared together	.60	5,546
Siblings reared together	.47	26,473
Siblings reared apart	.24	203
Single parent–child reared together	.42	8,433
Single parent–child reared apart	.22	814
Half-siblings	.31	200
Cousins	.15	1,176
Adopted/natural siblings	.29	345
Adopted/adopted siblings	.34	369
Adoptive parent–adopted child	.19	1,397
Spouses	.33	3,817

From Figure 1, Bouchard & McGue (1981), p. 1056. Used by permission.

scholars have attributed the greater IQ resemblance of MZ than DZ twins to unequal treatments, whereby MZ twins receive more equal IQ-relevant treatments than DZ twins and so become more alike in IQ. Although this argument is plausible on its face, recent evidence suggests that greater treatment similarities of MZ twins (such as dressing alike or sharing a room) fail to make them more alike in IQ (Loehlin & Nichols, 1976). Rather, greater similarity of MZ twins appears to be due to genetic similarity. Note the correlation of .72 for MZ twins raised apart (excluding Cyril Burt's MZ twins-apart data, which are under suspicion of fraud; Hearnshaw, 1979). Moreover, although various nongenetic explanations could be constructed for one relationship or another, the total pattern provides convincing evidence of genetic influence. Recent estimates place the heritability of IQ at about 50 percent (Henderson, 1982). A reasonable target range for IQ heritability is from 40 percent to 70 percent, which includes "real" differences in heritability, because the figure will change from one sample of people to another, as was mentioned earlier.

The field of developmental behavioral genetics is concerned with genetic influences over the period of biological maturation and aging, that is, over the life span (Plomin, 1983). This field concentrates on the potential of genetic factors to explain both change and constancy in development. The within-person stability of IQ is moderate, with correlations of about .70 between late childhood and adulthood. One reason we know that genes are important developmentally is that the IQ of an adult person—namely, a biological parent—will correlate with the IQ of an infant—namely, this parent's adopted-away child (Plomin, & DeFries, 1985). The only physical link between these two persons is their shared heredity. The IQ of the adult, however, represents effects of genes in a fifteen-to-twenty-five-year-old person; the IQ of the infant represents the action of copies of the same genes at one to three years of age. Thus, the correlation shows us that some of the same genes can produce IQ at both ages, the originals in the parent and their active copies in the child. Even late in life, heredity exerts a profound influence on IQ test scores. Jarvik, Blum, and Varma (1972), in a study of elderly twins, found that elderly MZ twins' IQs remained very similar.

Genetic inheritance also can create changes in personality traits (Rowe, 1987). Genetic changes can occur because genes turn on and off during development. Newly active genes may favor one person's IQ more than another person's IQ at a particular age. Ronald Wilson (1978) had the insight to pursue genetic determinants of change in a long-term study in which twins took IQ tests throughout infancy and childhood. He found that children's IQs shifted with age, with some children improving and others falling behind. More interestingly, he discovered that the whole profile of IQ change was heritable. This point is illustrated by figure 3.3, which compares two twin pairs, one MZ and the other DZ. The IQ scores of the MZ twins changed in tandem; the growth curves for the two DZ individuals were different. The complex patterns of IQ change, which vary widely from one twin pair to another, seem most easily interpreted genetically, because the patterns are unique to each twin pair, but they are more similar in MZ twins than in DZ twins. In addition, genetic influence appears to create spurts and lags in physical growth and development (Fischbein, 1977a; 1977b).

Although a variety of intellectual performances are heritable, one of the most heritable of all intellectual traits is vocabulary. It may come as a surprise that vocabulary is the most heritable trait, because it should be self-evident that people are not born with specific genes representing different words in the English language. If words must be learned, then how can they be inherited?

The answer to this seeming paradox is that the structure of the brain must influence how easily words are learned. For most words, children have a variety of opportunities to learn them. A child might learn "penguin" from a TV science program, from a teacher who reads aloud to the class, from a cartoon like the popular "Bloom County," or from other family members. For an exposure to be effective, however, a child must disengage the word from its context and recognize its referent, a process that is easier for a concrete noun like "penguin" than an abstract one like "justice." Too, the word must be placed in long-term memory and there integrated meaningfully with other concepts. Recent information processing views of intelligence indicate that even less complex mental operations, such as letter recognition time and working memory capacity, are crucial for a high IQ (see Hunt, Lunneborg, & Lewis, 1975). From these brief examples, we can understand that processes of word acquisition can be the genetically dependent component of vocabulary knowledge. Although vocabulary tests can be culturally biased, they are, within a particular culture, an excellent means of assessing heritable components of intellectual performance.

The emphasis on heredity thus far should not be misleading. Twin and adoption studies also verify the importance of family environments as another determinant of IQ scores. The correlation for the combined adopted/natural and adopted/adopted sibling pairings was .30, meaning that 30 percent of IQ variation can be attributed to differences among families in intellectual stimulation in the home (see table 3.3). This boost may be especially beneficial to children who are genetically bright. A part of IQ variation is due to the *passive correlation* of genes and family environment in that parents who give their children a

FIGURE 3.3

IQ Profiles for Monozygotic and Dizygotic Twins

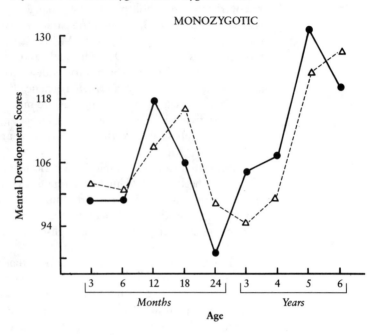

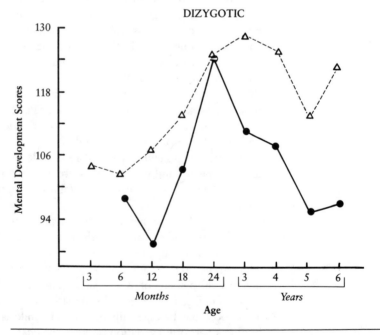

From Figure 1, Wilson (1978), p. 942. Copyright 1978 by the AAAS.

genotype favoring high IQ also provide for them the most intellectually stimulating environment. The effect of family environments, however, may be greatest when children are young. Scarr and Weinberg (1978) were surprised to discover that older (late teenage and early 20s) adoptive siblings were unalike in their IQs, that is, no more similar than children raised in different families. Although we should not emphasize a single result too much, it serves to remind us that environmental effects are not static. They may be important early in life, but they fade later when other environmental influences—such as schools and peer groups—come into prominence. Finally, good educational systems and cultural progress may benefit everyone. Flynn (1987) has obtained some evidence that IQ levels have increased historically. His observation was that students given an IQ test written in the 1920s or 1930s do better on it today than did the students who were given the same test originally. When a student is asked to take an IQ test, perhaps he should ask to be compared with the 1920 test norms! In the words of the President John Kennedy, "rising tides" of democratic social progress may raise all boats—children's IQs—yet they do not eliminate individual differences in IQ.

Abnormal Traits

In the DSM-IIIR, the manual of psychiatric diagnoses of the American Psychiatric Association (1987), criteria are given for diagnosing a number of different types of psychopathology, including the major mental illnesses of schizophrenia and manic depressive psychosis, anxiety disorders, and a number of personality disorders. The psychiatric association, with its emphasis on "all or none" diagnosis, takes a very different approach from most behavioral geneticists. If most traits are polygenic, then psychiatric disorders may represent extreme forms of normally (e.g., bell-curve-shaped) distributed behavioral tendencies. Indeed, subclinical forms of schizophrenic thought disorder may exist, such as schizophrenic spectrum disorders. Although it may be misleading to view psychopathology as "all or none," much research has come from this viewpoint. We mention in this section a few results on the inheritance of psychopathology, while admitting that the surface of this subject has barely been scratched.

The typical study of abnormal traits is a proband study. Such studies first involve the identification of *probands*—individuals known to have some form of psychopathology. Second, relatives of the proband are then found and checked to see whether they are also affected. The pairwise concordance of relatives is the percentage of relatives of the proband who are affected. For example, a study of schizophrenia might identify forty-one MZ twin individuals (the probands), admitted to a psychiatric hospital during successive years, who had received a diagnosis of schizophrenia. Next, the second twin of each pair, whenever possible, is located and similarly diagnosed using the same criteria as was used for the probands. If seven of these individuals are diagnosed as schizophrenic, then the concordance would be 17 percent (7/41).

Until 1966, considerable disagreement existed over the inheritance of schizophrenia. This disagreement was largely resolved with the first adoption study of schizophrenia. Heston (1966) discovered that children of schizophrenic parents, when adopted early and raised apart from their schizophrenic biological parents, developed the illness at about the same rate as children raised with their biological parent. In both groups of children, the concordance was about 10 percent. Adoption studies completed after this pioneering one support the idea that most of the family risk is a biological one (DeFries & Plomin, 1978). The implication is that the disposition to schizophrenia is inherited, and that family-environmental factors are not particularly relevant to its expression. Old notions such as the "schizophrenigenic mother," and other family environmental theories, are weakened by these findings. Adoption studies also produce considerable evidence for genetic risk to many other psychiatric diagnoses, such as manic depressive psychosis and, in childhood, diagnoses related to hyperactivity (conduct disorder, attention span problems).

Some intriguing results have been found for one behavioral problem: adolescent delinquency. Two researchers combined data from three adoption studies of adolescent delinquency (Cadoret, Cain, & Crowe, 1983). They looked at the interactive effects of environmental risk—namely, depression, sibling conflict, or divorce in the adoptive families—with biological risk. The latter referred to diagnoses of alcohol abuse or criminal behavior in the biological parent of the adoptees. Only when a child was exposed to the combined risk was he or she at an increased risk of committing delinquent acts. Such interaction effects are encouraging because they suggest that improving family environments may reduce levels of delinquent behavior. Work on adult criminality, however, tends to show stronger genetic influences.

How Heredity Can Be Disguised in Environmental Concepts

Social class, child-rearing styles, parental attitudes, and other concepts measured in psychological studies, although usually thought of as environmental, can in fact be an expression of heredity. Parental social class provides a good example. It is associated with a range of environmental differences; for example, poor people are less likely than wealthy people to have books and an enriching home environment, to afford adequate nutrition, to have good neighborhood schools, to live in low-crime communities, and so on.

The social class of individuals in any generation, however, is partly the result of individual differences in personality. Intelligence, achievement, sociability, persistence, and many other traits will contribute to the social standing a child will reach as an adult. This process of social mobility implies that people at different social class strata—in American society, in the 1980s—will probably differ genetically for the genes influencing these personality traits that, in turn, have contributed to their falling or rising in social status in comparison to their parents' statuses. Even siblings, although they have about the same environmental "head start" in life, often as adults will fall into different social class strata because of inherited personality differences. Hence, social class is a confounded variable: a higher social class is associated with both environmental advantages and with genetically transmissible traits.

We make a mistake, then, if we assume that social class effects are entirely environmental. For example, the higher IQs of upper class children will have resulted partly from their environmental advantages, but also from their IQ-relevant heredity. An adoption study can break apart the relative size of the two influences, but in a typical family study they would be completely indistinguishable. Given this, students should be aware of the limitation of family studies of environmental effects and seek additional information from behavioral genetic studies of the same topic. Heredity and environment are not in competition; but for the development of a particular trait, it is important to know their relative influence.

Further, environments and heredity can become correlated (related). First, there may be a passive matching of heredity and environment when parents transmit genetic traits that are reinforced by the family environment. Aggressive parents, for instance, might create chaotic home environments and at the same time genetically pass aggressive tendencies on to their children. The children could become even more aggressive as a result. Second, there may be a reactive correlation between heredity and environment in which genetic traits tend to elicit a particular environmental response. An attractive woman and a handsome man experience just this kind of gene–environment correlation when they are showered with social attention. Third, genetic dispositions may guide a person to pick particular environments over others. The tough, fearless, aggressive bully is more likely to hang out at a neighborhood street corner than a timid boy. Bright kids use the public libraries more than kids who find reading to be a chore. Achievement-oriented students get this far in this book chapter, while their lazier classmates are off having a soda. The ability of genes to make our environments may explain why MZ twins, when raised apart, are still able to experience so much of the world in the same way.

Postscript

The results of behavioral genetic studies are clear—everywhere, we find evidence of genetic influences on human personality traits. People are not the same; partly, they are different because of inborn differences regulated by genetic inheritance. Although we know *why* we are different, we do not always know "how"; that is, the particular genes influencing personality traits remain mysterious. The revolutionary advances in molecular biology have made it possible to find some genes, but they are usually genes for traits inherited in a simple way. One promissory note is that these advances may enable the discovery of some genes involved in complex, polygenic traits. The other gap in knowledge is between the complexities of personality description and physiology. Although the specific, biological bases for many personality traits are unknown, other chapters in this book document the remarkable progress that is being made.

The other, surprising result of behavioral genetics is that family environments are less important than was previously thought. One family can produce an aggressive child and a timid child, and a sociable child and a shy child. The environments of children may really be different because genes make people experience environments in different ways. The assumption that a family packages one "unit" of environmental influence seems to be wrong.

Genetic results, as those summarized in this chapter, worry many people concerned about egalitarian values. If people are really different, then they cannot be "equal" in the sense that each of us, given the proper opportunity, could with the same ease find a second derivative or dominate a group discussion. Concern for equality, however, must be melded with recognition of human differences. Even the champion of equality and human rights, John Locke, recognized that people were born with different temperamental traits. Recognition of individual differences means, in a country permitting people to have equal opportunities and rights before the law, that the "pursuit of happiness" can follow a course most satisfying to each individual. We can use the range of variation in personality to make a more exciting, varied, and productive society—there is no need to devalue personality differences.

Summary

A debate as old as psychology itself, and still profoundly important today, has focused on the relative effects of nature (meaning genetic heredity) and nurture (meaning all sorts of environmental influences) on personality differences. The conceptual and methodological tools for resolving this debate are contained in the field of behavioral genetics.

This chapter first covers the history of behavioral genetics, and in particular, the creative and inventive man, Francis Galton, who first saw how questions about heredity and environmental influences could be answered. In the next section, the chapter delves into the conceptual foundations of the field, including the idea of apportioning individual differences to genetic and environmental causes. The third section reviews data from family, twin, and adoption studies. Three domains of personality are surveyed briefly: normal personality traits, intellectual traits, and abnormal traits.

The chapter arrives at two conclusions from the evidence reviewed here. First, genetic variation can explain a substantial part of the individual differences in personality. Second, the family, although usually portrayed as the source of personality differences, is not really the main environmental influence for many traits. Instead, for most traits—especially for nonintellectual traits—the major environmental influences are ones outside of common experiences of the family unit.

SUGGESTED READINGS

Galton, F. (1865). *Hereditary genius: An inquiry into its laws and consequences.* London: Macmillan (Cleveland: World Publishing, 1962). Galton's family study of eminence introduces the student to the historical foundations of behavioral genetics.

Leahy, A. M. (1935). Nature-nurture and intelligence. *Genetic Psychology Monographs Supplement, 16,* 235–308. Alice Leahy's classic study produced evidence for the heritability of IQ and for the genetic mediation of some effects thought to be environmental. Written with forcefulness and clarity, this article shows an understanding of the issues that was ahead of its time.

Loehlin, J. C., Lindzey, G., & Spuhler, J. N. (1975). *Race differences in intelligence.* San Francisco: W. H. Freeman. Sponsored by the Social Science Research Council, this book evaluates the question of heritable racial differences in IQ with an even-handedness and thoroughness of analysis that sheds light on the question instead of adding more heat to an already overheated debate.

Loehlin, J. C., & Nichols, R. C. (1976). *Heredity, environment, and personality: A study of 850 sets of twins.* Austin: University of Texas Press. This massive twin study is a classic in design and execution. Loehlin and

Nichols try to pinpoint family environmental influences on personality, but find little evidence of them in the domain of (nonintellectual) personality traits.

Plomin, R., & DeFries, J. C. (1985). *Origins of* *individual differences in infancy: The Colorado Adoption Project.* New York: Academic Press. This book contains a wealth of findings from the largest prospective adoption study of behavior.

REFERENCES

American Psychiatric Association (1987). *Diagnostic and statistical manual of mental disorders.* (DSMIII-R). Washington, DC: APA.

Bouchard, T. J., Jr., & McGue, M. (1981). Familial studies of intelligence: A review. *Science, 212,* 1055–1059.

Cadoret, R. J., Cain, C. A., & Crowe, R. R. (1983). Evidence for gene–environment interaction in the development of adolescent antisocial behavior. *Behavior Genetics, 13,* 301–310.

Cattell, R. B. (1982). *The inheritance of personality and ability.* New York: Academic Press.

DeFries, J. C., & Plomin, R. (1978). Behavioral genetics. *Annual Review of Psychology, 29,* 473–515.

Eysenck, H. J. (1953). *The structure of personality.* London: Methuen.

Eysenck, S. B. G., & Eysenck, H. J. (1968). The measurement of psychoticism: A study of factor stability and reliability. *British Journal of Social and Clinical Psychology, 7,* 286–294.

Fancher, R. E. (1985). *The Intelligence Men: Makers of the I.Q. controversy.* New York & London: W. W. Norton.

Fischbein, S. (1977a). Onset of puberty in MZ and DZ twins. *Acta Geneticae Medicae et Gemellologieae, 26,* 151–158.

Fischbein, S. (1977b). Intra-pair similarity in physical growth of monozygotic and of dizygotic twins during puberty. *Annals of Human Biology, 4,* 417–430.

Flynn, J. R. (1987). Massive IQ gains in 14 nations: What IQ tests really measure. *Psychological Bulletin, 101,* 171–191.

Hay, D. A. (1985). *Essentials of behavior genetics.* Oxford: Blackwells.

Hearnshaw, L. (1979). *Cyril Burt: Psychologist.* Ithaca, NY: Cornell University Press.

Henderson, N. D. (1982). Human behavior genetics. *Annual Review of Psychology, 33,* 403–440.

Heston, L. L. (1966). Psychiatric disorders in foster home reared children of schizophrenic mothers. *British Journal of Psychiatry, 112,* 819–825.

Hunt, E., Lunneborg, C., & Lewis, J. (1975). "What does it mean to be high verbal?" *Cognitive Psychology, 7,* 194–227.

Jarvik, L. F., Blum, J. E., & Varma, A. O. (1972). Genetic components and intellectual functioning during senescence: A 20-year study of aging twins. *Behavior Genetics, 2,* 159–171.

Kolata, G. (1986). Manic depression: Is it inherited? *Science, 232,* 575–576.

Loehlin, J. C., & Nichols, R. C. (1976). *Heredity, environment, and personality: A study of 850 sets of twins.* Austin: University of Texas Press.

McCrae, R. R., & Costa, Jr., P. T. (1986). Clinical assessment can benefit from recent advances in personality psychology. *American Psychologist, 41,* 1001–1003.

Pedersen, N. L., McClearn, G. E., Plomin, R., & Friberg, L. (1985). Separated fraternal twins: Resemblance for cognitive abilities. *Behavior Genetics, 16,* 407–419.

Plomin, R. (1983). Developmental behavioral genetics. *Child Development, 54,* 253–259.

Plomin, R., & DeFries, J. C. (1985). *Origins of individual differences in infancy: The Colorado Adoption Project.* New York: Academic Press.

Plomin, R., DeFries, J. C., McClearn, G. E. (1980). *Behavioral genetics: A primer.* San

Francisco: W. H. Freeman.

Rowe, D. C. (1987). Resolving the Person-Situation Debate: Invitation to an Interdisciplinary Dialogue. *American Psychologist, 42,* 218–227.

Rowe, D. C., & Plomin, R. (1981). The importance of nonshared (E_1) environmental influences in behavioral development. *Developmental Psychology, 17,* 517–531.

Scarr, S. (1981). Race, social class, and individual differences in IQ. Hillsdale, NJ: Lawrence Erlbaum.

Scarr, S., & Weinberg, R. A. (1978). The influence of "family background" on intellectual attainment. *American Sociological Review, 43,* 674–692.

Tellegen, A., Lykken, D. T., Bouchard, T. J., Jr., Wilcox, K. J., Segal, N. L., & Rich, S. (1988). Personality similarity in twins reared apart and together. *Journal of Personality and Social Psychology, 54,* 1031–1039.

Watson, J. D., & Crick, F. H. C. (1953). Molecular structure of nucleic acids: A structure for deoxyribose nucleic acid. *Nature, 171,* 737–738.

Wilson, R. S. (1978). Synchronies in mental development: An epigenetic perspective. *Science, 202,* 939–948.

CHAPTER 4

Biological Approaches to the Study of Personality

RICHARD J. DAVIDSON

Introduction
Conceptual Issues in the Study of
    Biological Bases of
    Personality
  Three Approaches to the Use
    of Biological Measures in
    the Study of Personality
  Correlate or Substrate?
  Does Substrate Imply Cause?
Methodological Considerations in
    the Study of the Biological
    Bases of Personality
  Psychometric Considerations
  Resting or Task-Related
    Measures?
  Some Commonly Used
    Physiological Measures in
    the Study of Personality

An Empirical Example of the
    Biological Approach to
    Personality: Cerebral
    Asymmetry and Affective
    Style
  Introduction
  Individual Differences in
    Anterior Asymmetry and
    Affective Reactivity
ACTIVITY BOX: Measuring Your
    Hemisphericity
Summary
SUGGESTED READINGS
REFERENCES

Introduction

Inferences about personality have traditionally been made on the basis of self-reports and action. The use of biological measures in the study of personality has been comparatively less frequent, although many theorists have assumed that core personality traits were somehow rooted in underlying biology. For example, Gordon Allport (1966), one of the founders of modern personality psychology, explicitly suggested that traits were subserved by underlying biological processes. He (Allport, 1966) asserted that "traits are cortical, subcortical or postural dispositions having the capacity to gate or guide specific phasic reactions. It is only the phasic aspect which is visible; the tonic is carried somehow in the still mysterious realm of neurodynamic structure" (p. 3).

The assumption that core personality traits are products of underlying biological dispositions was one shared by a number of early influential workers including Freud and Pavlov. In his *Project for a Scientific Psychology* Freud (1895/1966) suggested that individuals may differ in certain neuronal properties that would in turn account for certain psychological differences. Pavlov (1928) introduced the concept of strength of the nervous system and indicated that pronounced individual variability exists in this property. His work laid the founda-

The research reported in this chapter was supported in part by NIMH grants MH40747 and MH43454, and by grants from the John D. and Catherine T. Mac-Arthur Foundation.

tion for an important tradition of research on the underlying biological substrates of introversion-extraversion (e.g., Eysenck, 1972).

These early theorists argued for the general importance of examining the underlying biological substrates of personality. They believed that personality traits were entities in the mind that were associated with and supported by specific patterns of biological activity. By examining these biological processes, these early theorists believed that a more direct measure of traits could be obtained. This enterprise, however, contains a number of thorny conceptual and methodological issues that merit some attention before we illustrate some of the more substantive areas.

Conceptual Issues in the Study of the Biological Bases of Personality

Three Approaches to the Use of Biological Measures in the Study of Personality

There are three ways in which biological measures have most often been used in the study of personality. The first way has been to complement measures obtained from other domains. For example, a psychologist might be interested in studying introverts and extraverts. In addition to examining how such groups differ in their behavior and self-reports, scientists have also asked how such groups might differ in their physiology. The British psychologist Hans Eysenck (1967) has explored this issue in considerable detail and has reported a number of interesting physiological differences between such groups. For example, he has reported that introverts and extraverts differ in global cortical arousal, with extraverts showing less arousal than introverts. He argued that the decreased arousal in the extraverts was actually a key factor that motivated such individuals to engage in extraverted behavior. Such behavior, Eysenck believed, served to increase their arousal to more optimal levels. On the other hand, introverts were found to show heightened global cortical arousal. Introverted behavior was thought to decrease their cortical arousal to more optimal levels. Thus, these differences in arousal were believed to be causal in producing the types of behavior that are characteristically associated with extraverts and introverts. Unfortunately, this model has been criticized as overly simplistic by some researchers (e.g., Gray, 1972).

A second way in which physiological information has been used in the study of personality is to examine relations among self-report, behavioral, and physiological measures of a hypothetical construct. For example, imagine an experiment in which we give a self-report measure of anxiety to a large group of subjects and select those who score low in anxiety for intensive study. If we present a moderately stressful stimulus to these subjects, we will likely find that some will show relatively little arousal in physiological measures that are thought to reflect anxiety, whereas other subjects will show heightened arousal on such measures. Remember that both of these groups reported little anxiety on the self-report measure that was administered. Thus, in one group, the physiological measures seem concordant with the self-report measures and, in the other group, the physiological measures are discordant with the self-report measures. Which measure should we believe? I wish to suggest that *both* measures are providing essential information and that what is most important in this example is the degree to which such measures are concordant or discordant.

The example just described is not entirely hypothetical. We and others have studied the type of persons who report themselves to be low in anxiety but respond both physiologically and behaviorally in ways that suggest heightened anxiety. We performed an experiment (Weinberger, Schwartz, & Davidson, 1979) in which subjects who scored very low on an anxiety scale were differentiated into two groups on the basis of a second self-report measure of repressive defensiveness. The subjects who scored low on *both* the anxiety measure and the measure of repressive defensiveness were considered to be truly low anxious subjects. The subjects who scored low on the anxiety measure but high on the measure of repressive defensiveness were considered to be "repressors." We presented neutral and emotional phrases in response to which subjects were requested to say the first word or phrase that came to mind. We found that in response to the emotional phrases, the repressors showed more arousal in several autonomic measures compared to the truly low anxious subjects. In fact, the level of arousal displayed by the repressors was comparable to (and, in some cases, even higher than) that displayed by a group of high anxious subjects who were also tested. This experiment illustrates the utility of measuring physiological activity in addition to self-report and action to provide a more complete account of personality. In this experiment the relationship of the physiological measures to other measures of personality was most important.

The two types of approaches to the use of biological indices in personality research just discussed both involve the use of physiological activity as *dependent variables*. In other words, groups are classified on the basis of some independent variable such as scores on a paper-and-pencil test and a study is performed to determine how such groups might differ on a physiological variable.

The third way in which biological measures have been used in the study of personality has been to use such indices as *independent variables*. In this strategy, subjects are not classified into groups on the basis of a traditional personality instrument such as a paper-and-pencil measure or a projective measure. Rather, they are classified on the basis of a physiological measure. Relations are then examined between subjects' scores on the physiological measure and relevant behavioral and/or self-report measures. Some scientists who have used the latter strategy have argued that, by selecting subjects on the basis of biological measures, they are not necessarily constrained by the existing categories that have developed within personality psychology. It is possible that individual differences in certain physiological measures will be discovered that do not have close analogs in the traditional personality psychology. The categories of individual differences that may emerge from using biological measures in this fashion may more closely reflect "natural" individual variation. At the present time, such arguments are very speculative. Although this line of reasoning has some intuitive appeal, there is little hard evidence toward which we can point to suggest that physiological measures should replace traditional personality measures as a way to assess individual differences.

Correlate or Substrate?

When physiological measures are examined in relation to behavior or personality traits, it is useful to inquire about whether the measure is being used as a substrate of the trait in question or as a correlate. In general, substrates can be considered an actual component of the trait whereas correlates are merely associated events that co-occur with the trait. If the physiological measure is taken to be a correlate of the trait, then experimental modification of the measure will not in any way alter the trait in question. For example, a number of researchers have examined individual differences in various measures of skin conductance. Skin conductance primarily reflects the degree of sweating on the skin and is usually measured from surface of the palms or fingers. In all likelihood, it is safe to conceptualize skin conductance differences between groups as *correlates* of an individual difference in behavior. If we were to peripherally block the skin conductance response with a locally applied pharmacological agent, we would not alter the trait in question.

Other physiological measures are assumed to reflect more "basic" differences between groups and are conceptualized as substrates of traits, rather than correlates. For example, some cardiac and respiratory changes associated with anxiety may, in certain circumstances, reflect substrates of this trait. In other words, if these autonomic processes were altered by a peripheral pharmacological agent, the construct of interest (i.e., anxiety) would also likely change. A specific example of this may be seen in social phobics who have been found to show heightened arousal in certain autonomic systems. One of the treatments of choice for this condition is the administration of a beta blocker, which blocks the expression of these autonomic changes and has been found to significantly attentuate anxiety. One of the most commonly used beta blockers to treat social phobias (atenolol) has the important property of not crossing the blood-brain barrier. This is significant because it allows us to conclude that the changes in behavior associated with the administration of this drug are due exclusively to the changes in peripheral autonomic activity and are not by-products of central changes. Thus, the autonomic changes that accompany this condition are properly conceptualized as substrates of the disorder, because altering the physiology changes the trait of interest.

It is useful to be explicit about one's conception of whether a particular physiological measure that is being recorded is to be regarded as a substrate or a correlate. If the physiological measure reflects a substrate, it may be informative with respect to the underlying psychobiology of the personality trait in question. In other words, we can potentially learn about the biological mechanisms that give rise to the trait. This type of information would be useful in advancing our understanding of basic brain-behavior relationships. When we measure a correlate, such information may have enormous practical utility in the prediction of behavior. However, because correlates are not directly related to underlying biological substrates, the contribution of such information to understanding of the biological bases of personality is necessarily less direct.

Does Substrate Imply Cause?

When biological substrates of personality are identified, students often assume that their presence implies a heritable cause. It is critical to underscore the fact that such an assumption is *unwarranted*. The finding of biological substrates of particular personality traits implies nothing about their cause. The issue of causality is an entirely separate issue. It certainly may be that the trait in question has heritable contributions, but it is not necessary that this be so. Biological differences among people occur for many reasons, only one of which is genetic. We know from extensive data in animals that the environment can significantly alter brain function and even structure. For example, rats raised in enriched environments have literally heavier brains and more extensive growth of neuronal processes (the axons and dendrites that make connections among neurons) (e.g., Rosensweig, Krech, Bennett, & Diamond, 1962). This is but one of many examples of dramatic environmental effects on the brain. It should not be assumed that, because two groups may differ in some aspect of biological function or structure, such differences are necessarily a product of heritable influences. The demonstration of heritable influences requires a different methodological strategy.

Methodological Considerations in the Study of the Biological Bases of Personality

Psychometric Considerations

Most of the psychometric considerations that apply to the measurement of personality with paper-and-pencil tests also apply to the study of individual differences in physiological measures. An important concern is the reliability of the measure. If individual differences in a physiological measure are examined, the measure must be stable, that is, show adequate test-retest reliability. Often, physiological measures are used as correlates of personality traits, with little attention paid to psychometric considerations. If a particular measure is not stable, it will less likely be found to relate to other individual difference measures that show adequate test–retest stability.

The validity of the physiological measure is also essential to demonstrate. In many ways, most of the research on physiological correlates of personality is an attempt to demonstrate the validity (both concurrent and predictive) of the physiological measures in question. For example, in Kagan's research (Kagan, Reznick, & Snidman, 1988) on the biological bases of childhood shyness, he is exploring the degree to which early measures of autonomic activity predict later behavioral manifestations of shy and wary behavior. The physiological measures are used to enhance the construct validity of the temperamental dimension under study. In addition, the research establishes the predictive validity of the physiological measures that are obtained.

Resting or Task-Related Measures?

Another very important methodological issue that is specific to the use of physiological measures concerns the situations during which they should be obtained. Here the basic choice is between resting measures and task-related measures. We can record most physiological measures during a baseline condition as well as in response to specific challenges. For example, we can compare introverts and extraverts on baseline measures of heart rate and brain activity. And we can obtain the same measures in response to specific tasks designed to challenge subjects in particular ways. There is no simple rule of thumb to use as a general guide in making this decision. It is certainly conceivable that differences between two groups of subjects will be uncovered only if physiology is recorded in response to specific challenges. This is not unlike the cardiac stress test that is used in the diagnosis of cardiac problems. There are some patients whose cardiac problems are not revealed in resting measures of cardiac function. Only when the system is challenged do differences become apparent. On the other hand, as will be illustrated, there are certainly some physiological indices that meaningfully vary across individuals in the resting state. It is often the case that an investigator will record the physiological measures during both a baseline period and in response to specific challenges.

In certain experimental contexts, the measurement of *baseline* physiology is really not possible. The very act of measurement is itself a challenge to the subject, particularly if the measurement procedure is complex and novel and especially in young children. For example, in studies of individual differences in temperament in young children, physiological measurement is itself a stressful challenge, particularly for subjects who are temperamentally wary to begin with. Thus, for these subjects, it is not really possible to obtain a measure of pure "resting" physiology. The physiological measures one obtains during a baseline period will inevitably reflect the interaction of the child's temperamental qualities and the stress of the measurement situation. The only way to minimize such influences is to acclimate the subject to the testing environment and have him or her return to the lab for a second testing session when the laboratory situation will be more familiar. One can then either use the data from the second session only, or compare the data from the first and second sessions.

Some Commonly Used Physiological Measures in the Study of Personality

Most of the physiological variables used in personality research fall under the rubric of what would be called "psychophysiological measures." Such measures are characterized by being recorded from surface electrodes on the subjects' body and are therefore totally noninvasive. This makes them ideally suited for studies of normal personality in which it would be difficult to justify the use of invasive measures. Although psychophysiological measures are the most commonly used, a number of other types of biological measures have also been used. These other measures vary in the degree to which they are invasive. This section will conclude with discussions of how several different psychophysiological measures have been used in personality research. It will also give several examples of how other types of biological measures have been used.

Electrodermal Measures

Electrodermal activity refers to the measurement of the electrical activity of the skin. There are several different types of electrodermal measurement (see Fowles, 1986, for a detailed discussion of this response system). Those most commonly used in personality research are based upon skin conductance (or its inverse, skin resistance). Skin conductance refers to the conductivity of the skin to a very small external current applied between two electrodes, usually on the palmar surface of the hand or fingers. The primary contributor to the variations in skin conductance is the degree of sweat in the sweat glands and on the surface of the skin. The more sweat, the greater is the conductivity. Researchers most commonly measure three different attributes of skin conductance. They are all somewhat intercorrelated, although they are thought to reflect partially independent response properties. The three attributes of skin conductance are: skin conductance level (SCL), skin conductance response (SCR) to an external stimulus, and spontaneous skin conductance responses (SSCR). The SSCR measure is usually the number of responses above a minimal threshold that occur in the absence of any defined external stimulus. Individual differences in all three types of measures have been studied in relation to different personality characteristics. For example, some investigators have studied individual differences in the rate at which the SCR to simple sensory stimuli habituates. A number of researchers have reported that extraverts habituate more rapidly than introverts (e.g., Crider & Lunn, 1971). Other investigators have reported that speed of habituation of the SCR is more related to anxiety or neuroticism (e.g., Coles, Gale, & Kline, 1971; see review by O'Gorman, 1983). Differences between depressed and nondepressed subjects in different aspects of electrodermal activity have also been studied. Depressed subjects consistently show lower SCL and smaller SCRs than nondepressed subjects (see Henriques & Davidson, 1989, for review).

Measures of Cardiovascular Activity

Heart rate and other measures of cardiovascular activity have been used in studies of personality for many years. A number of different indices of cardiac function have been measured. The most commonly used measures of cardiac activity are heart rate and heart rate variability. Other measures of cardiovascular function have been developed to provide additional information that is not readily available from simple measures of heart rate and heart rate variability (see Tursky & Jamner, 1982, for review). In his recent studies of childhood shyness,

Kagan and his colleagues (Kagan et al., 1988) have reported that shy or inhibited children have higher resting heart rates and less heart rate variability compared with uninhibited children. Those children who showed a stable temperamental disposition of wariness or inhibition from twenty-one months to 7.5 years had higher heart rate at every age measured. In this study, the original classification of the groups was made at age twenty-one months. In studies with adults, heart rate has also been used to examine individual differences. Hodes, Cook, and Lang (1985) reported that subjects with higher heart rates acquired a conditioned fear more readily than subjects with lower heart rates. Heart rate has also been found to be elevated among subjects with depression (Henriques & Davidson, 1989).

Measures of Brain Electrical Activity

Measures of brain electrical activity are ideally suited for studies of personality because they provide potentially useful information about central nervous system *substrates* of personality and they are noninvasive and relatively easy to record. Both spontaneous brain activity (EEG) and event-related potentials (ERPs) or evoked potentials (EPs) have been used in personality research. EEG refers to the ongoing background activity of the brain. It is usually measured either under resting conditions or while a subject performs a task. ERPs refer to brain activity that is specifically time-locked to some external event. ERPs are usually measured by averaging brain electrical activity for a short period of time just after a stimulus is presented. The activity that is specifically related to the event will be enhanced and the activity that is random with respect to the event will diminish. The averaging procedure is essentially a way to improve the signal-to-noise ratio of the measure. Both methods are useful in different contexts. Measurement of regional EEG activity can provide information on patterns of activation in different cortical regions. The use of EEG in personality research will be illustrated in the next section. ERPs have been used in a number of different ways in studies of individual differences.

One of the earliest applications of event-related potential (ERP) measures to the domain of personality was the study of individual differences in "augmentation/reduction." Augmentation/reduction refers to the degree to which a person tends to either augment or reduce the impact of sensory stimulation. This dimension of personality was first described by Petrie (1967/1978) in her book on individual differences in pain responsivity. Although Petrie did not use ERPs to measure augmentation/reduction, she described a number of fascinating differences between groups of people who were selected on the basis of their response to differing levels of sensory stimulation. The subjects were selected on the basis of a behavioral measure of this dimension that she developed. The essential principle of the measure was to determine subjects' perceived width of wooden blocks that they rubbed with their fingers. Reducers were those subjects who perceived the width of blocks to be thinner than they actually were, whereas augmenters were subjects who perceived the width of the blocks to be wider than they actually were. She found that reducers were more tolerant of pain and less tolerant of sensory monotony. Augmenters, on the other hand, were less tolerant to pain but were more tolerant of sensory monotony. Petrie also reported that drugs used to reduce pain, such as aspirin, tended to make augmenters more like reducers on her measure.

The logic behind the assessment of augmentation/reduction using ERPs is simple. If a subject shows increases in the amplitude of his or her evoked response to a stimulus with increases in intensity, the subject is said to be an augmenter. Alternatively, if a subject shows little change or an actual decrease in amplitude of the same component of the evoked response as stimulus intensity increases, the subject would be classified as a reducer. Buchsbaum and Silverman (1968) were among the first to report on this method to assess augmentation/ reduction. They randomly presented visual stimuli differing in intensity to subjects while brain electrical activity was measured from a number of scalp sites. They derived separate ERPs to the light flashes of each intensity level and computed the slope of the amplitude/intensity function for each subject. This slope reflects how steeply the amplitude of the response changes as a function of increases in stimulus intensity. Subjects with very large slopes would be considered augmenters, whereas those with small slopes or negative slopes would be considered reducers. They reported a correlation of .63 between their evoked potential method of assessing augmentation/reduction and the behavioral procedure used by Petrie. Subsequent research using the evoked potential procedure for measuring this characteristic has uncovered important genetic contributions to this trait (see Buchsbaum, Haier, & Johnson, 1983, for review). In addition, this trait has been linked to sensation seeking, with augmenters scoring more highly on one subscale of sensation seeking compared with reducers (e.g., Zuckerman, 1983).

Other Biological Measures

In addition to the psychophysiological measures just described, a number of other types of biological measures have been used in research on individual differences. An important class of measures are those used to provide information about regional brain activation. These are similar in purpose to EEG measures, but differ with respect to their spatial resolution. Spatial resolution refers to the precision with which such methods can accurately reflect brain activity in very localized regions. Techniques with good spatial resolution are those that reflect very localized activity. Two of the most common methods involve the measurement of regional cerebral blood flow and regional cerebral metabolism. The most common method for assessing regional cerebral metabolism involves the quantification of the amount of glucose used per unit time in a particular brain region. Because glucose is the main nutrient of the brain, increases in glucose in a particular brain region indicate increased activity in that region. The more active a brain region, the more glucose it will require. Both of these methods are based on the principle that brain regions that are most active require the most blood flow or metabolism. Therefore, differences between groups in regional brain activation can be inferred from patterns of regional blood flow or metabolism differences. The methods used to assess these parameters are complex and would take us beyond the scope of this chapter. The interested reader is urged to consult Trimble (1986) for a description of these new brain imaging procedures.

In addition to methods for the assessment of regional brain activation, other biochemical methods involving assays of either blood or saliva have been used in the study of individual differences. Individual differences have been studied in the levels of a number of different biochemicals. For example, several studies have been performed that have examined the personality correlates of individual differences in an enzyme—monoamine oxidase (MAO)—that regulates certain neurotransmitters in the brain (e.g., Buchsbaum, Coursey, & Murphy, 1976).

Other studies have used a measure that reflects overall activity in the hypothalamic-pituitary-adrenal axis in the study of individual differences. Cortisol levels in the saliva have been used for this purpose and have been found, for example, to be elevated in wary, inhibited children compared with uninhibited children (Kagan, Reznick, & Snidman, 1988).

An Empirical Example of the Biological Approach to Personality: Cerebral Asymmetry and Affective Style

Introduction

Although functional differences between the two cerebral hemispheres of the brain in the control of emotional behavior have been noted for over fifty years (e.g., Alford, 1933; Goldstein, 1939), there was relatively little systematic study of this problem prior to the past decade. A dramatic increase in research on this topic then occurred. The accumulating body of work encompasses a wide variety of methodological approaches. For example, neurological, psychiatric, and normal populations have all been studied extensively, and a range of assessment techniques have been used. They include self-report and behavioral indices of emotion, and behavioral, electrophysiological, and other indices of regional brain activity (for reviews, see, e.g., Davidson, 1984; Leventhal & Tomarken, 1986; Silberman & Weingartner, 1986; Tucker, 1981; Tucker & Frederick, 1989). In addition to this large corpus of new data in humans, animal findings consistent with the human data have been obtained, and promising animal models of the lateralization of emotion have been developed (for reviews, see, e.g., Denenberg & Yutzey, 1985; Glick & Shapiro, 1985).

One of the most significant extensions of basic research on laterality and emotion has been the study of relations between individual differences in particular indices of asymmetry and affective reactivity. After briefly discussing some relevant background literature, I will present an overview of some of our own recent findings in this area.

The literature on laterality and emotion supports two broad conclusions about the differential role of the two cerebral hemispheres in emotion. The first concerns the specialization of the *posterior* regions of the right hemisphere for the perception of emotional information. The second broad conclusion is that the *anterior* regions of the two hemispheres are differentially specialized for the experience and spontaneous expression of certain positive and negative emotions, with the left hemisphere playing a more active role in the former and the right hemisphere in the latter (see Davidson, 1984; Davidson & Tomarken, in press, for reviews). This latter specialization will be the central concern of the studies to be described.

Evidence from several sources supports the conclusion about the emotional specialization of the anterior regions of the hemispheres. Studies on the affective correlates of unilateral brain damage indicate that damage to the left anterior region is more likely to result in depressive symptomatology compared with comparable right hemisphere damage. In one of the first systematic studies to compare the emotional consequences of left- versus right-sided brain damage, Gainotti (1972) reported that left-lesioned patients had significantly more negative affect and depressive symptomatology than right-lesioned patients. Other more recent studies support this conclusion (e.g., Robinson, Kubos, Starr, Rao, & Price, 1984; Sackeim, Weiman, Gur, Greenberg, Hungerbuhler & Geschwind, 1982).

Electrophysiological studies on nonlesioned populations point toward a similar conclusion. Such studies have typically used measures of brain electrical activity to make inferences about patterns of regional activation. We and others (e.g., Ahern & Schwartz, 1985; Tucker, Stenslie, Roth, & Shearer, 1981) have reported in several studies that certain forms of negative affect are accompanied by selective activation of the right anterior region whereas positive affect is accompanied by selective activation of the left anterior region (see Davidson & Tomarken, in press, for review). A strong linkage between anterior regions of the cerebral hemispheres and affective experience is additionally consistent with evidence of the extensive neuroanatomical reciprocity between prefrontal and anterior temporal regions of the cerebral cortex and limbic circuits known to be directly involved in the control of motivation and emotion (e.g., Kelly & Stinus, 1984; Nauta, 1971).

Individual Differences in Anterior Asymmetry and Affective Reactivity

We have conducted a number of studies in normal and clinical populations on individual differences in anterior activation asymmetry. Anterior activation asymmetry refers to the relative difference in activation between the left and right cerebral hemispheres in the anterior brain regions. Activation is inferred from measuring brain electrical activity. The amount of brain activity between eight and thirteen cycles per second (known as alpha activity) in the adult (and somewhat slower in the infant) is inversely related to activation. Thus, the *less* alpha activity the greater the amount of activation. We therefore measure differences in the amount of alpha activity in the anterior regions of the cerebral hemispheres. These anterior brain regions, consisting predominantly of the anterior temporal and frontal regions, have extensive connections with other brain systems that lie below the cerebral hemispheres and that have been directly implicated in the control of certain aspects of emotion (see figure 4.1). In this section, I will summarize findings from studies that have focused on individual differences in anterior asymmetry in normal adults and infants, because this work is most relevant to the theme of this chapter. For extensions of this approach to psychopathology, the interested reader should consult Davidson (1988).

We have recently conducted several studies that indicate that patterns of baseline asymmetry can indeed *predict* affective reactions at a later point in time. These *baseline* patterns of brain asymmetry are measured during the resting state and tend to be fairly stable over time. Thus, an individual can be assessed on direction and magnitude of his or her anterior asymmetry and this measure can be considered to be a trait-like characteristic of the person. We have completed two studies to date in adults (Tomarken, Davidson, Henriques, Saron, Straus, & Senulis, 1989). These examined the relation between resting baseline

FIGURE 4.1

Diagram of the Major Areas of the Left Hemisphere of the Cerebral Cortex. The areas we have recorded over in our electrophysiological studies described in this chapter were: the left and right sides of the superior parietal lobule, middle temporal region, and middle frontal region.

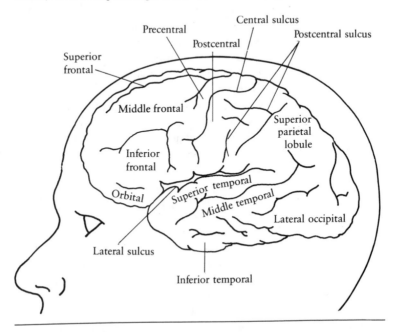

asymmetry measures obtained at the beginning of an experimental session and subjects' subsequent reactivity to short emotional film clips.

The design of each of the two studies was similar, although the subject samples were entirely independent and the film clips used in each study were different. In the first study, twenty-four right-handed females were assessed. Resting measures of EEG asymmetry from a thirty-second eyes-open period were recorded at the beginning of the session. Subjects were then presented with two positive film clips, followed by two negative film clips. The positive clips were designed to elicit happiness and amusement and the negative film clips were designed to elicit fear and disgust. The duration of each film clip was approximately two minutes. Following each baseline and film trial, subjects were asked to rate their emotional experience during the clip on a series of 0 to 8 rating scales.

The major issue addressed in this study was the relation between the resting measures of asymmetry taken at the start of the session and subjects' subsequent reports of their emotional responses to the film clips. The metric of asymmetry that was derived was right minus left hemisphere alpha power. Positive numbers on this index denote left-sided activation and negative numbers denote right-sided activation. We found that relative right frontal activation at rest significantly predicted fear responses to each of the two film clips ($rs = -.45$ and $-.43$, $ps < .05$) and composite (i.e., mean) fear responses across the two clips ($r = -.48$, $p < .025$). The correlations are negative in sign because *lower* numbers on the asymmetry metric are associated with more right-sided activation. The negative sign indicates that lower asymmetry scores (i.e., more right-sided activation) are associated with higher self-reports of negative affect. Correlations between frontal asymmetry and disgust responses were not significant, although trends in the predicted direction were evident. The results of several additional sets of analyses were also revealing. First, the correlations between resting anterior asymmetry and fear responses were not simply due to the confounding effects of preexisting mood at the time of the baselines. Resting EEG was uncorrelated with all individual mood scales assessed at the time of the baseline. In addition, it was uncorrelated with composite mood indices (e.g., composite negative affect). Consistent with the notion that anterior asymmetry is a state-independent marker indexing affective predispositions, we found that it predicted fear responses in this sample independent of concurrent mood state.

A second set of analyses focused on the relationship between anterior asymmetry and both positive and negative affective responses. In this sample, although the correlation was in the predicted direction, frontal asymmetry did not significantly predict happiness responses to positive films ($r = .18$). However, for both fear and disgust, frontal asymmetry was significantly correlated with the *difference* between negative affective responses to negative films and positive affective responses to positive films. The correlation between resting asymmetry and the disgust-happiness difference score was $-.41$ ($p < .05$) and the correlation between resting asymmetry and the fear-happiness difference score was $-.59$ ($p < .01$). This important finding suggests that resting anterior asymmetry may primarily index the individual's *relative balance* of positive and negative affective response tendencies.

That anterior asymmetry significantly predicted the *difference* between positive and negative affective responsivity also suggests that it does *not* index generalized emotional reactivity. This is an important observation given recent findings by Diener and his colleagues. This research group has identified stable individual differences in affective reactivity that are independent of the valence of emotion (e.g., Diener, Larsen, Levine, & Emmons, 1985; Larsen, Diener, & Emmons, 1986;

see also chapter 15, Emotion). To conduct a more direct test of a generalized affective reactivity interpretation of frontal asymmetry, we computed what might be considered a "generalized reactivity" index consisting of the *sum* of subjects' negative affective responses to negative films and positive affective responses to positive films. For both fear and disgust, frontal asymmetry was uncorrelated with this index (fear + happiness $r = -.10$; disgust + happiness $r = .09$). These data indicate that it is not affective reactivity per se that is indexed by anterior asymmetry but a valence-specific bias in reactivity.

One additional set of results in this study is also noteworthy. Specifically, for all analyses conducted, resting asymmetry in parietal sites was unrelated to any measure of affective reactivity (e.g., the correlation between parietal asymmetry and composite fear was .13). This observation once again underscores the regional specificity of the relationship between resting asymmetry and emotional responsivity.

In the second study in this series (Tomarken et al., 1989, Study II), subjects were fifteen right-handed females. As in the first experiment, EEG was recorded during a thirty-second eyes-open resting baseline, after which subjects completed a set of 0 to 8 scales assessing current mood. Subjects then watched two positive and six negative film clips selected from contemporary movies (i.e., *The Godfather*) and rated their emotional responses immediately after each clip. Film clips were different from those used in Study I. EEG was recorded from three sets of anterior sites: mid-frontal, lateral frontal, and anterior temporal. In addition, EEG was recorded from two posterior sites: posterior temporal and parietal.

We computed correlations between resting EEG asymmetry and composite fear and disgust responses across those four films that elicited at least moderate fear and disgust and we computed correlations between resting asymmetry and happiness ratings across those two films that elicited at least moderate happiness. As in the first study, greater relative right hemisphere activation in the mid-frontal site was associated with greater fear ($r = -.35$), although this correlation was not significant because of the small sample size ($N = 14$). Furthermore, resting asymmetry in both the mid-frontal and lateral frontal sites was highly correlated with disgust responses to negative films ($rs = -.62$ and $-.68$, respectively, $p < .025$). In addition, although resting frontal asymmetry did not predict happiness responses, anterior temporal asymmetry was significantly correlated with composite happiness ratings ($r = .52$) in the direction hypothesized (greater relative left anterior temporal activation associated with increased happiness).

As in Study I, resting anterior asymmetry predicted affective responses independent of concurrent mood at the time of the baselines. Resting asymmetry was either uncorrelated with baseline mood or correlated in a direction opposite to that which would be expected. Furthermore, when baseline mood was partialed out, correlations remained significant, and either identical or actually somewhat greater in magnitude (e.g., $r = .71$ between anterior temporal asymmetry and happiness). Finally, as in the previous study, EEG asymmetry in posterior sites failed to significantly predict any affective responses to films.

Although there were some inconsistencies across the two studies (e.g., the significant prediction of fear but not disgust in Study I, and the reversal of this pattern in Study II), the findings from these two studies indicate that in normal, unselected samples of adults, resting frontal asymmetry can predict positive and negative responses to affect elicitors. We have recently extended these findings and conclusions in a study examining the relation between individual differences in resting asymmetry and affective reactivity in infants (Davidson & Fox, 1989). In this study, resting EEG asymmetry was measured from fourteen female ten-month-old infants prior to their exposure to a brief episode of maternal separation. The episode was sixty seconds in duration unless the infant was judged by the experimenter to be extremely upset, at which point the episode was terminated. We focused on individual differences in response to this stressor because several researchers have noted the pronounced differences among infants of this age in response to maternal separation (e.g., Shiller, Izard, & Hembree, 1986; Weinraub & Lewis, 1977). Moreover, infants' response to maternal separation at this age period is one component of a constellation of behaviors that are associated with individual differences in vulnerability to distress. This is a dimension of temperament for which impressive longitudinal stability has been demonstrated (for a review, see Kagan, 1984).

From the videotaped record of the session, we coded infants' responses to the maternal separation challenge. Examination of these responses revealed that seven infants cried and seven did not cry. An infant was classified as a noncrier only if he or she showed no evidence of crying for the entire duration of the maternal separation episode. The classification of an infant as a crier or noncrier was done prior to any EEG analysis and was therefore completely blind.

In accord with our previous findings, we predicted that infants who responded with distress to maternal separation would show more relative right frontal activation during a baseline assessment of EEG than infants who were not distressed by the situation. The results indicated that infants who cried in response to maternal separation did in fact show greater right-frontal and less left frontal activation at rest than the noncriers. Consistent with our previous findings in adult subjects, parietal asymmetry recorded at the same time as the frontal asymmetry measures failed to discriminate between groups.

In order to examine the consistency of the group difference in frontal asymmetry on an individual subject basis, we computed a laterality difference score for each subject. Higher numbers on this metric indicate more relative left-sided activation. As shown in figure 4.2, every one of the criers fell below the mean score for the noncriers

FIGURE 4.2

Frontal Asymmetry Laterality Scores for Individual Infants in Response to a Brief Episode of Maternal Separation.
Note that all of the criers fell below the mean of noncriers and all of the noncriers fell above the mean of the criers.

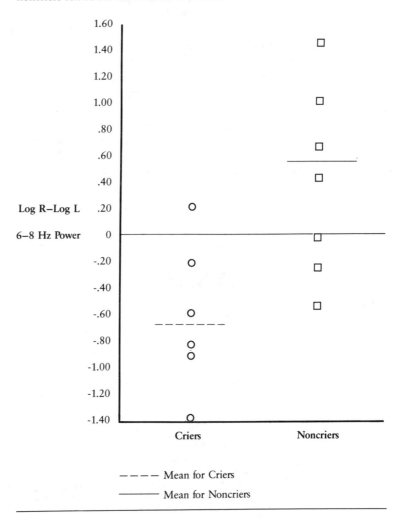

and every one of the noncriers fell above the mean score for the criers. Moreover, all but one of the criers had absolute right-sided frontal activation.

One concern that might be raised about these findings is that the difference in asymmetry between the two groups might simply reflect differences in preexistent mood, with the criers perhaps in a more irritable mood at the time of the resting baselines. In order to obtain data relevant to this issue, we coded infants' facial behavior during the resting baseline. Table 4.1 presents the duration in seconds of different facial signs of emotion during the baseline period. As indicated by this table, on all facial signs of emotion, the infants who subsequently cried in response to maternal separation failed to differ from those who did not cry. Although certainly not definitive, these findings do suggest that the two groups of infants were not in a different emotional state at the time that the EEG measures were recorded.

In sum, we have conducted two adult studies and one infant study, each of which assessed the relationship between resting EEG asymmetry and subsequent affective responses to an emotion elicitor. In each study, we found evidence that resting asymmetry recorded from anterior sites can predict affective responses to emotion elicitors. Furthermore, in each study, anterior asymmetry predicted affective responses independent of subjects' emotional state at the time of the baselines. Taken together, these two sets of findings suggest the following conclusions: (1) anterior asymmetry is a state-independent

TABLE 4.1

Facial Signs of Emotion During the Baseline Period

		Criers	Noncriers
Interest	M	9.5	11.3
	SD	8.6	7.8
No expression	M	17.0	15.1
	SD	8.2	8.9
Joy/Surprise	M	2.4	3.2
	SD	2.9	3.2
Negative affect	M	0.5	1.4
	SD	0.9	1.3

From Davidson & Fox (1989), p.130.

Note: Mean duration in seconds of facial affect for criers (N = 6) and noncriers (N =7) during the baseline period. The no expression category represents the mean number of seconds during which no facial signs of emotion were present. The negative affect category represents the mean number of seconds during which facial signs of any of the negative emotions (anger, fear, distress, sadness, and disgust) were expressed.

marker indexing the individual's readiness or predisposition for affective responsivity; and (2) this readiness is released only when the individual is exposed to a sufficiently potent affect elicitor. (The Activity Box provides a simple test for measuring your own hemisphericity.) In other words, baseline right frontal activation is not sufficient by itself for the production of negative emotion. Rather, in an individual who displays such a pattern, the threshold for eliciting negative emotion in response to a particular elicitor (such as a movie) will be lower. Finally, in each of these three studies, resting EEG asymmetry in posterior sites did not significantly predict subsequent affective responses. Thus, regional specificity is indicated.

One possible conceptualizion of the effects of such individual differences is that they represent differences in *thresholds* for affective responsivity. According to such a view, individuals with relative right anterior activation would require a less intense stimulus to elicit the same amount of negative affect that would be produced by a much more intense stimulus in an individual with left frontal activation. On the other hand, in an individual with left frontal activation, a less intense positive stimulus would be required to produce the same level of positive emotion as would be produced by a more intense positive stimulus in a subject with right frontal activation.

This conceptualization is consistent with recent evidence that individual differences in emotion or temperament are linked to altered thresholds for perception of, or responses to, affective stimuli (for a review, see Derryberry & Rothbart, 1984). Our interpretation is also consistent with infrahuman research indicating that activation of neural structures known to regulate important aspects of emotion does in fact produce lower thresholds for significant stimuli.

The research described illustrates how individual differences in one biological variable, anterior brain asymmetry, are related to affective reactivity. In the adult studies, the relations between the physiological measure of interest and measures of affective reactivity was obtained. In the infant study, subjects were classified on the basis of a behavioral measure (crying to maternal separation) and differences between groups were then examined in anterior asymmetry. Many questions remain to be answered in this line of research including the degree to which such measures of anterior asymmetry relate to the subsequent development of psychopathology and the underlying biological mechanisms that result in individuals with extreme asymmetry patterns showing biased affective reactivity. For example, do individuals who are particularly prone to depression and anxiety disorders show accentuated right anterior when they are children, prior to any overt expression of psychopathology? On the other hand, quite a few individuals exposed to very stressful environments when they are young do not

ACTIVITY BOX

Measuring Your Hemisphericity

Hemisphericity refers to individual differences in hemispheric activation. One way that individual differences in hemispheric activation have been assessed is to measure the direction of a person's gaze following a reflective question. In a right-handed person, eye movement to the left is associated with right-sided activation; eye movement to the right signifies left-sided activation (e.g., Gur & Reivich, 1980). Have a friend ask you the 10 questions that follow and note the direction of your first eye movement. If on seven or more of the questions you move your eyes to the same direction, you can infer that you are showing more activation on one side of your brain. Remember that this test is valid only for right-handed individuals. People who are left-handed have a more complicated pattern of hemispheric specialization and, without additional testing, it is not possible to unambiguously interpret their eye movement responses.

1. Tell me how you feel when you are anxious.
2. Visualize and describe the most upsetting photograph you have seen.
3. Imagine that you are relaxing in hot sulfur baths looking westward over the Pacific Ocean in California on a clear, sunny day. Your friend is peacefully resting with his back toward your right side. Approximately what direction is your friend looking out over?
4. Make up a sentence using the words "shock" and "anger."
5. When you visualize your father's face, what emotion first strikes you?
6. Tell me how you feel when you are frustrated.

develop any psychopathology. These individuals who are relatively invulnerable to stressful life events may be those with left-anterior activation, because this is the pattern we have predicted to result in heightened thresholds for experience of negative affect. Unfortunately, we do not have the answers to these important questions but we can look forward to future research in this area. Although this line of research is in its infancy, we hope to have illustrated its utility as a model of biological research in personality.

Summary

This chapter reviews some of the major conceptual and methodological issues in the study of biological bases of personality. Three

7. Picture and describe the most joyous scene you have recently been in.
8. Imagine that you are a veterinarian and must make a long and deep incision upon a dog. You must cut a straight line from the dog's left eye to his right, front shoulder. Visualize making the incision and tell me what parts of his face you would cut through.
9. Make up a sentence using the words rhapsody and pleasure.
10. Visualize and describe the most beautiful photograph you have recently seen.

These questions have been taken from the study by Schwartz, Davidson, and Maer (1975), which the interested reader may consult for additional details. This is not at all a conclusive measure of hemisphericity. Many factors unrelated to hemispheric activation affect a person's direction of lateral gaze following questions of this kind. Most people do not show consistent eye movements to one direction; rather, they show eye movements in different directions as a function of question content. If you do show consistent eye movements to the left or the right, you can decide whether you feel that you are more vulnerable to positive or negative affect. Research suggests that those who consistently move their eyes to the left should be more vulnerable to negative affect whereas individuals who consistently move their eyes to the right should be more vulnerable to positive affect.

approaches to the use of biological measures in personality research are identified: (1) the use of such measures as an additional correlate of a personality construct; (2) the use of such measures to examine individual differences in the relations among response systems that may all reflect different aspects of a single personality construct; and (3) the use of such measures as independent variables upon which to classify individuals. The question of whether to regard physiological indices of personality as correlates or substrates of the trait of interest is also discussed. A number of commonly used physiological measures in personality research are described. Following this overview, an example of a biological approach to personality from the author's own research is presented. Individual differences in baseline measures of brain asymmetry from the anterior regions of the hemispheres are shown to be related to affective reactivity in both infants and adults.

SUGGESTED READINGS

Davidson, R.J. (1984). Affect, cognition and hemispheric specialization. In C.E. Izard, J. Kagan, & R. Zajonc (Eds.), *Emotion, cognition and behavior* (pp. 320-325). New York: Cambridge University Press. This chapter presents a detailed review of research on hemispheric differences related to emotion, cognition, and individual differences.

Gale, A., & Edwards, J.A. (Eds.). (1983). *Physiological correlates of human behaviour: Vol. 3. Individual differences and psychopathology.* London: Academic Press. An excellent compendium of recent research on biological correlates of personality. Includes chapters on normal personality as well as certain forms of psychopathology such as anxiety, depression, and schizophrenia.

Levy, J. (1983). Individual differences in cerebral hemisphere asymmetry: Theoretical issues and experimental considerations. In J.B. Hellige (Ed.), *Cerebral hemisphere asym-*

metry, (pp. 465-515). New York: Praeger. A sophisticated and excellent treatment of the issue of individual differences in cerebral asymmetry and their relation to individual differences in cognitive and affective skills. Includes an important discussion of methodological issues in this area of research.

Nebylitsyn, V.D., & Gray, J.A. (Eds.). (1972). *Biological bases of individual behavior.* New York: Academic Press. A major collection of studies and theoretical papers emphasizing the work in the Soviet Union and other Eastern European countries in the Pavlov tradition.

Petrie, A. (1978). *Individuality in pain and suffering* (2nd ed.). Chicago: University of Chicago Press. This is a classic work on individual differences in augmentation/ reduction. This work forms the basis for a whole tradition of biologically oriented work on individual differences on this dimension.

REFERENCES

Ahern, G.L., & Schwartz, G.E. (1985). Differential lateralization for positive and negative emotion in the human brain: EEG spectral analysis. *Neuropsychologia, 23,* 745–756.

Alford, L.B. (1933). Localization of consciousness and emotion. *American Journal of Psychiatry, 12,* 789–799.

Allport, G.W. (1966). Traits revisited. *American Psychologist, 21,* 1–10.

Buchsbaum, M.S., Coursey, R.D., & Murphy, D.L. (1976). The biochemical high-risk paradigm: Behavioral and familial correlates of low platelet monamine oxidase activity. *Science, 194,* 339–341.

Buchsbaum, M.S., Haier, R.J., & Johnson, J. (1983). Augmenting and reducing: Individual differences in evoked potentials. In A. Gale & J.A. Edwards (Eds.), *Physiological*

correlates of human behaviour: Vol. 3. Individual differences and psychopathology (pp. 117–138). London: Academic Press.

Buchsbaum, M.S., & Silverman, J. (1968). Stimulus intensity control and the cortical evoked response. *Psychosomatic Medicine, 30,* 12–22.

Coles, M.G.H., Gale, A., & Kline, P. (1971). Personality and habituation of the orienting reaction: Tonic and response measures of electrodermal activity. *Psychophysiology, 8,* 54–63.

Crider, A. & Lunn, R. (1971). Electrodermal lability as a personality dimension. *Journal of Experimental Research in Personality, 5,* 145–150.

Davidson, R.J. (1984). Affect, cognition and hemispheric specialization. In C.E. Izard, J.

Kagan, & R. Zajonc (Eds.), *Emotion, cognition and behavior* (pp. 320-365). New York: Cambridge University Press.

Davidson, R.J. (1988). EEG measures of cerebral asymmetry: Conceptual and methodological issues. *International Journal of Neuroscience, 39,* 71–89.

Davidson, R.J., & Fox, N.A. (1989). Frontal brain asymmetry predicts infants' response to maternal separation. *Journal of Abnormal Psychology, 98,* 127-131.

Davidson, R.J., & Tomarken, A.J. (in press). Laterality and emotion: An electrophysiological approach. In F. Boller & J. Grafman (Eds.), *Handbook of neuropsychology.* Amsterdam: Elsevier.

Denenberg, V.H., & Yutzey, D.A. (1985). Hemispheric laterality, behavioral asymmetry and the effects of early experience in rats. In S.D. Glick (Ed.), *Cerebral lateralization in nonhuman species* (pp. 109–133). New York: Academic Press.

Derryberry, D., & Rothbart, M.K. (1984). Emotion, attention and temperament. In C.E. Izard, J. Kagan, & R.B. Zajonc (Eds.), *Emotion, cognition and behavior* (pp. 132–166). New York: Cambridge University Press.

Diener, E., Larsen, R.J., Levine, S., & Emmons, R.A. (1985). Intensity and frequency: Dimensions underlying positive and negative affect. *Journal of Personality and Social Psychology, 48,* 1253–1265.

Eysenck, H.J. (1967). *The biological basis of personality.* Springfield, IL: Charles C. Thomas.

Eysenck, H.J. (1972). Human typology, higher nervous activity, and factor analysis. In V.D. Nebylitsyn & J.A. Gray (Eds.), *Biological bases of individual behavior* (pp. 165–181). New York: Academic Press.

Fowles, D.C. (1986). The eccrine system and electrodermal activity. In M.G.H. Coles, E. Donchin, & S.W. Porges (Eds.), *Psychophysiology: Systems, processes and applications* (pp. 51–96). New York: Guilford.

Freud, S. (1895/1966). Project for a scientific

psychology. In J. Strachey (Ed.), *Standard edition of the complete psychological works of Sigmund Freud, Vol. 1* (pp. 281–397). London: Hogarth Press.

Gainotti, G. (1972). Emotional behavior and hemispheric side of lesion. *Cortex, 8,* 41–55.

Glick, S.D., & Shapiro, R.M. (1985). Functional and neurochemical mechanisms of cerebral lateralization in rats. In S.D. Glick (Ed.), *Cerebral lateralization in nonhuman species* (pp. 157–183). New York: Academic Press.

Goldstein, K. (1939). *The organism.* New York: Academic Press.

Gray, J.A. (1972). The psychophysiological nature of introversion-extraversion: A modification of Eysenck's theory. In V.D. Nebylitsyn & J.A. Gray (Eds.), *Biological bases of individual behavior* (pp. 182–205). New York: Academic Press.

Gur, R.C., & Reivich, M. (1980). Cognitive task effects on hemispheric blood flow in humans: Evidence for individual differences in hemispheric activation. *Brain and Language, 9,* 78–92.

Henriques, J.B., & Davidson, R.J. (1989). Affective disorders. In G. Turpin (Ed.), *Handbook of clinical psychophysiology* (pp. 357–392). London: Wiley.

Hodes, R.L., Cook, E.W., & Lang, P. (1985). Individual differences in autonomic response: Conditioned association or conditioned fear? *Psychophysiology, 22,* 545–560.

Kagan, J. (1984). *The nature of the child.* New York: Basic Books.

Kagan, J., Reznick, J.S., & Snidman, N. (1988). Biological bases of childhood shyness. *Science, 240,* 167–171.

Kelly, A., & Stinus, L. (1984). Neuroanatomical and neurochemical substrates of affective behavior. In N.A. Fox & R.J. Davidson (Eds.), *The psychobiology of affective development,* (pp. 1–75). Hillsdale, NJ: Erlbaum.

Larsen, R.J., Diener, E., & Emmons, R.A. (1986). Affect intensity and reactions to daily life events. *Journal of Personality and Social Psychology, 51,* 803–814.

Leventhal, H., & Tomarken, A.J. (1986). Emotion: Today's problems. In M.R. Rosenzweig & L.Y. Porter (Eds.), *Annual Review of Psychology* (Vol. 37, pp. 565–610). Palo Alto, CA: Annual Reviews, Inc.

Nauta, W.J.H. (1971). The problem of the frontal lobe: A reinterpretation. *Journal of Psychiatric Research, 8,* 167–187.

O'Gorman, J.G. (1983). Habituation and personality. In A. Gale & J.A. Edwards (Eds.), *Physiological correlates of human behaviour; Vol. 3. Individual differences and psychopathology* (pp. 45–61). London: Academic Press.

Pavlov, I.P. (1928). *Lectures on conditioned reflexes, Vol. 1.* New York: International Publishers.

Petrie, A. (1978). *Individuality in pain and suffering.* (2nd ed.). Chicago: University of Chicago Press.

Robinson, R.G., Kubos, K.L., Starr, L.B., Rao, K., & Price, T.R. (1984). Mood disorders in stroke patients: Importance of location of lesion. *Brain, 107,* 81–93.

Rosensweig, M.R., Krech, D., Bennett, E.L., & Diamond, M.C. (1962). Effects of environmental complexity and training on brain chemistry and anatomy: A replication and extension. *Journal of Comparative and Physiological Psychology, 55,* 427–429.

Sackeim, H.A., Weiman, A.L., Gur, R.C., Greenberg, M., Hungerbuhler, J.P., & Geschwind, N. (1982). Pathological laughter and crying: Functional brain asymmetry in the expression of positive and negative emotions. *Archives of Neurology, 39,* 210–218.

Schwartz, G.E., Davidson, R.J., and Maer, F. (1975). Right hemisphere lateralization for emotion in the human brain: Interactions with cognition. *Science, 190,* 286–288.

Shiller, V.M., Izard, C.E., & Hembree, E.A. (1986). Patterns of emotion expression during separation in the strange situation. *Developmental Psychology, 22,* 378–383.

Silberman, E.K., & Weingartner, H. (1986). Hemispheric lateralization of functions related to emotion. *Brain and Cognition, 5,* 322–353.

Tomarken, A.J., Davidson, R.J., Henriques, J.B., Saron, C.D., Straus, A., & Senulis, J. (1989). Anterior activation asymmetries predict emotional reactivity to film clips. In preparation.

Trimble, M. (Ed.). (1986). *New brain imaging techniques and psychopharmacology.* Oxford: Oxford University Press.

Tucker, D.M. (1981). Lateral brain function, emotion and conceptualization. *Psychological Bulletin, 89,* 19–46.

Tucker, D.M., & Frederick, S.L. (1989). Emotion and brain lateralization. In H. Wagner & T. Manstead (Eds.), *Handbook of psychophysiology: Emotion and social behaviour* (pp. 27–70). London: Wiley.

Tucker, D.M., Stenslie, C.E., Roth, R.S., & Shearer, S.L. (1981). Right frontal lobe activation and right hemisphere performance decrement during a depressed mood. *Archives for General Psychiatry, 38,* 169–174.

Tursky, B., & Jamner, L.D. (1982). Measurement of cardiovascular functioning. In J.T. Cacioppo and R.E. Petty (Eds.), *Perspectives in Cardiovascular Psychophysiology* (pp. 19–44). New York: Guilford.

Weinberger, D.A., Schwartz, G.E., & Davidson, R.J. (1979). Low anxious, high anxious and repressive coping styles: Psychometric patterns and behavioral and physiological responses to stress. *Journal of Abnormal Psychology, 88,* 369–380.

Weinraub, M., & Lewis, M. (1977). The determinants of children's responses to separation. *Monographs of the Society for Research in Child Development, 42* (Serial No. 172).

CHAPTER 5

Personality Development

PATRICIA L. WATERS AND JONATHAN M. CHEEK

Overview of Major Theories
Freud and the Psychoanalytic
    Tradition
    The Tripartite Structure of the
      Mind
    The Psychosexual Stages
    Defense Mechanisms
Attachment Research—
    A Neoanalytic Perspective
    Internal Working Models
    The Continuity of Internal
      Working Models
    Attachment and Intimacy
ACTIVITY BOX: Measuring Adult
    Attachment Patterns
Behaviorism and Social Learning
    Theory

Rogers and Humanistic
    Psychology
    The Fully Functioning Person
    Contemporary Research
      Applications
The Biosocial and Sociocultural
    Tradition
    Adlerian Individual Psychology
    Sullivan's Interpersonal
      Approach—Peer Influences
    The Sociocultural Approach of
      Horney
Future Directions: Toward a
    Transactional Theory of
    Personality Development
Summary
SUGGESTED READINGS
REFERENCES

The psychology of personality development addresses a very basic yet complex question: How did you become the person you are today? This is no idle philosophical musing. Views of personality development have a profound impact on choosing how to raise children, how schools are run, and how other government and social policy decisions are made. They also shape the approach therapists use when trying to help a person change and grow.

As you have seen in the preceding chapters, contemporary researchers are devoting a great deal of attention to genetics and the biological bases of personality. Traditional personality theorists did not have access to this emerging body of research. Some of them assumed that biology was of fundamental importance, whereas others preferred to focus on the influence of the social environment on personality development. In fact, the history of psychology is characterized by dramatic disagreements about the innate nature of human nature and the processes of psychological development. In this chapter we will examine the major theoretical approaches to personality development and link them to contemporary research topics.

Scientists usually agree that a good theory should be as simple as possible while still accounting for the phenomenon being explained. The preference for a theory requiring the fewest assumptions is called the law of parsimony. You probably only have to pause to think for a moment before you realize that a simple theory is unlikely to be able to account successfully for the variety and complexity of human personalities. Even simple assumptions about the innate nature of the infant will become complicated as they attempt to account for the change and growth that accompanies human development. Nevertheless, an overview of the basic assumptions of the major historically important theories of personality is a useful starting point.

Overview of Major Theories

Every reader of this book already has in his or her own mind elements of a personal theory of personality. Your views might be very explicit and well thought out. Or they might be a set of implicit assumptions that guide the ways in which you think about yourself and other people. In either case, you might want to compare your own views to the basic assumptions described in table 5.1.

As you can see, theorists vary in their root assumptions. Freud (1856–1939) believed that humans are innately selfish, subject to the will of powerful instincts. Freud believed that human behavior was largely motivated by intrapsychic conflicts—unconscious processes that dictate human behavior. Early experience, he believed, provides the subject matter of these conflicts.

The American behaviorist, John B. Watson (1878–1958) regarded Freud's theory as unscientific and needlessly pessimistic. Watson

TABLE 5.1

Overview of Basic Assumptions of Major Theoretical Approaches

	Innate quality of human nature: at birth, infants are inherently . . .	Inner/outer causes of behavior	Free will/ determinism	Importance of infant and early childhood experiences
Psychoanalytic (Freud)	selfish (sex and aggression motives)	inner/ unconscious	determinism	high
Behaviorism (Watson, Skinner, social learning theorists)	neutral (blank slate)	outer/ environmental	determinism	medium
Humanistic (Rogers)	good (self-actualization motive)	inner/ conscious	free will	low
Sociocultural and biosocial theorists (Adler, Horney)	mix of positive and negative motives	mix of inner and outer	free will	medium to varied

opposed the idea that inborn instincts shape personality and argued that learning experiences formed enduring habits of behavior. He also rejected the idea of the unconscious and the value of introspection about internal dynamics. Instead, he believed that behavior was shaped by the environment (external determinism) and the individual's learning history and was relatively optimistic about the possibility of unlearning bad habits and learning new good ones.

A third school of personality theory, humanistic psychology, is exemplified by another American, Carl Rogers (1902–1987). Rogers opposed Freud by asserting that the innate nature of human behavior is constructive and trustworthy. He opposed behaviorists such as Watson and Skinner by emphasizing internal causes of behavior such as the self-actualization motive. He regarded environmental pressures (conditions of worth) as a potential source of maladjustment and believed, if given unconditional positive regard, the infant will grow into a healthy and future-oriented individual.

Biosocial/cultural theorists (e.g., Adler [1870–1937]) tend to believe that extreme positions in arguments about good versus bad human nature, inner versus outer causes, and so on, fail to capture the complexities of personality (that these are false dichotomies). As contemporary research has become sophisticated, these more complex theories are becoming increasingly influential, as we shall see.

First, let's turn to a discussion of how the basic assumptions of the psychoanalytic, behaviorist, and humanistic theories have been elaborated as each theory tries to account for the processes of personality development, beginning with Freud and more recent examples of the psychoanalytic tradition.

Freud and the Psychoanalytic Tradition

Nearly every aspect of the field of psychology, and much of our everyday understanding of human personality, has been influenced by Freud's ideas. Freud provided the first and perhaps the most comprehensive theory of personality development. The very words he created to describe his observations have found their way into common use. References to "egotism" and slips of the tongue, for example, are testimony to the pervasiveness of his influence. In this overview we will focus on three areas of psychoanalytic theory that will help illustrate some of Freud's many contributions to our understanding of personality development: (1) the tripartite structure of the mind, (2) the psychosexual stages of development, and (3) the operation of defense mechanisms.

The Tripartite Structure of the Mind

Freud (1933) divided the adult mind into three parts: id, ego, and superego. The id is comprised of raw instincts such as hunger, sex, and aggression. It is ruled by the *pleasure principle,* which seeks immediate gratification of instinctual urges. Thus the id is unremitting in its pursuit of pleasure and avoidance of "unpleasure" (anxiety). The id is the source of all mental energy: it fuels the ego and the superego. However, the id operates on an unconscious, irrational level. The conscious ego differentiates from the id in early infancy. The ego operates on both conscious and unconscious levels. It is governed by the *reality principle* and it engages in a process of reality testing to bring satisfaction to the id. For example, an id instinct alerts the infant that he or she is hungry; however the ego tests reality—mouthing objects until an appropriate food supply is found.

The superego develops in the phallic stage of psychosexual development and is the embodiment of familial and cultural values. The superego introduces a conscience, or mechanism of punishment, into the system as well as provides an ego ideal. Like the id, the superego operates on a largely unconscious, irrational level. Thus it tends to consist of unrealistic extremes of "good" and "bad" that have not benefited from the tempering effect of the conscious mind. The superego draws its energy from the id. Yet it seeks to control the id by acting as a brake on the id's impulsive antics.

Freud's theory is based on the notion of internal, unconscious forces locked in conflict. The demands of the id and the superego are fundamentally at odds. The id says, "Do it *now*." The superego says, "*Never* do it." And the ego is left to mediate the debate. The ego serves three taskmasters: the id, the superego, and reality. The ego must balance the competing demands of these three. The ego provides the id with its only link to reality. One of the chief tasks of the ego is to create a diversion that will appease the id and alleviate the anxiety associated with frustration of instinctual impulses (see the discussion of defense mechanisms later in this section).

The Psychosexual Stages

Freud's training as a medical doctor resulted in a view of personality development that is closely tied to biological and maturational process-es. Thus, in part, Freud built the psychosexual stages around physiolog-ical features, such as the sucking instinct (early oral stage), the eruption of teeth (late oral stage), and the achievement of muscular control (anal stage). Freud's emphasis on instincts, particularly his theory of infantile sexuality, has been a source of much controversy.

Freud's infant is all id. He described infantile sexuality as polymorphously perverse: all areas of the body are experienced as sexually pleasing. Freud believed that at each stage instinctual needs seek a new outlet. He described personality development as a progressive shift from the polymorphous perversity of the newborn to focused zones of eroticism at each of the psychosexual stages. In Freud's view, patterns of frustration and satisfaction of instinctual (libidinal) urges at each stage contribute to the permutations we observe in adult personality.

The Oral Stage

In the *oral stage,* the mouth is the primary erogenous zone. In the early phase (up to approximately eight months) gratification is found in feeding and the pleasurable oral stimulation of sucking and swallowing. In the later months of the oral phase (during teething) the infant derives pleasure from biting and chewing.

According to Freud, satisfaction of oral impulses contributes to the individual's sense of trust and independence. However, frustration or excessive gratification during the oral stage may increase the traumatic impact of weaning and produce a *fixation* on oral issues. In describing fixation Freud likened the ego to an army: Becoming fixated at a stage is like leaving troops behind on a distant outpost (i.e., in the oral stage). The net effect is a weakening of the army (the ego). Fixations typically result from thwarted attempts to achieve gratification of an impulse, and they have consequences for later personality development (see table 5.2). For example, frustration of urges to bite and chew in the later half of the oral stage may contribute to an oral pessimistic style generally expressed in the belief that one's efforts are in vain. In contrast, excessive gratification of needs for sucking and swallowing in the early oral phase promotes unrealistic optimism—an assumption that all things are right with the world—based upon the early experience that one need only ask in order to receive (Kline, 1984).

Fixations in the early or late phases of the oral stage have been associated with other personality characteristics as well as seemingly mundane habits: chewing pencils, cigarette smoking, and a preference for soft, milky as opposed to hot, spicy foods (Kline, 1984). Interpersonal styles such as high sociability, and even the desire to acquire knowledge, have each been attributed to fixation in the early phase of orality.

The Anal Stage

In the *anal stage* the infant's attention shifts from the mouth to the anal region, as sphincter control becomes both a physiological possibility and a cultural mandate. Just as stimulation of the mouth is exciting to the one-year-old, a delight in defecation is typical in the toddler.

TABLE 5.2

Relationship Between Freud's Psychosexual Stages and Personality Characteristics

Stage name	Focus of libido	Satisfying behaviors	Outcome of gratification	Consequences of fixation
Early oral	mouth	sucking, swallowing	trust	gullibility, passivity, oral optimism
Late oral	mouth	biting, chewing	independence	oral pessimism, manipulativeness, sarcasm
Early anal	anus	expulsion of feces	self-control	obstinacy, cruelty, messiness
Late anal	anus	retention of feces	mastery	conscientiousness, punctuality, cleanliness
Phallic	genital organs	sexual curiosity, self-examination, and manipulation	sexual identity; superego (healthy conscience)	problems with authority figures, sexual maladjustment
Latency	—	—	—	—
Genital	genital organs and sublimation	sexual intercourse, intimacy; sublimation in work/art	capacity for unselfish love; fulfilling work, delay of gratification	—

Freud believed that the gratification of anal impulses resulted in healthy feelings of self-control and mastery over one's environment.

In many cultures, toilet training during the anal stage represents the first of society's numerous attempts to control instinctual impulses. As with the oral stage, the anal stage is subdivided into two phases: Libidinal pleasure is focused in the expulsion of feces in the early phase, and in retention in the later phase. Personality characteristics such as obstinacy, parsimony, excessive conscientiousness, orderliness, and cleanliness have all been linked to a preoccupation with issues of retention. Conversely, Freud associated fixation in the early, expulsive phase with cruelty, messiness, and destructiveness.

The Phallic Stage

You may have noticed that children between the ages of three and five often like to "play doctor." This is one of many expressions of the shift in focus from the anal zone to the genitals. Another is children's sudden "love affair" with their opposite sex parent. Until the phallic stage, both boys and girls view their mother as the primary object of their love and resent father's competition for their mother's affection. In boys this is expressed in the *Oedipus complex* as the unconscious desire to possess the mother and depose the father. However, sons fear retaliation by fathers (castration anxiety) and thus identify with their fathers as a defense against anxiety and as a vicarious source of instinctual gratification. In identifying with the same sex parent the child internalizes cultural and familial restrictions (i.e., against incest) and develops a superego that is part ego ideal and part conscience.

In girls, the realization that her genitals are different from boys' produces penis envy. In Freud's view, daughters become disenchanted with their mothers for depriving them of a penis and turn their affections towards a new love object—fathers. However, to possess the father, the daughter risks total loss of her mother's love. Freud contended that this was not as strong a prohibition as the fear of castration in boys. However, to defend against the threatened loss of love, daughters identify with their mothers.

According to Freud, the relatively weaker prohibition against incestuous longings in the female results in a weaker superego. However, numerous criticisms have been raised against Freud's perception of female development. For example, Horney (1967) asked whether penis envy in girls might not have a counterpart called "womb envy" in boys. Others have questioned Freud's emphasis on anatomy as destiny, suggesting that penis envy might better serve as a metaphor for power envy (Miller, 1976).

The Latency Stage

During latency, sexual instincts lie dormant, as the child undergoes a solidification of the superego formed during the phallic stage.

The Genital Stage

During the phallic stage, the child essentially abandons hope of possessing the opposite sex parent as a love object and replaces that loss with identification with the same sex parent. With the onset of puberty, sexual intimacy becomes a possibility and the individual seeks a new object of affection. Nearly all of us have observed friends or family members who have married someone who resembles their opposite sex parent. Freud used the phrase "object finding is object refinding" to describe the unconscious tendency to seek a sexual partner that is reminiscent of the lost one of childhood. The focus during the genital stage is on finding a new love object and learning to sublimate successfully other id impulses into productive channels (i.e., work)—striking a balance between love and work.

Defense Mechanisms

Recall that Freud viewed the infant psyche as a collection of polymorphously perverse and murderously aggressive id impulses seeking gratification. The goal of socialization is to gain control of these impulses. The individual achieves this by exercising the superego (conscience) and invoking a system of defenses against anxieties caused by frustration of the id or the conscious awareness of painful memories. Individuals do this in unique ways depending on their history of satisfaction and frustration at each stage of development. This history of frustrations or overgratifications (fixations), combined with the superego, form the individual's *character structure*. The dynamics of this character structure are visible in the defense mechanisms. Freud's daughter, Anna, provided a more complete elaboration of the defense mechanisms (Freud, A., 1958). Descriptions of a few of these follow.

- *Repression* protects the ego from consciously experiencing the anxiety of unacceptable thoughts. These thoughts can range from taboo id wishes to painful memories. The ego keeps these thoughts in the unconscious—away from conscious awareness—where they continue to exert an influence over behavior.
- *Displacement* is the replacement of one form of satisfaction of id impulses with another. For example, playing defensive tackle on a football team is an acceptable form of displacement for murderous aggression. When displacement takes a socially productive form it is called *sublimation.*
- *Projection* is ascribing unacceptable, anxiety-producing facts about the self to someone or something else. For example, "I can't dance" might be converted to "He is a terrible dance partner" or "This music has no beat."
- *Reaction formation* is the repression and transformation into its opposite of an objectionable thought. For example, a man who is drawn to sexual perversions may become a television evangelist preaching the wickedness of the flesh.

Attachment Research—A Neoanalytic Perspective

In spite of the criticism and controversies surrounding many aspects of Freud's theory, he succeeded in focusing attention on the crucial role of emotional development during infancy and early childhood. In stressing the importance of the ego from birth, *ego psychologists* have posited a less pessimistic view of infancy than Freud envisioned. In their view, the infant is not a mass of unconscious id impulses, but rather a social creature, with an innate urge to merge with others. This new conceptualization can be seen in Erikson's (1963) reinterpretation and extension of Freud's psychosexual stages into a psychosocial model of development. Winnicott (1960) described the newborn-caregiver relationship as a state of "fusion" in which mother and child experience such intense feelings of connection and attachment that the very boundary between them seems blurred.

Studies of early attachment patterns in other primates revealed that when given a choice between a wire "mother" with a bottle attached to it and a cloth "mother," the infant monkey sought out the wire mother only to satisfy hunger needs, but clung to the cloth mother for prolonged periods of time, presumably to satisfy needs for contact comfort (Harlow, 1958). Perhaps the most compelling evidence for the primacy of attachment in infancy has been drawn from observing the effects of maternal deprivation. In a study of the effects of institutionalization on young orphans, Spitz (1945) discovered higher infant mortality rates among infants whose physical needs had been met but whose needs for nurturance had been overlooked. Thus the availability of attachment figures affects the infant's survival on a profound level in a way Freud did not explore. The child's ability to "thrive" is placed in jeopardy in situations of caregiver deprivation.

Attachment research stresses the importance of the infant's experience of "felt security" (Bowlby, 1969). Felt security arises out of parents' sensitivity and responsiveness to infants' signals of distress, happiness, fatigue—in sum, the infants' affective cues. The quality of the caregiver-infant relationship has implications for the child's ability to explore freely the physical and social environment.

Indeed, many theorists argue that early attachment patterns may set the tone for basic personality styles such as the individual's emotional regulation in a variety of social settings (Kobak & Sceery, 1988). Through their observations of mothers and infants in the strange situation, Ainsworth and her colleagues identified three styles of caregiver-infant attachment patterns: secure, anxious/avoidant and anxious/resistant attachments (see Ainsworth, Blehar, Waters, & Wall, 1978, for review). Table 5.3 provides an overview of differences in approach to interpersonal relationships among children who had a secure or insecure (anxious/avoidant or anxious/resistant) attachment with their mothers.

When placed in an unfamiliar situation *securely attached* children demonstrate more freedom of movement and exploration, using their mother as a secure base of operations (Ainsworth, Bell & Stayton, 1974). Mothers of securely attached children tend to be sensitive to the needs and wishes of their toddlers and at the same time encourage their children's active exploration of the environment. As toddlers, securely attached children engage in social interactions with greater enthusiasm and delight and show greater persistence in solving cognitive problems. Similarly, as four-to-five-year-olds, children who had been classified previously as securely attached demonstrate greater ego resilience and

TABLE 5.3

Interpersonal Styles of Children with Different Attachment Histories

		Insecure	
	Secure	Anxious/Avoidant	Anxious/Resistant
Toddler	upon reunion with mother easily soothed by mother; seeks proximity to mother	upon reunion with mother looks or pulls away, ignores, or mixes proximity seeking with avoidance; as easily soothed by stranger as mother	upon reunion with mother mixes proximity seeking and resistance (hits, cries); cries, seeks contact prior to separation; inconsolable
3½ year old	greater persistence in problem solving; greater enthusiasm and affective sharing with peers; greater peer competence and ego strength than other attachment groups	less peer competence and ego strength than "secures"; less freedom in exploring environment	less peer competence and ego strength than "secures"; may passively resist exploring environment
4–5 year old	moderate ego control (flexibility in peer interactions); handles emotions of peers with greater ease, greater curiosity than other attachment groups	tends toward ego overcontrol (constrained); avoids contact with peers; low expression of emotion	tends toward ego undercontrol (high expression of distress, fear, anger); inappropriate affect in peer interactions (impulsive, helpless)
6 year old	in doll play, accepting, tolerant of other's imperfections; upon reunion, relaxed, responsive to parent (initiates positive interactions)	in doll play, defensive, dismissing of attachment; upon reunion, maintains distance from parent (ignores, continues to play)	in doll play, overt anger, hostility; upon reunion, may exaggerate dependency/intimacy, or spurn parent in overt or covert way (leaning against, then jerking away)

flexibility in their interactions with other preschoolers (Arend, Gove, & Sroufe, 1979), and they tended to smile more and interact with greater emotional expressiveness than their peers with different attachment histories (Waters, Wippman, & Sroufe, 1979). Preschool teachers' observations suggest that securely attached children not only demonstrate more positive (and less negative) emotions but seem to handle negative emotion in others with greater ease (Sroufe, Schork, Motti, Lawroski, & LaFrenier, 1984). Among six-year-olds, children with a history of secure attachment continue to be more curious in social situations and have higher levels of self-esteem than their peers (Main, Kaplan, & Cassidy, 1985). In interactions with mothers, secure six-year-olds are more relaxed, responsive, and willing to initiate positive interactions than their peers with other attachment histories (Main & Cassidy, 1988). Thus, enthusiasm and flexibility in problem-solving situations and greater freedom to explore the environment combine with greater social competence and higher levels of self-esteem to form a highly adaptive picture for the securely attached child.

Like those in the securely attached group, infants with *anxious/ avoidant* attachments have little difficulty separating to explore the environment and show relatively little avoidance of strangers while in the presence of their mothers. However, their interactions are marked by relatively little affective sharing and when distressed they are as easily consoled by a stranger as by their mother (see table 5.3). Upon reunion with their mothers after a brief separation period, infants with anxious/avoidant attachments generally ignore or turn away from their mothers, but may intermittently seek proximity (Sroufe, 1983).

As preschoolers, anxious/avoidant children tended to be ego overcontrolled. In their approach to others they are relatively constrained and conforming and tend to avoid ambiguous or inconsistent situations (Arend et al., 1979). Often lacking spontaneity in social situations, they are less demonstrative in displaying emotion than their securely attached peers (Sroufe, 1983). As six-year-olds, anxious/ avoidant children are dismissive of attachments in toy play (Cassidy, 1988) and maintain distance when reunited with their mothers after a brief separation. This distance seeking may be expressed subtly; the child may simply continue to be engrossed in toy play, ignoring the mother's reappearance (Main & Cassidy, 1988).

Infants with *anxious/resistant* attachments have the greatest difficulty separating to explore their surroundings and tend to be wary in the presence of strangers and in novel situations. Anxious/resistant infants appear to lack confidence in others. In times of distress, neither the mother nor a stranger can provide ready relief. Upon reunion infants with anxious/resistant attachments may react with extreme passivity or show angry ambivalence, alternating proximity seeking with aggressive emotional expressions such as kicking, hitting, or pushing away (see table 5.3).

At preschool age, these children continue to demonstrate a general wariness in exploring the environment and tend toward ego undercontrol. For example, they tend to react to stressful situations with a very high degree of emotional expressiveness, have difficulties delaying gratification, and are typically more distractible with interests and enthusiasms that are generally short-lived (Block & Block, 1980). As six-year-olds, anxious/resistant children display more angry/hostile emotions in toy play (Cassidy, 1988) and respond to reunions with parents after a brief separation by mixing exaggerated bids for dependency and angry expressions of rejection, first leaning against the parent, then jerking away (Main & Cassidy, 1988).

Internal Working Models

We have described some of the ways in which differences in caregiver-infant attachment patterns may be expressed in children's behavior in peer and school settings, but how does this process work? Many theorists believe that the child's experience of early attachment forms an *internal working model* that is integrated into the personality and invoked as a guide for behavior in subsequent social interactions (Bowlby, 1969; Main et al., 1985). As the phrase "internal working model" suggests, early attachment experiences are taken in, or internalized, by the child but are subject to change and elaboration as a result of new experience. Thus, they are considered to be "working," or in progress. Finally, they provide a general guide or template—a model—for interpersonal interaction. The notion of internal working models remains inferential. That is, researchers have not asked children how they structure their approach to others but have drawn inferences based upon the continuities observed between children's interactions with their primary caregivers and their interactions with peers and strangers.

The Continuity of Internal Working Models

Although the early evidence for continuity of internal working models is compelling, longitudinal study that extends beyond the early years of school will help clarify the relative stability or variation in an individual's interpersonal approach over the life course and thus test the significance of early attachments for personality development. In recent years, researchers interested in internal working models and patterns of attachment have begun to explore the relationship between adults' perceptions of their attachment with their own parents and their current attachment to their infants. Main and colleagues (1985) have identified secure, avoidant, and resistant attachment patterns using adults' self-reports of their early attachment histories. Interestingly, self-reports of parents' attachment to their own mothers were significantly correlated with their infants' behavior in the strange situation. For example, those women who reported a history of avoidant attachment to their mothers had children who similarly demonstrated an avoidant attachment. Their data suggest that patterns of attachment may be transferred across generations in the family. Thus, although internal working models may be subject to alteration and change across the life cycle, general patterns of early parent-child attachment described by adults tend to be reiterated in their own attachment patterns with their children.

ACTIVITY BOX

Measuring Adult Attachment Patterns

You might be interested in taking a closer look at how adult attachment patterns have been measured. Most measures of attachment in adulthood rely on semistructured interviews or questionnaires. Here are a number of items similar to those used on actual scales (Hazan & Shaver, 1987). Check only the items that accurately describe your feelings, or your general view about the course of romantic love over time.

1. The kind of head-over-heels romantic love depicted in novels and movies doesn't exist in real life.
2. It's easy to fall in love. I feel myself beginning to fall in love often.
3. Intense romantic love is common at the beginning of a relationship, but it rarely lasts forever.
4. I find it relatively easy to get close to others and am comfortable depending upon them [and having them depend on me].
5. I am somewhat uncomfortable being close to others; I find it difficult to trust them completely, difficult to allow myself to depend on them . . . often, love partners want me to be more intimate than I feel comfortable being.
6. I find that others are reluctant to get as close as I would like. I often worry that my partner doesn't really love me or won't want to stay with me.

The six items were adapted from Hazan and Shaver (1987). Used by permission.

Attachment and Intimacy

The implications of a persistent attachment style extend beyond the family and early peer group. Researchers studying later periods of personality development have used a variety of methods, ranging from retrospective self-reports to ratings by friends, to assess the coherence of attachment patterns across time and situations (see Activity Box; Hazen & Shaver, 1987; Kobak & Sceery, 1988). The incidence of each of the three attachment styles appears to be roughly the same in infancy and adulthood: Slightly over half (56 percent) of the adults in Hazan and Shaver's study (1987) were classified as securely attached. The remaining adults were nearly evenly distributed between anxious/ambivalent (resistant) (20 percent) and avoidant (24 percent) classifica-

---

Items such as the first three are designed to assess your "mental model" (or internal working model) of relationships. Individuals with avoidant attachment patterns, for example, tend to endorse items similar to 3, whereas "secures" endorse those like item 1 less often than either "avoidants" or "anxious/ambivalents." "Anxious/ambivalents" select items similar to 2 more often than any other group.

Hazan and Shaver (1987) were also interested in whether individuals could easily identify themselves as "secure," "avoidant," or "anxious/ambivalent" on the basis of a brief description. They asked participants to select the description that best matched their experiences and feelings in relationships. Excerpts from those descriptions are represented in items 4–6 (for complete descriptions, see Hazan & Shaver, 1987). Item 4 is most descriptive of a "securely" attached individual. Statements in item 5 best represent the opinion of individuals with avoidant attachments, and item 6 describes the opinion of those with anxious/ambivalent attachment patterns.

These items are meant to represent the type of questions used to identify attachment patterns and should not be viewed as a reliable assessment of your attachment style. The determination of attachment pattern is based on numerous items and, often, multiple measurement instruments (see Hazan & Shaver, 1987, for a good example of a complete scale).

tions. These proportions are similar to those obtained in infant research. For example, Campos, Barrett, Lamb, Goldsmith, and Stenberg (1983) identified 62 percent of the infants in their sample as secure, 15 percent as anxious/ambivalent, and 23 percent as avoidant.

Personality characteristics associated with each of the three attachment classifications in childhood appear to be consistent with descriptions of adults from the three attachment groups. Securely attached adults expect close relationships to endure and find others trustworthy. They tended to view themselves as likeable and were described by others as emotionally expressive (Hazan & Shaver, 1987; Kobak & Sceery, 1988). These patterns closely parallel the higher social competence and freedom of emotional expression noted earlier among securely attached children (Arend et al., 1979).

In an earlier study, Kobak (1985) noted that peers' evaluations of avoidant and anxious/ambivalent adults described them as less socially adept than secure adults. However, only the anxious/ambivalents described themselves as less socially competent. Main and her colleagues (1985) have suggested that avoidant individuals may deny the importance of attachments, favoring compulsive self-reliance, in a pattern reminiscent of the ego overcontrol of anxious/avoidant infants. Avoidant college students tended to be afraid of closeness and to doubt the existence or the durability of romantic love. Moreover, these individuals did not consider romantic love to be necessary for happiness.

In contrast, college students in the anxious/ambivalent attachment group described love as a preoccupation, viewing intimate relationships as "painfully exciting." You may recall that anxious/resistant preschoolers tended to be ego undercontrolled (i.e., highly spontaneous but unable to sustain interest and enthusiasm). Similarly, ambivalent college students have a personality style that enables them to fall in love more easily and more frequently than their peers, but they express difficulty in finding true love. They tend to be plagued by self-doubt and are at ease disclosing feelings of insecurity (Hazan & Shaver, 1987; Kobak & Sceery 1988).

The notion that our style of developing and maintaining attachments becomes integrated into the core of our personalities continues to be a topic of debate (Rutter, 1979). However, the parallels between mother-infant attachment patterns, peer interaction styles, and adult attachment styles suggest preliminary support for the importance of internal working models of attachment in personality formation. This topic will undoubtedly receive increasing attention from researchers in the 1990s.

Behaviorism and Social Learning Theory

John B. Watson (1878–1958) set out to change the definition of psychology from the study of mental life to the science of behavior. He wanted not only to exclude Freud's unconscious but also to omit any reference to the conscious mind, which he considered to be an unscientific philosophical abstraction. Instead, he proposed that the prediction and control of observable behavior should be the primary goal of psychology. Watson argued vehemently against the idea that instincts and heredity influence personality development and suggested that behavior patterns are learned entirely through experience with the environment. Even the word *personality* seemed too mentalistic to him, so he suggested that it be replaced by the term "habit system" (Watson, 1930).

Behaviorism is not a theory of personality but a general theory of behavior that rejects all explanations of the internal processes of the person. The preferred research method for behaviorism is laboratory experimentation that uses animals as well as people for research subjects. As we saw in table 5.1, Watson assumed that human infants are a blank slate at birth, and whether they become adults with good or bad habits will be determined by their environment. He tried to apply the law of parsimony in his theory by explaining most adult behavior as the result of a long history of the simplest kind of learning—classical conditioning (see table 5.4).

Classical conditioning is simple association learning. You may recall the famous example of Pavlov's dogs. After the sound of a tone

TABLE 5.4

Hierarchy of Learning

Theorist	Type of learning	Characteristics
Watson	classical conditioning	passive, association learning
Skinner	instrumental conditioning	active response selection through reinforcement and chaining of series of responses
Bandura	observational learning	modeling and vicarious reinforcement
Bandura and Mischel	learning rules and symbols	concepts, strategies expectancies

(the conditioned stimulus) was paired several times with the presentation of meat powder (the unconditioned stimulus), the dog responded by salivating when only the sound of the tone was presented. In his book advising parents how to raise their children, Watson (1928) explained how classical conditioning is crucial for human emotional development. An infant has no innate fear of a furry animal such as a rabbit, but does fear unexpected loud noises. By pairing a loud noise with presentation of a rabbit, Watson classically conditioned fear of the rabbit, and this learning generalized so that the infant feared other, similar objects such as a fur coat. Watson concluded that, over the years, such experiences accumulate into a complex set of emotional habits.

Watson believed that emotional dependency was the worst habit a person could develop. Therefore, he advised mothers never to kiss their infants, but to shake their hand and treat them as objectively as possible (just as a scientific behaviorist would!). He wanted to avoid "love conditioning" so that the child could grow up to be an efficient, self-reliant adult. Research on attachment contradicts Watson's now outdated advice, but it is worth noting that his child care manual was influential in the 1930s. Meanwhile, Watson's attempt to explain adult behavior through a history of classical conditioning came to be seen as too simplistic, and later behaviorists shifted the focus to more complex types of learning.

B.F. Skinner (1904–1990), a famous behaviorist, concentrated on instrumental or operant conditioning (see table 5.4). Rejecting the idea of free will, Skinner concluded that behavior is a function of its consequences. Humans and other animals are active organisms. Any particular response or behavior pattern that is rewarded will be selectively strengthened and whatever is ignored or punished will tend to be eliminated. By successively chaining a series of instrumental conditioning tasks, Skinner (1953) has demonstrated that even pigeons can learn remarkably complex behaviors. Instrumental conditioning can be applied in child-rearing practices, as in research showing that consistent punishment resulted in inhibition of aggression among elementary school boys (Parke & Devr, 1972). Skinnerian schedules of reinforcement also have been applied successfully in the treatment of autistic and mentally retarded children. However, the explanation of complex human behavior, such as learning to drive a car or speak a language, required psychologists to look at higher levels on the hierarchy of learning.

Albert Bandura helped to pioneer the transition from traditional behaviorism to social learning theory (see table 5.4). He studied the role of observational learning in the acquisition of human behavior. For example, children who saw a model being reinforced for acting aggressively behaved more aggressively than did children who saw a model punished for aggressive behavior (Bandura, 1965). This process is called *vicarious reinforcement,* the way we learn from watching the consequences of other people's behavior. What is observed is learned, but behavior we think will be positively reinforced is the most likely to be performed.

Bandura (1986) has recently extended his theory to focus on the most advanced, cognitive type of learning. Internalized goals, plans, strategies, and expectancies permit self-regulation of complex behavior. For example, Walter Mischel (1984) demonstrated that specific mental representations of potential rewards helped children to delay gratification in a laboratory test. Individuals use information such as repeated success or failure as a guide to adjust their behavior. A key determinant of self-regulated behavior is *perceived self-efficacy*—what the individual believes he or she is capable of accomplishing. Personal successes and failures, encouragement from others, and adequate role models are a few of the variables influencing the nature of the individual's *perceived self-efficacy*. Bandura now emphasizes self-efficacy expectancies as a central feature of personality. On the basis of their perceived self-efficacy, individuals develop a set of expectations for the self that have direct consequences on their behavior. For example, one cigarette smoker's *self-efficacy expectancies* may cause him or her to say, "I'd like to quit smoking, but it's hard, I've tried before and I don't think I can." Whereas, another smoker might say, "I'd like to quit smoking and I know if I really put my mind to it, I can." The expectation of success or failure influences the individual's persistence and, ultimately, shapes the outcome of his or her efforts (see chapter 9, Personal Efficacy, for a more complete discussion).

Cognitive social learning theory has come a long way from Watson's radical behaviorism, but Bandura and Mischel still focus on situationally specific behaviors in a way that puts them at odds with personality theorists who assume a more coherent and consistent integration within the individual personality. At least one author of a recent personality text, however, predicts that in the next decade cognitive social learning theory will emerge as a widely recognized, global theory of personality (Peterson, 1988).

Rogers and Humanistic Psychology

In the mid-1940s to 1950s, Carl Rogers introduced a new perspective on personality development. Considered to be the founder of humanistic psychology, Rogers holds an essentially optimistic view of human motivation and human nature. He believes that a central, organizing, or "master," motive guides human behavior—the actualizing tendency. The actualizing tendency is the natural human urge "to actualize, maintain, and enhance the experiencing organism" (Rogers, 1951, p. 487).

In contrast to Freud, Rogers believes in the innate goodness and basic integrity of human beings. Therefore, he suggests that the direction of the actualizing tendency is positive and growth promoting for the individual. In Rogers' view, the individual thrives when this propensity toward actualization is allowed to flourish, and it suffers when external influences exert excessive controls or restrictions. Therefore, he also opposed the external determinism of behaviorism.

Rogers takes an experiential approach to development. That is, he believes in the integrity of the individual's unique experiences. The course of development is largely contingent upon the person's ability to interpret his or her experiences without distortion. Although he suggests that "persons have a basically positive direction," Rogers concedes that human beings sometimes act in ways that are undesirable (Rogers, 1961). He attributes undesirable acts to distortions and defensiveness resulting from the conflict between a person's inner experience and tendency toward actualization, and the need to be held in positive regard by others.

In an ideal world, the need for positive regard would be satisfied, initially, by parents' unfailing expressions of acceptance, sympathy, warmth, and care for the child. In this state of "unconditional positive regard," the child learns to trust and rely upon its experience and evaluations of its feelings and experiences and behaves in ways that will allow movement toward fulfillment of innate potential. As the child matures, unconditional positive regard from others is internalized as unconditional positive *self*-regard. Positive self-regard, in turn, fosters a healthy self-concept that allows individuals to trust in their own experience and act on the basis of that trust.

In reality, most families extend "conditional positive regard" to their children. That is, the parents' acceptance of the child is partially dependent (conditional) upon the child's behaving appropriately. In conditional positive regard situations, "conditions of worth" are understood between the parent and child. For example, Amy knows that if she hits her little brother, her mother may get very angry and tell her she is bad. At the same time, Amy may really feel like hitting her little brother. Perhaps he's been teasing her all day. Confronted with the choice between hitting him (which would please her) and satisfying the conditions of worth (which would preserve her mother's acceptance and love), Amy experiences a classic conflict: "Shall I do what I want, or what I should do?"

Rogers suggests that, in most instances, children conform to the conditions of worth and act on the basis of "shoulds," because the need for positive regard is very strong. However, he views the urge to satisfy the need for positive regard as the most serious *obstacle* to the course of actualization. Why? In order to satisfy conditions of worth, the individual must deny or distort his or her experience. Thus, the price of conforming to conditions of worth, according to Rogers, is alienation from one's true self.

In the example of conditional positive regard noted earlier, Amy had only a few options to resolve the conflict. She could act as her evaluation of her experience dictated, and hit her little brother. But that would produce a withdrawal of positive regard and be damaging to her developing self-concept (i.e., "I am a bad person because I wanted to hit my brother"). Or she could distort her valuation of the experience, "I *love* my little brother and would never do anything to hurt him," and thus win her mother's conditional positive regard at the expense of alienating her genuine feelings.

In an ideal situation Amy's mother would continue to express unconditional positive regard, by acknowledging the child's aggressive feelings. She might suggest that "sometimes we all get very angry" and, although it may be understandable that Amy wants to hit her little brother and she loves Amy very much, she's pretty sure that the little brother does not want to be hit and he has a right to his feelings, too.

The Fully Functioning Person

According to Rogers, treating a child with unconditional positive regard provides the foundation for healthy personality development. Acknowledging children's right to evaluate their experiences in their own way and providing a democratic, mutually respectful family atmosphere are the keys to producing "fully functioning persons." In the fully functioning person, the self-concept is built upon trial and error evaluations of personal experience. Because they have developed unconditional positive self-regard, fully functioning individuals tend to trust their own judgment and have little need to distort or defend against experience. Thus they are typically able to correct their mistakes, because they perceive them clearly and without distortions, and they are notably free of the anxiety and confusion that plagues individuals who operate on the basis of "conditions of worth."

Contemporary Research Applications

✱ Child-Rearing Styles and Instrumental Competence

Contemporary research appears to support, with some modifications, Rogers' view that ideal parenting involves democratic family process as well as unconditional warmth and acceptance. For example, Baumrind (1967) found that children high on instrumental competence (self-assertive, independent, socially responsible) tended to have parents whose child-rearing practices combined nurturance and warmth with a modicum of discipline and clear parent-child communication strategies.

Baumrind identified three parenting styles—permissive, authoritarian, and authoritative—that produce distinctly different developmental outcomes. *Permissive* parents tend to exert low levels of control and place few maturity demands upon their children. At the same time, they are high on nurturance and warmth (what Rogers might call unconditional positive regard), and their communications with their children are characterized as very clear (see table 5.5). Thus, the permissive household is typified by the fewest external impingements upon the child. Despite this atmosphere of nurturing acceptance, however, children of permissive parents tend to be less self-reliant and self-controlled and more dependent upon their parents than their peers with authoritative parents.

In the *authoritarian* household, parenting practices are the reverse of permissive: the clarity of parent-child communications is low, there is little nurturance, and parental control and maturity demands upon the child are each high (see table 5.5). As Rogers might have suggested, this family environment does little to promote the child's actualizing tendency: Children of authoritarian parents are often lacking in vitality and self-assertion and are frequently shy and withdrawn and low in

TABLE 5.5

Baumrind's Three Parenting Styles

	Authoritarian	Authoritative	Permissive
Control/discipline	high	high	low
Clarity of parent–child communication	low	high	high
Maturity demands	high	high	low
Nurturance/warmth	low	high	high

Based on ideas in Baumrind (1967).

achievement motivation. Children raised permissively tended to engage in activities with greater vitality and a more positive mood than children raised in authoritarian households. However, apart from these differences, children of permissive and authoritarian parents behave in remarkably similar ways, exhibiting greater dependency upon their parents and less self-control in their interactions with others.

As in the case of Amy's mother, described earlier, *authoritative* parents combine warmth, nurturance, and clear communication strategies with relatively high levels of discipline and control (see table 5.5). Authoritative parents expect their children to act in mature ways, and their children respond accordingly. Children raised authoritatively tend to be self-assured, independent, highly motivated to achieve, and socially responsible—in essence, their "tendency toward actualization" is apparent.

Consistent with Rogers' view, it is clear that nurturance, warmth, and acceptance are vital to children's healthy personality development. It is less apparent that this acceptance must be "unconditional." Indeed, Baumrind's data suggest that an optimal child-rearing style couples warmth with clearly stated, realistic demands. Is unconditional positive regard antithetical to these demands? How might you combine the two?

Unconditional Positive Regard and the Development of Creativity

According to Rogers, a creativity-fostering environment provides (1) *psychological safety*, in which the individual experiences unconditional worth and no external evaluations are imposed, and (2) a sense of *psychological freedom*, in which the individual engages in "unrestrained symbolic expression" (Harrington, Block, & Block, 1987). In such a nonevaluative atmosphere, Rogers suggests, individuals develop the internal prerequisites for constructive creativity.

In recent years, efforts have been made to test empirically Rogers' assertions about the constituents of a creativity-fostering environment. Using data from their longitudinal study, Harrington, Block, and Block (1987) developed three indices measuring the extent to which parents' child-rearing techniques conformed to Rogers' descriptions of creativity-fostering environments. These indices were compared with a composite of children's creative potential drawn from assessments conducted during preschool and seven to eleven years later, during early adolescence. Parents who used Rogerian-style child-rearing practices with their preschoolers (such as warmth, support, and encouragement of children's independence) produced early adolescents who were higher on measures of creative potential than their peers. Even after accounting for initial differences in the intellectual abilities and creative potentials of the preschoolers, a history of Rogerian-style child-rearing increased the creativity of young adolescents. Children raised in more restrictive (authoritarian) or more chaotic (permissive) environments, in contrast, showed less creative potential as preadolescents.

The Biosocial and Sociocultural Tradition

In reviewing theory and research we have examined some key differences between the psychoanalytic, ego psychological, behavioral, and humanistic approaches to personality development. Alfred Adler, Harry Stack Sullivan, Karen Horney, and other interpersonally oriented theorists shifted attention away from instinct gratification (Freud's id) as the primary motive of human action, and toward the influence of the social and cultural context. In varying degrees, these theorists continued to emphasize the importance of early childhood experiences and psychodynamic processes. However, they focused on the role of social interactions and cultural expectations, rather than the primacy of biological motives, in the development of personality.

Adlerian Individual Psychology

Adler defined his theory as individual psychology, and he described an individual's striving for superiority as "the fundamental fact of life." However, as his ideas developed, he asserted that individual psychology was inextricably linked to social psychology: We are all in and of a social sphere and, as such, our strivings are not for ourselves alone, but for the perfection of society. We are born with the propensity for *social interest*—striving for cooperation with others toward the establishment of a superior society—and pathology is defined, in part, by a lack of social interest. Ideally, mothers encourage their children to develop their natural propensity for social interest by acting as the first link to the social world. In Adler's view the mother assists the child in extending this interest to others. The role of the father in Adler's view is to foster feelings of self-reliance and courage and to stress the need for establishing a career choice.

Adler believed that feelings of inferiority are a natural consequence of being a small, helpless infant. Children are aware of their parents' size and relative strength and much of their activity is centered around compensating for the feelings of inferiority that this engenders. Thus, in Adler's view, striving for superiority, excellence, and mastery is a natural propensity that can be enhanced or constrained depending on the circumstances of the child's life, especially his or her family environment.

In Adler's view, inferiority feelings have the potential to wreak havoc or inspire greatness in an individual's life. Depending upon how the child interprets them, inferiority feelings become the source for all human striving or the root of psychopathology. In optimum settings, the child uses feelings of inferiority as an impetus to grow and change. However, inferiority feelings may become accentuated, leading the child to feel overwhelmed and ineffectual, and creating an *inferiority complex.*

Inferiority complexes have a number of causes, most of which can be attributed to treatment of the child in the first five years of life. Adler identified three primary sources: (1) pampering, (2) neglect, and (3) organ inferiority. Pampering exacerbates feelings of inferiority by depriving the child of opportunities to develop his or her independence and initiative. In a pampered situation, the anticipation of the child's every need means that the child has few opportunities to overcome initial feelings of helplessness. An inferiority complex arises in which the child feels overwhelmed by his or her perceived inadequacies and is unable to develop strivings for excellence and mastery.

In instances of neglect, children are also prone to develop inferiority complexes, but for largely the opposite reasons: Believing themselves to be unloved and unlovable, neglected children may have little recourse but to renounce the necessity of love, often becoming hostile and/or withdrawn. Recall that in Adler's view it is the parents' role to nurture the child's social interest. Without this guidance, social interest gives way to self-centered strivings, resulting in a style of life that markedly lacks the capacity for concern for others. Compassion is replaced by the more mercenary "What can I get out of this situation?"

Adler identified physical or organic deficiencies as another risk factor in the development of an inferiority complex. Children born with cerebral palsy, for example, may have normal or superior mental capacities, but because their delivery systems are impaired, such talents may be underestimated. In such instances, a physiological impairment develops into a psychological one, with intensified feelings of inferiority impairing the individual's ability to strive for achievement.

The development of *organ inferiority* in response to a physiological impairment, or an *inferiority complex* in response to early childhood experiences, is not an inevitability. Although Adler believed that one's basic goals and personality characteristics are developed by the age of five, he acceded to the possibility of growth and change through concerted effort. Adler placed the true responsibility for striving and achieving superiority in the hands of the individual. "It is not the child's experiences which dictate his actions, it is the conclusions which he draws from his experiences" (Adler, 1958, p. 123).

There are other external factors that influence the child's personality. The constellation of the family may have a profound impact on the development of achievement motives, career choice, and interpersonal skills. Adler suggested that the first born child is likely to fall prey to pampering and thus have an increased chance of developing an inferiority complex. The birth of a sibling can prove to be a very painful dethroning and may further exacerbate the eldest child's feelings of inferiority. Personality characteristics of first borns may reflect this, early history: Adler suggested that among first borns there are higher instances of maladjustment with peers, neurotic tendencies, even criminality and alcoholism (Adler, 1958). On the other hand, they may assume a parental role with younger siblings and be more able to accept responsibility than their later born siblings (Ansbacher & Ansbacher, 1956). Firstborns tend to choose careers that involve a high degree of responsibility and that are relatively conformist (i.e., doctor, lawyer), perhaps reflecting their dislike for disruption of the status quo (Adler, 1969).

According to Adler, the middle child is in a favorable position, because he or she is unlikely to be pampered. Furthermore, the presence of an older sibling acts as an impetus to excel. In Adler's view, middle children tend to be highly competitive, socially adept, and able to assert themselves to overcome feelings of inferiority.

Although youngest children escape the pain of being "dethroned" by newly arriving siblings, they are in the unfortunate position of being pampered by both parents and older siblings, thus compounding their feelings of inadequacy. Whereas the presence of multiple older siblings may produce a high degree of ambition and a tendency to choose unique paths, pampering may deprive the youngest child of opportunities to set goals and strive for their achievement. Adler considered last born children to be the second highest risk group for inferiority complexes, but added that the stimulation provided by older siblings may, in some instances, inspire last borns to excel.

Only children are in the unique position of never being dethroned and may continue to be pampered by their parents. The result, in Adler's view, is that only children sometimes overestimate their own importance and may have difficulties interacting with peers (Adler, 1958).

Contemporary Research on Adler's Theory

The importance of birth order in Adler's theory of personality development stimulated much research. Is birth order as important to career choice or to the development of achievement motivation as Adler predicted? Perhaps, but not necessarily for the reasons that Adler suggested. It is well established that first borns, for instance, rather than appearing to suffer from debilitating inferiority complexes, are more likely than their siblings to achieve eminence in their professional lives, are more likely to seek higher education (Schachter, 1963), and tend to score higher on numerous standardized tests than their later born siblings (Eysenck & Cookson, 1969). There is evidence, however, that first borns are more obedient and willing to accept positions of responsibility in social situations than later borns (Sutton-Smith & Rosenberg, 1970). Hilton (1967) noted that mothers demanded more of their first borns, were more likely to withhold affection if they did not succeed on tasks, and yet were extremely warm and affectionate toward them when they did perform well. You may recognize, in this pattern, the key elements of the authoritative parenting style discussed earlier. Birth order appears to have a bidirectional effect: Both parent and child behaviors are modified by the birth of a sibling, and those changes are assimilated into the developing personality.

The situation with later borns is significantly more complex. Perhaps the second born is also the first girl in the family, or the youngest child happens to be the youngest of twelve, rather than the youngest of three, Does a general model of first, middle, and later born effects account adequately for such differences in family composition? What is the influence of socioeconomic status differences between families? Cultural differences? Attempts have been made to address these questions (for examples, see Sutton-Smith & Rosenberg, 1970; Zajonc & Markus, 1975). Despite these factors, birth order differences in people's ability to get along with others tend to persist; youngest children are perceived as more affable than either middle or first borns. And although first borns appear to initiate social interactions with greater frequency than their siblings, their attempts are not as successful as those of either middle or youngest children (Miller & Maruyama, 1976).

Sullivan's Interpersonal Approach—Peer Influences

Intrapsychic phenomena (i.e., Freud), attachment histories (i.e., Bowlby and others), parenting styles (i.e., Rogers), and birth order (i.e., Adler) each contribute in complex ways to the developing personality. Sullivan (1953), however, was among the first theorists to emphasize the critical role of peers in the definition and development of a unique personality. In Sullivan's view friendships formed in the preadolescent phase, particularly the development of a close same-sex friendship (or "chumship"), provide a new opportunity to amend and adjust maladaptive personality features developed in the context of early family interactions. Sullivan describes the chumship as a forum for the "clearing of warps" resulting from the unique treatment of the child in his or her early environment. In the context of a secure relationship, chums provide important feedback about the appropriateness and desirability of each others' actions and developing belief systems. The sharing of ideas, values, and opinions characteristic of a chumship acts as a mirror for adjusting and smoothing out the rough edges of one's personality. For example, children who were adored by their parents may develop a heightened sense of their own importance that may be less favorably received in the peer group. In the context of a trusting friendship such information can be shared and adjustments made without the threat of abandonment. A chumship provides individuals with the opportunity to note similarities and differences and make adjustments in their developing view of themselves and their place in the world.

The emergence of a chumship in preadolescence is made possible, in part, by increased cognitive capacities of the child (Piaget, 1960). Whereas toddler interactions tend to be centered around object play, shared interests, and "propinquity" (geographical convenience), friendships in later childhood involve increased intimacy, self-disclosure, mutual trust, and commitment (Bigelow, 1977; Mueller & Brenner, 1982; Youniss & Smollar, 1985). Although some of the interchanges between chums remain at a relatively concrete level (i.e., exchange of opinion about appearances), the creative work of the chumship lies in each individual's capacity to take the perspective of the other, making observations and assertions from the vantage point of sensing how it will be received by the other. This capacity for multiple perspective taking is both a cognitive accomplishment and an outgrowth of emotional development (i.e., the capacity for empathy). However, the individual's ability and willingness to adjust behaviors and beliefs as a response to mutual exchanges in a trusting relationship is largely the product of an emotional investment in the peer. Sullivan observes that a chumship differs from other friendships in intensity and level of commitment. In chumships, the individuals care as much or more for the welfare of the other as they do for themselves. Thus, emotional investment and mutual support are the core features enabling genuine personality transformation in the context of a preadolescent chumship.

The Sociocultural Approach of Horney

As we have seen, sociocultural and biosocial theories present a slightly more complex and multifaceted view of human motivation and personality development. In some instances, sociocultural perspectives have enhanced previous theoretical perspectives. Karen Horney (1885–1952), for example, influenced Rogers' view of conflict within the self. Like other neo-Freudians (e.g., Bowlby), Horney emphasized the importance of human relationships in personality development. In contrast to Freud, who believed that human disturbance is born of the conflict between environmental factors and repressed instinctual impulses, Horney believed that inner conflicts arose from contradictory needs. For example, an individual may experience a conflict between needs for comaraderie and equally compelling needs for privacy. The ability to negotiate disparate demands within the self stands as a hallmark of healthy adaptation in Horney's theory.

Horney (1945) identified three trends basic to all individuals: The tendency to (1) move toward others, (2) move away from others, or (3) move against others. Although present in everyone, these trends are essentially mutually exclusive, requiring the individual to negotiate competing urges within the self. In healthy individuals the tendency to move away, toward, or against others is largely dependent on the context. Thus, although it may be appropriate to move toward others in a new work environment, a normally functioning person has the flexibility to move away from or against an assailant on the street. In the neurotic personality, one trend has emerged as dominant and all interpersonal interactions are approached from that perspective.

Most of us have experienced individuals who might be called extreme in their tendency to move against others. Often regarded as troublemakers or bullies by teachers and peers, or as hostile or volatile by employers, the extreme "moving against" has a Machiavellian worldview, grounded in the need for control and a tendency to exploit others for self-serving ends. Conversely, an extreme "moving toward others" is often viewed as overly solicitous, compliant, and malleable in interpersonal interactions. Needs for love, approval, and affection are so pervasive among the extreme moving toward that all other urges are subjugated. Finally, individuals with extreme tendencies to "move away from others" are frequently identified as shy or withdrawn. The tendency toward isolation and detachment in the moving away from others is a source of both discomfort and solace to the individual who feels that it is perhaps best to fend for oneself because others cannot be relied upon to provide security. Each of these extreme stances, in Horney's view, is the result of differences in the child's early experience of security and safety in interpersonal relationships.

Contemporary Research on Horney's Theory

In a series of studies designed to examine the stability and consequences of extreme tendencies to move against others or move away from others, Caspi, Elder, and Bem (1987–1988) suggested that two parallel processes conspire to increase the stability of these personality characteristics. The first, *cumulative continuity,* involves a self-selection process; for example, in the case of "moving against the world,"

> the boy whose ill-temper leads him to drop out of school thereby limits his future career opportunities and selects himself into frustrating life circumstances that further evoke a pattern of striking out against the world. It is the progressive accumulation of their own consequences [that produces] cumulative continuity. (Caspi et al., 1988, 824)

The second, *interpersonal continuity,* involves the individual's expectations about interpersonal interactions. In a kind of self-fulfilling prophecy, the individual who expects to be treated with hostility may act in ways that evoke aggressive or hostile reactions in others.

Caspi, Elder, and Bem (1987) examined archival data from the Berkeley Guidance Study, identifying children (eight to ten years old) with explosive behavior patterns (moving against the world). During the 1940s, two follow-up interviews were conducted. Individuals with childhood histories of aggression (in their thirties and forties at follow-up) continued to exhibit aggressive behavior styles in adulthood and were more likely to be divorced than their even-tempered peers. Men with histories of aggressive behavior experienced a progressive deterioration of economic status, with work lives reflecting erratic employment. Women with explosive histories were likely to marry men from lower socioeconomic groups, tended to be ill-tempered in their interactions with their children, and often transmitted their explosive style to the next generation—their children (Caspi & Elder, 1988).

In a similar study Caspi, Elder, and Bem (1988) identified individuals with childhood histories of shyness (moving away from others). In adulthood, the consequences of shy behavior were most striking in males. Men with childhood histories of shyness delayed marriage and parenthood, had greater levels of marital disruption, and took a longer time establishing stable careers than their nonshy peers.

For women reaching mid-life in the 1940s, shyness did not affect the timing of marriage and childbirth. However, women identified as shy in childhood were more likely to conform to traditional marriage and childbirth patterns. Given that these data were collected in the 1940s, most of the women studied did not establish stable careers outside the home (outgoing women averaged nine years in the labor force, compared to six years for shy women) and the range of occupational status was slim. Shy women were more likely than nonshys to have no work history or to cease outside employment upon marriage or childbirth and not reenter the labor force.

Caspi and his colleagues suggest that childhood shyness expresses itself in later life situations that require taking the initiative (i.e., in negotiating career steps and proposing marriage). As the definitions of sex roles in society have broadened, the demands upon women to take the initiative, particularly in career settings, have increased. In a recent study of college women Kelly (1988) noted that shyness acted as a restraining barrier to women's career and educational aspirations. This very recent data on career patterns among shy women more closely mirrors findings observed in men's career aspirations in the 1940s. Thus the long-term consequences of shyness are determined, in part, by the expectations of the individual's cohort and society.

The development and stability of personality characteristics such as shyness and aggression are determined by a diverse constellation of factors. Culturally prescribed sex roles, the accumulation of consequences of the individual's behavior (cumulative continuity), and the expectations that individuals carry into their interactions with other people (interactional continuity) together influence the life course of personality characteristics.

Future Directions: Toward a Transactional Theory of Personality Development

If we look back at table 5.1, we can see that contemporary work in personality psychology is leaving behind the simple either-or assumptions underlying the psychoanalytic, behaviorist, and humanistic approaches to personality development. Rather than arguments about good versus bad human nature, inner versus outer causes of behavior, or free will versus determinism, we need a new model that accounts for the complex transactions between the person and the social environment. This model must explain how the biological building blocks of the individual become transformed through encounters with parents, siblings, peers, and the broader culture into the dynamic structure of adult personality. No one has yet constructed such a comprehensive theory, but the contemporary research in areas such as gender roles, self-concept, motives, traits, and situations described in the following chapters will inform you about the current status of the major elements of the personality equation.

Summary

This chapter examines four major theoretical approaches to the study of personality development: psychoanalytic, behavioral, humanistic, and sociocultural or biosocial. The psychoanalytic tradition began with Freud, who continues to influence personality theorists and researchers. Current research on attachment patterns in personality development represents a revision in the Freudian view of the primacy of the id instincts (i.e., sex and aggression) in personality formation. Ego psychologists and neoanalytic researchers such as Bowlby (1969) and Ainsworth et al. (1978) have included the need for "felt security" among the constellation of factors that motivate human behavior. The infant's feeling of felt security, arising out of early interactions with the primary caregiver, contributes to the development of an internal working model of attachment; that is, a template or guide for action in subsequent relationships.

Longitudinal research through the first six years of life suggest that such internal working models tend to persist at least through the early primary grades. Related research involving late adolescents and adults suggests that secure anxious/resistant and avoidant attachment patterns continue to be represented in roughly the same proportions as were found in toddler groups. Furthermore, adults' description of their own attachment with their parents tended to coincide with their attachment behavior with their infants in the strange situation. Thus, although longitudinal work has not been completed, there are provocative indications that attachment patterns may persist over the life course and across generations.

Behaviorism represents a radical departure from intrapsychic and ego psychological perspectives on personality development. Behaviorists view the external environment as the major determinant of personality and social behavior. Personality is shaped as a consequence of the selective reinforcement of behavior, through vicarious reinforcement (observing reinforcement of models) and through the establishment of self-efficacy expectancies. Current theorists (i.e., Bandura and Mischel) emphasize the roles of perceived self-efficacy—what the person thinks he or she can do; and self-efficacy expectancies—one's anticipation of success or failure, in determining behavior.

Humanistic psychology adopts an optimistic attitude toward personality development. Rogers asserts that unconditional positive regard in parent-child interactions promotes the development of a "fully functioning person"—one whose innate potential has been realized. Contemporary research on parenting styles and fostering creativity suggest that an authoritative child-rearing style—characterized by warmth, discipline, clear parent–child communications, and clear demands for the child's maturity—fosters confidence, exploration, and creative potential in the growing child.

Biosocial theorists stress the importance of social relationships (i.e., with parents, siblings, and peers) and the contributions of the social context to personality development. Adlerian theory suggests that individuals are aware of their relative helplessness and dependency in infancy and strive to overcome these feelings (striving for superiority).

Healthy social interest channels these strivings in directions that serve the society as well as the individual. Birth order contributes to individual differences in personality, influencing the level of "pampering" the child experiences and subsequently determining whether or not the child develops an inferiority complex.

Sullivan stressed the role of chumships in "clearing the warps" of early childhood experiences. Horney posited three neurotic interpersonal styles that result from the failure to provide the infant with safety and satisfaction of needs: moving toward (excessive compliance); moving away (withdrawal); and moving against (hostility). Hostile/explosive and withdrawn styles tend to persist across the life course, influencing marital and employment patterns (Caspi, Elder & Bem, 1987, 1988). Hostile patterns show continuity across generations as well (Caspi & Elder, 1988).

Current research and theory reflect an increasing awareness, among personality psychologists, of the complex interactions between biological, intrapsychic, interpersonal, and sociocultural factors contributing to personality development.

SUGGESTED READINGS

Damon, W. (1983). *Social and personality development.* New York: Norton. Excellent coverage of recent work on self-concept and social development.

Hazan, C., & Shaver, P. (1987). Romantic love conceptualized as an attachment process. *Journal of Personality and Social Psychology, 52,* 511–524. An interesting example of recent research on adult attachment styles.

Hogan, R. (1976). *Personality theories: The personological tradition.* Englewood Cliffs, NJ: Prentice-Hall. A comprehensive overview of the historically important theories of personality.

Horney, K. (1945). *Our inner conflicts.* New York: Norton. A theoretical overview of the development of neurotic interpersonal styles.

Main, M., Kaplan, N., & Cassidy, J. (1985). Security in infancy, childhood, and adulthood: A move to the level of representation. *Monographs of the Society for Research on Child Development, 50* (1 & 2, Serial No. 209), 66–104. An excellent summary of previous research in attachment and a presentation of the application of the attachment model to adulthood.

REFERENCES

Adler, A. (1958). *What life should mean to you.* New York: Capricorn Books.

Adler, A. (1969). *The science of living.* New York: Anchor Books.

Ainsworth, M.D.S., Bell, S.M., & Stayton, D.J. (1974). Infant–mother attachment and social development: Socialization as a product of reciprocal responsiveness to signals. In

M.P.M. Richards (Ed.), *The integration of the child into a social world* (pp. 99–135). London: Cambridge University Press.

Ainsworth, M.D., Blehar, M.C., Waters, E., & Wall, S. (1978). *Patterns of attachment.* Hillsdale, NJ: Erlbaum.

Ansbacher, H.L., & Ansbacher, R.R. (1956). (Eds.). *The individual psychology of Alfred Adler.* New York: Harper Torchbook.

Arend, R., Gove, F.L., & Sroufe, L.A. (1979). Continuity of individual adaptation from infancy to kindergarten: A predictive study of ego-resiliency and curiosity in preschoolers. *Child Development, 50,* 950–959.

Bandura, A. (1965). Influence of models' reinforcement contingencies on the acquisition of imitative responses. *Journal of Personality and Social Psychology 1,* 589–595.

Bandura, A. (1986). *Social foundations of thought and action.* Englewood Clifts, NJ: Prentice-Hall.

Baumrind, D. (1967). Child care practices anteceding three patterns of preschool behavior. *Genetic Psychology Monographs, 75,* 43–88.

Bigelow, B.J. (1977). Children's friendship expectations: A cognitive-developmental study. *Child Development, 48,* 246–253.

Block, J., & Block, J. (1980). The role of ego-development and ego-resiliency in the organization of behavior. In W.A. Collins (Ed.), *Development of cognition, affect, and social relations:* (Minnesota Symposium on Child Psychology, Vol. 13). Hillsdale, NJ: Erlbaum.

Bowlby, J. (1969). *Attachment and loss: Vol. 1. Attachment* (2nd ed.). New York: Basic Books.

Campos, J.J., Barrett, K.C., Lamb, M.E., Goldsmith, H.H., & Stenberg, C. (1983). Socioemotional development. In M. M. Haith & J. J. Campos (Eds.), *Handbook of child psychology: Vol. 2. Infancy and psychobiology* (pp. 783–915). New York: Wiley.

Caspi, A., & Elder, G. (1988). Emergent family patterns: The intergenerational construction of problem behaviour and relationships. In R. A. Hinde & J. Stevenson-Hinde (Eds.), *Relationships within families.* Oxford: Oxford University Press.

Caspi, A., Elder, G., & Bem, D. J. (1987). Moving against the world: Life-course patterns of explosive children. *Developmental Psychology, 23,* 308–313.

Caspi, A., Elder, G., & Bem, D. J., (1988). Moving away from the world: Life-course patterns of shy children. *Developmental Psychology, 24,* 824–431.

Cassidy, J. (1988). Child–mother attachment and the self in six-year-olds. *Child Development, 59,* 121–134.

Erikson, E. (1963). *Childhood and Society* (pp. 247–274). New York: Norton.

Eysenck, H. J., & Cookson, D. (1969). Personality in primary school children: 3. Family background. *British Journal of Educational Psychology, 40.* 117–131.

Freud, A. (1958). *The ego and the mechanism of defense.* New York: International Universities Press.

Freud, S. (1933). The dissection of the psychical personality. *New introductory lectures on psychoanalysis.* New York: Norton.

Harlow, H. F. (1958). The nature of love. *American Psychologist, 13,* 673–685.

Harrington, D., Block, J., & Block, J. (1987). Testing aspects of Carl Roger's theory of creative environments: Child-rearing antecedents of creative potential in young adolescents. *Journal of Personality and Social Psychology, 52,* 851–856.

Hazan, C., & Shaver, P. (1987). Romantic love conceptualized as an attachment process. *Journal of Personality and Social Psychology, 52,* 511–524.

Hilton, I. (1967). Differences in the behavior of mothers toward first and later born children. *Journal of Personality and Social Psychology, 7,* 282–290.

Horney, K. (1945). *Our inner conflicts,* New York: Norton.

Horney, K. (1967). *Feminine psychology.* New York: Norton.

Kelly, K. L. (1988). *Shyness and educational*

and vocational development at Wellesley College. Unpublished B.A. honors thesis, Wellesley College, Wellesley, MA.

Kline, P. (1984). *Psychology and Freudian theory.* London: Methuen.

Kobak, R. (1985). *Attitudes towards attachment relations and social competence among first year college students.* Unpublished doctoral dissertation. University of Virginia, Charlottesville, VA.

Kobak, R., & Sceery, A. (1988). Attachment in late adolescence: Working models, affect regulation and representations of self and others. *Child Development, 59,* 135–146.

Main, M., & Cassidy, J. (1988). Categories of responses to reunion with the parent at age 6: Predictable from infant attachment classifications and stable over a 1-month period. *Developmental Psychology, 24,* 415–426.

Main, M., Kaplan, N., & Cassidy, J. (1985). Security in infancy, childhood, and adulthood: A move to the level of representation. *Monographs of the Society for Research in Child Development, 50* (1 & 2, Serial No. 209), 66–104.

Miller, J. B. (1976). *Toward a new psychology of women.* Boston: Beacon Press.

Miller, N., & Maruyama, G. (1976). Ordinal position and peer popularity. *Journal of Personality and Social Psychology, 33,* 123–131.

Mischel, W. (1984). Convergences and challenges in the search for consistency, *American Psychologist, 39,* 351–364.

Mueller, E., & Brenner, J. (1977). The growth of social interaction in a toddler playgroup: The role of peer experience. *Child Development, 48,* 854–861.

Parke, R. D., & Devr, J. L. (1972). Schedule of punishment and inhibition of aggression in children. *Developmental Psychology, 7,* 266–269.

Peterson, C. (1988). *Personality.* New York: Harcourt, Brace, Jovanovich.

Piaget, J. (1960). *The child's conception of the world.* London: Routledge.

Rogers, C. (1951). *Client-centered therapy: Its current practice, implications and theory.* Boston: Houghton Mifflin.

Rogers, C. (1961). *On becoming a person.* Boston: Houghton Mifflin.

Rutter, M. (1979). Maternal deprivation, 1972–1978: New findings, new concepts, new approaches. *Child Development, 50,* 283–305.

Schachter, S. (1963). Birth order, eminence, and higher education. *American Sociological Review, 28,* 757–767.

Skinner, B. F. (1953). *Science and human behavior.* New York: Macmillan.

Spitz, R. A. (1945). Hospitalism: An inquiry into the genesis of psychiatric conditions in early childhood. In A. Freud (Ed.), *The psychoanalytic study of the child* (Vol. 1, pp. 53–74). New York: International Universities Press.

Sroufe, L. A. (1983). Infant–caregiver attachment and patterns of adaptation in preschool: The roots of competence and maladaptation. In M. Perlmutter (Ed.), *Minnesota symposium in child psychology* (Vol. 16, 41–81). Hillsdale, NJ: Erlbaum.

Sroufe, L. A., Schork, E., Motti, P., Lawroski, N., & LaFrenier, P. (1984). The role of affect in emerging social competence. In C. Izard, J. Kagan, & R. Zajonc (Eds.), *Emotions, cognition and behavior* (pp. 289–319). New York: Cambridge University Press.

Sullivan, H. S. (1953). *The interpersonal theory of psychiatry.* New York: Norton.

Sutton-Smith, B., & Rosenberg, B. G. (1970). *The sibling.* New York: Holt, Rinehart & Winston.

Waters, E., Wippman, J., & Sroufe, L. A. (1979). Attachment, positive affect, and competence in the peer group: Two studies in construct validation. *Child Development, 50,* 821–829.

Watson, J. B. (1928). *Psychological care of infant and child.* New York: Norton.

Watson, J. B. (1930). *Behaviorism* (rev. ed.). New York: Norton.

Winnicott, D. W. (1960). The theory of the parent-infant relationship. *International Journal of Psychoanalysis, 41,* 585–595.

Youniss, J., & Smollar, J. (1985). *Adolescent relations with mothers, fathers, and friends.* Chicago: The University of Chicago Press.

Zajonc, R. B., & Markus, G. B. (1975). Birth order and intellectual development. *Psychological Review, 82,* 74–88.

CHAPTER 6

The Person-Situation Debate: Do Personality Traits Really Exist?

DOUGLAS T. KENRICK AND DAVID C. FUNDER

Introduction
Hypothesis I: Personality
    Is in the Eye of
    the Beholder
  Errors of Judgment
  Lack of Agreement Between
    Judges
Hypothesis II: Agreement Is Due
    to Baserate Accuracy
ACTIVITY BOX: Comparing
    Personality Self-Ratings
    with Friends' Ratings
Hypothesis III: Agreement Is Due
    to Stereotypes Based on
    Obvious (but Erroneous)
    Cues
Hypothesis IV: Agreement Is Due
    to Discussion Between
    Observers

Hypothesis V: Agreement Is Due
    to Seeing Others in the
    Same Setting
Hypothesis VI: Compared with
    Situational Pressures,
    Cross-Situational
    Consistencies in Behavior
    Are Too Weak to Be
    Important
What Have We Learned?
  Person-Situation Interactions
  Combining Personality and
    Social Psychology
  Gene-Environment Interactions
Summary
SUGGESTED READINGS
REFERENCES

Introduction

Albert Einstein was brilliantly intelligent and humorous. John F. Kennedy was ambitious and charming. Frank Sinatra is aggressive and emotional. Or so their biographers tell us. But perhaps they are wrong. Perhaps Einstein, Sinatra, Kennedy, you, me, and your cousin Frederick are equally intelligent, humorous, aggressive, emotional, ambitious, and moralistic. Perhaps personality traits—the qualitative "individual differences" between us—are mere fictions. Because we are all accustomed to describing people's behavior in terms of traits like intelligence and aggressiveness, the idea that traits are fictions sounds a bit farfetched at first. According to the situationist position, however, internal traits are not an important cause of behavior. Instead, behavior is determined by the environment. Let your cousin experience the sudden rise to power and public scrutiny that Sinatra experienced, and he'd become aggressive and emotional too. Put Frederick into Einstein's life situation, and he'd act intelligent and humorous too.

During the 1960s, several psychologists began to lead a situationist attack on personality traits, leading to widespread disillusionment with the whole idea of consistent individual differences. In 1968, for instance, one social psychologist argued that:

> The prevalent view that the normal behavior of individuals tends toward consistency is misconceived [and the research evidence] . . . strongly suggests that consistency, either in thought or action, does not constitute the normal state of affairs. (Gergen, 1968, pp. 305–306)

150

In 1964, a behavioral psychologist stated that "I, for one, look forward to the day when personality theories are regarded as historical curiosities" (Farber, 1964, p. 37).

If these situationists were right, then the whole enterprise of psychology would have to be rethought. After all, whenever a clinical psychologist gives a test battery, he or she assumes there are some people who do have traits like "anxiety" or "depression" or "paranoia." Every time an organizational psychologist develops a personnel inventory, he or she assumes some people are more "responsible," "leader-like," or "ambitious" than others. Most of developmental psychology would have to be scrapped, because it is concerned with the development of individual differences in "aggressiveness," "intelligence," and so on. So the situationist critique of personality traits shook the discipline of psychology to its very roots and started a long and loud controversy.

Who started the war about personality traits, and why? Behaviorally oriented clinical psychologists led the attack on one front, and experimental social psychologists led on another. The clinicians were disappointed with the many findings showing that clinical judges often failed to agree with one another about who was "anxious," who was "depressed," and who was "hysterical" (e.g., Goldberg & Werts, 1966). At the same time, there were a number of findings in the domain of behavior modification showing that maladaptive behavior could be changed very radically simply by manipulating the environment. The social psychologists were also impressed with the fact that aggressive or leader-like or emotional behaviors could be produced in the laboratory with seeming ease. Furthermore, observers in some studies seemed to ignore the environmental pressures on people's behavior and mistakenly attribute the behavior to personality traits instead. Social psychologists concluded that this probably happened in everyday life. When we see cousin Frederick acting aggressively, we fail to consider how his present situation would be enough to make anybody feel hostile, and instead attribute the behavior to his trait of "aggressiveness" (Jones & Nisbett, 1971). Impressed with the power of the environment, then, behavior modifiers and laboratory experimentalists joined forces in a critical attack on personality traits.

The criticisms of personality traits that have been offered during the person-situation controversy can be organized into a progressive list of hypotheses, from most to least pessimistic (see table 6.1). The most pessimistic hypothesis is that personality is merely in *the eye of beholder*. This hypothesis assumes that people cannot even agree with one another about who is aggressive, who is ambitious, and who is intelligent; each of us lives in our own little world with unique fantasies about those around us. For example, the violent and emotional Frank Sinatra depicted in a recent biography written by a journalist that Sinatra fought with in court (Kelley, 1986) seems a very different man from the character in the biography written by his daughter (N. Sinatra, 1985). The next hypothesis, called the *baserate accuracy* hypothesis, assumes that we can reach agreement, but only because we all make similar guesses about what other people (in general) are like. To give an example of how baserate accuracy works, 90 percent of people might agree that your cousin Frederick does not have "murderous tendencies." But, in fact, they'd probably agree on that without even meeting him, because very few people have "murderous tendencies." Personality traits need to pass the tests of both consensus and discrimination; that is, we need to agree with one another about traits (consensus), and we need to be able to use them differently for different people (discrimination). Even if we can reach differential agreement, however, that doesn't prove there are traits. The *stereotype* hypothesis assumes that we do not really examine peoples' behavior before we apply trait labels to them; we simply classify them into a category and then apply a stereotypic list of traits that we mistakenly believe to fit their group. For instance, if cousin Fred is muscular and has a scar across his face, everyone may agree that he is "aggressive" (when he's really a mild-mannered altar boy who got the scar running away from a mouse in the sacristy). Another hypothesis assumes that differential agreement results from the fact that *observers are in cahoots with one another.* That is, people sit around and talk up a reputation for themselves and others, and that reputation sticks even though it may not have any basis in behavioral reality. According to this view, no one makes much of it when a man like Einstein acts humorless and unintelligent, but when he makes a brilliant quip, they say "Aha, isn't that just like Einstein." Two final hypotheses allow for consensus between observers, discriminations about who's got which traits, and even allow that observers really base their trait labels on behaviors, but still deny that people have internal traits. The *differential settings* hypothesis assumes we agree about people's traits because we see their behavior only in a small range of situations. If observers could have seen Frank Sinatra outside the fast-paced Las Vegas nightclub scene, or Einstein outside a lecture hall in Princeton, or John Kennedy outside of the demands of a political office, they could have seen that the three men did not have very different personalities after all. The final hypothesis assumes some behavioral consistency even across different situations, but presumes that, in comparison with the effects of situations, those *consistencies are too weak* to be of any real importance. For each hypothesis, the right-hand column in table 6.1 indicates the critical assumption about where traits fail.

TABLE 6.1

Hierarchy of Hypotheses from the Person-Situation Controversy, Arranged from Most to Least Pessimistic

Hypothesis	Critical Assumption
1. Personality is in the *eye of the beholder*.	People cannot agree in assigning traits to others.
2. Agreement between observers is due to *baserate accuracy* (our tendency to make similar guesses about what people in general are like).	People can agree, but don't distinguish between the people being rated.
3. Differential agreement is an artifact of the shared use of invalid *stereotypes*.	People can distinguish between the people being rated, but do not really observe behavior.
4. *Observers are in cahoots with one another*: their agreement results from discussion rather than accurate observation.	(same as above)
5. Raters see targets only within a *limited range of settings*, and mistake responses to situational pressures for traits.	People base trait ratings on behavioral observations, but the behavioral consistencies are not due to traits.
6. Compared with situational pressures, cross-situational *consistencies in behavior are too weak to be important*.	There are trait-like consistencies in behavior, but they are irrelevant.

In the past two decades, a great deal of research has addressed these different hypotheses. As we will show, the research suggests that each of these pessimistic hypotheses, in its pure form, can be rejected. It seems that behavioral clinicians and experimental social psychologists may have overstated how bad the case for traits really is. However, we will also attempt to show how the attack on personality traits has been instructive. Criticism and debate are essential to the scientific process. Without criticism, we would never explore the limitations on our knowledge and find out when and where we can expect our knowledge to apply. In the course of the person/situation debate, we have learned a great deal about when we can expect to find trait-like consistencies in behavior, and when and where we can expect not to find them. We have also learned not to be so overconfident about clinical judgments and psychological tests. All these lessons emerge from considering closely each of the hypotheses that have been used in the attack on personality traits.

Hypothesis I: Personality Is in the Eye of the Beholder

The first and most pessimistic hypothesis is this: Our perceptions of personality traits in our friends, acquaintances, and selves might be little more than a by-product of limitations and flaws in the way people think. In other words, as psychologists such as Gergen (1968) and Farber (1964) have claimed, personality might exist solely in the head and not in the external world. The eye of the beholder hypothesis assumes that we are all like the proverbial blind men who cannot reach consensus about whether the elephant is like a snake, a tree, or a lance. This possibility has to be considered first, because if it is true, then there is little use in inquiring further about where trait attributions come from.

Social psychologists often emphasize how easy it is to perceive personality traits even when objective evidence fails to support their existence:

> Unwitting evidence provided by countless personality psychologists shows how objectively low or nonexistent covariations (between personality and behavior) can be parlayed into massive perceived covariations through *a priori* theories and assumptions . . . The personality theorists' (and the layperson's) conviction that there are strong cross-situational consistencies in behavior may be seen as merely another instance of theory-driven covariation assessments operating in the face of contrary evidence. (Nisbett & Ross, 1980, pp. 109–112)

Research support for this "eye of the beholder" hypothesis has come from two types of studies: (1) demonstrations of how people make various "errors" when they try to process social information or (2) claims that different judges rating the same personality rarely agree with each other or with the person himself or herself.

Errors of Judgment

A number of studies have found that subjects frequently distort the information they are given in laboratory settings (for reviews, see Nisbett & Ross; 1980; Ross, 1977). People tend to jump to conclusions, biasing their judgments and their memories on the basis of their "implicit personality theories" (Schneider, 1973) or "scripts" (Abelson, 1976; Schank & Abelson, 1977). For example, we have a tendency to expect someone who is "friendly" to also be "honest." This tendency is so strong that we may decide a "friendly" person is "honest" even if we know nothing about how honest this person's behavior actually is, and we may even come to this conclusion when we have almost no information about the person at all.

Another example is the phenomenon called "overattribution." In a classic experiment on this topic, subjects read essays that either favored or opposed Fidel Castro. The subjects were told that the authors of the essays had been assigned, randomly, to take a particular side of the argument (Jones & Harris, 1967). Subjects tended to believe that the "pro-Castro" essays "must have been" written by authors who were "really" in favor of Castro, and that "anti-Castro" essays must have been written by authors who really opposed Castro. This was a false inference for subjects to make, because it ignores the information that the authors had no choice about the opinion expressed in their essays. Ross (1977) claims that these findings demonstrate a "fundamental attribution error," a widespread tendency for people to believe behavior is caused more by personality dispositions (such as traits and attitudes) than by the situation.

Findings like these clearly demonstrate how people have biased expectations and routinely go beyond the information they are given. However, the errors do not establish that personality resides solely in the eye of the beholder for two reasons. First, some of the errors are more a product of an unusual experimental situation than of a fundamentally biased cognitive process. For example, perhaps subjects in the "Castro" experiment assumed the experimenter would not give them misleading information, and for that reason believed the pro- and anti-Castro essays must be informative about their authors' true attitudes (Funder, 1987).

More important, just because people have judgmental *biases* does not necessarily mean they normally make *mistakes*. Biases demonstrated in laboratory tasks may actually help us make correct judgments in the real world (Funder, 1987). Many examples can be found in the field of visual perception, where a useful rule of thumb underlies every "optical illusion" (Gregory, 1971). The Ponzo, or railroad lines, illusion, for example, produces errors in the lab but correct judgments when applied to three-dimensional reality (see figure 6.1). Imagine the two horizontal lines in the figure as two logs on a photograph taken from the foot of a street. The lower one (which would be closer) would be smaller.

In the real world, perhaps "friendly" people do usually tend to be somewhat "honest," and making the inferential leap from friendliness to honesty is generally useful even when information on honesty is lacking. Sometimes the inference may be incorrect, but it may be correct enough of the time to be a worthwhile beginning assumption. Perhaps subjects in the "Castro" experiment are well-advised to base their attributions about attitude upon the behavior (e.g., essay writing) that they witness, because usually that practice will lead to correct attributions, even though sometimes behavior is caused solely by the situation and sometimes the attribution will be wrong. Even the "fundamental attribution error," if it exists (and that point is controversial), will lead to correct judgments to the extent that real people actually are somewhat consistent in their behavior. Albert Einstein was not randomly assigned to a chair in physics at Princeton University; his behavior fit the "brilliant" role long before he ended up there. Likewise, very few right-wing capitalists say positive things about

FIGURE 6.1

The Ponzo Illusion
The two horizontal lines in this figure are the same size. The one at the top appears larger because the two other lines appear to converge in the "distance" like railroad tracks. This leads to an incorrect inference of three dimensionality, and the perception that the lower line is closer than the one above it. This illusion reveals a rule that is normally correct in the natural world—parallel lines converge in the distance and give cues about depth. This illustrates that mistakes in laboratory judgments may not inform us about the accuracy of judgments in the real world.

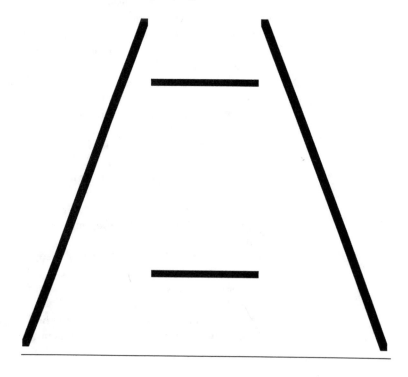

communist leaders like Castro. So when we see someone playing the role of a Princeton professor or of an advocate of Fidel Castro, it may be quite reasonable to assume that it gives us valid information about that individual's personality. In short, merely demonstrating errors in the laboratory is not informative, one way or the other, about how accurately people make judgments in real life (see also McArthur & Baron, 1983).

Lack of Agreement Between Judges

A different line of support for the "eye of the beholder" hypothesis has been the belief that people generally do not agree with each other when they judge the same personality. For example, one group of researchers asked children in a summer camp to describe each other and found that the traits the children used depended more on who was doing the ratings than on who was being described (Dornbusch, Hastorf, Richardson, Muzzy, & Vreeland, 1965). Studies like this do show that each of us has favorite terms and constructs for thinking about others. But other studies have found, again and again, that raters and ratees come to agree with each other more as they get a chance to know one another better (Funder & Colvin, 1988; Norman & Goldberg, 1966). And, when everybody is asked to use the same terms, people agree well about who is highest and lowest on each trait (Kenrick & Funder, 1988).

The Activity Box is included to give you a better feel for this type of research. It includes a number of dimensions for you to rate yourself on and then to compare with ratings made by your friends. The personality ratings are similar to ones that Jonathan Cheek (1982) used in his study of fraternity brothers at Johns Hopkins University. In that study, students rated themselves and were rated by other men who belonged to their fraternity. Cheek examined the extent to which these ratings were intercorrelated. If everyone was seeing the targets differently, the correlations would hover around zero, with some being positive by chance, but also some being negative. Cheek found that people's self-ratings and ratings by fraternity brothers were all correlated significantly beyond chance. Further, as the ratings were made more reliable (by grouping the three individual items in each set or by grouping ratings made by more than one member of the group), the correlations climbed steadily higher. As was discussed in chapter 2, correlations can range from 0 (which indicates no relationship) to 1.0 (which indicates a perfect relationship). In reviewing a number of studies that used methods like Cheek's, we found that ratings made by friends and relatives were above .50 when highly reliable ratings were

ACTIVITY BOX

Comparing Personality Self-Ratings With Friends' Ratings

Rate yourself on these dimensions, and ask a roommate, friend, or relative to rate you on the same dimensions. Do not discuss them. Just give the scale to the friend or relative and then leave the room until it is completed.

Rating of _____

Extraversion

Talkative	1	2	3	4	5	6	7	Silent
Sociable	1	2	3	4	5	6	7	Reclusive
Adventurous	1	2	3	4	5	6	7	Cautious

Agreeableness

Good-natured	1	2	3	4	5	6	7	Irritable
Mild/gentle	1	2	3	4	5	6	7	Headstrong
Cooperative	1	2	3	4	5	6	7	Negativistic

Conscientiousness

Responsible	1	2	3	4	5	6	7	Undependable
Neat/tidy	1	2	3	4	5	6	7	Careless
Persevering	1	2	3	4	5	6	7	Quitting/fickle

Emotional Stability

Calm	1	2	3	4	5	6	7	Anxious
Poised/relaxed	1	2	3	4	5	6	7	Tense/nervous
Composed	1	2	3	4	5	6	7	Excitable

Based on Cheek (1982).

---

used (Kenrick & Funder, 1988). Correlations that high indicate agreement rates that are not only beyond chance but quite substantial. In fact, the findings are more than sufficient to rule out the "eye of the beholder" hypothesis.

Hypothesis II: Agreement Is Due to Baserate Accuracy

Just because people can agree with one another's trait ratings does not mean that traits really exist. According to hypothesis II, raters can agree with one another because some traits have very stable and high baserates in the population at large (for example, "needs to be with other people" is true about almost everybody). Other traits have very low baserates ("has murderous tendencies" is true about hardly anybody). If you are trying to describe someone you do not know, you can achieve a certain degree of "accuracy" just by rating the first trait higher than the second: It is a good bet that a perfect stranger is more sociable than murderous. The baserate hypothesis allows for consensus between observers, but regards their judgments as "indiscriminate." Even if two people can agree that a third person is "sociable, but not murderous" their agreement is not necessarily based upon any specific knowledge about the person they are describing.

The baserate problem explains how astrology and other pseudoscientific prediction specialists can be so "accurate." They use "Barnum statements," or high baserate descriptions that apply to almost everyone. "As a Gemini, you are split. You have a great need to be with others, but at other times a completely opposite need to be alone." "As a Libra, you are well balanced, you love to be with others, but balance that with a need for occasional solitude." It is thus useful to beware of such glittering generalities in personality assessment. However, the baserate accuracy hypothesis cannot explain how judges distinguish *between* the targets they judge. To take a simple case, imagine that a group of sorority sisters is asked to rate one another as either "friendly" or "unfriendly." If "friendly" is chosen over "unfriendly" nine out of ten times, there could be a very high percentage of "agreement." However, the women's judgments would overlap even if there were absolutely no agreement about who the tenth unfriendly person is (see figure 6.2). The data in the figure have an 80 percent agreement rate; that is, there is an 80 percent chance that any two girls will agree on a rating (because almost all ratings are "F"—indicating "friendly"). However, a *correlation* calculated between judges would show no relationship at all. That is because a correlation requires discriminative agreement; that is, when a "U" shows up, it needs to show up in ratings of the same girl. When we calculated a correlation on the data in figure 6.2, for instance, we found it to be nonsignificant, and slightly negative (-0.11). Thus, baserate accuracy cannot explain the correlational agreement found in inter-rater studies (like Cheek's fraternity study in the Activity Box).

Summarizing thus far, we may say that neither the eye of the beholder hypothesis nor the baserate hypothesis can explain how two people can agree in their ratings when discriminating who is relatively more friendly, more aggressive, and so on. Does this prove that traits (such as friendliness and aggressiveness) really exist? No.

FIGURE 6.2

A Hypothetical Set of Ratings in which Ten Sorority Women Rated Themselves on Friendliness.

"F" refers to a rating of the target woman as friendly; "U" refers to a rating of the target woman as unfriendly. Woman 1 rated herself and eight other women as friendly (F) and categorized only woman 10 as unfriendly (U). Woman 2 had a similar pattern of ratings, except that she picked number 9 as unfriendly. Even though each of the women picked a different person as unfriendly, there is an 80 percent "agreement" rate because of the high likelihood of seeing another woman as friendly. This is an example of "baserate accuracy," or spurious agreement due to the relative commonness of one type of rating over another. A correlational analysis, however, indicates a nonsignificant negative relationship between the ratings made by any two women. Thus, baserate accuracy does not inflate correlations made about different targets on the same dimension.

		Ratings of:									
		1	2	3	4	5	6	7	8	9	10
Ratings by:	1	F	F	F	F	F	F	F	F	F	U
	2	F	F	F	F	F	F	F	F	U	F
	3	F	F	F	F	F	F	F	U	F	F
	4	F	F	F	F	F	F	U	F	F	F
	5	F	F	F	F	F	U	F	F	F	F
	6	F	F	F	F	U	F	F	F	F	F
	7	F	F	F	U	F	F	F	F	F	F
	8	F	F	U	F	F	F	F	F	F	F
	9	F	U	F	F	F	F	F	F	F	F
	10	U	F	F	F	F	F	F	F	F	F

Hypothesis III: Agreement Is Due to Stereotypes Based on Obvious (but Erroneous) Cues

Neither of the first two hypotheses required observers to really "observe" anything distinctive about the person they were describing. The stereotype hypothesis, however, does require that observers at least take a look at the target person—but assumes they hardly look much farther than the end of their noses, just enough to assign the target person to a general category. Two people see that Professor Einstein is a university professor with an unkempt hairdo and immediately assume he is absentminded. They see that John Kennedy is a millionaire's son, and a U.S. president, and immediately assume that he is ambitious. This use of stereotypes would lead the judges to agree even when their descriptions of these people were not accurate at all.

We do have stereotypes about other people, and we will use those stereotypes to generate guesses about them even when we know nothing about their actual behavior. The stereotypes help explain findings that people can agree about strangers. However, other findings show that people agree much better about people they know than about strangers. This suggests that, with acquaintance, we go beyond superficial stereotypes (e.g., Funder & Colvin, 1988; Monson, Tanke & Lund, 1980).

The stereotype hypothesis also has a difficult time explaining another set of findings. People's judgments about their friends' and relatives' traits can often be used to predict actual behaviors of those friends and relatives. For example, general personality descriptions made by parents and teachers predict how long a child will control himself when he is brought into a laboratory and seated in front of tasty candies or tempting toys (Bem & Funder, 1978; Funder, Block & Block, 1983; Mischel, 1984). Gormly and Edelberg (1974) used ratings by fraternity men to predict who would act most aggressively, and they found a strong relationship between teachers' ratings of dominance and a child's attempts to boss other children. These findings show that ratings by teachers, friends, and relatives are not simply based on empty stereotypes.

Stereotypes and personality traits are not unconnected. First of all, there is some truth to stereotypes. For instance, we expect attractive people to be more friendly, and research evidence indicates that they actually are (Goldman & Lewis, 1977). Stereotypes and traits may be related through the operation of self-fulfilling prophecies. If we expect attractive people to be friendly, we will respond more pleasantly to them, and they will begin to act friendlier (Snyder, Tanke & Berscheid, 1977).

In sum, stereotypes may tell us something about where traits come from, and they may explain how people can agree with one another about perfect strangers, but there are abundant findings that cannot be explained by the stereotype hypothesis. Stereotypes cannot explain why trait ratings relate to actual behaviors, nor why people agree much better about friends than about strangers.

Hypothesis IV: Agreement Is Due to Discussion Between Observers

We have just considered evidence that observers agree with each other better when they know the target person well. Is this because acquaintances have had more time to observe one another's behaviors, and are hence more truly accurate than strangers? Perhaps not. Maybe observers ignore the truly relevant nonverbal behaviors related to the friendliness or aggressiveness of the people they rate, but instead simply listen to what a person says about himself or herself and agree for this reason (cf. Funder, 1980; Funder & Colvin, 1988). Or maybe people get together and discuss one another's personalities and thus come to consensus (McClelland, 1972). That leads each of us to have a *reputation,* and our social reputation tells each of us what we are like. This idea was originally suggested by sociologist C.H. Cooley (1902) in his classical theory of the "looking glass self." Because we cannot see our traits in the mirror, we need to judge ourselves from the feedback we get from other people.

If social discussion were all there was to it, trait ratings would not relate to behaviors but only to other people's trait ratings. However, we just mentioned some of the evidence showing that trait ratings do relate to people's actual behaviors—to the things they do. Also, college students who know one another on campus can agree with ratings made by one another's parents, whom they have probably never met, much less discussed personalities with. One study examined college students in an isolated college town in Montana and found that friends' ratings agreed with parents "back home" (which, in Montana, may have been several hundred miles away from campus). Parents were unlikely to have met the friends (whose own hometowns may have been hundreds of miles in the opposite direction) (Kenrick & Stringfield, 1980).

Another important finding is that agreement is higher on traits that relate to observable behaviors (such as friendliness) than on traits that are less observable (such as emotionality). This is true not only across different traits (some traits, like "talkativeness," are more observable in everyone) but also within a single trait. That is, some people say their "emotionality" is observable; others say they hide it. Friends and relatives can agree substantially better about people when they say their behavior is publicly available (Amelang & Borkenau, 1986; Cheek, 1982; Funder & Colvin, 1988; Funder & Dobroth, 1987; Kenrick & Stringfield, 1980; McCrae, 1982). If judges simply manufacture a reputation for you, it would be as easy to agree about terms relating to your inner emotions as it would be to agree about terms relating to your friendly behaviors. Because people agree more about publicly observable traits, this suggests that they are really observing behavior, not simply words.

Several studies have directly examined the hypothesis that we pay attention to words and found that, when people's self-reports contradict their nonverbal behaviors, observers pay more attention to what is done than to what is said (Amabile & Kabat, 1982; Bryan & Walbek, 1970). For instance, subjects in one study watched a videotape of a woman who described herself as either "introverted" or "extraverted," and also watched her *behave* in either an introverted or extraverted fashion (Amabile & Kabat, 1982). The subjects' later judgments were much more strongly influenced by her actual behaviors than by the way she had described herself. If she claimed to be an extravert but acted like an introvert, subjects believed she was an introvert. It seems, then, that observers put more faith in behaviors than they put in self-descriptions.

Summarizing our arguments thus far, people can agree with one another in their trait ratings, and they can use trait terms differently for different people. For those we know well, at least, trait ratings are not based simply on stereotypes, nor merely on unfounded gossip. Are we therefore now compelled to allow some truth to the trait construct? Alas, the answer is still no, not necessarily.

Hypothesis V: Agreement Is Due to Seeing Others in the Same Setting

It is possible to allow for agreement and discrimination in the use of trait terms, and even to allow that observers are really and truly observing behavioral consistencies, without allowing that those behavioral consistencies come from factors that are "internal" to the person whose personality is being described. As William James noted a century ago:

> Many a youth who is demure enough before his parents and teachers, swears and swaggers like a pirate among his "tough" young friends. We do not show ourselves to our children as to our club-companions, to our customers as to the laborers we employ, to our masters and employers as to our intimate friends. (James, 1890, p. 294)

Club companions with whom a student drinks every Friday night might all agree that he or she is consistently rather "wild," whereas parents, who go to church with the student every Sunday, agree with one another, but think their offspring is quite "serious." Because the club companions and the parents live in "separate worlds," they can blissfully maintain their different mutual delusions. In reality, the student is doing what the social situations demand: when in a bar, orgy like the Romans, in a church, pray like a Christian. Because the people in the bar never see the student in church, and vice versa, neither group is aware of the power of the situation in maintaining the student's illusory consistency.

A good deal of the evidence we have already discussed argues against this hypothesis as a final explanation of rater agreement. Many of the studies of trait ratings use fraternity members or college roommates (e.g., Bem & Allen, 1974; Cheek, 1982; Funder, 1980; Funder & Dobroth, 1987, Kenrick & Stringfield, 1980). These fellow students see one another in bars, in classes, at parties, in the library, and in many other settings, so they get to see each other vary across situations. Yet they still agree well. Also, some of these studies examine agreement across peer and parent groups—who see the targets in very different situations. In the Kenrick and Stringfield (1980) study, for instance, peers knew the target as a college student (and perhaps fellow beer drinker), whereas parents knew the target as a child (and perhaps a ranch hand). Still, parents and peers were in significant agreement about traits.

Finally, personality ratings often correlate well with behavior measured in settings that neither the raters nor the subjects have ever seen before. For example, parents observe their children at home but their personality descriptions can be used to predict behavior in a completely unique experimental setting (Bem & Funder, 1978), even when the personality judgments were made years before the behavior was observed (Mischel, 1984).

The data require us to concede some degree of consensus, discrimination, and internality to the trait domain. Is it time, therefore, to give the store back to the "trait" position? Even with the distance we have come, the answer is still no. It is possible to argue that, although some true cross-situational consistencies in behavior may exist, they are too small to worry about.

Hypothesis VI: Compared with Situational Pressures, Cross-Situational Consistencies in Behavior Are Too Weak to Be Important

In what is often seen as the most important single attack on the notion of personality traits, Walter Mischel (1968) reviewed a number of studies and concluded that correlations between trait scores and behaviors and between different behaviors related to the same trait are seldom larger than about .30. The conclusions of Mischel's book hit the field of personality with devastating force because of two separable assumptions: (1) The coefficient .30 cannot be improved even with more accurate measurements; it is the true upper limit for the predictability of behavior from personality. (2) This upper limit is a small upper limit. It is necessary to accept both of these assumptions for Mischel's critique to have a major impact, and many initially did accept them.

Several personality psychologists (e.g., Block, 1977; Hogan, DeSoto, & Solano, 1977) challenged the first assumption, arguing that Mischel's review did not give a fair hearing to the better studies in the personality literature. Epstein (1979, 1983) argued that laboratory studies used unreliable samples of behavior. By observing someone's behavior in short laboratory experiments, researchers were making the same mistake someone would make who tried to measure IQ with a single item. For instance, what if I asked you, "Who wrote *Wuthering Heights?*" as my first measure of IQ. Later I time you as you solve a single math problem, like finding the square root of 8,281. I would find only a weak correlation (if any) between the likelihood of saying "Emily Bronte" and the speed of saying "91." Some would solve the math problem quickly, but not come up with the writer. Others would know the author, but labor for ten minutes over the square root. Even though some people would do well on both, the correlation would almost certainly be less than .30. Would I be justified in therefore discarding the concept of intelligence? No. A 100-item IQ test correlates about .40 with college grade point average—because both are reliable. Similarly, a combination of several measurements of a child's honesty correlate well with a combination of several other separate measurements, even though each single item of honesty is only weakly related to other single items (Hartshorne & May, 1928; Epstein & O'Brien, 1985).

Is a correlation of .30 or .40 too small to be useful? If it is, even experimental psychologists are in trouble. It is the equivalent strength of even powerful experimental manipulations like the ones used in Stanley Milgram's classic study of obedience to an authority who insisted that participants shock a fellow subject (Funder & Ozer, 1983). It is much stronger than the relationship between a professional baseball player's overall batting average and his likelihood of hitting the ball the next time at bat, yet batting averages are trusted enough to be used to dole out salary differentials of hundreds of thousands of dollars every season (Abelson, 1985). Even a test that correlates .30 with behavior can be very useful (Ozer, 1985). For instance, such a test of job performance could be used to save a corporation millions of dollars every year by hiring the top-scoring individuals.

The argument that personality's relationship to behavior is very small, then, applies only if we expect personality traits to predict single instances of behavior. In everyday life, we do not use personality traits to predict what someone will do in the next 20 minutes. Instead, we use trait ratings to make predictions over the long haul: Will this person be an agreeable friend? A reliable employee? An affectionate spouse? And so on. For these general predictions, the relationships between personality traits and behavior are not "too small" (Epstein, 1983).

What Have We Learned?

Table 6.2 summarizes the evidence against each of the six hypotheses we have discussed.

Although there is evidence against each of the critical hypotheses, it would be a mistake to conclude that each of them is simply a diversion and that personality psychologists would have been better off had the hypotheses not ever been considered. Before the controversy, personality researchers often wrongly assumed that they could make grand predictions from miniscule samples of behavior (like using an inkblot response to predict whether someone would repeat a violent crime). As with most controversies, the truth finally appears to lie not in the vivid black or white of either extreme, but somewhere in the less striking gray area. Personal biases, stereotypes, and personal reputations do impede our ability to make perfect traits ratings, and glittering

TABLE 6.2

Summary of the Evidence Against Each of the Critical Hypotheses

Hypothesis	Evidence that refutes it
1. Eye of the beholder	reliable agreement between observers
2. Baserate accuracy	agreement about where different people stand on same trait
3. Stereotypes	increasing agreement with acquaintance; ratings correlate with independent behavioral measures
4. Observers in cahoots	agreement between unacquainted raters; findings that behaviors speak louder than words
5. Limited range of settings	agreement between self and others known across settings; ratings predict behavior in completely novel settings
6. Consistencies too weak to be important	trait ratings and situations predict behaviors equally well; low correlations only with unreliable, unaggregated measures

generalities and situational consistencies may lead us to overestimate what we know about the specific characteristics of our friends and our family. Nevertheless, through all the noise, we can accurately discern something about the trait differences in our friends. Furthermore, we can use that something to predict behavior, only weakly if we want to make very specific, momentary predictions, but reasonably well if we want to be accurate over the long haul. In addition to the important distinction between specific and general effects of traits, the debate has brought out other lessons. We cannot decide that a personality trait rating is accurate simply because we find agreement between raters— they may be using invalid stereotypes. We should also assess the degree to which the ratings are able to predict behavior. And the evidence indicates that we can make better predictions if we stick to observable traits than if we focus on private, unobservable ones.

Person-Situation Interactions

An important lesson of the person–situation debate is that we cannot really separate the study of the person (the topic of personality research) and the study of the situation (the usual focus of research in social psychology). Although the "situational" hypothesis is often seen as an alternative to the trait position, they can be integrated. In recent years researchers have begun to examine how persons and situations interact (e.g., Bem & Funder, 1978; Kenrick & Dantchik, 1983; Magnusson & Endler, 1977; Snyder & Ickes, 1985). Some examples follow.

1. Specific *traits show up only in relevant situations* (Allport, 1966; Bem & Funder, 1978). If you are anxious, it is likely to show up only in situations that you find threatening, like a first date or a class presentation, not when you are sitting in front of the TV with a beer in your hand.

2. *All traits are more easily expressed in some situations* than others. People show their distinctive personalities more on a picnic than at a funeral (where *everyone* is reserved) (Monson, Keel, Stephens, & Genung, 1982; Price & Bouffard, 1974; Schutte, Kenrick, & Sadalla, 1985). Table 6.3 lists a number of situations, ordered from the most to least "constraining." Unfortunately, laboratory situations are probably more like churches and job interviews than they are like parks and private rooms. For that reason, laboratory experiments are probably not the best place to look for evidence of personality (Monson & Snyder, 1977; Wachtel. 1973).

3. A person's *traits can actually change a situation.* For instance, an

TABLE 6.3

Situations Arranged from High to Low in Behavioral Constraint

Degree of constraint	Situation
High (people likely to show little variation in behavior)	Church Job interview Elevator Family dinner Class Movies Restroom Sidewalk Bus Date Bar Football game Dorm lounge
Low (people likely to show most variation in behavior)	Park Own room

aggressive child can turn a previously peaceful playground into a brawl in a few minutes (Rausch, 1977).

4. *People choose different settings to match their traits* (Snyder & Ickes, 1985). For instance, highly sex-typed males are more likely to seek out sexually stimulating situations, while highly sex-typed females seem to avoid them (Kenrick, Stringfield, Wagenhals, Dahl, & Ransdell, 1980).

Combining Personality and Social Psychology

Research on the interaction between persons and situations is research that combines the traditionally separate fields of personality and social psychology. Research that cuts across these traditional boundaries is beginning to lead psychologists in some exciting new directions. One example is new research on accuracy in personality judgment (Funder, 1987; Kenny & LaVoie, 1984). This research examines how the judgments you make of your acquaintances' personalities are able to predict their behavior. One way to study this is to ask you to describe the traits you believe characterize your acquaintance, and then assess how well these ratings are able to predict his or her behavior in a social interaction. If your ratings do predict behavior successfully, then your judgments must have been accurate about something (Funder, 1987). In fact, instead of thinking of the six hypotheses we discussed as historical errors, accuracy researchers regard them as clues to different sources of noise that need to be considered in our search for accurate trait predictions (see table 6.4). Thus, accuracy research can capitalize on the lessons of the person–situation controversy.

Gene–Environment Interactions

If personality traits really do exist, then we are justified in asking where they come from. As chapter 3 has shown, there is increasing evidence that some aspects of personality are inherited. There are a host of interesting questions about how those inherited characteristics interact with the social environment (Kenrick, 1987; Kenrick & Trost, 1987). For instance, gender is related to a number of differences in hormones and body size (Kenrick, 1987). These differences lead to some direct effects on behavior; the male hormone testosterone is associated with aggressiveness and sexual interest, for instance. However, many of the effects of gender differences probably play out through indirect effects on the social environment. Males' slightly larger size and upper body physique is more likely to lead them to be rewarded for aggressive behaviors, for instance. Women's monopoly on pregnancy has a whole host of implications for their differential sexual and parental behaviors (Kenrick & Trost, 1987; 1989). Minor biological differences also have implications for how society constructs social roles, which further exaggerate gender differences in personality (Kenrick, 1987). The awareness of biological underpinnings connects the study of personali-

TABLE 6.4

The Lessons Contained in Each Hypothesis

Hypothesis	What it teaches us
1. Eye of the beholder	Individuals have unique biases in how they rate other. Strangers' ratings are especially prone to such biases.
2. Baserate accuracy	Accuracy is not enough. Beware of Barnum Statements that apply to everyone.
3. Stereotypes	Agreement is not enough. Just because two people agree does not prove they are right.
4. Observers in cahoots	Reputation can be a factor in agreement about trait ratings.
5. Limited Range of settings	Behavioral consistencies can be due to role and situational pressures.
6. Consistencies too weak to be important	Psychologists are often too glib about predicting behavior. Individual behaviors are too unreliable to be strongly related.

ty to evolutionary biology, and researchers at the interface of psychology and evolutionary biology have begun to test a number of hypotheses about the relationship between personality traits and mating behavior (Buss & Barnes, 1986; Kenrick & Trost, in press; Rushton, 1985; Sadalla, Kenrick, & Vershure, 1987). These theorists argue that, since differential reproduction and sexual selection were the two mechanisms that Darwin thought to be central to the evolutionary process, the social psychology of mate selection must be connected to the psychology of personality. From the evolutionary perspective, the selection of a mate is a search for adaptive personality traits that will benefit one's offspring.

Science seems to progress best when scientists use many different methods to address the same problem (Houts, Cook & Shadish, 1986). Each scientist usually has his or her own favorite method and is often critical of the methods used by other scientists. We have certainly seen this to be true of scientists involved in the person-situation debate. But such mutual criticism helps keep everyone on their toes. It often takes criticism from a scientific "opponent" to force a researcher to examine his or her methods closely and become fully aware of capabilities and limitations. Better still, when scientists who use different methods and have different biases begin to arrive at consensus about important issues, we can be increasingly confident that we have really learned something. The "opposing" scientists involved in the person-situation debate seem to be arriving at consensus about a number of important issues. That is why this controversy has been a good thing for psychology. As the smoke of the person-situation battle clears, we see only the strongest ideas left standing.

Summary

Before we can ask questions about how specific personality traits develop, we must be certain that traits actually exist. Although it seems "obvious" that there are differences between people in friendliness, aggressiveness, and emotionality, some psychological researchers have suggested that the obvious may be false. Various hypotheses have been suggested about how people might imagine traits when they really do not exist. For instance, we might simply judge people on physical stereotypes and fail to check out whether their behavior fits that stereotype. Psychologists who attacked the trait notion favored the view that most of our behavior is determined by our situation. This chapter discussed six critical hypotheses from the situationist school and showed how research evidence has ruled each one out. It also discussed how the critique of personality traits has taught us some valuable lessons. As a consequence of the person-situation debate, we have learned how to better specify the circumstances under which personality assessments will be useful, and when they will be useless.

SUGGESTED READINGS

Allport, G.W. (1966). Traits revisited. *American Psychologist, 21,* 1–10. A historical perspective on traits from the man most closely associated with the trait approach to personality.

Briggs, S.R. (1985). A trait account of social shyness. In P. Shaver (Ed.), *Review of personality and social psychology* (Vol. 6, pp. 35–64). Beverly Hills, CA: Sage. Makes a strong case that "shyness" is best regarded as a trait, using some of the same arguments we make in this chapter.

Epstein, S., & O'Brien, E. J. (1985). The person–situation debate in historical and current perspective. *Psychological Bulletin, 98,* 513–537. A review of several historically important studies from the trait–situation controversy, making the argument that personality traits show up only with repeated and reliable measures.

Funder, D. C. (1987). Errors and mistakes: Evaluating the accuracy of social judgment. *Psychological Bulletin, 101,* 75–90. A review of the evidence against hypothesis 1 in this chapter (personality is in the eye of the beholder).

Houts, A. C., Cook, T. D., & Shadish, W. R. (1986). The person-situation debate: A critical multiplist perspective. *Journal of Personality, 54,* 52–105. Places the debate in the context of philosophical inquiry, arguing that the radically different perspectives have been helpful in uncovering a set of facts that most can agree on.

Kenrick, D.T. (1987). Gender, genes, and the social environment. In P.C. Shaver & C. Hendrick (Eds.), *Review of personality and social psychology* (Vol. 8, Sex and Gender, pp. 14–43). Beverly Hills, CA.: Sage. A discussion of how gender-linked personality traits interact with the environment.

REFERENCES

Abelson, R. P. (1976). A script theory of understanding, attitude, and behavior. In J. Carroll & J. Payne (Eds.), *Cognition and social behavior.* New York, NY: Erlbaum.

Abelson, R. P. (1985). A variance explanation paradox: When a little is a lot. *Psychological Bulletin, 97,* 129–133.

Allport, G.W. (1966). Traits revisited. *American Psychologist, 21,* 1–10.

Amabile, T. M., & Kabat, L. G. (1982). When self-description contradicts behavior: Actions do speak louder than words. *Social Cognition, 1,* 311–335.

Amelang, M., & Borkenau, P. (1986). The trait concept: Current theoretical considerations, empirical facts, and implications for Personality Inventory Construction. In A. Angleitner & J. S. Wiggins (Eds.), *Personality assessment via questionnaire* (pp. 7–24). London: Plenum Press.

Bem, D. J., & Allen, A. (1974). On predicting some of the people some of the time: The search for cross-situational consistencies in behavior. *Psychological Review, 81,* 506–520.

Bem, D.J., & Funder, D.C. (1978). Predicting more of the people more of the time: Assessing the personality of situations. *Psychological Review, 85,* 485–501.

Block, J. (1977). Advancing the science of personality: Paradigmatic shift or improving the quality of research? In D. Magnusson & N.S. Endler (Eds.), *Personality at the crossroads: Current issues in interactional psychology* (pp. 37–63). Hillsdale, NJ: Erlbaum.

Bryan, J., & Walbek, N. (1970). Impact of words and deeds concerning altruism upon children. *Child Development, 41,* 747–757.

Buss, D.M., & Barnes, M. (1986). Preferences in human mate selection. *Journal of Personality and Social Psychology, 50,* 559–570.

Cheek, J.M. (1982). Aggregation, moderator variables, and the validity of personality tests: A peer-rating study. *Journal of Personality and Social Psychology, 43,* 1254–1269.

Cooley, C.H. (1902). *Human nature and the social order.* New York: Scribner's.

Dornbusch, S.M., Hastorf, A.H., Richardson, S.A., Muzzy, R.E., & Vreeland, R.S. (1965). The perceiver and perceived: Their relative influence on categories of interpersonal perception. *Journal of Personality and Social Psychology, 1,* 434–440.

Epstein, S. (1979). The stability of behavior: I. On predicting most of the people much of the time. *Journal of Personality and Social Psychology, 37,* 1097–1126.

Epstein, S. (1983). The stability of confusion: A reply to Mischel and Peake. *Psychological Review, 90,* 390–393.

Epstein, S., & O'Brien, E. J. (1985). The person–situation debate in historical and current perspective. *Psychological Bulletin, 98,* 513–537.

Farber, I. E. (1964). A framework for the study of personality as a behavioral science. In P. Worchel & D. Byrne (Eds.), *Personality change* (pp. 3–37). New York: Wiley.

Funder, D.C. (1980). On seeing ourselves as others see us: Self–other agreement and discrepancy in personality ratings. *Journal of Personality, 48,* 473–493.

Funder, D.C. (1987). Errors and mistakes: Evaluating the accuracy of social judgment. *Psychological Bulletin, 101,* 75–90.

Funder, D.C., Block, J., & Block, J. H. (1983). Delay of gratification: Some longitudinal personality correlates. *Journal of Personality and Social Psychology, 44,* 1198–1213.

Funder, D.C., & Colvin, C.R. (1988). Friends and strangers: Acquaintanceship, agreement, and the accuracy of personality judgment. *Journal of Personality and Social Psychology, 55,* 149–158.

Funder, D.C., & Dobroth, J. M. (1987). Differences between traits: Properties associated with inter-judge agreement. *Journal of Personality and Social Psychology, 52,* 409–418.

Funder, D.C., & Ozer, D.J. (1983). Behavior as a function of the situation. *Journal of Personality and Social Psychology, 44,* 107–112.

Gergen, K. J. (1968). Personal consistency and the presentation of self. In C. Gordon & K.J. Gergen (Eds.), *The self in social interaction* (pp. 299–308). New York: Wiley.

Goldberg, L.R., & Werts, C. E. (1966). The reliability of clinician's judgments: A multi-trait-multimethod approach. *Journal of Consulting Psychology, 30,* 199–206.

Goldman, W., & Lewis, P., (1977). Beautiful is good: Evidence that the physically attractive are more socially skilled. *Journal of Experimental Social Psychology, 13,* 125–130.

Gormly, J., & Edelberg, W. (1974). Validity in personality trait attributions. *American Psychologist, 29,* 189–193.

Gregory, R.L. (1971). Visual illusions. In R.C. Atkinson (Ed.), *Contemporary psychology* (pp. 167–177). San Francisco: Freeman.

Hartshorne, H., & May, M.A. (1928). *Studies in the nature of character* (Vol. 1). New York: Macmillan.

Hogan, R., DeSoto, C.B., & Solano, C. (1977). Traits, tests, and personality research. *American Psychologist, 32,* 255–264.

Houts, A.C., Cook, T.D., & Shadish, W.R. (1986). The person–situation debate: A critical multiplist perspective. *Journal of Personality, 54,* 52–105.

James, W. (1890). *Principles of psychology* (Vol. I). London: Macmillan.

Jones, E.E., & Harris, V.A. (1967). The attribution of attitudes. *Journal of Experimental Social Psychology, 3,* 2–24.

Jones, E.E., & Nisbett, R.E. (1971). *The actor and the observer: Divergent perceptions of the causes of behavior.* Morristown, NJ: General Learning Press.

Kelley, K. (1986). *His way: The unauthorized biography of Frank Sinatra.* New York: Bantam Books.

Kenny, D.A., & La Voie, L. (1984). The social relations model. In L. Berkowitz (Ed.), *Advances in experimental social psychology* (Vol. 18, pp. 141–182). Orlando, FL: Academic Press.

Kenrick, D.T. (1987). Gender, genes, and the social environment. In P.C. Shaver & C. Hendrick (Eds.), *Review of Personality and Social Psychology* (Vol. 8, Sex and gender, pp. 14–43). Beverly Hills, CA.: Sage.

Kenrick, D.T., & Dantchik, A. (1983). Interactionism, idiographics, and the social psychological invasion of personality. *Journal of Personality, 51,* 286–307.

Kenrick, D.T., & Funder, D. C. (1988). Profiting from controversy: Lessons from the person-situation controversy. *American Psychologist, 43.*

Kenrick, D.T., & Stringfield, D.O. (1980). Personality traits and the eye of the beholder: Crossing some traditional philosophical boundaries in the search for consistency in all of the people. *Psychological Review, 87,* 88–104.

Kenrick, D.T., Stringfield, D.O., Wagenhals, W.L., Dahl, R.H., & Ransdell, H. J. (1980). Sex differences, androgyny, and approach responses to erotica: A new variation on the old volunteer problem. *Journal of Personality and Social Psychology, 40,* 1039–1056.

Kenrick, D.T., & Trost, M.R. (1987). A biosocial theory of heterosexual relationships. In K. Kelley (Ed.)., *Males, females, and sexuality: Theory and research* (pp. 59–100). Albany: State University of New York Press.

Kenrick, D.T., & Trost, M.R. (1989). A reproductive exchange model of heterosexual relationships: Putting proximate economics in ultimate perspective. In C. Hendrick (Ed.), *Review of Personality and Social Psychology* (Vol. 10, Close relationships, pp. 92–118). Beverly Hills, CA: Sage.

Magnusson D., & Endler, N.S. (Eds.). (1977). *Personality at the crossroads: Current issues in interactional psychology.* Hillsdale, NJ: Erlbaum.

McArthur, L. Z., & Baron, R. M. (1983). Toward an ecological theory of social perception. *Psychological Review, 90,* 215–235.

McClelland, D.C. (1972). Opinions reflect opinions: So what else is new? *Journal of Consulting and Clinical Psychology, 38,* 325–326.

McCrae, R.R. (1982). Consensual validation of personality traits: Evidence from self-reports and ratings. *Journal of Personality and Social Psychology, 43,* 293–303.

Mischel, W. (1968). *Personality and assessment.* New York: Wiley.

Mischel, W. (1984). Convergences and challenges in the search for consistency. *American Psychologist, 39,* 351–364.

Monson, T.C., Keel, R., Stephens, D., & Genung, V. (1982). Trait attributions: Relative validity, covariation with behavior, and prospect of future interaction. *Journal of Personality and Social Psychology, 42,* 1014–1024.

Monson, T.C., & Snyder, M. (1977). Actors, observers, and the attribution process: Toward a reconceptualization. *Journal of Experimental Social Psychology, 13,* 89–111.

Monson, T.C., Tanke E. D., & Lund, J. (1980).

Determinants of social perception in a naturalistic setting. *Journal of Research in Personality, 14,* 104–120.

Nisbett, R.E., & Ross, L.D. (1980). *Human inference: Strategies and shortcomings of social judgment.* New York: Prentice-Hall.

Norman, W.T., & Goldberg, L.R. (1966). Raters, ratees, and randomness in personality structure. *Journal of Personality and Social Psychology, 4,* 681–691.

Ozer, D. J. (1985). Correlation and the coefficient of determination. *Psychological Bulletin, 97,* 307–315.

Price, R.H., & Bouffard, D.L. (1974). Behavioral appropriateness and situational constraint as dimensions of social behavior. *Journal of Personality and Social Psychology, 30,* 579–586.

Rausch, M.L. (1977). Paradox, levels, and junctures in person–situation systems. In D. Magnusson & N. S. Endler (Eds.), *Personality at the crossroads* (pp. 287–304). Hillsdale, NJ.: Erlbaum.

Ross, L. (1977). The intuitive psychologist and his shortcomings: Distortions in the attribution process. In L. Berkowitz (Ed.), *Advances in experimental social psychology* (Vol. 10). New York: Academic Press.

Rushton, J.P. (1985). Differential K theory: The sociobiology of individual and group differences. *Personality and Individual Differences, 6,* 441–452.

Sadalla, E.K., Kenrick, D.T., & Vershure, B. (1987). Dominance and heterosexual attraction. *Journal of Personality and Social Psychology, 52,* 730–738.

Schank, R.C., & Abelson, R.P. (1977). *Scripts, plans, goals, and understanding.* Hillsdale, NJ: Erlbaum.

Schneider, D. (1973). Implicit personality theory: A review. *Psychological Bulletin, 79,* 294–309.

Schutte, N. A., Kenrick, D. T., & Sadalla, E. K. (1985). The search for predictable settings: Situational prototypes, constraint, and behavioral variation. *Journal of Personality and Social Psychology, 49,* 121–128.

Sinatra, N. (1985). *Frank Sinatra: My father.* Garden City, NY: Doubleday.

Snyder, M., & Ickes, W. (1985). Personality and social behavior. In G. Lindzey & E. Aronson (Eds.), *Handbook of social psychology* (3rd ed., Vol II, pp. 883–948). Reading, MA: Addison-Wesley.

Snyder, M., Tanke, E.D., & Berscheid, E. (1977). Social perception and interpersonal behavior: On the self-fulfilling nature of social stereotypes. *Journal of Personality and Social Psychology, 35,* 656–666.

Wachtel, P. (1973). Psychodynamics, behavior therapy, and the implacable experimenter: An inquiry into the consistency of personality. *Journal of Abnormal Psychology, 82,* 324–334.

CHAPTER 7

Motives

DAN P. McADAMS

Four Traditions in the Study of Human Motivation
Optimism: People Are (Basically) "Good"
Pessimism: People Are "Bad" (and Usually Miserable)
Neutrality: People Are "Blank"
Diversity: People Are "Many Things"
Biology Versus Cognition in Human Motivation
Drive, Reward, Instinct
Expectancies, Schemas, Attributions

Individual Differences in Three Social Motives
ACTIVITY BOX: **Scoring Stories for Power and Intimacy**
Wanting to Do Better: The Achievement Motive
Wanting to Have Impact: The Power Motive
Wanting to Be Close: The Intimacy Motive
Summary
SUGGESTED READINGS
REFERENCES

The question of motivation may be the most fundamental question in all of personality psychology: *What do people really want?* The answer is not obvious. Indeed, a completely satisfactory answer to this question has probably never been provided, though some of the greatest scholars of history have offered intriguing possibilities. To address the question of motivation is to speculate on nothing less than human nature itself, for to ask what people really want is, in part, to ask what it means to be human.

But why do we ask this question? Why does motivation intrigue us? One of the central reasons for our interest in human motivation stems from our perception of our own lives and the lives of other human beings. What we invariably notice, and often take for granted, when we observe ourselves and others is that lives generally appear to be *organized and directed*. In short, people appear to *strive* toward desired ends. People seem to behave in accord with personal goals, desires, plans, wishes, concerns, and expectations. Though some of our behavior may seem random and chaotic, much of what we do appears to suggest that we, in fact, want something! And whatever it is that we want appears to *energize and direct* our behavior across different situations and over time. In very simple and general terms, human motives are recurrent "wants" that get us moving in certain directions in our lives. But what do we want?

Four Traditions in the Study of Human Motivation

There are at least four different ways that Western scholars have traditionally answered the question of what people want. Each of the four reflects a particular view of human nature and of the extent to which human beings are capable of living good lives versus bad lives, experiencing happiness versus misery, and obeying the dictates of reason versus irrationality. We may think of these four as the traditions of optimism, pessimism, neutrality, and diversity.

Optimism: People Are (Basically) "Good"

Most of us like to think that we are reasonable human beings who want what is *good*—good for ourselves and, in many cases, good for other people, too. We believe that we rationally evaluate our lives and our daily situations in order to make well-informed decisions about our behavior. We often believe that *reason* drives our behavior and guides our lives. Our belief is grounded in the general realization that human beings have been specially endowed with abilities for abstract thinking and rational decision making that sharply differentiate us from the rest of the animal kingdom.

Over two-thousand years ago, the Greek philosopher Plato (427?–347? BC) recognized the human person's privileged place in the world as the one being capable of reason. In *The Republic,* Plato presents one of the first motivational theories of human behavior on record. Human behavior is energized and directed, he argues, by three essential motives, each corresponding to a distinct portion of the mind. These are (1) the appetites, which are basic bodily needs and wants; (2) courage and fortitude, which motivate people, especially soldiers, to do heroic acts; and (3) reason, which motivates people to strive for "the Good." By contemplating the nature of reality in an abstract and rational manner, the human being may come to understand what is true, good, and harmonious. Reason is the great guiding light of human behavior, the motivational beacon of the virtuous life.

Hundreds of years after Plato, European poets and philosophers of "the Enlightenment," such as Alexander Pope (1688–1744) and Jean Jacques Rousseau (1712–1778), celebrated the enlightened status of the human being as a potentially reasonable and peace-loving creature. In Pope's view, human behavior is driven by self-love but guided by reason. Therefore, although selfish wants may energize us to act, rational thought tempers our selfishness and provides good direction for behavior. According to Rousseau, human beings are born into a state of natural goodness and perfection. Society, however, is capable of perverting human goodness and substituting destructive motives for benevolent and reasonable ones. Rousseau believed that only by ignoring modern (eighteenth century) society and returning to nature could human beings fully realize their own goodness.

The Platonic and Enlightenment views of human motivation have made their way into the twentieth century in a variety of forms. Modern psychology is replete with a number of *cognitive* approaches to human motivation that argue, as did Plato and Pope, that human behavior is guided by rational "plans," "scripts," and "schemas," and that human beings strive to match their behaviors to their reasonable understandings of the world (Kelly, 1955; Markus & Sentis, 1982). The optimistic tradition can be seen in many theories suggesting that people seek *cognitive consistency* in their lives. People are motivated to reduce "dissonance" or contradiction in their behavior and thought and to observe and make reasonable sense of what they do (Festinger, 1957; Kelley, 1973). In a relatedly optimistic vein, humanistic psychologists, like Maslow (1968) and Rogers (1951), portray human beings as potentially reasonable and creative organisms whose most noteworthy behavior is motivated by a fundamental drive toward perfecting the self, or *self-actualization*.

Pessimism: People Are "Bad" (and Usually Miserable)

In sharp contrast, the notion that men and women are inherently flawed, conflicted, and even evil—that we are all "sinners" at heart—is deeply ingrained in Judeo-Christian traditions. The Old Testament tells the story of the original sin of Adam and Eve and of many other instances in which the people created in God's image murdered, raped, destroyed, and disobeyed. In general, the Christian faith is premised on the basic assumption that people are born into sin and must, therefore, be redeemed through some kind of encounter with a benevolent deity. Human beings are motivated by nonrational forces, existing both within and outside the person. By and large, reason is not capable of controlling human behavior.

In the nineteenth century, Darwin and other scientists made a momentous contribution to the tradition of pessimism in developing the theory of the evolution of species. The implication of evolutionary theory is that human beings are ultimately motivated by the same forces that motivate all other animals: basic needs to *survive* and *reproduce*. Over thousands of years, natural selection has favored the basic human traits that promote the survival and procreation of the individual organism in the face of threatening environments containing limited resources and in the face of other threatening and competing individuals. Modern evolutionary theorists and sociobiologists such as Wilson (1978) assert that the most adaptive human wants are those that have maximized the individual's "fitness" in the environment over thousands of years. Human beings appear to have evolved to live in small social groups. Therefore, the most basic psychological motives may be those that enable the individual to prosper in group living, such as innate desires for social *acceptance* and *recognition* or status (Hogan, 1987).

In twentieth-century psychology, the most influential spokesman for the pessimistic tradition in human motivation has been Freud (1900/1953, 1930/1961). According to Freud's psychoanalytic view, (1) all behavior is *determined* (motivated) by forces over which we have little control; (2) these forces are in constant *conflict* with one another, which is why people suffer from persistent *anxiety*; and (3) the forces and conflicts that determine our behavior are *unconscious*. This third proposition asserts that we do not know, and except in extraordinary circumstances we cannot know, what we want. In other words, we do not know (consciously) our motives. If we were to know, however, we would probably shudder in disbelief and repugnance, for behavior is fundamentally driven by basic unconscious instincts of *sexuality* and *aggression*. Even the highest forms of human living—art, altruism, love, science—are ultimately motivated by primal, selfish wants. Like evolutionary theory, therefore, psychoanalysis emphasizes dark, instinctual, and egoistic forces as prime energizers and directors of human behavior, replacing the guiding light of reason with animalistic wants and desires.

Neutrality: People Are "Blank"

A third tradition in human motivation asserts that human beings are fundamentally neither good nor bad, happy nor miserable, rational nor irrational. Fundamentally human beings are blank, empty, unformed. In the famous terms of the Enlightenment philosopher John Locke (1632–1704), the person is at birth a *tabula rasa*, or "blank slate." Over time and with experience in the world, the person comes to receive the particular contents of human life, essentially *learning* from society what he or she should and should not want. A person's motives are shaped by the environment. A good and beneficent environment creates good, happy, rational, and sociable people, motivated to act in ways commensurate with the society's expectations and values. A bad, destructive, or oppressive environment breeds unhappiness, conflict, and depravity. We are what our worlds teach us to be.

The most influential spokesman for the motivational tradition of neutrality in twentieth-century psychology has been Skinner (1971). Skinner's brand of *operant behaviorism* looks for the motivators of human behavior in the environment rather than within the person. According to this view, psychologists should not make inferences about the internal needs, wants, desires, and expectations of the person, because these internal phenomena cannot be directly observed and precisely measured. Rather, the psychologist must examine carefully the particular environments within which behavior is displayed in order to understand how the environments reward or reinforce certain behaviors and punish or fail to reinforce others. Human behavior is virtually as malleable as are the environments in which it is exhibited.

Diversity: People Are "Many Things"

The traditions of optimism, pessimism, and neutrality tend to underscore ways in which all people are similar and thus behave in similar ways. A fourth tradition, however, takes a very different tack. The tradition of diversity emphasizes *individual differences* among persons. According to this very general view, we are probably unable to determine what *the* basic motives are for everybody, whether people are fundamentally good or bad, or what the possibilities of human happiness and misery really are. What we all do know, however, is that people differ from one another, sometimes in remarkable ways. Therefore, different people may want different things. Marked individual differences in the strength or prominence of various motives should be observed from person to person.

The appreciation of human diversity may be as old as the human species, but its discussion in psychological terms can be traced back at least as far as the personality typologies of ancient Greece and Rome. For instance, Hippocrates (460?–377? BC) classified human beings into four different temperament types: the sanguine (cheerful, robust), melancholic (sad, depressed), choleric (angry, irritable), and phlegmatic (cold, stoic). Aristotle (384–322 BC) and his student Theophrastus composed character sketches of different personality types of the day, such as the "Magnanimous Man" and the "Penurious Man" (in Allport, 1937). The implication of these primitive characterizations was that different people's lives are governed by different basic wants and desires. In this vein, twentieth-century psychologists like James (1890), McDougall (1908), and Murray (1938) have delineated classification systems for fundamental human motives. Murray's list of about 20 "psychogenic needs" has been especially influential and, as we will see later in this chapter, has generated a great deal of empirical research into individual differences in human motivation.

Biology Versus Cognition in Human Motivation

Biology and cognition denote two great poles of human existence. On the one hand, every person is an intricate biological mechanism that obeys the laws of physics and physiology. Like other members of the animal kingdom, we must meet the incessant demands of thirst and hunger, and we are completely beholden to the vagaries of pain, sickness, disease, and bodily breakdown. On the other hand, the human being is blessed with incomparable cognitive powers enabling one to reflect upon this biological condition, to ponder one's own mortality and imagine alternatives to it, to be conscious of one's own predicament, and to *think* about virtually anything at all. This essential dualism of biology and cognition influences our consideration of a wide range of human problems. It is no surprise, therefore, that the scientific study of human motivation embodies a tension between biology and cognition, body and thought. An adequate approach to the question of what people really want requires a consideration of both.

Drive, Reward, Instinct

Hull (1943) formulated a comprehensive and very influential theory of motivation and behavior that centered on the concept of generalized *drive*. According to Hull, drive refers to the sum total of forces within the organism arising from sexual desires, fear, hunger, thirst, and other basic *biologically* linked needs. Though various kinds of needs may contribute to an organism's current drive state, there is only one kind of drive, and it functions as a general *energizer* for behavior. An animal or human being in a strong drive state will act in a vigorous fashion to reduce the drive and thereby relieve the tension of the drive. The reduction of tension is rewarding in some sense, and as a result the behavior that successfully reduces the tension of strong drive is reinforced. The greater the drive reduction, the greater is the reinforcement. Therefore, responses that reduce high levels of drive should be learned more quickly and emitted more intensely than responses that reduce moderate to low levels of drive. Exactly what the organism will do to reduce drive, however, is not directly determined by drive. Rather, the *direction* of behavior is determined by other factors, most notably the habits or behavioral patterns that the organism has learned in the past under similar stimulus conditions. Hull referred to this factor as *habit strength*. In general, a behavioral response was conceived as a product of drive (energizer) and habit strength (director).

Although Hull derived his theory of drive and habit strength from animal studies, other researchers have applied the theory directly to human subjects. For instance, Spence (1958) proposed that every person is characterized by a particular level of *emotionality* that contributes directly to drive level. Taylor (1953) designed the Manifest Anxiety Scale (MAS) to assess individual differences in chronic anxiety, which was said to be a major source of emotionality. Research employing the MAS has shown that persons high in anxiety, and thus in a presumably higher drive state, perform better on simple tasks than less anxious subjects but do more poorly on difficult tasks, especially when the performance situation involves high levels of stress (Spence, Farber, & McFann, 1956; Spielberger & Smith, 1966). Therefore, the hypothesized energizing effect of high levels of drive, as operationalized on the MAS, appears to promote simple performance but interferes with more complex, stressful tasks.

Another application of drive theory to human behavior is research on *social facilitation.* A person's performance is often enhanced or facilitated in the presence of others, although sometimes the presence of others can have the opposite effect. Zajonc (1965) provided a Hullian explanation for social facilitation, essentially arguing that the presence of others increases a person's drive level, which in turn energizes "dominant" or readily available responses. Numerous studies have shown that the presence of others facilitates performance of well-learned responses but retards the learning of new ones. For instance, Hunt and Hillery (1973) showed that subjects were more effective during early attempts to solve a maze-learning task while working alone than when accompanied by others. Once the maze had become familiar through practice, however, the presence of others led to better performance than shown by isolated subjects. Why, however, social facilitation should increase drive remains a matter of speculation. Zajonc (1980) has suggested three possible answers: (1) the presence of others creates uncertainty about how the others will behave; (2) other people distract the subject; and (3) others may be seen as potential judges or evaluators of one's actions. In other words, drive may be increased by greater levels of uncertainty, distraction, or concern about social evaluation.

The past twenty-five years in psychology have witnessed a steady decline in the status of the concept of biologically based drive to explain human motivation. Hull's formulation has led to a great deal of empirical research, and numerous studies have suggested that (1) reinforcement often does *not* involve any kind of drive reduction and (2) the idea of a generalized and nonspecific drive that energizes all behavior seems untenable. Rather, reinforcement appears to be a much more complex matter than originally supposed, and behavior appears to be motivated by more specific processes than a generalized energizer. With respect to the issue of reinforcement, studies of electrical stimulation of animal brains reveal discrete "reward centers" that appear to have nothing to do with drive (Olds, 1977). Mild electrical stimulation of these cortical areas, located mostly in the brain's limbic system, is highly reinforcing, motivating rats and other animals studied to engage in a wide range of behaviors in order to obtain the stimulation.

Studies of brain stimulation offer a biological perspective on a proposition about motivation that is at least 2,000 years old: that organisms seek to maximize pleasure and minimize pain. An interesting twist on this idea has been proposed by Solomon (1980) in his *opponent-process* theory of motivation. According to Solomon, the brains of all mammals are organized to oppose or suppress certain types of emotional arousals. A highly positive or negative emotional process (Process A) automatically sets into motion an opposite emotional process (Process B). With repeated experiences, the intensity of Process A dissipates, but Process B continues to build up.

For example, a skydiver is likely to experience tremendous anxiety before his or her first jump. The anxiety dissipates rapidly just after the jump, however, and is followed by a rush of positive affect which, over time, slowly dissipates until the person is back to a kind of emotional steady state. According to Solomon, the anxiety (Process A) automatically sets into motion the euphoria (Process B), which overwhelms Process A and becomes the dominant emotional experience following the jump. With successive jumps, furthermore, Process A is likely to lessen in magnitude, but Process B continues to build up. Therefore, successive jumps are preceded by less and less anxiety but followed by greater and greater levels of positive affect. In this way, the novice parachutist gets "hooked on" skydiving over time. Similarly, a positive Process A can be opposed by a negative Process B, as in the case of drug addiction. For the novice drug user, the initial ingestion of, say, cocaine brings with it a highly positive pleasurable response that is followed by a relatively mild negative reaction once Process A has worn off. Repeated use of the drug may bring with it less and less positive pleasurable responses, requiring perhaps greater dosages to achieve a desired high, and greater and greater negative reactions as Process B continues to build up. Over time, therefore, the motivation for drug usage may become less a matter of seeking the positive results of Process A and more a matter of avoiding the highly distressing effects of Process B. Pleasure-seeking behavior is thus transformed, over time, into behavior motivated by the desperate avoidance of pain.

The opponent-process theory of motivation contends that the interplay of Processes A and B over time is a *natural* phenomenon, under innate biological control. As yet, the precise mechanisms within the brain and central nervous system that might specifically be involved have not been identified. However, the theory's emphasis on nature and biology reflects growing interest among scientists in the possible *instinctual* underpinnings of human motivation. Therefore, while the concept of a general biological drive has fallen into disfavor, the concept of particular biological instincts appears to be gaining momentum, at least among psychologists who adopt an evolutionary perspective on human motivation.

Modern instinct theories suggest a complex biological picture for higher mammals, primates, and human beings. Rather than innate drives, blind urges, or inflexible blueprints, instincts are understood more generally as biologically rooted motivational tendencies that have proven to be highly adaptive over thousands of years of evolution. Instincts give rise to particular urges, emotions, and behavioral plans that can be markedly influenced by the environment. While instincts may energize and direct fixed and stereotyped behaviors among certain animals, human instincts may generally "set boundaries or limits within which a good deal of variation may occur" (Breger, 1974, p. 24). Such universal human behavior patterns as aggression (Konner, 1983), altruism (Hoffman, 1981), and mother-infant attachment (Bowlby, 1969) may have instinctual foundations, ultimately coded in the genetic makeup of humans. By virtue of evolution, people may be naturally predisposed to seek out certain incentives (such as status, social acceptance, and stimulus novelty) and manifest certain kinds of behavior patterns (such as caring for infants and attacking an enemy) over the course of the human life span. Though learning and experience may exert a profound influence upon motivation and behavior, modern instinct theories make a compelling case for the existence of innate boundaries within which learning and experience operate and are given meaning.

Expectancies, Schemas, Attributions

Even during the heyday of Hull's influence, drive theory was pitted against a competing *cognitive* approach to motivation termed *expectancy-value* theory. Drawing on the early work of Tolman (1932) and Lewin (1936), this general approach contends that the basis for motivation is the anticipation of the consequences of behavior when those consequences have value for the person. The expectancy of being rewarded (or punished) for a particular response provides the individual with an *incentive* for behavior. Maximum incentive occurs when the individual is given the opportunity to perform behaviors for which he or she strongly expects (high expectancy) to receive highly valued rewards (high value) (Rotter, 1954).

The expectancy-value approach suggests that cognitions, such as expectancies about reward, are more important than biological drives in the motivation of behavior. Whereas Hull argued that reinforcement always involves the reduction of biological drive, expectancy-value theory holds that reinforcement shapes behavior by creating expectancies of additional reinforcements that have some value to the person. According to this view, the student who studies hard for a tough examination is motivated by the cognitive expectation of reinforcement for performance (e.g., a high grade), rather than by reduction of drive. In this example, the drive approach might focus instead on the reduction of anxiety (an aversive high-drive state) that studying for the test could bring.

Expectancy-value theory paved the way for a number of modern approaches to motivation emphasizing conscious thought and cognition. According to a wide variety of recent theories, human behavior is primarily energized and directed by such cognitive factors as (1) plans (Miller, Galanter & Pribram, 1960), (2) scripts (Abelson, 1981), (3) current concerns (Klinger, 1977), (4) personal projects (Palys & Little, 1983), and (5) personal strivings (Emmons, 1986). Table 7.1 defines these different but overlapping cognitive-motivational concepts. Another cognitive term that is frequently invoked in discussions of motivation is *schema*. A schema is an abstract knowledge structure that guides the processing of information. Particularly relevant for human motivation are *self-schemas*, which exist as cognitive "generalizations about the self derived from the repeated categorizations and evaluations of behavior by oneself and by others" (Markus & Sentis, 1982, p. 45). People tend to act in accord with their consciously construed self-schemas (Markus, 1977) or personified images of self (McAdams, 1985a). Thus, a man who consciously views himself as a kind and affectionate father is likely to engage in nurturant behavior that is consistent with this image. A hard-nosed drill sergeant will consciously cultivate a very different image of the self. In both cases, a self-schema serves to energize and direct certain forms of behavior. People seem to *want* to act in ways that are consistent with their own views of themselves.

Another class of cognitive variables assumed to exert some motivational influence on human behavior are *attributions*. Attributions are the casual explanations that people formulate for the behavior of others and for their own behavior. Attribution theorists have delineated a number of rules that people implicitly follow in assigning causes to behavior (Kelley, 1973). For instance, in explaining what causes the behavior of others, people often mistakenly cite stable and internal characteristics of the actors rather than unstable and external factors in the situation, a phenomenon that has been termed the *fundamental attribution error* (Jones, 1979). Therefore, in explaining why my students did poorly on the first examination in my Personality class, I am likely to attribute their performance to "low intelligence" or "general laziness"—factors that are internal (to them) and stable. The truth of the matter, however, may be that poor performance was more a function of external and unstable factors, such as boring lectures, an overly difficult examination, or some other situational determinant.

In general, attribution theory focuses more on the explanations

TABLE 7.1

Some Cognitive-Motivational Concepts

Plan	Hierarchical arrangement of goals that specifies the sequences of behaviors that are appropriate in particular situations. Plans guide behavior by providing a blueprint for action. (Miller, Galanter, & Pribram, 1960)
Script	Similar to plan, a script is a person's understanding of a simple and stereotyped event sequence. For instance, you may have particular scripts for "taking a shower" or "ordering from a menu" —each of which specifies what you typically do in each event and in what order. Like plans, scripts guide or direct behavior. (Abelson, 1981)
Schema	Any abstract knowledge structure. "Schema" is a very general concept that encompasses many different kinds of cognitive phenomena, including scripts and plans. A *self-schema* is a knowledge structure about the self. Self-schemas may guide and direct a person's behavior, in that he or she will strive to act in accordance with his or her cognitive understanding of the self. (Markus, 1977)
Imago	A personified and idealized image of the self that functions as a "main character" in a person's "life story." Imagoes are stock characters—such as "the care giver," "the clown," the "warrior" —that people adopt or develop as parts of themselves. McAdams (1985a) argues that power and intimacy motivation energize and direct behavior, in part, through imagoes. Thus, a person high in power motivation may develop a dominant image of self as a "warrior" or "adventurer" whereas a person high in intimacy motivation may develop a dominant imago of the"care giver" or "loyal friend."
Current concern	The state of the person between his or her initial commitment to a goal and either attainment or abandonment of that goal. To say that a person has a current concern with respect to a particular goal in his or her life is to say that he or she is currently oriented toward that goal and will continue to be so until the goal is either accomplished or abandoned. The current concern underlies his or her thought and affect with respect to the goal, but it is not synonymous with that thought and affect. (Klinger, 1977)
Personal Project	Extended sets of actions intended to achieve a personal goal. At any given time in a person's life, he or she may be involved in numerous personal projects. (Palys & Little, 1983).
Personal striving	What the individual is typically "trying to do" during a particular period in his or her life. Personal strivings unite discrete goals around a common quality or theme. For example, a young man's goal to obtain the grade of "A" in his biology class and his goal to read classic literature during summer break may both center on his more general personal striving to transform himself into a well-rounded scholar. (Emmons, 1986)

that people give for motivation—what energizes and directs certain behavior—than on motivation per se. However, explanations may themselves have motivational power. Attributions, once made, appear to influence the subsequent behavior of the person who made the attributions. For instance, persons who perennially explain negative events in their lives in terms of internal, stable, and global attributions (e.g., "Bad things happen to me because I am generally dumb, and I have always been dumb") tend to manifest depressive symptomatology, such as sad affect and low activity level. According to this attributional theory of depression, these cognitive explanations *precede* and *lead to* depressive behavior, thus serving as cognitive causes of and motivators for depression (Abramson, Seligman, & Teasdale, 1978; Peterson & Seligman, 1984).

Individual Differences in Three Social Motives

One of the most fruitful approaches to research on human motives and personality has focused on three recurrent social wants that energize and direct behavior: achievement, power, and intimacy motives. Pioneered by Murray (1938) and McClelland (1961), this approach seeks to assess individual differences in social motives by analyzing imaginative stories and fantasies that people tell for key motivational themes. The Murray-McClelland approach borrows liberally from a number of different theoretical trends already mentioned. By and large, the approach follows the "diversity" tradition in human motivation, maintaining that different people want different things and focusing, therefore, on individual differences in human motives. However, the approach also shares Freud's view, articulated within the "pessimism" tradition, that human beings do not consciously know what their motives are. Rather than ask people about their motives directly, therefore, this approach employs indirect methods of interpreting fantasies and imaginative narratives that are assumed to reveal less-than-fully-conscious wants and needs. In addition, the Murray-McClelland approach emphasizes the cognitive dimensions of human motives while sharing a certain affinity with modern instinct theory in suggesting that achievement, power, and intimacy motivation may ultimately be derived from basic natural incentives that are rooted in human evolution (McClelland, 1985).

Murray (1938) and his colleagues invented a number of different methods for measuring aspects of personality, like human motives, that do not appear to be fully conscious and amenable to self-report. The most well-known of these is the *Thematic Apperception Test (TAT)*. On the TAT, the person is asked to tell or write an imaginative story in

Scoring Stories for Power and Intimacy

To see how psychologists assess individual differences in the *power* motive and the *intimacy* motive, take ten minutes to do the following exercise. You need two sheets of paper and a pencil. The task is to write a story in response to each of the two pictures.

Look at the first picture briefly and then close the book. Take 5 minutes to write a short imaginative story. The story should say a little bit about what is going on in the picture now, what led up to this situation, and what may happen in the future. The story should also say something about what the characters are thinking and feeling. You should know that this is not a "test" in the sense that there are "right" or "wrong" stories. Any story you write is fine. The important thing is to

Based on Winter (1973) and McAdams (1980).

relax and be creative. Use the picture as a stimulus to get your imagination going. After five minutes, look at the second picture and repeat the procedure.

You are now ready to interpret the stories in terms of power and intimacy motivation. Detailed scoring manuals for both of these motives have been developed. Typically, a scorer would be trained with the detailed manual, going through over two hundred practice stories in order to learn the system. This procedure would require about seven to nine hours of work. Here, we will simply take a brief look at a few of the scoring categories that are used. This exercise is intended only to give you a feel for the general procedure; it is not a valid measure of your true power and intimacy motivation.

response to each of a number of ambiguous picture cues. Psychologists who employ the TAT, both in clinical work and in research, assume that the person's stories reveal important tendencies and themes in his or her life. The TAT is termed, therefore, a *projective test*, in that the subject is assumed to "project" onto the stimulus picture and into the story composed important needs, wishes, conflicts, and so on. In a standardized research setting, the subject is typically given about 5 minutes to write one story in response to each of 5 or 6 TAT pictures. Therefore, the entire procedure requires about half an hour to complete. Each story is an imaginative narrative that tells what is going on in the picture now, what led up to the current situation, what may happen in the future, and what the characters are feeling, thinking, and

ACTIVITY BOX (Continued)

Scoring Stories for Power and Intimacy

For each of the two motives, the scorer looks for certain *themes* or *categories* in the stories. Take a look now at your first story, in response to the picture of the two women in the laboratory. You may have power themes in this story. Let us consider four possible themes. For each you may check if the theme is present in the story or absent in the story. If it is present, you give yourself "1 point" for power; if it is absent, you give yourself "0 points" for power. Therefore, with respect to these four themes, the maximum score you could get in a story would be "4" (all four themes are present); the minimum would be "0."

- *Power theme 1: General power imagery.* A character in the story desires to have impact or make an impression on others. This may be accomplished through strong, forceful actions (like aggression), giving unsolicited help, or trying to control, persuade, or impress. *Examples*: "The woman on the left is trying to sabotage her colleague's experiment"; "She convinced her friend that she was right."
- *Power theme 2: Increased prestige.* The setting of the story or a character is described in ways that increase prestige or position. *Example*: "She was a world-famous scientist."
- *Power theme 3: Lower prestige.* The setting of the story or a character is described in ways that decrease prestige or position. *Example*: "The scoundrel was up to no good."
- *Power theme 4: Effect.* A power action produces a major, striking effect. *Example*: "The world was shocked by her bold words and brazen acts."

wanting. The researcher then scores the stories according to objective coding manuals developed for each of the three social motives. A feel for the general procedure is provided in the Activity Box.

Wanting to Do Better: The Achievement Motive

From an early age onward, most of us delight in "doing well." We strive to engage our environments in a competent, independent, and efficient manner, to be successful in our explorations and manipulations of the world. The developmental origins of our concern for successful performance may go back as far as the earliest months of life, at which time the infant experiences the basic human emotion of *interest-*

Now let us look at your second story, in response to the picture of two people sitting on a bench. You may have intimacy themes in this one. We will look at four of these themes. The scoring procedure is the same: you receive 1 point if the theme is present or 0 points if it is absent.

- *Intimacy theme 1: Positive affect.* A relationship among characters promotes positive feelings, such as joy, excitement, love, liking, and happiness. *Examples:* "She believes that she is in love with this strange man"; "The two good friends enjoy their day off."
- *Intimacy theme 2: Dialogue.* Characters in the story communicate with each other in a reciprocal and noninstrumental fashion. *Example:* "They talked all afternoon about anything that came to their mind."
- *Intimacy theme 3: Commitment or concern.* A character commits himself or herself to another or expresses humanitarian concern, as in helping another. *Example:* "Dan had pity on the old woman and spent the next hour trying to cheer her up."
- *Intimacy theme 4: Surrender of control.* Characters in the story find themselves in a relationship that they cannot control; they give up any attempts to control and let events transpire spontaneously. *Example:* "She could not help herself; the sympathy she felt for this spiteful character made her stay and talk to him, even though she knew better."

excitement (Izard, 1978). In the first months of life, infants find modest variety and discrepency in their environments to be especially interesting, and they will spend more time focusing their attention on these mild variations from expectancy than on stimuli that are too familiar or too novel. The adaptive function of such interest is "to focus and maintain attention and to motivate exploratory activity" (Izard, 1978, p. 397). Later, as they become able to walk and talk, babies explore their environments in more active ways, seeking out events that will elicit interest and excitement as they function with greater and greater levels of *autonomy* (Erikson, 1963). With respect to cognitive development, toddlers come to understand and appreciate the existence of primitive *standards* for "good" performance (Kagan, 1984). On a very simple but compelling level, they realize that "things work in a certain way." They seek to find out what these ways are and to master them.

According to some psychologists, early experiences of interest-excitement and subsequent exploration signal a biologically rooted and evolutionarily adaptive human tendency toward engaging the world as a curious and innovative achiever (McClelland, 1985). Although virtually all human beings may be endowed with this tendency, marked individual differences in its expression can be observed. Therefore, although virtually all adults want to do well in some sense and in some areas of their lives, some people have a stronger and more pervasive desire for achievement than do others. People with this strong desire have high achievement motivation. The achievement motive is a *recurrent preference or readiness for experiences of doing better and being successful,* and it is assumed to energize and direct behavior in certain situations. Individual differences in achievement motivation are assessed via the TAT. Persons composing TAT stories in which characters repeatedly strive for successful performance score relatively high in achievement motivation.

A substantial empirical literature suggests that people who score high on TAT achievement motivation behave in different ways than people who score low. For instance, people high in achievement motivation tend to prefer and show high performance in tasks of *moderate* challenge that provide immediate feedback concerning success and failure; they tend to be persistent and highly *efficient* in many kinds of performance, sometimes cutting corners or even cheating in order to maximize productivity; they tend to exhibit high *self-control* and a *future time-perspective;* and they tend to be restless, innovative, and drawn toward *change and movement* (McClelland, 1985; Winter & Carlson, 1988).

One of the most interesting lines of research on achievement motivation concerns how people who differ on this motive pursue careers and adapt to work settings. For many students, personal involvement in a career begins in college, where they take academic courses that are specially designed to prepare them for a certain career path. Research has shown that being high in achievement motivation, as assessed on the TAT, does not necessarily guarantee high grades in college courses (Entwisle, 1972). However, when the courses are perceived as directly *relevant* to their future careers, students high in achievement motivation (and low in fear of failure) earn higher grades than students low in achievement motivation (and high in fear of failure). Furthermore, students high in achievement motivation appear to have more realistic career aspirations. Mahone (1960) rated the career aspirations of students at the University of Michigan relative to the students' intelligence test scores, grade point averages, and major fields. Of the vocational choices made by students high in achievement motivation, 81 percent were rated as "realistic," compared to only 52 percent of the choices made by students low in achievement motivation. Therefore, students high in achievement motivation appear to understand better their own assets and liabilities with respect to future careers, choosing career paths that match their abilities and opportunities. In keeping with other research on achievement motivation, these students adopt a level-headed and pragmatic manner in career choice, settling on a path that is likely to offer *moderate* challenge and risk.

When they graduate from college and, in some cases, professional schools, how do people high in achievement motivation fashion and adapt to their careers? A nationwide survey of adults indicates that U.S. men high in achievement motivation report more job satisfaction, evaluate their jobs as more interesting, and prefer work to leisure, to a greater extent than do men low in achievement motivation (Veroff, 1982). The same relations, however, were not found among American women. With respect to career choice, young men high in achievement motivation tend to be drawn to careers in business. In one study, college men with a high need for achievement manifested patterns of personal interests and values very similar to those expressed by stockbrokers, real estate salesmen, advertisers, merchandise buyers, and factory managers (McClelland, 1961). In another study, men with high achievement motivation in college tended to become employed in small businesses years later (McClelland, 1965).

McClelland has argued that business is a good match for the achievement motive, because business requires that people take moderate risks, assume personal responsibility for their own performance, pay close attention to feedback in terms of costs and profits, and find new or innovative ways to make products or provide services. These hallmarks of *entrepreneurship* are precisely the same behavioral and attitudinal characteristics that laboratory studies have shown to "belong" to persons high in achievement motivation. In this regard, Wainer and Rubin (1969) showed that the heads of more successful small research and development companies had higher achievement motivation than heads of similar but less successful companies. Examining the performance of small knitwear firms in Finland, Kock (1965) found that increases in investment, gross value of output, and number of workers in the firm over time were positively associated with the achievement motivation of the owners and top executive. Following agricultural entrepreneurs over seven years, Singh (1978) found a significant positive correlation between achievement motivation and increased productivity.

Among men, then, high achievement motivation is associated with a number of indexes of success and productivity in business. Being high in the achievement motive, however, does *not* guarantee that a person will reach "the top" of a particular business organization. For instance, McClelland and Boyatzis (1982) found that achievement motivation in managers at the time of their entry into the American Telephone and Telegraph Company (AT&T) was associated with promotion up to Level 3 in the company after sixteen years, but not above that point. The managerial positions at Level 4 and above may have required skills and motives less associated with "doing better" and having more to do with "influencing people." McClelland suggests that in large hierarchical organizations high achievement motivation is likely to be instrumental in career advancement only up to a certain point. At the highest levels of prestige and influence, strong *power* motivation may prove more valuable.

In general, men and women do not differ in overall levels of achievement motivation (Stewart & Chester, 1982). Only a few studies, however, have examined the relation between achievement motivation and career striving in *women*. The results obtained are modestly consistent with findings for men (Stewart & Chester, 1982). For instance, Baruch (1967) and Stewart (1975) found that college women scoring high in achievement motivation tend to pursue more challenging careers than do college women low in achievement motivation. Bloom (1971) showed that adolescent girls aiming to combine career and family were higher in achievement motivation than girls who did not plan to pursue a career. There is very little research, however, on the topic of entrepreneurship and TAT achievement motivation among women already employed in the business world (Stewart & Chester, 1982).

Wanting to Have Impact: The Power Motive

Achievement and power can be very different experiences. Achievement involves doing better or performing well against an external or internal standard, whereas power involves influencing others, having an impact, and feeling *strong*. McClelland (1985) speculates that the developmental origins of power motivation may reside in early emotional experiences of *anger* as well as interest-excitement. Babies begin to express anger between four and six months of age (Izard, 1978). Though infants show wide individual differences in the intensity and range of anger responses, they are most likely to show anger when confronted with frustrations, restraints, and barriers. Anger likely serves an adaptive function. According to Izard (1978), "anger increases the infant's opportunities to sense self-as-casual-agent and hence to experience self as separate, distinct, and capable," and it contributes "to self-development through increasing the infant's sense of self-control and self-determination in the face of frustrating and distasteful situations" (p. 399). While anger, therefore, may intensify the infant's efforts to have a "big impact" on the environment, producing such impacts may also be intrinsically satisfying, eliciting positive emotions of excitement and joy in infants, children, and adults (McClelland, 1985; White, 1959). In general, "having an impact" may be viewed as an evolutionarily adaptive, natural incentive in human life, manifested in such widely varied behavior patterns as aggressive play, fighting, dominance, leadership, debate, and so on (McClelland, 1985).

The power motive is *a recurrent preference or readiness for experiences of having an impact and feeling strong,* and like the achievement motive it is assumed to energize and direct behavior in certain situations. A large number of studies have employed the TAT scoring system for assessing individual differences in power motivation, developed by Winter (1973). In these studies, power motivation has been positively associated with (1) holding elected offices, (2) exerting oneself in an active and forceful manner in small groups, (3) accumulating prestige possessions such as credit cards and fancy cars, (4) taking large risks in order to gain visibility, (5) getting into arguments, (6) choosing occupations in which one strongly directs the behavior of others (such as executive, teacher, and psychologist), and among men only (7) impulsive and mildly aggressive behavior (McAdams, 1985b).

A number of studies have shown that people who perennially adopt strong leadership roles and/or rise to positions of high influence tend to score relatively high on power motivation (McAdams, Rothman & Lichter, 1982). Some laboratory research has looked more closely at how the person high in power motivation actually exerts impact in a leadership role. Fodor and Smith (1982) investigated how students high in power motivation direct the behaviors of others in group decision making. Forty groups containing five students each met to discuss a business case study that concerned whether a company should market a new microwave oven. In each group, a leader was appointed. Half of the leaders had previously scored high in TAT power motivation and the other half had scored low. Observations of the group behavior indicated that students in the groups with high-power-motive leaders tended to present fewer proposals for consideration, to discuss fewer alternative plans, and to show less moral concern about the activities of their hypothetical company, compared to students in groups with low-power-motive leaders. The researchers interpreted these findings to mean that leaders high in power motivation encourage *groupthink*—a form of hasty decision making characterized by diffusion of responsibility, failure to consider long-term ramifications, and the *domination by a single strong leader whose opinion generally goes unchallenged*.

Support for this interpretation comes from another simulation experiment in which business administration students acted as supervisors directing the labors of a work crew (Fodor & Farrow, 1979). Supervisors high in power motivation were more likely than those scoring low in power motivation to react favorably to workers who curried favor with them and ingratiated themselves. High-power-motive supervisors also perceived themselves as exerting greater influence over the work group than did those low in power motivation, viewing subordinates as relatively unimportant and ineffectual. In this regard, it is interesting to note that college men high in power motivation tend to prefer friends who are *not* particularly popular or well known. Winter (1973) explains that such friends are attractive because they pose little threat to the power-motivated person's prestige.

What about the personal lives of people high in power motivation? On this topic, intriguing sex differences have been found. Perhaps surprisingly, men and women do not differ in overall levels of power motivation. However, high power motivation seems to be related to different patterns of love relationships for men and women. In the case of men, high power motivation has been associated with greater dissatisfaction in marriage and dating relationships, less stability in dating, more sexual partners over time, and higher levels of divorce (McAdams, 1984). For women, however, none of these negative outcomes has been observed as a function of power motivation. Rather, one study suggests that power motivation in women is positively associated with marital *satisfaction* (Veroff, 1982). Further, well-educated women high in power motivation tend to marry successful men (Winter, McClelland, & Stewart, 1981). Winter (1988) speculates that because women tend to be socialized to accept roles of caregiving in which they should be responsible for other people, a woman with high power motivation is likely to express the motive in more benevolent ways than is a man high in power motivation—ways that may promote rather than undermine intimate relationships.

Moving from love to health, recent research has suggested that power motivation may be implicated in a complex pattern of factors predicting susceptability to sickness and disease (Jemmott, 1987). Some evidence suggests that people high in power motivation are predisposed to show heightened activation of the sympathetic nervous system when faced with obstacles to or frustrations in the experience of feeling strong and having impact (Fodor, 1984, 1985). Because heightened sympathetic activity may, over time, exert an inordinate amount of stress upon the body's equilibrium, McClelland (1979) has argued that a strong power motive may increase a person's vulnerability to illnesses of various sorts *if the person's need for power is inhibited, challenged, or blocked*. Especially vulnerable may be individuals who show *all* of the following characteristics: (1) high power motivation, (2) low intimacy motivation, (3) high self-control (sometimes called "activity inhibition" and suggesting a tendency to "block" or "inhibit" one's own expression of power), and (4) high levels of power-related stresses.

In support of these ideas, McClelland and Jemmott (1980) administered the TAT to ninety-five students and obtained self-report measures of health problems and life stresses. They classified each life stress identified by a subject as either a power/achievement event, an affiliation/intimacy event, or "other." Examples of power/achievement events included troubles with an employer, a substantial academic disappointment, and participating in a major sports event. The results of the study indicated that the students with (1) relatively high power motivation, (2) relatively high activity inhibition (self-control), and (3) an above-average number of power/achievement stresses over the past year reported more physical illness in the previous six months than did other students. In addition, the illnesses they reported were more severe. The highly controlled and highly power-oriented person may "bottle up" his or her frustrations in such a way as to tax severely an internal physiological equilibrium. The result may be a greater number of colds, bouts of flu, and other physical maladies, especially during times of excessive power stress.

Wanting to Be Close: The Intimacy Motive

While our desires for achievement and power may motivate us to assert ourselves in effective and influential ways and to control, even master, our environments, our longings for close and warm relationships with other human beings pull us in a different direction, to the private life of intimate interpersonal communion (Bakan, 1966). The developmental origins of a general need for intimacy may reside in the joyful face-to-face play of three- to five-month-old babies and their caregivers (Stern, 1985) and the subsequent bond of love formed between the infant and caregivers in the second half of the first year of life, termed *attachment* (Bowlby, 1969). The dominant, biologically grounded emotion of the secure attachment relationship is *joy*—an emotion first expressed around the age of two months in initial smiling responses to faces, voices, and other social stimuli and to familiar events (Sroufe & Waters, 1976). Complexly related may be the emotions of *fear* and *sadness,* which tend to appear toward the end of the first year of life in response to strangers and separation. By the end of the first year of life, the infant knows the experiences of joyful communion with, fear of separation from, and sadness after the temporary loss of such primary caregivers as mother, father, and babysitter.

Bowlby (1969) has outlined how the caregiver-attachment bond is likely to have proven adaptive in the evolution of human beings, serving as a flexible but instinctually based behavioral system that assured mother-infant proximity and protection from predators in dangerous environments. Others have implied that a resultant need for close, warm, and communicative interaction with others may be considered an evolutionarily adaptive feature of human nature (Hogan, 1987). Human beings appear to have evolved as hunters and gatherers traditionally living in small groups, and such a fundamental human need is likely to have promoted cooperation and other key features of group living. Yet striking individual differences in a general need for intimacy may be observed, and these are readily assessed via the TAT.

The intimacy motive is a *recurrent preference or readiness for experiences of warm, close, and communicative interaction with others.* The person high in intimacy motivation desires intimacy in daily life at a relatively stronger level or to a greater degree than a person low in intimacy motivation. A small but growing number of studies show that people high in intimacy motivation (1) spend more time, over the course of a normal day, thinking about relationships with others; (2) engage in a greater number of friendly conversations and write more personal letters; (3) report more positive emotion in the presence of other people; and (4) laugh, smile, and make more eye contact when conversing with others (McAdams, 1982; McAdams & Constantian, 1983; McAdams, Jackson & Kirshnit, 1984). On the other hand, the person high in intimacy motivation may not be the "life of the party." The person high in intimacy motivation is not necessarily more outgoing, sociable, and extraverted. Instead, the high-intimacy person is likely to value close, one-on-one exchanges over boisterous group activities. When confronted with a large group, he or she is likely to promote group harmony and cohesiveness, viewing group activities as opportunities for everybody to get involved rather than for one or two people to dominate the action (McAdams & Powers, 1981). Partly for this reason, people high in intimacy motivation are rated by their friends and acquaintances as especially "sincere," "natural," "loving," "not dominant," and "not self-centered" (McAdams, 1980).

McAdams has undertaken a series of studies investigating relations between both intimacy and power motivation on the one hand and patterns of friendship on the other (McAdams, 1984). In one study, 105 college students wrote TAT stories and then described in some detail ten *friendship episodes* that occurred in their lives during the previous two weeks. A friendship episode was defined as any interaction with a friend that lasted for at least fifteen to twenty minutes. Students high in intimacy motivation tended to report friendship episodes involving one-on-one interaction with a single other friend rather than large-group interactions and to describe conversations in which the participants in the episodes disclosed personal information about themselves. Therefore, when they got together with their friends, students high in intimacy motivation were more likely (than those scoring low in intimacy motivation) to talk about and listen to their friends talk about their own fears, hopes, feelings, fantasies, and other highly intimate topics. Power motivation, on the other hand, was associated with large-group interactions and assertive friendship activities like making plans, initiating conversations, and helping others. In general, intimacy motivation is associated with a more *communal* friendship style that places prime importance on *being* together and *sharing* secrets with others, whereas power motivation is associated with an *agentic* friendship style that emphasizes *doing* things and *helping others*.

Two recent studies have examined the relations between intimacy motivation and overall psychological well-being. In the first, McAdams and Vaillant (1982) found that high intimacy motivation at age thirty among male graduates of Harvard College significantly predicted overall psychosocial adjustment seventeen years later, when the men were in their mid-forties. Those men high in intimacy motivation in early adulthood reported greater marital satisfaction, job satisfaction, and even a marginally higher income at mid-life compared to men scoring low in intimacy motivation.

In a second study, McAdams and Bryant (1987) drew upon a nationwide sample of over twelve hundred U.S. adults who were administered the TAT and a structured interview. High intimacy motivation *among women* was associated with greater overall *happiness* and *satisfaction* with life roles (such as roles of worker, mother, wife). Among *men,* on the other hand, intimacy motivation predicted *less strain* in life and *less uncertainty*. Though intimacy motivation appears to bring certain benefits for both men and women, the benefits do not seem to be exactly the same for both sexes. High-intimacy women are relatively happy and satisfied compared to low-intimacy women. On the other hand, high-intimacy men are *not* necessarily happier and more satisfied than low-intimacy men, but they do report the positive results of less strain in life and less uncertainty.

Finally, one other major sex difference has been found. Unlike achievement and power, where no consistent sex differences in overall levels of the motives have been observed, women tend to score higher on intimacy motivation than men (McAdams, Lester, Brand, McNamara & Lensky, in press). The difference is small but relatively consistent, and it is in keeping with the generally accepted view in American society that women tend to be more concerned with interpersonal relationships than are men (Gilligan, 1982).

Summary

The study of human motivation centers on the recurrent wants and needs that energize and direct human behavior and thereby provide human lives with organization, direction, and purpose. Western scholars have traditionally viewed human motivation from four different perspectives, suggesting either that (1) human beings are motivated by reason to attain the "good" and the "rational"; (2) human beings are motivated by "bad" internal forces that ultimately bring pain and misery; (3) motives are determined solely by environmental learning; or (4) there exists an indeterminate number of different motives upon which individuals vary widely. Among contemporary views of human motivation, those focusing on the biological bases of motives have emphasized generalized drives, the nature of reward, and the instinctual foundations of human behavior in the context of human evolution. Contemporary cognitive approaches to motivation, on the other hand, have emphasized the energizing and directing influences of such factors as expectancies, cognitive plans, schemas, scripts, conscious strivings, and attributions.

A research tradition pioneered by Murray and McClelland integrates various strands of historical and contemporary approaches to motivation, including both biological and cognitive concepts. This approach has focused on three important social motives: achievement, power, and intimacy motivation. Individual differences in these motives are assessed through content analysis of imaginative stories composed by people in response to the ambiguous pictures of the Thematic Apperception Test. A number of recent studies are reviewed showing significant relations between these three motives on the one hand and features of social behavior, career striving, leadership, personal relationships, adjustment, and health on the other.

SUGGESTED READINGS

Freud, S. (1900/1953). *The interpretation of dreams.* London: Hogarth. (Paperback edition published by Avon Books). One of the classics in modern psychology, Freud's book provides an overview of much of his early theorizing and focuses on how the psychologist may discern motivational themes in dreams.

Geen, R., Beatty, W.W., & Arkin, R.M. (1984). *Human motivation: Physiological, behavioral, and social approaches.* Boston: Allyn and Bacon. This textbook provides a very readable and balanced coverage of the entire field of human motivation, including biological and cognitive approaches.

McAdams, D.P. (1985). *Power, intimacy, and the life story: Personological inquiries into identity.* Chicago: Dorsey Press. (Reprinted in 1988 softcover by Guilford Press). Drawing on research into power and intimacy motivation, this book applies motivational theory to the study of the self and human identity.

McClelland, D.C. (1961). *The achieving society.* New York: The Free Press. This is McClelland's most well-known work, in which he analyzes the economic rise and fall of entire civilizations in terms of collective achievement motivation, as assessed through content analysis of popular literature, folk tales, and children's readers.

Wilson, E.O. (1978). *On human nature.* Cambridge, MA: Harvard University Press. In this Pulitzer-Prize-winning book, Wilson invokes modern instinct theory to argue for a sociobiological base for fundamental human motives that are manifested in aggression, sex, play, love, and altruism.

REFERENCES

Abelson, R.P. (1981). Psychological status of the script concept. *American Psychologist, 36,* 715–729.

Abramson, L.Y., Seligman, M.E.P., & Teasdale, J.D. (1978). Learned helplessness in humans: Critique and reformulation. *Journal of Abnormal Psychology, 87,* 49–74.

Allport, G.W. (1937). *Personality: A psychological interpretation.* New York: Henry Holt.

Bakan, D. (1966). *The duality of human existence: Isolation and communion in Western man.* Boston: Beacon Press.

Baruch, R. (1967). The achievement motive in women: Implications for career development. *Journal of Personality and Social Psychology, 5,* 260–267.

Bloom, A.R. (1971). Achievement motivation and occupational choice: A study of adolescent girls. Unpublished doctoral dissertation, Bryn Mawr College.

Bowlby, J. (1969). *Attachment.* New York: Basic Books.

Breger, L. (1974). *From instinct to identity: The development of personality.* Englewood Cliffs, NJ: Prentice-Hall.

Emmons, R.A. (1986). Personal strivings: An approach to personality and subjective well-being. *Journal of Personality and Social Psychology, 51,* 1058–1068.

Entwisle, D.R. (1972). To dispel fantasies about fantasy-based measures of achievement motivation. *Psychological Bulletin, 77,* 377–391.

Erikson, E.H. (1963). *Childhood and society* (2nd ed.). New York: Norton.

Festinger, L. (1957). *A theory of cognitive dissonance.* Stanford, CA: Stanford University Press.

Fodor, E.M. (1984). The power motive and reactivity to power stresses. *Journal of*

Personality and Social Psychology, 47, 853–859.

Fodor, E.M. (1985). The power motive, group conflict, and physiological arousal. *Journal of Personality and Social Psychology, 49,* 1408–1415.

Fodor, E.M., & Farrow, D.L. (1979). The power motive as an influence on the use of power. *Journal of Personality and Social Psychology, 37,* 2091–2097.

Fodor, E.M., & Smith, T. (1982). The power motive as an influence on group decision making. *Journal of Personality and Social Psychology, 42,* 178–185.

Freud, S. (1900/1953). The interpretation of dreams. In R. Strachey (Ed.), *The standard edition of the complete psychological works of Sigmund Freud* (Vols. 4 and 5). London: Hogarth.

Freud, S. (1930/1961). Civilization and its discontents. In R. Strachey (Ed.), *The standard edition* (Vol. 21). London: Hogarth.

Gilligan, C. (1982). *In a different voice: Psychological theory and women's development.* Cambridge, MA: Harvard University Press.

Hoffman, M.L. (1981). Is altruism part of human nature? *American Psychologist, 40,* 121–137.

Hogan, R. (1987). Personality psychology: Back to basics. In J. Aronoff, A.I. Rabin, & R.A. Zucker (Eds.), *The emergence of personality* (pp. 79–104). New York: Springer.

Hull, C.L. (1943). *Principles of behavior: An introduction to behavior theory.* New York: Appleton-Century-Crofts.

Hunt, P.J., & Hillery, J.M. (1973). Social facilitation in a coaction setting: An examination of the effects over learning trials. *Journal of Experimental Social Psychology, 9,* 563–571.

Izard, C.E. (1978). On the ontogenesis of emotions and emotion-cognition relationships in infancy. In M. Lewis & L.A. Rosenblum (Eds.), *The development of affect* (pp. 389–413). New York: Plenum.

James, W. (1890). *Principles of psychology.* New York: Holt, Rinehart, & Winston.

Jemmott, J.B. (1987). Social motives and susceptibility to disease: Stalking individual differences in health risks. *Journal of Personality, 55,* 267–298.

Jones, E.E. (1979). The rocky road from acts to dispositions. *American Psychologist, 34,* 107–117.

Kagan, J. (1984). *The nature of the child.* New York: Basic Books.

Kelley, H.H. (1973). The process of casual attribution. *American Psychologist, 28,* 107–128.

Kelly, G. (1955). *The psychology of personal constructs.* New York: Norton.

Klinger, E. (1977). *Meaning and void: Inner experience and the incentives in people's lives.* Minneapolis, MN: University of Minnesota Press.

Kock, S.W. (1965). *[Management and motivation].* English summary of a doctoral dissertation presented at the Swedish School of Economics, Helsinki, Finland.

Konner, M. (1983). *The tangled wing.* New York: Harper & Row.

Lewin, K. (1936). *Principles of topological psychology.* New York: McGraw-Hill.

Mahone, C.H. (1960). Fear of failure and unrealistic vocational aspiration. *Journal of Abnormal and Social Psychology, 60,* 253–261.

Markus, H. (1977). Self-schemata and the processing of information about the self. *Journal of Personality and Social Psychology, 35,* 63–78.

Markus, H., & Sentis, K. (1982). The self in social information processing. In J. Suls (Ed.), *Psychological perspectives on the self* (Vol. 1, pp. 41–70). Hillsdale, NJ: Erlbaum.

Maslow, A.H. (1968). *Toward a psychology of being.* New York: Van Nostrand Reinhold.

McAdams, D.P. (1980). A thematic coding system for the intimacy motive. *Journal of Research in Personality, 14,* 413–432.

McAdams, D.P. (1982). Intimacy motivation. In A.J. Stewart (Ed.), *Motivation and society* (pp. 133–171). San Francisco: Jossey-Bass.

McAdams, D.P. (1984). Human motives and personal relationships. In V. J. Derlega (Ed.),

Communication, intimacy, and close relationships (pp. 41-70). New York: Academic Press.

McAdams, D.P. (1985a). The "imago": A key narrative component of identity. In P. Shaver (Ed.), *Review of personality and social psychology* (Vol. 6, pp. 115-141). Beverly Hills, CA: Sage.

McAdams, D.P. (1985b). *Power, intimacy, and the life story: Personological inquiries into identity.* Chicago, IL: Dorsey Press. (Reprinted in 1988 softcover by Guilford Press).

McAdams, D.P., & Bryant, F.B. (1987). Intimacy motivation and subjective mental health in a nationwide sample. *Journal of Personality, 55,* 395-413.

McAdams, D.P., & Constantian, C.A. (1983). Intimacy and affiliation motives in daily living: An experience sampling analysis. *Journal of Personality and Social Psychology, 45,* 851-861.

McAdams, D.P., Jackson, R.J., & Kirshnit, C. (1984). Looking, laughing, and smiling in dyads as a function of intimacy motivation and reciprocity. *Journal of Personality, 52,* 261-273.

McAdams, D.P., Lester, R., Brand, P., McNamara, W., & Lensky, D.B. (in press). Sex and the TAT: Are women more intimate than men? Do men fear intimacy? *Journal of Personality Assessment.*

McAdams, D.P., & Powers, J. (1981). Themes of intimacy in behavior and thought. *Journal of Personality and Social Psychology, 40,* 573-587.

McAdams, D.P., Rothman, S., & Lichter, S.R. (1982). Motivational profiles: A study of former political radical and politically moderate adults. *Personality and Social Psychology Bulletin, 8,* 593-603.

McAdams, D.P., & Vaillant, G.E. (1982). Intimacy motivation and psychosocial adjustment: A longitudinal study. *Journal of Personality Assessment, 46,* 586-593.

McClelland, D.C. (1961). *The achieving society.* New York: The Free Press.

McClelland, D.C. (1965). Achievement and entrepreneurship: A longitudinal study. *Journal of Personality and Social Psychology, 1,* 389-392.

McClelland, D.C. (1979). Inhibited power motivation and high blood pressure in men. *Journal of Abnormal Psychology, 88,* 182-190.

McClelland, D.C. (1985). *Human motivation.* Glenview, IL: Scott, Foresman.

McClelland, D.C., & Boyatzis, R.E. (1982). The leadership motive pattern and longterm success in management. *Journal of Applied Psychology, 67,* 737-743.

McClelland, D.C., & Jemmott, J.B. (1980). Power motivation, stress, and physical illness. *Journal of Human Stress, 6* (4), 6-15.

McDougall, W. (1908). *Social psychology.* London: Methuen.

Miller, G.A., Galanter, E., & Pribram, K.H. (1960). *Plans and the structure of behavior.* New York: Holt, Rinehart & Winston.

Murray, H.A. (1938). *Explorations in personality.* New York: Oxford University Press.

Olds, J. (1977). *Drives and reinforcements: Behavioral studies of hypothalamic functions.* New York: Raven.

Palys, T.S., & Little, B.R. (1983). Perceived life satisfaction and the organization of personal project systems. *Journal of Personality and Social Psychology, 44,* 1221-1230.

Peterson, C., & Seligman, M.E.P. (1984). Causal explanations as a risk factor for depression: Theory and evidence. *Psychological Review, 91,* 347-374.

Rogers, C.R. (1951). *Client-centered therapy.* Boston: Houghton Mifflin.

Rotter, J.B. (1954). *Social learning and clinical psychology.* Englewood Cliffs, NJ: Prentice-Hall.

Singh, S. (1978). Achievement motivation and entrepreneurial success: A follow up study. *Journal of Research in Personality, 12,* 500-503.

Skinner, B.F. (1971). *Beyond freedom and dignity.* New York: Knopf.

Solomon, R.L. (1980). The opponent-process theory of acquired motivation: The costs of pleasure and the benefits of pain. *American Psychologist, 35,* 691-712.

Spence, K.W. (1958). A theory of emotionally based drive (D) and its relation to performance in simple learning situations. *American Psychologist, 13,* 131–141.

Spence, K.W., Farber, I.E., & McFann, H.H. (1956). The relation of anxiety (drive) level to performance in competitional and noncompetitional paired-associates learning. *Journal of Experimental Psychology, 52,* 296–305.

Spielberger, C.D., & Smith, L.H. (1966). Anxiety (drive), stress, and serial-position effects in serial-verbal learning. *Journal of Experimental Psychology, 72,* 589–595.

Sroufe, L.A., & Waters, E. (1976). The ontogenesis of smiling and laughter. *Psychological Review, 83,* 173–183.

Stern, D.N. (1985). *The interpersonal world of the infant.* New York: Basic Books.

Stewart, A.J. (1975). Longitudinal prediction from personality to life outcomes among college-educated women. Unpublished doctoral dissertation, Harvard University.

Stewart, A.J., & Chester, N.L. (1982). Sex differences in human social motives: Achievement, affiliation, and power. In A.J. Stewart (Ed.), *Motivation and society* (pp. 172–218). San Francisco: Jossey-Bass.

Taylor, J.A. (1953). A personality scale of manifest anxiety. *Journal of Abnormal and Social Psychology, 48,* 285–290.

Tolman, E.C. (1932). *Purposive behavior in animals and men.* New York: Appleton-Century.

Veroff, J. (1982). Assertive motivations: Achievement versus power. In A.J. Stewart (Ed.), *Motivation and society* (pp. 99–132). San Francisco: Jossey-Bass.

Wainer, H.A., & Rubin, I.M. (1969). Motivation of research and development entrepreneurs. *Journal of Applied Psychology, 53,* 178–184.

White, R.W. (1959). Motivation reconsidered: The concept of competence. *Psychological Review, 66,* 297–333.

Wilson, E.O. (1978). *On human nature.* Cambridge, MA: Harvard University Press.

Winter, D.G. (1973). *The power motive.* New York: The Free Press.

Winter, D.G. (1988). The power motive in women—and men. *Journal of Personality and Social Psychology, 54,* 510–519.

Winter, D.G., & Carlson, L. (1988). Using motive scores in the psychobiographical study of an individual: The case of Richard Nixon. *Journal of Personality, 56,* 75–103.

Winter, D.G., McClelland, D.C., & Stewart, A.J. (1981). *A new case for the liberal arts: Assessing institutional goals and student development.* San Francisco: Jossey-Bass.

Zajonc, R.B. (1965). Social facilitation. *Science, 149,* 269–274.

Zajonc, R.B. (1980). Compresence. In P.B. Paulus (Ed.), *The psychology of group process* (pp. 35–60). Hillsdale, NJ: Erlbaum.

PART TWO

TOPICS IN PERSONALITY RESEARCH

CHAPTER 8

The Unconscious

THOMAS HILL AND PAWEL LEWICKI

Personality and the Unconscious
ACTIVITY BOX: Nonconscious
    Perception
  The Psychoanalytic Tradition
  The Information Processing
    Model
Nonconscious Information
    Processing
Nonconscious Information
    Processing in Social
    Situations
Some Properties of Nonconscious
    Information Processing
    Algorithms

Applications to Personality
    Psychology
  Mere Exposure Effects
  The Self-Image Bias
    The Acquisition of
    Dispositions via
    Self-Perpetuation of
    Encoding Biases
Studying the Self-Perpetuation
    Mechanism
Concluding Remarks
Summary
SUGGESTED READINGS
REFERENCES

Personality and the Unconscious

"Most of what we do goes on unconsciously. It is the exception, not the rule, when thinking is conscious; but by its very nature, conscious thought seems the only sort. It is not the only sort; it is the minority" (Lachman, Lachman, & Butterfield, 1979, p. 207). Although many psychologists would agree with this statement, it may arouse skepticism in others. How can something that is not conscious influence behavior? For example, if I am terrified by little harmless spiders, then obviously there is some idea in my head that they are dangerous. Perhaps I cannot exactly recall where I have read about how dangerous spiders can be, but nevertheless I *know* and am consciously aware of their potential danger. Although there are many behaviors that are "automated" and do not require much conscious attention—such as driving a car, swimming, or riding a bike—we clearly were consciously aware of every aspect of those behaviors when they were learned. Thus, those behaviors should be labeled "well-learned behavior" or "overlearned behavior" rather than "unconscious."

Let us consider the possibility that all of our behavior, perceptions, and thoughts are indeed conscious, or at least that they were conscious at one time. Then how, for example, do we consciously determine that a face is attractive or unattractive; or how do we determine whether a face (without makeup and not showing any hair) is that of a male or

The preparation of this manuscript was supported by National Science Foundation Grant BNS-8504502 and National Institute of Mental Health Grant MH-42715 to Pawel Lewicki and Thomas Hill.

ACTIVITY BOX

Nonconscious Perception

The faces in figure 8.1 differ with regard to the proportion of the distances from the chin to the eyes and from the eyes to the top of the head. For the average face, this proportion is 1:1. Only the faces in the center column follow the average 1:1 proportion; the faces to the left and the right are slightly off. Most people are not consciously aware of the average proportions of the human face, or which particular aspect of the human face they pay attention to. Nevertheless slight violations of the basic proportions affect people's perception of faces, for example, the extent to which a face is considered attractive. Faces that violate the average proportions of the human face are usually rated as less attractive than those that do not violate those proportions.

Show the faces in figure 8.1 to a friend and ask him or her to rank them in terms of their attractiveness by assigning a 1 to the most attractive face, a 2 to the second most attractive face, and so on. It is important to instruct your "subject" to complete the ranking quickly without carefully scrutinizing the pictures. We suggest that you may make a copy of the faces and mix them up a little, so that your subject is not forced always to prefer the face presented in the center.

Most people in a sense "recognize" a disproportionate face when they see one (that is, find it less attractive), although few can express what exactly is "wrong" with the face. Thus this example demonstrates how people use, in their perception, inferential encoding algorithms that they are not consciously aware of.

female? Most of the time we have few problems making those decisions—but how do we actually do it? Lacking formal instruction on the proportions and sizes of the human physique, we may not even have a way of expressing how faces differ from one another. Most people do not know the basic proportions of the human face. For example, the average distance from the chin to the eyes, and from the eyes to the top of the head. Yet most everybody notices when this proportion is violated.

This was demonstrated in a simple experiment (from which the one in the Activity Box is adapted). Subjects were shown three drawings of faces, and they were asked to rate the attractiveness of each face and the intelligence of the persons depicted. There were three trials with different triplets of faces; thus, overall subjects were shown nine faces, as reproduced in figure 8.1. You may notice that some faces look very

FIGURE 8.1

Drawings of Faces That Subjects Rated for Attractiveness and Intelligence

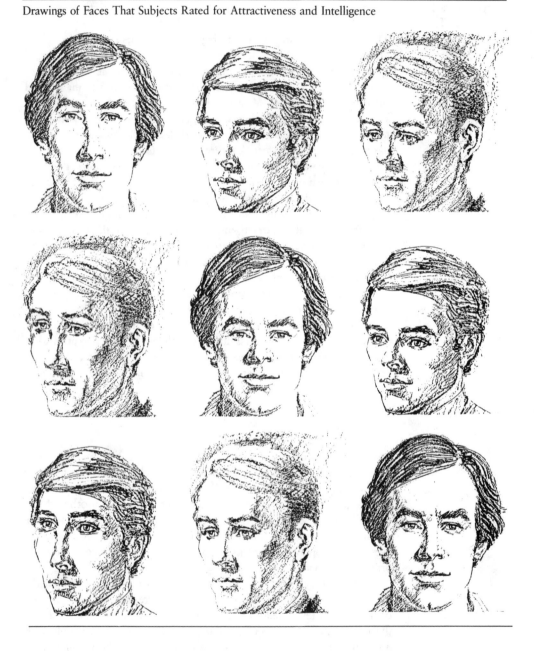

similar. In fact, these nine faces are variations of three faces that were slightly modified, so that either the face was too small relative to the forehead or the face was too long. Thus, two variations of the basic three faces slightly violated the average proportions of the human face. In the figure, the long faces are in the left-hand column, the average faces are in the center column, and the short faces are in the right-hand column. Figure 8.2 shows the average ratings of attractiveness and intelligence across the three faces.

Apparently, subjects clearly identified the "normal" face. Because familiar things tend to be perceived in a more positive manner (Zajonc, 1968), subjects rated the average face as more attractive and more intelligent than the long or short versions of the respective faces.

What were subjects consciously paying attention to when making their judgments? They were asked to write down all aspects of these faces to which they had paid attention when making their judgments. Almost all subjects mentioned some salient features of the face, such as the eyes or the mouth, or whether the person depicted "kind of had a

FIGURE 8.2

Average Ratings of Attractiveness and Intelligence for Long, Normal, and Short Faces

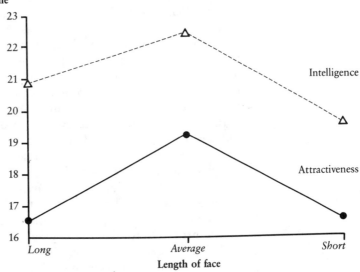

smile on his face." Not a single subject recognized the crucial feature that was manipulated, that is, the length of the face. Thus, in this study none of the subjects was consciously aware of the rule (or *algorithm*) that he or she used in order to determine whether a face was attractive and intelligent.

The average proportion of distances from the chin to the eyes and from the eyes to the top of the head is 1:1. Usually, (untrained) subjects will overestimate the first distance and guess this proportion to be closer to 2:1. Thus, subjects in this experiment were not only unaware of the algorithm that they used but, most likely, they would not have been able to describe accurately the algorithm had their conscious attention been directed to the crucial feature that was manipulated (i.e., the length of the faces).

In recent years, cognitive psychologists have accepted the view that most of our thoughts are nonconscious; or, put in the more technical terms of cognitive psychologists, most information processing follows algorithms (i.e., rules of procedure for solving problems) that are not accessible to conscious awareness. For example, we are not consciously aware of how we determine distances of objects in three-dimensional space or how we distinguish letters or symbols from random patterns printed on a page.

The Psychoanalytic Tradition

This way of thinking about nonconscious (or unconscious) processes is very different from the way in which Sigmund Freud (1966) and psychoanalysis viewed unconsciousness. A psychiatrist, Freud concluded from observations made on his patients that many personality characteristics and personal problems are rooted in basic drives (e.g., *eros*, the life instinct) and in early childhood experiences, neither of which is accessible to conscious awareness. Instead, "hidden" conflicts exist between one's unconsciously held beliefs about norms, values, sense of decency, and so on (contained in the so-called superego) and one's desires (e.g., sexual urges) contained in the so-called id. Presumably, the conscious part of our personality (the ego) attempts to deal with these conflicts; however, we are usually not consciously aware of their causes. Instead, the true nature of personal problems and psychological conflicts usually manifests itself indirectly, for example in dreams. The key then to successful psychotherapy, according to the psychoanalytic view, is to "bring out" these hidden conflicts, that is, to make a patient consciously aware of his or her conflicts and to help him or her resolve them.

Sigmund Freud's views of personality, in particular of the unconscious, have had a dramatic and lasting effect, not only on psychology but also on anthropology, sociology, literature, and many other fields. Some ideas have found their way into everyday language; for example, a "Freudian slip" is a slip of tongue that was unintended yet revealing of some true underlying, more or less unconsciously held belief, feeling, or motivation (e.g., someone calling her boyfriend by the wrong first name presumably reveals something about the person she was really thinking about). Although Freud's ideas are very appealing and inspiring, only some of his theoretical propositions have received empirical support from research (e.g., Eriksen, 1966). Thus, contemporary research on nonconscious processes follows a different orientation.

The Information Processing Model

Contemporary cognitive psychology looks at a person as a "black box" not unlike a computer. This black box has several input and output devices and in it many very complex programs are running to coordinate those devices. For example, a complex program is necessary to compose a three-dimensional color movie from the enormous number of signals that are received (i.e., input) by our eyes. The program must *encode* all incoming information; that is, it must translate the incoming signals so that we can recognize what we see as a dog, a table, and so on. To accomplish this task the program uses many complex *encoding algorithms,* that is, rules for translating incoming signals from the eyes into shapes, patterns, and so on, and ultimately into psychologically meaningful experiences. Other programs are responsible for producing adequate "output" such as speech. Those programs use complex *decoding* algorithms to translate ideas and knowledge that is stored in memory (e.g., thinking about a dog) into the corresponding representations in one's language (i.e., give the commands necessary to produce the word "dog").

Of those millions of different program steps and processing algorithms, actually only very few are available to consciousness. Intuitively, it is clear that only a relatively small number of items can be processed simultaneously in one's conscious awareness. Thus, the room for conscious thought can be considered a preciously scarce resource that is not to be occupied with the thousands of basic operations that must be performed every minute (e.g., coordinating movement, translating the changing retinal picture in the eye into a three-dimensional color movie, producing speech).

The goal of cognitive psychology is to reconstruct those cognitive processing algorithms and to find out how they are acquired (learned) and how they operate.

Nonconscious Information Processing

Because most cognitive processes are unconscious, subjects cannot tell us how their cognitive systems work (e.g., they cannot report on their memory retrieval processes or on how they go about generating judgments [Nisbett & Wilson, 1977]). Therefore, the reconstruction of these processes often requires indirect methods such as the measurement of response latencies.

For example, there are different theoretical models of how information is retrieved from memory. According to one model (Glucksberg & McCloskey, 1981), memory search is conducted in two stages. At the first stage, a person will scan the equivalent (in memory) of a "table of contents" to see whether there are any entries concerning an item. If not, then the memory search will terminate and the subject may respond "I don't know." However, if an entry is found, then the second stage of retrieval is initiated and the subject will attempt to locate the specific information that was filed under the entry found in the table of contents. Thus one can expect that, when a subject is asked to respond as quickly as possible to a series of questions, the answers to questions that the subject clearly does not know anything about will not trigger the second stage memory search; therefore, responding to those questions will require less time than responding to questions that require a second-stage memory search (Glucksberg & McCloskey, 1981). For example, consider the questions "Does Ronald Reagan use a blue toothbrush?" and "Is the city of Kiev in Russia?" Because most people do not know anything about Ronald Reagan's toothbrush (i.e., there is no such entry in the table of contents), a second-stage search will not be initiated, and a quick "I don't know" can be expected. However, most people have heard of Russia and of Kiev; therefore, there are entries for those entities in the table of contents and a second-stage search is initiated. The response to this question should thus require more time (even though the final answer may also be "I don't know"). Therefore, response times are an indirect measure of different cognitive processes involved in searching the memory.

Using such indirect methods, numerous studies have demonstrated that the cognitive system is capable of processing incomparably more information than people are consciously aware of, and that operations of considerable complexity can be performed without conscious awareness (Jacoby & Witherspoon, 1982; Kihlstrom, 1984; Kolers, 1976; Lewicki, 1986a; Lewicki, Czyzewska, & Hoffman, 1987; Reber, 1976, 1989; Seamon, Brody, & Kauff, 1983; Tranel & Damasio, 1985). These unconscious cognitive operations are not merely limited to "low level" processing in order to support and maintain conscious psychological activity (e.g., storage and retrieval of information), but they

include operations that one may believe to require conscious thinking
—activities such as drawing inferences or solving problems.

Even the most elementary perceptual operations, such as determining distances between objects in three-dimensional space, involve
complex inferential strategies and algorithms for problem solving
(Hochberg, 1978; Rock, 1975) that are beyond conscious control.
Similar observations have been reported in research on speech production (Chomsky, 1980). Most people are unable to articulate the
semantic and syntactic rules of the language they use (i.e., they do not
have a complete declarative knowledge of their language), although at
the same time they undoubtedly have a working (or procedural)
knowledge of those complex rules. For example, when asked by a
foreigner, native English speakers can almost always say whether a
particular sentence is correct but they usually cannot explain why,
other than that the correct sentence "sounds better" (Lewicki, 1986b).
The linguistic rules of one's first language are a good example of
complex procedural knowledge (Kolers & Roediger, 1984) that operates unconsciously.

An important characteristic of many of these automatically operating processing algorithms (like those involved in pattern recognition or
in speech production) is that they are not only unconscious, but that
they *never were* available to conscious awareness. In many cases, the
only way in which they could have been acquired is through unconscious learning (presumably through some process of unconscious
generalization of concrete instances; Lewicki, 1986b). For example,
most people cannot describe the many complex algorithms that are
involved in the recognition of shapes of objects (Hochberg, 1978) or
the estimation of distances in three-dimensional space; yet children
accomplish those tasks at a very early age. Another good example is the
complexity of the equations that describe how an object will appear in
three-dimensional space after it is rotated. Generally, school-age
children can perform "mental rotations" with relative ease and recognize, for example, a cube that stands on one of its corners.

Nonconscious Information Processing in Social Situations

So far, we have discussed unconscious processing algorithms that are
instrumental for performing many basic tasks—such as orientation in
space or speech production—in an efficient manner, that is, "without
thinking about it" and without understanding the complexities of the
algorithms involved. Now we will consider a study (Lewicki, 1985) that
was conducted to show how unconscious processing algorithms may

affect social behavior. In addition, this study sheds some light on how unconscious processing algorithms may be acquired. Specifically, it demonstrates how, through a single experience, people may acquire a processing algorithm that results in a biased (i.e., objectively not justified) perception of another person.

In this study, subjects participated in an experiment that consisted of two parts and involved the three experimenters shown in figure 8.3. Subjects first met experimenter A, who asked them some simple questions about their major, age, and so on. Then the experimenter asked the subject about his or her "birth order." All subjects asked for clarification of this question. In one experimental condition, the experimenter replied in a slightly impatient manner, asking "You really don't know what birth order means?" In the second experimental condition, the experimenter explained in a polite manner that birth order refers to whether the subject is a first born child, second born child, etc. Thus, in this experimental condition, the subject had a somewhat negative experience with experimenter A. In the other experimental condition (control condition), the subject did not have a negative experience with experimenter A.

At the conclusion of the first part of the experiment, experimenter A instructed subjects to go to another room for the second study and to "just choose whoever was available" among the experimenters. The

FIGURE 8.3

The Three Experimenters Who Conducted the Experiment on the Biasing Effects of Single Instances

A   B   C

subject found that two experimenters were available, namely, experimenters B and C shown in figure 8.3. The major dependent variable of interest was which one of the two experimenters the subject would approach.

As is apparent from figure 8.3, experimenter B looked similar to experimenter A, whereas experimenter C looked dissimilar to both. As expected, subjects tended to avoid experimenter B if they had previously had a negative experience with experimenter A. Thus, it appears that subjects "learned" that experimenters who look like experimenter A are not very polite and are likely to be unpleasant.

What were subjects' conscious reflections about the experiment and their choice of the second experimenter? The next part of the experiment was designed to explore this issue. Not a single subject was aware of the actual reason for his or her (biased) choice of an experimenter. Moreover, in an anonymous final questionnaire, subjects who had encountered the somewhat impatient experimenter did not actually rate their interaction with that (first) experimenter more negatively than subjects in the control condition. Thus, it is possible that, consciously, they did not experience this interaction as particularly unpleasant.

Two important conclusions can be drawn from this study. First, apparently people can acquire processing algorithms about relationships between variables (e.g., general appearance of the face and pleasantness) from just a single instance that does not have to be particularly salient (i.e., obvious). Second, these algorithms are not available to conscious awareness; and if they were they often would, as in this case, be considered undesirable and unreasonable (there is no rational reason to believe that all people who look like experimenter A will be unpleasant).

This general mechanism—that is, the nonconscious acquisition of knowledge about relationships (covariations) between variables—has been demonstrated in a large number of experiments (see Lewicki, 1986b, for a summary). Moreover, this research also has shown that people may acquire nonconsciously processing algorithms of such complexity that they could hardly be learned and used consciously (Lewicki, Czyzewska, & Hoffman, 1987). In other words, it appears that the nonconscious mode of acquiring and using knowledge is, in many respects, much more sensitive and capable than the conscious mode of learning. This ability to unconsciously acquire knowledge capable of automatically controlling subsequent perceptions constitutes a fundamental property of the cognitive system, and largely determines its overall performance.

Because of this "intuitive" knowledge, reality is often interpreted in a biased manner; that is, inferences are automatically drawn that are not warranted by the objective nature of the reality that one is encountering. For example, the previous experiment shows how the appearance of a person or his or her behaviors are much more "meaningful" for an observer than the observer can articulate. Based on this intuitive knowledge, most people (in laboratory and real-life conditions) easily form impressions of a stimulus person that go beyond their ability to articulate the rules responsible for their judgments. The interpretation of most social stimuli is based on processing (encoding) algorithms that are inaccessible to conscious awareness, and that were acquired via processes of unconscious learning analogous to those responsible for the acquisition of the processing rules aiding in the orientation in three-dimensional space (Hochberg, 1978) or the acquisition of a first language (Chomsky, 1980).

Some Properties of Nonconscious Information Processing Algorithms

The unconscious processing algorithms are unconscious in several respects. First they are unconscious in that they are invoked and used unconsciously. Their operation is initiated without the necessity to make any decisions or to give any conscious "commands." Second, these processes may automatically and without conscious awareness trigger respective behavioral or emotional reactions (e.g., liking or disliking). Third, the way in which these algorithms operate (i.e., their inferential rules) and their effects may actually be inconsistent with what a person would consciously consider reasonable, justified, or desirable. In other words, a person may find some of his or her "automatic categorizations" of people or other stimuli unreasonable or even clearly wrong and still be unable to modify them or to stop their emotional consequences.

This case is well illustrated by various kinds of so-called neurotic behavior. For example, a person may be perfectly aware of the fact that his or her strong negative affective reaction to being at home alone is unreasonable. Moreover, the person may be unable to explain the source of that fear, and may even be very motivated to overcome this uncontrolled cognitive process of encoding as dangerous something that is objectively harmless. Still, the person often cannot do anything about it. He or she cannot simply "convince" himself or herself that there is no cause for fear, that is, cannot modify the dysfunctional encoding algorithm that triggers anxiety in response to clearly safe stimuli.

This kind of independence or inconsistency of the encoding

algorithms (and behavioral reactions they automatically trigger) from perceivers' consciously controlled knowledge, attitudes, or preferences is by no means confined to cases of psychological disorders. The process appears to be general; it can be found in every individual and can be observed very often in everyday life. For example, some social stimuli are automatically categorized as emotionally "moving," and despite the fact that this may be inconsistent with what the person thinks on the consciously controlled level, the encoding algorithms responsible for generating those categorizations may automatically trigger respective behavioral reactions (e.g., crying). People usually cannot control this kind of reaction. Sometimes they are even surprised and wonder why they have responded this way, because they consciously classify the situation as unrealistic, naive, or melodramatic. For example, when watching soap operas such as "All My Children" or "Love Boat," people often recognize a primitive manipulation designed to affect viewers' feelings, but they still feel touched and they cannot stop their tears.

Emotional responses triggered by automatically operating information processing algorithms may be considered unreasonable by the person who is experiencing them, but they are not consciously controlled and cannot be simply modified by the person. He or she can only observe them as if it were another person who is experiencing the emotions.

Applications to Personality Psychology

The discussion so far has centered on the general processes that can explain how people nonconsciously learn algorithms for processing stimuli and how those algorithms—without conscious awareness—may trigger various behavioral or emotional responses. The central issue for personality psychology is, of course, to find out why and how people differ from one another in the way they behave. In addition, clinical psychology is particularly interested in learning why some people develop modes of responding to their environment that are maladaptive (e.g., why they develop neurotic behaviors).

First, genetic differences most likely cause some people to be more sensitive to particular types of stimuli and to more easily learn (unconsciously) complex rules and modes of responding. For example, some people learn to play the piano without formal instruction but simply by "playing" with it. There are even some individuals who generally have great difficulty learning in a consciously controlled manner (i.e., who are mentally retarded) but who acquire considerable musical skill with surprising ease. In other words, they learn easily—and clearly without conscious awareness of music theory—the rules that are necessary to coordinate the hands and fingers in order to produce coherent successions of notes that sound like music. Others do not master the piano even with extensive formal instruction. Such individual differences can probably be traced to genetic differences or differences in the environment during very early childhood. Most likely, the cognitive system of different people is sensitive to different types of stimuli; and those differences may account for some individual differences.

Exposure to different environments will also result in differences in personality. As described earlier, nonconscious information processing algorithms can be acquired with surprising ease, and it is obvious that being exposed to a particular environment with specific types of stimuli will cause a person to acquire—nonconsciously—very many complex information processing algorithms. For example, growing up in a family of musicians, being exposed to music every day, and playing with musical instruments will most likely stimulate the development of many complex algorithms pertaining to music. On the other hand, a person growing up in a household where music is produced only by radios will not acquire those algorithms.

Different environments may not only lead to differences in skills, but they may also cause different preferences (e.g., favorite color, preference for women with long hair, and so on). For example, in the experiment described earlier, subjects learned to avoid women (experimenters) who resembled experimenter A. Prolonged positive or negative experiences with particular stimuli could well lead to pervasive processing algorithms that cause strong and distinct preferences. For example, growing up in a family atmosphere that is tense, unpleasant, or even violent may lead to an "intuitive" disliking of family dinners or family reunions. Perhaps a person with those experiences may even be unable to maintain close relationships with others in general, because all family-like activities that friends or couples usually engage in, such as dinners or holiday activities (e.g., Thanksgiving dinners), are experienced in a negative manner and avoided.

One should not make the mistake of presuming that personality differences resulting from exposure to different environments will affect only children. There is ample research evidence, as well as evidence from everyday observations, that adult personality can also change. For example, McClelland (1965) succeeded in changing people's need for achievement. One of the main ingredients of his training method is to remove individuals from their common environments and to expose them to new situations and scenarios.

Mere Exposure Effects

The mere exposure to particular stimuli can increase one's preference for those stimuli, even when the exposure is very short. Again, this change in preference occurs without conscious awareness, sometimes even without awareness of the stimulus (i.e., when the exposure is subliminal). This was demonstrated in a study by Kunst-Wilson and Zajonc (1980). Subjects were subliminally exposed to a number of polygons (i.e., closed plane figures bounded by straight lines). Later, they were asked to select from a number of additional polygons those that were previously shown. Subjects were unable to discriminate between polygons that were unfamiliar and those that they had previously been exposed to (subliminally). Thus, subjects were not consciously aware of what they had previously seen.

However, when asked to select the polygons that they *preferred,* subjects were more likely to pick familiar shapes rather than unfamiliar (new) polygons. Thus, the mere exposure to particular stimuli caused a change in preference, even though the exposure was so brief that it was not registered consciously.

In real life, people are rarely exposed to subliminal stimuli. Although consumer advocates sometimes claim that advertisers like to "sneak in" subliminal messages into their advertisements, no evidence demonstrates that such messages are more effective than supraliminal (recognizable) messages—or that they are effective at all. In fact, the effect of mere exposure on preference is stronger when the exposure to the respective stimuli is salient (obvious) and repeated (Zajonc, 1968).

The mere exposure effect is another example of how people, without conscious awareness of the underlying mechanisms, may acquire a preference, that is, a stable disposition to prefer particular objects, types of music, or persons.

The Self-Image Bias

Sometimes existing individual differences may lead to further differentiation, without a person's awareness of such secondary effects. For example, once a person has acquired a particular skill (e.g., playing the piano) or considers himself or herself to be particularly intelligent, that person will weight those dimensions (i.e., being able to play the piano or possessing intelligence) more heavily when perceiving or judging other people (Lewicki, 1983). In other words, the skills and other positive characteristics that one believes oneself to possess are also more *central* (i.e., generally important) when forming impressions of other people. Characteristics or skills that are assigned greater weight in impression formation are called *central traits*. This effect is called the *self-image bias*.

As an example, a person who believes himself or herself to possess computer skills is likely to assign greater importance to those skills than people who do not believe they possess computer skills (Hill, Smith, & Lewicki, 1989). Subsequently, when evaluating others—for example, in a job interview—the person will base his or her judgments of others to a large extent on whether or not the other person also has computer skills. Thus, the initial individual difference (i.e., whether or not a person has computer skills) is now responsible for additional differences, namely, what one considers important and "looks for" when judging other people.

Research (Lewicki, 1984) has shown that the self-image bias becomes stronger when self-esteem is threatened. In a sense, the self-image bias protects and enhances self-esteem by painting a special picture of reality, in which all the "good guys" and "winners" have skills and characteristics that are similar to one's own.

Note that the biased processing algorithms (i.e., the rules one follows when forming impressions of others) underlying the self-image bias are not accessible to conscious awareness, and they would probably be deemed undesirable if they were conscious. Clearly, it is usually not justified to judge others by one's own yardstick, that is, to look mostly for the characteristics that one believes to possess oneself. Therefore, if people were aware of this bias, they would probably actively try to correct it in order to arrive at more objective judgments. The self-image bias is another example of an unconscious encoding algorithm that is counter to what one would consider justified or desirable.

The Acquisition of Dispositions via Self-Perpetuation of Encoding Biases

The mechanism discussed so far, that is, the unconscious acquisition of information processing algorithms, can explain how people learn the many complex rules that are necessary to function in everyday life, for example, to estimate distances, recognize objects, or produce language. However, how do people develop dispositions that are clearly dysfunctional rather than an effective adaptation to one's environment? For example, how do some people develop a fear of strangers and become shy (in the absence of very unpleasant encounters with strangers), or why do some people perceive themselves as overweight although they are objectively undernourished (e.g., anorexic)? If the mechanisms of nonconsciously acquiring information processing algorithms work in the way described so far, then those algorithms would always reflect the true relationships between variables in reality. For example, we acquire the algorithms necessary to estimate distances between objects in three-dimensional space through various experiences over time, and the resultant algorithm yields relatively good approximations of actual distances. If, for some reason, we have experienced several encounters in which someone who looked like experimenter A in figure 8.3 was impolite, a single instance of encountering such a person who is *not* impolite should lead us to abandon the respective processing algorithm (i.e., "people who look that way are impolite").

However, reality, especially social reality, is often ambiguous. Do we really know that our friend likes us? When seeing someone on the street whom we consider attractive, do we really know whether the person is not mean, aggressive, and without any manners at all? Or consider the three experimenters described earlier. Most subjects who had a somewhat unpleasant experience with experimenter A chose the dissimilar experimenter (C) for the second study. Thus, they never confirmed or disconfirmed the processing algorithm responsible for perceiving people who look like experimenter A as unpleasant. It is an interesting question to consider what might happen to a processing algorithm (i.e., will it strengthen or weaken?) when it is constantly used, but not confirmed or disconfirmed. For example, will the bias that led subjects in the experiment to perceive experimenter B as (probably) also unpleasant finally fade if not reaffirmed, or will it remain?

In more abstract terms, imagine that a subject has learned that whenever a person has feature A (e.g., looks like experimenter A), then he or she also has feature B (i.e., is unpleasant). Now the subject encounters a person with feature A, but has no information concerning B. The experiment suggests that the subject will "fill in the blank" and perceive the person as also having feature B (i.e., also being unpleasant). Thus, the subject has not only perceived reality, but the unconscious processing algorithm has *created* a reality that does not objectively exist (i.e., objectively it is not clear whether the person with feature A also has feature B). The processing algorithm has now confirmed itself, because reality appears consistent with the algorithm. In other words, once initiated, a processing algorithm may artificially *create* evidence supportive of itself and thus *self-perpetuate* and perhaps become stronger and stronger. As a result, a person may develop strong nonconscious processing algorithms that are independent of or even clearly at odds with reality. For example, a person who is objectively undernourished may conclude that "people are looking at me because I am so overweight"; a person who is frightened by strangers and objectively unreasonably shy may conclude after every encounter with a stranger that the stranger "was probably thinking all the time how to get me."

Encoding algorithms represent a working (i.e., *procedural*) but not articulable (i.e., *declarative*) knowledge. Although a perceiver uses them, they cannot be easily modified and they are not available to the perceiver's direct examination. Moreover, they can develop relatively independent of the perceiver's consciously controlled knowledge and, therefore, their inferential rules may even be inconsistent with the perceiver's preferences, attitudes, or consciously controlled standards of what is reasonable. This independent acquisition of encoding algorithms is a potentially powerful mechanism responsible for the development of various undesirable (and uncontrollable) cognitive dispositions.

The initial experiences capable of triggering such self-perpetuating development of a bias may in real life be conditions that are very difficult to identify because they may be incidental, nonsalient, and even not consciously remembered as meaningful events by a perceiver. Recent research demonstrates that surprisingly little consistent evidence is sufficient to produce an encoding bias, and, as shown in the previous experiment, in some circumstances even a single instance may be sufficient to nonconsciously influence the way in which a subsequently encountered relevant stimulus will be encoded (Lewicki, 1985, 1986b, chapter 7).

Studying the Self-Perpetuation Mechanism

The major focus of our current research program is to develop experimental paradigms that allow us to investigate the properties of the self-perpetuation mechanism. For example, are some people more prone to self-perpetuation of encoding algorithms than others? What is the relationship between the complexity of an encoding algorithm and the likelihood of its perpetuation? Are encoding biases pertaining to one's self-esteem or physical safety more likely to self-perpetuate than others?

In order to investigate these questions, it is first necessary to develop appropriate experimental paradigms in which self-perpetuation of encoding biases can be demonstrated. One such experimental paradigm is the so-called "matrix scanning procedure" (Lewicki, 1986b). Subjects are exposed to series of matrices of numbers that are shown on a computer screen. Figure 8.4 depicts an example of such a matrix of numbers.

Subjects are asked to search for a particular digit (target digit) in each matrix; for example, they may be asked to search for the number

FIGURE 8.4

Example Matrix of Numbers as Used in the Matrix Scanning Paradigm

```
5 1 3   8 4 7
4 9 7   1 6 0
7 8 2   4 5 2

9 0 3   4 5 1
3 2 5   8 0 9
1 9 8   9 2 7
```

6. In the example matrix the number 6 appears in the group of numbers in the upper right corner (i.e., the upper right quadrant). In order to make the task somewhat more difficult, the target digit is always displayed somewhere outside the area marked by the dashed line; thus, subjects have to scan all four quadrants of the matrix (and move their eyes). Subjects have a control box in front of them with four buttons, corresponding to the four quadrants of the matrix. After locating the target digit, they are instructed to push as quickly as possible the button that corresponds to the quadrant in which the target digit is located.

Unknown to subjects, each target location (i.e., the quadrant in which the target was located) is always paired with a particular matrix of numbers (which serves as the "background" against which the target is displayed). Thus, if a subject nonconsciously detects the relationship (i.e., acquires this processing algorithm), he or she does not have to search for the target digit. Rather, the subject only has to identify the particular background (matrix) that is shown in order to be able to push the right button. Therefore, if the subject learns this relationship, the resulting response times should become progressively shorter over a series of these matrix scanning trials. As a comparison group, some subjects are usually exposed to stimulus materials without any relationships between particular matrices and target locations. Thus, those subjects must always search each matrix for the location of the target digit.

In order to study self-perpetuation in this paradigm, subjects are exposed to several "guessing segments." Remember that self-perpetuation is likely to occur when reality is ambiguous. In this paradigm, subjects are shown a series of additional matrices, but each matrix is shown only for a very brief moment. Unknown to subjects, the matrices actually do not contain the target digit. Thus subjects are faced with a situation in which relevant stimuli are shown; that is, they are able to see the particular matrices. However, there is actually no target digit; therefore, the situation is ambiguous because subjects are not sure where the target is located. If subjects acquired a processing algorithm regarding the relationship between particular matrices and target locations, then they may use this algorithm to "fill in the blank" and believe that they actually located the target. Several experiments have shown exactly this effect (Lewicki, 1986b).

Of course, "filling in the blank" is only one (necessary) condition for demonstrating that self-perpetuation occurs. However, recent research (Hill, Lewicki, Czyzewska, & Boss, 1989; Lewicki, Hill, & Sasaki, 1989) has also shown that over a long sequence of guessing segments (over several days) subjects will make increasing use of the processing algorithm, as evidenced by their performance: They will make more and more responses that are consistent with the encoding algorithm, and those responses become faster and faster. Again, during final debriefing, subjects are not aware that they were following any particular strategy. In fact, subjects often respond with disbelief when fully debriefed about the study.

The process of self-perpetuation of encoding biases is a viable explanation of how people acquire cognitive dispositions that are not only independent from or inconsistent with what they "think" on the consciously controlled level, but also independent of the objective nature of the stimuli encountered.

Concluding Remarks

One of the fundamental properties of the cognitive system is its ability to unconsciously acquire procedural knowledge capable of automatically influencing subsequent perceptions, emotions, and behaviors. This unconscious procedural knowledge participates in both elementary (e.g., pattern recognition) and high level (e.g., social information processing by providing interpretive categories that encode stimuli into subjectively meaningful experiences. Although the final products of these encoding processes (e.g., impressions of encountered people, emotional responses, social preferences) are available to one's controlled cognition, the access to how they were generated is very limited. These cognitive processes determine not only one's orientation in the social environment but they also directly influence one's social adjustment. The nature and the dynamics of the development of these unconscious interpretive rules constitute crucial research problems for personality and social psychology.

Summary

Traditionally, the unconscious (or nonconscious) has mostly been studied by psychoanalytically oriented Freudian psychologists. Although today many psychologists disagree with Freud's view of the unconscious, few would deny its important role in human cognition and personality. In fact, if all behavior were rational, how could we explain why some people are frightened by (objectively harmless) spiders, or why a particular song can make us feel sad although there is no objective reason to experience that emotion?

In recent years, cognitive psychologists have discovered some general nonconscious personality processes and mechanisms that explain how we can learn—nonconsciously—new ways of processing and responding to stimuli in our environment. Researchers have demonstrated that nonconscious information processing plays a major role in the development of personality. Specifically, it has been shown in a number of experiments that people may nonconsciously acquire—even through very few experiences—new algorithms (i.e., rules) for interpreting and responding to new stimuli. These algorithms will subsequently be used to interpret similar stimuli, often in a biased manner. Thus, nonconsciously acquired algorithms may sometimes not only lead to mere interpretations of reality, but may *create* a (biased) "reality."

In this manner, (biased) algorithms for interpreting reality may confirm themselves, and through this self-perpetuation such algorithms may become increasingly stronger. This mechanism can explain how stable dispostions may develop, even if they are not rational or are "unwanted" by a person (e.g., phobias, shyness).

SUGGESTED READINGS

Anderson, J. R. (1985). *Cognitive psychology and its implications.* New York: Freeman. This is an introductory overview of the field of cognitive psychology. Although not directly related to the development of unconscious processing algorithms or the development of personality, the book addresses many of the relevant basic cognitive processes.

Freud, S. (1955). *The interpretation of dreams.* New York: Basic Books. (Originally published 1900). This was one of Freud's earliest influential books on the psychoanalytic view of the unconscious. In it, Freud provides fascinating analyses of dreams reported to him by some of his patients. In particular, Freud discusses the "hidden" meaning of dreams, that is, what they reveal about underlying unconscious conflicts and desires.

Lewicki, P. (1986). *Nonconscious social information processing.* New York: Academic

Press. This book presents in detail the theory of nonconscious information processing. In addition, a large number of experiments are presented that demonstrate how nonconscious information processing algorithms are acquired. These experiments involve not only abstract stimulus material (such as numbers of matrices) but also a wide variety of social stimuli (such as faces).

REFERENCES

Chomsky, N. (1980). Language and unconscious knowledge. In N. Chomsky (Ed.), *Rules and representations* (pp. 217-254). New York: Columbia University Press.

Eriksen, C. W. (1966). Cognitive responses to internally cued anxiety. In C. D. Spielberger (Ed.), *Anxiety and behavior* (pp. 327-360), New York: Academic Press.

Freud, S. (1966). *The standard edition of the complete psychological works of Sigmund Freud* (Vol. 1). London: Hogarth Press.

Glucksberg, S., & McCloskey, M. (1981). Decisions about ignorance: Knowing that you don't know. *Journal of Experimental Psychology: Human Learning and Memory, 7,* 311-325.

Hill, T., Lewicki, P., Czyzewska, M., & Boss, A. (1989). Self-perpetuating development of encoding biases in person perception. *Journal of Personality and Social Psychology, 57,* 373-387.

Hill, T., Smith, N., & Lewicki, P. (1989). The development of self-image bias: A real-world demonstration. *Personality and Social Psychology Bulletin. 15,* 205-211.

Hochberg, J. (1978). *Perception.* Englewood Cliffs, NJ: Prentice-Hall.

Jacoby, L. L., & Witherspoon, D. (1982). Remembering without awareness. *Canadian Journal of Psychology, 36,* 300-324.

Kihlstrom, J. (1984). Conscious, subconscious, unconscious: A cognitive perspective. In K. S. Bowers & D. Meichenbaum (Eds.), *The unconscious reconsidered* (pp. 149-211). New York: Wiley.

Kolers, P. A. (1976). Reading a year later. *Journal of Experimental Psychology: Human Learning and Memory, 2,* 554-565.

Kolers, P. A., & Roediger, H. L., III (1984). Procedures of mind. *Journal of Verbal Learning and Verbal Behavior, 23,* 425-449.

Kunst-Wilson, W. R., & Zajonc, R. B. (1980). Affective discrimination of stimuli that cannot be recognized. *Science, 207,* 557-558.

Lachman, R., Lachman, J. L., & Butterfield, E. C. (1979). *Cognitive psychology and information processing: An introduction.* Hillsdale, NJ: Erlbaum.

Lewicki, P. (1983). Self-image bias in person perception. *Journal of Personality and Social Psychology, 45,* 384-393.

Lewicki, P. (1984). Self-schema and social information processing. *Journal of Personality and Social Psychology, 47,* 1177-1190.

Lewicki, P. (1985). Nonconscious biasing effects of single instances on subsequent judgments. *Journal of Personality and Social Psychology, 48,* 563-574.

Lewicki, P. (1986a). Processing information about covariations that cannot be articulated. *Journal of Experimental Psychology: Learning, Memory, and Cognition, 12,* 135-146.

Lewicki, P. (1986b). *Nonconscious social information processing.* New York: Academic Press.

Lewicki, P., Czyzewska, M., & Hoffman, H. (1987). Unconscious acquisition of complex procedural knowledge. *Journal of Experimental Psychology: Learning, Memory, and Cognition, 13,* 523-530.

Lewicki, P., Hill, T., & Sasaki, I. (1989). Self-perpetuating development of encoding biases. *Journal of Experimental Psychology: General, 118,* 323-337.

Nisbett, R. E., & Wilson, T. D. (1977). Telling more than we can know: Verbal reports on mental processes. *Psychological Review, 84,* 231–259.

McClelland, D. (1965). Toward a theory of motive acquisition. *American Psychologist, 20,* 321–333.

Reber, A. S. (1976). Implicit learning of synthetic languages: The role of instructional set. *Journal of Experimental Psychology: Human Learning and Memory, 2,* 88–94.

Reber, A. S. (1989). Implicit learning and tacit knowledge. *Journal of Experimental Psychology: General, 118,* 219-235.

Rock, I. (1975). *Introduction to perception.* New York: Macmillan.

Seamon, J. G., Brody, N., & Kauff, D. M. (1983). Affective discrimination of stimuli that are not recognized: Effects of shadowing, masking, and cerebral laterality. *Journal of Experimental Psychology: Learning, Memory, and Cognition, 9,* 544–555.

Tranel, D., & Damasio, A. R. (1985). Knowledge without awareness: An index of facial recognition by propagnosia. *Science, 228,* 1453–1454.

Zajonc, R. B. (1968). Attitudinal effects of mere exposure. *Journal of Personality and Social Psychology Monograph Supplement, 9* (2, Part 2), 2–27.

CHAPTER 9

Personal Efficacy

JAMES E. MADDUX

Introduction
Basic Principles of Self-Efficacy
    Theory
  Basic Cognitive Processes
  Sources of Self-Efficacy
Personal Efficacy and
    Psychological Adjustment
ACTIVITY BOX: Increasing
    Self-Efficacy
Other Models of Personal
    Efficacy
  Effectance Motivation
  Level of Aspiration
  Expectancy-Value Theory
  Locus of Control
  Self-Concept and Self-Esteem
  Achievement Motivation

Research on Self-Efficacy Theory
  Relationships Between the Basic
    Components
  Linking Self-Efficacy Theory to
    Other Theories
Summary
SUGGESTED READINGS
REFERENCES

Introduction

People tend to engage in behaviors they believe will get them what they want and that they believe they can do. In other words, we all set goals in life (some short-term, some long-term), and much of our behavior is directed toward attaining those goals. The importance we place on certain goals and our beliefs about how to reach those goals strongly influence our choice of behaviors to attempt or initiate: our responses to obstacles that arise in pursuit of the goals; our emotional reactions, such as anxiety, sadness, and frustration; and our feelings of self-esteem and self-confidence.

The term *personal efficacy* is sometimes used for our sense of our ability to do the things that will get us what we want in life. People with a strong sense of personal efficacy are likely to set high goals for themselves and work hard to reach those goals. They also are likely to attempt new and untested ways of attaining their goals and to persist in the face of temporary setbacks. Thus, personal efficacy is an important aspect of personality. A strong sense of personal efficacy can be important to happiness and satisfaction in life. A number of psychologists have studied and written about personal efficacy. This chapter will look briefly at several areas of theory and research that are important to the concept.

A recent theory of personal efficacy that has been the topic of much research in social, clinical, and personality psychology is *self-efficacy theory*. This theory was introduced in 1977 by Albert Bandura, a psychologist who has made many important contributions to the study of personality through his research on modeling or observational learning and what is usually known as social learning

232

theory. Social learning theory—which includes self-efficacy theory—is an approach to the study of human behavior that assumes that the study of personality is best viewed as the study of social cognition (beliefs and attitudes about people) and interpersonal behavior. Social learning theory proposes that the most important determinants of our behavior are *cognitive mediators,* or the thoughts and beliefs we hold about our environment and our behavior. Social learning theory also assumes that we learn social cognitions and interpersonal behaviors by observing other people.

Self-efficacy theory maintains that psychological and behavioral changes can be best explained by examining our beliefs and expectations about our ability to achieve important goals, to deal effectively with obstacles that stand in the way of those goals, and to master or overcome the problems that come our way in life. In this chapter, I will use *personal efficacy* to refer to a person's general sense of his or her ability to achieve and attain important goals in life and his or her general sense of competence. On the other hand, I will use *self-efficacy* or *self-efficacy expectancy* to refer to a belief about performing a specific behavior in the pursuit of a specific goal. This chapter will provide an overview of self-efficacy theory, describe several other theories and concepts related to personal efficacy, and describe research on some basic problems and issues concerning self-efficacy theory.

Basic Principles of Self-Efficacy Theory

Basic Cognitive Processes

According to self-efficacy theory, two related expectancies influence our behavior in situations in which we are trying to achieve goals or cope with problems. An *outcome expectancy* is our belief that a certain behavior (or set of behaviors) probably will or will not lead to a certain outcome, goal, or consequence. A *self-efficacy expectancy* is the belief that we probably are or are not capable of performing this behavior or set of behaviors. For example, you may believe with some degree of certainty that strict adherence to Arnold Schwarzenegger's weight-lifting program or Jane Fonda's aerobic workout program will lead to such desired goals as improved physical fitness and increased physical attractiveness and sex appeal. If so, then you hold a *high outcome expectancy* for the behaviors in these programs and the desired outcomes that might result from regular practice of the behaviors described in these programs. If your outcome expectancy is low—if you do not believe that these programs are likely to lead to positive changes in your health and appearance—then you are unlikely to start a program.

High outcome expectancy alone, however, is probably not enough to convince you to start one of these programs. You must also believe that you are capable of doing the exercises in the program. In other words, you must have a *high self-efficacy expectancy* for the behaviors in the program. If you do not believe you will be able to do the exercises correctly—that is, if your self-efficacy expectancy is low for these particular behaviors—then you are not likely to give the program a try. Even if you do try to do the exercises, if your self-efficacy is low you are likely to give up easily when things get a little tough. But, if you believe that you will be able to do the exercises—high self-efficacy expectancy—then you are likely to make at least an initial attempt.

Three points about self-efficacy expectancy and outcome expectancy are important. First, the two expectancies always work together in influencing our decisions about what behaviors to attempt. Whatever the behavior in question, we always hold some expectations (possibly incorrect ones) about what the consequences might be and how capable we are of doing the behavior. Also, both these expectancies influence our behavior, and both must be fairly strong or high for us to want to attempt a behavior, especially a new or unfamiliar behavior in a new and threatening situation.

Second, these expectancies are defined in terms of *degrees* of probability or likelihood instead of in "either–or" or "yes and no" terms. We usually think about what the chances or "odds" are that a behavior will lead to a particular outcome and that we will be able to perform the behavior in question. Of course, sometimes we do hold either-or beliefs or expectancies, such as "either it will work or it won't work" or "either I can or I can't do it." In research, however, expectancies are measured as a thermometer measures temperature—in degrees.

Third, self-efficacy expectancies and outcome expectancies are not personality traits. They are relatively specific cognitions or thoughts that can be understood and defined only in relation to specific behaviors in specific situations or contexts. It would not make much sense to say "She has high self-efficacy" without specifying a particular behavior or set of behaviors. The same rule applies to outcome expectancy. It is necessary to talk about both a particular behavior or set of behaviors and a particular outcome or set of outcomes. For example, a person who generally feels very self-confident and in control (someone who has a lot of strong self-efficacy expectancies for a large number of behaviors) may have a low self-efficacy expectancy about his or her ability to quit smoking. The best way to predict success is to measure both self-efficacy expectancy for quitting and outcome expectancies for quitting (how he or she expects to benefit) rather than measure general self-confidence or self-esteem. Measuring self-efficacy expectancies for quitting smoking will be even more successful if we measure the person's expectations of being able to refrain from smoking under specific situations (e.g., while at a party, after eating, when around other smokers). The more we can relate self-efficacy expectancies and outcome expectancies to specific behaviors and specific situations, the better we will be able to measure these expectancies and predict behavior from them.

In addition to these two expectancies, a third type of cognition is important in our decisions about our behavior is an *outcome value*— that is the importance or value we place on certain goals or consequences. Before we are willing to work toward a goal and continue working toward it, we must value it or desire it. It was probably your desire to be healthier and more attractive that prompted you in the first place to consider enrolling in an aerobics class or begin a weight-lifting program. If you did not desire the possible results, then outcome expectancy and self-efficacy expectancy probably would not make much difference. Even if you believed the program would lead to thinner thighs or bigger biceps and believed that you could do the exercises, if you did not yearn for thinner thighs and bigger biceps you probably would not enroll in one of these programs.

The writers and researchers on self-efficacy theory have not paid much attention to outcome value. Bandura, for example, did not formally include outcome value as a component of self-efficacy theory. Most writers and researchers seem to assume correctly that outcome value needs to be high to begin with before self-efficacy expectancy and outcome expectancy will make any difference. In other words, we must desire something before we even care whether we will be able to attain it. A large number of studies on what is known as expectancy-value theory (described later in this chapter) have shown that the value of the potential outcomes of our behavior, sometimes called reinforcement value, has a powerful effect on our behavior. However, very little research has looked at the relationship between outcome value and these expectancies.

Sources of Self-Efficacy

Our feelings of self-efficacy come from four sources of information: performance experiences (what we do), vicarious experiences (what we see others do), verbal persuasion (what other people tell us), and emotional arousal (what we feel) (Bandura, 1977, 1986).

The most powerful sources of self-efficacy information are *performance experiences*—in particular, success or failure experiences. It seems only logical that what people actually see themselves do should have a powerful influence over what they think they are able to do. If they succeed at something, they are likely to believe that they will be able to succeed again at the same task or a similar task. If they fail, they probably will expect to fail again. Thus, success at a task, behavior, or skill strengthens self-efficacy expectancies, whereas failure diminishes self-efficacy expectancies. A person who once tried to quit smoking but failed will probably doubt his or her ability to quit in the future. On the other hand, a person who is able to go a full day without smoking may then have a high self-efficacy expectancy for going another day without smoking. Keep in mind that "success" and "failure" are personal and subjective judgments. Others may think we have succeeded at some task, and we may have met other objective criteria for success, but if we ourselves do not believe we have succeeded, then our self-efficacy will not be enhanced.

The second most powerful influence on self-efficacy expectancies is *vicarious experiences,* which are also referred to as modeling, imitation, and observational learning. In vicarious experiences, we learn by observing other people. We see what they do and what consequences result from their behavior. We then use this information to form expectancies about our own behavior. The effects of vicarious experiences depend on our perception of the similarity between ourselves and the "model" or person we are observing, the number and variety of models, and the perceived power of the models. For example, if you see people with whom you think you have much in common (similarities in skills and abilities), and these people are able to perform certain tasks or achieve certain goals, then you may come to believe that, because you are like them, you also are capable of the same accomplishments.

A common source of self-efficacy information in daily life is *verbal persuasion.* We frequently attempt to encourage our friends and family to try new behaviors or do things they are afraid of by telling them we have confidence in their ability ("I know you can do it!"). Other people try to encourage us in the same way. You can probably recall times when a friend or member of your family gave you a "pep talk" when you were feeling down or when your self-confidence was low. You may give yourself such talks on occasion to help get through tough situations in school or at work. As "The Little Engine That Could" discovered, "I think I can!" (high self-efficacy expectancy) can be one of the most powerful motivators of all.

Self-efficacy expectancies are also influenced by *emotional arousal.* Usually when you experience failure (or simply think you are doing poorly at something, like giving a talk in class), you also feel unpleasant emotions such as anxiety or sadness. Thus, unpleasant emotions become associated with failing or doing poorly. Even if you have learned to do something well, you may still have an unpleasant feeling like anxiety that accompanies your performance simply because it has been associated with it so often in the past. Thus, even when you are doing well at something—such as giving a talk you have given many times before, playing a musical piece you know well, or playing an important tennis match—you may experience a small amount of anxiety. If you become aware of this unpleasant feeling, you are more likely to doubt your abilities than if you were relaxed and comfortable.

These four sources of self-efficacy provide guidelines for organizing experiences that will increase your self-efficacy for a specific behavior or skill (see the Activity Box).

Personal Efficacy and Psychological Adjustment

Most theories of personality consider a strong sense of personal efficacy an important aspect of healthy psychological adjustment. People with a strong sense of personal efficacy typically have high self-esteem, set goals in life that motivate them toward achievement, and are effective in interactions with other people. A strong sense of personal efficacy helps one to persist at a task in the face of setbacks and to move steadily toward goals. Likewise, a general feeling of personal inefficacy is considered by many psychologists to be a hallmark of poor psychological and emotional adjustment.

People who seek help from psychotherapists and counselors usually do so because they feel inadequate, lack self-confidence and self-esteem, and feel that they are not able to do what others seem able to do to get what they want in life and be happy—a feeling of poor personal efficacy. Often people who see psychotherapists have recently experienced a major failure or series of failures (or what they believe are failures) in one or more important areas of their lives such as in their jobs, at school, or in relationships. Because of these perceived failures, these people usually have a poor sense of personal efficacy or general competence. They also hold a number of specific low self-efficacy expectancies about specific areas of life. These low self-efficacy expectancies may lead them to give up or stop trying to be effective in their lives.

For example, research has shown that low self-efficacy expectancies are an important feature of depression (see Stanley & Maddux, 1986a, for a review). Depressed people usually believe they are less capable than other people of performing effectively in their lives. Thus, they feel little or no control over what happens to them in life. Low self-efficacy is also important in problems with anxiety and fear. Much

Increasing Self-Efficacy

You do not need to be experiencing a serious psychological problem to be able to benefit from the principles of self-efficacy theory. The guidelines described here are highly general but will provide you with a basic plan for changing a behavior, improving a skill, or giving up a bad habit. Among the possibilities are cutting down on your smoking, eating a more healthy diet, losing weight, exercising more, improving your tennis game, becoming more assertive with others, improving your social life, earning a better grade in a class, improving your study habits, writing a term paper, or overcoming your fear of public speaking.

STEP ONE: SETTING A GOAL

The first step in making a productive change in some aspect of your life is setting a goal. The kind of goal you set is important because good goals encourage us to work harder and persist and enhance our feelings of self-efficacy, whereas poor goals discourage us and undermine self-efficacy. A good goal has three characteristics.

Specificity

A good goal is specific and fairly narrow rather than general and broad. For example, if you are concerned about your weight and want to lose a few pounds, you are more likely to experience success and enhance your self-efficacy if you set a specific goal such as "losing 5 pounds" rather than an ambiguous goal such as "losing weight" or "being thinner." If you want to improve your tennis game, a poor general goal would be "playing tennis better" whereas a good specific goal would be "improving my serve" or "improving my backhand."

Moderate Difficulty

A good goal is moderately difficult—that is, challenging but not over-whelming. Moderately difficult goals motivate us and give us a sense of hope and, when reached, give us a strong sense of self-efficacy. Goals that are too easy may be quickly and easily reached, but they may not give us much sense of accomplishment or enhance our feelings of self-efficacy sufficiently to spur us on to greater accomplishments. For example, if you smoke and want to stop, quitting smoking altogether is certainly an admirable and healthy goal, but it may seem so difficult that you never try or you give up when the going gets tough. On the other hand, reducing your cigarette consumption from 20 per day to 19 per day is probably not sufficiently challenging to motivate you to try or to give you a sense of accomplishment or the feelings of self-efficacy that would encourage you on to further success. However, an initial goal of cutting down from 20 to 15 may both challenge you and give you a reasonable chance for success. Succeeding is likely to give you a fairly strong sense of self-efficacy for reducing your smoking even further. Once this goal has been reached, you can set a new goal of cutting down to 10 cigarettes per day. Likewise, if you are flunking biology, then setting the goal of making an "A" in the course may not be realistic and could lead you to feel more discouraged. However, setting your sights on a "C" would be worthwhile, challenging, and realistic. In fact, you may even surprise yourself by surpassing your goal and getting a "B" or an "A," even though you are only "trying" to get a "C."

Divisibility

A good goal is divisible and can be broken down into short-term goals or smaller subgoals. Reducing cigarette consumption is accomplished one day at a time or even one hour at a time. Setting daily goals for cutting down on your smoking and then reaching these daily goals will increase the frequency with which you experience success and feel self-efficacious (i.e., you succeed *every day* you are able to smoke 15 instead of 20 cigarettes). Getting a "C" in a course is accomplished through your performance on specific tests and assignments. Studying for a specific test or working on a term paper can be an effective subgoal. Even the subgoal of getting a "B" on the next test can be broken down into smaller goals that include studying specific chapters for specific periods of time on specific days. In reaching any goal, "divide and conquer" is a cliché that works.

STEP TWO: SELF-EFFICACY ENHANCEMENT

The four sources of self-efficacy described in the text provide general guidelines for organizing experiences that will enhance your self-efficacy for a specific behavior or skill.

1. Performance Experience

Perform the new behavior for a short period of time or try it out in a situation in which success is all but guaranteed. For example, go without a cigarette for just an hour and then praise yourself for this accomplishment. Study for 15 minutes and enjoy even a small sense of accomplishment and self-efficacy. With a good friend, rehearse how to tell your of the work of Bandura and his associates has focused on understanding the role of self-efficacy in the development and treatment of extreme fears or phobias (Bandura, 1986). Self-efficacy also seems to be important in social or interpersonal anxiety (Leary & Atherton, 1986; Maddux, Norton, & Leary, in press). Research has also examined the importance of self-efficacy in many other problems such as cigarette

---

ACTIVITY BOX (Continued)

Increasing Self-Efficacy

parents that you have decided to change your major from pre-med to journalism. In some small way, *act.* Your self-efficacy expectancies may be enhanced by just a small amount, but you will be encouraged to then go forward with a more difficult task.

2. Vicarious Experience

Find a model and observe that person's behavior. Seeing someone who is similar to you experience success in an area in which you seek improvement will help convince you that you too can succeed. This kind of vicarious enhancement of self-efficacy expectancy is the goal of those "before and after" photographs and testimonials in weight-loss program advertisements. The message is: "Here is someone like you who was able to lose weight. If he/she can do it, so can you." In observing someone perform, you may learn a skill or technique (e.g., a new tennis serve) and you may come away with the sense that "If he/she can do it, then so can I!" Choose a model who is similar to you in as many ways as possible and whose level of skill is not too far above yours. Watching Martina Navratilova or Boris Becker is probably not a good way for a beginning tennis player to build his or her sense of tennis self-efficacy. Watching your sister or roommate (who is a little better than you) play may be more effective.

Reading inspirational books by people who have overcome obstacles or even tragedies or who have accomplished goals you would like to accomplish may enhance your sense of general personal efficacy and your self-efficacy expectancies for specific tasks or skills. Much of the success and popularity of Dale Carnegie's well-known books *How to Stop Worrying and Start Living* and *How to Win Friends and Influence People* can probably be attributed to Carnegie's use of personal examples from real people throughout the books—people who are just like you and me and who were able to learn to worry less, be happier, make friends, speak in public, or become better salespersons.

smoking, alcoholism, obesity, and eating disorders (e.g., bulimia). (More information about self-efficacy and these problems can be found in Maddux, Stanley, & Manning, 1987; DiClemente, 1986; and Maddux & Stanley, 1986.)

Most people who seek psychotherapy do so because of general feelings of low self-esteem, low self-worth, or low personal efficacy

3. Verbal Persuasion

Give yourself "pep talks" and have others do the same for you. As "The Little Engine That Could" demonstrated, "I think I can!" can be a highly motivating phrase; so can "I know you can!" when you hear it from someone you like and trust. In addition, you can make cards or signs that say "YOU CAN STOP SMOKING!" or "YOU CAN LEARN BIOLOGY!" and put them on your bathroom mirror, your refrigerator door, and the dashboard of your car. These can serve as "self-efficacy reminders" throughout the day.

4. Emotional Arousal

You can enhance your self-efficacy for a behavior or task by learning to associate positive feelings with the behavior. For example, imagine that you have achieved a goal or performed a behavior well and then feel the sense of pride and accomplishment that comes from the performance. You might imagine, for example, that you have just finished writing your psychology term paper a week before it is due. By doing so, you are learning to associate pleasant feelings (pride, relief, joy) with a task that probably has many unpleasant feelings associated with it.

You can also enhance your self-efficacy by reducing the unpleasant arousal associated with a task you fear (e.g., taking a test, making a phone call to ask for a date). For example, you can learn meditation or relaxation exercises and perform them while thinking about doing something about which you feel anxious. As you learn to feel less anxious and more relaxed while thinking about and rehearsing the behavior, your self-efficacy for the behavior is likely to increase. In addition, the feelings of relaxation are are likely to remain with you during an actual performance of the behavior. Learning to relax will help you develop stronger self-efficacy expectancies, and the stronger self-efficacy expectancies will then help you feel more at ease.

rather than because of specific low self-efficacy expectancies for one or two specific behaviors. However, in trying to understand and help people who are experiencing emotional or psychological problems, it is more useful to understand specific self-efficacy expectancies about specific behaviors and specific life goals than simply to examine a person's general sense of competence or effectiveness. Understanding specific self-efficacy expectancies about specific behaviors helps a psychotherapist or counselor determine exactly which beliefs and behaviors need to be changed to help the person experience success and begin to feel and be more effective, productive, and satisfied in his or her life.

Once a psychotherapy client begins to experience some success in one or two specific aspects of his or her life, the client begins to develop stronger self-efficacy expectancies for specific behaviors in specific areas of life. These higher specific self-efficacy expectancies then lead to a stronger sense of general personal efficacy. This initial success may be small. For example, an extremely shy client may be helped with calling a friend to arrange a lunch date, or a severely depressed person may be encouraged to simply get up and get dressed in the morning. According to self-efficacy theory, these small successes strengthen the client's sense of self-efficacy and his or her expectations for additional, more important successes. We can probably say that most popular and effective forms of psychotherapy and counseling have as their primary goal helping people experience success as a way of restoring high self-efficacy expectancies and a general sense of personal efficacy.

All four of the sources of self-efficacy information described earlier are important in psychotherapy. Many forms of psychotherapy rely strongly on verbal persuasion as a means of enhancing a client's sense of self-efficacy and encouraging clients to take small risks that may lead to small successes. Almost all psychotherapists and counselors rely initially upon their own powers of persuasion to convince clients that they indeed *can* make some small changes in their behavior that will lead to greater happiness or satisfaction. In what are known as cognitive and cognitive-behavioral forms of psychotherapy, the therapist engages the client in a discussion of the client's dysfunctional (ineffective or self-defeating) beliefs and attitudes and helps the client see the irrationality and self-defeating nature of such beliefs. Such kinds of psychotherapy are systematic attempts at changing self-efficacy expectancies by verbal persuasion. (See Hollon & Beck, 1986, for a review of cognitive and cognitive-behavioral psychotherapy.)

Some types of therapy use vicarious means for enhancing self-efficacy. For example, modeling films and videotapes have been used successfully to encourage socially withdrawn children to interact with other children. In such films, the socially withdrawn child observes another child encounter and then master problems similar to his or her own problems. The child model initially expresses some fear about approaching another group of children, but then takes a chance and starts talking to the children and joins in their play. The child watching the film sees the model child, someone much like himself or herself, experience success and comes to believe that he or she too can do the same thing (see Conger & Keane, 1981, for a review).

Biofeedback, relaxation training, and meditation are attempts to reduce emotional arousal (e.g., anxiety) and to reduce the association between this arousal and low self-efficacy. Finally, as noted earlier, actual performance of behaviors that lead to success is perhaps the most powerful way to enhance personal efficacy in psychotherapy. For example, the most effective treatment for phobias requires the client to practice thinking about and actually approaching the feared object (such as a spider in a glass case) in therapy sessions and between sessions as "homework" assignments.

Most psychotherapy and counseling approaches involve combinations of more than one source of self-efficacy information. For example, successful treatment with agoraphobic clients (people with extreme fears of leaving their homes and going out in public) requires intervention on all four levels: (1) emotional arousal—teaching the client to relax and feel less anxious when out in public; (2) verbal persuasion—encouraging the client to attempt feared behaviors and challenging the client's expectations of catastrophe; (3) vicarious experiences—observation of filmed or live models (such as the therapist) engaging in feared behaviors or participation in an agoraphobic group; and (4) performance experiences—actual practice in engaging in feared behaviors such as leaving one's home and approaching a feared situation or setting such as a supermarket.

Thus, like all good concepts and theories, the concept of personal efficacy in general and self-efficacy theory in particular can be of considerable practical value. Self-efficacy theory and research have contributed a lot to our understanding of how psychological and behavioral problems develop, how and why they persist, why people seek help, and how to develop more successful treatments for a number of important problems.

Other Models of Personal Efficacy

The study of personal efficacy or self-efficacy is not new. A number of psychologists have been concerned with our sense of personal mastery, ability, and achievement and with the effects of these beliefs on behavior (Kirsch, 1986). A discussion of several of these theories follows.

Effectance Motivation

Robert White (1959) wrote about the concept of "competence" and defined it as "an organism's capacity to interact effectively with its environment" (p. 297). The basic issue with which White dealt is how to explain human behavior that is not directed toward immediate biological goals such as satisfying hunger, thirst, and sexual desire. White proposed that human beings must be motivated by a different kind of goal, the goal of exploring, manipulating, and mastering the environment. White called this motivation "effectance motivation" and said that its satisfaction leads to a "feeling of efficacy." In other words, we are biologically driven to explore and master our environment, and we feel good when we explore new situations, learn about them, and deal with them effectively. White also believed that this feeling of efficacy is an aim in itself, apart from the practical value of the things we learn about the environment.

White's ideas are interesting and may seem to provide an explanation for much human behavior. It is convenient to refer to a basic biological motivation such as effectance and feelings of efficacy to explain behaviors that may otherwise be difficult to explain. Unfortunately, explanations that depend on internal drives are really not very helpful because these drives cannot be seen or observed directly. All we can see is the behavior that supposedly is motivated by the drive.

Level of Aspiration

Theory and research on "level of aspiration" are concerned with what people would like to achieve or what they "aspire to" and how their aspirations influence their behavior. Level of aspiration (what you would like to be able to do or achieve) is related to self-efficacy expectancy (what you think you will be able to do), but they are not the same thing. As Kirsch has stated, "Level of aspiration is concerned with the goals that people set for themselves, their intentions, and their hopes. . . . Self-efficacy concerns people's expected performance levels" (1986, pp. 340-341). In much of the early research on level of aspiration, however, investigators did not make this distinction very clear. Sometimes they asked people about what they would like to be able to do or achieve; other times they asked people what they expected to be able to achieve. The studies that made this important distinction found that peoples' levels of aspiration were usually greater than their expectancies for success. In other words, as we all learn in life, we often want more than we think we will be able to get.

Expectancy-Value Theory

Expectancy-value theories deal with the value we place on certain kinds of reward or reinforcement and with our expectations that we will be able to obtain those rewards. These theories have a long tradition in psychology. Probably the most influential expectancy-value theory has been Julian Rotter's "social learning theory" (1954). In his theory, Rotter proposed that the probability that a person will engage in a behavior is determined by the strength of the person's belief that some behavior will lead to a particular reward and the importance of that reward (or reinforcement) to the person. Rotter also proposed that success itself is a form of reinforcement. In this way, Rotter's ideas are compatible with White's, because White also stated that exploration, learning, and mastery are rewarding in themselves. Rotter's notion of "expectancy for success" is similar to Bandura's concept of self-efficacy expectancy.

Locus of Control

Perhaps Rotter's most well-known and well-researched idea is his notion of "locus of control" (Rotter, 1966; see also chapter 11, Control). Locus of control refers to the general belief that our behavior can have an impact on our environment and that we are capable of controlling outcomes through our own behavior. People who believe that their own behavior does control outcomes and that the environment is generally responsive to their behavior are said to have an *internal* locus of control. People who believe outcomes are determined by luck (good and bad) or powerful others (such as God) and that the environment is generally unresponsive to their own efforts are said to have an *external* locus of control (Rotter, 1966).

At first glance, locus of control may sound similar to self-efficacy expectancy. Bandura (1986), however, has argued that locus of control is really a kind of outcome expectancy because it is concerned with whether our behavior controls outcomes, not whether we can or cannot perform certain behaviors—behaviors that might or might not have an effect on our environment. For example, a highly religious person may have an external locus of control and believe that most of what happens in his or her life is determined by God, not by his or her own behavior. This person may believe that health is determined by God, not by actions (e.g., diet, exercise, wearing a seat belt), and thus may not engage in certain behavior that may help enhance or protect his or her health, not because the person believes he or she cannot do them (self-efficacy expectancy), but because of the belief that it will not do any good (because everything is decided by God). Also, locus of control is a generalized belief, almost like a personality trait. Self-efficacy theory, however, deals with specific expectancies about specific behavior and specific outcomes in specific situations. Studies have shown that measures of specific expectancies are better predictors of specific behaviors than are measures of general traits such as locus of control.

Self-Concept and Self-Esteem

Self-concept and self-esteem are two kinds of self-evaluations that have been given much attention by psychologists in the past several decades. Your *self-concept,* for example, consists of the sum total of your attitudes and beliefs about yourself, the kind of person you are, your likes and dislikes, and what you are capable or not capable of doing well. While self-concept is the set of beliefs you hold about yourself, *self-esteem* is your evaluation of those beliefs, or how you feel about these beliefs. Self-esteem is your assessment of your worth or value as a person—how much you like the kind of person you think you are. This evaluation is usually seen as independent of self-concept. Two people may have similar self-concepts—that is, they may hold beliefs about themselves that are very similar—yet one person may have high self-esteem and the other low self-esteem. For example, you may believe that you have little musical talent, but this belief will only affect your self-esteem if having musical talent is very important to you. If, however, you come from a family with many musically talented members but believe you do not have musical talent and very much wish you did, your self-esteem may be low.

Beliefs about personal efficacy are important aspects of self-concept. Also, personal efficacy beliefs may influence your self-esteem. If your self-efficacy for a skill or ability important to you is high, then this will contribute to high self-esteem (or low self-esteem if self-efficacy for the valued skill is low). Therefore, self-efficacy expectancies are related to and contribute to self-concept and self-esteem.

Achievement Motivation

The motivation to strive for achievement, success, and excellence is referred to as *achievement motivation* or *achievement need* (see also chapter 7, Motives). Work on achievement motivation was pioneered by David McClelland and his colleagues (McClelland, Atkinson, Clark,

& Lowell, 1953), and a large number of studies have been conducted to determine the characteristics of people who have high achievement motivation. This need to strive for success and excellence is similar to the concepts of effectance motivation and level of aspiration; each of these concepts deals with the tendency to set goals for ourselves and work toward these goals.

In self-efficacy theory, however, talking of a "need" or "motive" to achieve is not seen as very helpful in explaining and predicting actual achievement, especially achievement in a specific area (e.g., academic versus athletic, mathematics versus business). Self-efficacy theory would define a need as an outcome value and would measure achievement need by measuring the importance or value that the individual places on specific goals (e.g., getting an "A" in a specific course, earning a promotion or raise at work). Also, self-efficacy theory is more concerned with the role that expectancies play in determining and predicting achievement behavior. For example, you may have a strong overall need to achieve and a strong need to achieve in academics. This achievement need may be narrowed down to a specific situation such as the desire to get an "A" in my history course. According to self-efficacy theory, however, this need alone is not enough to motivate you to *try* to get an "A." In addition to this "need," you must believe there are things you can do that might help you get an "A" (such as study for a certain number of hours—an outcome expectancy). You must also believe that you will be able to do these things that might lead to an "A" (a self-efficacy expectancy). Thus, a sense of personal efficacy, defined in terms of self-efficacy expectancies, is important in achievement behavior, but is not the same thing as achievement need or achievement motivation.

Research on Self-Efficacy Theory

Dozens of studies on the basic concepts of self-efficacy theory have been published in the past decade. In addition, before Bandura described his theory, many studies were conducted on theories that are in some ways similar to self-efficacy theory. It would be impossible to summarize this tremendous body of research in this chapter. Instead, I would like to draw some broad and general conclusions about the research on self-efficacy theory.

Research on self-efficacy theory usually falls into one of four categories. Each category deals with a different "level" of self-efficacy theory or a different kind of question. The first category or level is research on the relationship between self-efficacy and behavior. A large number of studies have shown that self-efficacy expectancies are accurate predictors of a wide variety of behaviors (Bandura, 1977; Maddux & Stanley, 1986). The second category is research on how to best influence or change self-efficacy. Research has generally shown that enactive experiences (actual performance of a behavior) are the most powerful influences on self-efficacy expectancies. The third category includes research that looks at the relationship between self-efficacy and other kinds of "cognitive" variables such as outcome expectancies, outcome values, and intentions. A fourth kind of research is aimed at trying to identify similarities between self-efficacy theory and other theories from social psychology, personality psychology, and clinical psychology.

All four types of research are important in contributing to our understanding of personal efficacy, behavior, and personality. The studies I have conducted fall into the third and fourth categories. Many other researchers have pursued answers to the important questions of "How can we influence self-efficacy?" and "How does self-efficacy influence behavior?" I have been most interested in two questions: (1) What is the relationship between self-efficacy expectancy, outcome expectancy, and outcome value? and (2) How is self-efficacy similar to and different from other theories?

The first question is important because it is concerned with the basic concepts of self-efficacy theory. If we are to really understand and make good use of a theory, we need to understand its basic concepts and understand their relationships to one another. For example, self-efficacy theory assumes that self-efficacy expectancy and outcome expectancy are independent concepts. Is this assumption true? Do we need both of the concepts to understand and predict behavior? Does understanding outcome value add anything more to our understanding of behavior and personality? A related question concerns how to best *measure* these concepts. It may be logical to think of the concepts as different and independent, but can we devise ways of measuring them that reflect this idea? The question of measurement is very important because without measurements that we can trust, we cannot conduct research. Also, concepts that cannot be measured reliably are of little practical use.

The second question concerns the relationship between self-efficacy theory and other theories from social and clinical psychology. This question is important because a personality theory that is broad and can be used to explain and predict a wide variety of behaviors is better and more useful than a theory that is narrow and can be applied to only a relatively small range of behaviors. The more similarities we can find among theories, the closer we will come to the important goal of developing a comprehensive theory that explains a wide range of human behavior. Self-efficacy theory has shown some promise of being this kind of theory. Therefore, the more we understand about how self-efficacy theory is similar to and different from other theories, the better we will be able to bring these other theories together and *integrate* them into a more comprehensive and more useful theory of personality and behavior.

These two lines of research are not as separate as I make them seem. Most of the studies I will describe had more than one purpose. Several were designed to examine basic properties of self-efficacy theory, examine the relationship between self-efficacy theory and a similar theory, and to provide some understanding of a real-life problem. I have divided them into two categories for the sake of convenience.

Relationships Between the Basic Components

Self-efficacy theory assumes that self-efficacy expectancies and out-come expectancies are relatively independent. In this case, "independent" means that we cannot predict one from knowing the other. For example, knowing that your roommate expects losing twenty pounds will make him more attractive and healthier tells you little, if anything, about whether or not he believes he will be able to lose twenty pounds. Independence also means that each expectancy adds something important to our ability to predict behavior, over and above what the other expectancy predicts. For example, if you know the strength of your roommate's expectation that losing twenty pounds will make him healthier and more attractive (outcome expectancies) *and* you know the strength of his expectation that he will be able to lose those twenty pounds (a self-efficacy expectancy), then you will be better able to predict whether or not he will actually *try* to lose twenty pounds than if you know only about his outcome expectancy or his self-efficacy expectancy.

Logically, outcome value should also be independent of self-efficacy expectancy and outcome expectancy. It makes sense that the value or importance a person places in or attaches to specific goals or outcomes should not, for the most part, be influenced by beliefs concerning his or her ability to attain those goals. Of course, these relationships are not always this simple. Conventional wisdom, for example, says (and your own experience may provide evidence for this) that we often want most the things we think we cannot have, and we often lose interest in previously desired things or people once we believe they are within our reach. Research also supports this conventional wisdom. My interest, however, was not in determining whether or not people always are able to use self-efficacy expectancy, outcome expectancy, and outcome value independently in making decisions, but whether or not they sometimes are capable of doing so. In addition, some studies that had concluded that self-efficacy expectancy and outcome expectancy were not independent seemed, in my opinion, to contain some methodological errors that led to incorrect conclusions.

In our first study addressing this issue (Maddux, Sherer, & Rogers, 1982), we examined the relationship between self-efficacy expectancy and outcome expectancy and their effect on intentions to perform a specific behavior. We used intentions to behave as our dependent measure instead of actual behavior because we were primarily interested in the relationship between self-efficacy expectancy and outcome expectancy and not in their effect on behavior. A large number of studies have shown that intentions, when carefully measured, are good predictors of behavior. Therefore, we believed intentions would be useful and more convenient than measuring actual behavior in a real-life setting.

In this study, we recruited college students to take part in a study of "interpersonal effectiveness training." We told these students we were developing brochures to provide tips for solving interpersonal problems and that we wanted them to give us their opinions of these brochures. All the subjects read a brochure that described the "broken-record technique" that is often taught in assertiveness training courses. (In the broken-record technique, a person is taught to repeat a request or other verbal response in a calm manner instead of providing excuses or explanations or becoming angry—like a record when the needle is stuck. For example, if a friend asks to borrow money from you and refuses to take "no" for an answer, a broken-record response would be to simply reply "I'm sorry, I can't lend you the money" to your friend's repeated requests rather than continue to explain why you can't or won't lend him the money.) Some of the students read that the broken-record technique would be highly effective in dealing with people (high outcome expectancy), whereas others read that it would be ineffective (low outcome expectancy). In addition, some students read that the technique would be very easy to perform (high self-efficacy), whereas others read that it would be very difficult to perform (low self-efficacy). We asked these students, along with asking them a number of irrelevant questions to support our cover story, about their intentions to use the broken-record technique in their everyday lives.

As we expected, subjects who had read the high-outcome-expectancy brochures indicated stronger intentions to use the broken-record technique than subjects who had read the low-outcome-expectancy brochures. However, we found that the two self-efficacy brochures did not produce different levels of intentions to use the technique.

We decided to conduct another study that would try to replicate or repeat the results of the first study and that would address some additional questions. In this second study (Maddux, Norton, & Stoltenberg, 1986) we manipulated self-efficacy expectancy, outcome expectancy, *and* outcome value and looked at how well each of these manipulations affected and predicted behavioral intentions. The goal of this study, as before, was not to prove that people always make a distinction between self-efficacy expectancy, outcome expectancy, and outcome value, but to see whether or not people *can* make this distinction. This study used the same format as the above study (the "interpersonal effectiveness training" brochures that described the broken-record technique). Self-efficacy expectancy and outcome expectancy for the broken-record technique were manipulated, as before, by the use of written communications. We added a manipulation of outcome value by adding to the communications passages that described either positive outcomes (e.g., success with people, increased self-esteem) or negative outcomes (e.g., others will dislike you for being rude or pushy) that might result from using the broken-record technique. Again, the dependent measure was the subjects' intentions to use the broken-record technique in their everyday lives.

As before in Maddux et al. (1982), we found that the high-outcome-expectancy manipulation led to stronger intentions to use the technique than did the low-outcome-expectancy manipulation, but that our manipulations of self-efficacy expectancy did not produce differences between the groups on the intentions measure. We also found that the outcome-value manipulation influenced intentions. Subjects who were exposed to the high-outcome-value message indicated stronger likelihood of using the broken-record technique than did subjects exposed to the low-outcome-value message. We were not very confident, however, in this finding because we discovered (after having run the study!) some problems in the way we had manipulated and measured outcome value.

We were most interested, however, in the relationships of the self-efficacy expectancy, outcome expectancy, and outcome value measures with one another and whether they independently seemed related to intentions. We used a sophisticated correlational technique to look at these relationships. Correlation is concerned with the association between two measures and is not concerned with the question of which is causing a change in the other. Therefore, this correlational analysis included all the subjects in the study without regard to the experimental group to which they belonged.

Through this correlational analysis, we found that the self-efficacy expectancy and outcome expectancy measures were not strongly correlated, which meant that knowing one did not allow us to predict the other. We also found that the self-efficacy expectancy and outcome expectancy measures were both strongly and equally correlated with the intentions measure. Thus, the self-efficacy and outcome expectancy measures were each significant and independent predictors of the intentions measure. Although the outcome value measure was strongly correlated with intentions, it was also correlated with the self-efficacy and outcome expectancy measures. Thus, the outcome value measure was *not* a good independent predictor of the intentions measure. (It is important to keep in mind that a correlation looks at the relationship between one measure and another measure, not between an experimental manipulation and a measure. Thus, it is possible, as happened in this study, for the self-efficacy manipulations to fail to produce significant differences on the intentions measure, yet for the self-efficacy measure to be significantly correlated with the intentions measure when all the experimental groups are combined.)

This study provided support for the idea that self-efficacy may not always be the most important predictor of behavioral intentions. The results also gave evidence that outcome expectancy could be independent of self-efficacy expectancy and was important in its own right. We believed we had demonstrated that people can, under certain conditions, make a distinction between the effectiveness of a behavior (outcome expectancy) and their ability to perform the behavior (self-efficacy expectancy) and that these expectancies could be independent influences over the decisions people make about their behavior. In our study, compared to some other studies, our measures of self-efficacy expectancy and outcome expectancy made a clear distinction between expectations of being able to execute the behavior and expectations about the consequences of executing the behavior. The low correlation between self-efficacy expectancy and outcome expectancy indicates that we were successful.

We were confused over the results on outcome value, and we wanted to run another study that would be a better test of the role of outcome value in behavioral decisions. We were not as careful as we could have been in measuring outcome value. The high correlations between outcome value and self-efficacy expectancy and outcome expectancy reflected this. We still believed in the idea that outcome value was logically an independent factor in decisions about behavior —independent of outcome expectancy and self-efficacy—and that outcome value could be an equally important factor in decisions about behavior. Our next step, therefore, was to design another study to look at outcome value more carefully.

The first step in designing a new study was to look at what went wrong in the previous study. I especially wanted to look very closely at the outcome value manipulations and measures. When I did this, I realized that we had made some mistakes in the outcome expectancy and outcome value manipulations. The outcome expectancy manipulation in Maddux et al. (1986) had involved telling subjects that the broken-record technique was either very effective (high outcome expectancy) or ineffective (low outcome expectancy) in producing certain desirable results. However, in our attempt to manipulate the *value* that subjects attached to the outcome of performing the broken-record technique, we described two different sets of outcomes instead of describing one set of outcomes and trying to get subjects to attach either high or low value to them. In the high-value condition, subjects were told that performing the broken-record technique would produce increased success in problematic encounters with people, increased self-esteem, and greater life satisfaction. In the low-value condition, the opposite results were described—that is, different outcomes. Although outcome value may have been manipulated in these conditions, the manipulation clearly involved differences in the outcomes subjects could expect from engaging in the broken-record technique. The correct way to manipulate outcome value would be to convince people to find a particular outcome desirable or undesirable without describing two different sets of outcomes in the high- and low-value conditions.

We designed another study (Barnes, 1985) that attempted to solve these problems. This new study presented subjects with high and low levels of self-efficacy expectancy, outcome expectancy, and outcome value. In this study, college students (who were not aware of the true purpose of the study) read descriptions of what appeared to be a real part-time job (selling dictionaries over the phone) being offered by what appeared to be a real company. (Of course, both the job and the company were fictitious.) "Brochures" about the job and the company differed in their descriptions of the ease with which the firm's required sales pitch could be learned and used (high versus low self-efficacy expectancy), the probability that using the sales pitch would result in a sale (high versus low outcome expectancy), and the amount of commission paid to the salesperson for each dictionary sold (high versus low outcome value). Thus, self-efficacy expectancy, outcome expectancy, and outcome value were manipulated and measured in ways that reflected their logical differences. For example, the low outcome value manipulation did not introduce a set of outcomes different from the outcome described in the high outcome value manipulation. In each case, the outcome was the sale of a dictionary. What differed in the two conditions was the monetary value of a sale. Our main dependent measures in the study were (a) intentions to become a salesperson for the firm, (b) intentions to use the sales pitch if one became a salesperson, and (c) a "behavioral commitment" measure that asked the students to indicate whether or not they wanted to be contacted by the company and receive additional information about the job.

One of the most important findings was that we were successful in independently manipulating self-efficacy expectancy, outcome expectancy, *and* outcome value. None of these three measures was correlated with either of the other two. Thus, we were successful in showing that outcome value could be independent of both self-efficacy expectancy and outcome expectancy. In addition, we again demonstrated that self-efficacy expectancy and outcome expectancy were independent expectancies. A second important finding was that self-efficacy expectancy, outcome expectancy, and outcome value were each important and about equal predictors of intentions to become a salesperson for the company and of the behavioral commitment measure. Thus, we were also successful in demonstrating that outcome value could be an important factor in decisions about behavior.

Taken together, these studies strongly suggest (we shouldn't say "proved") that self-efficacy expectancy, outcome expectancy, and outcome value, as their definitions say, are relatively independent cognitions—that you cannot necessarily predict one from the other. The studies also suggest that each of these three cognitions is an important component of people's decisions about their behavior—or at least can be important under the right conditions.

Linking Self-Efficacy Theory to Other Theories

A second goal of our research with self-efficacy has been to explore the similarities and differences between self-efficacy and other theories that seem to contain similar ideas. We have looked at the relationship between self-efficacy theory and a theory of anxiety and a theory of health behavior.

Self-Efficacy Theory and Social Anxiety

Anxiety or discomfort during social or interpersonal situations is one of the most common psychological problems. A theory developed by Schlenker and Leary (1982), the *self-presentational model,* proposes that social anxiety is the result of our concern with how we are perceived and evaluated by others. In this model, social anxiety occurs when we are motivated to make a particular impression on others but do not believe we will be able to do so. A large number of studies support this model.

Just from this brief description, you may have noticed a similarity between the self-presentational model of social anxiety and self-efficacy theory. My colleagues and I saw similarities, also, and wanted to see if the two theories could be integrated or combined into a single theory that had the best features of both theories. We believed that beliefs about making impressions on others might be separated into outcome expectancies (beliefs that certain interpersonal behaviors, if performed competently, will lead to the desired impressions) and self-efficacy expectancies (beliefs that one is or is not capable of performing the necessary interpersonal behaviors).

We designed a study (Maddux, Norton, & Leary, in press) to see if this distinction was a useful one in understanding social anxiety. In this study, we asked college students to read a set of "scenes" that described interpersonal situations in which many or most people would feel some social anxiety or nervousness (for example, asking an angry professor to change an unfair grade, going on a job interview). We asked our subjects questions concerning (a) whether or not certain behaviors would be effective in helping them to make the right impression and achieve their goals (outcome expectancy), (b) whether or not they believed they could effectively perform the behaviors that would lead to making the right impression (self-efficacy expectancy), and (c) how important it was to them to make the right impression in the particular situation. We also asked them how anxious they would feel in the situation.

As predicted, we found that both self-efficacy expectancy and outcome expectancy were good predictors of the amount of anxiety subjects thought they would feel in the situations. Thus, we found that the distinction self-efficacy theory makes between these two expectancies was useful in understanding social anxiety and in improving the self-presentation theory of social anxiety. This distinction had not been made clearly in previous research on social anxiety, and outcome expectancies had been mostly ignored.

Models of Health Behavior

Health and medical care in our society has been gradually shifting its emphasis from an exclusive concern with the treatment of disease to the prevention of disease and the promotion of good health. Most preventive health care efforts involve changing behaviors (e.g., smoking, exercise, diet), and psychologists have much to offer toward our understanding of how and why people adopt healthy and unhealthy behaviors and how to change behaviors that affect health. The term "health psychology" is usually used to describe the branch of psychology concerned with theory and research on health behavior. Because self-efficacy theory is a broad theory of behavior change, it may have much to offer us in understanding and changing health behavior (see O'Leary, 1985, for a review).

My colleagues and I have conducted several studies that have attempted to use self-efficacy theory to understand how people make decisions about behavior that affects their health. In particular, we have tried to integrate self-efficacy theory with another theory of health behavior called "protection motivation theory" (Rogers, 1975). Protection motivation theory proposes that people's decisions to change from unhealthy to healthy behaviors are influenced mainly by their beliefs about the severity of a health problem for which they may be at risk, how much at risk or how vulnerable they believe they are, and how much they think changing their behavior will reduce this risk or vulnerability. As you can see, protection motivation theory is an expectancy-value theory because it is concerned with how important an outcome (e.g., a disease) is to an individual, his or her expectation that present unhealthy behavior may lead to this outcome, and the individual's expectation that changing the behavior may prevent this undesirable outcome.

If you look at this theory from the viewpoint of self-efficacy theory, you can see that protection motivation theory—at least in its original form—does not include a self-efficacy expectancy, or the individual's belief that he or she capable of changing from present unhealthy behaviors to new healthy behaviors (e.g., from a smoker to a nonsmoker, sticking to a low cholestoral or low salt diet). We were interested in seeing if self-efficacy expectancy could be integrated into protection motivation theory. In other words, we wanted to know if self-efficacy expectancies for health behaviors would influence peoples' decisions to change their health behaviors. Three studies examined the role of self-efficacy expectancies along with the components of protection motivation theory in influencing decisions about two different health-related behaviors: cigarette smoking and exercise. All three studies used the familiar format of presenting subjects with written information about the health behaviors in question. This information was used to vary the subjects' beliefs about self-efficacy expectancies, outcome expectancies, and outcome value.

Maddux and Rogers (1983) manipulated cigarette smokers' beliefs about the severity of the consequences of smoking such as lung cancer and heart disease (an outcome value), their vulnerability to the consequences (an outcome expectancy), the likelihood that quitting would reduce their risk or vulnerability (also an outcome expectancy), and their ability to quit smoking (a self-efficacy expectancy). As in the studies described earlier, we asked smokers about their intentions to quit smoking. (Keep in mind that intentions are usually good predictors of behavior.) Some subjects were told, through written persuasive communications, that the consequences of smoking were very serious, even fatal, whereas others were told that the effects of smoking had been exaggerated and were not as bad as they may have believed. Some subjects were also told that the risk for these consequences was not very great, whereas others were told that they were at great risk. Also, some subjects were told that quitting would greatly reduce their risk, whereas the rest were told that quitting would do very little to reduce their risk of serious disease. Finally, we convinced some subjects that quitting would be fairly easy (and this took a lot of convincing!), while we convinced others that quitting would be extremely difficult. (You can probably see now why we had to rely on subjects' intentions to quit as our dependent measure. We presented most of the subjects with incorrect information about smoking and could not let them leave without correcting this erroneous information.)

We found that subjects indicated greater intentions to quit if they believed they were at great risk for smoking-related diseases, if they believed that quitting smoking would reduce their risk, and if they believed they would be able to quit. The subjects' beliefs about the severity of the consequences of smoking did not influence their intentions to quit. As we expected, self-efficacy expectancy—beliefs about their ability to quit—was the best predictor by far of intentions to quit. Thus, we were successful in demonstrating that self-efficacy expectancy was a much-needed new component of protection motivation theory.

The second study (Stanley & Maddux, 1986b) examined the usefulness of the new and improved protection motivation theory (now with self-efficacy expectancy) in understanding exercise behavior. One important difference between this second study and the first is that the first study was concerned with preventing disease whereas this second study focused on improving the health of currently healthy people, or *health enhancement*. This may seem like a subtle distinction, but it is an important distinction in health psychology. Fear of a disease is usually seen as a more powerful motivation to change behavior than the desire to improve an already-healthy condition. In this study, college women were presented with information about a new exercise program that would be offered by the university they were attending. (This was our cover story. No such program was actually being offered.) They were told that the exercise program's activities would be either easy or difficult to do (high or low self-efficacy expectancy), that the program was either very likely or not very likely to lead to benefits such as improved health and physical appearance (high or low outcome expectancy), and that the possible benefits of the program were very important or not very important in our society (high or low outcome value). Our dependent measures were subjects' intentions to sign up for and participate in the program. We also gave subjects the opportunity to actually sign up for the program.

As predicted, we found that self-efficacy expectancy and outcome expectancy both influenced subjects' intentions to sign up and the rate at which they signed up. Outcome value did not influence intentions of sign-up. Although the study contained some problems, we were able to show that a theory that combined protection-motivation theory with self-efficacy theory could be a useful model of health behavior even when threats of a serious disease were not involved.

Our third study on health behavior (Wurtele & Maddux, 1987) was also concerned with exercise. This study used a format similar to the study just discussed. College women read descriptions of an exercise program and were asked about their intentions to make the behavioral changes described by the program. Most important, a follow-up was conducted two weeks after the study to see if participants changed their exercise behavior following the study. The information provided about exercise was written to change subjects' beliefs about their vulnerability to diseases that result from a sedentary lifestyle (lack of exercise), the severity of these diseases, the effectiveness of regular exercise in preventing these health problems, and their beliefs about their ability to do the exercises. We found that self-efficacy expectancy, vulnerability, and outcome expectancy (the effectiveness of the exercises) influenced intentions to change exercise behavior, although these influences were related in a rather complicated manner. Intentions to increase exercise behavior also were a significant predictor of changes in exercise at the two-week follow-up. Certainly additional research is needed to examine the role of self-efficacy in health behavior. In particular, the need is for studies of health behavior in real-life settings rather than just controlled studies with college students. Controlled studies such as these, however, are necessary for examining and testing the assumptions and predictions of a theory before the theory can be applied to the study of behavior outside of the laboratory. These three studies at least strongly suggest that a model that combines protection motivation theory and self-efficacy theory will be useful in understanding how people go about making decisions about behavior that affects their health in detrimental and beneficial ways.

Summary

Personal efficacy, the general sense that one is capable of dealing effectively with life's challenges and of achieving important life goals, is an important aspect of personality and has been the subject of study by psychologists for several decades. A recent theory of personal efficacy, self-efficacy theory, views personal efficacy not as a personality trait but as a set of specific cognitions (beliefs and expectations) that pertain to specific behaviors and specific situations or goals. These specific cognitions are (a) outcome value, the importance we attach to a specific goal; (b) outcome expectancy, our beliefs that certain behaviors may help us attain those goals; and, most important, (c) self-efficacy expectancy, our beliefs that we are capable or incapable of doing the things that we believe may help us attain the goals we want. Research has shown that self-efficacy theory can help us better understand a number of common psychological or behavioral problems and their treatment.

This chapter has described research on the relationships among the important components of self-efficacy theory and research on the relationships between self-efficacy theory and other psychological theories. The studies reported here suggest that self-efficacy expectancy, outcome expectancy, and outcome value are important factors in our decisions about our behavior. In addition, these studies suggest that we can understand and predict behavior better by measuring all three of these cognitions than by relying only on one or two of them. These studies have also suggested that self-efficacy theory has much in common with other theories and can be integrated with other theories to produce more powerful and useful theories.

The research on personal efficacy, self-efficacy theory, and related concepts such as effectance, achievement motivation, and locus of control would fill many volumes. In this chapter we were able to look only briefly at a small number of important issues. The articles, chapters, and books listed at the end of this chapter provide much useful information on many important issues and topics that could not be covered here.

SUGGESTED READINGS

Bandura, A. (1977). Self-efficacy: Toward a unifying theory of behavioral change. *Psychological Review, 84,* 191–215. Bandura's original and full description of self-efficacy theory; also an excellent review of studies on topics related to self-efficacy.

Kirsch, I. (1986). Early research on self-efficacy: What we already know without knowing we knew. *Journal of Social and Clinical Psychology, 4,* 339–358. A scholarly but readable review of pre-1977 research relevant to self-efficacy theory. Kirsch's main theme is that the concept of self-efficacy was investigated long before Bandura's 1977 article,

although previous theorists and researchers did not use the term "self-efficacy."

Maddux, J. E., & Stanley, M. A. (Eds.). (1986, Special Issue). Self-efficacy theory in contemporary psychology. *Journal of Social and Clinical Psychology, 4,* 249–373. Articles that review research on self-efficacy theory and a number of important issues in clinical, counseling, social, and industrial psychology.

Maddux, J. E., Stanley, M. A., & Manning, M. M. (1987). Self-efficacy theory and research: Applications in clinical and counseling psychology. In Maddux, J. E., Stoltenberg, C.

D., & Rosenwein, R. (Eds.), *Social processes in clinical and counseling psychology* (pp. 39–55). New York: Springer-Verlag. A review of theory and research on the use of self-efficacy theory in the assessment and treatment of emotional and behavioral problems.

O'Leary, A. (1985). Self-efficacy and health. *Behavior Therapy and Research, 23,* 437–452. A review of research on the use of self-efficacy theory in understanding and changing health-related behaviors.

REFERENCES

Bandura, A. (1977). Self-efficacy: Toward a unifying theory of behavioral change. *Psychological Review, 84,* 191–215.

Bandura, A. (1986). *Social foundations of thought and action.* New York: Prentice-Hall.

Barnes, J. (1985). *The relative utility of self-efficacy expectancy, outcome expectancy, outcome value, and behavioral intentions in explaining and predicting behavior.* Unpublished doctoral dissertation, Texas Tech University.

Conger, J. C., & Keane, S. P. (1981). Social skills intervention in the treatment of isolated or withdrawn children. *Psychological Bulletin, 90,* 478–495.

DiClemente, C. C. (1986). Self-efficacy and the addictive behaviors. *Journal of Social and Clinical Psychology, 4,* 302–315.

Hollon, S. H., & Beck, A. T. (1986). Research on cognitive therapies. In S. L. Garfield & A. E. Bergin (Eds.), *Handbook of psychotherapy and behavior change* (pp. 443–482). New York: Wiley.

Kirsch, I. (1986). Early research on self-efficacy: What we already know without knowing we knew. *Journal of Social and Clinical Psychology, 4,* 339–358.

Leary, M. R., & Atherton, S. C. (1986). Self-efficacy, social anxiety, and inhibition in social encounters. *Journal of Social and Clinical Psychology, 4,* 258–267.

Maddux, J. E., Norton, L. W., & Leary, M. R. (in press). Cognitive components of social anxiety: An investigation of the integration of self-presentation theory and self-efficacy theory. *Journal of Social and Clinical Psychology.*

Maddux, J. E., Norton, L. W., & Stoltenberg, C. D. (1986). Self-efficacy expectancy, outcome expectancy, and outcome value: Relative effects on behavioral intentions. *Journal of Personality and Social Psychology, 51,* 783–789.

Maddux, J. E., & Rogers, R. W. (1983). Protection motivation and self-efficacy: A revised theory of fear appeals and attitude change. *Journal of Experimental Social Psychology, 19,* 469–479.

Maddux, J. E., Sherer, M., & Rogers, R. W. (1982). Self-efficacy expectancy and outcome expectancy: Their relationships and their effects on behavioral intentions. *Cognitive Therapy and Research, 6,* 207–211.

Maddux, J. E., & Stanley, M. A. (Eds.). (1986, Special Issue). Self-efficacy theory in contemporary psychology. *Journal of Social and Clinical Psychology, 4,* 249–373.

Maddux, J. E., Stanley, M. A., & Manning, M. M. (1987). Self-efficacy theory and research: Applications in clinical and counseling psychology. In J. E. Maddux, C. D. Stoltenberg, & R. Rosenwein (Eds.), *Social processes in clinical and counseling psychology* (pp. 39–55). New York: Springer-Verlag.

McClelland, D. C., Atkinson, J. W., Clark, R. A., & Lowell, E. L. (1953). *The achievement motive.* New York: Appleton-Century-Crofts.

O'Leary, A. (1985). Self-efficacy and health.

Behavior Therapy and Research, 23, 437–452.

Rogers, R. W. (1975). A protection motivation theory of fear appeals and attitude change. *Journal of Psychology, 91,* 93–114.

Rotter, J. B. (1954). *Social learning and clinical psychology.* Englewood Cliffs, NJ: Prentice-Hall.

Rotter, J. B. (1966). Generalized expectancies for internal versus external control of reinforcement. *Psychological Monographs, 80* (1, Whole No. 609).

Schlenker, B. R., & Leary, M. R. (1982). Social anxiety and self-presentation: A conceptualization and model. *Psychological Bulletin, 92,* 641–669.

Stanley, M. A., & Maddux, J. E. (1986a). Self-efficacy theory: Potential contributions to understanding cognitions in depression. *Journal of Social and Clinical Psychology, 4,* 268–278.

Stanley, M. A., & Maddux, J. E. (1986b). Cognitive processes in health enhancement: Investigation of a combined protection motivation and self-efficacy model. *Basic and Applied Social Psychology, 7,* 101–113.

White, R. W. (1959). Motivation reconsidered: The concept of competence. *Psychological Review, 66,* 297–333.

Wurtele, S. K., & Maddux, J. E. (1987). Relative contributions of protection motivation theory components in predicting exercise intentions and behavior. *Health Psychology, 6,* 453–466.

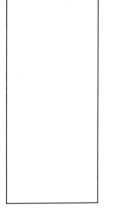

CHAPTER 10

Sex and Gender

BARBARA A. WINSTEAD, VALERIAN J. DERLEGA, AND
RHODA K. UNGER

Introduction
Differentiating Sex and Gender
Sex as a Subject Variable
    Antecedents of Sex Differences
    Limitations to the Use of Sex as
        a Subject Variable
Psychological Dimensions of
      Masculinity and Femininity
    Early Research Attempts
    Androgyny
    Gender Schema Theory

ACTIVITY BOX: **Avoidance of**
      Gender-Inappropriate
      Behavior
Sex as a Social Category
Summary
SUGGESTED READINGS
REFERENCES

Introduction

"Is it a boy or a girl?" For the parents as well as family and friends this is among the first questions asked upon the arrival of a new human being. (Currently, with technologies such as ultrasound and amniocentesis, this all-important question is often answered even before the birth of a child.) In hospital nurseries girls wear pink caps and lie in cribs with pink cards giving their names and birth dates. Boys, of course, are coded with blue. If a friendly passerby mistakes the sex of an infant dressed in a "neutral" color, she or he is quick to apologize: "Well, he's pretty enough to be a girl" or "She's strong enough to be a boy." Clearly, sex is an important aspect of who a person is in the minds of others and, usually, in a person's own mind. We tend to believe, even when we have no other information about a person, that if we know her or his sex we *do* know something about who that person is. That is, we have sex stereotypes, for example, girls are pretty, boys are strong.

Psychologists are intrigued by sex and sex stereotypes as ways of defining and understanding human behavior. In the past 20 years, there has been a proliferation of research on the topic of sex and gender (e.g., Deaux, 1984; Shaver & Hendrick, 1987; Spence, Deaux, & Helmreich, 1985; Stewart & Lykes, 1985a). In her analysis of research on gender Deaux (1984) identified three major approaches to this research: (1) sex as a subject variable; (2) individual differences in masculinity, femininity, and androgyny; and (3) sex as a social category. Using Deaux's three categories to organize the material, our chapter examines issues in the area of sex, gender, and personality.

Differentiating Sex and Gender

Writers often use the terms sex and gender interchangeably. We wish, however, to make a distinction between sex and gender that is important for understanding personality. *Sex* refers to the biological phenomena associated with being female or male. *Gender* refers to the psychological phenomena of being feminine or masculine, that is, having personal characteristics considered appropriate (in our culture) for women or men. Gender is culturally defined and, although every culture distinguishes (some more, some less) between females and males, the attributes that are assumed to belong to each sex vary across cultures.

Although sex and gender usually go together, at least in our minds (i.e., female = feminine, male = masculine), this need not be the case. An extreme example is transsexuals, individuals who feel so strongly that they are psychologically a member of the other sex that they have their physical selves (physique, genitals) altered to match their psychological selves. In other cultures, individuals who express feelings, thoughts, and behaviors that are characteristic of the other sex may be assigned special roles in the culture or honorary membership in that sex. In these cases, rather than expect gender to match sex, sex is altered, physically or socially, to match gender.

Sex, as defined here, is not a "good" *personality* variable. Although it is stable across time and situations, it is not a variable on which there is a broad range of individual differences. A person is either female or male. It is, however, a variable that has been used often to predict and understand personality differences. Or, one might say, personality variables have been used to understand what it means to be female or male in our culture. In either case, there is an enormous psychological literature on sex differences in personality and the first section of the chapter examines a small part of this literature.

Gender *can* be considered a legitimate personality variable. In general females are taught and encouraged (i.e., socialized) to be feminine and males are socialized to be masculine, but individuals vary in the degree to which they are feminine or masculine. (Consider, for example, a Southern belle versus Calamity Jane or Rambo versus Pee Wee Herman.) Also, females can have attributes considered masculine (e.g., aggression) and males can have attributes considered feminine (e.g., nurturance). The history and current study of masculinity and femininity, and criticisms of them, are presented in the second section of the chapter.

The third section of the chapter focuses on sex as a social stimulus. Knowing that a person is female or male influences the behaviors of persons interacting with her or him. A male, for example, might be seductive with a female and competitive with a male, but rarely vice versa. These behaviors of others influence the individual's behavior in ways that have little or nothing to do with her or his personality. This is perhaps a peculiar section for a textbook on personality. However, in attempting to understand how being female or male can influence personality it is useful to examine how sex can also limit the expression of personal dispositions by causing others to act toward a person in ways that limit her or his behavioral options.

Sex as a Subject Variable

A question that interests most people is: What difference does being female or male make in an individual's personality? From your own experiences and observations of people you may think the answer to this question is, "Not much; people vary but their differences don't seem to be related to their sex." On the other hand, you may say, "Men and women are very different; in some ways you can predict how people will behave just by knowing whether they are male or female." Studies that have investigated sex differences in human behavior have found that there are some differences between women and men that are reliably and repeatedly found, but there is more variability than most people expect there to be.

Research on sex differences has a long history. Hundreds of studies were conducted early in the twentieth century on such topics as color preferences, handwriting, memory for advertisements and movies, nervous behavior of children in nursery school, reading speed, credibility about fortune telling, stammering, reasoning skills, and even knowledge about psychology after taking an introductory survey course (Morawski, 1987). In this early research few if any sex differences were ever reported and studies finding differences often reported female superiority.

Studies of sex differences continued to be done but relatively little attention was paid to them. Psychologists were seeking general laws for human behavior. Although their subjects were frequently male undergraduates, they assumed their results could be generalized to all adults, including women. With the resurgence of feminism in the late 1960s, interest in what psychologists knew about sex differences was rekindled. In 1974 in the second edition of *The psychology of sex differences*, Maccoby and Jacklin summarized over fourteen hundred published studies on sex differences in a wide range of areas, such as cognitive functions, temperament, and social behaviors. To determine if sex differences in these variables were present Maccoby and Jacklin, and many others who have reviewed studies of sex differences, counted the number of studies finding statistically significant differences between females and males, taking into account the direction of the differences, and the number of studies not finding significant differences. Based on these tabulations, Maccoby and Jacklin concluded that few if any sex differences were documented. For cognitive abilities, however, they did report that males tend to be superior in mathematical and visual-spatial abilities while females are superior in verbal abilities. In one area of social behavior—aggression—it appeared that males are more aggressive than females.

In recent years, using a technique called meta-analysis that allows researchers to combine different studies and, thus, calculate the overall outcome of many studies, some psychologists have reexamined sex differences in behavior and suggested that they are more consistently present than Maccoby and Jacklin believed. For example, Eagly (1987) reported that men are more aggressive than women, but more so for aggressive behavior that produces physical harm than for aggression that produces psychological or social harm. She also found that men are more helpful, at least in emergency situations with strangers; that men conform less and are less easily influenced, at least when this behavior is being observed by the group; and that women are more skilled at nonverbal communication, especially for facial expressions. In social situations women are also more expressive and responsive to others. Men are also more likely than women to engage in behaviors aimed at accomplishing a group's task (Eagly, 1987).

These findings appear to fit stereotypes most people have about females and males: Females are person-oriented and agreeable and males are task-oriented and aggressive. An important aspect of these conclusions, however, is that it is not useful to make global assertions about sex differences in personality characteristics—that is, males are more aggressive than females—because what research demonstrates is that males are more aggressive *only* in some situations and for some types of aggressive behaviors. For sex differences, as for all other individual differences, the situation as well as personality influences behavior. The particular setting chosen to study a behavior will influence the degree and direction of the sex difference that is observed (Eagly, 1987; Unger, 1985). For example, although in many studies of helping behavior males are found to be more helpful than females, most of these studies use emergency situations with strangers in need of help and look at direct forms of helping (i.e., going to the aid of the stranger rather than seeking someone else's assistance). It may be precisely these circumstances in which women are less likely to help. In other situations such as helping in a nonemergency situation, women have been found to be more helpful than males (Pandey & Griffith, 1974) and women may use more indirect ways of helping than men do (Piliavin & Unger, 1985). Thus, where, how, and under what circumstances psychologists measure behavior affects whether or not a sex difference is observed in that behavior.

Sex is also related to how we view ourselves. Some studies have found that males are more self-confident than females (Crandall, 1969); that they take credit for their successes whereas females view their successes as due to luck or temporary factors, like lots of effort (Deaux & Farris, 1977); and that men prefer skill-determined tasks whereas females prefer chance-determined tasks (Deaux, White, & Farris, 1975). All of these findings suggest that men are self-assured and have high expectations for themselves and confidence in their skills. Women, on the other hand, appear to be uncertain about their abilities and unwilling to risk testing their skills. A closer look at these phenomena have revealed, however, that the *type of task* used in research makes all the difference in finding these sex differences in self-perception. Lenney (1977), surveying numerous studies, concluded that sex differences in self-confidence (men having more self-confidence than women) are likely to occur for tasks associated with the male role, but not for tasks associated with the female role. Deaux and Farris (1977) found that men compared to women had higher expectations for outcome and gave themselves higher ratings for ability, whereas women explained their outcomes in terms of luck *only* for "masculine" tasks (i.e., subjects were told that males excelled on the tasks). There were few sex differences for "feminine" tasks. Rosenfield and Stephan (1978) found that subjects' explanations for success were internal (e.g., ability) for males and external (e.g., luck) for females on a "masculine" task but just the opposite (i.e., internal for females and external for males) when the task was "feminine." Finally, Karabenick, Sweeney, and Penrose (1983) found that men (compared to women) preferred skill rather than chance tasks if the activity was masculine sex-typed (emphasizing physical skills). Women, however, preferred skill rather than chance tasks if the activity was feminine sex-typed (emphasizing social skills and a knowledge of children). Preferences for skill versus chance activities were primarily a function of the expectancies of success on the skill tasks.

Our exposure to and experience with different types of tasks is determined in part by our sex. There are girls' toys (e.g., dolls, toy kitchens, dress-up clothes) and boys' toys (e.g., action figures, toy garages, tool sets). Our self-confidence and our explanations for outcomes are bound to be related to familiarity and past experience with the task set for us or to our beliefs about how well females and males typically do at such tasks.

Previously we discussed the importance of considering the situation or circumstances in which behavior occurs in understanding sex differences in social behavior. Similarly, expectations for and explanations of performance are necessarily influenced by the nature of the task. The particular task chosen in a research study may determine whether a sex difference in expectancies or attributions does or does not occur.

Antecedents of Sex Differences

When a sex difference in behavior is found we want to know *why* it occurs. It is tempting with sex differences to assume that because sex is a biological difference between female and male, then the behavioral difference must also be in some way caused by biological factors. In fact, however, finding a relationship between sex and behavior (i.e., a sex difference) tells us *nothing* about what causes the sex difference to occur. A sex difference is always (because sex cannot be experimentally manipulated) the result of a study using a correlational design and, thus, conclusions about causation cannot be made (see chapter 2, Personality Measurement). Furthermore, we know that girls and boys, women and men are treated differently by others based on their sex, i.e., they are taught to behave differently. Unless we were to live in a culture that makes absolutely no distinction between females and males, we cannot know what sex differences in behavior would occur as a result of biological factors alone.

We will discuss in detail one example of a series of studies examining why a sex difference in self-explanations (generally called attributions) for success and failure might occur. These studies looked not only at differences in socialization experiences (teacher behavior, in this case) that might contribute to sex differences in attributional patterns; the studies also manipulated the socialization variables to show that they could affect children's perceptions of their outcomes. In the first study in the series Dweck, Davidson, Nelson, and Enna (1978) trained raters observed the behavior of fourth- and fifth-grade teachers and coded every instance of evaluative feedback they gave to their students during academic subjects. Girls and boys received comparable amounts of positive and negative feedback. However, the behaviors for which they received positive or negative feedback depended on their sex. For boys most of the negative feedback (67.5%) was for conduct and nonintellectual aspects of the work (e.g., messy work); whereas for girls most of the negative feedback (88.2%) was for intellectual aspects of the work (e.g., wrong answers). Conversely, boys received a greater proportion of praise (93.8%) than girls did (80.9%) for intellectual aspects of their work (e.g., correct answers). Praise for academic performance may encourage self-perceptions of ability, whereas negative feedback would encourage self-perceptions of lack of ability. Furthermore, if negative feedback is primarily for nonacademic behavior, as it is for boys, you may conclude that being messy or not listening to instructions is your problem and, thus, attribute poor academic performance to lack of effort or a picky teacher. If negative feedback is primarily for incorrect answers, as it is for girls, failure at academic tasks may mean only lack of ability.

Dweck et al. (1978) followed up the study on teacher behavior by conducting an experiment in which both girls and boys received negative feedback similar to that experienced by girls in the classroom (negative feedback exclusively for wrong answers) or negative feedback similar to that experienced by boys in the classroom (negative feedback for wrong answers and for messy work). All children received equal amounts of criticism. The results showed that most children who were criticized only for wrong answers attributed their failures to lack of ability; whereas three-quarters of the children who received mixed criticism perceived their failures as due to factors other than a lack of ability. These latter children, in a situation comparable to that of schoolboys, attributed their failures primarily to lack of effort. There were no sex differences in the study. In this case, children's attributions were determined by the type of feedback they received and were unrelated to sex. In real life, boys and girls apparently receive different types of feedback and, thus, may develop different attributional styles.

Limitations to the Use of Sex as a Subject Variable

The study of sex differences in behavior has major limitations. First, as was just explained, sex differences in behavior do not explain why these differences occur. Also, much research on the effects of sex differences has been conducted in psychology experiments. Using laboratory settings, we cannot know the type or degree of sex differences in behavior that would occur in more natural settings (Deaux, 1984). Recognizing the limitations of sex as a useful variable, psychologists have searched for core feminine and masculine personality characteristics that might lead to an understanding of the nature of females and males. It was assumed that feminine and masculine traits would be found differentially in females and males, and these personality concepts would provide a psychological explanation for sex differences in behavior.

Psychological Dimensions of Masculinity and Femininity

If we assume, and nearly all psychologists have, that women and men have on the average different personal attributes, then we ought to be able to define femaleness and maleness and measure the degree to which an individual possesses these traits. Femininity and masculinity, as such traits are generally called, were initially considered to be just *one* trait, masculinity–femininity, but they have more recently been considered two distinct traits. The history of attempts to measure and understand femininity and masculinity and the current status of these efforts provide insight not only into gender and personality, but also into how scientific knowledge is constructed by those who do science.

Early Research Attempts

In the early part of this century it was the potential utility of psychology to improve personal lives that kept research on sex differences and masculinity-femininity going. Psychologists were interested in promoting mental health and marital and family stability and they believed that a proper match between biological sex and psychological temperament was essential (Morawski, 1985). Researchers attempted to construct personality scales that would identify and measure the psychological attributes of females and males. Items on the scales were composed of characteristics that one sex was believed to have in greater abundance than the other sex. For instance, Lewis Terman and Catherine Cox Miles (1936) published a 910-item scale that was supposed to detect masculinity and femininity. It was called the Attitude Interest Analysis Test (AIST) in order to disguise its purpose from subjects. The criterion for including items on the test was the demonstration that women and men gave statistically different responses to the items. The sexes differed on the average by 127 points on the test and only about one person out of one hundred of each sex had a score that exceeded the mean of the other sex (Terman & Miles, 1936, p. 371, cited in Morawski, 1985).

The authors assumed that femininity and masculinity were personal qualities that could not be easily detected by observers but could be accurately assessed by scientific instruments, such as the AIST. They further assumed that such a measurement device would be useful in clinical settings for detecting homosexuality and female delinquency, because "inversion of temperament"—that is, masculinity in females or femininity in males—was believed to contribute to these psychological "abnormalities." Consider, however, the content of the items used to generate a masculine versus feminine score:

> Masculinity scores are gained by replying that you dislike foreigners, religious men, women cleverer than you are, dancing, guessing games, being alone, and thin women. Femininity points are accrued by indicating dislike for sideshow freaks, bashful men, riding bicycles, giving advice, bald-headed men, and very cautious people. (Morawski, 1985, p. 206)

Another assumption of the original scale developed by Terman and Miles was that the psychological attributes of femininity and masculinity are the two endpoints of a single, bipolar continuum. That is, feminine and masculine qualities (attributes more frequently displayed by one sex than the other) are assumed to be mutually exclusive and would not occur in the same individual. Most men were expected to score at the masculine extreme and most women were expected to score at the feminine extreme, with a few deviant individuals exhibiting cross-sex patterns of response. There was, however, little attention or interpretation given to scores that fell in the middle range of possible responses.

The importance of the AIST is that it served as a model for many subsequent attempts to measure femininity and masculinity and that the views of Terman and Miles on femininity and masculinity were similar to those of most psychologists at that time. The assumptions at the foundation of their views were (1) that women and men are essentially different in personality, (2) that a match between sex (female, male) and personal attributes (femininity, masculinity) is important for mental health, and (3) that masculinity-femininity is a single dimension. These assumptions were the result of the psychologists' own conceptualization of gender and not the product of a psychological "reality" that was being observed and explained.

Androgyny

In the early 1970s the feminist movement was beginning to influence psychology and other disciplines. Criticism was directed at the undimensional, bipolar conception of femininity and masculinity (Constantinople, 1973). Also the value of masculinity–femininity personality scales was being called into question because they had been validated simply by sex differences in item responses and offered no understanding of the development of the behavioral consequences of masculinity–femininity.

In response to this criticism, psychologists (Bem, 1974; Constantinople, 1973; Spence, Helmreich, & Stapp, 1974) developed a new conceptualization of gender. They argued that masculinity and femininity are two separate, unrelated dimensions. Possession of the traits characteristic of one sex does not necessarily mean the absence of traits characteristic of the other sex. Rather than view gender as a single dimension with feminine at one end and masculine at the other, these psychologists proposed that femininity and masculinity be viewed as separate traits. Thus, an individual could have both feminine and masculine attributes and behaviors, one or the other, or neither. If individuals have gender attributes commonly associated with their sex (i.e., femininity in females, masculinity in males) and few attributes associated with the other sex, they are referred to as *sex-typed*. If they have gender attributes associated with the other sex, but few associated with their sex (i.e., femininity in males, masculinity in females), they are referred to as *cross-sex-typed*. If they have both feminine and masculine attributes they are referred to as *androgynous;* if they have neither, they are referred to as *undifferentiated*. Bem also hypothesized that an androgynous person would be healthier psychologically and more flexible in coping with various situational demands than the feminine or the masculine person (whose behaviors are limited to sex-typed responses).

Various scales were developed to measure masculinity, femininity, and androgyny. These new scales included the Bem Sex Role Inventory (BSRI) (Bem, 1974, 1977) and the Personal Attributes Questionnaire (PAQ) (Spence, Helmreich, & Stapp, 1974; Spence & Helmreich, 1978). Both of these scales are self-report measures composed mostly or exclusively of items describing socially desirable traits that are believed to occur more frequently in one sex than the other. Recently Spence and Helmreich (1986) have extended the PAQ to include undesirable traits associated with female and male stereotypes. Items from the Extended Personality Attributes Questionnaire (EPAQ) are listed in table 10.1.

The new scales like the old scales measure gender-differentiating personality traits. Unlike the earlier bipolar, unidimensional scales, the new scales measure femininity and masculinity separately and allow for individuals to rate themselves as having one characteristic, both, or neither.

It is also important to note the change in the meaning of femininity and masculinity. Rather than assume that mental health corresponds with femininity in women and masculinity in men, the new ideal prescribes that women and men should be both feminine and masculine, that is, androgynous. The new scales stimulated an enormous amount of research examining connections between femininity, masculinity, androgyny, and mental health, and other variables. The connection between androgyny and mental health, however, is unclear.

TABLE 10.1

Extended Personal Attributes Questionnaire (EPAQ): A Measure of Gender-Related Differences in Personality

M+ Scale: Items that specify personality traits judged to be more characteristic of males than females and socially desirable for males and females.

Independent	Never gives up easily
Active	Self-confident
Competitive	Feels superior
Makes decisions easily	Stands up well under pressure

F+ Scale: Items that specify personality traits judged to be more characteristic of females than males and socially desirable for males and females.

Emotional	Kind
Devotes self to others	Aware of feelings of others
Helpful to others	Understanding of others
Gentle	Warm in relations with others

M−F+ Scale: Items representing the typical view of the ideal male and the ideal female. All items are high in social desirability for one sex but not the other. The ideal man falls toward the stereotypically masculine pole and the ideal woman toward the stereotypically feminine pole. The sex (M = male; F = female) of the ideal individual corresponding to the listed pole is indicated in parentheses.

Aggressive (M)	Needs approval (F)
Dominant (M)	Feelings easily hurt (F)
Excitable in a major crisis (F)	Cries easily (F)
Home-oriented (F)	Strong need for security (F)

M− Scale: Items are judged to be more characteristic of males than females and the content emphasizes self-assertiveness (paralleling the M+ Scale). But the content is low in social desirability for males and females.

Arrogant	Dictatorial
Boastful	Cynical
Egotistical	Looks out only for self; unprincipled
Greedy	Hostile

FC− Scale: Items are judged to be more characteristic of females than males and the content emphasizes an interpersonal- or communal-orientation (paralleling the F+ Scale). But the content is low in social desirability for males and females.

Spineless	Servile
Subordinates oneself to others	Gullible

FVA− Scale: Items are judged to be more characteristic of females than males (paralleling the F− Scale). But the content emphasizes a "neurotic, passive-aggressive" orientation and it is low in social desirability for males and females.

Whiny	Nags
Complaining	Fussy

Adapted from Spence and Helmreich (1986). Used by permission of Janet Spence and Robert Helmreich.

Although some evidence supports the assumption that androgyny promotes mental health, many studies have found that masculinity is the attribute most strongly related to psychological adjustment and self-esteem (see Spence, 1984a, pp. 70–77). The benefits of masculinity may reflect a capacity for self-assertion and positive self-expectations associated with masculinity or it may reflect cultural factors that place greater value on "masculine" characteristics, and, therefore, cause psychologists to include predominantly masculine attributes on measures of self-esteem.

Despite the frequent use of the BSRI and the PAQ in studies of gender, researchers disagree about what these scales actually measure. According to Spence (1984a, 1984b) a problem with the various masculinity–femininity tests is the false assumption that a collection of attributes that distinguish groups of males and females can be used to draw a picture of a typical person. No individual women or men are likely to display all of the attributes considered typical for their sex or that cultural stereotypes prescribe for them. Most women and men have several characteristics considered appropriate for their sex, but this collection varies from person to person, and men and women may also have characteristics that might be considered incompatible for their sex (e.g., men reporting that they are emotional or women reporting that they are aggressive).

Spence and Helmreich (the developers of the PAQ and EPAQ) state that their scales as well as Bem's BSRI measure only "self-assertiveness" and "interpersonal orientation" and that using labels such as femininity and masculinity suggests a simplicity to gender-relevant behavior that does not exist (Spence, 1984a, 1984b). In other words, while BSRI and PAQ scale scores do predict behaviors relevant to self-assertion and interpersonal qualities, they are poor predictors of other gender-relevant phenomena, such as preferences for stereotypically feminine or masculine recreational activities, vocational interests, social and dating behaviors, and marital behaviors (Orlofsky, 1981).

A criticism of the work on androgyny is that it continues to accept the basic assumption that female and male personality types (i.e., femininity and masculinity) exist (Morawski, 1985). This assumption that our personality is indelibly marked in some particular way by our sex is one we might question.

Gender Schema Theory

Recently Bem has shifted her focus from femininity and masculinity as attributes of the individual to gender as a category that individuals use to a greater or lesser extent in organizing information about themselves and others (called gender schema). People, she argues, learn gender-linked associations or gender schema from the language and behaviors of other members of their culture. For example, in our culture certain words (e.g., housewife, maid) indicate that domestic activities are female whereas assertive, protective activities (e.g., policeman, fireman) are male. If a culture through language, behavior, and roles emphasizes distinctions between women and men, then individuals growing up in that culture will learn to use gender to process information about the self, other people, and events around them; that is, a gender schema emerges. Having a gender schema also means having a culturally determined understanding of terms such as femininity and masculinity.

Individuals also learn to evaluate their adequacy and the appropriateness of behavior according to the gender schema. The gender schema thus serves as a guide or standard that motivates individuals to regulate their behavior according to culturally defined definitions of femaleness and maleness. According to Bem, "males and females behave differently from one another on the average because, as individuals, they have each come to perceive, evaluate, and regulate their own behavior and the behavior of others in accordance with cultural definitions of gender appropriateness" (Bem, 1984, p. 188). For instance, a gender schematic individual may be deciding on a career after college. The individual might consider how much income can be earned, flexibility of working hours, vacation time, and so forth. But the gender schematic individual would also consider the gender connotations of the job. Is this job for males or females? Does the job match up with what persons of my sex do for a living? I won't consider the job any further if it is more appropriate for the other sex. Gender schematic individuals may not even be aware that they are processing information on the basis of gender-related categories and so the gender schema may influence perceptions and behavior outside of conscious awareness.

Bem (1981, 1984) has conducted a number of studies testing whether gender schematic individuals (identified as "sex-typed" by the Bem Sex Role Inventory—"masculine" males and "feminine" females) organize information into gender-based categories more than androgynous or undifferentiated individuals. Gender schematic individuals, for example, should be more sensitive to cultural definitions of physical attractiveness for females and males. In one study (Anderson & Bem, 1981) subjects (either sex-typed or androgynous subjects of both sexes) participated in a getting acquainted telephone conversation with each of four partners. Subjects were shown pictures of their female and male partners and were led to believe that their partners were either attractive or unattractive.

The sex-typed persons were more likely than the androgynous persons to show interest and enthusiasm when talking with the attractive rather than the unattractive partners, and this differentiation was stronger when interacting with partners of the opposite sex. Gender schematic individuals' sensitivity to cultural definitions of physical attractiveness may lead them to encode information, particularly about opposite-sex persons, on the basis of physical attractiveness rather than other information that might be available.

Bem has also argued that gender schematic individuals are likely to maintain a high level of gender-stereotyped behavior. These persons are concerned about keeping their behavior consistent with the cultural definitions of gender-appropriate behavior. To test this idea, female and male subjects were divided into three groups: sex-typed, androgynous, and cross-sex typed. Subjects were told that their pictures were needed while performing various activities. The photos would ostensibly be used in another study in which people would be asked to make personality judgments based on the activities engaged in by the individual in the picture.

The activities were arranged into fifteen pairs. Subjects individually had to choose one activity from each pair that they would like to perform at the photo session that would occur next. In fact, the activities differed in their gender implications. Sometimes a masculine task (e.g., putting artificial bait on a fishhook) would be paired against a neutral activity (e.g., peeling oranges), a neutral task would be paired with a feminine task (e.g., preparing a baby bottle with formula), or a masculine activity would be paired with a feminine activity. Subjects were also told that they would be paid for being photographed doing the various activities. It was arranged that subjects would be paid more for engaging in the gender-inappropriate activities. (The Activity Box offers you the opportunity to sample a similar test.)

The results indicated that the sex-typed individuals were more likely to prefer activities that were consistent with their sex than were the androgynous or cross-sex-typed individuals. They were also more likely to select gender-appropriate than gender-inappropriate activities, even if engaging in the gender-inappropriate activity could have earned them more money. The sex-typed persons also felt worse when they performed gender-inappropriate behaviors compared to the other groups of subjects. For instance, they reported enjoying themselves less and they felt more peculiar and nervous after performing the sex-inappropriate task. Also, the sex-typed individuals rated themselves as less masculine (if they were males) and less feminine (if they were females) after performing the gender-inappropriate activities (Bem & Lenney, 1976). Thus, sex-typed individuals tended to avoid behaviors that do not fit cultural definitions of what is gender appropriate. This finding was predicted by gender schema theory.

Bem has used the BSRI to measure subjects' gender schemas.

Spence's criticisms of the instruments used to measure femininity, masculinity, and androgyny are relevant for their use in measuring gender schemas. It may be that individuals have self-schemas organized around the concepts of self-assertiveness and interpersonal orientation, but this does not imply that a global gender schema exists within the person that includes these dimensions plus others relevant to gender.

ACTIVITY BOX

Avoidance of Gender-Inappropriate Behavior

Imagine the following situation, based on procedures used in a study by Bem and Lenney (1976). You are asked to help in a study for which photographs are needed showing individuals participating in various activities. Specifically, you will pose for photographs to be shown to persons at another university (ensuring your anonymity), who will be asked to make personality judgments about the individual in the photograph on the basis of the activity he or she is seen to be performing. You are offered a small amount of money for each of four poses, ranging from 2 cents to 6 cents, depending on the activities you select.

Female readers should select one alternative from each of the following pairs:

Pair A: 1. Make simple paper or foil flowers from clear instructions. 3 cents
2. Set up the track for an electric train (from instructions). 6 cents

Pair B: 1. Polish silverware, using a cloth and polish paste. 2 cents
2. Toss horseshoes. 4 cents

Pair C: 1. Beat egg whites with sugar to make meringue, or pie topping. 3 cents
2. Set up a construction scene using toy trucks, sand, etc. 5 cents

Pair D: 1. Decorate a vase by painting flowers on it. 4 cents
2. Put on a football helmet and tackle a dummy. 5 cents

This material is used by permission of Sandra L. Bem.

Sex as a Social Category

Research on masculinity, femininity, and androgyny locates sex differences in behavior within the personality of the individual. The gender schema approach emphasizes how individuals learn to perceive themselves and others in terms of gender. Our behavior is influenced not

Male readers should select one alternative from each of the following pairs:

Pair A: 1. Attach the handlebars and seat to a child's tricycle (directions available). 3 cents
2. Sew a torn seam. 6 cents

Pair B: 1. Scrape old paint from boards. 2 cents
2. Decorate a vase by painting flowers on it. 4 cents

Pair C: 1. Oil squeaky hinges on a metal box. 3 cents
2. Prepare a baby bottle by mixing powdered formula with milk and reassembling the bottle. 4 cents

Pair D: 1. Drill holes into a board. 3 cents
2. Roll out dough and cut out cookies. 5 cents

The first alternative in each pair of items reflects a sex-typed activity for females (in the first set) and for males (in the second set). How many "sex-typed" or "cross-sex" behaviors did you choose from the four pairs of items? Gender schematic individuals are expected to make more sex-typed choices, even if barriers to gender-inappropriate behaviors have been removed (e.g., the situation might earn them more money by selecting the cross-sex behavior and anonymity is ensured). If you chose item 1 in any pair rather than item 2 (which was slightly more lucrative), was it because you preferred a gender-appropriate task? Do you believe that you use gender schemas as guides to your own behavior or your evaluations of the behavior of others. Also, regardless of your choices, if you were asked to be photographed in a cross-sex activity, would it cause you to be uncomfortable to do so?

only by our own gender schema but it may also be influenced by the gender schemas of others. This section of the chapter examines how sex differences in behavior may be influenced by social expectations and norms about appropriate behavior for females and males. The beliefs of others about how a woman or man should behave in a situation is communicated to the individual, who is then under some pressure, perhaps not consciously experienced, to conform to those expectations. To the extent that such social pressures exist and that women and men conform to them, there will be sex differences in behavior that are not entirely due to differences in the personalities of women and men (Spence, Deaux, & Helmreich, 1985).

Even if women and men have on the average the same personal dispositions and behavioral tendencies, they may differ in their self-presentations in order to conform to sex-role stereotypes that are held by influential others. For example, on an outing a man who feels as fearful of snakes as anyone else in the group may nevertheless be the one who removes a snake from the path and, thus, appears fearless because someone in the group says, "John, you're strong, you can take care of it." Or a woman who is as competitive and intelligent as her male companion may avoid skill games because she can see that her boyfriend does not like to lose, especially to her.

Zanna and Pack (1975) tested how women's behavior is shaped by the gender stereotypes that an attractive male is perceived to hold about them. A group of female Princeton students anticipated meeting an attractive male (he was portrayed as a six-foot, one-inch, twenty-one-year-old, Princeton senior who didn't have a girlfriend and who was interested in meeting female students). In one condition he was presented as holding traditional views about the ideal woman. For instance, he agreed with statements such as, "The ideal woman would be very emotional," ". . . be very soft," ". . . be passive." He would also disagree with statements such as "The ideal woman would be very independent," ". . . be very competitive," ". . . be very dominant"). In another condition, the attractive partner was presented as holding nontraditional views about the ideal woman, which were the exact opposite of these opinions. The female subjects were asked to prepare self-descriptions for the partner based on their agreement with various gender-related statements (e.g., "I am the kind of person who is not at all dependent on other people," ". . . not at all aggressive").

In comparison to self-descriptions that the women had provided at an earlier time, women who expected to meet the "sexist" male (with traditional views about females) described themselves as more feminine, whereas women who expected to meet the "nonsexist" male (with nontraditional views about females) described themselves as more masculine.

Subjects were also given an anagrams test that supposedly measured intelligence. Actual scores on this test were to be included in information to be given to the partner. Women who expected to meet an attractive, nontraditional male outperformed women who expected to meet the attractive, traditional male. This finding suggests that the women modified their performance (acted more or less "intelligent") to meet some unspoken standards the nontraditional or traditional males held for them.

Data were also collected from another group of female students who anticipated interaction with an unattractive male (who was portrayed as a five-foot, five-inch, eighteen-year-old, non-Princeton freshman who already had a girlfriend and who wasn't interested in meeting other female college students). There were no changes in the women's self-descriptions or performance on the anagram task for the undesirable male who held traditional or nontraditional views of women.

Individuals (either females *or* males) may act in ways to confirm another's expectations if they want to impress that person. Though Zanna and Pack's research documented how females are affected by the expectations that others hold, similar results would be predicted if the subjects had been males and the partner to be impressed had been female. If an attractive female held nontraditional views about men (e.g., the ideal male should *not* be competitive, aggressive, or dominant, but he should be emotional, home-oriented, and soft), her male partner may describe himself as more feminine.

Recent research on social influence indicates that males are more likely to use self-presentational strategies in some situations than women (Eagly, Wood, & Fishbaugh, 1981). For conformity behavior (i.e., the tendency to change one's opinions in the direction of those of other group members), females are unaffected by whether others will know (surveillance) or not know (no surveillance) if their opinions on campus issues are the same as the group's. Men, however, are less likely to conform with surveillance than no surveillance. Psychologists have traditionally assumed that women compared to men are more conforming partly to foster group cohesiveness and increase friendliness among group members. But women did not differ in their conformity in the surveillance and nonsurveillance situations, indicating that social rewards did not influence their behavior. In fact men conformed less than women only under the surveillance condition. The alleged conformity tendency of females might be better described as the "nonconformity tendency" of males. Males seem to be more concerned than females about presenting themselves to others as independent thinkers even though, when others are not watching, men are as much influenced by the opinions of others as women are.

This research illustrates the important role of gender stereotypes in determining the behavior of women and men. However, the influence of social factors on sex differences in behavior is not due entirely to gender differences in self-presentations (Deaux, 1984). People may use their gender stereotypes as a guide to regulating their social interactions with a woman or man, which then influence the other's behavioral options so as to generate *behavioral confirmations* for the stereotypes (Skrypnek & Snyder, 1982). One individual's stereotypes about the nature of the sexes may begin a chain of events that causes another person to act in agreement with these stereotypes.

Skrypnek and Snyder (1982) conducted a study documenting how social interactions contribute to the perpetuation of stereotyped beliefs about men and women. Pairs of males and females were asked to divide the labor for a series of work-like tasks that varied in their sex-role connotations. Some tasks were "masculine" (e.g., fixing a light switch), others were "feminine" (e.g., icing and decorating a birthday cake). In some cases, the male subjects in the study were led to believe that their partners were male; in other cases, the partners were believed to be female (which was always true). The male subjects were more likely to choose stereotypically masculine tasks for themselves and stereotypically feminine tasks for the partner when they thought their partner was a female. When women were subsequently given the opportunity to initiate choices, women were more likely to choose feminine tasks when her partner thought she was a female compared to when her partner thought she was a male. Thus, the females' behaviors confirmed the male partners' beliefs that they were female or male.

A study by Nyquist, Sawin, and Spence (cited in Spence, 1984a) provides another example of the power of sex roles to determine behavior regardless of personality traits. Pairs of individuals in which one was high and the other low on a measure of dominance were asked to choose a leader before working on a gender-neutral task. In same-sex pairs the high-dominant individual was chosen to be leader in the vast majority of cases. In the mixed-sex pairs, however, the personality trait, dominance, was less important than the sex of the individual. When the male was high-dominant and the female, low-dominant, the male was chosen as leader. When the female was high-dominant and the male, low-dominant, however, the male was still chosen to be the leader in about 75 percent of the pairs.

An individual's behavior is influenced by beliefs or observations about what others expect of a woman or man and, thus, of them and by behaviors directed toward them because of their sex. We might say that the individual's personality is in some situations *overridden* by the expectations or behaviors of others.

Summary

The chapter examines three major approaches to the study of sex, gender, and personality: sex as a subject variable; individual differences in masculinity, femininity, and androgyny; and sex as a social category.

Sex as a subject variable is embodied in research on sex differences in personality variables. Since the start of this century, psychologists have taken for granted that biological sex is an important variable and they have searched for its essential characteristics (Morawski, 1985, 1987; Stewart & Lykes, 1985b). Although few sex differences in personality are repeatedly and reliably found, those that do occur are sensitive to situational influences. For example, sex differences in causal attributions occur if the task is labeled as masculine or is more appropriate for males than females but not if the task is more appropriate for females.

Studies demonstrating sex differences in behavior do not tell us why these differences occur. In the case of sex differences in causal attributions, however, observations of teacher behavior in classrooms and an experimental study simulating the types of feedback given to girls and boys suggest that women and men differ in the explanations they give for their successes and failures because they have experienced different sorts of feedback in the classroom.

Researchers have also focused on the psychological attributes that would identify "core" masculine and feminine characteristics of males and females. Eventually, it was decided that masculinity and femininity could be studied as if they were unrelated to biological sex. High levels of both masculinity and femininity (called "androgyny") could be found in any individual—male or female. Furthermore, the androgynous person should be psychologically healthier and more flexible in coping with various situational demands than the feminine or masculine person. The work on androgyny has been criticized because it continues to accept the basic assumption that female and male personality types (i.e., femininity and masculinity) exist and because the connection between androgyny and mental health does not always receive empirical support.

Recently, attention has shifted from femininity and masculinity as attributes of the individual to gender as a category that individuals use to a greater or lesser extent to organize information about themselves and others (called gender schema). Gender schema may serve as a guide or standard that motivates individuals to regulate their behavior according to culturally determined definitions of femaleness and maleness.

Sex is also a social stimulus. Sex differences in behavior may be influenced by social expectations about appropriate behavior for females and males. To the extent that social pressures exist and women and men conform to them, there will be sex differences in behavior that are not entirely due to differences in the personalities of women and men.

SUGGESTED READINGS

Deaux, K. (1984). From individual differences to social categories: Analysis of a decade's research on gender. *American Psychologist, 39,* 105–116. A good overview of major personality and social psychological approaches that have been used to study sex differences in behavior.

Shaver, P., & Hendrick, C. (Eds.). (1987). *Sex and gender.* Beverly Hills, CA: Sage. An excellent collection of essays on sex-role socialization, gender schema theory, gender and communication, the sociobiological approach to gender, and epistemological issues in studying gender.

Sonderegger, T. (1984). Psychology and gender.

Nebraska Symposium on Motivation (Vol. 32). Lincoln, NE: University of Nebraska Press. Well-known psychologists present their theories and research about gender. Includes an essay by Sandra Bem on gender schema theory.

Spence, J. T. (1984). Masculinity, femininity, and gender-related traits: A conceptual analysis and critique of current research. In B. A. Maher and W. B. Maher (Eds.), *Progress in experimental personality research* (Vol. 13, pp. 1–97). A thorough review and critique of the research associated with the measurement of masculine (instrumental) and feminine (expressive) traits.

REFERENCES

Andersen, S. M., & Bem, S. L. (1981). Sex typing and androgyny in dyadic interaction: Individual differences in responsiveness to physical attractiveness. *Journal of Personality and Social Psychology, 41,* 74–86.

Bem, S. L. (1974). The measurement of psychological androgyny. *Journal of Consulting and Clinical Psychology, 42,* 155–162.

Bem, S. L. (1977). On the utility of alternative procedures for assessing psychological androgyny. *Journal of Consulting and Clinical Psychology, 45,* 196–205.

Bem, S. L. (1981). Gender schema theory: A cognitive account of sex typing. *Psychological Review, 88,* 354–364.

Bem, S. L. (1984). Androgyny and gender schema

theory: A conceptual and empirical integration. *Nebraska Symposium on Motivation, 32,* 179–226.

Bem, S. L., & Lenney, E. (1976). Sex typing and the avoidance of cross-sex behavior. *Journal of Personality and Social Psychology, 33,* 48–54.

Constantinople, A. (1973). Masculinity–femininity: An exception to the famous dictum? *Psychological Bulletin, 80,* 389–407.

Crandall, V. C. (1969). Sex differences in expectancy of intellectual and academic reinforcement. In C. P. Smith (Ed.), *Achievement-related motives.* New York: Russell Sage.

Deaux, K. (1984). From individual differences to

social categories: Analysis of a decade's research on gender. *American Psychologist, 39,* 105–116.

Deaux, K., & Farris, E. (1977). Attributing causes for one's own performance: The effects of sex, norms, and outcome. *Journal of Research in Personality, 11, 59–72.*

Deaux, K., White, L., & Farris, E. (1975). Skill versus luck: Field and laboratory studies of male and female preferences. *Journal of Personality and Social Psychology, 32,* 629–636.

Dweck, C. S., Davidson, W., Nelson, S., & Enna, B. (1978). Sex differences in learned helplessness: II. The contingencies of evaluative feedback in the classroom and III. An experimental analysis. *Developmental Psychology, 14,* 268–276.

Eagly, A. H. (1987). *Sex differences in social behavior: A social-role interpretation.* Hillsdale, NJ: Lawrence Erlbaum.

Eagly, A. H., Wood, W., & Fishbaugh, L. (1981). Sex differences in conformity: Surveillance by the group as a determinant of male nonconformity. *Journal of Personality and Social Psychology, 40,* 384–394.

Karabenick, S. A., Sweeney, C., & Penrose, G. (1983). Preferences for skill versus chance-determined activities: The influence of gender and task sex-typing. *Journal of Research in Personality, 17,* 125–142.

Lenney, E. (1977). Women's self-confidence in achievement settings. *Psychological Bulletin, 84,* 1–13.

Maccoby, E. E., & Jacklin, C. N. (1974). *The psychology of sex differences.* Stanford, CA: Stanford University Press.

Morawski, J. G. (1985). The measurement of masculinity and femininity: Engendering categorical realities. *Journal of Personality, 53,* 196–223.

Morawski, J. G. (1987). The troubled quest for masculinity, femininity, and androgyny. In P. Shaver and C. Hendrick (Eds.), *Sex and gender* (pp. 44–69). Beverly Hills, CA: Sage.

Orlofsky, J. L. (1981). Relationship between sex role attitudes and personality traits and the Sex Role Behavior Scale-1: A new measure of masculine and feminine role behaviors and interests. *Journal of Personality and Social Psychology, 40,* 927–940.

Pandey, J., & Griffith, W. (1974). Attraction and helping. *Psychonomic Society, 3,* 123–124.

Piliavin, J., & Unger, R. K. (1985). The helpful but helpless female: Myth or reality? In V. E. O'Leary, R. K. Unger, & B. S. Wallston (Eds.), *Women, gender, and social psychology.* Hillsdale, NJ: Lawrence Erlbaum.

Rosenfield, D., & Stephan, W. G. (1978). Sex differences in attributions for sex-typed tasks. *Journal of Personality, 46,* 244–259.

Shaver, P., & Hendrick, C. (Eds.) (1987). *Sex and gender.* Beverly Hills, CA: Sage.

Skrypnek, B. J., & Snyder, M. (1982). On the self-perpetuating nature of stereotypes about women and men. *Journal of Experimental Social Psychology, 18,* 277–291.

Spence, J. T. (1984a). Masculinity, femininity, and gender-related traits: A conceptual analysis and critique of current research. In B. A. Maher and W. B. Maher (Eds.), *Progress in experimental personality research* (Vol. 13, (pp. 1–97). New York: Academic Press.

Spence, J. T. (1984b). Gender identity and its implications for the concepts of masculinity and femininity. *Nebraska Symposium on Motivation, 32,* 59–96.

Spence, J. T., Deaux, K., & Helmreich, R. L. (1985). Sex roles in contemporary American society. In G. Lindsey and E. Aronson (Eds.), *Handbook of social psychology* (3rd ed.) (pp. 149–178). New York: Random House.

Spence, J. T., & Helmreich, R. L. (1978). *Masculinity and femininity: Their psychological dimensions, correlates, and antecedents.* Austin, TX: University of Texas Press.

Spence, J. T., & Helmreich, R. L. (1986). Personality Attributes Questionnaire (PAQ). Unpublished manuscript, University of Texas, Austin.

Spence, J. T., Helmreich, R. L., & Stapp, J. (1974). The Personal Attributes Questionnaire: A measure of sex role stereotypes and masculinity–femininity. *JSAS Catalog of*

Selected Documents in Psychology, 4, 43. (Ms. No. 617).

Stewart, A. J., & Lykes, M. B. (Eds.). (1985a). Conceptualizing gender in personality theory and research. *Journal of Personality, 53,* 93–405.

Stewart, A., & Lykes, M. B. (1985b). Conceptualizing gender in personality theory and research. *Journal of Personality, 53,* 93–101.

Terman, L. M., & Miles, C. C. (1936). *Sex and personality.* New York: McGraw-Hill.

Unger, R. K. (1985). Epilogue: Toward a synthesis of women, gender, and social psychology. In V. E. O'Leary, R. K. Unger, & B. S. Wallston (Eds.), *Women, gender, and social psychology* (pp. 349–358). Hillsdale, NJ: Lawrence Erlbaum.

Zanna, M. P., & Pack, S. J. (1975). On the self-fulfilling nature of apparent sex differences in behavior. *Journal of Experimental Social Psychology, 11,* 583–591.

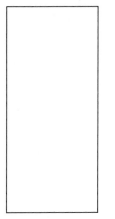

CHAPTER 11

Control

JERRY M. BURGER

The Impact of Perceived Control
  Positive Aspects of Perceived
    Control
  Negative Aspects of Perceived
    Control
**Individual Differences in
  Perceived Control: Locus of
  Control**
  Some Differences Between
    Internals and Externals
  Issues in Locus of Control
    Research

**Individual Differences in
  Motivation for Control:
  Desire for Control**
ACTIVITY BOX: **The Desirability
  of Control Scale**
  Cognitive Responses
  Motivational Responses
  Affective Responses
Summary
SUGGESTED READINGS
REFERENCES

Lord, give me
The strength to change the things that I can,
The patience to accept the things that I cannot,
And the wisdom to know the difference.

During the past several years I have seen the above quote in various forms attributed to an old Jewish prayer, an old Dutch saying, an old German saying, Thomas Jefferson, Abraham Lincoln, and Mark Twain. The widespread credit for this sentiment suggests that it may strike at the heart of a concept central to the lives of many people. There are some things in life that we can and probably should do something about. Exercising control over our environment allows us to meet our needs, to avoid or end experiences we dislike, and to feel generally competent. However, there also are severe limitations on what we can do about who we are and what happens to us. Although we all recognize some obvious limitations (e.g., we cannot flap our arms and fly), there is a large gray area of events over which we may or may not have any influence. As the saying suggests, having the wisdom to know when we can make a difference and when we should accept things as they are would seem to be one of the keys to happiness and personal adjustment.

It should not be surprising, therefore, that most major personality theorists have in one way or another wrestled with the question of how much control people have over their environment and how this affects behavior. Debates among personality theorists have often centered around the question of control. B. F. Skinner (1971), for example, has argued that people incorrectly attribute their behavior to their own free choices. He urges us to acknowledge that our behavior is largely controlled by the environment and to abandon the illusion of personal control that most people now maintain. Carl Rogers (1961), on the other hand, has emphasized the importance of free choice in his theory of personality. He encourages people to recognize the extent to which they are personally responsible for what happens to them and to stop attributing their actions to forces outside of their control.

Other theorists have focused on how the perception of personal control influences personality development and behavior. Alfred Adler, for example, centered his theory of personality around the notion of a *striving for superiority* (Ansbacher & Ansbacher, 1956). Some people, Adler argued, are highly motivated to overcome feelings of inferiority. Their behavior is driven by a need to overcome life's obstacles and achieve. Adler identified other people who have incorrectly accepted their inferiority, overwhelmed by their inability to control their fate. Still other psychologists have centered their descriptions of human personality around the concept of personal control. White (1959) and deCharms (1968), for example, have argued that a need to control the events in one's life is perhaps the primary human motive.

Over the past two decades the concept of personal control also has been embraced by a large number of personality researchers. The bulk of this research has been concerned with responses to *perceived* control, rather than actual control. That is, how much a person can actually influence events is not as important as the amount of control that person believes he or she has. If I perceive no control over my ability to do well on a test, then I probably will do nothing to improve my score. If I believe I can control the outcome of the test, I might study and work a little harder. But whether or not I actually can control the test outcome is relatively unimportant in determining my behavior. Of course, how people react when they find their perceptions of control are in error is an interesting issue (e.g., Taylor, 1983). However, the research reported here is concerned with the effects of perceiving that one is or is not in control.

We will begin exploring this question by examining the various reactions people have to changes in their level of perceived control. Next, the role of two relevant individual difference variables will be examined. These are locus of control, the extent to which we typically see ourselves in control of what happens to us, and desire for control, the extent to which we generally are motivated to control the events in our lives. Where people fall on each of these personality dimensions will have an impact on a large number of behaviors.

The Impact of Perceived Control

Before looking at some specific personality variables associated with personal control, it is useful to examine how changes in a person's level of perceived control affect his or her behavior. Another way of looking at this is to ask if the perception of personal control is good or bad. Most of the theories of personality mentioned earlier seem to assume that the more control a person has, the better off that person is.

Positive Aspects of Perceived Control

A strong case can be made that feeling in control of events is tantamount to good personal adjustment and mental health (e.g., Lefcourt, 1980, Seligman, 1975). Much of the research that supports this conclusion is concerned with the debilitating effects that are found when people are deprived of control over important events. This has been well demonstrated in research designed to test the theory of *learned helplessness* (Abramson, Seligman, & Teasdale, 1978; Seligman, 1975). Learned helplessness begins when we perceive an inability to control some important aspect of our lives. For example, you may conclude that nothing you do is going to help you to get into medical school. This would be a reasonable conclusion for many people to draw, and understanding the limits of our abilities is probably a sign of good adjustment. However, people sometimes incorrectly generalize these feelings of no control to other situations over which they might exercise some control. Thus, the frustrated pre-med student might also decide that he or she is unable to do well at any type of job, unable to make friends, or incapable of succeeding at other personal challenges. In essence, the person has learned (incorrectly) that he or she is helpless to do anything about the problems and opportunities that life throws his or her way. The result is a decline in motivation and productivity. If nothing is done to break this thinking, the person is a likely candidate for depression.

The development of learned helplessness has been demonstrated in a large number of laboratory investigations (cf. Peterson & Seligman, 1984). The standard procedures (e.g., Hiroto & Seligman, 1975) present subjects with several trials of an aversive stimulus, such as blasts of irritating noise. Some subjects can do something to stop (control) the noise, such as solving a simple word puzzle. Other subjects can do nothing to stop the noise. Following their exposure to controllable or uncontrollable noise, subjects typically are given a different type of task to work on, and perhaps a measure of depression. People subjected to the uncontrollable aversive noise tend to inappropriately generalize their perception of no control to this second task. They perform more poorly than subjects in the controllable-noise condition and often report higher levels of depression.

Langer and Rodin (1976) conducted research to explain why helplessness-like behavior often occurs among residents of old-age homes. Residents on one floor of a retirement home were instructed to take more control of their own lives. They were encouraged to recognize the influence they could have over the course of daily events at the home. Activities on the floor were arranged to emphasize the role of residents' personal responsibility. Another floor of the home served as a comparison group. These residents were given no control-enhancing instructions nor any increased opportunities for control. The investigators found that the residents who were given the increased personal control became more active, more well-adjusted, and healthier than the group not given this perception. A follow-up investigation at the same residence found that the positive effects of the control-enhancing instructions were still present eighteen months later (Rodin & Langer, 1977).

Other research has found that decreases in perceived (and sometimes actual) control are related to increased feelings of crowding in congested areas (Schmidt & Keating, 1979), poorer academic performances (Dweck & Licht, 1980), and destructive behavior (Allen & Greenberger, 1980). On the other hand, increases in perceived control have been associated with progress in a weight-loss program (Mendonca & Brehm, 1983) and better performance on achievement tasks (Perlmuter & Monty, 1977). In short, there is much research to suggest that control is a very positive commodity.

Negative Aspects of Perceived Control

Does this mean that the more control we have in our lives the better? Some recent research suggests that this is not always the case. At least three features of increased personal control may make it less than desirable for some people sometimes (Burger, 1989). First, when we are given control over a situation, it also means that we typically are held more responsible for its outcome. This increase in responsibility can then lead to an increase in concern for what others will think of us, and a subsequent increase in anxiety. For example, the business executive who is promoted to a position of increased power may enjoy his or her ability to control the direction the company takes, but also recognizes that he or she will be held responsible in the event of a poor company performance.

This effect was demonstrated in a laboratory experiment (Burger, Brown, & Allen, 1983). Some subjects were given increased feelings of control by being allowed to select which of three tasks they wanted to be tested on. This choice seemingly would allow them to select the task they would do best on, and thereby make them feel better about their chances of performing well. However, these subjects reported *higher* levels of anxiety before working on the task than subjects who were not given this choice. Apparently the increase in concern for how they would be evaluated increased for the subjects who had been given control over the choice of tasks. In support of this interpretation, when a new experimenter unaware of the subject's choice was used to administer the task (thereby reducing the subjects' concern for what the experimenter would think of them), no increase in anxiety was found.

Sometimes people become so concerned about their public image they engage in *self-handicapping* behavior (cf. Arkin & Baumgardner, 1985). That is, fear of looking bad in the event of failure becomes so powerful people sometimes intentionally reduce their control over the outcome (e.g., take performance-inhibiting drugs). This action results in an increased likelihood of failure, but because the person has less control over the situation, he or she can take less responsibility for the outcome.

A second consequence of increased control is an increase in predictability. Having control over an event usually means an increase in understanding what things will happen and when they will happen. Although many theorists have talked about how preferable predictable events are to unpredictable events (e.g., Kelly, 1955), the research in this area is quite mixed (cf. Averill, 1973; Miller, 1981; Thompson, 1981). Knowing when something will happen may be desirable, but sometimes people prefer not to know. Watching a clock count down the seconds to an electric shock, for example, has been found to generate more anxiety than not knowing when the shock is coming (Monat, Averill, & Lazarus, 1972). This may be why most people prefer to have someone else take a blood sample from them, rather than having to prick their own finger (Burger, McWard, & LaTorre, 1986).

Third, sometimes being in control of a situation increases rather than decreases the chances of experiencing something aversive. There are many situations that are likely to turn out worse if I am given control instead of someone who might be more competent. This is why people usually are willing to give control of their health care to a doctor they trust, and why people who have been drinking are, hopefully, willing to allow someone else to drive them home from a party. In an empirical demonstration of this effect, Miller (1980) gave people the choice of performing a reaction-time task themselves or of turning control of the task over to a partner. She found that most people preferred to relinquish control when they believed their partner would do better on the task and avoid an electric shock for both of them.

In summary, perceiving that one is in control sometimes is desired and results in positive outcomes (e.g., lowered anxiety, better health). However, at other times increasing the amount of control a person has over a situation is not preferred and may result in some negative reactions. In all of these cases, however, there are important differences among people. For example, even though most people prefer to have someone else administer a blood sample, there are those who still prefer to do it themselves. Although some people tend to give up and avoid challenging tasks, others find challenges stimulating and rise to the occasion. How can we account for these differences? This is a question of individual differences.

The remainder of this chapter is concerned with two individual difference variables that help to explain some of the differences in reactions to changes in personal control. One of these, locus of control, is concerned with the extent to which people generally see themselves as in control or not in control of the things that happen to them. The second variable, desire for control, is concerned with the extent to which people typically are motivated to control the events in their lives. As will be described, where you fall on each of these personality dimensions may have important implications for such things as how well you do in school, how well you cope with stress, and how susceptible you are to depression.

Individual Differences in Perceived Control: Locus of Control

We often encounter situations in which the amount of control we can exercise is not entirely clear. Is getting a good job up to you, or is it the result of luck or knowing the right person? Can you make friends if you want to, or do you have to be in the right circumstances? When your car breaks down, is there something you could have done to prevent it, or are such problems inevitable? How you respond to these questions probably is indicative of your own locus of control level. As will be described whether or not you generally feel as if you can exercise some control will have an impact on how you respond to these types of situations.

The concept of individual differences in perceived personal control evolved out of Julian Rotter's (1954) social learning theory of personality. A key concept for predicting behavior in Rotter's model is the extent to which a person expects that his or her behavior will be reinforced. Generally we rely on our past experiences in similar situations when making these estimates. If, for example, you have been reinforced with a good grade when you stayed up all night studying for an exam, then the likelihood of doing this the next time you find yourself in a night-before-the-big-test situation is quite high.

But how do we make these estimates in new situations? Rotter proposed that people will use fairly stable *generalized expectancies* about their likelihood of reinforcement in these cases. Individual differences in these expectancies usually are referred to today as differences in *locus of control*. At one end of this dimension are those people who believe that almost everything that happens to them is under their control. They tend to take credit for their successes, blame for their failures, and believe there are actions they can take to overcome obstacles and prevent future problems from developing. Rotter called these people *internals*. At the other extreme are those who believe that most of what happens to them is caused by forces outside of their control. These people are likely to attribute their successes and failures to such things as luck or the actions of powerful forces (e.g., "administrators" or "the system"). People who generally hold this orientation are called *externals*.

Most people, of course, fall somewhere between these two extremes. Like other individual difference variables, locus of control should be thought of as a continuum of points along a dimension ranging from extreme internals at one end and extreme externals at the other. Rotter (1966) developed a scale to measure the extent to which people tend to perceive their amount of control in an internal or external manner. Externals, for example, tend to agree with statements such as "Many of the unhappy things in people's lives are partly due to bad luck," whereas internals tend to agree with statements such as "People's misfortunes result from the mistakes they make." Like other trait-like measures, scores on this scale tend to be fairly stable. That is, unless your life is suddenly changed in a manner that causes you to rethink how much control you exercise over events, your locus of control level as measured today probably will be very similar to your score if measured a month or even a year from now.

Some Differences Between Internals and Externals

Since Rotter (1966) introduced the locus of control concept, thousands of studies have been conducted comparing internals and externals on nearly every behavior and personality dimension that you could think of (see Phares, 1976, and Lefcourt, 1982, for reviews). Some have suggested that interest in locus of control, particularly at its peak of popularity in the late 1960s and early 1970s (during the Vietnam War and the civil rights movement), was a reflection of the concern about personal control and the influence of powerful social and political forces. Then again, it is difficult to think of many situations for which the question of personal control is not an important one. How much effort I put into trying to influence a situation certainly is a reflection of how much control I believe I have. It should not be surprising, therefore, that much of this research has been successful in demonstrating the role of locus of control. Naturally, to review even a small part of this research is not possible here. Instead, let's look at the relationship between locus of control and two well-researched behaviors: academic achievement and coping with stress.

Academic Achievement

Who is more likely to do well in school, an internal or an external? Imagine an internal and an external college student both enrolled in a class that is reputed to be difficult and taught by a professor who is known to be a tough grader. The internal may approach the class with the idea that with enough work it is possible for him or her to beat the odds and get a good grade out of this professor. The external, on the other hand, is more likely to conclude that there is no way to do well in this class no matter how hard he or she studies. Given the different approaches to the class, it seems reasonable to expect that the internal will study more, do better on the tests, and get the higher grade. In fact, this generally is what is found in research with college students (Nord, Connelly, & Daignault, 1974; Prociuk & Breen, 1975).

The impact of locus of control on academic performance is not limited to college students, however. Researchers have examined this relationship in classes ranging from young elementary students to graduate students. Reviews of this research find that while there are some exceptions, there tends to be a fairly consistent relationship between internality and higher academic achievement (cf. Bar-Tal & Bar-Zohar, 1977; Findley & Cooper, 1983; Lefcourt, 1982).

Why do internals appear to perform consistently better than externals? One reason has already been mentioned. Internals are more likely than externals to believe that there are actions they can take to do well on a particular task. In addition, internals appear better able than externals to plan and work toward long-term goals, such as a grade at the end of the semester or a degree after several years of work (Lefcourt, 1982). Internals also are better able to establish reachable goals for themselves and tend to take more credit for their academic successes (Gilmor & Reid, 1978, 1979). Thus, internals seem to have a better idea than externals about what they can do and probably are more motivated by success to work toward those goals. One note of caution should be mentioned, however. These studies cannot demonstrate the order of this relationship. That is, it is possible that some students develop a belief that there is little they can do to improve their grades (an external orientation) *because* they have not done well in school.

Coping with Stress

All of us, internals and externals, occasionally experience stressful events. Stress results from the perception that the demands a situation places on us are much greater than we believe we are capable of dealing with (Lazarus & Folkman, 1984). Among those situations often cited as stressful are high pressure situations at school or on the job (such as final exams or annual reports), interpersonal difficulties (such as problems with dating partners or parents), and negative life events (such as personal losses, health or financial problems). Researchers have long recognized that not everyone reacts the same to these situations. Some people respond to even mild stress with anxiety, depression, loss of sleep, and low productivity. Others appear able to pass through stressful periods with a minimal amount of pain. One variable that may account for these differences is the person's locus of control level.

For many years researchers have found that externals are more likely to react to stressful events with anxiety and depression than are internals (cf. Benassi, Sweeney, & Dufour, 1988; Lefcourt, 1980). This finding is consistent with the laboratory research on control presented earlier. Generally, although there are exceptions, people who believe they have some control over aversive laboratory events show fewer problems than those who do not hold this belief. It is not important that the subjects in these experiments actually have control, but rather that they believe they do (Glass & Singer, 1972). Internals, therefore, who are more likely to see themselves in control of a given stressful situation, should suffer less than the externals, who do not often share this belief.

However, real-world stressful events typically last longer and are of a more serious nature than the relatively mild stressors used in laboratory investigations. Therefore, some researchers have examined the long-term impact of serious negative life events. Anderson (1977), for example, compared the reactions of internal and external business-men who had suffered through a hurricane and subsequent flooding more than three years after the incident. He found that internals reported using more effective coping strategies (e.g., problem-solving approaches) and experienced less stress compared to the externals.

Another team of investigators compared the long-term and short-term coping of internals and externals (Lefcourt, Miller, Ware, & Sherk, 1981). Subjects were asked about their experiences with a number of negative life events (e.g., death of a loved one, severe illness) at various points in their lives and how well they had coped with them.

The results indicated that internals and externals have similar reactions to severe events soon after the event has occurred. Internals appeared to gain the advantage, however, in the long-run. After experiencing the death of a loved one, for example, internals seem better able to overcome their grief and readjust their lives during the recovery stage (sometimes as long as two or three years later) than do externals.

Lefcourt et al. (1981) speculate that the internals' superior coping with stress may be caused by their tendency to develop new goals and concentrate on new challenges and situations. Externals, on the other hand, may retreat from challenges, thus continuing their feelings of helplessness. This reasoning is consistent with other research indicating that internals generally learn to utilize more effective coping strategies (Parkes, 1984). For example, some research (Lefcourt, Martin, & Saleh, 1984; Sandler & Lakey, 1982) indicates that internals make more efficient use of social supports than do externals. Internals may benefit more from hearing the advice of friends and family members who encourage them to avoid blaming themselves and get on with living their lives. For all these reasons, it seems that the internal perspective allows for more efficient coping with stressful events, particularly long-term coping with severe negative life experiences.

Issues in Locus of Control Research

Two issues that confront personality trait researchers are the questions of unidimensionality and specificity. *Unidimensionality* refers to the extent to which an individual difference construct, or more particularly the measure used to assess the construct, is comprised of a single concept. That is, when subjects complete the items on Rotter's (1966) Locus of Control Scale, are all of the items measuring the same thing, or are they perhaps measuring several personality variables that are somewhat similar, yet conceptually distinct? The issue of *specificity* concerns the number of situations to which it is useful to apply the concept. For example, is it useful to think of one's locus of control level as a fairly stable degree of internality or externality that applies equally to achievement situations, interpersonal relationships, and political involvement? Or would it be better to increase our ability to predict behavior in, for example, academic settings, by measuring specifically the extent to which a person believes he or she has control over his or her class performance? Each of these issues will be addressed.

Unidimensionality

Many researchers have argued that locus of control, at least as conceived of and measured by Rotter, is comprised of more than one personality concept. Most of these investigators have utilized a statistical concept called factor analysis to determine the extent to which the Locus of Control Scale measures one or more than one personality variable (e.g., Collins, 1974; Levenson, 1974; Paulhus, 1983). Although there is not always agreement on how many or which dimensions make up the overall locus of control score, there seems to a general consensus that more than one dimension can be identified and measured. Because the various dimensions are only slightly related to one another, it is possible to be internal about some matters of your life, such as whether or not you will get a desired job, and external about other parts of your life, such as your ability to make and develop satisfying interpersonal relationships.

Paulhus (1983; Paulhus & Christie, 1981) has identified three "spheres" for which locus of control scores can be measured. The first of these is the *personal efficacy* sphere. People who are internals in this sphere of their lives believe they have a great deal of control over the outcome of personal achievement situations. They believe that how well they do in school, in sports, or even when working on a crossword puzzle is the result of their own efforts and abilities. Next, there is the *interpersonal control* dimension. If you are internal on this dimension, then you generally believe that your ability to develop friendships and maintain pleasant relationships is largely under your control. Finally, Paulhus identifies the *sociopolitical control* sphere. People with test scores falling in the internal end of this dimension tend to believe that they can have an influence on the outcome of political decisions and some of the larger societal forces that shape our lives.

The value of assessing three different locus of control dimensions lies in the increased predictability that comes from matching the locus of control sphere with the behavior of interest. For example, Paulhus (1983) surveyed college students about their participation in a recent election. We might expect that, because they generally believe in their ability to influence important events, internals would be more likely than externals to vote. Paulhus found support for this prediction, but only when looking at the subjects' locus of control scores from the sociopolitical sphere scale. Scores from the other two locus of control spheres were not related to whether or not the students had voted. Thus, people can be internal about one part of their lives and act accordingly, but remain external about other parts of their lives.

Specificity

A recent trend in locus of control research is to identify a person's locus of control level for a specific type of behavior or for a specific type of situation or problem. One example of this is locus of control about one's health (cf. Strickland, 1978; Wallston & Wallston, 1981). Health professionals often observe that some patients take an active role in their treatment and in the prevention of future health problems, whereas others act as if there is nothing that they can do to improve their health. The extent to which the patient believes he or she can control his or her health would seem to account for these differences.

People who generally believe that there is something they can do to improve their health should engage in behaviors that will make them healthier than those who do not. We would expect, therefore, that those who score on the internal end of the Health Locus of Control Scales (Wallston & Wallston, 1981) would be healthier than those scoring on the external end. Although there are exceptions, research generally supports this conclusion. For example, internals have been found to be more likely than externals to seek out information about potentially dangerous health risks (Wallston, Maides & Wallston, 1976), to succeed at efforts to stop smoking (Kaplan & Cowles, 1978), and to request specific medications from medical professionals for their illnesses (Krantz, Baum, & Wideman, 1980). Internals also generally expect that their medical treatment is going to work, even with cancer (Marks, Richardson, Graham, & Levine, 1986). Finally, Krantz et al. (1980) found internal college students reported to the health clinic fewer times than did externals. In short, the extent to which a person believes that he or she can control his or her health is related to health behaviors and eventually to one's health.

When researchers compare the Health Locus of Control Scale with Rotter's general Locus of Control Scale, the more specific scale almost always does a better job of predicting health behavior (Wallston & Wallston, 1981). However, there is a price to pay for this. Knowing that someone is highly internal about health behavior tells us very little about how he or she might behave in, for example, academic situations. A more general locus of control score, however, will provide some information about both health behavior and academic performance, albeit less than two measures designed to specifically assess locus of control in each of these areas. When deciding whether to use a general or specific measure of locus of control, a researcher must weigh the value of increased predictability against the advantage of increased generalizability of his or her results.

Individual Differences in Motivation for Control: Desire for Control

Many personality theorists have proposed that people are motivated to exercise control (e.g., deCharms, 1968; White, 1959). Influencing important events in our lives is said to make us feel competent and masterful. However, the strength of this motive is not the same for all people. There are relatively stable individual differences in the extent to which people prefer to see themselves in control (Burger & Cooper, 1979). That is, some people have a strong need to control what happens to them, and other people do not. Like other personality trait variables, this individual difference is assumed to be stable across time as well as across situations. Although there naturally will be fluctuations in the

ACTIVITY BOX

The Desirability of Control Scale

To get an idea of your own level of desire for control, you can take the following personality test. Using a 7-point scale, indicate the extent to which each of the following statements applies to you. That is, if the statement always applies to you, place a 7 in the appropriate space. If the statement doesn't apply to you at all, answer 1. Use the numbers 2 through 6 to indicate degrees of partial agreement.

_____ 1. I prefer a job in which I have a lot of control over what I do and when I do it.

_____ 2. I enjoy political participation because I want to have as much say in running government as possible.

_____ 3. I try to avoid situations in which someone else tells me what to do.

_____ 4. I would prefer to be a leader than a follower.

_____ 5. I enjoy being able to influence the actions of others.

_____ 6. I am careful to check everything on an automobile before I leave for a long trip.

_____ 7. Others usually know what is best for me.

_____ 8. I enjoy making my own decisions.

_____ 9. I enjoy having control over my own destiny.

_____ 10. I would rather someone else take over the leadership role when I'm involved in a group project.

_____ 11. I consider myself to be generally more capable of handling situations than others are.

_____ 12. I'd rather run my own business and make my own mistakes than listen to someone else's orders.

_____ 13. I like to get a good idea of what a job is all about before I begin.

_____ 14. When I see a problem, I prefer to do something about it rather than sit by and let it continue.

extent to which we are motivated to control events, over time there should emerge a typical level of this need that affects many important aspects of our lives.

Before reading further, complete the personality inventory found in the Activity Box. This is the Desirability of Control (DC) Scale

---

_____ 15. When it comes to orders, I would rather give them than receive them.

_____ 16. I wish I could push many of life's daily decisions off on someone else.

_____ 17. When driving, I try to avoid putting myself in a situation in which I could be hurt by someone else's mistake.

_____ 18. I prefer to avoid situations in which someone else has to tell me what it is I should be doing.

_____ 19. There are many situations in which I would prefer only one choice rather than have to make a decision.

_____ 20. I like to wait and see if someone else is going to solve a problem so that I don't have to be bothered with it.

To determine your score, reverse the values you gave items 7, 10, 16, 19, and 20 (i.e., 1 = 7, 2 = 6, 3 = 5, 4 = 4, 5 = 3, 6 = 2, 7 = 1). Then add the 20 values together. The higher the score, the higher is your desire for control. You can compare your score with those of other college students who have taken this test by looking at the following norm table:

	Mean	Standard Deviation
Males	102.7	11.31
Females	97.3	11.64
Combined	99.1	11.80

From Burger and Cooper (1979), pp. 384-85.

These norms should be used for comparison and descriptive purposes only. It would be inappropriate to diagnose oneself as, for example, prone to depression, with this information alone.

developed by Burger and Cooper (1979). The DC Scale identifies the extent to which people typically are high or low in their motivation for control. People who score high on the scale (high-DC people) are described as "decisive, assertive, and active. They generally seek to influence others when such influence is advantageous" (Burger & Cooper, 1979, p. 383). High-DC people are highly motivated to manipulate events to avoid unpleasant situations or failures. They are likely to become the leaders in group situations. In contrast, those who score low (low-DC people) are described as "generally nonassertive, passive, and indecisive. These people are less likely to attempt to influence others and may prefer that many of their daily decisions be made by others" (p. 383).

Scores on the scale have been found to be only slightly related to scores on measures of locus of control (Dembroski, MacDougall, & Musante, 1984). Thus, the extent to which a person prefers to be in control is not necessarily related to the extent to which that person sees himself or herself in control. Although men typically score slightly higher than women in their desire for control, the difference is small. The framework presented in figure 11.1 has been developed to explain how a person's desire for control level will interact with the amount of control he or she perceives in a given situation to influence the response to that situation. Three general types of responses can follow: cognitive responses, motivational responses, and affective responses. Examples of each will be described.

FIGURE 11.1

Model for Desire for Control and Situation Interaction

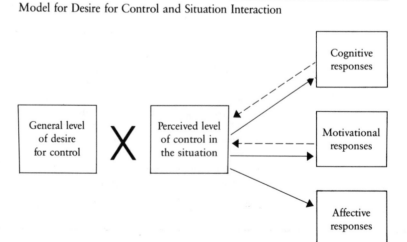

Cognitive Responses

What happens when a person with a high desire for control encounters a situation over which he or she has relatively little control? The person may reinterpret the situation in a manner that satisfies the need to see himself or herself in control. This reaction is possible because in many situations the extent to which we are able to control events is rather vague. For example, how much of your performance in a class (i.e., your grade) is determined by you and how much is the result of a good or bad professor? A person high in desire for control is likely to assume there is something that can be done to affect his or her grade.

But what about situations in which the amount of control one has over events is less ambiguous? For example, would people high in desire for control also distort their perceived amount of control over something as obviously chance-determined as flipping a coin or rolling a pair of dice? A series of investigations suggests that people high in desire for control may even distort their perceptions of control over these types of events, and that this distortion may be related to gambling behavior.

Under certain circumstances people will succumb to what has been called the *illusion of control* (Langer, 1975). Sometimes people believe they have some influence over events that a rational observer would easily recognize as chance-determined. The illusion of control is likely to develop when the chance-determined event is made to resemble a skill-determined event. For example, people who are allowed to throw the dice often feel more control over the outcome of a dice game than those who simply watch another person throw the dice or those who throw the dice without knowing what the winning number will be (Strickland, Lewicki, & Katz, 1966). Although the dice thrower cannot possibly influence the outcome of the game, somehow having the dice in one's hand gives the feeling of being able to shoot for the winning number and thereby control the game.

Given this observation, people high in desire for control should be more likely than lows to succumb to the illusion of control. High-DC people are more motivated to control this situation (especially if money is at stake) than low-DC people. They may interpret a chance-determined situation as one they can exercise some control over, satisfying the need to feel in control.

Several studies have found support for this prediction. Burger and Cooper (1979) placed high- and low-DC college students in a simulated gambling game. Some of the subjects were allowed to throw the dice in this game knowing what the winning number would be, whereas others had to make their bets and throw the dice without knowing the number that they were shooting for. The high-DC subjects bet more when they knew the number to shoot for than when they did not, the illusion of control effect. The subjects with low DC scores showed no tendency to increase their bets when in the illusion of control situation. When they did not know the winning number ahead of time, the high-DC subjects did not bet any more than did the lows. Another investigation (Burger & Schnerring, 1982), in which subjects either did or did not know the winning card in a card-drawing game, found the same effect, but only when the outcome of the game was important (i.e., prizes could be won).

Other studies have found that high-DC people are more likely than lows to fall for the illusion of control when playing with familiar rather than unfamiliar cards, and when they are led to believe that they have guessed correctly during most of the initial trials in a "heads or tails" coin-toss game (Burger, 1986). In the latter example, high-DC college students who had an early string of luck in guessing if a coin would come up heads or tails actually predicted that on the average they would be able to guess the outcome of nearly 60 percent of future coin tosses. Finally, compulsive gamblers with a high desire for control bet more and are more likely to gamble on games with a high amount of illusion of control than are lows (Burger & Smith, 1985).

This research suggests that people with a high desire for control often selectively interpret information in a manner that satisfies their general need for control. Ironically, by convincing themselves that they are able to control events they in fact cannot, high-DC people may be decreasing their amount of control. Believing incorrectly that one can control the outcome of a dice game or the outcome of a final exam may cause the high-DC person to engage in inappropriate behaviors that eventually could lead to losing one's money or inefficiently expending one's efforts.

Motivational Responses

One way to deal with an uncontrollable situation is to reinterpret the situation in a manner that satisfies the desire for control. Another option is to change the situation so that it comes in line with our need to feel in control. What does a high-DC person do, for example, when he or she comes upon a problem at work that at first seems too difficult to resolve? Giving up, admitting that this problem is too difficult, or asking someone else for help all seem inconsistent with the description of a high desire for control. More likely, a difficult task might be perceived as a challenge. Overcoming this challenge should prove very satisfying in reaffirming the high-DC person's perception of personal competence and mastery. Based on the model presented in figure 11.2, people with high and low desire for control differ in their achievement-

FIGURE 11.2

Model for Desire for Control and Achievement-Related Behavior

	Aspiration level	Response to challenge	Persistence	Attributions for success and failure
Theoretical relationship with high DC as compared with low DC	Select harder tasks; set goals more realistically	React with greater effort	Work at difficult task longer	More likely to attribute success to self and failure to unstable source
High-DC benefit	Higher goals are achieved	Difficult tasks are completed	Difficult tasks are completed	Motivation level remains high
High-DC liablity	May attempt goals too difficult	May develop performance-inhibiting reactions	May invest too much effort	May develop an illusion of control

From Burger (1985). Used by permission of the American Psychological Association.

related behavior in at least four ways (Burger, 1985). First, high-DC people may have higher and more realistic aspirations levels than do low-DC people. High-DC subjects in fact do predict they will do better and chose to work on harder tasks than lows when working on number and word puzzles (Burger, 1985). In addition, the high-DC subjects were better able to adjust their predictions in a realistic manner when they found that their initial estimates were too high. Undergraduate students have been found to approach their classes in a similar manner. High-DC students predict they will obtain higher grades than low-DC students. This higher aspiration was found when asking about an upcoming test, the final grade for a specific class, this quarter's grade-point average, and this year's grade-point average (Burger, 1987a; 1987b).

The second difference between high-DC and low-DC people concerns how they react to challenging tasks. Because admitting one's inability to master a task is more threatening to high-DC people, it is not surprising that high-DC subjects did better than lows when given a very difficult proofreading task (i.e., correcting errors in a manuscript while counting the number of proper nouns and the number of times the word *the* appeared). When the task was relatively easy (just correct errors), the two groups did not differ (Burger, 1985).

High-DC people also are more persistent when working on a difficult task than are lows. Burger (1985) gave undergraduates some word puzzles to work on. In reality, all of the puzzles were impossible to solve. Low-DC subjects were quick to give up on a puzzle and move on to the next one. The high-DC subjects were more likely to stay with the impossible puzzle, even though they were obviously making no progress. It should come as no surprise that high-DC people are more likely to accomplish difficult tasks. However, as this study illustrates, this persistence in the face of a task that eventually proves too difficult may not result in efficient achievement striving.

Desire for control level has been related to the explanations people give for their successes and failures in an achievement situation. High-DC people tend to explain their performances on tasks in terms that help them to maintain a sense of control (Burger & Hemans, 1988). High-DC subjects who succeed tend to attribute success to their own efforts and abilities (Burger, 1985, 1987a), which allows them to maintain a sense of continued ability to control the outcome of the situation. High-DC subjects who fail have been found to attribute the failure in a way that does not force them to admit to a lack of control. Winning a tennis game might be attributed to superior ability, whereas losing the game might be attributed to some lucky breaks for the opponent. Low-DC subjects show these same general self-serving tendencies, but to a lesser degree than highs. The high-DC attributional pattern has the advantage of maintaining a high level of motivation for the next game, regardless if one wins or loses. The negative side of this is that the high-DC person may tackle tasks well beyond his or her capabilities.

Do desire for control scores predict achievement? The answer seems to be yes. High-DC subjects appear to perform better on most laboratory tasks, if the tasks are made challenging (Burger, 1985, 1987a). In addition, Burger (1987b) found a significant correlation between a student's desire for control score at the beginning of the term and his or her final grade in a psychology course. In a second investigation, high-DC students were found to have higher overall grade point averages than low-DC students for a 2-year period following the DC testing. Not surprisingly, the high-DC students reported that good grades were more important to them than did the low-DC students. Finally, high-DC students are more likely to become motivated when they performed poorly on a task than are lows (Burger, 1987a).

In summary, one response that high-DC people make to a situation that challenges their perception of control is to work harder to reassert their competence and mastery. In research on achievement tasks, high-DC people respond with a number of behaviors designed to satisfy their need for control. In research on conformity, high-DC subjects are also less willing than lows to conform to social pressure (Burger, 1987c). Apparently the need to feel self-determined is stronger in high-DC people than the need to go along with one's peers.

Affective Responses

Even high-DC people may occasionally encounter situations they cannot control. Efforts to change some situations are bound to fail and the ability to convince oneself that a situation is controllable must have limits. The next question, therefore, is how high-LDC and low-LDC people differ when faced with the perception of no control.

The perception that one has no control over events has long been associated with depression. Research on learned helplessness has found that people who perceive an inability to control important events in their lives are likely candidates for many of the symptoms of depression. A key element in learned helplessness is the assumption that failure to control *important* events precipitates depression. Surely few people become depressed because they cannot control a long traffic light or the songs played by their favorite radio station. However, there are people who generally are more interested in controlling events than others are, that is, those high in desire for control. Compared to lows, high-DC people probably wish to control more situations, and whether or not they can control these situations is more important to them. Thus, we would expect that high desire for control people are more susceptible to depression than are lows.

Burger and Arkin (1980) placed high-DC and low-DC undergraduates in a typical learned helplessness laboratory situation. Subjects either could or could not do something to control the onset and offset of fifty trials of aversive noise. Subjects then were given a measure of their mood and were administered a short memory task. Consistent with the predictions, high-DC subjects receiving the helplessness induction reported higher levels of depression and performed more poorly on the memory task than did the low-DC subjects. Burger, Oakman, and Bullard (1983) also found that high-DC people were more likely to feel crowded in a highly congested area. Presumably this is because their ability to act as they pleased was limited, and they found this more uncomfortable than did the low-DC subjects.

In another study, undergraduates were given measures of desire for control and locus of control at the beginning of the school year (Burger, 1984). By dividing the subjects into high and low halves on each of the measures, a group could be identified that was high in desire for control but external in locus of control. These people enter situations with a high level of motivation to control events, but with the perception that they can do little to influence what happens; they are similar to subjects in a learned helplessness experiment who want to control the situation but find that they cannot. It was reasoned that high desire for control combined with external locus of control would be related to susceptibility to depression.

Subjects were contacted six months later—toward the end of the school year—and asked to report about their current level of depression as well as several indicators of how depressed they had felt during the school year. Subjects with a high desire for control and an external locus of control were more likely than those in the other groups to seek out help from others for a problem they had found depressing, and they reported having been depressed on more days during the six-month period. In addition, a surprisingly large number of these students reported that they had thought about the possibility of suicide during that time.

In summary, individual differences in desire for control interact with a person's perception of control to determine cognitive, motivational, and affective responses. People with a high need for control who find themselves in a situation they have little control over may convince themselves they have some control, or they may work to reassert their control. If these fail, high-LDC people may be more susceptible than lows to negative affective responses, most notably depression.

Summary

The extent to which a person perceives himself or herself in control of events influences that person's reactions to the events. People who perceive a large amount of control often feel masterful and competent, whereas perceiving a loss of control can result in depression and poor performance on subsequent tasks. However, there are times when the perception of control is not desirable. People may become anxious about the increased responsibility, the increased predictability of aversive stimuli, and the increased likelihood of an unwanted outcome.

Individual differences in the extent to which people generally perceive themselves to be in control of what happens to them have been found to affect a large number of behaviors. People who generally perceive personal control (internals) tend to perform better on academic tasks than those who do not hold this perception (externals). Internals also appear to cope with stress better than externals.

Individual differences in the extent to which people generally are motivated to control events also influence many important behaviors. People with a high desire for control are more likely than those low on this dimension to perceive they are able to influence events they in reality cannot control, to respond to challenging tasks in a manner that increases the likelihood of success, and to succumb to depression when they find they cannot exercise control.

SUGGESTED READINGS

deCharms, R. (1968). *Personal causation: The internal affective determinants of behavior.* New York: Academic Press. DeCharms presents a theory of human motivation centered around the concept of personal control. He describes the need for control as our "primary motivational propensity."

Langer, E. J. (1983). *The psychology of control.* Beverly Hills, CA: Sage. A collection of some of Langer's work with the concept of personal control, including her research on the illusion of control and the effects of control-enhancing intervention in an old-age home.

Lefcourt, H. M. (1982). *Locus of control: Current trends in theory and research* (2nd ed.). Hillsdale, NJ: Erlbaum. A review of research on the concept of locus of control and some of the many areas to which individual differences in locus of control have been applied, including achievement, coping, and cognitive activity.

Lefcourt, H. M. (Ed.). (1981–1984). *Research with the locus of control concept* (Vols. 1–3). New York: Academic Press. Three edited volumes on current locus of control research. The three volumes are divided into chapters dealing with assessment of locus of control, the application of locus of control to social problems, and extensions and limitations of the locus of control construct.

REFERENCES

Abramson, L. Y., Seligman, M. E. P., & Teasdale, J. D. (1978). Learned helplessness in humans: Critique and reformulation. *Journal of Abnormal Psychology, 87,* 49–74.

Allen, V. L., & Greenberger, D. B. (1980). Destruction and perceived control. In A. Baum & J. E. Singer (Eds.), *Advances in environmental psychology. Vol 2: Applications of personal control* (pp. 85–109). Hillsdale, NJ: Erlbaum.

Anderson, C. R. (1977). Locus of control, coping behaviors and performance in a stress setting: A longitudinal study. *Journal of Applied Psychology, 62,* 446–451.

Ansbacher, H. L., & Ansbacher, R. R. (Eds.) (1956). *The individual psychology of Alfred Adler.* New York: Basic Books.

Arkin, R. M., & Baumgardner, A. H. (1985). Self-handicapping. In J. H. Harvey & G. Weary (Eds.), *Attribution: Basic issues and applications* (pp. 169–202). New York: Academic Press.

Averill, J. R. (1973). Personal control over aversive stimuli and its relationship to stress. *Psychological Bulletin, 80,* 286–303.

Bar-Tal, D., & Bar-Zohar, Y. (1977). The relationship between perception of locus of control and academic achievement. *Contemporary Educational Psychology, 2,* 181–199.

Benassi, V. A., Sweeney, P. D., & Defour, C. L. (1988). Is there a relationship between locus of control orientation and depression? *Journal of Abnormal Psychology, 97,* 357–367.

Burger, J. M. (1984). Desire for control, locus of control, and proneness to depression. *Journal of Personality, 52,* 71–89.

Burger, J. M. (1985). Desire for control and achievement-related behaviors. *Journal of Personality and Social Psychology, 48,* 1520–1533.

Burger, J. M. (1987a). Effects of desire for control on attributions and task performance. *Basic and Applied Social Psychology, 8,* 309–320.

Burger, J. M. (1987b). *Desire for control and*

academic performance by college students. Unpublished manuscript.

Burger, J. M. (1987c). Desire for control and conformity to a perceived norm. *Journal of Personality and Social Psychology, 53,* 355–360.

Burger, J. M. (1989). Negative reactions to increases in perceived personal control. *Journal of Personality and Social Psychology, 56,* 246–256.

Burger, J. M., & Arkin, R. M. (1980). Prediction, control and learned helplessness. *Journal of Personality and Social Psychology, 38,* 482–491.

Burger, J. M., Brown, R., & Allen, C. K. (1983). Negative reactions to personal control. *Journal of Social and Clinical Psychology, 1,* 322–342.

Burger, J. M., & Cooper, H. M. (1979). The desirability of control. *Motivation and Emotion, 3,* 381–393.

Burger, J. M., & Hemans, L. T. (1988). Desire for control and the use of attribution processes. *Journal of Personality, 56,* 531–546.

Burger, J. M., McWard, J., & LaTorre, D. (1986). *Relinquishing control over aversive stimuli.* Paper presented at the annual meeting of the Western Psychological Association, Seattle.

Burger, J. M., Oakman, J. A., & Bullard, N. G. (1983). Desire for control and the perception of crowding. *Personality and Social Psychology Bulletin, 9,* 475–479.

Burger, J. M., & Schnerring, D. A. (1982). The effects of desire for control and extrinsic rewards on the illusion of control and gambling. *Motivation and Emotion, 6,* 329–335.

Burger, J. M., & Smith, N. G. (1985). Desire for control and gambling behavior among problem gamblers. *Personality and Social Psychology Bulletin, 11,* 145–152.

Collins, B. E. (1974). Four components of the Rotter Internal–External Scale. *Journal of Personality and Social Psychology, 29,* 381–391.

deCharms, R. (1968). *Personal causation.* New York: Academic Press.

Dembroski, T. M., MacDougall, J. M., & Musante, L. (1984). Desirability of control versus locus of control: Relationship to paralinguistics in the Type A interview. *Health Psychology, 3,* 15–26.

Dweck, C. S., & Licht, B. G. (1980). Learned helplessness and intellectual achievement. In J. Garber & M. E. P. Seligman (Eds.), *Human helplessness: Theory and applications* (pp. 197–221). New York: Academic Press.

Findley, M. J., & Cooper, H. M. (1983). Locus of control and academic achievement: A literature review. *Journal of Personality and Social Psychology, 44,* 419–427.

Gilmore, T. M., & Reid, D. W. (1978). Locus of control, prediction, and performance on university examinations. *Journal of Consulting and Clinical Psychology, 46,* 565–566.

Gilmore, T. M., & Reid, D. W. (1979). Locus of control and causal attribution for positive and negative outcomes on university examinations. *Journal of Research in Personality, 13,* 154–160.

Glass, D. C., & Singer, J. E. (1972). *Urban stress.* New York: Academic Press.

Hiroto, D. S., & Seligman, M. E. P. (1975). Generality of learned helplessness in humans. *Journal of Personality and Social Psychology, 31,* 311–327.

Kaplan, G. D., & Cowles, A. (1978). Health locus of control and health value in prediction of smoking reduction. *Health Education Monographs, 6,* 129–137.

Kelly, G. A. (1955). *The psychology of personal constructs.* New York: Norton.

Krantz, D. S., Baum, A., & Wideman, M. V. (1980). Assessment of preferences for self-treatment and information in health care. *Journal of Personality and Social Psychology, 39,* 977–990.

Langer, E. J. (1975). The illusion of control. *Journal of Personality and Social Psychology, 32,* 311–328.

Langer, E. J., & Rodin, J. (1976). The effects of choice and enhanced personal responsibility for the aged: A field experiment in an institutional setting. *Journal of Personality and Social Psychology, 34,* 191–198.

Lazarus, R. S., & Folkman, S. (1984). *Stress, appraisal, and coping.* New York: Springer.

Lefcourt, H. M. (1980). Locus of control and coping with life's events. In E. Staub (Ed.), *Personality: Basic aspects and current research* (pp. 200–235). Englewood Cliffs: Prentice-Hall.

Lefcourt, H. M. (1982). *Locus of control: Current trends in theory and research* (2nd ed). Hillsdale, NJ: Erlbaum.

Lefcourt, H. M., Martin, R. A., & Saleh, W. E. (1984). Locus of control and social support: Interactive moderators of stress. *Journal of Personality and Social Psychology, 47,* 378–389.

Lefcourt, H. M., Miller, R. S., Ware, E. E., & Sherk, D. (1981). Locus of control as a modifier of the relationship between stressors and moods. *Journal of Personality and Social Psychology, 41,* 357–369.

Levenson, H. (1974). Activism and powerful others: Distinctions within the concept of internal–external control. *Journal of Personality Assessment, 38,* 377–383.

Marks, G., Richardson, J. L., Graham, J. W., & Levine, A. (1986). Role of health locus of control beliefs and expectations of treatment efficacy in adjustment to cancer. *Journal of Personality and Social Psychology, 51,* 443–450.

Mendonca, P. J., & Brehm, S. S. (1983). Effects of choice on behavioral treatment of overweight children. *Journal of Social and Clinical Psychology, 1,* 343–358.

Miller, S. M. (1980). Why having control reduces stress: If I can stop the roller coaster, I don't want to get off. In J. Garber & M. E. P. Seligman (Eds.), *Human helplessness: Theory and applications* (pp. 71–95). New York: Academic Press.

Miller, S. M. (1981). Predictability and human stress: Toward a clarification of evidence and theory. In L. Berkowitz (Ed.), *Advances in experimental social psychology (Vol 14,* pp. 203–256). New York: Academic Press.

Monat, A., Averill, J. R., & Lazarus, R. S. (1972). Anticipatory stress and coping reactions under various conditions of uncertainty. *Journal of Personality and Social Psychology, 24,* 237–253.

Nord, W. R., Connelly, F., & Daignault, G. (1974). Locus of control and aptitude test scores as predictors of academic success in graduate school. *Journal of Educational Psychology, 66,* 956–961.

Parkes, K. R. (1984). Locus of control, cognitive appraisal, and coping in stressful episodes. *Journal of Personality and Social Psychology, 46,* 655–668.

Paulhus, D. (1983). Sphere specific measures of perceived control. *Journal of Personality and Social Psychology, 44,* 1253–1265.

Paulhus, D., & Christie, R. (1981). Spheres of control: An interactionist approach to assessment of perceived control. In H. M. Lefcourt (Ed.), *Research with the locus of control construct. Vol 1: Assessment methods* (pp. 161–188). New York: Academic Press.

Perlmuter, L. C., & Monty, R. A. (1977). The importance of perceived control: Fact or fantasy? *American Scientist, 65,* 759–765.

Peterson, C., & Seligman, M. E. P. (1984). Causal explanations as a risk factor for depression: Theory and evidence. *Psychological Review, 91,* 347–374.

Phares, E. J. (1976). *Locus of control in personality.* Morristown, NJ: General Learning Press.

Prociuk, T. J., & Breen, L. J. (1975). Defensive externality and academic performance. *Journal of Personality and Social Psychology, 31,* 549–556.

Rodin, J., & Langer, E. J. (1977). Long-term effects of control-relevant intervention with the institutionalized aged. *Journal of Personality and Social Psychology, 35,* 897–902.

Rogers, C. R. (1961). *On becoming a person: A therapist's view of psychotherapy.* Boston: Houghton-Mifflin.

Rotter, J. B. (1954). *Social learning and clinical psychology.* Englewood Cliffs, NJ: Prentice-Hall.

Rotter, J. B. (1966). Generalized expectancies for internal versus external control of reinforcement. *Psychological Monographs, 80,* (1, Whole No. 609).

Sandler, I. N., & Lakey, B. (1982). Locus of control as a stress moderator: The role of control perceptions and social support. *American Journal of Community Psychology, 10,* 65–80.

Schmidt, D. E., & Keating, J. P. (1979). Human crowding and personal control: An integration of the research. *Psychological Bulletin, 86,* 680–700.

Seligman, M. E. P. (1975). *Helplessness: On depression, development and death.* San Francisco: Freeman.

Skinner, B. F. (1971). *Beyond freedom and dignity.* New York: Bantam.

Strickland, B. R. (1978). Internal–external expectancies and health-related behaviors. *Journal of Consulting and Clinical Psychology, 46,* 1192–1211.

Strickland, L. H., Lewicki, R. J., & Katz, A. M. (1966). Temporal orientation and perceived control as determinants of risk-taking. *Journal of Experimental Social Psychology, 2,* 143–151.

Taylor, S. E. (1983). Adjustment to threatening events: A theory of cognitive adaptation. *American Psychologist, 38,* 1161–1173.

Thompson, S. C. (1981). Will it hurt less if I can control it? A complex answer to a simple question. *Psychological Bulletin, 90,* 89–101.

Wallston, K. A., Maides, S., & Wallston, B. S. (1976). Health information seeking as a function of health related locus of control and health value. *Journal of Research in Personality, 10,* 215–222.

Wallston, K. A., & Wallston, B. S. (1981). Health locus of control scales. In H. M. Lefcourt (Ed.), *Research with the locus of control construct. Vol. 1: Assessment methods* (pp. 189–243). New York: Academic Press.

White, R. (1959). Motivation reconsidered: The concept of competence. *Psychological Review, 66,* 297–330.

CHAPTER 12

Self-Awareness and Self-Consciousness

MARK H. DAVIS AND STEPHEN L. FRANZOI

**Past and Present Concepts Related
    to Private Self-Awareness**
**Past and Present Concepts Related
    to Public Self-Awareness**
**Current Self-Awareness and
    Self-Consciousness Theories**
Self-Awareness Versus
    Self-Consciousness
The Self-Consciousness Scale
ACTIVITY BOX: **The
    Self-Consciousness Scale**

The Texas Connection
Wicklund's Approach:
    Objective Self-Awareness
Buss's Approach:
    Self-Consciousness Theory
Carver and Scheier's Approach:
    A Control-Theory Model
Concluding Remarks
Summary
SUGGESTED READINGS
REFERENCES

How well do you know your emotional state right now? That is, if you were asked to describe your feelings of happiness or anxiety on a 10-point scale, how sure would you be about your answers? How well do you know your own motives? Do you ever do things and yet find yourself later unable to figure out why?

How well do you know the image of yourself that comes across to other people? For example, what sort of impression do you think your really close friends have about your level of intelligence? How affectionate and caring would your sister or brother say you are? How would the last person you dated rate you on a 10-point scale of self-confidence?

What all of these questions have in common is that they refer to your knowledge about yourself, what psychologists often refer to as *self-awareness* or *self-consciousness*. The purpose of this chapter is to consider some of the ways in which social and personality psychologists have studied this topic, where the fundamental ideas have come from, and the different kinds of self-knowledge that people can have. As we proceed, we will see that some of the questions about self-awareness with which psychology is wrestling today are very similar to questions that have been around for centuries. In a way, that can be seen as a disappointment—after all, why are we still dealing with the same old issues? Haven't we made any progress in hundreds of years? Another way to look at this is more encouraging. For these issues to have remained unsolved for so long tells us how complicated they must be;

The authors gratefully acknowledge the useful comments by Linda Kraus on an earlier version of this chapter.

for us to still be *interested* in them after all this time certainly tells us how important and fascinating they are.

Before going on, it is necessary for us to make an important distinction, one that will help us to understand how self-awareness has been studied. This is the distinction between private self-awareness and public self-awareness. *Private self-awareness* refers to a psychological state in which we are aware of the aspects of ourselves that are hidden from public view—our thoughts, feelings, attitudes, wishes, dreams, and fantasies. When we become aware of internal emotional and physiological states such as happiness and hunger, when we think about our innermost fears and hopes, when we try to figure out why in the world we behave the way we do, we are in a state of private self-awareness. *Public self-awareness* refers to a psychological state in which we are aware of those aspects of ourselves that are observable by other people—our physical appearance, public words and actions, and expressions of emotions. When we think about how we look to others, when we examine ourselves in a full-length mirror at the clothing store, when we rehearse our end of a phone call before dialing the number, we are in a state of public self-awareness.

This differentiation between public and private self-awareness is a very fundamental one. In fact, it has been suggested that the public-private distinction may be an example of a more general and very fundamental concept in social and personality psychology, what has been termed the *inner–outer* metaphor (Hogan & Cheek, 1983). This inner–outer metaphor shows up in many ways. For example, Jung's (1923) theory of personality emphasizes the concept of introversion-extraversion—the idea that people differ in terms of whether they characteristically turn psychic energy inward toward the inner world or outward toward the external world. More recent approaches to personality, exemplified by such characteristics as field dependence-independence (Witkin, Lewis, Hertzman, Machover, Meissner, & Wapner, 1954), locus of control (Rotter, 1966), and self-monitoring (Snyder, 1974) echo this distinction between attention to and knowledge of internal matters and attention to and knowledge of external forces. From this perspective, the distinction between awareness of public and private self-aspects can be viewed as one more instance of a powerful and recurring theme in personality theory. The reason this theme is persistent is probably that it is so useful to us in making sense of our personalities. Later in the chapter we will examine some of the findings that illustrate this usefulness.

Although it is widespread today, we should note that this distinction between private and public aspects of self may actually be a relatively recent development in human history. For example, Roy Baumeister (1986) argues that in earlier times (such as in medieval

Europe) public and private aspects of the self may have been viewed as equivalent. The widespread realization today that private aspects of the self can be separate and distinct from public behavior and appearances has gradually evolved over the past few centuries. In the twentieth century, though, this distinction between private and public self is a strong one; let us turn our attention therefore to a separate consideration of some modern concepts related to each.

Past and Present Concepts Related to Private Self-Awareness

Although many modern theorists have contributed to our knowledge about the private self, one of the single strongest influences was made by Sigmund Freud. His major contributions were made early in this century, and modern psychology takes many exceptions to his theory, but his emphasis on the unseen, internal, private world of the self has had a huge effect on later attempts to understand the self. In particular, Freud placed heavy emphasis on the *difficulty* people have in being aware of their true motives and desires. Because many of our impulses and motives are too threatening for us to acknowledge consciously, they are relegated to the unconscious.

This emphasis on the unconscious raises some very interesting questions regarding our ability to be aware of our private selves. For example, if so many of our true motives and desires are concealed, how accurate can our self-understanding ever be? Indeed, Freud believed that, because so much about true motives is not consciously available to the individual, a person's self-understanding is always, necessarily, inaccurate. Another matter of importance to Freud is clearly related to the first: the issue of *self-deception*. In Freud's view, a primary reason that people have inaccurate views of self is that they deliberately, although unconsciously, deceive themselves about their true feelings, desires, and wishes. Freud in fact catalogues a long list of techniques, called *defense mechanisms*, that we use to hide unpleasant and threatening information from ourselves.

The issues of accuracy and self-deception have generated contemporary research in an effort to discover whether Freud's ideas are tenable. As one example, Gur and Sackheim (1979) have attempted to demonstrate self-deception through an intriguing experiment. First, they define self-deception as consisting of three elements: (1) the individual must simultaneously hold two contradictory beliefs; (2) the individual is not aware of holding one of these beliefs; and (3) the reason that the person is not aware of one of the beliefs is that he or she is *motivated* not to know it (that is, the person does so because it is more pleasant for him or her to not be aware). Gur and Sackheim attempted to find evidence for the existence of self-deception by presenting subjects with audio recordings of a number of different voices, including their own. The key result was that the subjects' physiological responses (a measure of physical arousal) were much stronger when they heard their own voices than when they heard someone else's, *even when they did not consciously recognize the voice as their own.* That is, at the very same time that subjects were saying "No, that isn't my voice," measures of their physical arousal indicated that they *did* recognize it. Gur and Sackheim interpret this as evidence of self-deception—evidence that people at least some of the time are not consciously aware of private information that they possess. Thus, research seems to indicate that private self-awareness may exist at more than just the conscious level.

Past and Present Concepts Related to Public Self-Awareness

Whereas Freud's work has had a considerable influence on modern views about private self-awareness, it has had much less impact on conceptions of public self-awareness. Freud's theory, after all, was largely concerned with how the private, hidden parts of personality developed and functioned. The ideas that have shaped modern views of public self-awareness have tended to come instead from other sources, including the psychologist William James (1890) and the sociologist George Herbert Mead (1934). The ideas generated by these and other writers all revolve around a common theme: In addition to any awareness people may or may not have about their inner selves, people are quite acutely aware of their *outer* selves. In particular, they are quite aware of how their appearance and behavior are seen and judged by other people, and this awareness has some crucial implications for how we act.

Sociologist Charles Cooley (1902) used the term *looking-glass self* to describe the fact that we form our own images of ourselves by using the reactions that others have toward us. Just as we use a mirror to understand what our outward appearance is like, we use other people as mirrors to understand what kind of people we are. Does everyone laugh at our jokes? Then we must have a pretty good sense of humor. Do friends frequently tell us what a good and attentive listener we are? We must therefore be warm and sympathetic. According to this view, our self-concept is directly shaped by the ways in which we come across to others.

The writings of Cooley and Mead were further developed by others in sociology and came to be known as the theory of *symbolic interactionism*. This approach, rather than emphasize a direct knowledge of one's inner self, advances the idea that knowledge of inner self only *results from* an awareness of our outer, public selves. It thus places primary importance on humans as social beings and stresses the importance to us of audiences—other people who witness our behavior.

One modern outgrowth of this perspective on the self has been the development of the *impression management* viewpoint in social psychology. Impression management has been defined as *"the conscious or unconscious attempt to control images that are projected in real or imagined social interactions.* When these images are self-relevant, the behavior is termed *self-presentation"* (Schlenker, 1980, p. 6). This approach therefore focuses on the many, many ways in which we try to influence the way others perceive and judge us. In essence, this viewpoint takes the basic symbolic interactionist idea that we are strongly affected by others' judgments of us, and extends the concept to a consideration of what that must mean for our behavior. What it seems to mean, according to the evidence, is that in a multitude of ways we strive mightily to influence how others will judge our attitudes, personalities, behaviors, families, possessions, appearance, and values.

Over the past twenty-five years, social psychologists have catalogued a number of different techniques people use for this purpose. One such technique is *ingratiation,* or attempts to increase one's attractiveness in the eyes of others. This can be accomplished through a variety of means, including exaggerating one's own positive characteristics (e.g., Goldstein, 1971), or flattering the audience (e.g., Aronson & Linder, 1965). Other common techniques come into play when we find ourselves in danger of being viewed negatively by others. In such situations, we may have to offer *excuses,* which are attempts to convince an audience that we are not responsible for some event that threatens our public self-image. For example, someone's image as a good student can be threatened by failing miserably on an exam on which others performed well. An excuse ("I mistakenly studied the wrong chapter") offers an alternative explanation for the otherwise threatening event.

In 1974, psychologist Mark Snyder took a different and quite fascinating approach to impression management. Previously, the assumption had been that everyone engaged in self-presentation techniques. Snyder's view was that while everyone at times probably uses these techniques, there are some people who may use them much more frequently and successfully than other people. That is, there may be differences between individuals in terms of their characteristic tendency to engage in impression management. The term Snyder used to describe this characteristic tendency or skill is *self-monitoring* (Snyder, 1974, 1987).

A considerable amount of research has supported Snyder's approach. For example, one implication of self-monitoring is that high self-monitors will not always act in accordance with their own internal attitudes, because they so often use the situation to guide them. Low self-monitors would usually act more in accordance with their internal attitudes, because they do not let the situation guide them. Indeed, this seems to be the case (Snyder & Swann, 1976; Snyder & Tanke, 1976). Another implication of self-monitoring is that high and low self-monitors should have different types of social relationships. Because high self-monitors tend to act in ways that are appropriate to particular situations, they may be more likely to choose as friends and activity partners people who are especially skilled in the particular situation in question. That is, high self-monitors may be likely to have several separate groups of friends, some to play tennis with, some to study with, some to dine with, some to discuss music with, and so forth. In fact, Snyder, Gangestad, and Simpson (1983) found exactly that. While high self-monitors reported having much more "segmented" social worlds, the low self-monitors paid less attention to the demands of the particular activity or situation and tended to have one consistent set of friends with whom they engaged in a wide variety of activities.

Current Self-Awareness and Self-Consciousness Theories

The remainder of this chapter will focus in more detail on a specific line of research, very influential in recent years, that deals specifically with the causes and consequences of paying attention to private and public aspects of the self. This line of research has spawned literally hundreds of empirical investigations and continues to be a fertile source of inspiration for research efforts. Several different terms have been used to describe the key variables and processes that are central to this approach, and we will attempt to identify them as we proceed. Let us begin with one of the most important distinctions in this area: the distinction between self-awareness and self-consciousness.

Self-Awareness Versus Self-Consciousness

For the remainder of this chapter, the term *self-awareness* will refer to the actual psychological state of being attentive to oneself—the temporary condition of focusing attention on the self. Our earlier distinction between private self-awareness and public self-awareness still remains in effect. Thus, *private self-awareness* is the temporary state of being aware of one's hidden, private self-aspects; *public self-awareness* is the temporary state of being aware of one's public self-aspects.

In contrast, *self-consciousness* is a personality trait; it refers to a relatively permanent tendency on the part of the individual to spend more or less time in the *state* of self-awareness. Again, the private-public distinction still holds. *Private self-consciousness* is the chronic tendency to engage in private self-awareness; *public self-consciousness* is the chronic tendency to engage in public self-awareness. Although it may be confusing at first, the research we are about to discuss makes clear distinctions between states and traits and uses the awareness/consciousness terminology to reflect this distinction. Before discussing the actual theories of self-awareness and self-consciousness, however, let us examine the assessment device that is used to measure the personality characteristics of private and public self-consciousness.

The Self-Consciousness Scale

In the early 1970s, Allan Fenigstein, Michael Scheier, and Arnold Buss began work on the development of an individual difference measure to assess the chronic tendency to engage in self-awareness. In developing this measure, they decided to concentrate on the following seven basic content areas of self-consciousness: (1) preoccupation with past, present, or future behaviors; (2) recognition of one's own positive and negative attributes; (3) sensitivity to inner feelings; (4) introspective behavior; (5) a tendency to visualize oneself; (6) awareness of one's own appearance and style of presentation; and (7) concern over the appraisal of others. From these areas they constructed a list of thirty-eight items and administered them to college students. Using a statistical procedure called factor analysis they subsequently reduced the list to twenty-three items, which were then separated into three factors or scales. These scales, known collectively as the Self-Consciousness Scale (SCS), appear in the Activity Box.

Fenigstein and his colleagues (1975) named the first scale, which consists of ten items, *private self-consciousness,* because a person who agrees with these items would be one who habitually looks inside the self, fantasizes, and examines moods, motives, and mental processes. The second scale, containing seven items, was named *public self-consciousness.* People who agree with these items would be habitually aware of and concerned about their appearance, social behavior, and the general impression they make on others. Finally, the third scale consists of six items and was named *social anxiety.* Social anxiety is considered to be a possible by-product of high public self-consciousness, and a person who agrees with these items would generally be shy, easily embarrassed, and anxious in social situations.

A number of studies have found the SCS to be a valid measure of these three personality traits (e.g., Carver & Glass, 1976; Fenigstein, 1979; Franzoi & Brewer, 1984; Hass, 1984; Riggio, 1986; Turner, Scheier, Carver, & Ickes, 1978). The scale has been translated into a number of foreign languages (e.g., Merz, 1984; Sugawara, 1984; Vleeming & Engelse, 1981), and today it is used by personality researchers throughout the world to investigate a wide variety of issues. Recently, Michael Scheier and Charles Carver have introduced a revised version of the scale (Scheier & Carver, 1985) that is designed for use with noncollege populations. The original scale, however, remains the most popular version.

One final comment about the scale is in order. Although all investigators who study the personality traits of private and public self-consciousness use the SCS to measure these traits, they do not all share the same assumptions about those traits. Thus, as you will discover shortly, different theories offer different interpretations of what the scores on this measure represent. In fact, one theory (the first one we will discuss) has little if any use at all for the SCS!

The Texas Connection

It seems safe to say that much of the research and theorizing concerning self-awareness and self-consciousness got its start at the University of Texas at Austin in the early 1970s. As we shall see in a moment, this line of research received its initial impetus in 1972 from the work of Robert Wicklund and Shelley Duval, both at Texas, concerning the *state* of self-awareness. Soon after that, another set of Texas investigators (Fenigstein, Scheier, & Buss, 1975) turned the focus onto the trait rather than the state of self-awareness. One of those investigators, Arnold Buss, has presented a detailed theory concerning these issues (Buss, 1980). Another one of the men, Michael Scheier, and his collaborator, Charles Carver, both of whom were graduate students at Texas during this time, have formulated their own theoretical explanation regarding self-awareness and self-consciousness (Carver, 1979; Carver & Scheier, 1981). We will examine each of these approaches in more detail in a moment.

The fact that the theories we are to discuss got their start at the same school at roughly the same time has some important consequences. One of these is that the three approaches we will present have some obvious similarities. To be sure, there are also some important differences, but you will be able to discern a clear "family resemblance" among these approaches as they are presented. A second

The Self-Consciousness Scale

The Self-Consciousness Scale (SCS) is a self-report questionnaire designed to measure three different kinds of dispositional self-consciousness. The first of these is *private self-consciousness*, the tendency to pay attention to private, internal aspects of the self. The second is *public self-consciousness*, the tendency to be aware of and concerned about aspects of the self that others can perceive. The third is *social anxiety*, the tendency to be anxious and ill at ease in social settings. The items here come from the SCS.

To take the SCS, read each item carefully and then indicate how well each statement describes you. Use the 0–4 response scale for your answers. After answering each item as honestly and accurately as possible, refer to the scoring information at the end of this Activity Box.

Response scale: For each item, please choose the number from 0 to 4 that best indicates how well the item characterizes you. The choices are:

0 = extremely uncharacteristic (not at all like me)
1 = uncharacteristic (somewhat unlike me)
2 = neither characteristic nor uncharacteristic
3 = characteristic (somewhat like me)
4 = extremely characteristic (very much like me)

_____ 1. I'm always trying to figure myself out.
_____ 2. I'm concerned about my style of doing things.
_____ 3. Generally, I'm not very aware of myself.
_____ 4. It takes me time to overcome my shyness in new situations.
_____ 5. I reflect about myself a lot.
_____ 6. I'm concerned about the way I present myself.
_____ 7. I'm often the subject of my own fantasies.
_____ 8. I have trouble working when someone is watching me.
_____ 9. I never scrutinize myself.
_____ 10. I get embarrassed very easily.
_____ 11. I'm self-conscious about the way I look.
_____ 12. I don't find it hard to talk to strangers.
_____ 13. I'm generally attentive to my inner feelings.
_____ 14. I usually worry about making a good impression.
_____ 15. I'm constantly examining my motives.
_____ 16. One of the last things I do before I leave my house is look in the mirror.
_____ 17. I sometimes have the feeling that I'm off somewhere watching myself.

_____ 18. I feel anxious when I speak in front of a group.
_____ 19. I'm concerned about what other people think of me.
_____ 20. I'm alert to changes in my mood.
_____ 21. I'm usually aware of my appearance.
_____ 22. I'm aware of the way my mind works when I work through a problem.
_____ 23. Large groups make me nervous.

TO SCORE THE SCS

Several of the SCS items are reverse-scored; that is, for these items a lower rating (toward the "uncharacteristic" end of the scale) indicates a higher level of self-consciousness. Thus, when scoring these items you should first recode your responses to them so that 0 = 4, 1 = 3, 3 = 1, and 4 = 0. A response of 2 remains the same. The items to be recoded are indicated with asterisk (*).

- *Private self-consciousness.* To calculate your private self-consciousness score, add up your responses to the following items (taking care to reverse the coding on the appropriate items): 1, 3*, 5, 7, 9*, 13, 15, 17, 20, and 22.
- *Public self-consciousness.* To calculate your public self-consciousness score, add up your responses to the following items: 2, 6, 11, 14, 16, 19, and 21.
- *Social anxiety.* To calculate your social anxiety score, add up your responses to the following items: 4, 8, 10, 12*, 18, and 23.

To give you some idea of how to interpret your SCS scores, consider the following. Fenigstein, Scheier, and Buss found when they developed the SCS in 1975 that the mean score of college students on the private self-consciousness scale was about 26; for the public self-consciousness scale it was about 19; and for the social anxiety scale it was about 13. The higher your score is above one of these values, the more of this type of self-consciousness you probably possess. The lower your score is below one of these values, the less of this type of self-consciousness you probably possess.

You should remember, however, that this test was not developed to study the self-consciousness levels of *individuals*, but was designed to measure these levels for different *groups* of people. As a result, any individual person's scores on these scales are far from perfect as indicators of that person's "true" self-consciousness levels. The SCS is included here to give you a sense of how this construct is usually measured by researchers and not to provide a reliable measure of your own personality.

consequence—one that could lead to some confusion—is that some of the same names will appear repeatedly as we discuss the evidence for these three theories. Frequently, in fact, research that was carried out to test one theory will turn out to provide support for another theory as well. Because so much similar research was being done simultaneously, a degree of overlap like this was probably inevitable. In any event, the reader should not be surprised to find that a study done by Carver or Scheier, for instance, is used to illustrate the evidence for Wicklund's or Buss's theory. In fact, as we shall see, a considerable amount of Carver and Scheier's early research was carried out to test the ideas of Wicklund and Buss; eventually, however, Carver and Scheier were to develop their own views about self-awareness and self-consciousness. In the beginning, however, modern self-awareness research got its start with the ideas of Robert Wicklund.

Wicklund's Approach: Objective Self-Awareness

Before the development of the Self-Consciousness Scale, and before there was any interest in self-consciousness as a trait, Shelley Duval and Robert Wicklund wrote a book entitled *A Theory of Objective Self-Awareness* (1972). This book outlined a theory—concerned with the state of self-awareness—that triggered much of the recent interest in the issues of self-awareness and self-consciousness. Since the publication of the book, Wicklund has been much more active than Duval in promoting and defending this viewpoint, and for that reason most discussions, including ours, refer to this simply as Wicklund's theory.

The theory of objective self-awareness (OSA) takes as its starting point the assumption that a person's conscious attention can be focused in only one of two directions: either internally toward the self or externally toward the environment. When attention is turned toward the self, an important sequence of events is set into motion. Wicklund assumes that self-focused attention leads us almost invariably to a critical self-evaluation—that is, we begin to judge ourselves as soon as our attention is focused inward. This raises a question, however: *What* is it about ourselves that we judge? That is, once attention is focused inward, what specifically do we examine? Wicklund believes that we tend to focus on whatever dimension of the self is most important or *salient* (noticeable) to us at the time. Thus, if you become self-aware while taking the SAT exams, the most salient aspect of self may well be your intelligence; if you become self-aware while getting ready for a big date, you may focus instead on your physical attractiveness.

In any event, once attention is focused on some salient aspect of self, the theory makes an important assumption. It assumes that there is a difference between our *real self* on that dimension (that is, how intelligent or physically attractive we perceive ourselves to be) and our *ideal self* (how intelligent or physically attractive we desire to be). In fact, Wicklund proposes that we almost always fall short of our ideal self, and thus self-focused attention makes us uncomfortably aware of our shortcomings. This uncomfortable feeling is aversive to us; we desire to be rid of it. As a result, we are motivated to somehow reduce the negative feeling. For this reason, Wicklund's theory is referred to as a *motivational* theory.

How can we reduce this unpleasant motivational state? There are two basic ways, according to the theory. One way is to escape the self-aware state; after all, if focusing attention on the self causes this negative feeling in the first place, then focusing attention back on the environment again should stop it. The other way to reduce the unpleasant state is to somehow *reduce* the discrepancy between the real and ideal states. Because what makes us uncomfortable is the distance between what we are and what we desire to be, one way to feel better would be, for instance, to reduce that distance by bringing the real self more into line with the ideal self. Of course, at some times and circumstances it may be relatively easy to change the real self to bring it closer to the ideal, and at other times it may be much more difficult.

Before discussing some evidence regarding the theory, we must mention one more issue. We have said that focusing attention on the self is what initiates the self-evaluative process; however, what makes someone focus attention on the self in the first place? Wicklund believes that there are certain stimuli in the environment that have the effect of reminding us of ourselves—that is, they make us aware of ourselves as objects in the world. For example, seeing a photo of ourselves tends to focus our attention back on ourselves rather than outward toward the environment; it makes us see ourselves in the way that others do. Hearing our own voice on a tape recording has the same effect. However, the stimulus that may most directly create self-focused attention is a mirror. Seeing ourselves in a mirror quite clearly makes us self-aware; our attention is literally turned back on us by the reflective properties of the mirror. It is not surprising, then, that many of the experiments designed to test this theory used mirrors to create self-focused attention among the subjects.

Research has provided considerable evidence in support of the theory. For example, Duval, Wicklund, and Fine (1971) carried out a study to test the notion that people will seek to escape self-focused attention when the discrepancy between the real and ideal selves is negative. Student participants were given false information about their levels of creativity and intelligence, supposedly on the basis of personality questionnaires they had filled out at the beginning of the semester. Half of the students were told that they had done quite well on the tests, scoring in the upper 10 percent of their class; for these students, then, their real selves are quite successful. The other half of the participants were told that they had not done so well on the tests, scoring in the lower 10 percent of the class; thus, these students were led to believe that their real selves were not very successful. Remember, of course, that this information was false, but the participants did not know it at the time.

The participants were next led to a separate room, ostensibly for a second and unrelated experiment. For half of them, the room contained a mirror that faced them and a television camera that pointed toward them; for the other half, the mirror was turned around so that its nonreflecting side was facing the students, and the television camera was also pointed away from them. Thus, half of the participants should be engaging in self-focused attention (due to the mirror and camera), and the other half should not. The participants were then told to wait there for the second experimenter, but that if he did not show up in five minutes, to go look for him in another room. The dependent measure in the experiment was simply how long the students were willing to wait in the room.

The theory would predict that one group should be especially likely to leave the room quickly. Those students who believed that they had done poorly on the personality tests (high discrepancy between real and ideal selves) *and* who were facing a mirror and television camera (self-focused attention) should be feeling the most discomfort because they were being made aware of their shortcomings. The other three groups were either not focusing attention on the self or had less real-ideal discrepancy. Thus, only the high discrepancy/self-focused attention group should be motivated to escape the room. As table 12.1 indicates, this is exactly the pattern that was found.

TABLE 12.1

Mean Number of Seconds Spent in the Experimental Room Before Leaving

	High discrepancy	Low discrepancy
Mirror	383	468
No mirror	487	492

Based on data in Duval, Wicklund, and Fine (1971), p. 19.

TABLE 12.2

Mean Level of Shock Administered to the "Learner" (on a 1 to 10 Scale)

	Antishock attitudes	Proshock attitudes
Mirror	3.01	4.75
No mirror	3.53	3.38

Based on data in Carver (1975), p. 515.

What about the prediction that people who focus attention on the self will try to bring the real self into line with the ideal self? Carver (1975) provided evidence for that prediction in the following way. First, he pretested students at the beginning of a semester with a questionnaire that included items asking whether they thought the use of strong punishment in teaching is justified. Carver used these answers to select a group of students with strong pro-punishment attitudes and a group with strong anti-punishment attitudes. Later in the semester, members of these two groups had the opportunity to play the role of a teacher in an experiment, and also had the power to use electric shock on another student (the "learner") in order to improve his learning. Although the students thought they were delivering real shocks to another person, in actuality no shocks were delivered.

For half the students, there was a mirror in front of them as they delivered the shocks; for the other half, there was no mirror. According to the theory, those with a mirror in front of them should be experiencing self-focused attention, and should be aware of the discrepancy between the ideal self (the attitudes they expressed earlier in the semester) and the real self (what kind of shocks they actually delivered). In order to keep the real-ideal discrepancy low, these students should strive to act in accordance with their attitudes; that is, they should try to make the real self conform to the ideal self. Those who were not facing a mirror should not be aware of themselves and thus should feel less pressure to match behavior to attitudes. As table 12.2 reveals, this is the pattern that was found. Participants with "pro-shock" attitudes who were facing a mirror administered the most intense shocks of all; those with "anti-shock" attitudes facing a mirror administered the weakest shocks of all. This general pattern has been found repeatedly with a variety of other attitudes and behaviors (see Gibbons, 1983).

All told, there has been a considerable accumulation of evidence that supports this approach. However, there have also been empirical criticisms of the theory, one of which has been a challenge to Wicklund's contention that self-awareness inevitably leads to the experience of negative affect. A number of investigations (e.g., Carver & Scheier, 1978; Franzoi & Brewer, 1984; Hull & Levy, 1979; Steenbarger & Aderman, 1979) have failed to support this prediction. In response to such criticism, Wicklund has slightly changed his original position. His current view (Wicklund & Frey, 1980) is that self-awareness may not actually lead to negative affect in every single instance; however, because human beings are so easily dissatisfied with themselves when they engage in self-evaluation, self-awareness quite frequently *does* produce unpleasant affect. We shall return to this point later on, in our discussion of Carver and Scheier's theory.

Buss's Approach: Self-Consciousness Theory

In the mid-1970s, as research spurred by Wicklund's theory began to accumulate, Arnold Buss was developing his own theoretical viewpoint regarding self-awareness and self-consciousness. While there is some similarity between Buss's approach and Wicklund's, Buss's theory in many ways is quite different. One important difference is the strong emphasis Buss places on distinguishing between private self-awareness or self-consciousness and public self-awareness or self-consciousness, a distinction that Wicklund ignores. Another difference is that Buss's theory essentially makes no use of the concept of an ideal self, or behavioral standard, which is the centerpiece of Wicklund's approach. Instead, Buss uses another way to conceptualize the processes of private and public self-awareness—one that does not pay much attention to such ideals. Thus, his theory will have a very different "feel" to it, one that is clearly distinguishable from the position of Wicklund.

Because the foundation of Buss's self-consciousness theory is the distinction between private and public self-aspects, let us consider each one in turn.

Private Self-Aspects

Buss holds that, when attention is focused on private aspects of the self, two processes result: intensification of affect and clarification of knowledge. *Intensification of affect* means that any positive or negative feelings present during private self-awareness will be intensified. As Buss (1980) says, private self-attention serves "to deepen melancholy, to heighten elation, to make pain more painful and pleasure more pleasurable" (p. 14). Thus, engaging in private self-awareness will serve to exaggerate whatever affect we feel; however, it will *not* intensify a private event that is affectively neutral. Because an affectively neutral event *has no* affect, there is nothing to intensify. To illustrate this, consider your feelings of anger after being insulted; this is a negatively charged affective event, and focusing attention on the private self will serve to intensify your feelings of anger. Similarly, your feelings of happiness after doing well on an exam are affectively charged (positively) and will be intensified by private self-focus. In contrast, your memory of what your elementary school looked like is probably an affectively neutral event because it does not produce any emotional reaction. As a result, there can be no intensification of affect regarding that memory.

However, the second consequence of private self-focus does apply to neutral private events. *Clarification of knowledge* means that during private self-focus all private events, whether affectively charged or not, become clearer and more distinct. In effect Buss claims that paying attention to the private self leads us to have clearer and more accurate knowledge about the private self. Private self-awareness will therefore make us more clearly aware of an aching muscle, will let us more accurately know our attitudes, and will bring our memories or fantasies more sharply into focus. It does not matter whether the private event is affectively charged or affectively neutral; all internal events are more clearly experienced as a result of private self-focus.

What would cause someone to focus attention on the private aspects of the self? Buss argues that keeping a diary is one activity that should focus attention on the private self, because doing so forces us to think about our feelings, motives, and reasons for acting—all things that are private. Some kinds of instructed meditation can also induce private self-awareness. Finally Buss holds that a certain type of mirror will also create private self-focus: a small mirror of the type found on bathroom cabinets, one that provides an image of the head and shoulders. Small mirrors, but not large ones, are said to produce this private self-focus because the image they provide us with is so familiar; after literally *thousands* of exposures to our images in bathroom mirrors, they eventually tell us nothing especially new about how we look to others. As a result, the ability of small mirrors to make us publicly self-aware is usually quite weak. Instead, what small mirrors do is direct our attention back toward ourselves and eventually produce in us an attention to our private, unseen aspects. Larger mirrors provide us with less familiar images of ourselves and have a different effect, according to Buss; we shall return to that effect shortly.

Finally, Buss makes quite explicit the difference between self-awareness and self-consciousness. When some stimulus in the environment, like a diary or a mirror, focuses our attention on the private self, that focus is only temporary. This transient state is called private self-awareness. For some people, there is also a tendency to engage in private self-awareness even in the absence of an inducer like a small mirror. This permanent tendency to engage in private self-awareness is called private self-consciousness, and it is measured by scores on the private self-consciousness portion of the SCS. However, the effect of engaging in private self-focus, whether caused by dispositions or inducers, is the same: It leads to intensification of affect and clarification of knowledge. Table 12.3 presents an outline of the basic elements in Buss's view of private self-awareness.

What sort of evidence is there for Buss's theory concerning attention to private self-aspects? One body of evidence supports his prediction that private self-focus will lead to intensification of affect. It has been found that people scoring high on the private self-consciousness scale, and thus dispositionally high on the tendency to attend to private self-aspects, do tend to react more intensely to stimuli that produce an affective response. For example, Scheier and Carver (1977) exposed college men to enjoyable slides (photographs of beautiful nude women) and unpleasant slides (such as photographs of dead bodies). The men high in private self-consciousness rated the enjoyable slides more positively, and also rated the unpleasant slides more negatively, than did those low in private self-consciousness. Thus, the feelings produced by the slides, both positive and negative, were intensified by a disposition to focus on the private self. In that same investigation, similar effects were found when the men viewed the slides in front of a small mirror or not. Viewing the slides in front of a mirror led to an intensification of affect, just as Buss's theory would predict. A number of other investigations have resulted in similar support for the intensification hypothesis (see Buss, 1980, for a review of this research).

Evidence also supports the prediction that private self-focus will lead to clearer and more distinct self-knowledge. For example, Scheier, Buss, and Buss (1978) carried out an experiment based on the following

TABLE 12.3

Outline of Buss's Theory Regarding Private Self-Attention

Inducers	Focus	Result
Introspection	Body processes	Clearer self-knowledge
Keeping a diary	Moods	
Meditation	Emotions	Intensification of affect
Small mirror	Motives	
Private self-consciousness		

Based on Buss (1980).

proposition: If people high in private self-consciousness have clearer self-knowledge, then their descriptions of themselves should be more accurate than those low in private self-consciousness. To test this, a number of college students were tested early one semester about their aggressive tendencies. They answered a number of questions concerning how frequently they had aggressive thoughts or engaged in aggressive behavior. Several weeks later they took part in an experiment in which they were given the opportunity to deliver (so they thought) painful electric shocks to another student. The intensity of the shocks administered by the students was the primary dependent variable.

From the standpoint of Buss's theory, what should be the pattern of results? Those high in private self-consciousness should have had clearer self-knowledge and thus reported more accurately about their aggressive tendencies earlier in the semester; consequently, when they later had a chance to display their aggressive tendencies through actual behavior, that behavior should have corresponded closely to their earlier self-report. Those low in private self-consciousness should have been less accurate in their early self-descriptions and thus should have later acted in ways that may not have corresponded very closely to their relatively inaccurate self-report. This is exactly what was found. When self-reported levels of aggressiveness were correlated with the intensity of the actual shocks they delivered, those low in private self-consciousness showed very little correspondence between self-report and behavior (correlation was .09). Those high in private self-consciousness, on the other hand, showed a very strong correspondence between their self-reports and actual behavior (correlation was .66). Thus, it appears that persons high in private self-consciousness *do* possess clearer and more accurate self-knowledge. Very similar findings have also been reported when the initial questionnaire was completed in front of a small mirror or not; correlations between self-reports and behavior are much higher when those self-reports are made in front of a mirror, apparently as a result of the greater private self-awareness during the self-report (Pryor, Gibbons, Wicklund, Fazio, & Hood, 1977; Experiment 1).

Another body of evidence also supports Buss's views concerning the degree of self-knowledge possessed by those high in private self-consciousness. If such people really possess more clear and distinct knowledge based on their frequent attention to the private self, they might be expected to have a more extensive and detailed self-concept. Indeed, Turner (1978) and Franzoi (1983) found that high private self-conscious individuals provide more extensive self-descriptions than do those low in private self-consciousness, and Nasby (1985) found that they have more articulated self-schemata or self-concepts. Franzoi and Davis (Davis & Franzoi, 1986; Franzoi & Davis, 1985; Franzoi, Davis,

& Young, 1985) have also found that both high school and college students who are high in private self-consciousness are more likely to disclose private self-information to friends and to romantic partners than are their low private self-consciousness counterparts. This is consistent with Buss's theory if it is assumed that persons who possess the most self-knowledge will therefore have the most to disclose to others.

Public Self-Aspects

According to Buss, the effects of being publicly self-aware depend on the particular inducer that leads to the awareness. Therefore, let us turn our attention to the things that can make us aware of our public selves. First and foremost, according to Buss, other people make us publicly self-aware, particularly groups of other people, and especially strangers. Thus, to find a group of strangers staring at us is a very powerful inducer of public self-attention, and it leads us to question whether our appearance and behavior are appropriate. As Buss notes, a *lack* of attention from others may also induce public self-awareness; if your friends suddenly ignore your presence, this will also trigger an intense awareness of your public self.

Another kind of inducer of public self-awareness that has similar effects is a recording device such as a still camera, tape recorder, or video camera. Such devices in effect are mechanical "substitutes" for live audiences and thus make us aware of ourselves in the same way that live audiences do. What both of these classes of inducers have in common is that, in each one, the individual is *being observed*, either by a live audience or by a mechanical substitute. As a result, both of these classes of inducers will have similar effects on the individual.

There is another class of inducers as well. These inducers provide *perceptual feedback* to the individual—that is, they actually show us how we look or sound to other people. Unlike cameras or audiences, which simply make us aware that we are being observed, this kind of inducer presents us with information about how we are actually perceived by others. Examples of this class of inducer would be photographs or videotapes, audiotapes of our voices, or the sight of ourselves in three-piece, full-length mirrors like those found in clothing stores. In each case, we are faced with an image of ourselves to which we are not accustomed, and this makes us publicly self-aware. Large mirrors are said to make us publicly rather than privately self-aware, then, because the image they provide is novel and unusual.

According to this theory, public self-awareness leads to different effects, depending on whether it is induced by observation from others or from perceptual feedback. Buss describes the effects of being observed as uneasiness and discomfort; when other people (or mechanical substitutes) are watching us, we become uncomfortably aware of ourselves. According to Buss, we have come to learn through painful experience that scrutiny from other people (such as teachers, parents, and peers) usually means that we are doing something unusual or wrong; thus, when we become aware that others are observing us, our immediate reaction is to become vaguely uncomfortable and wonder what it is about our appearance that is causing this unwanted attention.

The effect of perceptual feedback is slightly different. When we suddenly come across a photograph or recording of ourselves or see ourselves in a full-length clothing mirror, we see aspects of ourselves in a way that is novel and unexpected. Quite literally, we become self-aware about some specific feature of our public image that the perceptual feedback presents to us. For example, people are typically surprised when they hear recordings of their voices because the sound is so different from what they are used to hearing. Seeing yourself in a full mirror also presents you with a view that you rarely see, although *other people* see that view all the time. Thus, you suddenly become aware of an aspect of yourself (voice, hair, weight) in the way that other people are aware of it. Buss also assumes that this new awareness is almost always less than flattering; voices sound tinny, figures look less attractive, hairlines seem to recede more than expected. As a result of perceptual feedback, then, we become aware of a discrepancy between our imagined public self and the actual public self; this awareness will lead to a temporary loss of self-esteem. In summary, then, being observed leads to a general uneasiness and apprehension about public self, while perceptual feedback leads to an awareness of a specific aspect of public self, and an accompanying loss of self-esteem. Table 12.4 illustrates in outline form Buss's theory regarding public self-awareness.

Just as Buss made a distinction between the state of private self-awareness and the trait of private self-consciousness, he makes a similar distinction with regard to the public self. The temporary, transient state of focusing attention on the public self is called public self-awareness. The chronic tendency that some people have to be aware of the public self is referred to as public self-consciousness, and is assessed by scores on the public self-consciousness portion of the SCS. Buss also points out that most of the time even those high in public self-consciousness will not focus attention on the public self without some kind of inducer. What distinguishes high public self-consciousness people from low public self-consciousness people is their *reaction* to inducers; those high in public self-consciousness will react more strongly to an audience, whereas those low in public self-consciousness will be less likely to become self-aware as a result of an audience.

TABLE 12.4

Outline of Buss's Theory Regarding Public Self-Attention

Inducer	Focus	Result
Being Observed		
Audience	Unspecified public	Discomfort and
Shunning situation	aspects of self	inhibition
Still cameras		
Video cameras		
Perceptual Feedback		
Large mirrors	Physical appearance	Drop in self-
Photographs	Physical appearance	esteem result-
Videotape	Physical appearance,	ing from dis-
	style, voice	crepancy be-
Tape recording	Voice	tween imagined
		and real self-
		image

Based on Buss (1980).

Relatively less research has explicitly examined situationally in-duced and habitual attention to public self-aspects than has examined private self-aspects. However, a number of studies are relevant to Buss's predictions. Allan Fenigstein, for example, conducted a study (Fenig-stein, 1979) that directly compared the reactions of high and low public self-conscious individuals in a social situation. In that experiment, three college women waited in a room for an experiment to begin; unbe-knownst to the third woman, the other two were working for the experimenter and only pretending to be participants in the experiment. Sometimes these two accomplices acted in a normal and friendly manner to the real subject—they neither stared at her nor ignored her. Other times the two accomplices deliberately *shunned* her; that is, they ignored her and spoke only among themselves. If she spoke to them directly, they responded as briefly as possible and seemed quite uninterested in her.

What effect should this have on the real subject? According to Buss, this obvious *lack* of attention from others should produce public self-awareness, just as open staring by the accomplices would have. As a result, the women in the "shunning" condition should be uneasy and uncomfortable. However, individuals high in public self-consciousness should be especially likely to react this way because of their greater sensitivity to inducers such as audiences. To measure this discomfort, Fenigstein did an interesting thing. He separated the three women and then told them that in the experiment itself they would have a choice of continuing with the same two women they had shared the waiting room with or continuing with a new pair of subjects. Choosing to stay with the original two women would indicate some satisfaction with them, whereas choosing to switch to a new pair would indicate dissatisfaction. Fenigstein found that the high public self-conscious women reacted most strongly to the shunning manipulation, as expected. For the women low in public self-consciousness it did not matter very much whether they were shunned or not; 50 percent of the shunned women chose to stay with the same two women who had shunned them, as did 70 percent of the nonshunned women. For the women high in public self-consciousness, shunning made a big difference: if they were not shunned, 75 percent chose to keep the original partners, but if they had been shunned, only 15 percent did so. Thus, those high in public self-consciousness showed the predicted strong reaction to an inducer of public self-awareness.

Much of the recent research dealing with public self-consciousness has also investigated private self-consciousness at the same time (e.g., Carver & Humphries, 1981; Carver & Scheier, 1981; Froming & Carver, 1981). The reason is that in many situations it would seem that private and public self-awareness should lead to different, and sometimes opposite, behaviors; in particular, it would seem that private self-attention should often lead us to act in keeping with our private beliefs whereas public self-attention should lead us to act in ways that we think others approve, regardless of our private beliefs. According to this logic, then, Buss's theory would predict that people who are high on private self-consciousness and low on public self-consciousness should be the ones most likely to act in accord with their true attitudes; they would know their true attitudes better (clarification) and they would be relatively unconcerned about how they appear to others. The other combinations of private and public self-consciousness should show much less consistency between private attitudes and public behavior. Those low in private self-consciousness would not have the clear accurate knowledge of their attitudes necessary to act consistently with them, whereas those high in private self-consciousness *and* high in public self-consciousness would have the necessary knowledge but might not act consistently because of a concern about the judgment of others.

Michael Scheier (1980) directly tested this idea. Scheier first used a questionnaire to measure students' private attitudes toward the use of physical punishment as a learning technique. Several months later some of these same people came to the laboratory in groups of two, three, or four and were told that they would be writing an essay on the use of punishment in child rearing *and* that they would later publicly discuss their views with the other group members. The essays were later evaluated by independent raters as to how favorable they were toward the use of punishment. Thus, Scheier had a measure of private attitude (the questionnaire responses) and a measure of a public expression of that attitude (the essay). How consistent were the students' responses from the first measure to the second? As expected, those high in private and low in public self-consciousness showed a very strong correlation (.64) between their initial attitudes and later essay; those with any other combination of private and public self-consciousness showed almost no correlation. Thus, it appears that even when people have an accurate self-knowledge resulting from high private self-focus, being simultaneously high in public self-consciousness can lead to behavior that does not reflect that self-knowledge; the concern over evaluation by others is too strong.

Carver and Scheier's Approach: A Control-Theory Model

The final approach to the issue of self-consciousness and self-awareness that we will discuss is one proposed by Charles Carver and Michael Scheier. Both men were graduate students at Texas during the time that Wicklund and Buss were formulating their theories; in fact, several of the experiments that we have mentioned so far as support for Wicklund's or Buss's views were carried out by one or both of them. In recent years, however, Carver and Scheier have developed an interpretation of self-focused attention that differs from the ones discussed thus far. This approach, which has been termed a *cybernetic,* or *control theory* model, is in some ways identical to Wicklund's theory but is in at least one way very different. In order to explain this model, a little background is necessary.

In formulating their view of self-awareness and self-consciousness, Carver and Scheier have borrowed some ideas and terminology from cybernetics, which is the science of communication and control. Although this field can often be confusing and complex, the fundamental ideas relevant to Carver and Scheier's theory are actually quite straightforward. Perhaps the easiest way to explain this theory is to start with the concept of a TOTE unit (Miller, Galanter, & Pribram, 1960). TOTE is an acronym that stands for Test-Operate-Test-Exit, which are the steps taken during the execution of a TOTE unit. Figure 12.1 displays the processes making up a TOTE unit.

In essence, a TOTE unit is a sequence of activities that serve to control some behavior. The first step in the sequence is the *test* phase,

FIGURE 12.1

The TOTE Unit

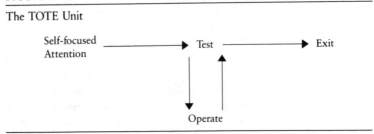

Based on Miller, Galanter, & Pribram (1960).

which is a comparison between an existing state and some predetermined standard. If this comparison reveals that there is a discrepancy between one's present state and the standard, then the next phase in the process, the *operate* phase, is initiated. Generally speaking, the operate phase has the effect of altering the existing state in some fashion. Once this has been completed, the *test* phase is initiated again, and a comparison of the present state and standard again determines whether a discrepancy exists. The test and operate phases thus alternate until there is no discriminable difference between the present state and standard. At this point a new phase—*exit*—is initiated, which ends the sequence.

Perhaps a practical everyday example will help to make this clearer. A very simple example of a TOTE unit would be a room thermostat connected to an air conditioner. A thermostat measures the temperature of the air in the room (the existing state) and compares it to the temperature that has been preset (the predetermined standard). This is the *test* phase. If there is a difference between the two, then a signal is sent to the air conditioner, which begins cooling the air (the *operate* phase). Eventually there is another test, and if the temperature in the room is now the same as the preset value, the air conditioner is turned off *(exit)*.

Carver and Scheier believe that human behavior is controlled by a very similar kind of process. Our behavior is said to be guided by predetermined standards of behavior that are represented in our minds. These behavioral standards take many forms. Our attitudes, for example, are a kind of behavioral standard, because our positive or negative attitudes toward someone or something often imply how we should act toward them. Our wishes and desires are a form of behavioral standards, because they imply a desired type of behavior. Instructions that have been given to us are also a form of standard.

Carver and Scheier argue that everyone (at least part of the time) compares their actual behavior to their standards (test), and when discrepancies exist they attempt to change their actions in order to bring themselves into line with the standards (operate). Thus, human behavior is said to be controlled by a process identical to that of the thermostat. Where does self-awareness fit into this scheme? According to the theory, the comparison or test phase *results from* a focusing of attention on the self. Greater self-directed attention is said to lead to "more frequent comparisons, or a more thorough comparison, between present behavior and the standard" (Carver & Scheier, 1981, p. 144). This greater degree of comparison results then in a greater tendency to alter behavior so that it matches the standard. Thus, focusing attention on the self should lead ultimately to greater attempts to act in accordance with our standards of behavior.

The observant reader may be wondering at this point what the difference is between this theory and Wicklund's theory. After all, Wicklund also proposes that self-awareness leads to an attempt to bring an existing state (the real self) into line with a predetermined standard (the ideal self). Aren't both theories saying the same thing? To a large degree they are. However, one key difference between the two theories is their explanation of *why* a discrepancy between existing state and standard leads to behavior change. Wicklund claims that the discrepancy leads to an unpleasant motivational state; in order to get rid of this unpleasant feeling, we strive to reduce such discrepancies. Thus, Wicklund's theory is a motivational theory. Carver and Scheier claim that such discrepancies do *not* necessarily lead to an unpleasant motivational state. That is, simply being aware that there is a discrepancy between one's ideal and real self does not mean that a person will necessarily experience any negative feelings. As a result, there is no pressure to get rid of those feelings by reducing the real-ideal discrepancy. Instead, Carver and Scheier believe that the shifting of behavior to bring it into line with standards occurs almost automatically; as they describe it, the shift is simply "a natural consequence of the engagement of a discrepancy-reducing feedback loop" (i.e., a TOTE unit). Thus, they do not believe that behavior is produced by a desire to reduce unpleasant motivational states; their theory is not a motivational theory in the same way that Wicklund's is.

At one level, of course, this difference between the two theories really doesn't matter. The motivational and nonmotivational approaches still generally make the same predictions about *how* people will act; they only differ as to exactly *why*. In fact, the vast majority of the research that supports the Wicklund approach also supports the Carver and Scheier approach because both approaches make the same predictions so much of the time. Carver and Scheier do believe, however, that there is some research indicating that their approach is superior. Specifically, they point to the prediction of the Wicklund theory that becoming self-aware almost always leads to negative affect because of the real-ideal self discrepancy. As noted earlier, there are several studies (e.g., Carver & Scheier, 1978; Franzoi & Brewer, 1984; Hull & Levy, 1979; Steenbarger & Aderman, 1979) that have failed to find that the state of self-awareness produces unpleasant feelings. If self-focus invariably leads to a negative motivational state, why didn't these studies find it? Carver and Scheier's explanation is that there is only *one* kind of situation in which self-awareness will lead to negative affect— when the discrepancy between the existing state and the standard cannot be reduced. That is, only when we become aware of a shortcoming that cannot be overcome will unpleasant feelings result; people facing such a situation might also be likely to seek escape from self-awareness more quickly, as subjects did in the Duval, Wicklund, and Fine study discussed earlier.

Two other differences between these two theories may be more important than the question of motivation. First, although Wicklund's theory does not deal with the question of individual differences, Carver and Scheier explicitly acknowledge that not only can stimuli in the environment (such as mirrors) serve to focus attention on the self, but some people are simply more likely to spontaneously turn attention on the self. Thus, unlike Wicklund but similar to Buss, Carver and Scheier are concerned not only with the state of self-awareness but also with the trait of self-consciousness as assessed by the SCS. Carver and Scheier also believe that the process resulting from both the state and trait is the same: Attention to the self, whether resulting from dispositions or cues, instigates the comparison process of the TOTE unit, which in turn produces behavioral change. In fact, Carver and Scheier have frequently carried out their experiments twice—once manipulating self-attention with a mirror and the second time measuring dispositional private self-focus with the SCS—and they have consistently found identical patterns of results with each approach (Carver & Scheier, 1978; Scheier, 1976; Scheier & Carver, 1977; Scheier & Carver, 1980; Scheier, Carver, & Gibbons, 1979).

The other difference between the two approaches is that Carver and Scheier, unlike Wicklund (but again like Buss), clearly distinguish between private and public self-awareness as well as between private and public self-consciousness. For Carver and Scheier, the difference between private and public self-awareness is simple but important; being privately self-aware produces a comparison between an existing state and a *private* standard (for example, one's own values), whereas being publicly self-aware produces a comparison between an existing state and a *public* standard (for example, one's belief about what other people value). In either case, however, this comparison then leads to a behavior shift designed to bring the existing state into line with the standard.

As an example of how this works, consider a clever experiment conducted by Froming, Walker, and Lopyan (1982, Experiment 1). In order to fully demonstrate how *private* standards can differ from *public* standards, these researchers pretested a large number of college students regarding their attitudes toward physical punishment. From this large group, a smaller number with a particular set of attitudes were then selected: These students personally felt that physical punishment was rarely justified, but they believed that most other people felt that such punishment *was* justified. That is, these people had a private standard (anti-punishment) that differed from what they thought the public standards were (pro-punishment). Several weeks later, these students took part in the experiment that required them to serve as a "teacher" and administer electric shocks to another person (in reality, a confederate of the experimenters) as part of an attempt to help that other person learn. Because the students could control the intensity of the shocks they delivered, the dependent variable was simply the average shock intensity chosen by the student.

In essence, the question is this: To which standard—private or public—will the participants adhere? Will they follow their own private views, or will they act in the way they believe most others favor? Froming and his colleagues thought that students might follow either standard, depending upon the kind of self-awareness they were experiencing. Therefore, some students administered shocks while facing a small mirror, which should have the effect of increasing private self-awareness. Other subjects administered the shocks not in front of a mirror, but with a two-person audience present; they were told that these two people were there to observe the experiment and to rate the student's "effectiveness as a teacher." The presence of the audience, rather than increase awareness of private standards, was expected to heighten the students' public self-awareness—that is, enhance their awareness of how they would look to the audience. Finally, a control group of students administered the shocks with neither a mirror nor an audience present.

What pattern of results would you expect in this experiment? Froming and his colleagues predicted (as would Carver and Scheier) that, compared to the control group, the students facing a mirror would behave in accordance with their private standard and give weak shocks. That is exactly what happened. In contrast, those faced with an audience were predicted to be more aware of the public standard they believed to exist—that is, other people favor the use of shocks. Thus, it was expected these students, compared to the control group, would administer stronger shocks; again, that is what occurred. In short, the *kind of self-awareness,* either private or public, had important consequences for behavior. Attention to private standards led to behavior consistent with those standards; attention to public standards led to behavior that conformed to those standards.

In summarizing the Carver and Scheier position, we can say that considerable evidence supports its predictions; of course, much of that evidence supports the Wicklund and Buss positions as well. Where the Carver and Scheier approach seems to have a clear advantage over Wicklund's is in distinguishing between private and public self-awareness and self-consciousness. Because Wicklund's theory does not make a distinction between private and public, it is poorly equipped to make sense of findings like those of Froming et al. (1982). As a result, it seems limited in its ability to accurately explain as wide a range of situations as Carver and Scheier's approach.

It should be clear by now that Carver and Scheier's theory is more similar to Wicklund's approach in some ways, but more similar to Buss's approach in others. Like Buss, Carver and Scheier emphasize the public–private distinction and the difference between the state of self-awareness and the trait of self-consciousness, both of which Wicklund essentially ignores. Like Wicklund, however, Carver and Scheier emphasize the comparison of an existing state to a predetermined standard as the chief mechanism for governing behavior, a position with which Buss takes issue. In a way, then, and this is an oversimplification, Carver and Scheier have provided a new way of understanding self-attention processes that is a synthesis of Wicklund, Buss, and concepts from control theory.

Concluding Remarks

Our discussion of these theories will end by offering two conclusions. First, regardless of the specific theoretical mechanism said to produce it, attention to private aspects of the self clearly has the effect of making people act in ways that are consistent with their attitudes, beliefs, and values, whereas attention to public self-aspects results in people being more inclined to behave in ways consistent with social standards or relevant reference groups. These findings should not be underemphasized. One of the most durable controversies in social and personality psychology has concerned the degree to which internal factors, like attitudes, versus external factors, like reference groups, actually guide overt behavior (Abelson, 1972; LaPiere, 1934; Wicker, 1969). The fact that the two different kinds of self-focused attention produce different responses to social pressure is a notable accomplishment.

A second conclusion concerns one possible direction for future research in this area. An issue that has been almost totally ignored to date has been a consideration of how individual differences in private and public self-consciousness develop. As we have seen, the effects of such individual differences are sometimes powerful and have been clearly documented. An important task, it would then seem, is to account for the development of those individual tendencies in the first place. Buss (1980) has done the most along these lines, speculating about some possible causes of individual differences in self-consciousness. He has suggested, for example, that children who are socially isolated may be more likely to develop a tendency toward private self-consciousness, partially as a compensation for the lack of social activity. Likewise, children who experience chronic health problems may also learn to pay extra attention to internal bodily states and thus develop a permanent tendency toward private self-scrutiny. To our knowledge, however, no research has been done to test these ideas, and this seems clearly to be a valuable avenue to explore in coming years.

Over the past fifteen or twenty years, research interest in self-awareness and self-consciousness has grown at a phenomenal pace; a conservative estimate is that over 290 published articles dealing primarily with issues of self-awareness and self-consciousness appeared between 1972 and 1986 (Franzoi, 1986). One of the reasons for this interest should be obvious: Self-awareness and self-consciousness have proven to have considerable impact on important human behaviors. The evidence reported here illustrates just how successful the self-awareness and self-consciousness concepts have been, and in psychology as in any other field, interest follows success. However, it seems to us that this area has attracted intense attention for another reason as well: people—psychologists included—are simply intrigued by questions of self-knowledge. How much do we know about ourselves? How accurate is that knowledge? What do we do with such knowledge? These questions have fascinated psychologists, sociologists, and the population at large for centuries, and continue to do so today. Thus, recent theories dealing with these issues are exciting at least in part because they offer us new ways to satisfy an age-old curiosity. Perhaps it should not surprise us, therefore, to find that these fresh perspectives on fundamental questions are as attractive as they are. Happily, if the evidence thus far is any indication, the attention given to these approaches has not been misplaced, and all indications are that these lines of research will remain vital and productive for years to come.

Summary

For hundreds of years, humans have distinguished between the private, nonvisible aspects of self and the public, observable ones. In recent years modern psychology has expended considerable energy in attempts to understand the awareness that people have (or lack) concerning these different aspects of self. This chapter has presented three current theories dealing with the issues of self-awareness and self-consciousness.

Robert Wicklund's theory of objective self-awareness was the first of these modern theories to be formulated. According to this theory, when something in the environment (like a mirror) directs our attention back toward ourselves, it makes us aware of the discrepancy that typically exists between our actual behavior and the idealized standards of behavior we possess. Becoming aware of our shortcomings then produces an unpleasant affective state, which leads either to attempted escape from the self-focused attention or to efforts directed toward a reduction of the real–ideal discrepancy. One common outcome of self-awareness, then, is said to be a closer correspondence between one's actual behavior and one's behavioral standards. Considerable research evidence supports this theory.

A second modern view of self-awareness comes from Arnold Buss. Buss essentially discards the notion of ideal behavioral standards. He instead makes the claim that self-focused attention simply brings people to know themselves better as a result of the increased attention to their private aspects. Thus, persons with greater self-awareness may behave in ways more consistent with their internal attitudes, but for reasons different from those proposed by Wicklund. Too, Buss distinguishes between attention to private aspects of self and public aspects of self and claims that different kinds of behavior will follow from the different types of awareness. In addition, and unlike Wicklund, Buss acknowledges that individuals may differ among themselves in terms of their ongoing dispositional tendency to be self-aware.

The third modern approach is in some ways a hybrid of the two foregoing views. Charles Carver and Michael Scheier have recently proposed a cybernetic model of self-attention, which holds that behavior is regulated by a set of internal processes that compare one's current behavioral state with a preset behavioral standard and then strive to minimize the differences between these two states. Although this view clearly has some similarities to Wicklund's approach, it differs in its rejection of unpleasant affect as the motivator of behavior change. In addition, Carver and Scheier's view is similar to Buss's with regard to its emphasis on distinguishing between public and private self-attention as well as in its differentiation between the state and trait of self-focused attention.

SUGGESTED READINGS

Buss, A.H. (1980). *Self-consciousness and social anxiety.* San Francisco: Freeman. This is a highly readable account of Buss's ideas concerning self-awareness and self-consciousness, and how he sees his views in relation to other theorists.

Carver, C.S., & Scheier, M.F. (1981). *Attention and self-regulation: A control-theory approach to human behavior.* New York: Springer-Verlag. This is a comprehensive presentation of Carver and Scheier's cybernetic view of self-attention, intended for a professional audience, but still accessible for an undergraduate reader.

Duval, S., & Wicklund, R.A. (1972). *A theory of objective self-awareness.* New York: Academic Press. This is the original presentation of objective self-awareness theory, intended for a professional audience.

Hull, J.G. (1981). A self-awareness model of the causes and effects of alcohol consumption. *Journal of Abnormal Psychology, 90,* 586–600. This is an interesting extension of modern self-awareness theories, in which Hull argues that alcohol consumption tends to decrease one's degree of privately self-focused attention, and that this might in fact be one reason that people choose to drink.

Snyder, M. (1987). *Public appearances/private realities.* New York: Freeman. An interesting presentation of Snyder's ideas and research on the topic of self-monitoring, especially tailored for a student audience.

REFERENCES

Abelson, R.P. (1972). Are attitudes necessary? In B.T. King & E. McGinnies (Eds.), *Attitudes, conflict, and social change* (pp. 19–32). New York: Academic Press.

Aronson, E., & Linder, D. (1965). Gain and loss of esteem as determinants of interpersonal attractiveness. *Journal of Experimental Social Psychology, 1,* 156–171.

Baumeister, R. F. (1986). *Identity: Cultural change and the struggle for self.* New York: Oxford University Press.

Buss, A.H. (1980). *Self-consciousness and social anxiety.* San Francisco: Freeman.

Carver, C.S. (1975). Physical aggression as a function of objective self-awareness and attitudes toward punishment. *Journal of Experimental Social Psychology, 11,* 510–519.

Carver, C.S. (1979). A cybernetic model of self-attention processes. *Journal of Personality and Social Psychology, 37,* 1251–1281.

Carver, C.S., & Glass, D.C. (1976). The self-consciousness scale: A discriminant validity study. *Journal of Personality Assessment, 40,* 169–172.

Carver, C.S., & Humphries, C. (1981). Havana daydreaming: A study of self-consciousness and the negative reference group among Cuban Americans. *Journal of Personality and Social Psychology, 40,* 545–552.

Carver, C.S., & Scheier, M.F. (1978). Self-focusing effects of dispositional self-consciousness, mirror presence, and audience presence. *Journal of Personality and Social Psychology, 36,* 324–332.

Carver, C.S., & Scheier, M.F. (1981). *Attention and self-regulation: A control-theory approach to human behavior.* New York: Springer-Verlag.

Cooley, C.H. (1902). *Human nature and the social order.* New York: Scribner's.

Davis, M.H., & Franzoi, S.L. (1986). Adolescent loneliness, self-disclosure, and private self-consciousness: A longitudinal investigation. *Journal of Personality and Social Psychology, 51,* 595–608.

Duval, S., & Wicklund, R.A. (1972). *A theory of objective self-awareness.* New York: Academic Press.

Duval, S., Wicklund, R.A., & Fine, R.L. (1971). Avoidance of objective self-awareness under conditions of high and low intra-self discrepancy. In S. Duval & R.A. Wicklund, *A theory of objective self-awareness* (pp. 16–21). New York: Academic Press.

Fenigstein, A. (1979). Self-consciousness, self-attention, and social interaction. *Journal of Personality and Social Psychology, 37,* 75–86.

Fenigstein, A., Scheier, M.F., & Buss, A.H. (1975). Public and private self-consciousness: Assessment and theory. *Journal of Consulting and Clinical Psychology, 43,* 522–527.

Franzoi, S.L. (1983). Self-concept differences as a function of private self-consciousness and social anxiety. *Journal of Research in Personality, 17,* 275–287.

Franzoi, S.L. (1986). Self-consciousness and self-awareness: An annotated bibliography of theory and research. *Social and Behavioral Sciences Documents, 16,* listing 2744.

Franzoi, S.L., & Brewer, L.C. (1984). The experience of self-awareness and its relation to level of self-consciousness: An experiential sampling study. *Journal of Research in Personality, 18,* 522–540.

Franzoi, S.L., & Davis, M.H. (1985). Adolescent self-disclosure and loneliness: Private self-consciousness and parental influences. *Journal of Personality and Social Psychology, 48,* 768–780.

Franzoi, S.L., Davis, M.H., & Young, R.D. (1985). The effects of private self-consciousness and perspective taking on satisfaction in close relationships. *Journal of Personality and Social Psychology, 48,* 1584–1594.

Froming, W.J., & Carver, C.S. (1981). Divergent influences of private and public self-consciousness on a compliance paradigm. *Journal of Research in Personality, 15,* 159–171.

Froming, W.J., Walker, G.R., & Lopyan, K.J. (1982). Public and private self-awareness: When personal attitudes conflict with societal expectations. *Journal of Experimental Social Psychology, 18,* 476–487.

Gibbons, F.X. (1983). Self-attention and self-report: The "veridicality" hypothesis. *Journal of Personality, 51,* 517–542.

Goldstein, I.L. (1971). The application blank: How honest are the responses? *Journal of Applied Psychology, 55,* 491–492.

Gur, R.C., & Sackheim, H.A. (1979). Self-deception: A concept in search of a phenomenon. *Journal of Personality and Social Psychology, 37,* 147–169.

Hass, R.G. (1984). Perspective taking and self-awareness: Drawing an E on your forehead. *Journal of Personality and Social Psychology, 46,* 788–798.

Hogan, R., & Cheek, J. (1983). Identity, authenticity, and maturity. In T.R. Sarbin & K.E. Scheibe (Eds.), *Studies in social identity* (pp. 339–357). New York: Praeger.

Hull, J.G., & Levy, A.S. (1979). The organization functions of the self: An alternative to the

Duvall and Wicklund model of self-awareness. *Journal of Personality and Social Psychology, 37,* 756–768.

James, W. (1890). *The principles of psychology.* New York: Holt, Rinehart, & Winston.

Jung, C.G. (1923). *Psychological types.* New York: Harcourt, Brace.

LaPiere, R.T. (1934). Attitudes versus actions. *Social Forces, 13,* 230–237.

Mead, G.H. (1934). *Mind, self, and society.* Chicago: University of Chicago Press.

Merz, J. (1984). The self-consciousness scale of Fenigstein, Scheier, and Buss: Empirical results. *Psychologische Beitrage, 26,* 239–249.

Miller, G.A., Galanter, E., & Pribram, K.H. (1960). *Plans and the structure of behavior.* New York: Holt, Rinehart, & Winston.

Nasby, W. (1985). Private self-consciousness, articulation of the self-schema, and recognition memory of trait adjectives. *Journal of Personality and Social Psychology, 49,* 704–709.

Pryor, J.B., Gibbons, F.X., Wicklund, R.A., Fazio, R.H., & Hood, R. (1977). Self-focused attention and self-report validity. *Journal of Personality, 45,* 514–527.

Riggio, R.E. (1986). Assessment of basic social skills. *Journal of Personality and Social Psychology, 51,* 649–660.

Rotter, J.B. (1966). Generalized expectancies for internal versus external control of reinforcement. *Psychological Monographs, 80,* 1–28.

Scheier, M.F. (1976). Self-awareness, self-consciousness, and angry aggression. *Journal of Personality, 44,* 627–644.

Scheier, M.F. (1980). Effects of public and private self-consciousness on the public expression of personal beliefs. *Journal of Personality and Social Psychology, 39,* 514–521.

Scheier, M.F., Buss, A.H., & Buss, D.M. (1978). Self-consciousness, self-report of aggressiveness, and aggression. *Journal of Research in Personality, 12,* 133–140.

Scheier, M.F., & Carver, C.S. (1977). Self-focused attention and the experience of emotion: Attraction, repulsion, elation, and depression. *Journal of Personality and Social Psychology, 35,* 625–636.

Scheier, M.F., & Carver, C.S. (1980). Private and public self-attention, resistance to change, and dissonance reduction. *Journal of Personality and Social Psychology, 39,* 390–405.

Scheier, M.F., & Carver, C.S. (1985). The self-consciousness scale: A revised version for use with general populations. *Journal of Applied Social Psychology, 15,* 687–699.

Scheier, M.F., Carver, C.S., & Gibbons, F.X. (1979). Self-directed attention, awareness of bodily states, and suggestibility. *Journal of Personality and Social Psychology, 37,* 1576–1588.

Schlenker, B.R. (1980). *Impression management: The self-concept, social identity, and interpersonal relations.* Monterey, CA: Brooks/Cole.

Snyder, M. (1974). Self-monitoring of expressive behavior. *Journal of Personality and Social Psychology, 30,* 526–537.

Snyder, M. (1987). *Public appearances/private realities: The psychology of self-monitoring.* New York: Freeman.

Snyder, M., Gangestad, S., & Simpson, J.A. (1983). Choosing friends as activity partners: The role of self-monitoring. *Journal of Personality and Social Psychology, 45,* 1061–1072.

Snyder, M., & Swann, W.B., Jr. (1976). When actions reflect attitudes: The politics of impression management. *Journal of Personality and Social Psychology, 34,* 1034–1042.

Snyder, M., & Tanke, E.D. (1976). Behavior and attitude: Some people are more consistent than others. *Journal of Personality, 44,* 510–517.

Steenbarger, B.N., & Aderman, D. (1979). Objective self-awareness as a nonaversive state: Effect of anticipating discrepancy reduction. *Journal of Personality, 47,* 330–339.

Sugawara, K. (1984). An attempt to construct the self-consciousness scale for Japanese. *Japanese Journal of Psychology, 55,* 184–188.

Turner, R.G. (1978). Consistency, self-consciousness, and the predictive validity of typical and maximal personality measures. *Journal of Research in Personality, 12,* 117–132.

Turner, R.G., Scheier, M.F., Carver, C.S., & Ickes, W. (1978). Correlates of self-consciousness. *Journal of Personality Assessment, 42,* 285–289.

Vleeming, R.G., & Engelse, J.A. (1981). Assessment of private and public self-consciousness: A Dutch replication. *Journal of Personality Assessment, 45,* 385–389.

Wicker, A.W. (1969). Attitudes vs. actions: The relationship of verbal and overt behavioral responses to attitude objects. *Journal of Social Issues, 25,* 41–78.

Wicklund, R.A., & Frey, D. (1980). Self-awareness theory: When the self makes a difference. In D.M. Wegner and R.R. Vallacher (Eds.), *The self in social psychology* (pp. 31–54). New York: Oxford University Press.

Witkin, H.A., Lewis, H.B., Hertzman, M., Machover, K., Meissner, P.B., & Wapner, S. (1954). *Personality through perception.* New York: Harper.

CHAPTER 13

Self-Concept and Identity

ROY F. BAUMEISTER

Introduction
Self-Concept
    Formation of the Self-Concept
    Self-Esteem: Evaluating the Self
ACTIVITY BOX: Measuring Your
    Self-Esteem
    Research on Self-Esteem
    Other Aspects of Self-Concept
    Maintaining Self-Concept and
        Self-Esteem

Identity
    Structure and Functions of
        Identity
    Identity Crises
Summary
SUGGESTED READINGS
REFERENCES

Introduction

What is the self? When asked that question, small children answer by indicating their bodies. Self starts with body, in the sense that people first develop a notion of self that is based on the physical self.

Older children and adults, however, have notions of selfhood that go far beyond the physical self. These notions include social identity, reputation, personal values, and other factors. They think of the self as something that exists "inside," that is, somewhere not visible to physical inspection and something separate from the palpable, physical body.

If you are asked to identify yourself, you might respond in quite different ways depending on what you were doing and who was asking. Feelings about the self may also change from time to time. There is probably a stable core to the self, but different parts or versions of the self are apparent in different circumstances. Moreover, selves do change over time in fundamental ways so that even the most stable core of the self may not be fixed and constant. You can see why it has proven difficult for psychology to come up with firm answers about the nature of the self, for the self includes stability and change, visible manifestations and inner phenomena, ideas and feelings, and other complexities.

In this chapter we will be concerned with one large region of the self, namely, self-concept and identity. Self-concept and identity refer to ideas about the self, to definitions placed on the self. This part of the self is constructed out of *meaning*. Unlike the body, which is made out of biochemical substances, the self-concept is made of meaning, which is a symbolic, social, linguistic phenomenon. Without symbols or language, there would be no self-concepts. Another way of putting this is that the self-concept is a network of interrelated ideas.

"Self" is perhaps the broadest term. It has been used in many different ways, referring to many parts of a whole set of experiences and thoughts. Sometimes it is used to refer to the whole set. Some related terms are ego, identity, self-concept, self-schema, proprium. Because the term self has many meanings, different theorists have used it in different ways, which generates some confusion. It is not always safe to assume that what one writer means by "self" is the same as what another writer means by it.

In this chapter, we will use "self" pretty much the same way the word is used in ordinary language. Your self is the totality of you, including your body, your sense of identity, your reputation (how others know you), and so on. It encompasses both the physical self and the self that is constructed out of meaning.

Self-Concept: Your Idea(s) About Yourself

The self-concept is the individual's beliefs about himself or herself, including who and what the self is, and including the person's attributes. The self-concept includes many things that might not be part of one's identity. For example, a person's self-concept might include many personality attributes, such as being friendly or talkative.

Self-Esteem: How You Evaluate Yourself

An important part of the self-concept is self-esteem. A self-concept is not merely an abstract summary or notion of the self, but it is full of evaluations, that is, of perceptions of the self as good, bad, or mediocre. Self-esteem refers to the person's broadest evaluation of himself or herself. Of course, people also have levels of specific self-esteem for specific domains. Someone may regard herself, for example, as an excellent tennis player, a mediocre student, and a poor cook.

Identity: Who You Are

Identity is a definition placed on the self. Your sense of identity refers to your knowledge of who you are. Identity always answers the question, "Who are you?" Self-concept, in contrast, may contain answers to other questions like "What kind of person are you?" and "How good are you?"

Identity may contain material that is not part of the self-concept, because identity is not fully contained inside the person's own mind. To use an extreme example, newborn babies do not have self-concepts, but they do have identities: They belong to a certain family, they soon have a name, and so on.

The concept of identity rests on two notions, sameness (continuity) and difference. Identity means being the same person you were yesterday or ten years ago; it also means being different from someone else. The task of eyewitness identification is to decide which person in the police lineup is the person who committed some crime. This means identifying someone as being the same person who performed some other deed and differentiating that person from other, innocent people. Likewise, a campus identification card links your identity across time (you have the same card for a period of time) and differentiates you from other people (for example, only people with such cards are permitted to use campus facilities).

Self-Concept

This section will cover current knowledge about the self-concept. First, we will examine what is known about the formation of the self-concept in children. Second, we will look closely at self-esteem, because that is the aspect of the self-concept that has received the greatest amount of research. The final section will, however, examine several approaches to the self-concept other than self-esteem.

Formation of the Self-Concept

Although psychology still has much to learn about how self-concepts form and develop, there is a reasonable amount of information available. Psychologists have recently devised several very clever strategies to study self-concepts in very young children.

The first step in forming a self-concept is learning to distinguish between one's own body and the rest of the world. The infant learns that some things are always there, whereas others come and go. The bed, like Daddy, is only present at certain times, but hands and feet are always there. Gradually the infant learns the boundaries of its own body. For a long time, self is equated with body.

How early does sense of self start? There is no way to be certain, but the signs suggest that it starts very early in life. By the time an infant is three months old, it likes to look at itself in the mirror, presumably because it can see that its own body movements "magically" produce movements in the image (Lewis & Brooks-Gunn, 1979). Recognizing oneself on the basis of facial features—such as recognizing a photograph rather than a moving image in a mirror—happens during the second year of life.

During this second year of life, children begin to understand that they need to conform to external standards and rules, and they begin to evaluate their own actions against external standards (Kagan, 1981). This is a big step in the growth of self-awareness. Children learn to evaluate their actions as good or bad, and they develop some concept of *mastery,* as in knowing how to do things. Obviously, at this age, there are many things one cannot do, but the child's mastery of simple skills brings pleasure and satisfaction. One sign of that is that children will smile when they successfully accomplish something (Kagan, 1981). This suggests a feeling of self as capable of performing up to certain external standards.

The proper beginnings of a self-concept seem to occur around fifteen months of age. At this point, children are able to identify themselves (and others) on the basis of gender and age (Damon & Hart, 1982; Lewis & Brooks-Gunn, 1979). Of course, this is not numerical age, but merely the difference between children and adults. Thus, age and gender seem to be the first ingredients of the self-concept. Familiarity is also important, implying that children's self-concepts also soon incorporate some sense of belonging to a certain family group.

During the second year of life, the child's self-concept begins to include active skills. Perhaps the first such skill to have a major impact on self-concept is the ability to walk (Erikson, 1968; Mahler, Pine, & Bergman, 1975). From ages three to five, self-concepts of children seem to emphasize skills and abilities. The self is understood in terms of what it can and cannot do (Keller, Ford, & Meacham, 1978). The child's concept of self revolves around whether the child can brush its teeth, tie its shoes, ride a tricycle or bicycle, tell time, and so on.

From ages six to twelve, the child's sense of competency and control normally tends to increase in a steady fashion (e.g., Brim, 1976; Erikson, 1968). Children begin to see their competencies in more complex ways than simply what they can versus cannot do. In particular, they begin to compare their competencies against others and to measure them by hierarchies of standards. To the young child, the issue is simply whether one can ride a bike or not. The older child is concerned with riding a bike faster, farther, or better than other children (Damon & Hart, 1982).

Another development of the period from age six to age twelve is the beginning of a conception of self as something inner or hidden. If you ask a young child about the self, the child will point to the body, for the young child has no other way of thinking about the self. Older children begin to develop notions of a more psychological self, including thoughts, feelings, and intentions, that go beyond the mere physical self (Mohr, 1978). The idea of an inner self is difficult for children at first, and they tend to accept whatever their parents (or other authority figures) tell them. Indeed, eleven-year-old children, when asked, "Who knows best what kind of person you really are, deep down inside, your mother or father or yourself?" tend to say that the mother or father knows the child better than the child knows himself or herself (Rosenberg, 1979). The idea of knowing one's own self better than anyone else—the principle of *privileged access* to one's inner self—does not become firm until adolescence.

The self-concept undergoes further refinements during the teen years. Increases in mental abilities greatly improve the child's capacity to consider himself or herself from other, outside perspectives. In particular, teenagers are much better than younger children at imagining how they appear to someone else. As a result, self-consciousness increases greatly around age twelve or thirteen (Simmons, Rosenberg, & Rosenberg, 1973; Tice, Buder, & Baumeister, 1985). Moral issues and dilemmas become important, and the adolescent seeks to ground the self-concept in a firm set of values, often in the form of universal or abstract principles. The self-concept comes to include ideological beliefs such as religious, political, and philosophical views (Montemayor & Eisen, 1977). Many people undergo identity crises at this age (Erikson, 1968). We shall return to the nature of identity crises at the end of this chapter.

Self-Esteem: Evaluating the Self

Of all the aspects of the self-concept, one of the most important is self-esteem. When researchers set out to study the self-concept, they usually end up studying self-esteem. This is partly because self-esteem is so important (Greenwald, 1981). Self-esteem affects many different actions and reactions.

What is the best way to conceptualize self-esteem? One important early approach was to think of it as a comparison between goals or standards and achievements. William James defined self-esteem as one's successes divided by one's pretensions (i.e., one's goals or aspirations). Carl Rogers stated a similar idea in regarding self-esteem as the discrepancy between one's *real self* and one's *ideal self*. For example, imagine two men who measure their worth by how much money they earn and who both earn an annual salary of $25,000. Suppose, however, that one of them holds the ambition of reaching a $75,000 salary whereas the other's ambition is to earn around $30,000.

According to James and Rogers, the first man will have lower self-esteem than the second, because he is farther away from his goal.

Today, most researchers have abandoned this notion of self-esteem. They found that the goal level or ideal self contributed little to understanding self-esteem (Wylie, 1974). The two men who both measure their worth by their salary and who earn the same salary probably have about the same level of self-esteem, despite the difference in their eventual ambitions. Indeed, the man with the higher goal might well turn out to be the one with the slightly higher self-esteem, because people with higher levels of self-esteem sometimes set higher goals for themselves (see, e.g., Coopersmith, 1967). The best way to measure self-esteem is to find out just how good someone thinks he or she is; it is not necessary to bother with measuring how good the person wants to be.

Thus, goals and ideals have not been found to be an important factor in measuring self-esteem. Partly this is because most people want to be good and successful. Partly it's because low aspiration levels tend to indicate the irrelevance of the dimension rather than produce high self-esteem. That is, if someone does not have high goals and ambitions in a certain area (e.g., athletic skills), it is likely that the person simply views that area as irrelevant to his or her self-esteem. Consider a traditional male who doesn't feel he needs to be able to cook well, beyond being able to fry himself a hamburger once in a while. According to the theory of James and Rogers, his success at frying hamburgers equals his goal level, so he should have high self-esteem with respect to his cooking ability. More likely, however, he simply regards cooking as irrelevant to his self-esteem, and frying hamburgers makes no difference in his overall self-esteem.

An important principle associated with self-esteem is the desire for high esteem. People are reluctant to lose esteem, such as by failing publicly or being humiliated. Most people rate themselves as above average, even on self-esteem scales (Baumeister, Tice, & Hutton, 1987). Even people with low self-esteem generally regard themselves as having some quality or ability that marks them as above average on a dimension they consider important (Swann, Pelham, & Krull, 1987). People go to great lengths to support their favorable opinions of themselves and to avoid loss of esteem.

The desire for high esteem can be subdivided into two motives, called self-enhancement and self-protection. Self-enhancement means increasing esteem, whereas self-protection means avoiding the loss of esteem. Although sometimes these go together, at other times they can operate in a conflicting fashion. For example, suppose someone challenges you to a tennis game, and you can either accept or decline the challenge. Self-enhancement would say you should accept the challenge, for you can increase your esteem as a tennis player by winning. In contrast, the self-protection motive might tell you to make some excuse and decline to play, for that is the safest way to avoid the reduction in esteem that might occur if you lose the game.

Different situations emphasize the enhancement and protection motives differently. Suppose the person challenging you to a tennis match is only twelve years old. The enhancement motive becomes irrelevant here, for it will not boost your reputation much to win a game against a smaller, weaker, younger opponent. If a twelve-year-old defeats you, however, you may be embarrassed and lose esteem. Thus, a challenge from such a child invokes the self-protection motive but not the self-enhancement one.

In contrast, suppose the person who challenges you is a first-rate player—someone clearly better than you, perhaps someone who has played professionally. If you lose to this person, you do not lose much esteem. If you happen to win, however, you will gain much. A challenge of this type invokes the enhancement motive but not the protection motive.

ACTIVITY BOX

Measuring Your Self-Esteem

Most measures of self-esteem rely on asking the person to rate himself or herself on various dimensions. Here are some sample items that are similar to those used on actual scales. Try to rate yourself on each one, giving yourself a numerical rating from 0 to 6 (0 = very often, or very much; 6 = almost never, or not at all).

1. How often do you feel superior to most other people?
2. How often do you think that one day you will accomplish great things?
3. Do you worry about making a good impression on other people?
4. Do you frequently fear that other people will dislike you or think badly of you?
5. When you complete an assignment or test, do you usually have the feeling that you did a poor or inadequate job?
6. Do you consider yourself more physically attractive than the average person you know?
7. How often do you do things that seem clumsy or uncoordinated?

Research on Self-Esteem

Measuring Self-Esteem

How does one measure self-esteem? The usual way is to ask the subject to rate himself or herself on a series of questions or statements expressing views about the self.

There is no single measure of self-esteem that is used by everyone. Rather, there are many such measures, partly because the topic is quite important and partly because researchers criticize one another's ways of measuring it. As already noted, one approach was to look for discrepancies between real self and ideal self. Another way is to ask a series of simple questions about global self-regard (e.g., Rosenberg, 1965). The most common approach is to ask a series of questions about different attributes and add them up. The problem is that such a measure might not lend the right importance to the various attributes or dimensions. Most of the common self-esteem measures tend to emphasize social self-esteem, for example. To get an understanding of this approach, please consult the Activity Box.

Self-esteem is scored by computing a total based on the number of points per item. For questions 3, 4, 5, and 7, your rating (0 to 6) is your score. The other three items (1, 2, and 6) are *reverse scored*; that is, you compute your score by subtracting your rating from 6. For example, if you responded to question 2 by rating yourself 5, your score would be 1 $(6 - 5)$.

These questions refer to various areas or facets of self-esteem. Questions 1 and 2 refer to "global self-esteem," that is, an overall appraisal of self. Questions 3 and 4 measure social self-esteem, that is, feeling of confidence or inhibition about getting along with other people. Question 5 refers to school (intellectual) abilities (confidence in the ability to do good work). Questions 6 and 7 refer to body image: 6 is concerned with attractiveness and 7 with physical skills and ability.

Because most self-esteem scales use more items than these (see Fleming & Courtney, 1984, for a good example of a complete scale), you should not place much trust in the reliability of your score based on these few items. Still, you can get a rough idea of how self-esteem is measured by considering these items and similar ones.

The results of these self-esteem measures yield a continuum of scores. Although everyone speaks of high and low self-esteem as if these were distinct types, they are not types in the sense of distinct clusters of scores. Rather, there is a continuum and people may range anywhere along it. Dividing the scores into high and low self-esteem groups is done for the sake of conceptual convenience (i.e., it makes results easier to talk about). Sometimes researchers divide their scores into two groups for analyzing their data, that is, comparing the typical behaviors of high versus low self-esteem groups. There are some minor statistical problems with that approach (for example, it ignores the fact that the highest score in the low-esteem group is probably closer to the lowest score in the high-esteem group than to the lowest score in the low-esteem group), but these can safely be overlooked in making rough comparisons.

Another important factor in looking at self-esteem scores is where the distribution lies. Most distributions of self-esteem scores are skewed toward the high end. That is, rather few people actually score at the low end of a self-esteem scale. The group that is called "low self-esteem" is actually low only in a relative sense. In an absolute sense, they typically rate themselves around the middle of the scale. In other words, the main difference is between people who rate themselves very positively and people who rate themselves medium or average. Although the latter are typically called "low self-esteem" because their scores are lower than the first group, they may be different from those few individuals who really describe themselves in negative, unflattering terms.

It is also necessary to mention the pattern of "defensive high self-esteem" (e.g., Schneider & Turkat, 1975). These are people who exaggerate how favorably they regard themselves because they think that that will make them look good. Given a self-esteem scale, they will score high, but these high scores do not indicate a genuinely favorable appraisal of themselves. Rather, they simply rated themselves very positively and favorably so that whoever reads their responses will think favorably of them. Defensive high self-esteem appears to derive from some inner insecurity and a strong need for the approval of others.

Performance and Persistence

In many respects, the performances of high and low self-esteem groups are similar. Self-esteem is not intelligence, and although there may sometimes be a connection, it is quite possible to be both stupid and conceited—or to be both intelligent and insecure. Abilities in general are not *strongly* related to self-esteem, although there is some relationship between them.

Still, self-esteem does sometimes affect performance. In general, high self-esteem signifies greater overall confidence, and confidence can help one to achieve success. Global self-esteem does not have a strong effect on each individual performance, for an individual performance may involve a very specific ability. But there is some general tendency for people with high self-esteem to expect to do better in general, and this confidence has some positive effects.

Many researchers have found differences in response to success and failure. Although high and low self-esteem individuals may perform at the same level at first, they respond differently to feedback, especially failure. Initial failure can be upsetting and discouraging, and a person's level of self-esteem is an important factor in determining how the person responds to it—whether the person gives up or tries again harder.

After an initial failure, people with high self-esteem tend to persist longer than people with low self-esteem (Shrauger & Sorman, 1977). The person with low self-esteem is more likely to give up. In many cases, this will mean that the person with high self-esteem will ultimately do better than the person with low self-esteem. Persisting and trying harder after failure may often bring success, whereas quitting leaves the project as a failure. Thus, the responses of people with high self-esteem may often lead to the best outcome.

On the other hand, sometimes persistence can be fruitless. It is important to know when to quit. If you invest some money in a certain stock, and its price drops, you have a choice between cutting your losses (selling, and reinvesting elsewhere) versus persisting and hoping for improvement. If you refuse to give up on a losing stock, you may end up losing even more money. Persistence is not always good. Indeed, in the long run you may be worse off by persisting at something you are untalented at rather than devoting your efforts to something you might be better at. In a sense, then, the issue is whether you know when it's best to quit.

One investigation examined how self-esteem predicted persisting in a futile endeavor (McFarlin, Baumeister, & Blascovich, 1984). People in this experiment had a limited time in which to solve as many problems as they could, and some of the problems were actually unsolvable. Thus, an individual might try one of the unsolvable problems, and of course his efforts would meet with failure. The optimal strategy would be to abandon this problem and move on to a solvable one. Persistence was actually counterproductive, for it wasted time that could have been spent more fruitfully on other problems. The results of this investigation showed that people with high self-esteem showed greater persistence on the unsolvable problems, whereas the people with low self-esteem tended to move along to other, more solvable problems. As a result, people with low self-esteem ended up performing better.

In fact, even when the experimenter gave subjects advice not to get stuck persisting on one problem, the pattern remained: High self-esteem subjects persisted longer than those with low self-esteem. Apparently the people with high self-esteem tended to disregard this helpful (and actually very sound) advice. They remained confident they could solve the problem.

The tendency of high self-esteem people to persist after failure seems very broad and general. It occurs regardless of whether persistence is good or bad, and regardless of whether the person gets advice to the contrary. High self-esteem appears simply to be associated with the belief that one will succeed soon at whatever one chooses to work on. In short, high self-esteem seems to lead to favorable expectancies for one's performance.

The operation of expectancies was demonstrated in another investigation (McFarlin & Blascovich, 1981). In this study, people were given either an initial success or an initial failure experience, and then they were asked to predict how well they would do the next time. People with high self-esteem were more confident—that is, they predicted better performances the next time around—than people with low self-esteem. Those with low self-esteem *wanted* to perform well, but they were less confident that they could successfully do so. An intriguing result from this study was the fact that high self-esteem people made more optimistic predictions after initial failure than after initial success. Apparently the initial failure made them all the more determined to succeed the next time, and they expressed this determination by predicting strongly that they would perform well.

In these studies, people were always required to perform again after initial success or failure. The results seem to indicate that people with high self-esteem are determined to succeed after initial failure. Perhaps this is because they want to succeed at everything—or perhaps they simply hate to fail. What happens if they are given the chance to withdraw totally from the situation?

Persistence in a free-choice situation was studied by Baumeister and Tice (1985). In this study, subjects received initial success or failure. They were then left alone in the room with some materials for that task on which they had just succeeded or failed. The experimenter said she would return shortly and the subject could do whatever he or she wanted. In fact, the subject was secretly observed in order to ascertain whether the subject chose to work with that same task some more.

Strong effects of self-esteem emerged. This time, however, it was the people with low self-esteem who went back to working at the same task after failure. People high in self-esteem only chose to spend their own free time pursuing the same task if they had initially succeeded. Apparently people with high self-esteem hate to fail. If required to perform again after initial failure, they will try extremely hard to avoid a second failure, but they would prefer simply to abandon the entire area and not perform any more at the task on which they failed. People with low self-esteem put in more work on the task after failing it than after succeeding at it.

To understand the results of this study, it is useful to consider the different goals and feelings associated with different levels of self-esteem. People with low self-esteem are probably accustomed to a certain amount of failure. They wish to avoid humiliating experiences associated with the inadequacies they perceive in themselves, and they do not expect to perform extremely well at very many things. Their goal in general may be simply to find out their deficiencies and try to remedy them, so as not to stand out in a bad way. Initial failure at some task gives them a signal that they have some area of deficiency, and they respond by feeling that they should try to improve, to come up to an adequate or passable level. Success, in contrast, tells them they are doing fine in that area and that they don't need to devote themselves to improvement. Indeed, they might sometimes prefer not to pursue something on which they have initially succeeded, for to do so would risk a failure that would discredit their earlier success. Preferring to quit while they're ahead, they turn away from tasks on which they have initially succeeded.

People with high self-esteem, in contrast, think very well of themselves. They aren't concerned with remedying their deficiencies so as to become merely adequate. Rather, they want to stand out in a positive way—they want to excel. Initial failure tells them that they don't have much aptitude in that particular area, and their reaction may well be a desire to forget the whole affair. By avoiding that task, they can prevent further failures. After all, they think, they are good at plenty of things, so it doesn't matter if they fail at one thing. Initial success, on the other hand, tells them that they have some promising ability, and they may want to cultivate this so as to become truly outstanding.

To sum up: People with high self-esteem hate to fail, and they desire to be exceptionally good at things. They respond to initial success with increased interest and effort. Initial failure inclines them to avoid the task so as to prevent further failures. If they must perform again after initial failure, however, they show an intense determination that leads to extremely high levels of effort and persistence—even, in some cases, persistence that may be wasteful and counterproductive. Low self-esteem people, in contrast, wish to be adequate and are satisfied with a moderate level of performance. They respond to initial failure by trying to improve, although they may easily become discouraged and give up when further difficulties are encountered. They are happy when they succeed, and they do not feel the need to follow up initial success with further, even greater successes.

Situationality and Influence

There is a fair amount of evidence that low self-esteem people are more malleable. They yield more easily to external influence than people with high self-esteem, and their behavior is more guided by external forces and cues. People with high self-esteem tend to describe themselves as consistent, and they act on their internal beliefs and values, regardless of external influences.

Thus, for example, one study asked people to indicate their personality traits. For each dimension, the person could choose a trait or its opposite to describe how he or she normally acted—or the person could say, "It depends on the situation." People with low self-esteem were most likely to say that their behavior depended on the situation (Goldberg, 1981). In a word, people with low self-esteem are more *situational* than others—their behavior varies with the immediate situation.

A related finding is that people with low self-esteem have less elaborate self-concepts than people with high self-esteem (Campbell, 1986). If you ask them to describe themselves, they have less to say than people with high self-esteem.

Part of these patterns may be due to a reluctance to call attention to oneself. Earlier, we talked about self-enhancement and self-protection, and there is some evidence that people with low self-esteem lean heavily toward self-protection rather than self-enhancement (Baumeister, Tice, & Hutton, 1987). They make fewer claims about the self and are more willing to go along with the group or the situation because that is the safest strategy—the one least likely to risk embarrassment, failure, or humiliation.

Much of the evidence for the greater malleability of people with low self-esteem comes from studies of persuasion (e.g., Janis, 1954, 1955; Janis & Field, 1959). Researchers would present two subjects with identical persuasive messages, such as a speech or essay. In most cases, the person with low self-esteem expressed greater attitude change in response to the message. People with low self-esteem are more easily persuaded.

Prejudice

On the surface, it seems that people with low self-esteem are more prejudiced than people with high self-esteem. Many studies have shown, for example, that people with low self-esteem give more negative ratings to minority group members and other stereotyped groups. But one must recall that low self-esteem means giving *oneself* a negative rating. To examine prejudice, one must ask: Do people with low self-esteem rate others worse than themselves?

The answer appears to be no. People with low self-esteem rate themselves, members of their own group, and members of other groups all about the same (Crocker & Schwartz, 1985). All of these ratings tend to be somewhat negative, relative to the ratings given by people with high self-esteem. But the negativity does not reflect any selective prejudice, for it applies to everyone. People with low self-esteem are apparently more critical of everyone—including minority groups and themselves.

False Consensus, False Uniqueness

An interesting question about self-concepts is this: Do people think they are unique, or do they think that they are similar to others? Past research has shown support for both views under different circumstances. Studies of *false consensus* have shown that people overestimate the percentage of others who would agree with their opinions and share their habits (Ross, Greene, & House, 1977). For example, high school boys who smoke cigarettes estimate that over half of their fellow male students smoke, but nonsmokers estimate that only about 38 percent smoke (Sherman, Chassin, Presson, & Agostinelli, 1984). Likewise, college students tend to overestimate the proportion of students who share their attitudes about drugs, abortion, hamburgers, the President's performance, and many other issues (Nisbett & Kunda, 1985). In short, people tend to believe that their preferences are widely shared—they assume that the consensus favors their opinion more than it actually does.

Other research has found, however, that people like to believe themselves to be unique, at least with regard to their most important abilities (Suls & Wan, 1987). People are eager for the recognition that their achievements mean something special, and they are loathe to hear that "anyone else could have done that just as well." In short, people tend to underestimate how many other people can do the things that they can do.

Thus, people systematically distort the way they see other people (in comparison to themselves). Sometimes these distortions make the person feel more unique, and other times they make the person feel more like everyone else. Recent work has revealed the key factors that determine which distortion is likely to occur (Campbell, 1986). People tend to overestimate consensus on matters of opinion—they tend to think that many people would agree with their views. With abilities (rather than opinions), it depends on whether the person's own ability level is high or low. People tend to overestimate the proportion of others who share their incompetencies (e.g., "I know I'm not very good at math, but not very many people are"), but they underestimate the proportion who share their expertise ("No one else can do this as well as I can"). The more important the domain is to one's self-esteem, the more people distort. That is, false consensus and false uniqueness effects are small on trivial matters, but when an important facet of the self-concept is involved, people show much greater errors in estimating consensus. Lastly, all these effects are stronger among people high in self-esteem than among people with low self-esteem.

It appears, then, that these distortions in perceiving others occur in the service of maintaining self-esteem. People like to believe their opinions are shared by many others, because that suggests that they are correct. They like to believe that many other people cannot do the things they cannot do, because that reduces feelings of inferiority. They like to believe their abilities are unique, because that makes them feel superior. People who show these self-flattering distortions most strongly are the ones with the most favorable views of themselves—namely, people with high self-esteem.

Other Aspects of Self-Concept

We will now examine some aspects of the self-concept that are not directly involved in self-esteem. After all, there is more to the self-concept than evaluation.

Spontaneous Self-Concept

Is the self-concept stable, or does it change and fluctuate from day to day? Many people think it fluctuates, but most researchers have found self-concepts to be quite stable. Attempts to raise or lower self-esteem often have weak or negligible effects.

One reason for this discrepancy between popular wisdom and research beliefs is that the self-concept is very large and complex, and although the entire structure of self-concept may remain rather stable, the parts of it that come to mind immediately may fluctuate. On the surface, self-concepts may seem to change from day to day, even from hour to hour, as different features of the self come to the forefront of one's mind. The concept of self is not really changing; rather, different parts of it are coming to light.

What is changing, then, is that part of the self-concept that happens to be present on one's mind at a given moment. This is sometimes called the "spontaneous self-concept" or the "phenomenal self."

There is indeed evidence that the spontaneous self-concept changes, even though self-esteem and the deeper aspects of the self-concept appear to be quite resistant to change. The immediate social context brings out different features of the self, causing the spontaneous self-concept to change.

Changes in the spontaneous self-concept have been shown in a series of clever studies by McGuire and his colleagues (McGuire & McGuire, 1982; McGuire, McGuire, Child, & Fujioka, 1978; McGuire, McGuire, & Winston, 1979). They reasoned that people will become aware of their attributes that make them stand out in a given situation. For example, being an American may not come to mind readily when you think about yourself here in America, because everyone else is an American too. But if you travel alone overseas, you may often be quite conscious of being an American, for it sets you apart from most of the people you encounter.

The researchers tested this idea by asking schoolchildren to describe themselves in writing. They were tested in groups, and the researchers made sure that each group was composed of either all boys except for one girl, or of all girls except for one boy. The child who was the only one present of his or her sex was much more likely to mention that fact in describing the self. In other words, a girl was much more likely to mention being a girl as part of her self-concept if she was the lone girl in a group of boys than if she was in a group of girls. Likewise, boys were more conscious of being boys when they were alone in a group of girls. Thus, the spontaneous self-concept changed in response to the social context.

It is important to remember that these changes occurred only on the surface of the self-concept, that is, only at the level of the features of the self that are on one's mind at a given time. McGuire and his colleagues were certainly not claiming that a boy in a group of boys ceases to consider himself as a boy. If you asked him whether he is a boy, he would certainly say yes. But if nobody asks him, he is not likely to be paying much attention to the fact that he is a boy. Being surrounded by girls, however, will make him very aware of being a boy. The immediate social context brings out certain features of the self and makes others seem temporarily unimportant, minor, or irrelevant.

In short, not all of one's self-concept is present in one's mind at any given moment. Indeed, some researchers have suggested that the self-concept is like a large, complex set of files, and current events cause people to pull out one drawer or another of these files. People may "scan" their files in different ways depending on the immediate context and recent experiences. One study has even found that a surface level of self-esteem can fluctuate, depending on recent experiences (Jones, Rhodewalt, Berglas, & Skelton, 1981). Acting in a positive way can remind you of your good traits and make your surface level of self-esteem rise, whereas acting in a negative fashion can bring your bad traits to mind and cause a temporary drop in self-esteem. These effects tend to be temporary, and most evidence indicates that people's evaluations of themselves change only very slowly, but there are indeed surface fluctuations.

Self-Schemas

Another important approach to the self-concept rejects the notion that each person has one single, integrated self-concept. Rather, it may be that people have a loose collection of specific ideas about themselves. For example, someone may regard herself as intelligent, friendly, lazy, talkative, helpful, dependent, sympathetic, and sensitive. Perhaps the important thing is not how all these traits fit together to compose a single "self-concept" with a given level of global self-esteem. The important thing may be the individual pieces: being intelligent, friendly, and so forth. In this view, each trait or attribute about oneself is a "self-schema." A self-schema is thus a concept of some particular attribute of the self. Instead of one large self-concept, this approach emphasizes many small concepts of parts and features of the self (Markus, 1977).

One important feature of the self-schema approach is that it makes it easier to understand changes in self-concept. The person may feel that he or she remains pretty much the same across time, although specific schemas about the self may change. Another important implication of the self-schema approach is that on some dimensions, many people simply don't have self-schemas. Thus, for example, some people may think of themselves as talkative, others may think of themselves as quiet and reticent, but many other people may not think of themselves as characteristically being either one. It is not that they regard themselves as somewhat or moderately talkative; rather, they may think that in some circumstances they are extremely talkative, while in other situations they are extremely shy and quiet. Or perhaps they have simply never thought about themselves in terms of talkativeness or quietness.

Thus, not all self-concepts are made out of the same ingredients. Dimensions or traits that may be extremely important to some self-concepts may simply be irrelevant to others. Each individual self-concept is made up of several self-schemas on certain dimensions, but other dimensions are left out.

Possible Selves

Another important concept is that of *possible selves* (Markus & Nurius, 1986). The self-concept may refer to who you are *now*, but people also have fairly elaborate ideas about who they might become. Possible selves are defined as concepts of the self in the future; not just any way of imagining the self, but specific, individually significant hopes, fears, and fantasies. Possible selves are people's ideas of what they might become, what they would like to become, and what they are afraid of becoming (Markus & Nurius, 1987).

People's actions may be guided by their possible selves. Indeed, Markus and Nurius (1986) describe possible selves as mental bridges between the present and the future. They prescribe how one might change, for better or for worse. A struggling young student, for example, might persevere through the stress, poverty, and humiliation of medical or law school because of the appeal of a guiding image of self as a successful, well-respected professional. Or the child of an alcoholic might refuse even an occasional glass of beer because of the feared image of self ending up as a broke, drunk, Skid Row loser. These possible selves—successful professional physician or lawyer, or pathetic alcoholic—guide and shape the behavior of the present, actual self.

Research on possible selves is only beginning, but there is some evidence that people are affected by different types of possible selves. It appears that juvenile delinquents, although they may have high self-esteem, have rather narrow ranges of possible selves. They see themselves as becoming ordinary laborers or criminals; relatively few other possibilities seem realistic to them. Nondelinquent adolescents, in contrast, often see a wide range of possible selves, both good and bad (Oyserman & Markus, 1986). Likewise, as people get older, they tend to have more negative (feared) possible selves, which are associated with a feeling that one's life is not fully under one's own control. People who feel responsible for other people who depend on them tend to have fewer *positive* possible selves than other people, for commitment and responsibility to others reduce one's options (Markus & Nurius, 1987).

Higgins (1987) has explored the basic types of possible selves. He distinguishes between the "ideal self," which is the way you would like yourself to be, from the "ought self," which refers to the way others might like you to be. The ideal self is composed of wishes, fantasies, and aspirations, whereas the ought self is composed of duties and obligations.

Some evidence indicates that these different possible selves are associated with different emotions. A discrepancy between how you see yourself and your ideal self—that is, not reaching your goals such as career success—will tend to make you feel sad and depressed. In contrast, a discrepancy between how you see yourself and your ought self—failing to fulfill obligations and responsibilities—will tend to make you feel agitated, upset, and perhaps guilty (Higgins, Klein, & Strauman, 1987).

Maintaining Self-Concept and Self-Esteem

Most theorists believe that people generally desire to maintain stable concepts of themselves, with some exceptions. In simple terms, people try to avoid changing their self-concepts. One reason for this is a general tendency for the human mind to prefer to hold on to its ideas (Fiske & Taylor, 1983). That is, once a person has formed some belief or opinion, the person is very reluctant to change it. If contradictory evidence arises, the person may often react by trying to explain away this evidence or by trying to fit it into preconceived notions, rather than change the belief or opinion. These general patterns certainly apply to the self-concept as well.

An obvious example of this tendency is people's reluctance to accept any loss of self-esteem. People strongly resist experiences or events that will embarrass them, humiliate them, discredit them, or in other ways cause loss of esteem. Countless studies have shown this effect.

When there is a chance of increasing esteem, however, things become more complicated. Gaining prestige means changing the self-concept on a positive dimension. Two competing motives come into play. The consistency motive, which encompasses a reluctance to change the self-concept at all, would oppose such changes. But the self-enhancement motive, which is a desire to have a highly favorable self-concept, would eagerly embrace any gain in esteem. The two motives agree with each other in opposing any possible loss of esteem, but they conflict about the desirability of gaining esteem.

Undoubtedly, many people leap at the chance to gain fame and recognition—that is, to gain esteem, such as by a powerful and important public success experience. There is evidence, however, that not everyone does. In the late 1960s and early 1970s, for example, some researchers suggested that women had a "fear of success" (Horner, 1972), which meant that they were reluctant to change their self-esteem in an upward direction because they feared negative repercussions for being too successful. Some researchers argued more generally that people with low self-esteem would tend to "reject success," because they wanted to maintain their low opinions of themselves (Maracek & Mettee, 1972).

These research findings on fear of success and rejection of success have not stood the test of time very well, and today most researchers have severe doubts that people actively sabotage their own performances in order to maintain a negative view of self (see Baumeister & Scher, in press). At most, some people may avoid certain kinds of *public* success because they don't want others to start expecting too much from them (Baumgardner & Brownlee, 1987).

The crux of the consistency versus enhancement issue concerns people with low self-esteem. Do they prefer success (which raises esteem) or failure (which confirms a low opinion of self)? That is, would they rather remain consistent with their negative views of themselves, or change their self-concepts toward more positive views?

Many studies have examined this question, and they do not all agree, but a consensus is slowly emerging (e.g., Swann, Griffin, Predmore, & Gaines, 1987). First, it is apparent that most people think pretty well of themselves, so there are only a few people who have sufficiently low self-esteem to make failure appealing in any sense. Second, it is necessary to differentiate cognitive from emotional preferences. On a cognitive, rational basis, the mind prefers consistency, because this makes life stable and predictable. On a more emotional level, however, people generally desire to think well of themselves, and so they prefer success. Thus, given a choice between success and failure, people with low self-esteem may be more likely to expect failure but they are happier with success (Shrauger, 1975). Failure may appeal to the purely rational part of the mind that likes a stable, predictable world, but success appeals to the emotions and feelings. Thus, people who have strong patterns of low self-esteem may feel a conflict between the desire to succeed and the cognitive, rational expectation for failure. If you tell such a person that he is terrific, he might like this very much on an emotional level, but on a rational, cognitive level he may reject it and think it is untrue.

Still, most people hold generally favorable views of themselves, and so they desire success and positive feedback to confirm and enhance their favorable self-concepts. Confronted with negative feedback, most people actively try to reject it so as to avoid losing esteem. There is a wide variety of techniques people use to avoid losing esteem when confronted by failure or threat. We have already seen some of these techniques: exaggerating the uniqueness of one's good traits and seeing one's shortcomings as widespread and typical, responding to failure by trying extra hard or by avoiding the task, and so forth. Other techniques include remembering the good things and forgetting the bad ones, overestimating one's performance and good qualities, and many more (e.g., Goleman, 1985; Greenwald, 1980). It is obvious that people spend a lot of time and energy sustaining favorable opinions of themselves because they have so many strategies of doing so!

Identity

Although the terms "identity" and "self-concept" have some things in common, they are different. A self-concept exists only in one person's mind, whereas identity is essentially social. That is, identity rests on a definition of the self that is shared by the person himself or herself, other people, and society at large.

Structure and Function of Identity

Identity, as we said earlier, is a definition of the self. It is actually a composite definition made up of several partial definitions. The components of identity are these partial definitions. Any answer to the question "Who are you?" is an identity component, for to answer that question is to give a partial definition of oneself. Examples of identity components include being an employee of a certain company, a lawyer, a student, someone's nephew, a member of the swim team, and so on.

If identity is a definition, then there have to be certain criteria used for defining it. There are two major *defining criteria* of identity, namely, continuity and differentiation. *Continuity* means sameness over time. Part of having an identity is being the same person today as yesterday, last week, and last year. People do change in various ways, but they retain some continuity of identity, as signified by having the same name and other things. *Differentiation* refers to the things that distinguish someone from other people. Being identified with a certain family or organization, for example, marks one off as distinct from nonmembers.

Anything that furnishes continuity and differentiation thus helps to define identity. A strong sense of identity arises from having many sources of continuity and differentiation. A stable home, strong family ties, a secure job, an established reputation, and such things make identity secure, and someone with all those things is not likely to have identity problems. One reason for the increased concern over identity in modern life is that many things that once provided continuity and differentiation no longer do so (Baumeister, 1986). For example, in previous centuries many people would live their entire lives in the same locale, even having the same neighbors and friends, but now people are much more mobile, and so home and friendship networks are no longer the sources of stability that they once were.

The makeup of each individual identity is different, but there are certain broad common features. Identity seems to include at least three major types of things. First, it includes one's interpersonal self: how others know you, your interpersonal style, your reputation, and so forth. Second, it includes some concept of potentiality, that is, of what you may become. Third, it includes some general values, principles, and priorities.

Identity Crises

The notion of an "identity crisis" appears to be a modern phenomenon. People in the Middle Ages, for example, do not seem to have had identity crises or anything resembling them. Likewise, there is not much evidence of identity crises in cultures very different from our own. Probably identity crises are fostered by some of the unique features of modern Western cultures (see Baumeister, 1986).

The term "identity crisis" was coined by Erik Erikson in the 1940s. It was quickly adopted and used by many people, which suggests that it named an experience that was already common and widespread. Erikson thought that nearly everyone has an identity crisis during adolescence, although in many cases this could be an unconscious crisis so the person would be unaware of it. Erikson believed that the identity crisis resulted from the need to separate oneself emotionally from one's parents (cf. Blos, 1962) and to make basic decisions about one's values, goals, and ambitions in life.

In the 1960s, psychologists started to do research on identity crises. They soon abandoned Erikson's original theory that everyone goes through an identity crisis. Instead, they began to think that some people go through life without ever having such a crisis, although many others have important crises. Researchers became interested in comparing people who had identity crises against people who did not have them.

James Marcia (1966, 1967) developed a typology of people based on identity crises. Four types of people were distinguished, based on two dimensions: (1) Has the person ever had an active period of identity crisis? and, (2) Does the person have a stable identity based on firm commitments? Here are the four types:

Identity Achieved: Crisis Plus Commitment

People who have had an identity crisis and resolved it are classified as identity-achieved. They are typically regarded as being mature, capable individuals, whose identity is solidly based on the outcome of a personal struggle.

Moratorium: Crisis But No Commitment

When there is evidence of an identity crisis but firm commitments are lacking, the individual is classified as having "moratorium" status. In most cases, this means that the identity crisis is currently in progress. These people are thus currently, actively struggling to form an identity.

They are often thoughtful individuals, open to experimenting with new ideas and lifestyles. They sometimes seem to change their personalities and styles from day to day. Part of this process of change results from their efforts to try out different ways of being in order to see how these feel and what reactions they get. The term "moratorium" comes from Erikson's term *psychosocial moratorium*, which he used to refer to the modern status of adolescence in which the individual is psychologically grown up in many respects but is not well integrated into society—rather, the person is left for several years (such as in college) with minimal social obligations and commitments so as to be free to try out different ways of forming an identity.

Foreclosure: Commitment Without Crisis

When the person has a stable, committed identity but there is no sign of having had a period of crisis, he or she is classified as foreclosure status. In most cases, these are people who have remained close to how their parents brought them up, perhaps with minor modifications (usually ones that the parents would approve). Children are almost all classified as having "foreclosed identities" up until an identity crisis starts, and if no crisis ever happens the person simply remains in the foreclosed status.

Foreclosure status is a complex one. On the surface, these people tend to seem unusually mature, often having adult values, plans, and opinions while still in their teens. But this is partly an illusion, for these signs of maturity are simply accepted from the parents rather than acquired personally. Upon closer inspection, many people with foreclosed identities turn out to be rigid and inflexible, defensive, even insecure. They are often the exact opposite of the "moratorium" status individuals who are open to trying out new things; foreclosures tend to be uninterested in new ideas or experimental lifestyles. The rigidity of the foreclosed individual may cause problems when the person comes under stress or tries to form intimate relationships.

More recent evidence suggests, however, that foreclosure status is a reasonably healthy one for females (e.g., Damon, 1983; Waterman, 1982). Apparently, females can grow up to be normal and capable without an identity crisis. In our culture, maturity may require the male to reject parental teachings and find his or her own identity, but a female may do just fine to remain close to the values and goals her parents taught her. Given the rapid recent changes in the feminine sex role and woman's places in society, these results are likely to change from one generation to the next. For the present, though, most of the disadvantages of the foreclosure status are mainly true for males.

Identity Diffusion: Neither Crisis Nor Commitment

The last category refers to people who have neither had an identity crisis nor remained foreclosed in the commitments they were brought up with. These "identity diffuse" people lack a stable, committed identity, but they do not seem to mind this, and they are not engaged in any struggle to form one. Identity diffusion can border on psychopathology. This may be because the mentally ill do not tend to have and resolve identity crises and are most comfortable with a vague, uncommitted position in society. At best, individuals with diffuse identities tend to be "perpetual teenagers," people who seem to thrive on the uncommitted lifestyle of adolescence and who may seek to prolong it long after others have formed adult identities. They may shun long-term relationships that might lead to marriage, and they postpone career choices and other decisions that solidify the adult identity.

Perhaps surprisingly, most of the research suggests that identity crises are good for you, even though they may be unpleasant. Research shows that people who experience identity crises—especially people who successfully resolve them and reach identity-achieved status—are superior to others on many things, including academic performance at college, motivation and ambition, ability to adapt and perform under stress, and ability to form mature, intimate relationships (Bernard, 1981; Bourne, 1978). Many of the studies providing this evidence used males only, so it is less clear whether identity crises are good for females. There is some suggestion that women with foreclosed identities are just as capable and mature as those with achieved identities, although identity-diffuse females are worse off (e.g., Marcia & Scheidel, 1983). There is almost nothing to suggest that identity crises have negative effects on males or females. The best conclusion at present, then, is that identity crises are beneficial for males and either beneficial or neutral for females.

What is an identity crisis like, and how does it happen? When researchers attempted to answer this question, they came to the conclusion that all identity crises are not the same. There appear to be at least two major types of identity crises, which follow quite different patterns and processes. These two types of identity crisis may be called *identity deficit* and *identity conflict* (Baumeister, 1986; Baumeister, Shapiro & Tice, 1985). Let's take a look at these two types of identity crisis.

Identity deficit is just what it sounds like; that is, the person does not have "enough" identity to deal with life and make major decisions. This type of identity crisis may be caused by reaching a point in life at which major decisions need to be made, but the person does not have a satisfactory inner basis for making them. Adolescence is a prime example, for in our culture adolescents need to make the choices that will shape their adult identities—especially choosing a career and a spouse—but such decisions are enormously difficult because one lacks information and there are many possible options. As a result, the person often feels a need to look inside himself or herself to find the basis for making these decisions. Sometimes a person will "look inside" and immediately feel a strong preference for one course of action, but in many other cases there is nothing inside to make the choice. That is called an identity deficit.

Identity deficits arise when people reject some beliefs or values or ambitions that they have been taught or have long held. Adolescents, for example, are often in the process of rejecting many things their parents taught them. Evidence suggests that adolescent identity crises may be more common in males than females, probably because males tend to make more drastic breaks with their parents than females (e.g., Blos, 1962). There is also evidence that adolescents are more likely to have an identity crisis if they attend college than if they go right to work out of high school (Morash, 1980), because college presents one with many new ideas and opinions that encourage the individual to question parental teachings.

The individual who rejects many of his or her beliefs, values, and goals thus creates an inner vacuum that constitutes the identity deficit. This inner vacuum often causes an active search for new views to replace the discarded ones. People having identity deficit crises are often very interesting people, for they are busily exploring and trying out many new ideas and new ways of relating to others. They are also more vulnerable to influence than other people are, probably because the inner vacuum makes them receptive to new views. Recruiters for religious cults, for example, may often have their best success with people in the midst of identity deficit crises.

The emotional side of an identity deficit may seem like a roller-coaster ride from despair to euphoria and back again, in rapid succession. People having such crises may feel depressed and bewildered at times, and the lack of certainty about where their lives are going may seem alternately like an exhilarating breadth of opportunity and freedom, and a dispiriting, confusing meaninglessness.

Not everyone has an identity crisis at adolescence, of course, and not everyone who does have one manages to resolve it. But for those who do, the resolution of an identity deficit seems to be a two-step process. First, the person resolves the fundamental issues of value and meaning. That is, he or she decides on basic, abstract principles, such as what is important in life. The second step is to translate these abstract values and convictions into concrete, realistic ambitions. For example, someone may first struggle to reach the decision that what he wants out of life is to help others and to earn a comfortable salary; in the second stage, these general values are elaborated into a specific desire, such as becoming a physician or psychotherapist. Once this is done, the identity crisis is ended, and the person begins to work toward fulfilling these goals.

Identity crises are most common at adolescence, but there may be a second set of them at mid-life (Levinson, 1978). Some evidence indicates that many men grow dissatisfied with their lives around the age of forty. They often feel that things have not turned out the way they had envisioned them. They come to realize that the goals that guided them ever since adolescence are either not going to be reached—or, if they do reach them, this will not bring satisfaction and fulfillment. As a result, many men begin to discard, downplay, or reject these goals, and an identity deficit is the result. Males with mid-life crises show many of the same signs and symptoms of adolescent identity crises. They may detach themselves from their family, experiment with new opinions and lifestyles, rethink their career ambitions or even change careers, and so forth. Most often, they change their priorities among career, family, religion, and other involvements, such as by deciding to work less hard and spend more time with their wives and children. Although this initial research has used only male subjects, there may well be comparable patterns for women.

If identity deficit means having too little identity to make vital life decisions, identity *conflict* is the opposite problem. An identity conflict is an inconsistency or incompatibility between two parts of the self. In most cases, these parts of the self were not initially in conflict, but circumstances brought them into conflict (such as by forcing a decision that affects both parts). Identity conflict means that the person has several identity components that disagree about the best decision to make. For example, a working mother who is offered a promotion that would entail increased responsibility and travel may be torn between her work identity (which tells her to accept the promotion) and her identity as a mother (which may tell her not to take time away from her family). This form of identity crisis also occurs among immigrants, who want to remain loyal to their old culture while embracing the new one. It can also occur in marriages between people who come from strong but different religious backgrounds, especially if there is pressure to convert. Loyalty to spouse may then conflict with holding to one's most deeply held beliefs.

We saw earlier that identity deficits can be an emotional roller coaster, with both exhilarating and depressing phases. Identity conflicts do not appear to have these fluctuations, for there is little that is positive or pleasant about identity conflict. People having such crises tend to

[margin note: Similar Dollard & Millers approach approach conflict]

suffer, to feel like they are being a "traitor" who is "betraying" some important part of self and others as well. They do not tend to show the openness to new ideas or the exploration and experimentation typical of identity deficits. Also, unlike identity deficits, there is nothing to suggest that identity conflicts are good for you.

Resolving an identity conflict is a difficult matter. Sometimes the person simply has to renounce some important part of himself or herself. In other cases, there are various compromise solutions. The person may choose one of the conflicting parts of identity but find some way of retaining something of the "loser" of this inner struggle. Some people compartmentalize; that is, they try to keep two rigidly separate spheres of their lives, to prevent the two parts of their identity from coming into open conflict.

Identity crises, whether deficit or conflict, are difficult periods in life. They involve changing the self to adapt to new circumstances. Although they may be depressing and even painful, most people apparently come through them quite well in the end. In many cases, the person is better off for having had the crisis.

Summary

The self is a large, complex structure. Self-concept refers to how the person thinks of himself or herself, that is, the person's own beliefs and ideas about this self. Identity refers to definitions of the self that are created jointly by the individual, relatives and acquaintances, and society.

Children's self-concepts begin with awareness of their bodies and with knowing that they are male or female children belonging to a particular family. Around age two, self-concept begins to be heavily based on knowledge of what the child can and cannot do. The emphasis on competency and control grows steadily through the later phase of childhood and increasingly involves comparing one's own abilities against those of other children. Older children also gradually begin to develop a notion of the self as something inner, including thoughts and feelings.

Self-esteem is a very important and influential aspect of the self-concept. Most people think well of themselves and desire to increase their esteem (self-enhancement) and avoid loss of esteem (self-protection). Self-esteem is measured by asking people to rate themselves on various evaluative dimensions. One problem with this approach is the group of people whose scores indicate defensive high self-esteem: Although insecure, they rate themselves favorably to make a good impression.

People with high self-esteem hate to fail. After initial failure, they prefer to avoid that task, but if required to perform again they show high levels of persistence, as compared with people who have low self-esteem. People with high self-esteem are less easily swayed or persuaded by external influence than those with low self-esteem. People with low self-esteem are critical toward others as well as themselves, which is sometimes mistaken for prejudice. High self-esteem is sustained in part by thinking one's abilities are unique, one's flaws are common, and one's opinions agree with the majority. People with low self-esteem are sometimes torn between a tendency to expect failure and believe bad things but another tendency to wish for success. The desire to maintain a stable self-concept can conflict with the desire to raise one's self-esteem.

Other aspects of the self-concept include the spontaneous self-concept, a surface level of self-concept that fluctuates depending on immediate circumstances; possible selves, which are clear images of the self in future states; and self-schemas, which are concepts of specific attributes of the self.

Identity consists of a set of partial definitions of the self, each of which is one answer to the question, "Who are you?" Identity is defined according to continuity across time and differentiation from others. It has three functional aspects: an interpersonal aspect (social roles and reputation), a potentiality aspect, and a values aspect.

Not everyone has identity crises, but many people do. The two main types of crisis include identity deficit, in which an inner vacuum is created by rejecting some important parts of the self, and identity conflict, in which two or more parts of the self disagree about the best course of action. Identity deficits occur most commonly at adolescence and mid-life; they appear to have beneficial effects on males, and perhaps for females as well. Identity conflicts can occur at any point in life. They are difficult to resolve and seem to have little positive value for the individual.

SUGGESTED READINGS

Baumeister, R. F. (1986). *Identity: Cultural change and the struggle for self.* New York: Oxford University Press. This recent, interdisciplinary work covers current knowledge about identity, drawing on studies of identity crises, history and literature, studies of brainwashing, child development, and more.

Damon, W., & Hart, D. (1982). The development of self-understanding from infancy through adolescence. *Child Development, 53,* 841–864. This is the most important source of the formation of self-concept during childhood, although it is written primarily for specialists in the area.

Erikson, E. (1968). *Identity: Youth and crisis.* New York: Norton. This is one of the classic works on identity, in which Erikson explains his seminal theory of identity based on clinical observations.

Goleman, D. (1985). *Vital lies, simple truths.* New York: Simon & Schuster. Goleman's book explains the psychology of self-deception in clear yet sophisticated terms.

Suls, J., & Greenwald, A.G. (1982, 1984, 1986). *Psychological perspectives on the self* (3 volumes). Hillsdale, NJ: Erlbaum. A recent collection of chapters by leading researchers on various topics about the self.

Yardley, K., & Honess, T. (1987). *Self and identity: Psychosocial perspectives.* Chichester, England: Wiley. This book contains 24 chapters by different authors, covering a wide range of discussion of self and identity. Some chapters are difficult reading, but others provide good, clear summaries of current research on the self.

REFERENCES

Baumeister, R.F. (1986). *Identity: Cultural change and the struggle for self.* New York: Oxford University Press.

Baumeister, R.F. (1987). How the self became a problem: A psychological review of historical research. *Journal of Personality and Social Psychology, 52,* 163–176.

Baumeister, R.F., & Scher, S.J. (1988). Self-defeating behavior patterns among normal individuals: Review and analysis of common self-destructive tendencies. *Psychological Bulletin, 104,* 3–22.

Baumeister, R.F., Shapiro, J.J., & Tice, D.M. (1985). Two kinds of identity crisis. *Journal of Personality, 53,* 407–424.

Baumeister, R.F., & Tice, D.M. (1985). Self-esteem and responses to success and failure: Subsequent performance and intrinsic motivation. *Journal of Personality, 53,* 450–467.

Baumeister, R.F., Tice, D.M., & Hutton, D.G. (1987). Self-presentational interpretation of individual differences in self-esteem. Unpublished manuscript, Case Western Reserve University, Cleveland, OH.

Baumgardner, A.H., & Brownlee, E.A. (1987). Strategic failure in social interaction: Evidence for expectancy disconfirmation processes. *Journal of Personality and Social Psychology, 52,* 2525–2535.

Bernard, H.S. (1981). Identity formation during late adolescence: A review of some empirical findings. *Adolescence, 16,* 349–357.

Blos, P. (1962). *On adolescence.* New York: Free Press.

Bourne, E. (1978). The state of research on ego identity: A review and appraisal. Part II. *Journal of Youth and Adolescence, 7,* 371–392.

Brim, O.G. (1976). Life-span development of the theory of oneself: Implications for child development. In H. Reese (Ed.), *Advances in child development and behavior* (Vol. 2, pp. 241–251). New York: Academic Press.

Campbell, J.D. (1986). Similarity and uniqueness: The effects of attribute type, relevance, and individual differences in self-esteem and depression. *Journal of Personality and Social Psychology, 50,* 281–294.

Coopersmith, S. (1967). *The antecedents of self-esteem.* San Francisco, CA: Freeman.

Crocker, J., & Schwartz, I. (1985). Prejudice and ingroup favoritism in a minimal intergroup situation: Effects of self-esteem. *Personality and Social Psychology Bulletin, 11,* 379–386.

Damon, W. (1983). *Social and personality development.* New York: Norton.

Damon, W., & Hart, D. (1982). The development of self-understanding from infancy through adolescence. *Child Development, 53,* 841–864.

Erikson, E.H. (1968). *Identity: Youth and crisis.* New York: Norton.

Fiske, S.T., & Taylor, S.E. (1983). *Social cognition.* Reading, MA: Addison-Wesley.

Fleming, J.S., & Courtney, B.E. (1984). The dimensionality of self-esteem: II. Hierarchical facet model for revised measurement scales. *Journal of Personality and Social Psychology, 46,* 404–421.

Goldberg, L.R. (1981). Unconfounding situational attributions from uncertain, neutral, and ambiguous ones: A psychometric analysis of descriptions of oneself and others. *Journal of Personality and Social Psychology, 41,* 517–552.

Goleman, D. (1985). *Vital lies, simple truths: The psychology of self-deception.* New York: Simon & Schuster.

Greenwald, A.G. (1980). The totalitarian ego: Fabrication and revision of personal history. *American Psychologist, 35,* 603–613.

Higgins, E.T. (1987). Self-discrepancy: A theory relating self and affect. *Psychological Review, 94,* 319–340.

Higgins, E.T., Klein, R.L., & Strauman, T.J. (1987). Self-discrepancies: Distinguishing among self-states, self-state conflicts, and emotional vulnerabilities. In K. Yardley & T. Honess (Eds.), *Self and Identity: Psychosocial perspectives* (pp. 173–186). Chichester, England: Wiley.

Horner, M. (1972). Toward an understanding of achievement-related conflicts in women. *Journal of Social Issues, 28*(2), 157–176.

Janis, I.L. (1954). Personality correlates of susceptibility to persuasion. *Journal of Personality, 22,* 504–518.

Janis, I.L. (1955). Anxiety indices related to susceptibility to persuasion. *Journal of Abnormal and Social Psychology, 51,* 663–667.

Janis, I.L., & Field, P. (1959). Sex differences and personality factors related to persuasibility. In C. Hovland & I. Janis (Eds.), *Personality and persuasibility* (pp. 55–68 and 300–302). New Haven, CT: Yale University Press.

Jones, E.E., Rhodewalt, F., Berglas, S.C., & Skelton, A. (1981). Effects of strategic self-presentation on subsequent self-esteem. *Journal of Personality and Social Psychology, 41,* 407–421.

Kagan, J. (1981). *The second year: The emergence of self-awareness.* Cambridge, MA: Harvard University Press.

Keller, A., Ford, L.H., & Meacham, J.A. (1978). Dimensions of self-concept in preschool children. *Developmental Psychology, 14,* 483–489.

Levinson, D.J. (1978). *The seasons of a man's life.* New York: Ballantine.

Lewis, M., & Brooks-Gunn, J. (1979). *Social cognition and the acquisition of self.* New York: Plenum.

Mahler, M.S., Pine, F., & Bergman, A. (1975). *The psychological birth of the human infant: Symbiosis and individuation.* New York: Basic Books.

Maracek, J., & Mettee, D. (1972). Avoidance of continued success as a function of self-esteem, level of esteem certainty, and responsibility for success. *Journal of Personality and Social Psychology, 22,* 98–107.

Marcia, J.E. (1966). Development and validation of ego-identity status. *Journal of Personality and Social Psychology, 3,* 551–558.

Marcia, J.E. (1967). Ego identity status: Relationship to change in self-esteem, "general maladjustment," and authoritarianism. *Journal of Personality, 35,* 118–133.

Marcia, J.E., & Scheidel, D.G. (1983). *Ego identity, intimacy, sex role orientation, and gender.* Presented at the annual meeting of the Eastern Psychological Association, Philadelphia, PA.

Markus, H. (1977). Self-schemata and processing information about the self. *Journal of Personality and Social Psychology, 35,* 63–78.

Markus, H., & Nurius, P.S. (1986). Possible selves. *American Psychologist, 41,* 954–969.

Markus, H., & Nurius, P.S. (1987). Possible selves: The interface between motivation and the self-concept. In K. Yardley & T. Honess (Eds.), *Self and identity: Psychosocial perspectives* (pp. 157–172). Chichester, England: Wiley.

McFarlin, D.B., Baumeister, R.F., & Blascovich, J. (1984). On knowing when to quit: Task failure, self-esteem, advice, and nonproductive persistence. *Journal of Personality, 52,* 138–155.

McFarlin, D.B., & Blascovich, J. (1981). Effects of self-esteem and performance feedback on future affective preferences and cognitive expectations. *Journal of Personality and Social Psychology, 40,* 521–531.

McGuire, W.J., & McGuire, C.V. (1982). Significant others in self space: Sex differences and developmental trends in social self. In J. Suls (Ed.), *Psychological perspectives on the self* (Vol. 1, pp. 71–96). Hillsdale, NJ: Erlbaum.

McGuire, W.J., McGuire, C.V., Child, P., & Fujioka, T. (1978). Salience of ethnicity in the spontaneous self-concept as a function of one's ethnic distinctiveness in the social environment. *Journal of Personality and Social Psychology, 36,* 511–520.

McGuire, W.J., McGuire, C.V., & Winton, W. (1979). Effects of household sex composition on the salience of one's gender in the spontaneous self-concept. *Journal of Experimental Social Psychology, 15,* 77–90.

Mohr, D.M. (1978). Development of attributes of personal identity. *Developmental Psychology, 14,* 427–428.

Montemayor, R., & Eisen, M. (1977). The development of self-conceptions from childhood to adolescence. *Developmental Psychology, 13,* 314–319.

Nisbett, R.E., & Kunda, Z. (1985). Perceptions of social distributions. *Journal of Personality and Social Psychology, 48,* 297–311.

Oyserman, D., & Markus, H. (1986). Delinquency and possible selves. Unpublished manuscript, University of Michigan.

Rosenberg, M. (1965). *Society and the adolescent self-image.* Princeton, NJ: Princeton University Press.

Rosenberg, M. (1979). *Conceiving the self.* New York: Basic Books.

Ross, L., Greene, D., & House, P. (1977). The false consensus effect: An egocentric bias in social perception and attribution processes. *Journal of Experimental Social Psychology, 13,* 279–301.

Schneider, D.J., & Turkat, D. (1975). Self-presentation following success or failure: Defensive self-esteem models. *Journal of Personality, 43,* 127–135.

Sherman, S.J., Chassin, L., Presson, C.C., & Agostinelli, G. (1984). The role of the evaluation and similarity principles in the false consensus effect. *Journal of Personality and Social Psychology, 47,* 1244–1262.

Shrauger, J.S. (1975). Responses to evaluation as a function of initial self-perceptions. *Psychological Bulletin, 82,* 581–596.

Shrauger, J.S., & Sorman, P.B. (1977). Self-evaluations, initial success and failure, and improvement as determinants of persistence. *Journal of Consulting and Clinical Psychology, 45,* 784–795.

Simmons, R., Rosenberg, F., & Rosenberg, M. (1973). Disturbances in the self-image at adolescence. *American Sociological Review, 38,* 553–568.

Suls, J., & Wan, C.K. (1987). In search of the false uniqueness phenomenon: Fear and estimates of social consensus. *Journal of Personality and Social Psychology, 52,* 211–217.

Swann, W.B., Griffin, J.J., Predmore, S.C., & Gaines, B. (1987). The cognitive-affective crossfire: When self-consistency confronts self-enhancement. *Journal of Personality and Social Psychology, 52,* 881–889.

Swann, W.B., Pelham, B.W., & Krull, D.S. (1987). *The ray of hope: Averting the conflict by avoiding the choice.* Unpublished manuscript, University of Texas.

Tice, D.M., Buder, J., & Baumeister, R.F. (1985). Development of self-consciousness: At what age does audience pressure disrupt performance? *Adolescence, 20,* 301–305.

Waterman, A.S. (1982). Identity development from adolescence to adulthood: An extension of theory and a review of research. *Developmental Psychology, 8,* 341–358.

Wylie, R.C. (1974). *The self-concept.* Vol 1: A *review of methodological considerations and measuring instruments.* Lincoln, Nebraska: University of Nebraska Press.

CHAPTER 14

Moral Character

NICHOLAS EMLER

Moral Character: The Fall and
   Rise of a Concept
  The Psychology of Moral
   Character—An Historical
   Introduction
  Rule-Breaking: The Reality of
   Individual Differences
Discovering and Accounting for
   Character
  The Consistency of Conduct
  Individual Differences in
   Character: How Well Do
   Existing Theories Do?

ACTIVITY BOX: Deviance and
   Attitudes to Authority
  The Visibility of Conduct and
   the Anonymity of Society
Moral Character: Some Final
   Thoughts on Pinning
   Down Explanations
Summary
SUGGESTED READINGS
REFERENCES

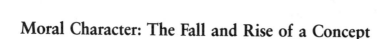

Moral Character: The Fall and Rise of a Concept

Imagine you are the manager of a store and you wish to hire a new assistant to work in the warehouse. There are several promising applicants. You have their filled-out applications giving details of education and previous employment history. But what else might you want to know about them that this information will not tell you, and how might you find out? Employers in this position may obtain references from the applicants' previous employers covering such matters as work record, skills, and qualifications. But directly or indirectly they could also offer an estimation of the person's character: Is this person reliable, responsible, conscientious, honest, hardworking, willing to follow instructions? In other words, these references may indicate some of the virtues and vices the respondent believes this person to possess.

Everyone involved—employers, applicants, and the people who provide character references—might be somewhat surprised to learn that many psychologists have regarded them as a waste of time. The use of references in making employment decisions is inappropriate, according to this view, not because respondents have conflicting interests and

The research program on which this chapter draws was supported by Grant No. HG 11/24/11 from the Economic and Social Research Council of Great Britain. Thanks are due to Julie Dickinson, Derek Honour, Julie Pehl, Andrew Ross, and especially Stanley Renwick and Stephen Reicher, for their assistance in this research program.

cannot be relied upon to give candid assessments. Nor is it inappropriate because people cannot make these kinds of judgments very reliably. These would be reasonable objections to the practice if true, but psychologists have come up with an altogether more serious difficulty: the concept of character may have no foundation in fact. This concept implies, indeed requires, that people differ in the degree to which they possess moral virtues and vice, and that these differences are both consistent across a range of circumstances and stable across occasions. This means that if Arthur Jones is more conscientious than the average warehouse foreman today or in this job, he will be tomorrow, next week, and probably next year too. He will also do a more conscientious job as a janitor or truck driver or mechanic than the average person. The objection is that this kind of consistency and stability in people's conduct simply does not exist. Arthur Jones is as likely to be conscientious one minute, irresponsible the next, honest in one job, dishonest in another. How he behaves will depend on the circumstances in which he finds himself at that moment and not on any general inclination he has to be honest or conscientious in everything he does.

In this chapter I shall explore the concept of moral character and I shall argue that it does after all have some psychological reality. Individuals are to a considerable degree consistent from one occasion to the next in the moral qualities they display. Thus, for example, individual differences in moral character *can* potentially serve as a useful predictor of a person's integrity in a job situation. I shall examine criticisms of the concept of moral character in psychology, tracing these first to assumptions that were made about the nature of deviance and second to difficulties of measurement. I will then look at the strengths and weaknesses of different ways of assessing character. In the second part of the chapter I will examine the evidence for consistency of character and ask how this consistency can best be explained.

There are many kinds of moral virtue. Robert Havighurst and Hilda Taba (1949), in their detailed study of adolescent character, examined five different virtues—honesty, responsibility, loyalty, moral courage, and friendliness—and one can doubtless think of others. But I shall devote most of this chapter to just one, albeit quite basic, example: willingness to abide by rules of social conduct. I have in mind here the inclination to abide by those rules, often also laws, proscribing conduct that injures the person, dignity, or property of others. The breaches of these rules have more familiar labels, such as "theft," "assault," and "vandalism." For the moment this will serve as my working definition of moral character. Later I shall have more to say about its derivation, and its justification.

The Psychology of Moral Character—
An Historical Introduction

The idea that *Homo sapiens* is preeminently a moral or rule-following animal has become almost a cliché in social science. Human social arrangements, so the argument goes, depend on the members of a society abiding by its various rules of conduct—tell the truth, keep promises, don't betray trusts, return favors, respect the interests of others, defer to the legitimate authority of the group, and so on. Precisely what the rules should be, and even what they are, is a matter of continuing debate in every known society. But it also cannot have escaped notice that rules get broken from time to time. So the questions arise: Who breaks these rules, when, and why? To understand the answers that psychology itself has produced to these questions it is necessary to look at a little history.

Until the late 19th century theories of crime were dominated by the ideas of Jeremy Bentham (1748–1842) and Cesare Beccaria (1738–1794). Both men believed that humans make decisions based on rational calculations of the personal costs and benefits of each line of action. They further assumed that people must be naturally inclined to break rules because the activities these rules outlaw are inherently attractive and rewarding. They will be deterred only if the anticipated costs of punishment outweigh the rewards of transgression.

During the 19th century incidents of crime and civil disorder increased rapidly in the new industrial cities of Europe and America. Social theorists initially made sense of this by arguing that the industrial revolution had swept away the kind of society in which punishment for crime was more certain. This was supposedly a society of small-scale communities in which everyone knew everyone else's business and so it was difficult to get away with anything without being found out. In cities, by contrast, the pattern of social life was anonymous and impersonal. And this anonymity made crime a more rational choice. It provided more opportunities than ever before for breaking rules covertly and secretly, and remaining undetected and unpunished. Under these conditions it would be rational for people to pursue self-interest and ignore the rules.

There was, however, a flaw in this neat analysis. It required far more lawlessness than actually occurred. The entire population was not after all running riot, committing mayhem, or indulging their lusts while the backs of their rulers were turned. Many people were keeping to the rules even when transgression could not possibly be detected, in other words, when it was irrational to do so. The obvious conclusion, to which Freud and others came, was that behavior in general is not under rational control. Furthermore, because no external threat or inducement could be permanently present in the anonymity of city life to discourage these people from the gratifications of misbehavior, purely internal control of conduct must be commonplace. And this internal control must be immune to or independent of reason.

Freud's own view of the childhood sources of internal control (e.g., Freud, 1930) is now of mainly historical interest. It has been superceded by other theories of moral development, variously emphasizing the styles of discipline and control employed by parents, processes of conditioning or imitative learning, or the consequences of cognitive development. Textbooks in developmental psychology will describe these theories and document their differences. What they may not do is emphasize their very considerable similarities. Almost all accept that moral development is a process in which controls over conduct are internalized. And almost all imply the process is generally successful. Only quite abnormal adults are assumed to lack internal controls and only these pathological individuals consistently break the rules.

So from Freud onward "moral character" in psychology has referred to the inner resources with which childhood had equipped the individual to resist solitary temptations. However, the very abnormality of crime suggested that its perpetrators were different in kind and not just degree from other people. The concept of moral character thus began to seem less relevant to this distinction, but its wane in popularity in psychology probably had more to do with the *social* psychology of deviance.

This social psychology appears, superficially at least, directly to contradict developmental theories. While the latter have been predicting that most adults will be well-socialized, social psychologists have set about demonstrating just how fragile and situation-contingent their good behavior is. Moreover, a common theme runs through the history of this social psychology down to the present day: Individuals will abandon standards of civilized behavior when they find themselves in groups or crowds.

This idea was first articulated by Gustav Le Bon (1903) as an explanation for the civil disorder that afflicted industrial France in the 1800s. He attributed the destructive effects of mobs to a kind of hypnosis that crowds produce in their members. Nonetheless, this and many similar arguments remained largely speculative interpretations until the 1950s and 1960s. During this period a succession of experimental studies revealed that individuals will indeed frequently deny, by word or deed, what is true or good or sensible or decent when in the presence of others doing the same. These studies confirmed, moreover, the powerful influence of the situation on conduct: Circumstances it seemed, rather than individual character, determine behavior. Finally, many social psychologists argued that the presence of a group has this immoralizing effect on conduct because it actually increases individual anonymity (e.g., Latané & Darley, 1970; Zimbardo, 1970). The group, in other words, has been social psychology's metaphor for the city.

Rule Breaking: The Reality of Individual Differences

I shall argue that orientation to social rules is a personality characteristic; individuals differ in the degree to which they are inclined to abide by or break social rules. These differences are generalized in the sense that this disposition applies to rules as a broad category, and not just to very specific kinds of rules. These differences are also relatively stable. I am suggesting therefore that crime is not some special or pathological characteristic but that it is continuous with more moderate levels of rule breaking; it is simply the extreme of a continuum. Crime is only rare or unusual in the sense that relatively very high or low levels of intelligence are rare.

Many psychologists believe that the idea of moral character—or any theory that posits stable, generalized individual differences in antisocial behavior—has been so thoroughly discredited that it barely deserves discussion. For instance, writing in 1976, Walter Mischel concluded: "The data on self-control and moral behavior do not support the existence of a unitary, intrapsychic moral agency like the superego nor do they support a unitary trait of conscience or honesty" (p. 461). Mischel's argument was aimed at a much larger target than theories of moral character: he was attacking the entire enterprise of personality assessment as traditionally conceived. But by far the strongest evidence for his general case does concern moral character, and it is to the practicalities of assessing moral character that we must now turn.

There have been four solutions to the problem of measuring moral character: experimental tests of character, the recorded judgments of law courts, reputational evidence, and self-reports.

Experimental Tests

Almost from the beginning psychologists were attracted by the idea of submitting people to tests of character under the scientifically controlled conditions of the laboratory. But there was a difficulty. Psychologists' theory of deviance told them the true test of character is to resist temptations and uphold moral standards even when there is no external inducement to do so, no possibility of detection, or sanction if one succumbs. How do you observe the unobservable?

Hugh Hartshorne and his colleagues, in their study of childhood character education (Hartshorne & May, 1928), solved the problem in the following way. They realized it was necessary only to create a convincing illusion for individuals that they could transgress without possibility of detection. Children would be tempted to cheat on typical classroom tasks of intelligence, numerical ability, or physical capacity. In every case the individual child under assessement is given the impression that he or she can cheat and get away with it. Thus if any child did not cheat it could only be because he or she had been restrained by internal controls. In fact, of course, the experimenters were able to detect cheating by various ingenious tricks, such as ensuring that the task could not be solved by honest means, or that certain levels of performance were improbable without cheating, or by surreptitious recording of true performance levels.

The results were surprising. Children's moral behavior was highly inconsistent. It was seldom the same child who cheated the most on different tests, and seldom the same child who behaved most honestly. Furthermore, the average amount of cheating varied considerably from one test to another. It is precisely this kind of evidence that Mischel and others have found so compelling. It seemed to justify the social psychologist's preference for situational explanations of deviance, and by the same token it seemed to rule out explanations of behavior in terms of character.

I do not believe that Hartshorne's evidence can support the conclusions customarily derived from it, for at least four reasons. The first is that the behaviors sampled by the various tests represent rather trivial kinds of transgression, if they can be thought of as transgressions at all. They hardly belong in the same league as theft, assault, or the destruction of others' property. What is true of trivialities need not be true of more serious offenses, and we shall see later that the most trivial forms of misconduct tend to be the least representative of an individual's moral conduct as a whole.

A second, related and perhaps more significant point concerns the moral ambiguity of experimentally induced transgressions. The very methodology places the experimenter in a dilemma. To create conditions under which more serious offenses might occur would be to connive in them. Moreover, matters regarded as truly serious normally give rise to precautions, obstructions put in the way of rule breaking. For a person to fail to take precautions would be regarded as both foolish and bizarre. The absence of precautions in Hartshorne and May's tasks must tell the children who take them that the experimenter does not regard these as serious matters.

A third and even more serious objection is that the steps necessary to construct an adequate measure of individual differences were not taken. When writers say that Hartshorne and May's data indicate the situational specificity of conduct, what they usually have in mind is that these data indicate positive but only modest correlations between honesty in one test and honesty in another, an average correlation over all the tests of a little over .2. But no psychological attribute can be accurately assessed on the basis of a single sample of behavior. Psychometric practice requires at the very least that measurements should be based on the combination or "aggregation" of a number of separate observations or tests. Even the individual tests that make up measures of intelligence correlate on average .15 with one another, which is lower than Hartshorne's figure. (For a more detailed discussion of these issues as they relate to the assessment of conduct, see Emler, 1984.) Some of these weaknesses could be overcome. It would in principle be quite possible to develop scales based on a number of individual tests that satisfy the necessary psychometric criteria. In practice, however, tests of this kind are cumbersome to set up and conduct, and so they have rarely been used in large enough numbers and with sufficiently large samples to allow the construction of proper scales.

However, there is a fourth reason to suspect that Hartshorne's data do not provide a good test of the hypothesis that there are individual differences in rule breaking. It is that the concept of character that their tests operationalize is inappropriate. Like many others before and since, they construed character in terms of covert and private conformity to rules—for example, continuing to work conscientiously even when you are alone and no one could possibly know if you were not working. I shall argue later that conformity to rules *per se,* whether in private or in public, is the more relevant test of character. Thus, do you work conscientiously at all, whether or not anyone else is watching?

Official Records

In modern societies records are kept of certain kinds of rule breaking and rule breakers—for example, the criminal records kept by the government. Could these not be used as evidence of character? This clearly overcomes the problem of triviality, but there are others.

Crimes are relatively rare events and most people do not have criminal records. Using officially recorded convictions as a measure of rule breaking would therefore result in a highly skewed distribution; most people would score zero on this measure. This would be quite acceptable if the world really were divided into a small minority who break the rules (criminals) and a large majority who do not. But I doubt this is an accurate description of reality.

Another difficulty is that many things intervene between committing a crime and receiving a conviction, of which detection is only one. Convictions only represent a small proportion of all the actions that would formally qualify as crimes, and they are likely to be in many ways a biased selection (see Box, 1981). Perhaps the most reasonable view is that crime represents the extreme of a continuum. As such it can be a useful source of information about rule breaking and rule breakers in general but one to be used with caution and always checked against evidence from other sources.

Researchers most frequently use this official evidence of character in the following way. They compare the psychological characteristics of people who are officially of good character—they have no criminal record—with those who do have a criminal record. In practice it is easier to compare people who are currently incarcerated in penal establishments with those who are not, and assume that this amounts to the same thing. The problem is that conviction and incarceration are likely to have psychological effects of their own and these will be confounded with any psychological qualities that may have produced the criminal activity in the first place.

Reputational Measures

Many people would probably regard this as the obvious solution. If you want to know about a person's character, ask some of the other people who know him or her. This is precisely what reputational measures involve, albeit in a more systematic form. Parents, teachers, or employers might be asked to rate the individual concerned, either for qualities of character (punctuality, reliability, courage, and so on) or for the occurrence of specified behaviors (how often this person arrives late for appointments, gets into fights, does work for charity, and so on).

Despite its simplicity, this solution became unfashionable in psychology for a variety of reasons. First, if the natural reflex of sinners is concealment, there will necessarily be much misconduct about which observers could not know. Second, if Hartshorne and others were right, there could be no stable core to character that people could make ratings of. This objection appeared more plausible when research in person perception revealed that people are very unreliable judges of others' character, prone to imagine more consistency than actually exists, and liable to make the world fit their own implicit models of personality (e.g., Cronbach, 1955). Thus, if the method suggested individual differences in character, this was merely an illusion in the minds of perceivers.

It now appears that the criticisms were much overstated. When ratings are provided by people acquainted with the targets and when ratings are aggregated from different sources, very satisfactory levels of reliability and validity can be achieved (e.g., Moskowitz & Schwartz, 1982). Observer ratings specifically of moral conduct or character have been used successfully in a number of studies (Gold, 1970; Havighurst & Taba, 1949). What is perhaps more interesting is what this success should tell us about the nature of rule breaking, a point to which I shall return.

Self-Reports

This method relies on people reporting upon their own degree of conformity or nonconformity with a variety of rules. If you want to know what rules people have broken, you simply ask them. So, if there are individual differences in rule breaking, do self-reports of behavior provide a good way of measuring them? In practical terms this comes down to questions about scaling and validity. Can scales be constructed, and do the scores such scales provide accord with independent evidence of these individual differences?

Short and Nye (1957) are credited with the first systematic use of this strategy as a means of assessing conduct. Their inventory included questions about twenty-three different kinds of misbehavior—minor crimes, acts of disobedience, and breaches of regulations. Since that time self-reports have become widely used in sociological research, initially to answer questions about the extent of unrecorded crime, but eventually as a way of assessing individual deviance (Hindelang, Hirschi, & Weis, 1981). Its advantages are obvious. It can sample a large number of different kinds of conduct economically and the sample need not be limited to trivial misbehavior.

In psychology it has been shunned and for reasons many psychologists probably regard as obvious: People cannot be expected to report honestly, accurately, or objectively upon their own rule breaking. Quite apart from the natural tendency to conceal one's sins, so the argument might run, there will be serious distortions arising from the sheer fallibility of human memory, distortions quite possibly compounded by defensive needs.

The short answer to this is that scales based on self-reports of rule violation can provide valid and highly reliable measures of relative degrees of actual misconduct. Reliability coefficients between .88 and .96 are common, and these are very high by the standards of psychological measurement generally. There are also several indications of the validity of self-reports. Incarcerated young offenders obtain much higher scores than their peers who are still at liberty (Emler, Heather, & Winton, 1978). This constitutes admittedly a rather crude test of validity. More direct validation is possible by checking acts that have resulted in convictions against self-reports of these same actions, as in the study by Gibson, Morrison, and West (1970). Yet another test has been to include direct questions about police contacts and convictions in the self-report. Each of these, however, is vulnerable to the same criticism: A person might be expected to be candid about matters that can be checked in official records anyway while continuing to deny any misdemeanors that have thus far remained undetected. To get around this objection Martin Gold (1970) attempted to corroborate self-report claims with evidence from respondents' acquaintances. The results were largely comparable.

Discovering and Accounting for Character

Now that we have considered the relative merits of different forms of measurement, what do these reveal about the basic question, namely, do people differ in moral character in a consistent and coherent way? In this second part I will examine this and a further question: To the extent that there are such differences, can any existing theory account for them? To answer these questions I will, where relevant, draw upon a program of research into moral conduct in which I have been involved.

This research has concentrated on a particular period of life, adolescence. There are many indications that adolescents are more likely than any other age group to break social rules. This has led to the speculation that bad character may just be a passing phase, a further question for us to consider. The research program has also relied on self-report evidence of conduct as the most useful for testing hypotheses about conduct and character. However, at every point it is proper to ask whether findings based on this kind of evidence converge with that from other reliable sources.

The Consistency of Conduct

One form of consistency is generalization: How generalized is the tendency to break or respect rules? Do people who break one kind of rule break other kinds, and conversely are the people who respect one kind of rule also those most likely to respect other kinds of rule? Hartshorne and May's (1928) answer as we saw was "no"; even in the specific case of cheating, different forms were unrelated to one another. But if responses in different tests are aggregated and the proper statistical procedures followed, consistency does emerge. Burton (1963) reanalyzed the Hartshorne data and found a general factor accounting for between 35% and 43% of the variance in test scores.

Our own approach has been to use self-report inventories that sample a large number of different kinds of rule breaking and then to examine relations between admissions of these different kinds. In one study we asked 214 boys, fifteen to seventeen years of age, about thirty-eight different kinds of misbehavior. We found a general factor accounting for just over 33 percent of the total variance. In a similar study of 440 boys and girls, twelve to fifteen years of age, a general factor accounted for 31 percent of the variance in responses (Emler & Reicher, 1989).

In a more intensive study of a smaller group of fourteen to fifteen-year-old boys (N = 40) we asked in more detail about an even larger range of misbehaviors, sixty-eight in all (Emler, Reicher, & Ross, 1987). This procedure allowed us to create scales for different categories of misbehavior and then to examine the relationships between these categories. Table 14.1 describes the correlations between the scales formed in this way. These relationships are uniformly positive and in most cases strong, suggesting that one form of rule breaking is consistently related to others.

It was also possible to factor analyze scale scores, as Burton had done with the Hartshorne data (in our other factor analyses the variables had been individual questions rather than scales). The first factor accounted for 62 percent of the variance. This indicates a very strong general factor underlying these diverse forms of behavior. On the question of generalization, therefore, self-report and experimental evidence converge, as they do with evidence from official records (Klien, 1984).

Klien (1984) also confirms that people do not specialize in particular forms of rule breaking—in effect, being of good character in all respects but one. If they break one kind of rule they are likely to break others. It seems there is one general dimension to which most of the common forms of misconduct are related.

The self-report evidence helps to clarify certain other questions about this dimension, in particular the types of conduct and misconduct that are particularly representative of this dimension and those that are less representative. Most representative are various forms of

TABLE 14.1

Intercorrelations Among Subscales of Rule-Breaking Behavior

Subscale	Theft	Aggression	Vandalism	Status	Minor/Nuisance
Drugs	.48***	.41**	.43**	.17	.36*
Theft		.75***	.77***	.76***	.46***
Aggression			.83***	.66***	.47***
Vandalism				.56***	.52***
Status					.18*

N = 40 (boys aged 14 to 15).

Status = forms of behavior proscribed only by virtue of the person's age, such as drinking alcohol in bars or driving a motor vehicle.

*p < .05.   **p < .01.   ***p < .001.

From Emler, Reicher, & Ross (1987), p. 102.

theft, getting into fights in public and using weapons, malicious damage to property, and defying representatives of authority. Rather less representative is whether a person smokes, gambles, drinks, or uses illegal drugs. This dimension is defined, therefore, more strongly by rule breaking that has victims or targets than by rule breaking that does not. It is also more strongly defined by relatively more serious forms of misbehavior, activities of the kind normally regarded and treated as criminal offenses. In other words, it confirms that a person's tendency to engage in or avoid serious misconduct is more representative of that person's conduct as a whole than whether or not he or she misbehaves in trivial ways. Finally, as official records would also lead one to expect, boys are more likely to have "bad character" in this sense than girls; and the more serious the misconduct, the greater is the difference between males and females.

The other common meaning of behavioral consistency is stability across time. There is a difficulty and an apparent contradiction here. Both self-reports and official records indicate that criminal misbehavior of the kind we are talking about rises to a peak at about fourteen or fifteen years of age and gradually declines thereafter. Does this mean that moral conduct is not stable across time? No, the disposition to break or respect rules, *relative to others of the same age,* is relatively stable. Those most likely to break rules at eleven or twelve are generally those most likely to do so at fourteen or fifteen and these in turn are the people most likely to do so at seventeen or eighteen.

Therefore, although absolute levels of rule breaking do change with age, rule breaking at different ages will be correlated. Among twelve- to sixteen-year-olds we found high correlations in the range .6 to .8 between self-report scores over an eighteen-month period. Others have found similar degrees of stability over even longer periods.

The Activity Box provides an opportunity to test yourself on conduct and attitudes.

Individual Differences in Character: How Well Do Existing Theories Do?

Both of the general views of deviance we considered earlier can now be seen to have overstated their respective cases. First, socialization is not as successful as developmental psychology implies and criminal misconduct is not confined to a small, abnormal minority. Rather, rule breaking is commonplace and serious crime is perhaps only the extreme of a continuum whose middle range is represented by moderate degrees of moderately serious rule breaking. Thus, a very small minority of the population has committed robbery with violence and many, perhaps the majority, have breached minor regulations at some time in their lives, while a proportion somewhere in between these extremes will have gotten into fights, committed minor thefts, or written on walls with spray paint.

ACTIVITY BOX

Deviance and Attitudes to Authority: Self-Concept and Reputation

There is hardly anyone who has never broken any rule and hardly anyone believes that authorities are perfect in every respect. Both, like so much else in life, are matters of degree. Where do you think you stand on these dimensions? Do you believe that on balance you are more law abiding or honest than most people of your acquaintance, or less? And do you think your views about authority are more positive or more critical or negative than those of most people you know? Equally important, what do other people think about you, and does their assessment agree with your own?

This Activity Box contains various questions about misbehavior— some trivial, some less so—and various statements about authority. Make two copies (for later use) and then answer the questions for yourself.

SELF PERCEPTIONS

Check TRUE if you have ever engaged in the activity described, FALSE if you never have.

1. I have torn up or thrown on the floor things belonging to other people.   TRUE   FALSE
2. I have smashed, slashed, or damaged things in public places—in streets, cinemas, dance halls, trains, buses, and so on.
   TRUE   FALSE
3. I have carried some kind of a weapon (knife, razor, etc.) in case it was needed in a fight.   TRUE   FALSE
4. I have annoyed, insulted, or fought strangers in the street.
   TRUE   FALSE
5. I have thrown things such as stones at other people.
   TRUE   FALSE
6. I have driven a car or motorbike under the influence of drink or drugs.   TRUE   FALSE
7. I have taken money from home with no intention of returning it.
   TRUE   FALSE
8. I have obtained money by false pretenses.   TRUE   FALSE

The implication of this analysis is that we do not need one kind of explanation for the moral conduct of most people and quite another for the criminal conduct of the few, any more than we need different kinds of explanation for normal and exceptional intelligence, for they are not

---

9. I have stolen things from department stores, supermarkets, and so on, while the store was open.   TRUE   FALSE
10. I have fought someone in a public place.   TRUE   FALSE
11. I have switched price tags on things before buying them.   TRUE   FALSE
12. I have deliberately traveled on a train or bus without a ticket or paid the wrong fare.   TRUE   FALSE
13. I have witnessed an incident in which the law was broken and failed to report it to the police.   TRUE   FALSE

Scoring: To obtain your total score, simply count the number of times you have checked TRUE.

An average score for males is about 5. If you are male and your score is 8 or above, you are definitely more delinquent than the average student. If it is 2 or less, you are distinctly less delinquent than the average. If you are female, all the above values should be halved.

Attitudes: For each statement, indicate whether you strongly agree (SA), agree (A), are undecided (U), disagree (D), or strongly disagree (SD) by circling the appropriate letters.

1. Laws are made for the benefit of everyone in society.
   SA   A   U   D   SD
2. The police are often unnecessarily brutal to people.
   SA   A   U   D   SD
3. Rules in schools and colleges are made just for the benefit of the staff, not the students.   SA   A   U   D   SD
4. The police do treat everyone the same on the whole.
   SA   A   U   D   SD
5. A lot of laws are not to help ordinary people but purely to restrict their freedom.   SA   A   U   D   SD
6. Most policemen are honest.   SA   A   U   D   SD

categorically different. Finally, conduct is not, as some social psychologists have argued, entirely a function of the situation. In situations in which rules sometimes get broken, the same people tend to break them.

ACTIVITY BOX (Continued)

Deviance and Attitudes to Authority: Self-Concept and Reputation

7. The main purpose of the law is to keep things as they are in a society that favors the rich.   SA   A   U   D   SD
8. You should always do what the police tell you.
   SA   A   U   D   SD
9. It can be OK to break the law if it is to help a friend.
   SA   A   U   D   SD
10. The police exist to make society a better place for everyone to live in.   SA   A   U   D   SD

Scoring: For questions 1, 4, 6, 8, and 10, score 5 for SA, 4 for A, 3 for U, 2 for D, 1 for SD. For the remaining questions score 1 for SA, 2 for A, 3 for U, 4 for D, 5 for SD.

The average total score for males is about 24, for females about 26. Scores of 30 and above are distinctly more positive than the average for males and females. Scores of 18 and below are more negative than the average for males, 22 and below for females.

How did your scores for conduct and attitudes compare? Were they in the same direction? Behavior and attitudes may not always coincide; sometimes people may be hostile to authority but not at all delinquent. However, it would be very unusual to be highly delinquent and have very positive opinions about authority.

REPUTATION

This exercise could be developed by asking your friends to guess your replies. For example, give one of the two copies to a friend who knows you very well and the other to someone who knows you less well, possibly a recent acquaintance, and ask them to guess how you responded. You might expect the first person to be more accurate than the second but there are other possibilities. When they make errors, in which direction do these tend to be? Do both make errors in the same direction? Do they make errors in different directions for attitudes and conduct respectively? If a good friend makes a lot of errors, it is worth asking why this should be; have you got a better or a worse reputation than you deserve?

What then can explain this consistency? In our research program we have looked at two popular explanations, Eysenck's (1964) theory of criminality and Kohlberg's (1984) theory of moral development.

Neurotic Extraverts

Eysenck's (1964) theory ingeniously integrates learning processes with genetic factors. Eysenck argues first that adult conduct is normally controlled by an internal mechanism based on conditioned anxiety. Anxiety responses to certain stimuli (temptations) are acquired in childhood by a process of Pavlovian or classical conditioning. A small boy may be about to draw on the living room wall when his mother shouts angrily at him. If she does this often enough under the same circumstances, he will automatically begin to flinch every time he approaches a wall with a writing implement.

Conditioned responses of this kind, however, are not equally strong in every case. And those in whom they are weakest are the most likely to act antisocially. The relative strength or weakness of these responses will depend on two things: the extent to which parents provided the appropriate socialization experiences in childhood and the extent to which the individual is constitutionally conditionable. Eysenck regarded the latter, genetically determined factor as the more important source of individual differences. This quality of conditionability is reflected in two features of personality, extraversion-introversion and neuroticism-stability. Neurotic extraverts are the least conditionable and so the most prone to antisocial behavior.

The most popular way of testing this hypothesis has been to compare the personalities of incarcerated offenders with those of controls. Support for the hypothesis has been mixed at best (Cochrane, 1974) but, given the problems of interpretation raised by this kind of comparison, self-reports of antisocial behavior should provide a better test of the hypothesis. Here the results have been more conclusive (Emler, 1984). In very few studies is a strong relationship reported between antisocial behavior and neuroticism. Extraversion emerges as a significant correlate of misbehavior in some samples of older (late adolescent, young adult) males but in few of younger males and virtually none of the female samples. Our own research confirms this picture (e.g., Emler, Reicher, & Ross, 1987).

Deficient Moral Insight

In a highly influential theory, Lawrence Kohlberg (1984) proposed that moral development is much like the development of intelligence. Acting morally means finding solutions to problems where interests or obligations conflict. Not only are some moral problems more complex and difficult to resolve than others, the solutions we come up with can be more or less complete. As we develop we construct successively more adequate intellectual means for solving these problems. Kohlberg believed this development can best be described as a sequence of steps or stages. Each stage is a moral theory, a way of reasoning about problems and choosing between competing moral demands. The first is rather simple, inadequate for coping with most moral problems and providing very imperfect solutions. The second is a little more complex and it overcomes some of the limitations of the first, but it still has many shortcomings so that we go on to construct a third, and so on. Kohlberg believed that there are potentially six stages of this kind, each a more complex and adequate theory than the one it replaces.

This number is only potential because hardly anyone completes all six stages. Indeed, most adults in Western society have come to a halt after only three or four. Moreover, just as intelligence develops at different rates in different individuals so people move through this sequence more or less quickly. How might this help explain differences in moral character?

Kohlberg himself had little time for the idea of moral character, agreeing with Hartshorne and May that "you cannot divide the world into honest and dishonest people." Nonetheless, he also believed there would be a connection between stage of moral reasoning and conduct: Higher stages of moral reasoning produce better moral decisions, so we should expect better behavior of people who have achieved higher stages than those who have not.

There is an intuitive appeal in this idea. It makes sense that an individual who lacks insight into the nature of moral obligations will be more likely to violate rules of social conduct than someone who grasps the obligations those rules reflect. The theory also suggests an explanation for the age pattern of rule breaking, as follows. A considerable degree of external control is still in place for children at the start of adolescence; they are extensively supervised by parents, teachers, and other adults. Well-developed internal control is not yet much needed and its absence has few serious effects. But as the years pass the external controls slacken. If moral insight develops at different rates in different individuals, it may still have only reached an early stage among some young people when they are beginning to experience less external control. Are adolescent rule breakers therefore individuals in a hiatus between external and internal controls, after the police have left but before a fully developed conscience has arrived?

Unfortunately, there is as yet no convincing evidence to support this hypothesis. Most researchers have compared the moral reasoning levels of criminal offenders with nonoffenders of the same age. Jennings, Kilkenny, and Kohlberg (1983) review the results from several studies in which this comparison has been made, and all show the predicted negative relation between moral reasoning and this criterion of character, namely, whether or not one has been imprisoned by the courts. This is less impressive than it seems. The relations are never strong, but more important they are potentially contaminated by the fact that the offenders are or have been incarcerated. When we compared the moral reasoning of incarcerated boys and controls we found the same relationship (Emler, Heather, & Winton, 1978). But when we looked at self-reports of delinquency, we found no link with moral reasoning level, either within or between these groups.

The Visibility of Conduct and the Anonymity of Society

Eysenck and Kohlberg, though in very different ways, both explain variations in conduct in terms of the strength of internal controls. Thus both reflect the long-standing assumption that external constraints are insufficient to account for good conduct. The assumption rests on the twin beliefs that (1) rule breaking normally occurs under conditions of anonymity and (2) such anonymity is readily and frequently available in contemporary society. I wish to suggest that both beliefs are false.

Conduct, both good and bad, is typically visible, and there are at least four indications of its visibility. First, many forms of transgression are by definition unconcealed, at least from the victim, for example, acts of direct aggression. Second, reputational measures of conduct work and they can only do so because people's conduct is visible to observers. Third, self-reports work; concealment is apparently not the natural reflex of sinners, for they are at least willing to make researchers privy to their past misconduct.

The determined critic could probably think of objections to each of these arguments. Aggressors could still be protected by the cloak of anonymity to the extent that their victims are strangers. Observer ratings could still underestimate concealed rule breaking. And researchers typically guarantee the confidentiality of answers to self-reports. The fourth indication of visibility is that there are almost always direct witnesses to rule breaking in the form of accomplices (Emler, Reicher, & Ross, 1987), but even this is open to dispute. Social psychologists have been saying for years that people behave more badly when in groups and do so because the group context renders them more, not less, anonymous. In other words, these companions in crime could be strangers to one another.

There are answers to each of these objections. Aggressors are more often than not known to their victims. Observer ratings predict concealable forms of deviance—theft, vandalism, drug use—as successfully as they predict less concealable forms such as aggression or confrontations with authority. Guarantees of anonymity have little effect on self-report responses. Accomplices in crime are not strangers to one another. And offenders are no more likely to associate in groups than nonoffenders.

But there is a more fundamental reason why most conduct is public knowledge, why observer ratings are valid, and why it is difficult to conceal deviance. The anonymous society is largely a myth. Despite the tremendous social changes brought on by industrialization and urbanization, the vast majority of individuals continue to live in worlds populated by people who know them. Whether we live in small villages or large cities, most of the significant business of our lives is conducted with and in the presence of acquaintances, not strangers. Furthermore, given the connectedness of our personal worlds, the fact that so many of the people we know and talk to also know and talk to one another, there is very little of any significance that we do, good or bad, that is not likely to become public knowledge. This suggests a straightforward explanation for rule following. Good character has social guarantees. People behave well, not just to the degree that they are committed to standards they have internalized, but because they wish to preserve their good name in the social worlds they inhabit. Why then does anyone still break the rules? One possibility is that the conditions that sustain the visibility of conduct—and so a concern with good character—are not present to the same degree for everyone all the time.

Travis Hirschi (1969) has put forward a theory of conduct that makes just such an interpretation. People will conform to the extent that they have direct personal ties to the conventional order of society, ties that lead them to believe they will be found out if they transgress and that this will be personally costly. Good conduct in other words is guaranteed by attachments to other people one cares about, often but not necessarily parents, and by investments in the system, most obviously investments in education or a career, which misconduct would put at risk. When these ties and investments are temporarily or more permanently weakened, one will feel free to break rules.

An attraction of Hirschi's theory is that the strength of those conditions that contain misconduct could be relatively stable features of a person's circumstances. Attachments and investments may remain at the same level for years at a time, thereby explaining stability in an individual's conduct. On the other hand, these are just the kind of circumstances liable to change in adolescence. One major investment, education, fails to pay off for many people during this period and it may be a few years before alternative investments in jobs or recognized roles in the community are made. And the social bonds may be temporarily weakened for adolescents as contact with parents declines but before they acquire new attachments through employment and families of their own.

Are the rule breakers therefore those individuals who have temporarily or more permanently slipped through the web of informal controls? This cannot be the whole answer, for the following reason. If it were we would expect rule breakers to be relative social isolates, lacking friends and lacking regular contact with acquaintances. Yet it has now been extensively and convincingly documented that rule breakers are no less likely to have friends or regular social contacts than anyone else (Emler & Reicher, 1989).

Perhaps then immunity to social control is subjective rather than objective. Do rule breakers chronically miscalculate the visibility of their conduct or the damage it will do to their reputations? Or do they simply lack the skills to construct a good name for themselves? Our own and other research forces us to rule out these possibilities too. The views of chronic rule breakers may differ from those of more conforming peers on some points of detail, but they largely agree about the implications of rule breaking for character. And there has as yet to be a convincing demonstration that rule breakers lack any of the social skills or insights rule followers possess. Finally, far from being unaware that their misdeeds will be noticed, we have found that delinquent adolescents actually prefer an audience to witness the deed. We are forced to the conclusion that a reputation for bad behavior is a deliberate choice on the part of the individual concerned.

Moral Character: Some Final Thoughts on Pinning Down Explanations

It seems we are little closer to explaining moral character. Many promising hypotheses have had to be ruled out, but this is no reason for pessimism; we have actually made a lot of progress as should be clear if we briefly take stock. We know that there is a consistent core to character and that it is most directly defined by the way an individual behaves in relation to rules about respecting the person and property of others. Serious violations of these rules are rare, but less serious violations are commonplace. They are also unconcealed. We know that the people in society most likely to violate these rules are adolescent boys, and that those who do so are not ignorant of the consequences for their public reputations. The question that remains is why people choose to pursue different kinds of reputation.

In this last section I shall sketch out a preliminary answer. It begins with the view that social life involves extensive regulation of affairs by various authorities who both make and enforce rules and regulations and issue various instructions and orders. At the beginning of our lives this authority is most likely to be represented to us by our parents, but increasingly it is encountered in other, often more impersonal and symbolic forms—teachers and school principals, policemen and other officials of the state, employers and bosses. Each of us has to arrive at some kind of accommodation with authority, and there are reasons to believe this starts early, probably in the family. The kind of accommodation we reach has far-reaching and relatively enduring effects on conduct.

One justification for making this intimate link between accommodation to authority and moral conduct comes from studies of the relation between rule breaking and attitudes toward institutional authorities. Table 14.2 summarizes some of the evidence from our research program. The correlations are so strong and consistent as to suggest not that attitudes predict conduct but that attitudes and conduct are really two facets of the same relationship—that between the young person and authority. The verbal and subjective facet of that relationship is to be found in what people say and believe about authority, the behavioral facet in how they conduct themselves in relation to those standards that authority supports.

But a negative relation with authority not only puts the individual at odds with its demands, it also puts that individual outside its protection. Rule breaking may then become a defensive strategy, providing informal means for settling grievances, given that formal

TABLE 14.2

Relations (Based on Correlation Coefficients) Between Negative Attitudes Toward Formal Authority and Self-Reported Rule Breaking

Sample	Males	Females
12 to 14-year-olds, working-class background (Emler and Reicher, 1987)	.60 (N = 45)	.68 (N = 50)
13-year-olds, lower middle- and working-class backgrounds (Reicher and Emler, 1985)	.68 (N = 55)	.76 (N = 53)
15 to 17-year-olds, middle- and working-class backgrounds (Emler and Reicher, 1987)	.76 (N = 16)	.42 (N = 53)
College students, mean age 20 (Emler and Reicher, 1987)	.42 (N = 42)	−.01 (N = 25)

Note: More negative attitudes are associated with higher levels of rule breaking.

Data taken from Emler & Reicher (1987) and Reicher & Emler (1985).

remedies are believed to be unavailable. And it offers informal protection by virtue of the kind of reputation it does convey, a reputation for being the sort of person it is dangerous to victimize or offend. One can see therefore why rule breakers might want their mayhem to be known, particularly to potential enemies. And as might also be expected, they present themselves in personality tests as wild and reckless but also tough, unemotional, and indifferent to the suffering of their victims.

However, it would be a mistake to assume that rule breakers are in every respect unpleasant people. They may be as generous, helpful, and loyal to their friends as anyone else (otherwise it is unlikely they would have any), though the world may be more sharply divided for them into friends and enemies.

As to the greater prevalence of males among the rule breakers, we can see that a positive accommodation to authority competes with several cultural expectations—for independence, assertiveness, toughness—that are stronger for boys than for girls. By the same token the rule breaker's reputation as hard, strong, unemotional, and cruel is less compatible with traditional images of femininity.

We have yet to address one of the most striking features of misbehavior: It is overwhelmingly a collective rather than a solitary activity. Precisely what this tells us about the causes of misconduct is still unclear but I am currently inclined to the view that people who are disposed to break the rules only do so when they find themselves in like-minded company (see Emler, Reicher, & Ross, 1987). Company does not make people bad or good; it only releases dispositions that are already present, and only when the company is similarly disposed.

This could make sense of the greater prevalence of criminal misbehavior in adolescence. The period combines an increase in opportunities with an increased probability of finding like-minded company. The latter arises with the move from small elementary schools to large high schools and the tendency of these schools to sort young people in ways that are sensitive to their delinquent inclinations. And this brings me to the consequences of character.

Moral conduct as defined in this chapter is closely associated with educational performance. Why should this be? Is it because they are both influenced by a more basic attribute of the person, namely, intelligence? There is not the space here to explore this controversial issue in the detail it deserves, but I will mention one difficulty about explaining differences in conduct in terms of differences in intelligence. Involvement in delinquent misbehavior increases between ages ten and fourteen. So, in absolute terms, does intellectual ability. It is hard to see why increases in intelligence should produce increases in delinquency. On the other hand, intellectual ability undoubtedly is related to educational performance positively, as is delinquency negatively. The conclusion this suggests, to me at least, is that the young person's orientation to authority influences his or her educational career rather than the reverse. This does make some sense. It implies that doing well at school is not just a matter of being intellectually able. It also depends on deferring to the authority of teachers, abiding by the various rules of classroom procedure, and following instructions. More generally, it suggests that moral character has consequences for those prospects in one's life that derive from educational qualifications.

Finally, almost everyone who has thought deeply about moral questions has recognized that occasions sometimes arise in which the more moral course is to resist authority. About the special qualities of character such resistance requires I have said nothing. I have claimed that an important quality of character is the inclination to follow the rules of social conduct supported by the established authorities in society. Whether those who most persistently defy such authority in the service of their own interests would also prove the most resistant when authority becomes corrupt and unjust we do not yet know.

Summary

Psychologists started to think seriously toward the end of the nineteenth century about the forces that cause people to behave morally. They were curious as to how people are restrained from transgressing when they are alone, particularly as the mass society of the cities seemed to create so much anonymity. The general conclusion, common to a number of different theories, was that individuals must be restrained by some form of control that they have internalized in childhood. However, the concept of moral character all but disappeared from the psychological literature after the 1920s, psychologists by then being convinced that people do not possess any stable trait of honesty. This fitted with social psychology, which interpreted behavior as resulting from characteristics of situations rather than individuals.

One major difficulty for research in this area has been the development of effective measures of character. The experimental tests of character, evidence from which had done so much to discredit the very concept of moral character, have a number of limitations. Other methods have consequently grown in popularity, including observer ratings and particularly self-report measures.

Evidence from these sources now supports the view that there is a stable core to moral character. People do consistently differ in their inclination to abide by various rules. However, the same evidence also raises questions about a number of popular psychological explanations of rule breaking, including those that have attributed it to certain genetically based personality differences, immaturity of moral insight, and low intelligence.

More interestingly, it appears that transgressions of the rules are not typically concealed and that most rule breaking occurs in the company of acquaintances. Indeed the very notion that modern society is anonymous and allows many opportunities for covert misbehavior seems to have been in error. This raises the possibility that people are deterred from breaking rules by a concern for their reputation or good name within the communities to which they belong. The intriguing question is then why anyone should deliberately behave in such a way as to create a bad name. A tentative answer is that relatively early in life some individuals find it difficult to accommodate to the demands of authority, particularly the formal authority encountered in settings like the school. Then they encounter others with the same difficulties and together their opposition is translated into action. They develop an antiauthority ethos and work out informal solutions to the hazards of life in which a bad reputation has certain attractions and advantages.

SUGGESTED READINGS

Emler, N. (1984). Differential involvement in delinquency: Toward an interpretation in terms of reputation management. In B.A. Maher & W.B. Maher (Eds.), *Progress in experimental personality research* (Vol. 13, pp. 173–239). New York: Academic Press. Provides a more technically detailed statement of many of the arguments to be found in this chapter.

Empey, L. (1978). *American delinquency.* Homewood, Ill.: Dorsey. An excellent and thorough textbook treatment of theory and research on delinquency.

Havigurst, R., & Taba, H. (1949). *Adolescent character and personality.* New York: Wiley. A classic study based primarily on "reputational" measures of character.

Mars, G. (1982). *Cheats at work: An anthropology of work-place crime.* London: Unwin. A highly readable and entertaining argument for a circumstantial interpretation of rule breaking. People break the rules largely because of the circumstances in which they find themselves and not because they are persons of bad character.

REFERENCES

Box, S. (1981). *Deviance, reality and society.* New York: Holt.

Burton, R.V. (1963). Generality of honesty reconsidered. *Psychological Review, 70,* 481–499.

Cochrane, R. (1974). Crime and personality: Theory and evidence. *Bulletin of the British Psychological Society, 27,* 19–22.

Cronbach, L.J. (1955). Processes affecting scores on "understanding others" and "assumed similarity." *Psychological Bulletin, 52,* 177–193.

Emler, N. (1984). Differential involvement in delinquency: Toward an interpretation in terms of reputation management. In B.A. Maher & W.B. Maher (Eds.), *Progress in experimental personality research* (Vol. 13, pp. 173–239). New York: Academic Press.

Emler, N., Heather, N., & Winton, M. (1978). Delinquency and the development of moral reasoning. *British Journal of Social and Clinical Psychology, 17,* 325–331.

Emler, N., & Reicher, S. (1987). Orientations to institutional authority in adolescence. *Journal of Moral Education, 16,* 108–116.

Emler, N., & Reicher, S. (1989). *The social psychology of delinquency.* Oxford: Blackwell.

Emler, N., Reicher, S., & Ross, A. (1987). The social context of delinquent conduct. *Journal of Child Psychology and Psychiatry, 28,* 99–109.

Eysenck, H.J. (1964). *Crime and personality.* London: Routledge & Keegan Paul.

Freud, S. (1930). *Civilization and its discontents.* New York: Norton.

Gibson, H., Morrison, S., & West, D.J. (1970). The confession of known offences in response to a self-report delinquency schedule. *British Journal of Criminology, 10,* 277–280.

Gold, M. (1970). *Delinquent behavior in an American city.* Belmont, CA: Brooks/Cole.

Hartshorne, H., & May, M.A. (1928). *Studies in the nature of character. Vol. 1. Studies in deceit.* New York: Macmillan.

Havighurst, R., & Taba, H. (1949). *Adolescent character and personality.* New York: Wiley.

Hindelang, M., Hirschi, T., & Weiss, J.G. (1981). *Measuring delinquency.* Beverley Hills, CA: Sage.

Hirschi, T. (1969). *Causes of delinquency.* Berkeley, CA: University of California Press.

Jennings, W.S., Kilkenny, R., & Kohlberg, L. (1983). Moral development: Theory and practice for youthful and adult offenders. In W. Laufer & J.M. Day (Eds.), *Personality theory, moral development and criminal behavior* (pp. 281–355). Toronto: Lexington Books.

Klien, M. (1984). Offence specialisation and versatility among juveniles. *British Journal of Criminology, 24,* 185–194.

Kohlberg, L. (1984) *Essays on moral development.* Vol. 2. *The psychology of moral development.* New York: Harper and Row.

Latané, B., & Darley, J. (1970). *The unresponsive bystander: Why doesn't he help?* New York: Appleton.

Le Bon, G. (1903). *The crowd: A study of the popular mind.* London: Allen & Unwin.

Moskowitz, D.S., & Schwartz, J.C. (1982). Validity comparison of behavior counts and rating by knowledgeable informants. *Journal of Personality and Social Psychology, 42,* 518–528.

Mischel, W. (1976). *Personality and assessment* (2nd. ed.). New York: Wiley.

Reicher, S., & Emler, N. (1985). Delinquent behavior and attitudes to formal authority. *British Journal of Social Psychology, 24,* 161–168.

Short, J.F., & Nye, F.J. (1957). Reported behavior as a criterion of deviant behavior. *Social Problems, 4,* 296–302.

Zimbardo, P. (1970). The human choice: Individuation, reason and order versus deindividuation, impulse and chaos. In W.J. Arnold & D. Levine (Eds.), *Nebraska symposium on motivation* (pp. 237–307). Lincoln, NE: University of Nebraska Press.

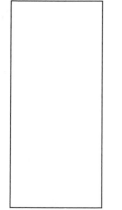

CHAPTER 15

Emotion

RANDY J. LARSEN

Introduction and Issues
Emotional States Versus
    Emotional Traits
Emotional Content Versus
    Emotional Style
  Emotional Content
  Emotional Style

ACTIVITY BOX: Affect Intensity
    Measure
Concluding Remarks
Summary
SUGGESTED READINGS
REFERENCES

Introduction and Issues

How can emotion be useful to an understanding of personality? Emotions are useful to the extent that they provide an understanding of individual lives as well as provide us with useful distinctions between persons. Emotions can help us understand individual lives by telling us what is important to people, what motivates them, and what behaviors or responses we can expect certain persons to exhibit. Emotions also help us distinguish between different persons by providing characteristics of emotional life that are helpful in describing different personalities. To the extent that these emotion-related characteristics are stable and enduring, they will be useful for characterizing differences between individual personalities. Emotion is a large and diverse area of research, just as personality is a large and diverse area of research. These two fields do overlap, however, and it is precisely this area of overlap that we will focus on in the remainder of this chapter. But how can we conceive of emotions as stable and enduring personality characteristics, when common sense suggests that emotions are really states that come and go?

Emotional States Versus Emotional Traits

Emotions are typically thought of as states that occur and go away depending on various circumstances and situations, for example, "I'm anxious *because* of the final exam." And yet, when we describe someone's personality, we may refer to consistencies in his or her emotional states or typical emotional responses, for example, "John is typically an anxious sort of person." How can it be that we use emotions to describe both states and traits of people? To answer this question we need to know the differences between states and traits.

States are understood to be transient; they occur and go away in usually a short amount of time. States are also thought to be caused mainly by environmental conditions, and so we say that states are situationally determined and specific to the particular conditions that bring them about. For example, a state of high arousal might be caused by a noisy and stimulating environment or perhaps by drinking lots of coffee. In these cases the arousal that a person feels is a state that has a specific cause *outside* of the person and so will eventually go away over time (in the case of coffee) or when the person leaves the situation (in the case of the stimulating environment).

Traits, on the other hand, are understood to be longer lasting patterns of behavior or experience. In addition, traits are understood to be caused by forces "internal" to the person and are not necessarily due to situational or environmental forces outside the person. In a sense, persons "carry around" their traits, and so behaviors determined by traits should be stable over time, somewhat consistent from situation to situation, and useful for describing differences between people. Arousal, as in the earlier example, could alternatively be viewed as a trait, perhaps calling it *arousability* to refer to a stable and consistent tendency of some people to become easily "worked up" and for other people to remain calm almost no matter what the circumstances.

Emotions thus represent a peculiar hybrid category of responses that can be viewed as either states or traits. We can talk about a person who is in a state of fear, or talk about fearfulness as a trait. We could talk about a person who is happy on some occasion (state) or talk about happy persons (trait). We can talk about anxiety as a state, or anxiety-proneness as a trait. For emotions to be relevant to the understanding of personality, it will be necessary to conceive of emotions as trait-like in nature. As a brief matter of terminology, I will sometimes use the term affect instead of emotion. Affect technically refers to the specific feeling state that a particular emotion provokes. For the most part, however, affect and emotion can be considered as interchangeable terms, especially because our focus is on trait-like aspects of emotion (i.e., characteristic patterns of emotional experience).

Emotional Content Versus Emotional Style

When emotions are viewed as traits we can make certain useful distinctions. For example, we can distinguish between the content of a person's emotional life and the style with which the person experiences those emotions. Both of these aspects of emotion—content and style—exhibit trait-like properties (e.g., consistent over time and situations and useful for making distinctions between people). Thus we shall consider each of these aspects of emotional life in some detail.

Emotional Content

Every person has an emotional life, and the content of that emotional life is a topic of interest to personality psychologists. By content we refer to the characteristic or typical emotions the person is likely to experience over time. For example, someone whom we might characterize as an angry or hot-tempered person should have an emotional life that contains a good deal of anger. Or someone else whose emotional life contains a lot of positive affect is someone we might characterize as a happy sort of person. Thus the notion of content leads us to consider the *types* of emotions a given person is most likely to experience over time. Before we inquire about different types of emotional content we need to have some understanding of the variety of emotions that humans in general are capable of experiencing. That is, what are the primary dimensions of emotional experience?

There are over 550 terms that describe different emotions (Averill, 1975). This leads to a good deal of complexity in trying to understand the emotional lives of humans. Consequently, researchers have tried in various ways to reduce this complexity by defining or discovering the primary or basic dimensions of emotional experience. Attempts to reduce the large set of emotion terms to a manageable collection of more fundamental emotions have taken two different approaches.

One approach has been to use theory to determine which emotions are fundamental. In this approach, a theory is used to establish some criteria for including an emotion within the category of fundamental emotions. For example, Tomkins (1980) suggests that the fundamental emotions are those that result in unique facial expressions. He concludes that, because there are nine unique facial emotion display patterns, there are nine fundamental emotions. These nine emotions are: interest, enjoyment, surprise, distress, fear, shame, contempt, disgust, and anger. In discussions of these emotions, Tomkins (1980) broadly categorizes these nine emotions as positive and negative categories, suggesting that positive and negative experiences may be an even more fundamental level for understanding emotions.

Another example of using theory to determine the primary dimensions of emotional experience is the work of Izard (1977). Izard suggests that the primary emotions are distinguished by their unique motivational properties. That is, emotions are understood to guide behaviors by motivating the person to take specific adaptive actions. For example, fear is included as a primary emotion because it motivates the person to avoid danger and seek safety. Interest is similarly a fundamental emotion because it motivates the person to learn and acquire new skills. Izard's criteria result in a list of ten primary emotions that are essentially the same as Tomkins' list, with the addition of guilt as a primary emotion. Also similar to Tomkins, Izard (Izard & Buechler, 1980) broadly categorizes the primary emotions into positive and negative affects, again suggesting that positive and negative emotional experiences may be an even more fundamental category of emotion.

The second approach to determining the primary dimensions of emotional experience has been to address the problem empirically. That is, researchers gather data from subjects who rate emotional experiences using a large set of emotion terms. Then the researcher uses sophisticated statistical techniques to search the data and determine if the emotions cluster into a smaller number of distinct primary dimensions.

A good example of this empirical approach is the work of Russell (1978, 1980, 1983). Russell typically has a large number of subjects rate a variety of emotion adjectives in terms of how similar the feelings described by those adjectives are. He then uses statistical techniques to explore the resulting data set to see if it is structured along primary dimensions. His results suggest that subjects categorize emotions using two primary dimensions: positive versus negative affect, and high versus low arousal. This structural arrangement is depicted in figure 15.1.

FIGURE 15.1

Dimensions of Emotion

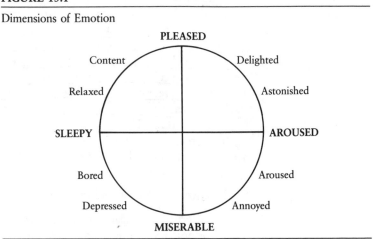

Adapted from Russell (1980), p. 1167.

The major dimension of emotional experience runs from positive/pleased to negative/miserable. The second dimension refers to the degree of arousal, or the intensity, of the particular positive or negative emotional experience. For example, a person may be positive in a very aroused sort of way (delighted) or positive in a very unaroused sort of way (content). Thus positive versus negative affect appears as the primary emotion dimension, which then varies in terms of the degree of arousal or the intensity of the positive or negative affect.

Another empirical approach to determining the primary structure of emotions has been simply to have subjects describe how they are feeling using a large number of emotion rating scales. These self-ratings are then statistically analyzed to see which emotions tend to occur together in the same person at the same time. Emotions that frequently occur together are understood to define some fundamental common dimension of emotional experience. In this approach, people rate their emotions in terms of how they feel, not in terms of which emotions they think are similar, as in much of Russell's work. Thus the results of this line of research refer more to how people *experience* their emotions than how they think about their emotions. A good representative of this line of research is the work by Watson and his colleagues (Watson & Clark, 1984; Watson, Clark, & Tellegen, 1984; Watson & Tellegen, 1985). In this approach the subjects use mood adjective rating scales to report how they feel, with some studies asking about "right now," others asking about "today," and still others looking at longer time frames such as "during the past week." In some of these studies, subjects reported how they felt each day for a month or longer, keeping an emotion diary.

Results from analyzing the data from many such studies (Watson & Tellegen, 1985) suggest there are two dimensions of self-reported emotional experience: positive affect and negative affect, with both types of emotions ranging from high to low. High positive affect consists of such feelings as elated, excited, and enthusiastic, whereas low positive affect consists of such feelings as calm, relaxed, and placid. High negative affect consists of such feelings as distressed, fearful, and hostile, whereas low negative affect consists of such feelings as drowsy, sluggish, and dull. These two general dimensions of positive and negative affect, ranging as they do from high to low in intensity, incorporate the arousal dimension suggested by Russell.

Positive and Negative Emotion

Based on these research findings we can conclude that the most general or primary emotions are positive and negative affect. Certainly there are many distinct emotions, such as guilt, joy, anger, contentment, and so on. However, they can all be described as specific variations of either positive or negative affect. In terms of our own emotional lives what seems to make the most difference to us is whether we are feeling positive or negative at any given time, or whether we are having a good or bad day, or a good or bad week, and so on. In other words, based on research results and our own intuitive understanding, positive and negative affect emerge as being the most important general categories of emotions that are experienced. As a consequence, researchers in the area of personality and emotion focus their studies mainly on positive and negative affect.

Now that we have established positive and negative affect as the primary dimensions of emotional experience we can return to our discussion of the content of people's emotional lives. For emotions to be useful to personality psychologists they must help us understand individual lives and how and why these individuals are different from one another. We said earlier that people differ in terms of the *content* of their emotional lives. Now we know that the major dimensions that describe the content of individual emotional lives are positive and negative affect. People differ in terms of *how much* positive or negative affect they have in their lives over time. Such differences are also associated with a variety of other personality characteristics, as we will see later on. But before we discuss these differences it would be good to illustrate how psychologists measure or assess the content of their subjects' emotional lives.

Assessing the Content of Emotional Life

In order to find out about the content of a person's emotional life it is necessary to ask the person to describe how he or she feels or usually feels. There are two ways to go about this. One way is to use a questionnaire that inquires about the person's past emotional experiences. The other way is to have the person keep a record of emotions over a relatively long time period, at least several weeks or longer. Because both of these assessment methods are widely used and have their own particular strengths and weaknesses, they will be discussed separately.

Questionnaire Measures of Emotional Content

There are several questionnaire measures that exist for assessing the degree of positive and negative affect in a person's life. Larsen, Diener, and Emmons (1985) provide a description and evaluation of many of these measures. One measure that was found to be particularly good was a questionnaire developed by Fordyce (1978). This measure simply asks:

> What percent of the time do you feel happy?
> What percent of the time do you feel unhappy?
> What percent of the time do you feel neutral?

The subject is required to estimate these percentages in such a way that they add up to 100 percent. Larsen et al. (1985) found that subjects were generally quite accurate in estimating the percentages of positive affect and negative affect in their lives. That is, when subjects kept daily records of their emotions, the Fordyce % Happy and % Unhappy scores predicted quite well the percentage of positive and negative days they experienced over a two-month period. Thus the Fordyce questions appear to be quick and relatively accurate ways to assess the content of someone's emotional life.

Other questionnaire measures were also evaluated by Larsen et al. (1985). For example, Campbell, Converse, and Rodgers (1976) developed an eight-item scale on which the subject rates his or her life in general on such affect dimensions as interesting-boring and worthwhile-useless. Bradburn and Caplovitz (1965) developed a ten-item true–false questionnaire that yields separate positive and negative affect scores. Gurin, Veroff, and Feld (1960) have used the question, "Taking all things together, how would you say things are these days?" There are three response choices: "very happy," "pretty happy," and "not too happy."

Because all of these measures assess the subjects' long-term emotional life, many of them are called Subjective Well-Being measures. Subjective well-being is often defined as the experience of more positive affect than negative affect in a person's life over time (Diener, 1984). Thus, to assess subjective well-being you would want to know the relative amounts of positive and negative emotional content in a person's life. Subjective well-being is a personality characteristic that refers mainly to the content of a person's emotional life. As we'll see later, many other personality characteristics are related to the relative levels of positive and negative affect in a person's life.

Questionnaire measures of emotional content are efficient ways to quickly assess the amount of positive and negative affect in a person's life. There are a few weaknesses to these questionnaire measures however. The most serious weakness concerns distortions that might arise when a person is asked to remember or recall emotions. We know that memories are sometimes inaccurate, and cognitive psychologists have shown that emotions influence our memories in various ways (Bower, 1981). It thus seems likely that memory for emotions might contain errors, especially if the person is experiencing an emotion while being asked to remember. Instead of using such retrospective measures (asking subjects to remember their emotional experiences), many researchers are now starting to use contemporaneous measures (having subjects keep ongoing records of their emotions as they experience them).

Contemporaneous Measures of Emotional Content

In using this strategy for assessing emotional content the subjects are asked to record their emotional experiences at regular intervals for a relatively long time period. Subjects record the degree to which they have experienced a variety of emotions. Typically subjects make their ratings at least once a day, and continue to keep such records for anywhere from several weeks to several months. The researcher thus obtains a fairly representative sample of the subject's emotional life.

A classic example of this contemporaneous approach to emotion–personality research is the work of Wessman and Ricks (1966). In their study they had twenty-one Radcliffe women and seventeen Harvard men keep daily mood records for six consecutive weeks (forty-two days). Each night before retiring the subject completed a "Daily Record of Personal Feelings." On this daily record the subject reported how much of each of a variety of emotions they felt that day. For example, subjects indicated how elated versus depressed they were that day by checking off a 10-point scale on which 10 equaled "complete elation, joy, and ecstasy," 5 equaled "feeling . . . just so-so," and 1 equaled "utter depression and gloom, completely down." Many other mood scales were also included, such as harmony versus anger, tranquil versus anxious, energy versus fatigue, and outgoing versus withdrawn.

Wessman and Ricks (1966) found that the primary dimension of daily mood was a broad positive versus negative affect factor. A person who was above average on the elation scale tended to also score in the positive direction on the other emotion scales as well. Thus each day for each person could be characterized in terms of the degree of "positive versus negative mood" reported. Also, when the entire forty-two-day report period was examined for each subject, Wessman and Ricks could characterize each subject in terms of the overall level of positive mood or negative mood reported during the six-week period.

The average level of good mood or bad mood reported by each subject over the entire forty-two-day period forms what Wessman and Ricks called a "hedonic level" score and represents how characteristically happy or unhappy the subject was. In fact, based on these scores, Wessman and Ricks classified their subjects as either happy, average, or unhappy persons. If the content of a subject's emotional life was primarily represented by positive emotions, he or she was described as a happy person; if primarily negative, an unhappy person. In this way emotional content served to describe an aspect of personality that is stable and consistent over time. Wessman and Ricks went on to ask the important question: In what other ways do happy and unhappy people differ and why? Their book reports many results and extensive case study reports of happy and unhappy persons. What follows is a summary of the major personality differences between happy and unhappy persons documented by Wessman and Ricks and other researchers.

Findings on Happy and Unhappy People

In the Wessman and Ricks' study happy subjects exhibited a good deal of optimism and positive outlook toward themselves and their future. They tended to have high levels of self-esteem and were confident in their abilities. Happy persons were better able than unhappy persons to cope with the minor stresses, frustrations, and hassles of daily life. Happy persons appeared to possess the ability to "roll with the punches" rather than get upset, discouraged, and give up when things were not going well. Happy subjects reported being more satisfied with their interpersonal relationships (e.g., friends and family), as well as more successful in making friends. Happy subjects possessed a gratifying sense of identity, accepting who they were and being satisfied with themselves. Happy subjects also tended to have purpose and goals in their lives and organized their efforts to attain these goals.

Unhappy subjects, on the other hand, were found to be much the opposite in many respects. They were found to be pessimistic and had lower self-esteem and lower self-confidence. Unhappy subjects tended to be more dissatisfied in their relationships and, in fact, often viewed their interpersonal relationships as sources of anger, guilt, and anxiety. Unhappy people appeared less capable of coping with stress and were usually dissatisfied with their identities. Unhappy subjects also had less continuity among the goals in their lives and approached their goals in a less organized manner.

When happiness is conceived as a personality trait defined by the content of a person's emotional life we can see that this emotion trait is associated with many other personality characteristics. Although knowing these associations helps us understand and recognize happy and unhappy people, this knowledge is still basically descriptive. Beyond knowing what happy and unhappy people are like, it would be important to know how they got that way and what keeps them the way they are.

Wessman and Ricks offer some speculation about the origins of happiness and unhappiness as emotional traits. Their data do not point to a single cause, in terms of a specific event or crisis, that could account for the development of a happy or unhappy disposition. Rather, these authors suggest that gradual development in a warm and supportive home environment provides the general long-term life experiences that culminate in the trait of happiness. I will list some of the life experiences thought to be important, but want to stress that no single experience is crucial. Rather it is the cumulative nature of these experiences that seems to result in the development of happiness or unhappiness as an emotional trait. Also, these results are based on recollections of early life by currently happy and unhappy persons. It is quite possible that these results are biased by differences in what happy and unhappy persons tend to remember or in how their memories might distort their past. Nevertheless, the results are at least suggestive of possible early life differences between persons who became either happy or unhappy as young adults.

The happier subjects in Wessman and Ricks studies appeared to have many success experiences in childhood, experiences in which they mastered some challenge and were rewarded in some way. These challenges could be as simple as learning the alphabet or coloring a picture without going outside the lines of the coloring book. The important point is that these success experiences were noticed by the adults in the child's life, who then praised the child and acknowledged these successes. Through these repeated success experiences, Wessman and Ricks suggest, the child develops a sense of competence and expectations for future successes. Also, the happy subjects in Wessman and Ricks' studies reported having role models in childhood that they respected, imitated, and often identified with at various stages of development. Such identifications favor the establishment and development of a sense of the self as worthwhile and valuable. While these identifications with role models usually begin in the family, happy subjects appeared to continue this process through childhood, adolescence, and into young adulthood as they moved out into the world. Transitions to behaviors appropriate at each age level appeared to have been more gradual and smoother for the happier subjects. They were gently encouraged, not pushed, by their parents to exercise their developmental abilities at the appropriate times.

More recent research has also used the longitudinal method to explore the relationship between personality and the emotional content of individuals' lives. For example, Larsen and Diener (1985) had seventy-six college-aged subjects keep daily mood records for eighty-four consecutive days. The daily report form used in this and similar studies is reproduced in figure 15.2. Subjects completed this form each evening before going to bed. On it they summarized the emotions they

FIGURE 15.2

Daily Mood Form Used in the Studies of Larsen and Diener

Daily Mood Form

Name _____ Day # _____ Date _____

Please indicate how much of each emotion you felt today.

Not at all	Very slight	Some-what	Moderate amount	Much	Very much	Extremely much
1	2	3	4	5	6	7

_____ Happy   _____ Angry/Hostile
_____ Depressed/Blue   _____ Enjoyment/Fun
_____ Joyful   _____ Worried/Anxious
_____ Pleased   _____ Unhappy
_____ Frustrated

Adapted from Larsen & Diener (1987).

felt that day. To ensure that subjects were following instructions and actually completing the forms on time, they were required to turn in their completed forms the following day.

Based on statistical analysis of the responses to this daily mood report, Larsen and Diener (1985) conclude that a major content factor underlying the subjects' responses is positive versus negative affect. Larsen and Diener (1986) call this dimension "frequency of positive affect" or "hedonic tone" because it is so similar to the Wessman and Ricks primary dimension. To score the daily mood reports for frequency of positive affect it is first necessary to compute a positive affect score and a negative affect score. Positive affect is computed as the average of the ratings on "happy," "joyful," "pleased," and "enjoyment." Negative affect is similarly computed as the average of the ratings on "depressed," "unhappy," "frustrated," "angry," and "worried." Then the negative affect score is subtracted from the positive affect score for each day for each subject to give a global daily mood score. If this score is greater than zero, the subject reported more positive affect than negative affect; if it is less than zero, the subject reported more negative affect than positive affect that day. In other words, the daily mood score tells us whether the person's emotional life that day consisted of predominantly positive or predominantly negative affect, or whether the mood that day was somewhere in between.

The reader may wish to make several copies of figure 15.2 and keep his or her own daily mood record for several days. The reader may then score the report forms for frequency of positive affect or perhaps plot daily mood scores over the days mood was recorded. To compute a frequency of positive affect score, the number of positive days is divided by the total number of days on which reports were made. This ratio represents the proportion of days the subject reports more positive than negative affect. The average frequency of positive affect score among college students is 72 percent, meaning that, for example, out of one hundred days the average college student feels predominantly positive on seventy-two of those days and feels predominantly negative on the remaining twenty-eight days. Even though we find that the average is 72 percent, we also find a wide range of frequency of positive affect scores, ranging from 20 percent to 99 percent.

Figures 15.3a and 15.3b present the results from two subjects in the Larsen and Diener study. Subject A had a predominance of positive affect in his emotional life over the three month reporting period. In fact, with the exception of a few negative days at the beginning of the semester, this subject reported primarily positive affect. The frequency of positive affect score for subject A was 95 percent. On the other hand, subject B had a frequency of positive affect score of 22 percent, indicating that during the three month reporting period over three quarters of his days were predominantly negative.

The frequency of positive affect score is a fairly direct measure of the content of a person's emotional life in terms of the relative amounts of positive and negative affect. Larsen and Diener (1985) provide some validity evidence for the frequency of positive versus negative affect score. The parents of a group of college-age subjects were contacted and asked how happy their child was. These parental ratings of happiness were then found to be strongly related to the subjects' self-reported frequency of positive affect scores, suggesting that the frequency score predicts ratings of emotional life made by other people who know the subject well (i.e., their parents).

A study by Diener, Larsen, Levine, and Emmons (1985) found that frequency of positive affect scores related to a variety of traits indicative of psychological well-being and positive adjustment (e.g., high self-esteem, feelings of harmony, cheerfulness, self-confidence, and satisfaction with one's life). Other studies have looked more at the relationship between daily emotion content and personality variables. For example, Costa and McCrae (1980) found that positive affect was strongly related to the personality trait of extraversion (defined as the tendency to be outgoing, friendly, and enjoy being with other people). Negative affect, on the other hand, was found to be related primarily to the personality dimension of neuroticism (defined as the tendency to worry and get upset easily). These relationships were found even when the mood measures were taken ten years after the personality measures,

FIGURE 15.3a

Data from "Subject A"

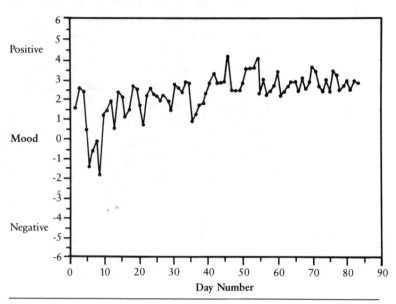

Adapted from Larsen (1987).

FIGURE 15.3b

Data from "Subject B"

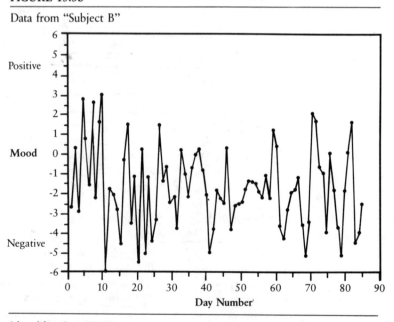

Adapted from Larsen (1987).

suggesting a good deal of stability in how mood relates to personality. These results also fit well with Gray's (1981) theory that extraverts are more sensitive to rewarding experiences than punishing experiences, where neurotics are more sensitive to punishing experiences than rewarding experiences. Consequently, extraverts should have more positive affect in their lives whereas neurotics should have more negative affect in their lives over time.

Emotional Style

We can say that content refers to the *what* of a person's emotional life, whereas style refers to the *how* of that emotional life. That is, content refers to *what* emotions are typically experienced, and style refers to *how* those emotions are typically experienced. The content versus style distinction, which has been useful in other areas of psychology, also proves useful in understanding emotion and personality.

Intensity as an Emotional Style

When we think about *how* emotions are experienced, probably the major stylistic distinction is one of intensity. This intensity dimension is suggested by the work of Russell discussed earlier. We also know from experience with our own emotional reactions that, beyond the positive versus negative content distinction, emotions also vary in terms of their intensity or strength. As you will see, in order to characterize the emotional style of a person's life we have to inquire about the stability and consistency of the intensity of their emotional experiences. In other words, for emotional intensity to be useful to personality theory we must first establish that it describes a stable characteristic of persons that is also useful for making distinctions between persons.

Affect intensity can be defined by a description of persons who are either high or low on this dimension (see Larsen & Diener, 1987). High affect intensity individuals typically experience their emotions strongly and are emotionally reactive and variable. We might say that high affect intensity subjects usually go way up when they are feeling "up" and go way down when they are feeling "down." They also alternate between these extremes more frequently and rapidly than low affect intensity individuals. The low affect intensity individuals, on the other hand, typically experience their emotions only mildly and with only gradual fluctuations and minor reactions. Such persons are stable and usually do not suffer the troughs of negative emotions. But they also tend not to experience the peaks of strong positive affect either.

In this description of high and low affect intensity persons I make use of the qualifying terms of "typically" or "usually." This is because certain life events can make even the lowest affect intensity person experience relatively strong emotions. For example, winning a lottery for a million dollars, or the death of a loved one, can cause intense emotions in almost anyone. The point is that such events are fairly rare and so we want to know what people are "usually" or "typically" like or how they *characteristically* react to the normal sorts of everyday emotion-provoking events in their daily life.

A picture here will help illustrate these differences between high and low affect intensity individuals. Figures 15.4a and 15.4b present daily mood data for two subjects, again from the Larsen and Diener (1987) study. Recall that these subjects kept daily records of their moods for 84 consecutive days. It can be seen here that Subject C is fairly stable and does not depart too far from his baseline level of mood over the entire three-month reporting period. Subject D, on the other hand, exhibits extreme changes in mood over time. This subject is hardly ever near the baseline level of mood. Instead, Subject D appears to have a lot of strong positive affect and a lot of strong negative affect. When he goes "up" he characteristically goes way up, and when he goes "down" he characteristically goes way down. Also note that Subject D alternates between these extremes frequently and rapidly. This means that the intense person also exhibits a good deal of variability in daily moods, fluctuating back and forth between positive and negative affect from day to day.

Assessing Emotional Intensity and Variability
In early studies of affect intensity (e.g., Diener et al., 1985) this characteristic of emotional life was assessed using the longitudinal method. That is, data were gathered much like that presented in Figure 15.4. Researchers would then compute a total score for each subject to represent how intense or variable the subjects were over the time period that records were kept. For example, Larsen and Diener (1985) took an average mood score on *just those days* on which the subject reported more positive than negative affect. This was called the positive affect intensity score because it represented how high up the subjects typically went on those days when they were primarily "up." A similar negative affect intensity score was computed by averaging across *only those* days on which the subject reported more negative than positive affect. This score similarly represents how low the subject typically goes down when he or she is feeling "down." As it turns out, these positive and negative affect intensity scores are strongly related, meaning that the higher up a subject typically goes when "up," the lower the subject typically goes down when "down." The converse also holds true— subjects who don't go up much typically don't go down much either. Because positive and negative affect intensity scores are so strongly

FIGURE 15.4a

Data from "Subject C"

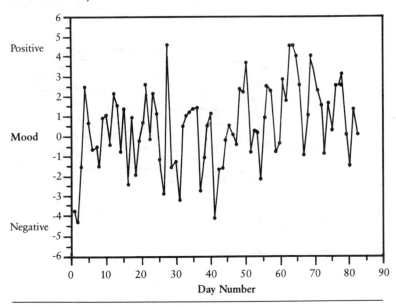

Adapted from Larsen (1987).

FIGURE 15.4b

Data from "Subject D"

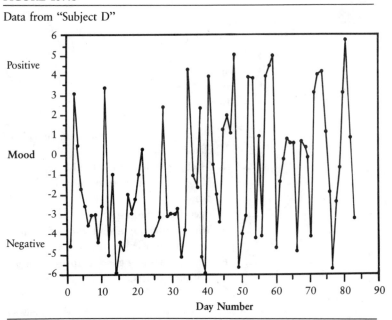

Adapted from Larsen (1987).

related, it makes sense to simply combine them into a total score to represent the subjects' general, overall level of affect intensity.

This longitudinal method of assessing affect intensity makes a good deal of sense because it is so straightforward and represents the idea of affect intensity quite well. However, it takes several weeks or longer of daily mood reports to obtain enough data to generate a reliable affect intensity score for each individual. Consequently, a questionnaire measure of affect intensity has been developed that allows a relatively quick assessment of a person's emotional style in terms of intensity. This questionnaire is called the Affect Intensity Measure (AIM) and the full item set and details of its construction can be found in Larsen and Diener (1987). The Activity Box provides fifteen items from the AIM so

ACTIVITY BOX

Affect Intensity Measure

The following questions refer to the emotional reactions in typical life situations. Please indicate how *you* react to these events by placing a number from the following scale in the blank space preceding each item. Please base your answers on how *you* react, not on how you think others react or how you think a person should react.

1 = Never
2 = Almost Never
3 = Occasionally
4 = Usually
5 = Almost Always
6 = Always

_____ 1. When I accomplish something difficult I feel delighted or elated.

_____ 2. I feel pretty bad when I tell a lie.

_____ 3. My emotions tend to be more intense than those of most people.

_____ 4. I get overly enthusiastic.

_____ 5. When I'm happy it's a feeling of being untroubled and content rather than being zestful and aroused.

_____ 6. When something good happens, I am usually much more jubilant than others.

the reader can have some experience with this questionnaire and obtain a preliminary indication of his or her standing on the emotion trait of affect intensity.

It should be pointed out that the Affect Intensity Measure is used primarily in research that compares scores for groups. This test is generally not used to interpret individuals' scores and is not used for clinical purposes. The Activity Box is used in this chapter to give you some experience with how an aspect of emotional life is assessed for research purposes, and to give you a chance to think about the questions on the test and the answers that you gave.

An important aspect of the affect intensity trait is that we really cannot say whether it is good or bad to be high or low on this trait.

_____ 7. The sight of someone who is hurt badly affects me strongly.
_____ 8. "Calm and cool" could easily describe me.
_____ 9. When I get angry it's easy for me to still be rational and not overreact.
_____ 10. When I know I have done something very well, I feel relaxed and content rather than excited and elated.
_____ 11. When I do feel anxiety it is normally very strong.
_____ 12. When I am excited over something I want to share my feelings with everyone.
_____ 13. I would characterize my happy moods as closer to contentment than to joy.
_____ 14. My friends would probably say I'm a tense or "high-strung" person.
_____ 15. When I am nervous I get shaky all over.

Scoring: Some of the above items are reverse-keyed, meaning that a high response indicates low affect intensity. So the first thing to do is reverse your answers to these items. Items numbered 5, 8, 9, 10, and 13 are reversed; change your answers to _these_ items as follows: change a 6 to a 1, a 5 to a 2, a 4 to a 3, a 3 to a 4, a 2 to a 5, and a 1 to a 6. Now simply add up your responses to all the questions to obtain a total score. An average score would be in the range of 45 to 65. Below 45 is considered fairly low in affect intensity and above 65 is considered fairly high. To understand the meaning of high and low scores on this questionnaire please refer to the text.

That is, there are both positive and negative consequences to being high on this trait, as well as other positive and negative consequences for being low on this trait. For example, the high-scoring person gets a lot of zest out of life, enjoying peaks of enthusiasm, joy, and positive emotional involvement. On the other hand, when things are not going well, the high-scoring person is prone to strong negative emotional reactions, such as sadness, guilt, and anxiety. In addition, because the high-scoring persons have frequent experiences of extreme emotions (both positive and negative), they tend to suffer the physical consequences of this emotional involvement. Emotions activate the sympathetic nervous system, making the person aroused or keyed up. Even strong positive emotions cause activity in the sympathetic nervous system. Because of the regular activation of their sympathetic nervous system, high-scoring persons tends to exhibit physical symptoms that are due to their emotionally activated lifestyle. We know that high-scoring persons report higher levels of such emotion-related symptoms as muscle tension, stomachaches, headaches, and fatigue. An interesting finding is that, even though they report more of these symptoms, high-scoring persons are not particularly unhappy or upset by these symptoms. In other words, it seems that high-scoring persons are willing to pay the price for their emotionally intense lifestyle. In interviewing high-scoring persons, I have found that they usually have no desire to change their level of emotional intensity. They seem to prefer the emotional involvement, the ups and downs, and the physiological arousal that accompanies their intense style of emotional life.

The low-scoring individual, on the other hand, is fairly stable and does not typically get upset very easily. Even when negative events happen to them they maintain an even emotional state and thus avoid the troughs of negative affect. They are reliable in the sense that we know their moods will usually be about average. The price they pay for this emotional stability, however, is a failure to experience their positive emotions very strongly. That is, although they appear to be protected from strong negative affect, they also appear to be inhibited from experiencing strong positive affect as well. Thus they lack the peaks of zest, enthusiasm, and joy that energize the lives of high affect intensity individuals. The low affect intensity individual, however, does not pay the price of the physical symptoms that the high affect intensity person does.

So we see that it is difficult to put an evaluation on the affect intensity dimension because there are both good and bad things about being either high or low in terms of this emotional style. Usually people like their emotional lives the way they are. This suggests that having strong emotional experiences is rewarding to the high affect intensity person, whereas maintaining an even and stable emotional life is rewarding to the low affect intensity person. Consequently, such individuals tend to seek out or create a general lifestyle that fosters the kind of emotional experiences that they desire. High affect intensity individuals create an active and emotionally involving lifestyle, whereas low affect intensity individuals create an orderly, routine, and self-controlled lifestyle. Such high and low affect intensity persons also differ in a number of other important ways, as we will see in the next section.

Research Findings on Intense and Nonintense People

In a daily study of mood, Larsen, Diener, and Emmons (1986) had subjects record the events in their daily lives that most influenced their positive and negative emotions. Sixty-two subjects recorded their life events for fifty-six consecutive days, resulting in almost six thousand event descriptions. The subjects also rated these events each day in terms of how *subjectively* good or bad they thought the events were. Then the event descriptions were rated by a team of raters for how *objectively* good or bad they were for the average college student. You would think that these objective and subjective ratings of the same events should match fairly well. Indeed, there was a moderately strong relationship between these two scores over all the days of the study. However, the subjects high on the affect intensity dimension rated their life events as significantly *more* severe than the low affect intensity subjects. That is, events that were rated as only *moderately* good by the objective raters (e.g., receiving a compliment from a professor) were rated as *very* good by the high affect intensity subjects. Similarly, events that were rated as only *moderately* bad by the objective raters (e.g., losing a favorite pen) tended to be rated as *very* bad by the high affect intensity subjects. Thus high affect intensity subjects tend to evaluate the events in their lives—both good and bad events—as having significantly more emotional impact than the low affect intensity subjects. When the *number* of severe events was analyzed, the high affect intensity subjects were found not to have more frequent severe events in their lives than the low affect intensity subjects. Thus, even though the same types of events are happening with equal frequency in their lives, the high affect intensity subjects (compared to the low affect intensity subjects) interpret these events as provoking stronger emotions. It is in this sense that the style of emotional life is different between high and low affect intensity individuals. High affect intensity individuals are more reactive to the emotion-provoking events in their lives.

An interesting aspect of these results is that high affect intensity individuals are more reactive to *both* positive and negative events in their lives. If we assume that good and bad things happen randomly, then we should expect to find that the moods of high affect intensity individuals should be going up and down randomly with those events. This is another way of saying that high affect intensity individuals should exhibit more mood variability or more fluctuations in their emotional life over time. Larsen (1987) recently found that individuals high on the affect intensity dimension do in fact exhibit more frequent changes in their moods and these changes tend to be larger in magnitude than the mood changes of low affect intensity individuals. Thus the concept of affect intensity contains mood variability in addition to the tendency to experience strong positive and strong negative emotions on a day-to-day basis.

Wessman and Ricks (1966) also found mood variability to be a stable characteristic of the emotional lives of the subjects in their studies. These authors found that day-to-day variability in mood was related to a variety of personality characteristics. Highly variable subjects were found to score high on such measures as self-sufficiency, imagination, and conflict. High variability subjects were found to be creative, outgoing, and energetic, but they also tended to spread themselves too thinly and had difficulty fulfilling their ambitions. Low variability subjects, on the other hand, were more cautious, quiet, controlled, objective, and not given to imagination or flights of fancy. Low variability subjects were serious and reserved, placing more value on work and productivity than originality and creativity. Wessman and Ricks (1966) also do not attach an evaluation of whether it is better to be high or low on mood variability, recognizing that society needs people of lively passions as well as people of solid character.

The concept of emotional intensity, containing as it does the notion of mood variability, is a general and broad characteristic of emotional life. Affect intensity has been found to relate to a variety of standard personality variables. For example, Larsen and Diener (1987) report that affect intensity relates to the personality dimensions of high activity level, sociability, and arousability. High affect intensity individuals thus tend to have a vigorous and energetic lifestyle, they tend to be outgoing and enjoy being with others, and seek out stimulating and arousing things to do in their daily life. During an interview a high affect intensity subject reported that, to her, the worse thing in life is to be bored. She reported that she often did things to liven up her life, such as playing practical jokes on her roommates. Although such activities sometimes got her into trouble, she felt that it was worth it to obtain the stimulation. Another high affect intensity subject described himself as an "intensity junkie," hooked on the need for an emotionally stimulating lifestyle. It should be mentioned that the life events of the high intensity person may not appear that different from those of the low intensity person. The idea is that the high intensity persons get more emotional impact out of the events that do occur in their life, or they engage in events—available to everyone—that have a greater potential for emotional involvement if one so desires, for example, attending sports events where one could either be highly involved and obtain strong emotional activation or could remain uninvolved and consequently not experience much emotion regardless of whether one's team won or lost. Once again, subjects who are high or low on the affect intensity dimension typically like their emotional lifestyles and usually report no motivation to change.

Concluding Remarks

An interesting aspect of the two dimensions—positive versus negative affect and affect intensity—is that they are *unrelated* to each other in frequency. This means that we can find people who have frequent positive affect of low intensity and others who have frequent positive affect of high intensity. Similarly we can find people who have frequent negative affect of low intensity and others who have frequent negative affect of high intensity. In other words, frequency of positive versus negative affect interacts with affect intensity to produce specific types of emotional life that characterize different personalities. The effects of this interaction of frequency of positive versus negative affect and affect intensity in creating emotional life are illustrated in figure 15.5.

According to this figure, you can see that individuals high and low on the affect intensity dimension will typically experience happiness

FIGURE 15.5

Quality of Emotional Life as a Function of Frequency of Positive Versus Negative Affect and Affect Intensity

	Low affect intensity	High affect intensity
Frequent positive affect	Emotional life experienced as contentment, easygoing composure, serenity, and tranquil calmness.	Emotional life experienced as exuberance, animated joyfulness, and zestful enthusiasm.
Frequent negative affect	Emotional life experienced as chronic melancholia, mild but persistent unhappiness, dejection, and discontent.	Emotional life experienced as acute and agitated negative affect, distress, aggravation, depression, and severe episodes of negative emotions.

and unhappiness in very different ways. The person low in affect intensity will have an emotional life that is characterized by its enduringness, evenness, and lack of fluctuation. If such a person also happened to be a happy person (i.e., more positive than negative emotional content in his or her life), then he or she would experience this happiness as a placid sort of enduring contentment. If he or she happened to be an unhappy type of person (i.e., less positive than negative emotional content in his or her life), then his or her emotional life would consist of a chronic and somewhat annoying or irritating level of negative affect over time. The person high on the affect intensity dimension, on the other hand, would have an emotional life that is characterized by its abruptness, changeableness, and volatility. If this kind of person also happened to be a happy person, then he or she would experience this happiness as enlivened and animated spikes of enthusiasm and exhilaration. If this high affect intensity person were instead an unhappy person, then he or she would tend to experience troughs of a variety of negative emotions, such as anxiety, guilt, depression, and loneliness.

The frequency of positive versus negative affect determines the content of a person's emotional life, and the affect intensity dimension determines the style of that emotional life. These two emotion-relevant dimensions help us understand personality functioning because they provide us with a description of individual lives as well as provide us with the ability to make useful distinctions between persons. Future research will tell us more about how the emotional lives of individuals develop, what keeps people the way they are, and how they might change if they so desire.

Summary

In this chapter we have discussed how emotion can be used to understand personality. We have focused on the primary dimensions of positive and negative affect. People are understood to differ from each other both in terms of the relative frequency of positive versus negative emotional content in their lives over time, and in terms of the stylistic intensity of their emotional experiences. The relative frequency of positive versus negative emotions and the intensity of emotion are trait-like concepts that have the largest impact on the emotional lives of individuals. That is, in trying to understand emotional life as an aspect of personality, it appears that the two dimensions of frequency of positive versus negative affect and affect intensity provide a good deal of descriptive and explanatory power. The frequency of these two dimensions of emotional experience are also unrelated to one another.

SUGGESTED READINGS

Diener, E. (1984). Subjective well-being. *Psychological Bulletin, 95,* 542–575. An excellent overview of research on happiness and life satisfaction, including measurement, demographic and personality influences on happiness, and theories of happiness.

Larsen, R. J., & Diener, E. (1987). Affect intensity as an individual difference characteristic: A review. *Journal of Research in Personality, 21,* 1–39. A recent review of research on the intensity and variability of emotion as aspects of personality.

Watson, D., & Clark, L. A. (1984). Negative affectivity: The disposition to experience aversive emotional states. *Psychological Bulletin, 96,* 465–490. In addition to highlighting the associations between chronic negative affect, personality, social behavior, and health, this paper is also a good example of the dispositional approach to emotions.

Wessman, A. E., & Ricks, D. F. (1966). *Mood and personality,* New York: Holt. An older but classic work that continues to stimulate researchers in this area. Easy to read and available in paperback.

REFERENCES

Averill, J. R. (1975). A semantic atlas of emotional concepts. *JSAS catalogue of selected documents in psychology, 5,* 330, (Ms. No. 421).

Bower, G. H. (1981). Mood and memory. *American Psychologist, 36,* 129–148.

Bradburn, N.M., & Caplovitz, D. (1965). *Reports on happiness.* Chicago: Aldine.

Campbell, A., Converse, P.E., & Rodgers, W. L. (1976). *The quality of American life.* New York: Sage.

Costa, P.T., & McCrae, R.R. (1980). Influence of extraversion and neuroticism on subjective well-being: Happy and unhappy people. *Journal of Personality and Social Psychology, 38,* 668–678.

Diener, E. (1984). Subjective well-being. *Psychological Bulletin, 95,* 542–575.

Diener, E., Larsen, R. J., Levine, S., & Emmons, R.A. (1985). Frequency and intensity: The underlying dimensions of affect. *Journal of Personality and Social Psychology, 49,* 1253–1265.

Fordyce, M. W. (1978). *Prospectus: The self-descriptive inventory.* Unpublished manuscript, Edison Community College, Fort Myers, Florida.

Gray, J. A. (1981). A critique of Eysenck's theory of personality. In H. J. Eysenck (Ed.), *A model of personality* (pp. 246–276). New York: Springer-Verlag.

Gurin, G., Veroff, J., & Feld, S. (1960). *Americans' view of their mental health.* New York: Basic Books.

Izard, C. E. (1977). *Human emotions.* New York: Plenum.

Izard, C. E. & Buechler, S. (1980). Aspects of consciousness and personality in terms of differential emotion theory. In R. Plutchik and H. Kellerman (Eds.), *Emotion: Theory, research, and experience, Vol. 1, Theories of emotion* (pp. 165–186). New York: Academic Press.

Larsen, R. J. (1987). The stability of mood variability: A spectral analytic approach to daily mood assessments. *Journal of Personality and Social Psychology, 52,* 1195–1204.

Larsen, R. J., & Diener, E. (1987). Affect intensity as an individual difference characteristic: A review. *Journal of Research in Personality, 21,* 1–39.

Larsen, R. J., Diener, E., & Emmons, R. A. (1985). An evaluation of subjective well-being measures. *Social Indicators Research, 17,* 1–18.

Larsen, R. J., Diener, E., & Emmons, R. A. (1986). Affect intensity and reactions to daily life events. *Journal of Personality and Social Psychology, 51,* 803–814.

Russell, J. A. (1978). Evidence of convergent validity on the dimensions of affect. *Journal of Personality and Social Psychology, 36,* 1152–1168.

Russell, J. A. (1980). A circumplex model of affect. *Journal of Personality and Social Psychology, 39,* 1161–1178.

Russell, J. A. (1983). Pancultural aspects of the human conceptual organization of emotions. *Journal of Personality and Social Psychology, 45,* 1281–1288.

Tomkins, S. S. (1979). *Affect, imagery, and consciousness (Vol 3).* New York: Springer-Verlag.

Tomkins, S. S. (1980). Affect as amplification: Some modifications in theory. In R. Plutchik and H. Kellerman (Eds.), *Emotion: Theory, research, and experience. Vol. 1. Theories of emotion* (pp. 141–164). New York: Academic Press.

Watson, E., & Clark, L. A. (1984). Negative affectivity: The disposition to experience aversive emotional states. *Psychological Bulletin, 96,* 465–490.

Watson, D., Clark, L. A., & Tellegen, A. (1984). Cross-cultural convergence in the structure of mood: A Japanese replication and a comparison with U.S. findings. *Journal of Personality and Social Psychology, 47,* 127–144.

Watson, D., & Tellegen, A. (1985). Toward a consensual structure of mood. *Psychological Bulletin, 98,* 219–235.

Wessman, A. E., & Ricks, D. F. (1966). *Mood and personality,* New York: Holt.

CHAPTER 16

Human Sexuality

SUSAN S. HENDRICK AND CLYDE HENDRICK

Overview
  Sex Researchers
**Research on Personality and
  Sexuality**
  Sociocultural Influences
  Interpersonal Influences
  Personality Variables and
    Sexuality
  Gender and Sexuality
  Sexual Preference
  Sexual Variants
  Sexual Dysfunction

The Study of Sexual Attitudes
  Measurement of Sexual
    Attitudes
  Sexual Attitudes and Related
    Constructs
**ACTIVITY BOX: Sexual Attitudes
  Scale**
  Gender Differences Revisited
  Integrating Sex with Love
Summary
SUGGESTED READINGS
REFERENCES

Overview

"Sex is primarily a bodily function, like eating." "At its best, sex seems to be the merging of two souls." How do you react to these two statements? Do you agree or disagree with them? Or do you agree with one statement and not the other?

Each of these items is taken from a questionnaire assessing attitudes toward sexuality (Hendrick, Hendrick, Slapion-Foote, & Foote, 1985). Attitudes are frequently assessed as part of the study of personality. In fact, many questionnaires that measure aspects of personality may be considered as measures of attitudes and beliefs. The attitudes and beliefs happen to be about one's self; for example, how well you like or dislike yourself. Thus, your attitudes about self are part of your personality. You might therefore expect that your answer to such sexual attitude questions would reveal aspects of your personality that both influence and are influenced by your sexuality. Our sexuality encompasses our early childhood experiences, parental and societal norms, and our own resulting emotions about sex (does it make us happy or depressed or scared?), our attitudes toward sex (do we think it is good or bad?), and our actual sexual behavior (do we practice contraception, do we engage in oral sex?).

The fact that sexuality encompasses our past experience and our ongoing life leaves much room for inconsistency in various aspects of sexuality. For example, how do you feel about masturbation? If your parents told you not to "touch yourself" when you were a child, but your school's sex education materials said that masturbation is normal, then you might have mixed feelings about it. You might believe that it is okay to masturbate (that is your attitude), yet feel guilty when you do so (that is your emotion). Thus you might rarely engage in masturbation (the actual behavior), but when you do, you feel emotionally guilty but physically good. Such "mixed feelings" are frequent as we study personality and sexuality, a diverse topic that includes attitudes, cognitions, emotions, and behaviors.

The scientific study of sexuality has involved professionals from a number of different disciplines (e.g., sociology, anthropology, medicine), but the specific focus on personality and sexuality has been of particular interest to psychologists. This chapter first presents a historical overview of the study of personality and sexuality and then focuses on some of the diverse factors affecting human sexuality, including environmental/cultural, personality, and gender influences. Some of the negative aspects of sexuality (e.g., sexual perversions, sexual dysfunction) are also discussed. The remainder of the chapter concentrates on an original research program assessing sexual attitudes and their relations to other relevant variables, including aspects of personality.

Sex Researchers

Although literary and artistic descriptions of human sexuality go back thousands of years, systematic research on sexuality is quite recent. Henry Havelock Ellis (1859–1939), an Englishman, is acknowledged by many scholars as the first contemporary scientific figure to legitimize the study of human sexuality (Brecher, 1971). Ellis studied the available information on sexuality since ancient Greek civilization and closely observed his Victorian and post-Victorian contemporaries. Although his scholarly work was considerable, one of his greatest legacies was his acceptance of the *infinite variety* of sexual attitudes and behaviors that cross the boundaries of time, geography, and culture.

Another major figure in the study of sexuality is Sigmund Freud (1856–1939), an Austrian, who developed his influential theories of personality and psychopathology with a central focus on sexuality. His concepts included castration anxiety (males), penis envy (females), and adult anxiety neurosis that resulted from childhood sexual trauma (either real or imagined) (Freud, 1949). One of Freud's most significant insights was that the influence of feelings, fantasies, and experiences retained from childhood survive in our unconscious to mold our adult feelings and behavior (both sexual and nonsexual).

The individual considered to be the American pioneer in studying sexuality is Alfred Charles Kinsey (1894–1956), who spent nearly his whole career at Indiana University. Kinsey, a biologist, used his rigorous training in studying gall wasps to study as precisely as possible the sexual histories of thousands of American men and women. His goal was to describe *what* people do, *when,* and *with whom,* and his scientific contribution consisted of several major volumes on Americans' sexual lives as well as an approach to interviewing that may have been one of the most thorough ever developed (Brecher, 1971).

Even a very brief list of major sex researchers would not be complete without William Masters and Virginia Johnson, whose Reproductive Biology Research Foundation in St. Louis has become famous for the study of human sexual response and treatment of sexual inadequacy. Though their impact on present knowledge of the sexual response cycle has been tremendous, one of their most important single accomplishments has been to convince a whole society that sexual problems can be successfully treated.

Although the scientific study of human sexuality is relatively new (all the work just discussed was conducted within the past one hundred years), it has gained considerable momentum in recent decades. It has received attention as a scholarly area, with books and articles on adolescent sexual behavior (e.g., Sorenson, 1973), homosexuality (e.g., Bell & Weinberg, 1978), and sex and aging (e.g., George & Weiler, 1981) that have earned at least acceptance by the wider academic/scientific community. The study of sexuality has also taken the form of more popularized, media-conscious work such as The Hite Report (Hite, 1976), which appeals to a substantial percentage of the wider lay population. This acceptance has been hard won, however, because sex researchers have often presented easy targets to any persons wanting to stigmatize the whole topic of sex (see Bullough, 1985). In fact, a few scholars have explored the ideology and politicization that seem to have always surrounded human sexuality (e.g., Davis, 1983).

Apparently, many human beings have almost a love/hate relationship (Freud referred to it as ambivalence) with their own sexuality, though other people accept sex as a natural and basic part of existence. The differences between individuals—and cultures—in their orientations toward sexuality is an extremely important topic.

Research on Personality and Sexuality

Sociocultural Influences

It is natural for each of us to view the world from our own unique vantage point—and then imagine that everyone sees it in much the same way. Havelock Ellis was clear in stating that people experience sexuality differently and that we shouldn't assume that other people are like us.

Many sexuality books discuss cultural differences in sexuality. For example, Crooks and Baur (1987) illustrate such differences by contrasting the sexually open Mangaians of Polynesia, who encourage sexual pleasure and sexual activity beginning in childhood, with the sexually avoidant inhabitants of Inis Beag (an island off Ireland), who actively punish childhood sexual expression and believe that female orgasm is a deviant sexual response. An important new book by sociologist Ira Reiss (1986) explores some of the major themes in sexuality (e.g., sexual jealousy, gender roles, normality, homosexuality, erotica), using available information on industrialized societies and on 186 nonindustrialized cultures. The author concludes that "among societies, differences in sexuality will be due to sociological forces" (p. 210).

Such conclusions from a respected scholar of human sexuality are meant to keep the reader aware that although the focus of this chapter is on sexuality and personality, intrapsychic explanations of sexuality are fully useful only when considered within the context of wider sociological explanations.

Interpersonal Influences

Within the general sociocultural/environmental context, interpersonal influences on sexuality are increasingly viewed as important. In everyday life, certain individuals (or groups), personally relevant to us, can and do have an impact on our sexual attitudes and behavior. Typically such individuals are family members and friends. Although parents influence sexual behavior by rule setting as well as by modeling sexual values, peer influence is one of the most consistently important influences on adolescents as they make major sexual decisions, such as the move from virginity to nonvirginity (e.g., Billy & Udry, 1985; Jessor & Jessor, 1975). Peer influence is only one of several determinants of sexual attitudes and behaviors. In a recent, statistically sophisticated study, Newcomb, Huba, and Bentler (1986) ascertained that of eight major determinants of adolescent sexual and dating behaviors, only the measure "importance of dating" showed a direct influence on the category of dating and sexual behavior. Because dating importance reflects the desire and motivation of the individual to date other people, these findings point out that beyond sociocultural and interpersonal influences lies our own internal motivation system, part of our personality that helps to govern our sexuality.

Personality Variables and Sexuality

Our primary interest in this chapter is in "normal" personality variables, and how variation in personality is related to various aspects of sexuality. Self-esteem is one example of such a personality variable. Everyone has a self-attitude about how much he or she is "worth." Some people have high self-esteem most of the time; others have low self-esteem. Many questions can be asked about how self-esteem relates to sexuality. For example, have people with high self-esteem had more sexual partners by age twenty-five than people with low self-esteem? Do people with low self-esteem have more problems in achieving orgasm than people with high self-esteem? The research questions are practically endless.

Outgoingness is another "normal" personality variable. Some people are very shy, whereas others are very outgoing. The personality variable of introversion–extraversion represents this normal variation in shyness or outgoingness. Several questions immediately suggest themselves with respect to how introverted people might differ from extroverted people on aspects of sexuality.

It will be useful and interesting to review several such personality variables as they have been studied in relation to facets of sexuality. Research is still quite sketchy in this area, but enough exists to provide an overview. Our focus will be on the variables of self-esteem, introversion–extraversion, sensation seeking, and self-monitoring.

Self-Esteem

Self-esteem is related to a number of different variables, including physical attractiveness, past successes or failures, and popularity with a peer group. Self-esteem is also related to one's sexual behavior. Stratton and Spitzer (1967) studied a sexually conservative group of females in which only one-fourth of the women approved of premarital intercourse. Among this group, women who were sexually permissive had lower self-esteem than nonpermissive women. The authors proposed that in any given society there will be rules, or norms, prescribing "correct" sexual behavior and beliefs. Most people internalize these sexual norms while growing up. Violation of these norms may cause negative feelings, or low self-esteem. Therefore, in a sexually conservative culture, greater sexual liberality may be related to lower self-esteem. In a study related to the one just described, Perlman (1974) found that when a social group was divided evenly in attitude (half permissive, half conservative), self-esteem was unrelated to sexual permissiveness. In another very liberal sample of unmarried students, Perlman found that subjects high in self-esteem had significantly more previous coital partners than subjects low in self-esteem.

Such research demonstrates the links between self-esteem, an aspect of personality, and sexuality. Self-esteem is indeed related to sexual permissiveness, but the type of relationship depends upon the norms for permissiveness within one's social group.

Introversion-Extraversion

One approach to personality is the assumption that it can be described by a large set of traits. Some approaches view these traits as clustering into a few broad dimensions. Introversion-extraversion is such a dimension (Eysenck, 1976). An extravert is defined by traits such as sociable, impulsive, activity-oriented, carefree, and so on. An introvert is generally low on these traits. Eysenck's theory is that there is a desirable level of arousal or brain stimulation. Extraverts have a naturally low level of arousal and consequently must engage in many activities (i.e., extraverted behavior) to achieve an optimal level of arousal. In contrast, introverts have a naturally high level of arousal, and they avoid strong social stimulation in order to reduce their high arousal level to an optimal level. In general, extraverts seek increased levels of sensation and introverts avoid such increases.

This theory led Eysenck (1976, pp. 12–13) to propose that extraverts will have sexual intercourse earlier, more frequently, with more partners, and in more varied positions than will introverts. Some support was found for these predictions. Barnes, Malamuth, and Cheek (1984) followed up on Eysenck's work with a sample of college-age males. They found that extraverts acquired sexual knowledge at a younger age than introverts. In terms of sexual attitudes, extraverts were more pleasure-oriented and sought novelty more than did introverts. Extraverts were also somewhat disposed toward an interest in a wider range of sexual activities (except homosexuality) than introverts. Therefore the results were in general agreement with Eysenck's predictions. Schenk and Pfrang (1986) also found that extraversion–introversion was a strong predictor of sexual behavior among young unmarried males. Extraverts had intercourse at a younger age, had more sexual partners, and had intercourse more frequently during the previous six months than introverts.

Among married couples, however, Schenk, Pfrang, and Rausche (1983) studied a sample of 631 German couples who had been married an average of ten years. These researchers found almost no relation between extraversion–introversion and the couples' degree of satisfaction with their sexual relations. Qualities of general interaction between partners were much more strongly related to sexual satisfaction than were personality traits.

It appears that introversion–extraversion is related to facets of sexuality. But it appears to be related only for young people, before they are attached in a long-term sexual relationship. Once such attachment occurs, characteristics of the relationship are overwhelmingly more important.

Sensation Seeking

We noted earlier that extraverts have a stronger tendency than introverts to seek out stimulation. In fact, sensation seeking itself has been defined as a personality variable, and a questionnaire (Sensation Seeking Scale, described in detail in a later section) has been devised to measure this variable (Zuckerman, Kolin, Price, & Zoob, 1964). One relevant study examined the effects of a human sexuality course on sexual attitudes and behavior (Zuckerman, Tushup, & Finner, 1976). A great many questionnaires were given to the students, including the Sensation Seeking Scale. The results showed that students higher in sensation seeking tendencies were more permissive in sexual attitudes, and they had more heterosexual experiences, partners, and orgasmic experience than students who were low in sensation seeking tendencies. This study suggests that sensation seeking is strongly related to several aspects of sexuality.

Self-Monitoring

Some people are very responsive to appropriateness of social cues during their interactions with others. Such people modulate their behavior in ongoing interaction, according to such cues, rather than according to their own private attitudes and opinions. Such people may be described as high in self-monitoring tendencies. Other people behave in interactions in line with their own attitudes and opinions. Such people are low in self-monitoring tendencies.

Snyder (1974) designed the Self-Monitoring Scale to measure these different tendencies. Self-monitoring has been related to a great many social variables. As one example, Snyder and Simpson (1984) found that high self-monitors were more uncommitted in dating relationships than low self-monitors. That is, high self-monitors were more willing than low self-monitors to date people other than their current partner, and in fact high self-monitors had dated more people during the preceding year.

Snyder, Simpson, and Gangestad (1986) wondered whether this uncommitted orientation to dating by high self-monitors might also hold true for sexual relations. They conducted a study and confirmed this conjecture. High self-monitors, more than low self-monitors, were willing to engage in sex with partners with whom they were not psychologically close, had a larger number of different sexual partners during the preceding year, and anticipated more sexual variety over the next five years. Snyder et al. (1986) speculated that differences in self-monitoring may actually be based on genetic differences. Further, such genetic differences may be related to genetic differences in reproductive strategies. Some species have mating strategies based on colorful self-displays and attention seeking tactics. In humans, such displays may be analogous to high self-monitoring. Other species (and low self-monitors) establish a long-term bonding relation with one other mate. Both strategies may lead to success in the transmission of the individual's genes. This theorizing is very interesting but will require considerable research.

This brief review suggests that personality variables are indeed related to sexuality. The relationships are often moderated by social and cultural factors, as illustrated by self-esteem and introversion-extraversion. Other personality variables, such as sensation seeking and self-monitoring, may be linked more directly to sexual behavior.

Gender and Sexuality

The specific impact that gender has on our sexuality is an important consideration. Of course our biological sex (whether we are male or female) has tremendous implications for our sexuality, because all the socialization in the world is unlikely to change the fact that women have babies and men produce erections. Beyond our biological sex, however, is our socialization into the adult world of maleness and femaleness. Most people would agree that boys and girls are raised somewhat differently, even in contemporary society (if you don't agree, then go into the home of an acquaintance who has children and see if you can guess the sex of the children by looking at how their rooms are decorated). Thus certain activities are considered more appropriate for one sex or the other, and this includes sexual activities.

A carryover from the Victorian era included the idea that women are less sexually responsive than men and, consistent with that idea, hold more conservative sexual attitudes. Although we now know that women can be as behaviorally sexual as men, similarity between men's and women's sexual attitudes is a bit less clear. In studies among undergraduate college students (e.g., Jurich & Jurich, 1974) and across several Western countries (e.g., Luckey & Nass, 1969), women have typically reported more conservative sexual attitudes than have men. However, some scholars believe that women are becoming more liberal, and Bell and Chaskes (1970) found that their female college sample increased in sexual activity and decreased in sexual guilt relative to a similar sample assessed a decade earlier. While some researchers believe that males and females are *converging* in their sexual attitudes (e.g., DeLamater & MacCorquodale, 1979), others have concluded that women have become much more permissive because they were so conservative initially that liberalization was inevitable (e.g., Walsh, Ferrell, & Tolone, 1976). A recent study of reported sexual behaviors of West German college students (Clement, Schmidt, & Kruse, 1984) indicated that, compared to a 1966 student sample, their 1981 sample showed decreased gender differences in masturbation (though incidence was still higher for males), reversal of participation in coitus (females now more active than males), a disappearance of earlier differences in tendency to change partners or to have sexual relations outside a steady relationship, and a change from similar male-female attitudes toward sexuality (in 1966) to greater female liberality in 1981. In a questionnaire study of reported sexual activity, daydreaming, and sexual fantasies (Knafo & Jaffe, 1984), gender differences were found in "type" though not in amount of fantasy. "Women had more submission fantasies, whereas men reported more performance fantasies. This difference was interpreted as reflecting social sexual stereotypes" (p. 451). In still another questionnaire study, Carroll, Volk, and Hyde (1985) found gender differences in approval of casual sexual intercourse (males approved more), importance of particular sexual behaviors (more males said orgasm, more females said feeling loved and needed), and whether an emotional involvement was a necessary prerequisite for a sexual encounter (more females said "yes"). A recent study by the present authors and their colleagues (Hendrick et al., 1985) found some similarities but considerable differences between males and females across several sexual attitude dimensions. Female subjects reported themselves to be more responsible, conventional, and idealistic, whereas male subjects indicated that they were more permissive, instrumental, and control- and power-oriented. The verdict is apparently not yet in on gender differences in sexuality.

Although it may be that both women and men are becoming less conservative (for a different perspective, see Gerrard, 1987), with women moving at a more rapid rate, both biology and socialization are undoubtedly strong enough to maintain some behavioral and attitudinal gender differences. In any case, such liberalization may well be halted or at least slowed by pressure from political and religious conservatives and by increasing fears of sexually transmitted diseases, such as AIDS (e.g., Davis, 1983; Emmons, Joseph, Kessler, Wortman, Montgomery, & Ostrow, 1986).

Sexual Preference

Homosexuality is a sexual preference and lifestyle choice that has not yet been accepted within the societal mainstream. The topic of homosexuality has become politicized in recent years. However, our interest is in how personality may relate to homosexuality, either as "cause" or "effect."

One of the most comprehensive studies was conducted by Bell, Weinberg, and Hammersmith (1981), who intensively interviewed hundreds of homosexual and heterosexual persons and compared them on a number of indices. The results of this study dispelled a number of widely held stereotypes about the origins of homosexuality (e.g., that homosexuals dated less during high school [they dated the same amount] or that people became homosexuals after being seduced by older homosexuals [most homosexual first encounters occurred with a same-age peer]). Although family dynamic theories about male homosexuality being induced by a dominant, overprotective mother and a passive and distant (or absent) father have been popular, no single pattern of family interaction appears to be responsible for homosexuality (Grant, 1976). An interesting study conducted by the authors and colleagues (Adler, Hendrick, & Hendrick, 1987) examined sexual attitudes (and love attitudes) of homosexual and heterosexual males in Texas and New York. Results indicated that there were *no* significant differences between the two groups on the sexual attitudes that were measured.

Unidimensional causal theories are always appealing, and indeed, explanations for homosexuality have been sought in both psychosocial and biological data. However, to date, "It seems more appropriate to think of the continuum of sexual orientation as influenced by a variety of psychosocial and biological factors, which may be unique for each person, than to think in terms of a single cause for sexual orientation" (Crooks & Baur, 1987, p. 320). Although aspects of personality as *effects* rather than causes of homosexuality have been explored, no "general" personality traits can be ascribed to homosexuals. And because no particular psychopathology can be linked to homosexuality, it has been removed from the category of mental illness by the American Psychiatric Association.

Sexual Variants

The topic of atypical sexual behaviors will be considered briefly, because there are few consistent data on personality in relation to sexual variants. Three frequently expressed variants include exhibitionism (exposing one's genitals to an involuntary observer), obscene phone calls, and voyeurism ("Peeping Tomism"). Feelings of personal inadequacy and insecurity are frequent among people who express these variants. Sadomasochism, or SM, (giving and/or receiving mental or physical pain in connection with sexuality), another variant, is not uncommon and may range from "love bites" during sex play to the use of the much-stereotyped whips and chains. Although extreme practitioners of SM may actually harm themselves or a partner, most participants probably just want to widen their sexual repertoire in a departure from conventionality. Additional sexual variants include transvestism (obtaining sexual excitement from putting on the clothes of the other sex), and variants of the object of one's sexual gratification, such as fetishism (becoming sexually aroused by an inanimate object or a part of the human body), zoophilia (sexual contact between humans and animals), and so on. Although certain behavior patterns may be more common among those who practice such variants, few personality correlates have been identified (Crooks & Baur, 1987).

Beyond sexual variants, which typically do not involve physical harm to anyone, lie various forms of sexual victimization, such as rape, pedophilia (child molestation), and incest. In each type of victimization, various psychosocial factors are implicated. For instance, socialization that emphasizes extreme macho, aggressive male behavior may exert influence on male rapists along with individual personality characteristics of the rapist (Crooks & Baur, 1987). For those who sexually victimize children, however, the causes may be more personal, such as feelings of inadequacy in dealing with others, unassertiveness, fear of evaluation by others, and additional problems such as marital problems or alcoholism (e.g., Crooks & Baur, 1987; Overholser & Beck, 1986). It appears that no single personality or psychosocial variable can identify those who engage in coercive sexual activity (Overholser & Beck, 1986).

Sexual Dysfunction

If dysfunction can be thought of as cognitive and emotional as well as behavioral, it seems reasonable to discuss sexual guilt and anxiety, as well as actual performance dysfunction. Although "sexual guilt" has been defined as negative sexual attitudes and value systems, whereas "sexual anxiety" includes performance anxiety and fears (Janda & O'Grady, 1980), neither is a desirable concomitant of sexual interaction. Extensive research on sex guilt, a concept developed in the work of Donald Mosher (e.g., 1965), has shown sex guilt to be negatively associated with self-reported sexual experience and sexual arousal in response to erotica. More recently, Green and Mosher (1985) have developed a causal model to test the presumed negative effects of sex guilt on sexual arousal.

Sexual anxiety (including performance anxiety) has been more closely linked with sexual dysfunction. Although there are numerous reasons for sexual dysfunction (Kaplan, 1974), fears or anxieties about the acceptability of being sexual in general or the specific acceptability of one's own sexual performance can lead to a host of sexual problems, from avoidance of sex to orgasmic dysfunction in females and erectile dysfunction in males. A substantial component of human sexuality is psychological, rather than physical, so that ultimately psychological feelings of sexual guilt or anxiety can have detrimental physical/sexual effects. In addition, sexual dysfunction can be a cause as well as an effect of psychological/personality problems. For instance, in a study of couples with and without sexual dysfunction, Rosenheim and Neumann (1981) found males experiencing erectile and/or ejaculatory difficulties to have higher levels of self-punishment, hostility, guilt, sensitivity to rejection, and external locus of control. Interestingly, such personality attributes may precede the dysfunction or may be caused by it—or may be *both* cause and effect.

One sexual difficulty that has been increasingly studied in recent years is Inhibited Sexual Desire (ISD), which refers to a syndrome in which individuals fail to initiate or respond to sexual cues (Rosen & Leiblum, 1987). Determinants of sexual desire disorders have been largely classified into internal (e.g., hormonal) or external (e.g., sociocultural) determinants, with some attention paid to intrapsychic conflicts such as performance anxiety, fear of intimacy (and perhaps subsequent rejection), and so on. Rosen and Leiblum's (1987) comprehensive approach to the assessment and treatment of desire problems is multidimensional, taking into account health history, presence of depression, previous sexual trauma, interpersonal difficulties, and intrapsychic (i.e., personality) problems (e.g., "fears of intimacy and commitment, conflicts around dependency issues, concerns about loss of control, and guilt around sexual pleasure" [p. 156]). Thus, personality is seen as a major influence (though not the only influence) on human sexual behavior.

This first section of the chapter serves as an overview of existing theory and research on human sexuality and personality. It serves as prelude to the next section, which describes a program of research concerned in part with relating sexual attitudes to various sociocultural and personality variables.

The Study of Sexual Attitudes

Measurement of Sexual Attitudes

In 1982 we began an original program of research on attitudes toward love and attitudes toward sexuality. Our work on love resulted in the development of a forty-two-item Love Attitudes Scale that is discussed in detail elsewhere (Hendrick & Hendrick, 1986). At the same time, we searched the literature for a measure of sexual attitudes that would include such topics as premarital sexuality, contraceptive behavior, the "double standard," and so on. However, sex attitude scales have typically been designed to focus on a particular topic area rather than on sexual attitudes in general. Thus, Reiss's (1964) twelve-item Guttman scale, a widely used assessment instrument, evaluates the construct of sexual permissiveness. The Sexual Opinion Survey (Fisher, Byrne, White, & Kelley, 1988) is used to assess subjects' responses to erotic materials along a dimension of erotophobia (disliking erotic material) to erotophilia (liking erotic material); and the Revised Mosher Guilt Inventory (Green & Mosher, 1985) is a measure of sexual guilt. Although there are also a number of other measures of sexual attitudes, these are among the most popular. Because we couldn't find the kind of wide-ranging scale we were seeking, we decided to develop one.

As we initially constructed the scale, we took no items from existing scales but rather chose to generate a large pool of items that we felt reflected a variety of attitudes, values, and orientations toward sex. Our initial pool of 150 items was very diverse, reflecting topics such as permissiveness, premarital sex, birth control, and power and dominance, and we subsequently reduced this pool to a 102-item measure. The measure was administered (as part of a longer questionnaire) to 813 students at the University of Miami (Florida) during 1982. Factor analyses resulted in five factors (58 items) that were retained for additional analyses and scaling work. This shortened sex attitude questionnaire was again part of a longer questionnaire administered to 807 Miami students during the academic year 1983–1984. Although factor analyses and reliability analyses (test-retest; alpha reliability) indicated that the scale was quite sound, an essentially confirmatory analysis was conducted with nearly 600 students at Texas Tech University in the fall of 1984. All analyses resulted in values very similar to those of the preceding study and indicated that the scale was psychometrically sound. (A detailed report of these studies can be found in Hendrick et al., 1985; Hendrick & Hendrick, 1987a). The final version of the Sexual Attitudes Scale contains four factors (subscales) composed of 43 items. Although Permissiveness (open, casual sexuality) is the longest subscale (21 items), the other three subscales add needed multidimensionality to the scale. Sexual Practices (7 items) represents responsible, tolerant sexuality; Communion (9 items) denotes emotional, idealistic sexuality; and Instrumentality (6 items) portrays sex as egocentric and very biological. The complete Sexual Attitudes Scale is shown in the Activity Box.

Because the Sexual Attitudes Scale had been constructed without particular theoretical underpinnings, we conducted additional studies, including a criterion validity study employing our scale, the Sexual Opinion Survey (Fisher et al., in press), the Revised Mosher Guilt Inventory (Green & Mosher, 1985), and the Reiss Male and Female Premarital Sexual Permissiveness Scale (1964). (A criterion validity study in this case involved seeing how our new questionnaire related to other, more established questionnaires, called the "criterion" measures.) Three of the four subscales of the Sexual Attitudes Scale related to the other three scales in logical ways. For instance, Permissiveness was quite strongly related to Reiss's permissiveness scale. It turned out that our new scale was similar enough to existing scales to show that it truly measured sexual attitudes, yet different enough to be a real addition to the area.

The task of developing a good measuring instrument is important —but not very exciting, so we have described the development of the sex attitudes scale only briefly. It is much more interesting, however, to consider how sexual attitudes are related to various sociocultural and personality variables, and to consider gender differences in sexual attitudes.

Sexual Attitudes and Related Constructs

Sociocultural Variables

We examined sexual attitudes in relation to a number of variables, across several studies, and the most interesting sociocultural findings resulted for strength of religious belief, ethnicity, number of times in love, and whether a person was currently in love. Rather consistently, subjects who described themselves as "very religious" also reported themselves to be less sexually permissive, instrumental, and endorsing of Sexual Practices on the attitude scale. Their opposites on most of these scales were the relatively nonreligious subjects. In an additional study, the very religious subjects were also less endorsing of Communion. Thus, across studies, religious subjects were less favorable to all aspects of sex assessed than were other subjects. These findings are congruent with existing literature on the topic (Hendrick & Hendrick, 1987b).

Ethnic differences appeared only for Florida subjects, who were much more ethnically diverse than were Texas subjects. Anglos were more permissive and endorsing of Sexual Practices than were other groups, and along with Hispanic subjects, more strongly endorsed Communion. Oriental subjects were more instrumental. Although these findings are very preliminary, they are interesting and are being explored further.

The number of times a subject had been in love produced

Sexual Attitudes Scale

Several statements that reflect different attitudes about sex are listed below. For each statement fill in the response that indicates how much you agree or disagree with that statement. Some of the items refer to a specific sexual relationship, whereas others refer to general attitudes and beliefs about sex. Whenever possible, answer the questions with your current partner in mind. If you are not currently dating anyone, answer the questions with your most recent partner in mind. If you have never had a sexual relationship, answer in terms of what you think your responses would most likely be.

For each statement:
1 = strongly agree with the statement
2 = moderately agree with the statement
3 = neutral—neither agree nor disagree
4 = moderately disagree with the statement
5 = strongly disagree with the statement

_____ 1. I do not need to be committed to a person to have sex with him/her.

_____ 2. Casual sex is acceptable.

_____ 3. I would like to have sex with many partners.

_____ 4. One-night stands are sometimes very enjoyable.

_____ 5. It is OK to have ongoing sexual relationships with more than one person at a time.

_____ 6. It is OK to manipulate someone into having sex as long as no future promises are made.

_____ 7. Sex as a simple exchange of favors is OK if both people agree to it.

_____ 8. The best sex is with no strings attached.

_____ 9. Life would have fewer problems if people could have sex more freely.

_____ 10. It is possible to enjoy sex with a person and not like that person very much.

_____ 11. Sex is more fun with someone you don't love.

_____ 12. It is all right to pressure someone into having sex.

_____ 13. Extensive premarital sexual experience is fine.

_____ 14. Extramarital affairs are all right as long as one's partner doesn't know about them.

_____ 15. Sex for its own sake is perfectly all right.

_____ 16. I would feel comfortable having intercourse with my partner in the presence of other people.

_____ 17. Prostitution is acceptable.

_____ 18. It is OK for sex to be just good physical release.

_____ 19. Sex without love is meaningless.

_____ 20. People should at least be friends before they have sex together.

_____ 21. In order for sex to be good, it must also be meaningful.

_____ 22. Birth control is part of responsible sexuality.

_____ 23. A woman should share responsibility for birth control.

_____ 24. A man should share responsibility for birth control.

_____ 25. Sex education is important for young people.

_____ 26. Using "sex toys" during lovemaking is acceptable.

_____ 27. Masturbation is all right.

_____ 28. Masturbating one's partner during intercourse can increase the pleasure of sex.

_____ 29. Sex gets better as a relationship progresses.

_____ 30. Sex is the closest form of communication between two people.

_____ 31. A sexual encounter between two people deeply in love is the ultimate human interaction.

_____ 32. Orgasm is the greatest experience in the world.

_____ 33. At its best, sex seems to be the merging of two souls.

_____ 34. Sex is a very important part of life.

_____ 35. Sex is usually an intensive, almost overwhelming experience.

_____ 36. During sexual intercourse, intense awareness of the partner is the best frame of mind.

_____ 37. Sex is fundamentally good.

_____ 38. Sex is best when you let yourself go and focus on your own pleasure.

_____ 39. Sex is primarily the taking of pleasure from another person.

_____ 40. The main purpose of sex is to enjoy oneself.

_____ 41. Sex is primarily physical.

_____ 42. Sex is primarily a bodily function, like eating.

_____ 43. Sex is mostly a game between males and females.

Scoring: For each of the following subscales, add up your responses and divide by the number of items in the subscale.

- _Permissiveness:_ items 1–21 (Items 19, 20, and 21 are reverse scored, which means 1 = 5, 2 = 4, 3 = 3, 4 = 2, 5 = 1.)
- _Sexual Practices:_ items 22–28
- _Communion:_ items 29–37
- _Instrumentality:_ items 38–43

You will get four subscale scores; an overall scale score is not computed.

significant differences on all four sex scales in the Florida studies and on two scales in the Texas study. Subjects who had been in love several times were consistently more endorsing of Permissiveness and showed some tendency toward Instrumentality. Responding to a question that asked "Are you in love now?" subjects currently in love were less permissive and instrumental and more endorsing of Communion than subjects who were not currently in love. It appears that being in love has an influence on several relationship characteristics.

Personality Variables

Constructs that seem to be more in the realm of personality and that showed some interesting relationships with sexuality included self-esteem, self-disclosure, and sensation seeking.

Self-esteem produced findings that varied somewhat. In Florida, subjects who were highest in self-esteem were most endorsing of Permissiveness, Sexual Practices, and Communion. In Texas, there were no differences. These findings can be at least partially explained on the basis of work by Perlman (1974), who found self-esteem to be related to group sexual norms. Thus in "liberal" Florida, sexuality was related to higher self-esteem, while in more moderate Texas, sexual activity and self-esteem were unrelated.

Another study (Hendrick & Hendrick, 1987c) explored relationships between the sex scale and both self-disclosure and sensation seeking. "Self-disclosure" typically refers to verbally revealing aspects of one's inner or "real" self to another person, and it has proved to be an important aspect of interaction with intimate others (Hendrick, 1981; Morton, 1978) and strangers (Derlega, Winstead, Wong, & Hunter, 1985). We measured both the subject's self-reported *giving* of disclosure to a love partner and the subject's ability to *elicit* self-disclosure from others (Miller, Berg, & Archer, 1983). Correlations between sexual attitudes and disclosure were modest, but consistent with what we expected. Permissiveness and Instrumentality were either unrelated or negatively related to disclosure, whereas Sexual Practices and Communion were positively related to disclosure.

The Sensation Seeking Scale (Zuckerman et al., 1964) was noted previously. It emphasizes affective and sensory attitudes and experiences that seem particularly relevant to sexuality. Its four subscales include: Disinhibition (social nonconformity), Experience seeking (desiring a wide variety of sensory and aesthetic experiences), Boredom susceptibility (tending to become bored and restless easily), Thrill and adventure seeking (desiring physical excitement), and a total sensation seeking score composed of the four subscale scores. Not surprisingly, Permissiveness showed the highest correlation with sensation seeking, relating to three of the four subscales and the total scale score. The

Permissive person appears to be relatively unconforming to social norms and is easily bored (also moderately seeking of experiences). Sexual Practices was related to Disinhibition and Experience seeking, thus revealing both tolerance for and interest in a variety of sexual practices and other life experiences. Idealistic Communion showed no significant relationships with any of the scales. Instrumentality was related to both Disinhibition and Boredom susceptibility. Permissive and instrumental relationship partners appear to have a restless need for sexual variety and fulfillment, without any particular regard for societal norms.

Gender Differences Revisited

We earlier noted some gender differences found in initial studies using the Sexual Attitudes Scale. In subsequent studies with the revised, four-factor scale, gender differences appeared consistently on Permissiveness and Instrumentality (males more endorsing of both) and appeared in Texas studies also on Sexual Practices and Communion (females more oriented to both). We have noticed some thematic consistencies between our work and previous work in the way that females seem to approach relationships. "Women seem oriented to a love/sexuality pattern that is relatively practical and conventional . . . but that can also encompass idealistic and highly affective attitudes. . . . Men, on the other hand, identify more with a casual, less conventional, and more manipulative approach" (Hendrick & Hendrick, 1988).

Although the primary focus of this chapter is on personality and sexuality, because one of our original goals in studying sex was to theoretically and empirically link sex with love, we will briefly discuss those two closely interwoven phenomena.

Integrating Sex With Love

For several of the studies we conducted using our full questionnaire (demographic items, love scale, sex scale), we examined patterns of correlations (e.g., relationships) between the four sexual attitude subscales and six subscales measuring different orientations to love. These six subscales reflect six love *styles* developed by Lee (1973) and scaled by the authors (Hendrick & Hendrick, 1986). The six styles are *Eros* (passionate, romantic love), *Ludus* (game-playing love), *Storge* (love based on friendship), *Pragma* (practical love), *Mania* (possessive, dependent love), and *Agape* (altruistic love). We found definite relationships among the six love subscales and four sex subscales, and although the patterns of correlations differed somewhat across the three studies we examined, certain central relationships were consistent. We then examined all ten subscales by a factor analysis to see which scales would relate to one another and which would not (discussed in detail in Hendrick & Hendrick, 1987a). Three factors resulted. Ludus, Permissiveness, and Instrumentality loaded positively on *Factor 1*, and Agape loaded negatively. Because these first three scales are all somewhat oriented to game-playing, mechanistic love/sex relationships, they are all positively related to one another and negatively related to the scale embodying altruistic, idealistic love. For *Factor 2*, Eros, Mania, Agape, Sexual Practices, and Communion all loaded positively. Eros, Mania, and Agape are all strongly emotional, committed love orientations, and although they are qualitatively different, it is not surprising that they load on the same factor. Sexual Practices and Communion are aspects of sexuality that are both responsible and idealistic, and are oriented to the "relationship" aspects of sexuality. They fit logically in this factor. *Factor 3* showed strong positive loadings by Pragma and Storge, a modest positive loading by Mania, and a modest negative loading by Permissiveness. This factor could probably be called a "stability" factor, because both Storge and Pragma are solid, steady love styles. Casual, free-ranging Permissiveness had an expectedly negative relationship with the other two. Mania's appearance on this factor may reflect the manic tendency to steadily and single-mindedly focus on a love partner. The way the sex and love scales were linked on the three factors supports the idea of common links between love and sex. Although sex and love don't always go together, relations between these two kinds of scales, and the phenomena they represent, reflect the fact that love and sex are often intertwined. Love serves as the motive force for much of our sexual interaction, and sex serves as an intense medium for expressing love, with personality presenting a backdrop to both.

Summary

Sexuality is an important aspect of human experience, and it both influences and is influenced by, one's individual personality. A number of factors influence our sexuality. These include sociocultural influences (e.g., societal norms for sexual behavior), interpersonal influences (e.g., how our family and friends feel about sex), gender influences (these include both our biological sex *and* the ways we have been socialized as a female or a male), and personality influences (e.g., the relationship between our styles of presenting ourselves to others and the ways we express ourselves sexually). These multiple influences continue to shape our sexual attitudes and behavior during childhood and on into adult life. Among the more controversial topics within the sexual sphere are issues of sexual preference, sexual variants, and sexual dysfunctions.

The study of sexual attitudes connects sexuality with personality, and this chapter details the recent development of a multidimensional Sexual Attitudes Scale. Also presented are some of the findings of recent research studies employing this scale. These findings include the influences of such variables as religious commitment and sensation seeking on sexuality, and sexual attitude differences between men and women. Attention is also given to the links between sexuality and love. There are a number of factors that affect the relationship between sexuality and personality, and it is important that we continue seeking new information about this significant topic.

SUGGESTED READINGS

Davis, M. S. (1983). *Smut: Erotic reality/obscene ideology.* Chicago: University of Chicago Press. This book gives a historical sociological perspective on why sexuality has been and continues to be controversial.

Grant, V. W. (1976). *Falling in love: The psychology of the romantic emotion.* New York: Springer. An interesting volume, easy to read. Argues that sexual attraction is an aesthetic impulse, different from sexual desire. Much evidence is cited, e.g., young children can experience passionate love long before they are capable of sexual experience.

Morrison, D. M. (1985). Adolescent contraceptive behavior: A review. *Psychological Bulletin, 98,* 538–568. This excellent review article gives an interesting and provocative overview of adolescents' use (and nonuse) of contraceptives.

Reiss, I. L. (1986). *Journey into sexuality: An exploratory voyage.* Englewood Cliffs, NJ: Prentice-Hall. This volume surveys certain basic sexual phenomena such as power, and homosexuality, through sociological/anthropological comparisons of numerous nonindustrialized and industrialized societies.

Robinson, P. A. (1976). *The modernization of sex.* New York: Harper & Row. Devotes chapters to each of the major figures, and others, described in this chapter who were important in helping develop a scientific approach to sexuality. An interesting short volume.

REFERENCES

Adler, N. L., Hendrick, S. S., & Hendrick, C. (1987). Male sexual preference and attitudes toward love and sexuality. *Journal of Sex Education and Therapy, 12* (2), 27–30.

Barnes, G. E., Malamuth, N. M., & Cheek, J. V. P. (1984). Personality and sexuality. *Personality and Individual Differences, 5,* 159–172.

Bell, A., & Weinberg, M. (1978). *Homosexualities: A study of diversity among men and women.* New York: Simon & Schuster.

Bell, A., Weinberg, M., & Hammersmith, S. (1981). *Sexual preference: Its development in men and women.* Bloomington, IN: Indiana University Press.

Bell, R. R., & Chaskes, J. B. (1970). Premarital sexual experience among coeds, 1958 and 1968. *Journal of Marriage and the Family, 32,* 81–84.

Billy, J. O. G., & Udry, J. R. (1985). The influence of male and female best friends on adolescent sexual behavior. *Adolescence, 20,* 21–32.

Brecher, E. M. (1971). *The sex researchers.* New York: Signet.

Bullough, V. L. (1985). Problems of research on a delicate topic: A personal view. *The Journal of Sex Research, 21,* 375–386.

Carroll, J. L., Volk, K. D., & Hyde, J. S. (1985). Differences between males and females in motives for engaging in sexual intercourse. *Archives of Sexual Behavior, 14,* 131–139.

Clement, U., Schmidt, G., & Kruse, M. (1984). Changes in sex differences in sexual behavior: A replication of a study on West German students (1966–1981). *Archives of Sexual Behavior, 13,* 99–120.

Crooks, R., & Baur, K. (1987). *Our sexuality* (3rd ed.). Menlo Park, CA: Benjamin/Cummings Publishing.

Davis, M. S. (1983). *Smut: Erotic reality/obscene ideology.* Chicago: The University of Chicago Press.

DeLamater, J., & MacCorquodale, P. (1979). *Premarital sexuality: Attitudes, relationships, behavior.* Madison, WI: University of Wisconsin Press.

Derlega, V. J., Winstead, B. A., Wong, P. T. P., & Hunter, S. (1985). Gender effects in an initial encounter: A case where men exceed women in disclosure. *Journal of Social and Personal Relationships, 2,* 25–44.

Emmons, C. A., Joseph, J. G., Kessler, R. C., Wortman, C. B., Montgomery, S. B., & Ostrow, D. G. (1986). Psychosocial predictors of reported behavior change in homosexual men at risk for AIDS. *Health Education Quarterly, 13,* 331–345.

Eysenck, H. J. (1976). *Sex and personality.* Austin, TX: University of Texas Press.

Fisher, W. A., Byrne, D., White, L. A., & Kelley, K. (1988). Erotophobia–erotophilia as a dimension of personality. *The Journal of Sex Research, 25,* 123–151.

Freud, S. (1949). *An outline of psychoanalysis* (J. Strachey, Trans.). London: W. W. Norton. (Original work published 1940).

George, L., & Weiler, S. (1981). Sexuality in middle and late life. *Archives of General Psychiatry, 38,* 919–923.

Gerrard, M. (1987). Sex, sex guilt, and contraceptive use revisited: The 1980s. *Journal of Personality and Social Psychology, 52,* 975–980.

Grant, V. W. (1976). *Falling in love: The psychology of the romantic emotion.* New York: Springer.

Green, S. E., & Mosher, D. L. (1985). A causal model of sexual arousal to erotic fantasies. *The Journal of Sex Research, 21,* 1–23.

Hendrick, S. S. (1981). Self-disclosure and marital satisfaction. *Journal of Personality and Social Psychology, 40,* 1150–1159.

Hendrick, C., & Hendrick, S. (1986). A theory and method of love. *Journal of Personality and Social Psychology, 50,* 392–402.

Hendrick, S., & Hendrick, C. (1987a). Multidimensionality of sexual attitudes. *The Journal of Sex Research, 23,* 502–526.

Hendrick, S., & Hendrick, C. (1987b). Love and sex attitudes and religious beliefs. *Journal of Social and Clinical Psychology, 5,* 391–398.

Hendrick, S. S., & Hendrick, C. (1987c). Love and sexual attitudes, self-disclosure, and sensation seeking. *Journal of Social and Personal Relationships, 4,* 281–297.

Hendrick, S. S., & Hendrick, C. (1988). Love and sex attitudes: A close relationship. In W. H. Jones & D. Perlman (Eds.), *Advances in personal relationships* (pp. 141–169). Greenwich, CT: JAI Press.

Hendrick, S., Hendrick, C., Slapion-Foote, M. J., & Foote, F. H. (1985). Gender differences in sexual attitudes. *Journal of Personality and Social Psychology, 48,* 1630–1642.

Hite, S. (1976). *The Hite report: A nationwide study of female sexuality.* New York: Dell Books.

Janda, L. H., & O'Grady, K. E. (1980). Development of a sex anxiety inventory. *Journal of Consulting and Clinical Psychology, 48,* 169–175.

Jessor, S. L., & Jessor, R. (1975). Transition from virginity to nonvirginity among youth: A social-psychological study over time. *Developmental Psychology, 11,* 473–484.

Jurich, A. P., & Jurich, J. A. (1974). The effect of cognitive moral development upon the selection of premarital sexual standards. *Journal of Marriage and the Family, 36,* 736–741.

Kaplan, H. (1974). *The new sex therapy: Active treatment of sexual dysfunctions.* New York: Brunner/Mazel.

Knafo, D., & Jaffe, Y. (1984). Sexual fantasizing in males and females. *Journal of Research in Personality, 18,* 451–462.

Lee, J. A. (1973). *The colors of love: An exploration of the ways of loving.* Don Mills, Ontario: New Press.

Luckey, E. B., & Nass, G. D. (1969). A comparison of sexual attitudes and behavior in an international sample. *Journal of Marriage and the Family, 31,* 364–379.

Miller, L. C., Berg, J. H., & Archer, R. L. (1983). Openers: Individuals who elicit intimate self-disclosure. *Journal of Personality and Social Psychology, 44,* 1234–1244.

Morton, T. L. (1978). Intimacy and reciprocity of exchange: A comparison of spouses and strangers. *Journal of Personality and Social Psychology, 36,* 72–81.

Mosher, D. L. (1965). Interaction of fear and guilt in inhibiting unacceptable behavior. *Journal of Consulting Psychology, 29,* 161–167.

Newcomb, M. D., Huba, G. J., & Bentler, P. M. (1986). Determinants of sexual and dating behaviors among adolescents. *Journal of Personality and Social Psychology, 50,* 428–438.

Overholser, J. C., & Beck, S. (1986). Multimethod assessment of rapists, child molesters, and three control groups on behavioral and psychological measures. *Journal of Consulting and Clinical Psychology, 54,* 682–687.

Perlman, D. (1974). Self-esteem and sexual permissiveness. *Journal of Marriage and the Family, 36,* 470–473.

Reiss, I. L. (1964). The scaling of premarital sexual permissiveness. *Journal of Marriage and the Family, 26,* 188–198.

Reiss, I. L. (1986). *Journey into sexuality: An exploratory voyage.* Englewood Cliffs, NJ: Prentice-Hall.

Rosen, R. C., & Leiblum, S. R. (1987). Current approaches to the evaluation of sexual desire disorders. *The Journal of Sex Research, 23,* 141–162.

Rosenheim, E., & Neumann, M. (1981). Personality characteristics of sexually dysfunctioning males and their wives. *The Journal of Sex Research, 17,* 124–138.

Schenk, J., & Pfrang, H. (1986). Extraversion, neuroticism, and sexual behavior: Interrelationships in a sample of young men. *Archives of Sexual Behavior, 15,* 449–455.

Schenk, J., Pfrang, H., & Rausche, A. (1983). Personality traits versus the quality of the marital relationship as the determinant of marital sexuality. *Archives of Sexual Behavior, 12,* 31–42.

Snyder, M. (1974). The self-monitoring of expressive behavior. *Journal of Personality and Social Psychology, 30,* 526–537.

Snyder, M., & Simpson, J. A. (1984). Self-monitoring and dating relationships. *Journal of Personality and Social Psychology, 47,* 1281–1291.

Snyder, M., Simpson, J. A., & Gangestad, S. (1986). Personality and sexual relations. *Journal of Personality and Social Psychology, 51,* 181–190.

Sorenson, R. (1973). *Adolescent sexuality in contemporary America.* New York: World.

Stratton, J. R., & Spitzer, S. P. (1967). Sexual permissiveness and self-evaluation: A question of substance and a question of method.

Journal of Marriage and the Family, 29, 434–441.

Walsh, R. H., Ferrell, M. L., & Tolone, W. L. (1976). Selection of reference groups, perceived reference group permissiveness, and personal permissiveness attitudes and behavior: A study of two consecutive panels (1967–1971; 1970–1974). *Journal of Marriage and the Family, 38,* 495–507.

Zuckerman, M., Kolin, E. A., Price, L., & Zoob, I. (1964). Development of a sensation seeking scale. *Journal of Consulting Psychology, 28,* 477–482.

Zuckerman, M., Tushup, R., & Finner, S. (1976). Sexual attitudes and experience: Attitude and personality correlates and changes produced by a course in sexuality. *Journal of Consulting and Clinical Psychology, 44,* 7–19.

CHAPTER 17

Aggression

HAL S. BERTILSON

Introduction
Definitional Issues
  Personality
  Aggression
Longitudinal Stability of
    Aggression
ACTIVITY BOX: Defining
    Aggression
Heritability of Aggressiveness
  Behavioral Genetics
  Temperament
A Coercion Model: The
    Development of Antisocial
    Behavior

Anger and Aggression
Catharsis
  Emotional Catharsis
  Behavior Catharsis
Aggressive Habits
Rational Aggression
Summary
SUGGESTED READINGS
REFERENCES

Introduction

The power of a charismatic leader, a provocative insult, an out-of-control mob, or a physical attack to stimulate aggressive behavior may be so great that it often seems as if aggression is "caused" exclusively by social factors. Accordingly, one may ask if personality processes play any important role in influencing aggressive behavior.

But there are violent people—individuals who recurrently do harm to other people and/or who display lifelong patterns of violence. Toch (1984) describes some of these people, all men, in his extensive interview study of violence in sixty-nine prison inmates and parolees. Analyses of these data led Toch to suggest personality categories of violent men. The *self-image promoter*, for example, is a man who works hard at manufacturing the impression that he is not to be trifled with—that he is formidable and can't be intimidated. His fights are demonstrations designed to impress the audience. He butts into the affairs of others as a means of proving his own self-worth. One self-image promoter described himself as attacking any individual who insulted him. Upon his first arrival at the prison yard, he was whistled at by fellow inmates. After brooding for a while he sought out the offenders, forcing them to confess and then seriously thrashing each one. He often purposefully maneuvered others into positions where he could justify attacking them. He was unconcerned about others' welfare and expressed no remorse over knifing his father and killing his father's common-law wife in an argument.

The *bully*, another category of Toch's violent men, goes out of his way to be unfair, unmerciful, and inhumane in his violence. He takes advantage of people whenever they are in a weakened position. And then when the victim gives some indication of weakness (e.g., begging

458

for mercy), the bully accelerates his violence. He resorts to any number of clearly cruel actions like walking over the victim's chest or stomping on his face. The pattern of bullying episodes begins with boyhood escapades and then becomes adult felony assaults.

Toch vividly describes other aggressive personalities. *"Rep-defenders"* are individuals who occupy special positions within gangs. Their reputation and position depend upon demonstrating their violence. *Norm enforcers* act as one-man posses. They feel they know the rules, when the rules have been violated, and how violators must be dealt with. *Self-image defenders,* like self-image promoters, act aggressively out of profound feelings of insecurity and low self-esteem. Whereas self-image promoters deal with their insecurity by manufacturing a formidable image, self-image defenders react to implications of other people's actions. Any possible threat to their integrity or manliness leads to a violent reaction. *Self-defenders* react to other persons as sources of physical danger. They are afraid that if they do not strike first, they will become victims themselves. *Pressure removers* lack interpersonal skills. When they find themselves in situations that they are unable to handle they may explode. *Exploiters* persistently manipulate others into being a source of pleasure or convenience for them. When others resist, exploiters react with violence. *Self-indulgers* behave as though the only purpose of other people is to cater to them in every possible way. Unlike exploiters, there is no intent to deliberately manipulate. They simply proceed as though their own welfare is the primary concern. *Catharters* use aggression to discharge accumulated internal pressure and moods. (For interesting case histories that provide the evidence for these categories, see Toch [1984].)

The point is that there clearly are aggressive personalities. The purpose of this chapter is to describe some of what we know about the processes that produce these individuals. The first major theme will deal with developmental processes. How do aggressive personalities develop? The discussion will include behavioral genetics, temperament, coercive interactions, and longitudinal stability of aggressive tendencies. The second major theme will deal with different processes that mediate aggressiveness. Which processes differ in aggressive personalities from nonaggressive personalities? The discussion of this theme will include anger, catharsis, habits, and rational processes.

Definitional Issues

Personality

Investigators who are interested in the effects of personality on aggressive behavior usually have in mind four related aspects of personality. One aspect emphasizes *internal* processes such as anger, hostility, and irritability. These personality processes *mediate* between the actions of other people and the aggressive person's responses to those actions. Toch sees the self-image promoter as driven by fear. In the language of mediation, the presence of others is interpreted by the self-image promoter as a threat that produces fear. Fear leads those in this personality category to try to enhance their image through violence. Or in the case of anger, the angry person is very easily "set off." An insult touches off anger that "mediates" angry aggression. Emotions, attitudes, motives, and traits are all included as mediators in theories of aggressive personality processes.

A second aspect of personality refers to different kinds of people who are likely to act aggressively. Some boys are known to be bullies. Others are self-indulgers. Still others are norm enforcers. These are examples of aggressive personalities in the *individual differences* sense.

To say that aggressiveness is a personality trait also conveys the notion that aggressiveness is something carried by individuals from *situation to situation* and influences their behavior in a wide range of settings. Self-image promoters, for example, continue to try to create a favorable impression by challenging a man on the street, in prison, or on the job.

Finally, aggressiveness is carried by individuals from *time to time* and influences their behavior over a long period of time. As will be seen, some individuals rated as aggressive at age 8 were more likely than those not rated as aggressive to be convicted of a crime 22 years later at age 30 (Huesmann, Eron, Lefkowitz, & Walder, 1984).

For the purposes of this chapter, the study of *personality* is defined as concern with "inferred mediating processes that account for organization in the behavior of the individual person" (Shontz, 1965, p. 7). Such a definition is intended to include mediation, individual differences, and consistency in behavior from situation to situation and from time to time. *Trait* is generally used to refer to "any distinguishable, relatively enduring way in which one individual varies from another" (Guilford, 1959, p. 6). Impulsiveness, for example, is one trait that could mediate aggressive behavior.

Aggression

Aggression is defined as behavior intended to harm or injure another person who is motivated to avoid injury (Baron, 1977). Note several aspects of this definition. Aggression is a *behavior,* for example, stabbing a victim. Aggression is *not* an emotion (anger), a motive (revenge), or an attitude (hate), although these variables may cause or enhance aggressive behavior. Aggression involves *intent*. The intent may be to seek revenge. The intent may be to rob a convenience store. If the clerk is shot as part of the robbery, we judge the act as aggressive. But if it is purely an accidental hurt, then intent is lacking and we are not inclined to label it as an aggressive act. When a child plays with a gun as if it is a play gun and it accidently goes off and seriously hurts someone, we think of this as a terrible tragedy but not as aggression. Aggression involves intention to harm or injure, but the injury *need not* be physical. *Verbal* criticism and public embarrassment produce harm and injury as well. Revealing to the press evidence that an election campaign opponent has made false claims about his or her qualifications for City Council is considered aggressive behavior according to this definition.

Aggressive behavior may be assigned to several categories based upon theoretically important criteria. If such an analysis allows us to highlight different processes that cause aggression, it may aid in our understanding, prediction, and control of aggression. A classic distinction is one between hostile and instrumental *motives*. *Hostile* aggression refers to instances in which the goal is to cause the victim to suffer. Toch's bully is a case in point. In contrast, *instrumental* aggression refers to instances in which the aggressor's principal motive is to obtain money, prestige, or other incentives—for example, the armed robbery of the convenience store in which a clerk is shot.

Stuart Taylor (1986) offers a recent distinction that will be used in this chapter. Instead of emphasizing motives, he emphasizes the process of initiating *action*. This distinction has the advantage of separating attitude (e.g., hostility) from behavior (aggression). It conceptualizes the initiation of action as impulsive or rational. *Impulsive aggression* is "essentially reactive, impulsive, and irrational." *Rational aggression* is "reflective, rational, and self-regulated." Many aggressive acts are comprised of both impulsive and rational components. Some aggressive acts will be mostly impulsive—for example, in the heat of argument. Other aggressive acts will be mostly rational, as in premeditated murder. (The Activity Box provides descriptions of seven aggressive acts for analysis.)

A further advantage of Taylor's distinction based on action is that it characterizes two of the major laboratory research programs. The work of Leonard Berkowitz and his colleagues generally concentrates on impulsive aggression. The research of Stuart Taylor and his colleagues concentrates on rational aggression. A full understanding of human aggression requires the integration of findings from both laboratory research approaches.

Longitudinal Stability of Aggression

Research methods vary in what they are able to tell us about human aggression (Bertilson, 1983). The case study method used by Toch is

ACTIVITY BOX

Defining Aggression

Traditional methods of measuring aggression have relied on distinctions between different motives such as hostility and instrumentality. Considerable theory and research have been stimulated by such an approach. Stuart Taylor (1986) takes the position that distinctions based upon action may be more useful. It will take time to see if his distinction stimulates additional theory and research. The author of this chapter believes that it will and has organized the chapter along the lines of Taylor's definitions.

Listed below are a series of aggressive acts. Read each carefully and indicate your judgment:

1 = Impulsive aggression
2 = Mostly impulsive aggression, with some degree of rational aggression
3 = Both impulsive and rational aggression
4 = Mostly rational aggression, with some degree of impulsive aggression
5 = Rational aggression

Explain the factors that led you to define the act in the way you did.

1. Johnny O. attended a party with neighborhood friends in Vancouver, British Columbia. After much music and alcohol a stranger became rowdy and insulting. When the stranger referred to Johnny's girlfriend as a "whore," Johnny hit the stranger over the head with his guitar.
2. A series of robberies in South Philadelphia seemed to follow a similar pattern. It now seems evident that they were perpetrated by Willy K. Willy was arrested yesterday for a robbery of a convenience store. Two employees were tied up and shot to death.
3. A twelve-year-old girl in Laramie, Wyoming, was arrested for poisoning her parents with rat poison. The method was similar to a poisoning incident shown on television the evening before. Neighbors were not surprised. The family was notorious for conflict, violence, and hostility.
4. Kenneth P. was promoted to store manager of an independent hard-

excellent for describing experience in the sometimes dangerous real world and suggesting new research and theory. But the case study method lacks systematic, quantifiable procedures necessary for confirming theory. The alleged importance of personality processes in

ware store in South Bend, Indiana. Before the promotion he was friendly and relatively timid. Immediately after his promotion, Kenneth's personality seemed to change dramatically. He was excitable, constantly hostile, often angry, and very demanding of his subordinates. Instructions to subordinates contained threats and insults.

5. Alice Q. was a member of a teenage gang. She was from a working-class family in South Chicago. Her parents worked long hours and were often not at home. Her own self-esteem was low and she did many things to gain the approval of her gangland peers including the stabbing homicide of a helpless derelict.

6. Mary B. was the frequent victim of spouse abuse from her alcoholic husband. He would come home drunk and without provocation beat her unmercifully. Recently as a precaution she decided to keep a handgun near her bed. When her husband came home last night he began beating her. She broke away long enough to grab the handgun and shot him to death.

7. Cynthia S. is a secretary for the biology department of a large regional university. One male faculty member is notorious for his sexual harassment of female students and staff. Cynthia has tried ignoring his advances without success. Friday, he patted her on the derriere. She responded by slapping him in the face. Over the weekend she couldn't get the incident out of her mind and Monday morning she filed a formal complaint against the errant faculty member with both the department chairperson and the affirmative action office of the university. She felt a responsibility to prevent future harassment of herself and others. Did you rate the slap on the face as the same type of aggression as you rated the formal complaint? Explain.

Aggressive act 1 is the clearest example of rating "1 = Impulsive aggression." The formal complaint in item 7 is the clearest example of rating "5 = Rational aggression." Each of the others might best be described as a mixture of impulsive and rational aggression.

causing aggressive behavior would be strengthened if systematic, quantifiable methods were used to demonstrate that individuals' characteristic aggressive patterns persist over time.

Such evidence is found in the results of recent research that focuses on the longitudinal stability of aggressiveness. If out of a sample of one hundred individuals Frank, Howard, and Phil are judged to be among the ten most aggressive at four years of age and among the ten most aggressive at nine years of age, longitudinal stability has been observed. The nature of aggressiveness at age four (e.g., taking a toy from a playmate) may be different from aggressiveness at age nine (e.g., physical fighting). Nevertheless an individual's relative position on the general dimension of aggressiveness is inferred to be relatively stable.

Dan Olweus (1984) conducted longitudinal studies of aggressiveness in adolescent boys in Sweden with peers providing ratings of the boys' aggressive tendencies. Ratings included unprovoked physical aggression against peers ("He starts fights with other boys at school") and verbal aggression ("When a teacher criticizes him, he tends to answer back and protest"). The subjects of the study were two hundred boys from eighteen school classes who were rated at the end of grade six (when their median age was thirteen) and three years later at the end of grade nine (when their median age was sixteen). Correlations demonstrated that boys who were verbally aggressive in grade six were also verbally aggressive in grade nine. Boys who were physically aggressive in grade six were also physically aggressive in grade nine.

This study offers a relatively stringent test for persistence in aggression for the following reasons: the aggressive behaviors were separated by three years, each ninth-grade class was composed of boys from a mix of different sixth-grade classes, the ninth-grade classes were in different school buildings than the sixth-grade classes, and there were new teachers in all the classes. Thus a high correlation between aggression scores at grades six and nine cannot be explained away as representing, say, the same social context (which causes the boys to be aggressive). The social situation was different in grades six and nine, but aggressive behavior persisted over this time period.

Olweus' conclusions were confirmed by other studies. For instance, Block (1971) investigated the stability of judgments by clinical psychologists on persons' tendencies to be "overreactive to minor frustrations," "irritable," and "rebellious and nonconforming." These judgments were collected as part of longitudinal research studying individuals between junior high and high school and between high school and adulthood (when subjects were in their mid-thirties). Results provided evidence for considerable stability in aggressive behavior across two decades. These results are even more impressive when one realizes that considerable environmental change had occurred in the lives of subjects between high school and the adult follow-up.

Huesmann and associates (1984) reported positive correlations between peer-nominated aggression at age eight with measures of aggressiveness twenty-two years later. Both females and males high in peer-nominated aggression at age eight were found to be more than twice as likely to be convicted of a crime in New York State before the age of thirty than were females and males low in peer-nominated aggression at age eight. Both females and males high in peer-nominated aggression at age eight were more than twice as likely to use strong punishment on their own children than were females and males low in peer-nominated aggression. Aggression scores at age thirty derived from selected scales of the Minnesota Multiphasic Personality Inventory (MMPI) (Hathaway & McKinley, 1951) were also more than twice as great for females and males high in peer-nominated aggression at age eight than females and males low in peer-nominated aggression.

For males there was additional evidence of longitudinal stability over time. There were impressive positive correlations between peer-nominated aggression at age eight and spouse abuse by age thirty and between peer-nominated aggression at age eight and driving while intoxicated by age thirty. These later two relationships did not appear in the female sample.

Heritability of Aggressiveness

Behavioral Genetics

What processes account for the tendency of individuals like those just described to develop into aggressive personalities? Some promising leads are now emerging from behavioral genetics. As indicated in the chapter on heredity (chapter 3), genetic variation can explain a substantial portion of individual differences in personality.

Rushton, Fulker, Neale, Nias, and Eysenck (1986) provide evidence about the effects of heredity on aggressive behavior. Five hundred seventy-three twin pairs from the University of London Institute of Psychiatry Twin Register filled out an aggressiveness questionnaire containing items asking people to indicate agreements with statements such as "Some people think I have a violent temper." One of the techniques used by Rushton et al. (1986) to analyze the inheritance of aggression with this data was the classic twin design (see chapter 3). A higher correlation for monozygotic than for dizygotic twins indicates a genetic component to the behavior.

The combined correlation for both females and males of aggressiveness between monozygotic twins was substantially above chance (r = .40) while the correlation between dizygotic twins was only chance (r = .04). The genetic component to aggressive behavior was evident for both females and males. For females the correlation between monozygotic twins was above chance (r = .43) while the correlation between dizygotic twins was chance (r = .00). For males the correlation between monozygotic twins was also above chance (r = .33) and the correlation between dizyotic twins was substantially less (r = .16).

These genetic influences become even more powerful influences on aggression via the emergence of environments that reinforce genetic effects (Rushton et al., 1986). *Passive genotype-environment correlations* occur when parents who are genetically disposed to aggressiveness pass on a social environment as well as genes favorable to aggressiveness. Parents pass on their genes and, because of their aggressive disposition, reinforce and model aggressive behavior. The aggressive social environment in the home as well as the inherited genes may make the children more likely to be aggressive themselves. *Evocative genotype-environment correlations* refer to the responses aggressive people evoke from others. Individuals who are aggressively disposed are more likely to elicit reciprocal aggressive responses from others. Aggressive responses often evoke hostility, defensiveness, and retaliatory aggression in others around them. *Active genotype-environment correlations* refer to the creation and selection of social environments. Aggressive individuals select other aggressive people to associate with, as friends and as marriage partners. These friends may initiate aggressive interchanges and respond aggressively to inept communication and assertive actions (Rushton et al., 1986).

Temperament

The Rushton et al. (1986) research reported genetic effects in samples of adults. Can these genetic effects be observed in children? The evidence is suggestive, particularly if one is willing to speculate about the effects of temperaments as well as genotype-environment correlations. Arnold Buss and Robert Plomin (1984, p. 84) define temperaments as "inherited personality traits present in early childhood" that develop into broad and influential adult traits. Buss and Plomin present convincing evidence that three of these traits—emotionality, activity, and sociability (EAS)—are the major dimensions of personality in infancy and childhood.

Temperaments may partially account for individual differences in aggressiveness observed in studies like Rushton et al. (1986). Temperaments may influence aggressive behavior by leading people unintentionally to modify their environments to match their EAS pattern. For example, people high in emotionality tend to exaggerate the impact of the environment. A minor irritant may be reacted to as a major insult. Emotional people also tend to make situations more tense. Others become nervous and irritable because the emotional person acts nervous and wary. It seems likely that some of these temperamental patterns may make impulsive and angry aggression more likely. These temperamental patterns may also be one of the factors contributing to lifelong patterns of violence described by Toch (1984).

A Coercion Model: The Development of Antisocial Behavior

Aggression and related antisocial behaviors are also learned. According to the *coercion model,* aggressive personalities develop out of family interaction sequences. Interaction between a relatively unskilled parent and a child with a difficult temperament is hypothesized to develop into patterned exchanges of aggressive behaviors. The exchanges are such that the members train each other to become increasingly punitive (Patterson, 1986).

The coercion model was developed from several decades of field clinical studies in homes and schools with antisocial boys and their families. Antisocial behaviors include such things as hitting, teasing, whining, and yelling. The coercion model has several stages. Initially antisocial behavior and noncompliance develop from coercive family interaction sequences. One such sequence occurs when the child whines and the mother responds to the whining with an expression of disapproval. Unfortunately the expression of a disapproval serves as an *accelerator* of whining. Thus two people are caught in accelerating coercive interaction sequences (Patterson, 1974).

Noncompliant and coercive behaviors in turn make it difficult for parents, siblings, teachers, and peers to teach the antisocial boy social skills. The child's antisocial, aggressive behaviors then lead to rejection by peers, academic failure, and low self-esteem, which all lead to an increasing spiral of problems in interpersonal relationships and sustained antisocial behaviors.

As can be seen, this model is quite consistent with the developmental patterns we have described. Genetics may determine difficult temperaments. Interaction between a child with a difficult temperament and a relatively unskilled parent may produce training for antisocial behavior. Antisocial behavior leads to rejection by peers, academic failure, and low self-esteem, which were reflected in the genotype-environment correlations discussed by Rushton et al. (1986). Subsequent problems in interpersonal relationships as well as the continued antisocial behavior may account for the longitudinal stability of aggression described by Olweus (1984), Block (1971), and Huesmann et al. (1984).

Anger and Aggression

So far we have been discussing developmental issues—processes involved in the development of aggressive personalities. Let us now turn to issues of dynamics—what we have defined as *mediation*. One such mediator is the emotion of anger. Anger has been traditionally defined as an energizing emotional response that is characterized by diffuse activation of the autonomic nervous system accompanied by facial and skeletal reactions. Anger is regarded as one of the drive states that lead to aggression (Buss, 1961).

In the past an intimate relationship has been assumed between anger, frustration, and aggression. It was said that frustration leads to (instigates) aggression. Several versions of this *frustration-aggression hypothesis* have been proposed. In these hypotheses, frustration refers to an interference or thwarting of goal-directed activity.

According to one theory, frustration produces anger, and it is the anger that creates a readiness for impulsive aggression (Berkowitz, 1962). During the 1960s Berkowitz argued that two factors were necessary for impulsive aggression to occur. Figure 17.1 illustrates this theory of aggression, in which both anger and aggressive cues are

FIGURE 17.1

Frustration, Anger, and Impulsive Aggression

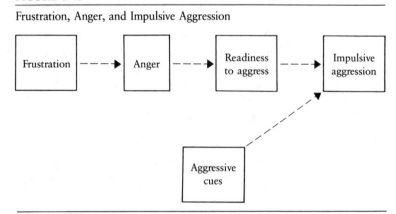

Adapted from Berkowitz (1962).

FIGURE 17.2

Aversive Events, Negative Emotions, and Impulsive Aggression

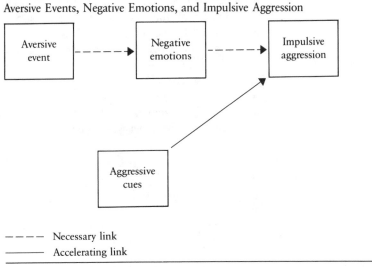

———— Necessary link
———— Accelerating link

Adapted from Berkowitz (1983), pp. 103-4.

necessary before impulsive aggression can occur. Imagine a husband and wife who are having an argument. They are both very angry (readiness to aggress). The husband glances at an open drawer containing a kitchen knife (aggressive cue). The knife generates ideas, images, and emotional responses associated with memories of aggression. The anger coupled with aggressive cues elicits the violent act (Berkowitz, 1978, 1983). Berkowitz refers to the concept of aggression resulting from the association between anger and aggressive cues as *neoassociative theory*.

Since 1969 Berkowitz has made two modifications to his neo-associative theory. First, frustration and anger are not necessary antecedents for impulsive aggression to take place. Any kind of aversive event (producing a negative emotion) can lead to impulsive aggression. Frustrations and insults may provoke aggression because they are unpleasant and thus generate negative affect. It is not the exact nature of the aversive event that is important, but how unpleasant it is. Second, aggressive cues, while powerful in producing impulsive aggression, are not now viewed as always necessary. If the negative emotional response is strong enough, aggression will occur in the absence of aggressive cues (Berkowitz, 1978, 1983). These changes to Berkowitz's theory are depicted in figure 17.2.

Two additional elaborations of Berkowitz's (1983) recent theory

are depicted in figure 17.3. First, he holds that it is not the objective
nature of the frustration, pain, or insult that is important in determining
the strength of the negative affect and instigation to aggress. The
subjective experience of the event is what is important. The perception
of a stimulus is a *construction* created by the behaving person. What
determines the aversiveness of an event is the meaning it has for the
person. A severe criticism given to a person with a confident and
positive self-image may have little effect. The same criticism to
someone with a damaged self-concept may be perceived as terribly
threatening and have devastating effects.

FIGURE 17.3

Aversive Events, Negative Emotions, Perception, Impulsive Aggression, and
Anger

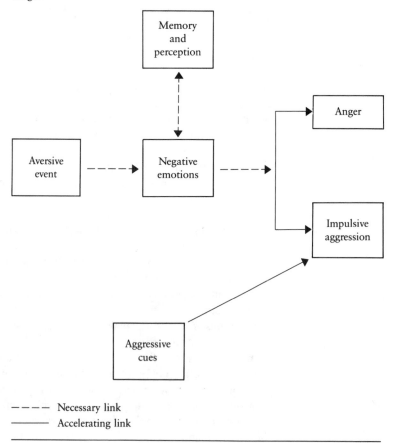

Adapted from Berkowitz (1983), pp. 103-34.

Anger was once thought to serve as a "necessary mediational link" between frustration and subsequent aggression. No longer. As we have seen, any kind of aversive event is believed to produce aggression. The importance of anger as a determinant of aggression is discounted for two other reasons. First, some people will respond to frustration, not with anger, but with feelings unrelated to aggression (Berkowitz, 1983). Some individuals may respond with self-deprecation (e.g., "I failed at this important event"), others with ingratiation (e.g., "How may I get you to like me?"). One is not likely to act out aggressively while engaging in self-deprecation or ingratiation. Further, the same individual may respond with anger at one time but at another time may be experiencing a mood incompatible with anger. The setting, recent thoughts, and other influences will affect the behaving person's response to an aversive event and may be incompatible with anger (Baron, 1983).

A second process that mitigates any "necessary link" between anger and aggression is that anger may be an end in itself and it may not necessarily be followed by aggressive behavior. Anger may act as a way of *communicating* to and influencing people (Averill, 1982; Tavris, 1982). Often gentle hints and persistent kindnesses go unheard by an irritating spouse or coworker. In those instances anger may be functional in reducing irritation from one's spouse or coworker. Anger in this sense is a conscious choice to use an emotional expression to obtain desired goals. We find it works and so are likely to use anger again; it is reinforced. We may use it with no intent to follow anger with aggression.

As depicted in figure 17.3, Berkowitz (1983) views anger as a "parallel process." Aversive conditions instigate aggression, and anger may or may not also occur. The exact relationship between anger and aggression is mediated by aggressive cues, the meaning the aversive event has for the behaving person, behavioral preferences that people bring with them to cope with aversive situations, and whether anger is a relatively automatic emotional response to an aversive event or purposely chosen to serve as an interpersonal influence attempt in its own right. According to this view anger may occur with aggression; however, there will be times when anger occurs without aggression and aggression occurs without anger.

Catharsis

The current view of anger has implications for a corollary of the frustration-aggression hypothesis. That corollary is catharsis: the assumption that giving *angry people* the opportunity to "act out" their aggression, to "blow off steam" in some safe, noninjurious manner will weaken their tendency to engage in overt acts of harmful aggression (Breuer & Freud, 1961). Dollard, Doob, Miller, Mowrer, and Sears (1939) proposed that covert behaviors such as aggressive fantasies, noninjurious behaviors such as pounding one's fist on the table, and indirect behaviors such as destroying an adversary's personal property were acts that would lower the instigation to subsequent aggression. Actually the concept of catharsis has two components. *Emotional catharsis* predicts that expressions of aggression will lead to a decrease in anger and its physiological components such as blood pressure. *Behavioral catharsis* hypothesizes that expressions of aggression will lead to a decrease in subsequent overt aggression (Baron, 1977; Quanty, 1976).

Emotional Catharsis

A number of studies have been conducted on emotional catharsis with varying results. Following cathartic-like situations some studies have found reductions in physiological responses; others have shown just the opposite effect, that is, increases in physiological arousal (Quanty, 1976). The catharsis concept was developed as part of the older view that there is a "necessary link" between anger and aggression. As we have seen, that position is no longer defensible. What other theoretical approach is available as an aid in making sense of these mixed results?

According to the *social learning* view (Bandura, 1973), learning experiences shape the way we think about situations. The reinforcement and modeling of our parents and peers, experience in combat sports like boxing, experience in military service, and other social experiences influence our judgments about when a peaceful response, an aggressive response, and retaliation are appropriate and will be approved by ourselves and others. Whether physiological tension decreases or remains elevated is determined by these *learning experiences and what one thinks* as well as what one does. In addition, thoughts that dwell on past provocations or anticipate future hostilities generate high states of arousal. Thoughts that divert one's attention or induce relaxation tend to decrease physiological arousal. Counting to ten after provocation takes advantage of this process by allowing time to calm down.

Emotional catharsis conceptualized as a "necessary link" between expressions of aggression and decreases in emotional arousal is no longer defensible, because the way we think about emotional experiences determines our physiological responses to those experiences. The same objective situation leads to increases in arousal one time but decreases in arousal another time because different thoughts were occurring (see Hokanson, Willers, & Koropsak, 1968; Quanty, 1976).

Behavioral Catharsis

It should come as no surprise that there are also problems with the notion of behavioral catharsis. In several reviews, Baron (1977, 1983) has shown that behavioral catharsis occurs only under highly specific circumstances and will not be observed in many other situations. The opportunity to aggress does not lead to a decrease in the probability of subsequent aggression if the aggressor is not angry. Even when angry, decreased aggression may occur only when angry individuals either witness harm occurring to persons who provoked them or cause harm to the persons who provoked them. In addition, the effects of behavioral catharsis, when they do occur, are usually short term in nature.

Decreased aggression does not occur when harm is caused to inanimate objects (e.g., pounding one's fist into a pillow) or persons who were not the source of frustration or anger. In fact, the opposite (an increase in aggression) is likely. Observing violence, participating in violence against inanimate objects, and engaging in verbal aggression or "sounding off" about one's anger often increase the probability of subsequent violence through such processes as imitation, practice, and justification of violence. There is considerable evidence favoring this social learning approach to catharsis (Bandura, 1973).

Another way to conceptualize catharsis and aggression is suggested by an elaboration of Berkowitz's (1983) neoassociative theory—the recent view that impulsive aggression is caused by aversive events. He applied Howard Leventhal's (1980) *perceptual-motor theory* of emotion to impulsive aggression. According to this analysis emotion is understood as a "subjective perceptual experience." When a person encounters an exciting event, he or she becomes aware, interprets, and responds to it through schematic memories. *Schemata* are cognitive structures that represent organized knowledge about concepts (Fiske & Taylor, 1984). Such schemata may be generalized from memories of times when a bully cornered us in the school yard and gave us a thorough thrashing or a teacher ridiculed us in front of our classmates. Memories of concrete events and episodes such as these are linked so that perceptions of new events are interpreted by this memory network. Our interpretation in turn determines our response to it. Whether or not behavior in a particular situation demonstrates a cathartic-like or

FIGURE 17.4

Cognitive Neo-Associative Theory

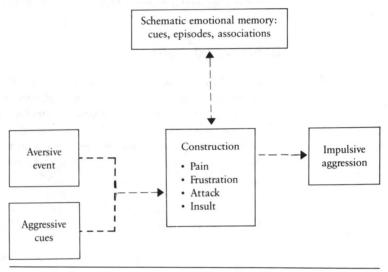

Adapted from Berkowitz (1984), pp. 410-27.

an aggression-facilitating effect depends upon which memories are dominant at the time or are more easily aroused by our awareness of the exciting event (see figure 17.4).

In summary, the concept of catharsis, emotional or behavioral, no longer seems serviceable. The "conceptual baggage" that implies a "necessary linkage" between anger and aggression is at considerable variance with present evidence and theory. Reductions in physiological arousal and decreases in aggression following angry retaliation are best understood as the result of thoughts, expectations, social learning, and schematic memory networks.

Aggressive Habits

As we saw when discussing Patterson's (1986) coercion theory, learning causes the development and pervasiveness of aggressive and antisocial behavior patterns. Learning has also been described as important in our understanding of frustration, anger, and catharsis. Such habits are important mediators of behavior and have been the source of much theory and research.

Bandura's social learning theory (1973) proposes that aggressive habits are learned in two somewhat different ways: (1) observation of aggressive models and (2) direct reinforcement of aggressive responses. Observing others behaving in an aggressive manner leads to the acquisition of novel and new aggressive behaviors; for example, the use of a knife as weapon where one previously had only thought of it as tool. The term observation is used globally to include reading about or hearing about violence as well as actually seeing it.

The strength of aggressive responses is also learned through direct reinforcement in aggressive interactions (e.g., Geen & Pigg, 1970). Reinforcement may take many forms including, for example, approval from peers, satisfaction at retaliating at the source of one's anger, and acquiring a desired possession. Learned aggressive responses may then generalize to other settings and other responses. For example, reinforced verbal aggression may generalize to increases in physical aggression as well as other verbal aggression. Furthermore, reinforcement doesn't have to be direct to have an effect. If one *expects* approval for engaging in aggression, such behavior is likely to increase. Expectations were tested by Borden (1975) by placing an observer in an aggression experiment with a subject. If the observer wore a jacket indicating membership in the university karate club, subjects were more aggressive than if the jacket showed membership in a world peace organization.

Social learning theory distinguishes between *performance* and *learning*. Once learned, aggressive behavior may remain *inhibited* because of fear of disapproval from important others or oneself. Through socialization we learn that it is inappropriate to harm an innocent person. However, observing others engaging in antisocial behavior has the effect of disinhibiting those behaviors. *Disinhibition* refers to removal of the restraints that we feel concerning the expression of taboo behaviors. By learning that others violate these restraints, the restraints in ourselves may be weakened (disinhibited). For example, Phillips (1983) reported that widely publicized heavyweight championship prize fights between 1973 and 1978 were typically followed by an increase in homicides throughout the United States. It was reasoned that publicizing these prize fights communicated the message that fighting might be acceptable under certain circumstances, thus removing restraints (disinhibition).

As depicted in figure 17.4, *cognitive neoassociative* theory (Berkowitz, 1984) emphasizes memory associations. Memory is regarded as a collection of networks of thoughts and feelings that are interconnected through associative pathways. This theory reconceptualizes disinhibition in terms of aggressive thoughts that have been *primed* via exposure to violent events such as championship prize fights. Priming occurs when a thought is brought into awareness and the thought activates associative pathways to other thoughts in memory. Theoretically, aggressive ideas suggested by prize fights, violent movies, vivid newspaper accounts of violence, and other compelling stimuli can prime semantically related thoughts.

It is furthermore believed that, once priming has occurred, the concept that has been activated has an increased likelihood of coming to mind again. It is as though there remains residual excitation at that memory location. The more thoughts of violence that are aroused, the greater is the priming of aggression.

According to these analyses, the likelihood that an aggressive act will be performed is the function of both that person's enduring learning history and contemporary contextual factors. Contemporary factors include such processes as disinhibition, priming of memory networks, and expectations for approval.

Rational Aggression

Many of the types of aggression discussed in this chapter contain elements of both impulsive and rational aggression. Some types of aggression seem to be mainly impulsive—for example, those involving neoassociative and cognitive neoassociative processes. Other types of aggression seem to be mainly rational. Recall that rational aggression was defined as reflective, rational, and self-regulated. Rational aggression components seem apparent in our discussions of Toch's violent men, Patterson's coercion model, and social learning theory.

Taylor (1986) and his colleagues have systematically investigated several processes that influence rational aggression. One of these processes is *social anxiety,* which refers to anticipation of criticism from others (Dengerink, 1976). Individuals high in social anxiety regulate their behavior in order to minimize the unpleasant state of social anxiety. Persons high in social anxiety are substantially less aggressive than those who are low in social anxiety, particularly at low to moderate levels of provocation (physical attack). One of the most potent causes of aggression is the perception that one has been physically attacked. In keeping with this general finding in aggression research, at high levels of physical attack there were no differences in the aggressiveness of high and low anxious persons (Dengerink, 1971).

Approval motivation refers to a dependency on the positive evaluation of others. Individuals high in need for approval are believed to possess a negative perception of themselves and seek positive evaluations from others in order to enhance their self-image (Crowne & Marlowe, 1964). Such individuals are unlikely to engage in strongly disapproved behaviors such as aggression. Instead they regulate their behavior to avoid aggression. Persons high in *need for approval* are significantly less aggressive than those who are low in need for approval. The differences between persons high and low in need for approval persisted through all levels of provocation tested (Taylor, 1970).

Other research has shown that *attribution of intent* is an important rational mediator of aggression. Under conditions of attack from an adversary, the victim's response is a higher level of aggression when the victim attributes intent to the attack than when the attack is viewed as unintentional (Dengerink, 1976).

Summary

Violence is all around us. Our newspapers, magazines, and television are replete with accounts of murder, rape, family violence, terrorism, and war. Something as pervasive as aggression may be caused by many factors. Indeed, it is the consensus among social scientists that aggression is multiply determined. Social psychological forces such as attack, peer pressure, and violence in the media are important determinants of aggressive behavior.

Many personality factors influence aggressive behavior as well. A few representative ones have been selected for discussion in this chapter. Personality was defined as concern with inferred mediating processes that account for organization in the behavior of the individual person.

Aggression was defined as behavior intended to harm or injure another person who is motivated to avoid injury. Distinctions such as hostile versus instrumental aggression and impulsive versus rational aggression are helpful in understanding motives, functions, and causes of aggression.

Aggressive patterns of behavior do persist in some individuals from childhood into adulthood. Many factors contribute to long-term stability of aggression. Two that were reviewed were inheritance of aggressive predispositions and learning within coercive family interactions.

Initially it was held that frustration produced anger, which invariably caused aggression. More recently any negative emotional response is thought to increase the likelihood of impulsive aggression. At the same time, though, the role of anger in aggression is seen as much more problematical. People respond to aversive events with many emotions other than anger. Furthermore, anger is often used as a rational strategy to influence others.

It has been widely believed in our culture that the opportunity to engage in indirect, symbolic aggression reduces the potential of subsequent overt harmful aggression. However, evidence provides no support for either emotional or behavioral catharsis. Instead, social learning and perceptual-motor theories of emotion appear to better account for the evidence. There is, for example, no necessary link between anger and aggression. Anger may occur with aggression. However, there will be times when anger occurs without aggression and aggression occurs without anger.

The strength of the instigation to aggress is a function of learning experiences through both observation of aggressive models and direct reinforcement of aggressive responses. Actual performance of learned aggressive behavior depends upon additional factors such as expectations, disinhibition, and priming.

Most aggression contains both impulsive and rational components. Impulsive components are particularly evident in our discussion of temperaments and neoassociative perspectives on anger, catharsis, and memories of violence. Rational components are evident in our discussions of Toch's violent men, Patterson's coercion model, Averill's constructivist view of anger, social learning theory, social anxiety, approval motivation, and attribution of intent.

SUGGESTED READINGS

Berkowitz, L. (1983). The experience of anger as a parallel process in the display of impulsive, "angry" aggression. In R. Geen & E. Donnerstein (Eds.), *Human aggression: Theoretical and empirical reviews* (Vol. 1, pp. 103–133). New York: Academic Press. This chapter provides an excellent review of impulsive aggression.

Bertilson, H. S. (1983). Methodology in the study of aggression. In R. Geen & E. Donnerstein (Eds.), *Human aggression: Theoretical and empirical reviews* (Vol. 1, pp. 213–245). New York: Academic Press. This chapter provides a comprehensive review of research methods and issues in the area of human aggression.

Patterson, G. R. (1984). Siblings: Fellow travelers in coercive family processes. In R. J. Blanchard & D. C. Blanchard (Eds.), *Advances in the study of aggression* (Vol. 1, pp. 173–215). New York: Academic Press. This chapter provides a description of coercive interactions of siblings and parents that lead to antisocial behavior in the aggressive child. It is based upon an impressive systematic program of research.

Tavris, C. (1982). *Anger: The misunderstood emotion.* New York: Simon & Schuster. This paperback presents a highly readable discussion of anger as a means of communication and influence.

Taylor, S. P. (1986). The regulation of aggressive behavior. In R. J. Blanchard & D. C. Blanchard (Eds.), *Advances in the study of aggression* (Vol. 2, pp. 91–119). New York: Academic Press. This chapter provides an excellent review of social and cognitive determinants of aggressive behavior.

Toch, H. (1984). *Violent men.* Cambridge: Schenkman. This paperback uses the case history method to develop hypotheses about habitually aggressive men.

REFERENCES

Averill, J. R. (1982). *Anger and aggression: An essay on emotion.* New York: Springer-Verlag.

Bandura, A. (1973). *Aggression: A social learning analysis.* Englewood Cliffs, NJ: Prentice-Hall.

Baron, R. A. (1977). *Human aggression.* New York: Plenum Press.

Baron, R. A. (1983). The control of human aggression: A strategy based on incompatible responses. In R. Geen & E. Donnerstein (Eds.), *Human aggression: Theoretical and empirical reviews* (Vol. 2, pp. 173–190). New York: Academic Press.

Berkowitz, L. (1962). *Aggression: A social psychological analysis.* New York: McGraw-Hill.

Berkowitz, L. (1978). Whatever happened to the frustration–aggression hypothesis? *American Behavioral Scientist, 21,* 691–708.

Berkowitz, L. (1983). The experience of anger as a parallel process in the display of impulsive "angry" aggression. In R. Geen & E. Donnerstein (Eds.), *Human aggression: theoretical and empirical reviews* (Vol. 1, pp. 103–134). New York: Academic Press.

Berkowitz, L. (1984). Some effects of thoughts on anti- and prosocial influences of media events: a cognitive-neoassociation analysis. *Psychological Bulletin, 95,* 410–427.

Bertilson, H. S. (1983). Methodology in the study of aggression. In R. Geen & E. Donnerstein (Eds.), *Human aggression: Theoretical and empirical reviews* (Vol. 1, pp. 213–246). New York: Academic Press.

Block, J. (1971). *Lives through time.* Berkeley, CA: Bancroft.

Borden, R. J. (1975). Witnessed aggression: Influence of an observer's sex and values on aggressive responding. *Journal of Personality and Social Psychology, 31,* 567–573.

Breuer, J., & Freud, S. (1961). *Studies in hysteria.* Boston: Beacon Press.

Buss, A. H. (1961). *The psychology of aggression.* New York: Wiley.

Buss, A. H., & Plomin, R. (1984). *Temperament: Early developing personality traits.* Hillsdale, NJ: Erlbaum.

Crowne, D. P., & Marlowe, D. A. (1964). *The approval motive.* New York: Wiley.

Dengerink, H. A. (1971). Anxiety, aggression and physiological arousal. *Journal of Experimental Research in Personality, 5,* 223–232.

Dengerink, H. A. (1976). Personality variables as mediators of attack-instigated aggression. In R. G. Geen and E. C. O'Neal (Eds.), *Perspectives on aggression* (pp. 61–98). New York: Academic Press.

Dollard, J., Doob, L., Miller, N., Mowrer, O., & Sears, R. (1939). *Frustration and aggression.* New Haven, CT: Yale University Press.

Fiske, S. T., & Taylor, S. E. (1984). *Social cognition.* Reading, MA: Addison-Wesley.

Geen, R. G., & Pigg, R. (1970). Acquisition of an aggressive response and its generalization to verbal behavior. *Journal of Personality and Social Psychology, 15,* 165–170.

Guilford, J. P. (1959). *Personality.* New York: McGraw-Hill.

Hathaway, S. R., & McKinley, J. C. (1951). *Minnesota Multiphasic Personality Inventory* (rev. ed.). New York: Psychological Corporation.

Hokanson, J. E., Willers, K. R., & Koropsak, E. (1968). The modification of autonomic responses during aggressive interchange. *Journal of Personality, 36,* 386–404.

Huesmann, L. R., Eron, L. D., Lefkowitz, M. M., & Walder, L. O. (1984). Stability of aggression over time and generations. *Developmental Psychology, 20,* 1120–1134.

Leventhal, H. (1980). Toward a comprehensive theory of emotion. In L. Berkowitz (Ed.), *Advances in experimental social psychology* (Vol. 13, pp. 140–208). New York: Academic Press.

Olweus, D. (1984). Development of stable aggressive reaction patterns in males. In R. J. Blanchard and D. C. Blanchard (Eds.), *Ad-*

vances in the study of aggression. (Vol. 1, pp. 103–138). New York: Academic Press.

Patterson, G. R. (1974). A basis for identifying stimuli which control behaviors in natural settings. *Child Development, 45,* 900–911.

Patterson, G. R. (1986). Performance models for antisocial boys. *American Psychologist, 41,* 432–444.

Phillips, D. (1983). The impact of mass media violence on U. S. homicides. *American Sociological Review, 48,* 560–568.

Quanty, M. B. (1976). Aggression catharsis: Experimental investigations. In R. G. Geen and E. C. O'Neal (Eds.), *Perspectives on aggression* (pp. 99–132). New York: Academic Press.

Rushton, J. P., Fulker, D. W., Neale, M. C., Nias, D. K. B., & Eysenck, H. J. (1986). Altruism and aggression: The heritability of individual differences. *Journal of Personality and Social Psychology, 50,* 1192–1198.

Shontz, E. C. (1965). *Research methods in personality.* New York: Appleton.

Tavris, C. (1982). *Anger: The misunderstood emotion.* New York: Simon & Schuster.

Taylor, S. P. (1970). Aggressive behavior as a function of approval motivation and physical attack. *Psychonomic Science, 18,* 195–196.

Taylor, S. P. (1986). The regulation of aggressive behavior. In R. J. Blanchard & D. C. Blanchard (Eds.), *Advances in the study of aggression* (Vol. 2, pp. 92–119). New York: Academic Press.

Toch, H. (1984). *Violent men.* Cambridge: Schenkman.

CHAPTER 18

Stress and Illness

CHARLES K. PROKOP

Introduction
Historical Overview
Definitions of Stress and Illness
Personality, Stress, and Illness
　Type A Behavior Pattern and
　　Hostility
　Approach and Avoidance
ACTIVITY BOX: Scale of College
　Stresses

　Optimism and Pessimism
Hardiness
Summary
SUGGESTED READINGS
REFERENCES

Introduction

The belief that stress increases the risk of illness has become a part of the commonsense knowledge of today's culture. Although there is some basis for this assumption, a little reflection reveals that there are many ambiguities and inconsistencies in the relationship between stress and illness. All of us know some friends or family members who became ill after experiencing some psychologically distressing event, yet we also know others who seem to tolerate high levels of stress without becoming ill. Why is it that some persons seem resistant to illness in the face of stress, whereas others become ill with relatively low levels of stress? Indeed, the more thought we give to questions about stress and illness, the less clear the relationship between the two is likely to be. Do all persons experience similar levels of stress when faced with the same events, or are there differences in how various persons react to presumably stressful events? Although stress is typically thought of as a reaction to negative events, pleasant or positive events may also lead to stress. A promotion and raise in pay at work may be quite desirable. However, the adjustments to the new job and changes in lifestyle the increased salary allows may be stressful. Is stress an environmental event, such as marriage or job pressures, or may stress be better defined by how an individual reacts to events? Some psychological reactions to life events, such as anxiety and depression, often include physical symptoms such as tension headache and sleep disorders. If a person is anxious about the security of his or her job and develops tension headaches, should this be considered as evidence for an association between stress and illness or is it merely a reflection of the fact that increased arousal is a common feature of anxiety and this arousal may include increased muscle tension?

A great deal of psychological research has been devoted to studying the stress-illness relationship, and the results of the investigations have varied depending upon the answers given to questions such as the ones just noted. This chapter examines the evidence accumulated to date regarding the relationship between stress and physical illness, with emphasis on the personality factors suggested to be important in determining whether or not a person is likely to experience illness in reaction to stress. Particular attention is given to the personality dimension of hardiness. Persons high in hardiness believe that life has purpose, feel a sense of control over events, and view change as an opportunity for personal growth. Hardiness has been proposed as one of the major personality resources that may reduce the probability of illness in response to stress.

Historical Overview

The suggestion that personality may be an important determiner of physical symptoms that develop as a person attempts to cope with life events has exerted a significant force on psychological and psychiatric thinking during the twentieth century. Sigmund Freud was trained as a physician, and his experience treating patients suffering from physical disorders with little or no apparent physical cause played a major role in the development of psychoanalytic theory. Freud's experiences with these patients led him to the conclusion that persons who tended to deal with threatening psychological material by repressing emotional reactions or denying the presence of emotional disturbance were at risk for the development of physical symptoms (Freud, 1905/1953). Repressed psychological distress, particularly distress related to sexuality, appeared in the form of physical symptoms through the defense mechanism of conversion.

According to Freud, conversion operates by converting psychological distress into a physical symptom, and the symptom provides a clue to the nature of the psychological conflict. For example, a person might become blind after witnessing a traumatic event such as a serious accident in which his or her loved ones died. By becoming blind, the person indirectly expresses the distress the accident caused, as if he or she were saying "I cannot bear to see if I must see people die." At the same time, the blindness allows the person to avoid psychological distress about death, as the focus of attention shifts away from feelings about the accident and the loss of loved ones to feelings about blindness and efforts to cure it. An individual not prone to relying on repression and denial might witness the same accident and experience psychological consequences such as depression, but not develop physical symptoms. Instead, the sources of the distress—the sudden loss of loved ones and thoughts about the accident and death—would be directly expressed in the depression.

Psychoanalytic theorists after Freud remained interested in the relationship between personality and illness. Their interests converged in the field of psychosomatic medicine. Psychosomatic disorders differ from conversion disorders in that a psychosomatic disorder is the result of the normal physiological changes occurring with emotions. For example, increased blood pressure is a normal correlate of anger, and if a person frequently experienced excessive and inhibited anger, high blood pressure might develop (Alexander, 1939/1948). Psychosomatic disorders are therefore not symbolic expressions of emotional states, but instead are related to the consistent experience of a particular emotion and its biological consequences.

Specific diseases were thought to be associated with specific personality styles. If a child feared separation from her or his mother, asthma might develop. The choking and gasping characteristic of asthmatic attacks was interpreted as a repressed cry for mother's attention, as the asthmatic was choking back urges to cry out. Alexander and French (1948) presented discussions of a wide variety of diseases thought to be psychosomatic in origin, including disorders as diverse as peptic ulcer, bronchial asthma, essential hypertension (high blood pressure), and diabetes. A particular type of psychological conflict was suggested for each of these disorders, and whenever environmental events occurred that triggered these conflicts, the symptoms of the illness were expected to appear as the emotional reactions to the events stimulated biological changes leading to the symptoms. Personality structure thus determined which events were likely to be experienced as stressful and also determined the nature of the physiological arousal to be expected under stress.

Evidence gradually accumulated suggesting that such specific relationships between personality structure and the development of illness were the exception rather than the rule. For example, it is doubtful that psychological influences may cause the physiological symptoms of asthma and it has been argued that asthma should not be considered as a psychosomatic disease. Personality differences between asthmatics and persons without asthma are more likely to be effects of suffering from a chronic disease rather than the causes of asthma (Alexander, 1981). Similarly, it has been found that only one-third to one-half of ulcer patients secrete high levels of gastric acid (Weiner, 1977); psychosomatic theory suggested that ulcer patients had high levels of gastric acid secretion in reaction to psychological conflicts regarding dependence upon others. Diabetes was also suggested to be related to frustrated wishes for dependence (Meyer, Bollmeier, & Alexander, 1945), but it is now recognized that psychological difficulties are much more likely to be a consequence rather than a cause of diabetes (Ezrin, 1977). As will be discussed later in this chapter, the relationship between hypertension and anger is probably the best supported of the psychosomatic hypotheses. High blood pressure is a risk factor for heart disease, and hostility and anger have been found to be related to the development of heart disease (Barefoot, Dahlstrom, & Williams, 1983). On balance, it appears that the relationship between personality and illness is not as specific or direct as early psychosomatic theory suggested.

As the search for specific personality factors related to specific diseases declined, attention turned toward a more generalized conception of stress as a precursor of illness. Current conceptualizations of conversion disorders do not emphasize the converting of psychological conflict into physical symptoms, but instead stress the fact that the physical symptoms allow a person to escape a stressful situation without having to acknowledge responsibility for doing so (Carson, Butcher, & Coleman, 1988). Research into the stress-illness relationship has been complicated by several factors, including such basic issues as how stress should be defined and how illness should be measured.

Definitions of Stress and Illness

Stress has been defined in a variety of ways, dependent upon whether the focus is on the stressor (the environmental event to which an organism is attempting to adapt), or upon the responses of the organism as it combats the stressor. Each approach has its own advantages and disadvantages, its own assets and limitations.

Hans Selye (Selye, 1982) has done more than any other single researcher to bring the concept of stress out of the world of casual speculation into the realm of scientific study. During Selye's medical training he became interested in the similarities between patients suffering different diseases. All patients showed symptoms such as loss of appetite and weight, lowered muscle strength, and absence of ambition. In later experimental work Selye noted consistent physical changes that occurred whenever the body was attempting to deal with attacks from toxic substances, infection, trauma, heat and cold, and other stimuli.

These physical changes were identified by Selye as the General Adaptation Syndrome (GAS), a three-stage process representing the attempts of the body to cope with the demands of adjusting to change. In the alarm stage of the GAS the body mobilizes its resources to combat the stressor. The outer layer, or cortex, of the adrenal glands enlarge and become hyperactive, the thymus and lymph nodes shrink, and bleeding ulcers may appear in the stomach and upper intestines. If the stressor continues to assault the body and the organism survives, the body enters the second, or resistance, stage of the GAS. During resistance physiological reactions stabilize as the body attempts to adapt to the stressor.

The resistance stage is in many ways the opposite of the alarm stage. The adrenal cortex shrinks and lymph nodes return to normal size. However, the organism is also more sensitive to stressors as physiological arousal remains high. If this high level of arousal continues, bodily resources are eventually depleted and the exhaustion stage of the GAS is entered. The organism becomes fatigued and less able to deal with stressors. All of us cycle through the alarm and resistance stages repeatedly throughout life as we attempt to deal with commonly encountered stressors. However, the exhaustion phase is entered only when stressors are unremitting, uncontrollable, and/or extremely intense.

The GAS illustrates a definition of stress that focuses on the organism's responses to stressors rather than upon the stressors themselves. Selye defined stress as "the *nonspecific* [that is, common] *result of any demand on the body*, be the effect mental or somatic" (Selye, 1982, p. 7, italics in original). The demand to which the body is attempting to adapt may be positive or negative, it may be a promotion at work or the death of a family member. The important element is that the event demands change, and the result of the demand may be seen in the body's physiological responses. This type of definition has some advantages, particularly in that it offers a clear sign of the presence of stress. If the biological events characteristic of the GAS are present, stress is present. However, a definition of stress such as Selye's also suffers from the practical limitation that large-scale research studies into the relationship between stress and disease may be hampered by the need to document the physiological reactions of each subject to determine the presence or absence of stress. One method of dealing with this problem has been to define stress by the presence or absence of events that require change in lifestyle and thus would be expected to stress most people.

The best-known and most influential study of stress as defined by the presence or absence of stressors was conducted in 1967 by Holmes and Rahe. These investigators studied the medical records and life event reports of over five thousand hospital patients and determined that certain life events often coincided with the development of illness.

These events were collected into the Social Readjustment Rating Scale (SRRS) (Holmes & Rahe, 1967). This questionnaire includes forty-three events such as the death of a spouse, marriage, work changes, beginning or ending school, and vacations. A subject is asked to indicate which events have occurred to him or her during a specified period of time, usually six to twenty-four months. Each event is weighted according to the amount of life change it is expected to require, so the death of a spouse receives 100 points whereas a vacation receives only 13 points. The final stress score is determined by totaling the weights of the events a subject has experienced in the specified time period. The higher an individual scores on the SRRS, the more at risk he or she should be for the development of illness.

The Social Readjustment Rating Scale and similar instruments measuring life events simplify the study of stress, and a great many studies have been conducted investigating the relationship between presumably stressful life events and illness. The results of these studies consistently point to the conclusion that there is a relationship between the experience of stressful life events and illnesses as diverse as tuberculosis, heart disease, cancer, depression, and schizophrenia (Perkins, 1982). Correlations between reports of stressful life events and illness are typically in the .2 to .3 range, suggesting a reliable but not exceptionally powerful correspondence between stress and illness. However, the validity of assessing stress by accumulating life events has been questioned, as has the existence of a true relationship between life events and illness.

Some criticisms have been directed at the nature of the events surveyed by the Social Readjustment Rating Scale. Some of the events, such as changes in sleeping or eating habits and sexual difficulties, may occur in response to illness. In fact, personal injury or illness is one of the items on the SRRS. For this reason, some of the apparent association between life change and illness may be due to the fact that preexisting illness may elevate life change scores, so that life change may be a consequence rather than a cause of illness. It is therefore important to eliminate stressful events that may be a result of illness in research projects attempting to demonstrate that stress may lead to illness. Recent studies that have relied only on non-illness-related life events have reported that a correlation does exist between stressful events and illness (Maddi, Bartone, & Puccetti, 1987; Schroeder & Costa, 1984).

Another criticism that has been advanced is that the illness reports typically used in stress research are based on the memories of the subjects in the study. For example, subjects may be asked to complete a life stress inventory for the past year, and then indicate the illnesses that they have suffered during the same year. These retrospective accounts may be subject to several types of bias. Subjects may not recall illnesses accurately, or they may be prone to reinterpreting the past year as stressful in an effort to explain to themselves why they became ill. The first bias may be dealt with by using more objective indicators of illness, such as physician diagnoses, hospitalization, work days missed, or death. Physician diagnoses have been used relatively little because of the difficulty involved in obtaining such data. However, Kobasa, Maddi, and Courington (1981) compared physician diagnoses to self-reports of illness and found 89 percent agreement between the two sources of data. It thus appears that self-report may not be a perfect indicator of illness, but it does generally agree with physician diagnosis and also may allow for reports of illnesses that the subjects did not feel were serious enough to demand medical care, such as headaches, colds, or influenza.

The second bias may be reduced by using a prospective research design, in which reports of stress are gathered at the beginning of a study and the health status of the subjects is then followed for a period of time to see who becomes ill and who does not. Reports of stress levels are thus less likely to be influenced by illness or by a tendency to over-report stress to justify illness. A prospective study of navy seamen found physician reports of illness to correlate only .12 with stressful events prior to a six-month tour of sea duty (Rahe, 1974). Two other prospective studies have reported no significant association between stressful life events and the objective illness criteria of death, hospitalization, and time missed from work (Goldberg & Comstock, 1976; Theorell, Lind, & Floderus, 1975). The lack of associations between stress and illness found in these studies may be related to the fact that although the illness measures used are indeed objective, they also are insensitive. Many illnesses do not require a physician visit, time off work, or hospitalization, and death is clearly the result of only the most serious illnesses or accidents. Other prospective studies have demonstrated the presence of a relationship between stressful life events and illness when self-report measures have been used (Maddi et al., 1987).

The assessment of stress by life event reporting has also been criticized because it contains the assumption that certain events are stressful to all people and that the degree of stress each event involves is relatively consistent across persons. People may vary greatly in the degree of subjective stress they experience when confronted with life changes, and it may be as important or more important to determine how an individual interprets an event and reacts to it as to note that the event has occurred. This has led to a call to define stress by referring to both the individual involved and the environmental events with which the person is attempting to cope. Stress is thus experienced when environmental or internal demands are judged to tax or exceed the individual's coping resources (Holroyd & Lazarus, 1982). This definition of stress invokes the need to consider personality structure in studies of stress and illness, as personality may be a major determinant of when a person perceives that the environment is placing demands upon him or her and when he or she believes coping resources are exceeded or taxed.

The relatively low correlations commonly found between stress and illness in combination with the increasingly recognized need to consider individual differences in when persons experience stress have generated a significant body of research examining the impact of personality factors on the stress-illness relationship. Despite continuing debate (Maddi et al., 1987; Schroeder & Costa, 1984) most studies are retrospective and rely upon life event reports and self-reports of illness. In many ways, current research into the relationships between personality, stress, and illness may be seen as attempts to refine and integrate the environmental focus of life event research and the focus on the individual represented by the psychosomatic model. The following section surveys the problems and promises of current psychological investigations of this complex area.

Personality, Stress, and Illness

Type A Behavior Pattern and Hostility

The best-known personality/behavior style associated with illness is the Type A Behavior Pattern (TABP). The TABP concept developed out of the work of Friedman and Rosenman, two cardiologists who became interested in the possibility that emotional reactions to the stresses of modern life might be related to the increase in the incidence of coronary heart disease (CHD) during the twentieth century. In particular, Friedman and Rosenman wondered if the rapid pace of modern life may be an important factor in the development of CHD.

Friedman and Rosenman had noted that their CHD patients consistently showed higher cholesterol levels than did their patients without CHD, yet the differences in cholesterol levels could not be accounted for by dietary differences. In order to test the hypothesis that a sense of time urgency affects cholesterol levels, the team tested the cholesterol levels and blood clotting time of a group of tax accountants every two weeks for five months. The accountants were also questioned as to the sense of time urgency they felt. Cholesterol levels rose and blood clotting time decreased in association with a sense of time urgency (Friedman & Rosenman, 1959).

Their own observations and similar results in other studies led

Friedman and Rosenman to suggest that a particular behavioral style might be important in the development of CHD. They labeled this behavioral pattern the TABP, and described TABP as involving six primary features: (1) a pervasive drive to reach usually poorly defined goals, (2) a powerful desire to compete, (3) an enduring need for recognition and advancement, (4) constant involvement in varied tasks involving deadlines and time pressure, (5) an enduring tendency to speed up mental and physical tasks, and (6) high levels of mental and physical alertness. All of these behaviors combine to create "an enhanced performance designed to assert and maintain control over the environment when this control is challenged or threatened" (Rosenman, 1986, p. 23).

TABP is most accurately assessed by means of the Structured Interview (SI) (Rosenman, 1978). The SI is a ten- to fifteen-minute interview with a specific set of carefully worded questions with challenging follow-ups. For example, after asking whether or not the interviewee would be likely to show up for a date on time, the interviewer asks if the interviewee's answer is always or never true, if he or she resents being kept waiting and says something about it after being kept waiting, and why the interviewee would or would not say anything. The interviewer also interrupts the interviewee and in one question speaks very slowly in an effort to elicit impatience. The intent of the SI is to create a challenging interview situation that will elicit Type A behavior if it is present in the subject. In order to maintain this atmosphere, the interviewer's style is "coldly professional," although it has also been described as hostile, confrontive, or businesslike (Chesney, Eagleston, & Rosenman, 1981). The Structured Interview is scored as much or more for how the interviewee behaves during the interview as for the content of the answers to the questions. Impatience, hostility, competitiveness, and explosive, emphatic, and rapid speech are particularly noted.

Several paper and pencil self-report measures of Type A Behavior Pattern have also been developed. The most frequently used questionnaire is the Jenkins Activity Survey (JAS), developed by constructing test items that reflect the content of the SI and clinical experience with CHD patients (Jenkins, Rosenman, & Friedman, 1967). The JAS divides Type A behavior into three components: job involvement, speed and impatience, and hard-driving tendencies. However, many Type As are not aware of their Type A tendencies (Rosenman, 1986). The Structured Interview thus appears to be the most accurate method of assessing TABP (Chesney et al., 1981).

Although not all studies have found TABP to be a predictor of CHD, many more investigations have documented the presence of a significant relationship between the two (Chesney et al., 1981; Dembroski & Costa, 1987; Rosenman, 1986). The area is quite difficult to investigate, and the contradictory results of different studies are probably due to variations in how TABP has been measured, difficulties in a uniform definition of CHD, the frequent lack of healthy control subjects, and the fact that the samples used in different studies are strongly influenced by uncontrollable fluctuations in the characteristics of CHD patients who may be available for study at any particular time (Chesney et al., 1981; Dembroski & Costa, 1987; MacDougall, Dembroski, Dimsdale, & Hackett, 1985). In addition, psychological states such as depression have been found to be related to CHD (Booth-Kewley & Friedman, 1987), so a perfect TABP-CHD relationship should not be expected.

Recent research has attempted to identify the "toxic" factor in TABP. It may be that some components of TABP are more important than others in the development of heart disease, and the prediction of CHD could be improved if these important components were isolated. The leading contender for the toxic factor in Type A behavior is hostility/anger. Williams et al. (1980) reported that hostility was a better predictor of the presence of blocked coronary arteries in patients with the symptoms of CHD than was TABP, and Barefoot, Dahlstrom, and Williams (1983) found that hostility predicted which medical students were likely to develop heart disease during a twenty-five-year follow-up period. Potential for Hostility and Anger-in, the tendency to keep angry feelings to oneself, have also been found to be significantly associated with the number of blocked coronary arteries in heart disease patients (MacDougall et al., 1985).

These results are particularly impressive because different methods for assessing hostility and anger were used in the studies. Williams et al. (1980) and Barefoot et al. (1983) measured hostility with a paper and pencil measure, the Hostility Scale of Cook and Medley (1954). This scale contains few items that ask directly about the expression of hostility and anger, but instead provides an indicator of a cynical and mistrustful attitude toward others (Costa, Zonderman, McCrae, & Williams, 1986). MacDougall et al. (1985) measured Potential for Hostility and Anger-in from the Structured Interview responses of their subjects. Potential for Hostility was reflected in responses indicative of hostile responses to frustration, such as reports of blowing a car's horn whenever other drivers are going too slow, the use of obscenity during the interview, and the presence of rudeness, argumentativeness, and arrogance. Anger-in was assessed by the presence of reports of holding anger in and not letting other people know about feelings of anger.

In summary, Type A behavior, particularly as assessed by the SI, does seem to be a contributor to the development of heart disease. However, it does not appear that all aspects of TABP are risk factors for

CHD. Instead, the consistent presence of hostility and suppressed anger increases the risk for heart disease, probably because of the high level of arousal associated with always living as if one is on guard and defending oneself against hostile or incompetent others. Indeed, this sense of needing to protect oneself is consistent with Rosenman's view of TABP as a response to maintain control in the face of a threatening environment. The Type A individual appears to create an unremittingly stressful environment by approaching his or her world as an enemy to be dealt with rather than as an ally to be collaborated with.

Approach and Avoidance

Type A behavior appears to be a personality style that creates the perception of a stressful environment. The stress-illness relationship may also be affected by how a person copes with stressful events. For example, an individual may attempt to cope with stress by approaching or avoiding the perceived stressor. Consider the case of a deteriorating marriage or other long-term relationship. The partners may try to work out their problems by talking to one another or seeking couples therapy, or they may avoid topics of conversation and activities that they have learned may lead to conflict. In the first case they are approaching the problem by confronting the stressor in an effort to change the interpersonal environment, whereas in the second they are avoiding the problem and withdrawing from the conflict. As Roth and Cohen (1986) have noted, the relative advantages of approach and avoidance for coping with stress have been studied at least since the early twentieth century. Freud's description of repression and denial in conversion disorders illustrates avoidance mechanisms, as focusing on physical symptoms provides a means of avoiding the true source of the stress: psychological conflict.

The Activity Box presents some examples of approach and avoidance solutions for two stresses that may be encountered at college. Read each of the situation descriptions and evaluate your own likelihood of using all of the coping solutions listed under each situation. After completing the exercise, look at the key at the bottom. The key indicates which items are approach responses, in which you attempt to change the situation by engaging in an interaction with the problem, and which items are avoidance or withdrawal responses. If you wish, you may separately sum your engagement item ratings and your withdrawal item ratings to get an indication of your engagement and withdrawal tendencies in response to the two events. These two situations by no means allow you to evaluate your general tendency to use approach or avoidance because of the limited range of events the situations represent. However, they should give you a better idea of the difference between engagement and withdrawal responses.

The use of approach or avoidance responses has been found to be related to illness complaints in responses to stress. Collins, Baum, and Singer (1983) studied persons living near the nuclear plant at Three Mile Island. There was a major accident at this nuclear plant in Pennsylvania, followed by a long period of uncertainty regarding how much radiation, if any, had escaped and how damaging the consequences of any escaped radiation might be. Collins et al. studied residents in the Three Mile Island area for two years following the accident to determine what effects the chronic stress of living with this uncertainty might have, and if differences in health status might be related to how residents coped with the event.

Residents who avoided thinking about the event by relying upon denial reported more physical complaints two years after the accident than did residents not using denial. Correspondingly, residents using reappraisal to cope with the event reported fewer physical symptoms than did residents not using reappraisal. Reappraisal is a coping strategy in which a person engages with a stressor by considering the event and attempting to reevaluate it in a way that allows it to be more manageable and thus less stressful. A Three Mile Island resident using denial might tell himself or herself that nothing serious really happened and avoid reading the newspaper or listening to televised news reports about the possibility of escaped radiation. A resident using reappraisal might seek out information so as to evaluate the risk of any escaped radiation and make a decision as to what, if anything, he or she might do to reduce personal risk. The use of reappraisal was also associated with lower levels of norepinephrine in urine samples; a high level of urinary norepinephrine is a biological sign of a high level of physiological arousal.

The relative advantages of approach and avoidance may be determined by the duration of a stressor. Approach may be more appropriate for longer lasting stressors than for brief, time-limited stressors (Collins et al., 1983). The Three Mile Island accident is an excellent example of a continuing stressor, as uncertainty and potential effects of the accident may continue for years after the accident itself. Briefer stressors may be dealt with adequately through denial. Wilson (1981) studied patients recovering from the brief stress of surgery and found that patients using denial recovered more quickly and required less pain medication than did patients who did not use denial. A patient using denial would be likely to tell himself or herself that the surgery is not a serious medical problem and might thus ignore many physical sensations because they would be interpreted as normal reactions to surgery. A patient not using denial would be more likely to attend closely to physical sensations and interpret them as possible signs of surgical complications. The longer a stress lasts, the more likely it becomes that denial will become more and more difficult, and the less useful denial is likely to become.

ACTIVITY BOX

Scale of College Stresses

Two stressful situations college students may experience are described below. After each situation several possible ways of handling the situation are listed. Read each situation carefully and imagine yourself in it, including how you would feel, what you would think, and what you would be likely to do. If you have experienced the situation, recall how you handled it.

Rate each possible way of handling the situation according to the likelihood that you would actually choose that way of behaving. Rate all of the ways of coping that are listed; people often cope with stress in more than one way. There are no right or wrong answers. Put down what *you* would be most likely to do.

Use the following scale to rate your likelihood of using each way of coping:

1 = Very unlikely I would behave that way
2 = Unlikely I would behave that way
3 = Just as likely as unlikely I would behave that way; about 50-50
4 = Likely I would behave that way
5 = Very likely I would behave that way

Write the appropriate rating in the blank next to the item number for each possible way of coping.

SITUATION ONE

You are talking to family members or close friends about how things are going at school. They don't seem to be listening to you or to be understanding how you feel and what you are trying to let them know. You would:

Optimism and Pessimism

Whether a person approaches or avoids a stressor may be related to the outcome she or he expects to result from the confrontation. The belief that things will work out for the best, or optimism, has been suggested to be an important factor in health and happiness for decades (e.g.,

---

    ____ 1. Stop talking.

    ____ 2. Tell them you feel they aren't listening.

    ____ 3. Tell them what you think they want to hear, even if it isn't really how you feel.

    ____ 4. Change the subject.

    ____ 5. Repeat what you are saying more forcefully and emotionally.

    ____ 6. Try to impress on them that you feel it is important for them to understand what is happening at school.

SITUATION TWO

You are taking a course you are interested in, but the course is not required for graduation. Class participation is a large part of the grade. The instructor unexpectedly calls on students to answer questions, seems to you to humiliate students when they don't know the answers, and grades participation in a way that seems unfair to you. You would:

    ____ 7. Talk to the instructor about your concerns about the course.

    ____ 8. Study extra hard so you're ready for questions in class.

    ____ 9. Complain to your friends about the class.

    ____ 10. Go to class only on exam days.

    ____ 11. Talk to the other students in the class and see if they will go with you and talk to the instructor as a group.

    ____ 12. Drop the course.

Key

Engagement items: 2, 5, 6, 7, 8, and 11
Withdrawal items: 1, 3, 4, 9, 10, and 12

Peale, 1956). This belief has been based more on impressionistic and inspirational literature than upon scientific data, but recent research has confirmed that this popular idea may have some merit. More important, the mechanisms associating optimism and pessimism with health and illness are beginning to be clarified.

Scheier and Carver (1985) studied college students during the final four weeks of a semester, a period that all readers of this chapter probably view as stressful. Optimism was measured by administering the Life Orientation Test (Scheier & Carver, 1985), and subjects indicated to what degree they had been bothered by thirty-nine physical symptoms during the preceding two weeks. Both the Life Orientation Test and the symptom checklist were administered at the beginning and end of the final four weeks of the semester. Optimism was associated with lower levels of physical symptoms at both administrations. In addition, higher levels of optimism at the beginning of the study predicted the presence of fewer symptoms at the conclusion of the study even when the level of symptoms at the start of the study was taken into account. That is, the association between good health and optimism was not due to the possibility that poor health reduces optimism and simultaneously increases symptoms. Optimism was an independent predictor of good health.

Other studies have reported similar results. Optimists have been found to show better recovery from coronary bypass surgery and optimism has been found to be more important than hostility in predicting physical symptoms in undergraduates (Scheier & Carver, 1987). A pessimistic style of explaining why bad events occur has been found to increase the risk of infectious illness over a one-year period. Pessimism was defined as explaining bad events as being due to stable and global causes, causes that are likely to occur again in the future and that affect more than one area of life (Peterson & Seligman, 1987).

One of the more interesting examinations of the effect of pessimism on health examined newspaper quotes from members of the Baseball Hall of Fame (Peterson & Seligman, 1987). Newspaper interviews between 1900 and 1950 were examined for how players explained good and bad events, such as winning and losing games. Players who explained losses as due to internal, stable, and global causes ("I just can't get motivated to practice batting the way I know I need to, and it shows in my playing") lived shorter lives than players who attributed losses to external, unstable, and specific causes ("The other team was just lucky yesterday.") When wins were explained as due to external, unstable, and specific causes, such as "We hit all those home runs because of that high wind blowing to center field, and we can't expect that to be true every game," players lived shorter lives.

Optimism and pessimism appear to affect health status by means of the different ways optimists and pessimists cope with stressful and challenging events. Scheier, Weintraub, and Carver (1986) administered the Life Orientation Test to a group of college students, and asked them to describe their probable responses to five hypothetical stressful situations similar to those presented in the Activity Box. Optimists tended to respond by confronting the situation and reinterpreting the event in a positive light so as to make it seem less stressful. Pessimists were more likely to withdraw from the situation and to express their feelings. Optimists may thus remain more healthy in the presence of stress because they are more likely to engage with the stressor and try to solve or reinterpret the problem. Pessimists are more likely to withdraw and thereby reduce the probability of problem solution. Thus, an optimist at Three Mile Island might be more likely to use reappraisal and remain healthy, whereas a pessimist may use denial and increase the risk of illness.

Hardiness

A significant body of research during the past decade has focused on the personality disposition of hardiness as a moderator of the effects of stressful life events on illness. The research involving hardiness will be described in detail because it illustrates how many of the problems that arise in studying personality, stress, and illness may be dealt with in a series of research projects extending over several years. A hypothesis originally tested in one sample of subjects is evaluated multiple times in samples differing on important variables, such as sex, age, and occupation. Some studies investigate illnesses occurring during a brief period, such as several months, while other studies look at illnesses over a span of several years. Some investigators may use a retrospective design, in which subjects are asked to recall stressful events and illnesses in the past. Others may use a prospective design, in which personality and stress are measured at the beginning of the study and illness is measured at a later date. The collective results of all the studies allow for more certain statements about the relationships between personality, stress, and illness, and they frequently lead to some refinements and changes in the understanding of the personality disposition under study. The investigations of hardiness in the review that follows provide an excellent illustration of the steps in such a research program.

Much of the hardiness research has been conducted by Suzanne Kobasa and her colleagues. Kobasa (1979) originally described hardiness as a multifaceted concept involving three characteristics: (1) commitment, or a clear sense of purpose, involvement with others, and the ability to recognize personal values, goals, and priorities; (2) control, or the ability to choose among courses of action, incorporate events into an ongoing life plan, and feel motivated to achieve; and (3) challenge, or a feeling that change is a positive experience, an opportunity to integrate life goals into new situations. Kobasa's initial study will be described in detail because it is the base upon which most later studies of hardiness were built.

Kobasa (1979) studied a group of 161 male middle and upper level executives at a large public utility company. The 161 executives were selected from an initial pool of 837 because of their levels of stress and illness during the preceding three years. Seventy-five reported high levels of stress and high levels of illness, while 86 reported high levels of stress and low levels of illness. A subject was classified as experiencing high levels of stress if he scored above the median (in the top half) of the entire sample of 837 subjects on a modified version of the Social Readjustment Rating Scale. High illness subjects scored above the median on a modified version of the Seriousness of Illness Rating Scale (Wyler, Masuda, & Holmes, 1968). This questionnaire contains a list of 126 illnesses ranked according to seriousness. Each illness receives a seriousness score, with more serious illnesses receiving higher scores. Low illness subjects scored below the median on the Seriousness of Illness Rating Scale. The subjects selected for study had experienced sufficient stress during the three-year period to have an 80 percent likelihood of developing a serious illness in the near future, and had experienced a moderate level of illness during that time, equivalent to the development of a peptic ulcer or high blood pressure.

The subjects were mailed personality questionnaires within three months after completing the stress and illness surveys. Hardiness was measured with six standardized psychological tests, and subjects provided information on how stressful they thought seven aspects of their lives were, including such areas as work, finances, family, and interpersonal relationships. After the questionnaires were returned, each group was subdivided into two equal samples. The first sample (the test subjects) was used to test the hypothesis that hardiness might moderate the effect of stress on illness. The second sample was used to confirm, or cross-validate, the results derived from the first sample.

The personality test scores of the test subjects were analyzed by a discriminant function procedure. Discriminant function analysis determines the variables that differentiate between groups of subjects, and it provides an indication of which variables are most important in the differentiation. For example, if the height, weight, and age of a group of jockeys and a group of professional basketball players were entered into a discriminant function analysis, height and weight would likely emerge as significant discriminators between the groups. Age would be less likely to emerge as a significant discriminator.

The high stress/low illness test subjects could be discriminated from the high stress/high illness test subjects by their scores on the hardiness questionnaire. Low illness subjects scored higher on commitment, control, and challenge than did high illness subjects. They were particularly more committed to self, more vigorous in their approach to life, found life to be more meaningful, and had a more internal locus of control. Persons with an internal locus of control believe that personal efforts are strongly related to reinforcements (Rotter, 1966). More information on locus of control may be found in chapter 11. Low illness subjects also found their personal life to be less stressful than did high illness subjects. A similar pattern of results was found in the second sample of subjects, indicating that the differences found in the test subjects were unlikely to be due to chance factors.

Based on these results, Kobasa (1979) suggested that hardiness might act to reduce the risk of illness in response to stress. Hardy executives would be more likely to approach change with a clear sense of personal values and capabilities and become actively involved with the environmental changes they must deal with. Life changes would be seen as stimulating challenges, and the opportunities that change provided would be used to further personal and family goals. An internal locus of control would allow the hardy executive to feel confident that his own actions would lead to desirable results. Executives low in hardiness would be more likely to view life changes as threats to life plans, and would be at risk for passively acquiescing and not exerting personal effort to cope with the changes.

These initial results provided encouraging evidence that hardiness might be an important personal resource for reducing illness risk. However, several methodological and conceptual problems with the study make this conclusion tentative. Kobasa (1979) dealt with two of these problems in her study. First, because physician reports or other physiological measures were not available, the illness scores were based entirely on self-reports. It might be argued that the reports of illness in the high illness subjects were not indicative of actual illness, but instead reflected a desire to be treated as if they were ill. Illness reports could then justify withdrawal from a stressful situation. However, Kobasa noted that although this could be true for vague complaints such as headaches or indigestion, this explanation was much less likely for serious illnesses such as heart attacks and high blood pressure. The high illness subjects reported suffering from these more serious health problems, and so self-report bias could not adequately explain the results.

Second, it might be that the personality differences in hardiness were not the causes of illness, but instead were results of illness. It is easy to imagine that a serious illness might reduce a person's sense of control, change might be seen as more of a threat, and life goals might begin to seem less meaningful as illness threatens life plans. This type of interpretation reflects the problems common with a retrospective study, and the best test of this hypothesis would be a prospective study in which hardiness and stress are assessed and subjects are then followed for several years to see who falls ill and who does not. However, Kobasa pointed to a group of low stress/high illness subjects not involved in her published study. The hardiness scores for these subjects were midway between those of the high stress/low illness and high stress/high illness subjects. If illness had decreased hardiness, the hardiness scores of the low stress/high illness subjects should have been closer to the hardiness scores of the high stress/high illness subjects.

Other questions were raised by the Kobasa (1979) study. All of the subjects were male executives, and most were between forty and forty-nine years old, married with two children, college educated, regular Protestant church attenders, and had a wife not working outside the home. Such a homogeneous sample raises the question that the effects of hardiness might be restricted to a relatively small portion of the general population. In addition, the test and cross-validation subjects were all under high levels of stress. What effect might hardiness have in persons not experiencing high levels of stress? It is also reasonable to wonder if some aspects of hardiness might be more important health enhancers than others. Indeed, the results of Kobasa's (1979) discriminant function analysis suggested that this might be true. In addition, might it be that hardiness operates by encouraging health enhancing behaviors, such as exercise and a good diet? It is certainly reasonable to speculate that a person with a vigorous approach to life and an internal locus of control might exercise more and follow a lifestyle that the evidence suggests may lead to better health. Later studies of hardiness have investigated these questions.

Two studies have used a prospective research design to investigate the effects of hardiness on the stress-illness relationship. Kobasa, Maddi, and Kahn (1982) studied a group of male managers quite similar to the executives in Kobasa's original study. Hardiness, and stress and illness during the preceding three and one-half years were measured in two initial surveys. These two surveys will be referred to as the Time 1 measures. Stress and illness measures were administered again a year later (Time 2), and a third time after the passage of another year (Time 3).

The results indicated that hardiness at Time 1 reduced the risk of illness at Times 2 and 3. Low hardy subjects with high levels of stress at Time 2 and Time 3 experienced more illness at Time 2 and Time 3 than other subjects. Similarly, low hardy subjects with high levels of stress at Time 1 experienced more illness at Times 2 and 3, but the effect of Time 1 stress was less pronounced than the effects of stress at Times 2 and 3. In other words, the longer ago the stress occurred, the less important it was in predicting illness. Hardiness exerted its most powerful effect when stress was high. Subjects reporting low stress reported relatively little illness, without regard to levels of hardiness.

A shorter term prospective study (Wiebe & McCallum, 1986) investigated the effects of hardiness, stress, and health practices on illness in male and female undergraduate college students. Subjects were assessed at three one-month intervals; hardiness was measured only at the first assessment and stress, illness, and health practices were measured at all three. Health practices surveyed included diet, substance abuse, exercise, hygiene, and recklessness. Stress appeared to influence health by reducing healthy behavior. When subjects were stressed, they reported engaging in fewer health practices, and the reduction in health-enhancing behavior apparently led to illness. Hardiness once again served to reduce the risk of illness. High hardiness was related to good health practices, and high hardiness was also related to lower levels of illness.

Wiebe and McCallum's (1986) data suggested that hardiness reduces the risk of illness partly because hardy individuals are more likely to maintain good health practices when under stress. However, although hardiness may influence health because it is associated with healthy behavior, this is not the complete explanation for why hardiness reduces the risk of illness. Wiebe and McCallum noted that health practices could not totally explain the association between hardiness and good health, and Kobasa, Maddi, and Puccetti (1982) found no relationship between exercise habits and hardiness in male business executives. Their data indicated that hardy executives did not tend to exercise more than low hardy executives, but hardiness and exercise both exerted independent protective effects against illness. The degree to which the combination of high hardiness and high levels of exercise protected against illness was remarkable. For executives low in hardiness and low in exercise, the correlation between stress and illness was .64. For executives high in hardiness and high in exercise, the stress-illness correlation was nonsignificant (-.08). High hardiness/low exercise and low hardiness/high exercise executives showed an intermediate relationship between stress and illness (correlations of .33 and .39, respectively) (Kobasa, Maddi, & Puccetti, 1982).

The different relationships between hardiness and health practices in these two projects may be due to differences in the subjects studied, as Kobasa et al. studied male executives and Wiebe and McCallum studied a mixed sex sample of undergraduates. Alternatively, it may be that hardiness is related to general health practices, but not to a single health practice such as exercise. Although high and low hardy individuals may exercise equally, high hardy persons may put healthy practices into action in broader areas of their lives.

The relationship between hardiness and other personality and social variables has also received research attention. Kobasa and Puccetti (1983) studied yet another sample of male executives, assessing stress, illness, hardiness, and perceived support from boss and family members. Hardiness was once again found to decrease the risk of illness, and stress was found to increase the risk of illness. Support from boss and family members showed varying effects. When stress levels were high, executives who felt that their boss supported their efforts at work reported lower levels of illness than executives who did not feel their boss was supportive. However, family support could actually act to *increase* the risk of illness. Executives low in hardiness with high levels of family support reported more illness, and if a low hardy executive with high family support was under high levels of stress, the risk of illness was even greater. This confusing pattern of relationships was interpreted as indicating that low hardy executives are likely to be those who feel a lack of commitment to their job, feel little control over events at work, and see changes at work as threatening. When these executives confront a stressful work situation and simultaneously have support at home, they may show little motivation to try to confront and resolve problems. They may thus continue to be exposed to stress at work and be encouraged at home to focus on their distressing psychological and physical feelings. Illness thus may become more likely.

Type A behavior has also been studied in association with hardiness. In the first such study, Kobasa, Maddi, and Zola (1983) used their standard procedure to measure hardiness, stress, illness, and Type A behavior in male executives. Stress and illness were reported retrospectively for each six months during the previous two years, and Type A behavior was measured by the Jenkins Activity Survey. Although the authors acknowledged that the Jenkins Activity Survey is not the best measure of Type A behavior, the Structured Interview could not be administered in the mail survey used in this study. Type A and hardiness were found to be uncorrelated with one another. As would be expected, stress increased illness and hardiness decreased illness. Type A behavior had no independent effect on illness. However, Type A, stress, and hardiness interacted in such a way that Type A individuals reported the most illness when they were also low in hardiness and under high levels of stress.

Hardiness has been found to be independent of Type A behavior in two other studies (Nowack, 1986; Schmeid & Lawler, 1986). Schmeid and Lawler assessed Type A behavior by both the Structured Interview and the Jenkins Activity Survey; both methods yielded no significant correlation between hardiness and Type A behavior. Nowack did not study the association between stress and physical illness. However, Schmeid and Lawler reported a surprising finding: although stress was associated with illness, hardiness had no impact on illness. Hardiness scores of high stress/high illness groups and high stress/low illness groups were equivalent.

Schmeid and Lawler (1986) discussed several possible reasons for the lack of association between hardiness and health. First, they studied female secretaries in Tennessee, a much different sample than Kobasa and colleagues' usual samples of male executives from the Midwest. In fact, they go on to point out that studies of females and hardiness have typically used mental health, not physical illness, as the dependent variable. Thus, hardiness may be more important to mental than physical health in women. The authors also suggested that hardiness may be more important to the physical health of executives than to persons in clerical occupations. However, it is important to remember in this regard that Wiebe and McCallum (1986) did find an association between hardiness and physical health in a mixed-sex sample of undergraduates. Gender and occupational differences are therefore unlikely to be the total explanation for Schmeid and Lawler's findings.

There are other indications that Schmeid and Lawler's sample differed in important ways from other groups studied. Age, marital status, and years of education all correlated significantly with hardiness in their sample; these variables have typically been unrelated to hardiness in samples used by Kobasa and her colleagues. The hardy secretaries tended to be older, married, and better educated. As Schmeid and Lawler suggested, successfully weathering stressful events in the course of aging may lead to greater feelings of commitment, control, and challenge. In total, Schmeid and Lawler's findings highlight the need to study hardiness in more varied samples than those used in most of the research projects to date. Larger numbers of female subjects, more diverse occupational groups, and studies of the associations between hardiness and factors such as age and education could be particularly illuminating.

The most critical study of hardiness is a recent contribution by Hull, Van Treuren, and Virnelli (1987). The structure of hardiness was examined in a sample of 1,004 college students. Information on the sex and age distribution of the sample was not provided. The authors were particularly interested in evaluating the wisdom of combining the commitment, control, and challenge aspects of hardiness into a single score, as has been commonly done in most other studies. Their data suggested that although commitment, control, and challenge were accurate descriptions of the dimensions that make up hardiness, commitment is measured more adequately than are control or challenge. In addition, total hardiness, and particularly commitment, was associated with optimism. Finally, challenge tended to be the weakest of the three dimensions of hardiness. Test-retest reliability for challenge was poorer than for commitment and control, and challenge showed relatively low correlations with total hardiness, commitment, and control. Hull et al. therefore suggested that the illness protective properties of commitment and control be investigated independently of total hardiness scores, and that challenge be discarded as an important ingredient in hardiness.

In summary, there is a substantial body of accumulated data from both prospective and retrospective studies indicating that hardiness may reduce the risk of illness. However, more prospective studies emphasizing the power of hardiness to reduce the risk of future illness are needed and several questions remain open for future investigation. More data regarding how hardiness operates in females and in males not holding managerial or executive positions would be useful. Further investigation of the association between hardiness and other variables related to health status, such as optimism and health behaviors, is also warranted. Perhaps most important, the relative importance of commitment, control, and challenge in reducing illness risk deserves additional study. It may be that their relative importance varies dependent on variables such as gender, occupation, and age. Commitment and control may be more important in persons holding jobs allowing for creativity and self-direction than in persons holding jobs not allowing for such personal expression. Finally, more illness data based on sources other than self-report would be reassuring. Even though Kobasa, Maddi, and Courington (1981) reported 82 percent to 93 percent agreement between physician records and self-reports of illness, additional verification of this association is needed.

Summary

A substantial body of psychological research has documented an association between stress and illness. However, although the relationship is reliable, it is also relatively small. Personality factors affecting the stress–illness relationship have been studied in an attempt to explain why some people remain healthy when stressed and others are more likely to become ill.

Type A behavior has been found to increase the risk of heart disease, but it appears that the most damaging feature of Type A behavior is the sense of chronic anger and hostility experienced by many Type A persons. A tendency to approach stressful situations and either solve problems or reevaluate their meaning has been found to reduce the risk of illness in response to stress. Approach is more useful for long-term than short-term stresses. An optimistic outlook also appears to reduce the risk of illness. Optimists seem more likely to approach stresses and solve problems, whereas pessimists may be more likely to avoid stresses and thus reduce the likelihood of successful coping.

Hardiness, or an attitude of commitment to life goals, an internal locus of control, and viewing change as a positive challenge, has also been associated with reduced risk of illness. Hardiness may increase the frequency of health-enhancing behaviors, but it also appears to exert an influence on health over and above that due to good health practices alone. Commitment and control appear to be the most reliable features of hardiness. Studies of potential sex- and occupation-related differences in hardiness are needed.

SUGGESTED READINGS

Goldberger, L., & Breznitz, S. (Eds.). (1982). *Handbook of stress.* New York: Free Press. A detailed review of theoretical and methodological issues in stress research by leading investigators in the field.

Maddi, S. R., & Kobasa, S. C. (1984). *The hardy executive: Health under stress.* Chicago, IL: Dorsey. An excellent summary of theoretical and methodological issues in hardiness by the most influential researchers in the field.

Roth, S., & Cohen, L. J. (1986). Approach, avoidance, and coping with stress. *American Psychologist, 41,* 813–819. An integrated look at many concepts relevant to approach and avoidance coping styles.

Schmidt, T. H., Dembroski, T. M., & Blumchen, G. (Eds.). (1986). *Biological and psychological factors in cardiovascular disease.* New York: Springer-Verlag. A comprehensive overview of current research on Type A behavior and other psychological issues relevant to cardiovascular disease.

Suls, J., & Rittenhouse, J. D. (1987). Personality and physical health [Special issue]. *Journal of Personality, 55*(2). More extensive coverage of issues reviewed in this chapter, with special emphasis on personality concerns.

REFERENCES

Alexander, A. B. (1981). Behavioral approaches in the treatment of bronchial asthma. In C. K. Prokop & L. A. Bradley (Eds.), *Medical psychology: Contributions to behavioral medicine* (pp. 373–394). New York: Academic Press.

Alexander, F. (1948). Emotional factors in essential hypertension: Presentation of a hypothesis. In F. Alexander & T. M. French (Eds.), *Studies in psychosomatic medicine* (pp. 289–297). New York: Ronald Press. (Original work published in 1939.)

Alexander, F., & French, T. M. (Eds.). (1948). *Studies in psychosomatic medicine.* New York: Ronald Press.

Barefoot, J. C., Dahlstrom, W. G., & Williams, R. B. (1983). Hostility, CHD incidence, and total mortality: A 25-year follow-up study of 255 physicians. *Psychosomatic Medicine, 245,* 59–63.

Booth-Kewley, S., & Friedman, H. S. (1987). Psychological predictors of heart disease: A quantitative review. *Psychological Bulletin, 101,* 343–362.

Carson, R. C., Butcher, J. N., & Coleman, J. C. (1988). *Abnormal psychology and modern life* (8th ed.). Glenview, IL: Scott, Foresman.

Chesney, M. A., Eagleston, J. R., & Rosenman, R. H. (1981). Type A behavior: Assessment and intervention. In C. K. Prokop & L. A. Bradley (Eds.), *Medical psychology: Contributions to behavioral medicine* (pp. 19–36). New York: Academic Press.

Collins, D. L., Baum, A., & Singer, J. E. (1983). Coping with chronic stress at Three Mile Island: Psychological and biological evidence. *Health Psychology, 2,* 149–166.

Cook, W., & Medley, D. (1954). Proposed hostility and pharisaic-virtue scales for the MMPI. *Journal of Applied Psychology, 38,* 414–418.

Costa, P. T., Jr., Zonderman, A. B., McCrae, R. R., & Williams, R. B. (1986). Cynicism and paranoid alienation in the Cook and Medley HO scale. *Psychosomatic Medicine, 248,* 283–285.

Dembroski, T. M., & Costa, P. T., Jr. (1987). Coronary prone behavior: Components of the Type A pattern and hostility. *Journal of Personality, 55,* 211–235.

Ezrin, C. (1977). Psychiatric aspects of endocrine and metabolic disorders. In E. D. Wittkower & H. Warnes (Eds.), *Psychosomatic medicine: Its clinical applications* (pp. 280–295). New York: Harper & Row.

Freud, S. (1953). Three essays on sexuality. In J. Strachey (Ed. and Trans.), *The standard edition of the complete psychological works of Sigmund Freud* (Vol. 7). London: Hogarth Press. (Original work published 1905).

Friedman, M., & Rosenman, R. H. (1959). Association of a specific overt behavior pattern with increases in blood cholesterol, blood clotting time, incidence of arcus senilis and clinical coronary artery disease. *Journal of the American Medical Association, 169,* 1286–1296.

Goldberg, E. L., & Comstock, G. W. (1976). Life events and subsequent illness. *American Journal of Epidemiology, 104,* 146–158.

Holmes, T. H., & Rahe, R. H. (1967). The social readjustment rating scale. *Journal of Psychosomatic Research, 11,* 213–218.

Holroyd, K. A., & Lazarus, R. S. (1982). Stress, coping, and somatic adaptation. In L. Goldberger & S. Breznitz (Eds.), *Handbook of stress* (pp. 21–35). New York: Free Press.

Hull, J. G., Van Treuren, R. R., & Virnelli, S. (1987). Hardiness and health: A critique and alternative approach. *Journal of Personality and Social Psychology, 53,* 518–530.

Jenkins, C. D., Rosenman, R. H., & Friedman, M. (1967). Development of an objective psychological test for the determination of the coronary-prone behavior pattern in employed men. *Journal of Chronic Diseases, 20,* 371–379.

Kobasa, S. C. (1979). Stressful life events, personality, and health: An inquiry into hardiness. *Journal of Personality and Social Psychology, 37,* 1–11.

Kobasa, S. C., Maddi, S. R., & Courington, S. (1981). Personality and constitution as mediators in the stress–illness relationship. *Journal of Health and Social Behavior, 22,* 368–378.

Kobasa, S. C., Maddi, S. R., & Kahn, S. (1982). Hardiness and health: A prospective study. *Journal of Personality and Social Psychology, 42,* 168–177.

Kobasa, S. C., Maddi, S. R., & Puccetti, M. C.

(1982). Personality and exercise as buffers in the stress–illness relationship. *Journal of Behavioral Medicine, 5,* 391–404.

Kobasa, S. C., Maddi, S. R., & Zola, M. A. (1983). Type A and hardiness. *Journal of Behavioral Medicine, 6,* 41–52.

Kobasa, S. C. O., & Puccetti, M. C. (1983). Personality and social resources in stress resistance. *Journal of Personality and Social Psychology, 45,* 839–850.

MacDougall, J. M., Dembroski, T. M., Dimsdale, J. E., & Hackett, T. P. (1985). Components of Type A, hostility, and anger-in: Further relationships to angiographic findings. *Health Psychology, 4,* 137–152.

Maddi, S. R., Bartone, P. T., & Puccetti, M. C. (1987). Stressful events are indeed a factor in physical illness: Reply to Schroeder and Costa (1984). *Journal of Personality and Social Psychology, 52,* 833–843.

Meyer, A., Bollmeier, L. N., & Alexander, F. (1945). Correlation between emotions and carbohydrate metabolism in two cases of diabetes mellitus. *Psychosomatic Medicine, 7,* 335–341.

Nowack, K. M. (1986). Type A, hardiness, and psychological distress. *Journal of Behavioral Medicine, 9,* 537–548.

Peale, N. V. (1956). *The power of positive thinking.* Englewood Cliffs, NJ: Prentice-Hall.

Perkins, D. V. (1982). The assessment of stress using life events scales. In L. Goldberger & S. Breznitz (Eds.), *Handbook of stress* (pp. 320–331). New York: Free Press.

Peterson, C., & Seligman, M. E. P. (1987). Explanatory style and illness. *Journal of Personality, 55,* 237–266.

Rahe, R. H. (1974). The pathway between subjects' recent life changes and their near-future illness reports: Representative results and methodological issues. In B. S. Dohrenwend & B. P. Dohrenwend (Eds.), *Stressful life events: Their nature and effects* (pp. 73–86). New York: Wiley.

Rosenman, R. H. (1978). The interview method of assessment of the coronary-prone behav-

ior pattern. In T. M. Dembroski, S. M. Weiss, J. L. Shields, S. G. Haynes, & M. Feinleib (Eds.), *Coronary-prone behavior* (pp. 55–70). New York: Springer-Verlag.

Rosenman, R. H. (1986). Current and past history of Type A behavior pattern. In T. H. Schmidt, T. M. Dembroski, & G. Blumchen (Eds.), *Biological and psychological factors in cardiovascular disease* (pp. 15–40). New York: Springer-Verlag.

Roth, S., & Cohen, L. J. (1986). Approach, avoidance, and coping with stress. *American Psychologist, 41,* 813–819.

Rotter, J. B. (1966). Generalized expectancies for internal versus external control of reinforcement. *Psychological Monographs, 80* (1, Whole No. 609).

Scheier, M. F., & Carver, C. S. (1985). Optimism, coping, and health: Assessment and implications of generalized outcome expectancies. *Health Psychology, 4,* 219–247.

Scheier, M. F., & Carver, C. S. (1987). Dispositional optimism and physical well-being: The influence of generalized outcome expectancies on health. *Journal of Personality, 55,* 169–210.

Scheier, M. F., Weintraub, J. K., & Carver, C. S. (1986). Coping with stress: Divergent strategies of optimists and pessimists. *Journal of Personality and Social Psychology, 51,* 1257–1264.

Schmeid, L. A., & Lawler, K. A. (1986). Hardiness, Type A behavior, and the stress-illness relationship in working women. *Journal of Personality and Social Psychology, 51,* 1218–1223.

Schroeder, D. H., & Costa, P. T., Jr. (1984). Influence of life events stress on physical illness: Substantive effects or methodological flaws? *Journal of Personality and Social Psychology, 46,* 853–863.

Selye, H. (1982). History and present status of the stress concept. In L. Goldberger & S. Breznitz (Eds.) *Handbook of stress* (pp. 7–17). New York: Free Press.

Theorell, T., Lind, E., & Floderus, B. (1975). The relationship of disturbing life-changes and emotions to the early development of myo-cardial infarction and other serious illnesses. *International Journal of Epidemiology, 4,* 281–293.

Weiner, H. (1977). *Psychobiology and human disease.* New York: Elsevier.

Wiebe, D. J., & McCallum, D. M. (1986). Health practices and hardiness as mediators in the stress–illness relationship. *Health Psychology, 5,* 425–438.

Williams, R. B., Haney, T. L., Lee. K. L., Kong, Y., Blumenthal, J., & Whalen, R. (1980). Type A behavior hostility and coronary atherosclerosis. *Psychosomatic Medicine, 242,* 539–549.

Wilson, J. F. (1981). Behavioral preparations for surgery: Benefit or harm? *Journal of Behavioral Medicine, 4,* 79–102.

Wyler, A. R., Masuda, M., & Holmes, T. H. (1968). Seriousness of Illness Rating Scale. *Journal of Psychosomatic Research, 11,* 363–374.

CHAPTER 19

Personality and Relationships
WARREN H. JONES

The Psychology of Relationships
  Definition
  Importance of Studying
    Relationships
  Methodological Issues in
    Studying Relationships
  Relationship Development and
    Processes
  Some Conceptual Issues
Personality and Relationships
  Relationship Influence in the
    Development of Personality

Personality Influences on the
  Development of
  Relationships
**ACTIVITY BOX: Experience of
  Loneliness in Various
  Situations**
Concluding Remarks
Summary
SUGGESTED READINGS
REFERENCES

Most everything we do, think, and feel involves, to a significant degree, other people. Most of us spend most of our time with others representing a variety of relationships and even when we are alone we spend much of that time thinking about the significant others in our lives: fondly musing about them, worrying about them, being proud of them, lusting after them, brooding about their absence, or plotting against them. Because of this, relationships comprise not only one of the most important aspects of our lives, but understanding relationships—how they are formed, how they change a person's life, how they dissolve, their benefits and limitations—constitutes one of the more critical issues in several areas of psychology and, in part, it is this topic that ties various subdisciplines together. For example, the topic of relationships is at the juncture of personality, clinical, developmental, and social psychology; increasingly, questions concerning the variety and quality of relationships have received research and theoretical attention in these areas.

The Psychology of Relationships

Before considering personality and relationships, it is useful to focus on relationships generally, that is, what we mean by the term, something about what is known about relationships, and why they are important —in other words, the psychology of relationships.

Definition

At the simplest level of analysis one could say a relationship exists when people are seen repeatedly to interact. Ordinarily, however, we use the

510

term relationship to mean a state of mutual awareness and interdependence. A relationship exists when two people are aware of each other's existence and, more important, both persons believe a relationship exists and both feel some sort of commitment or emotional bond toward the other. The bond is not always positive although typically it is; however, relationships can also be based on competition, distrust, and even hatred. Furthermore, there can be asymmetric relationships when only one person feels an emotional bond, although completely asymmetric relationships of long duration are presumably less common than mutually conceived relationships.

The degree of commitment and the types of bonds vary considerably across relationships, of course. For example, some of the more common relationships to which we belong include friendship, marriage, dating relationships, the relationships among "blood" relations as well as in-laws (parent–child, siblings, cousins, sisters-in-law, grandparent–grandchild, etc.), and the various relationships that emerge in conjunction with other activities in life such as supervisor–worker, teacher–student, roommates, and so on.

Importance of Studying Relationships

Why are relationships important in the study of personality? One reason, suggested in the opening sentence of this chapter, is that so much of what an individual does is related to his or her relationships; they are ubiquitous in human experience. For example, think for a moment about how much of your time is spent meeting, talking, arguing, sharing, and simply being with your friends and family. Psychologists who study this issue report that about 75 percent of the waking time of college students is spent with other people (Larson, Csikszentmihalyi, & Graef, 1982). Thus, interactions with others and the relationships that emerge from such interactions are important because of their frequency in the experience of most people. To understand the role of personality in our lives we must also understand the relationships in which we participate.

Second, even when what we are doing is not directly related to a particular relationship, our experiences unfold, as it were, in the context of our relationships and are shaped by them. For example, part of what makes a clumsy action or a foolish statement so embarrassing is not the action or statement itself, but having someone whose opinion we value observe such behaviors (Miller, 1986). Similarly, what creates the joy of an accomplishment? To some extent it derives from the personal satisfaction of knowing we have done something well. In addition, however, much of the sense of elation derives from the reactions of friends and loved ones to the accomplishment. Thus, relationships comprise part of the social context in which other aspects of our experience take place and this context adds texture and meaning to these experiences.

A third reason that relationships are important in the study of personality derives from research findings regarding the criticality of satisfactory relationships for many areas of functioning that have long been of interest to personality psychologists. For example, one of the major factors in the psychological and emotional health of an individual is the quality and status of that individual's close relationships. It has been known for a long time that one of the best predictors of mental illness among adults is marital status (cf. Hafner, 1986). Generally speaking, single adults are overrepresented among persons undergoing psychiatric treatment and hospitalization relative to their proportion in the population. This does not mean that marriage necessarily reduces psychological problems. Persons predisposed to mental illness may be simply less likely to marry. It does suggest, however, a fundamental linkage between the ability to relate effectively to other people in marriage and vulnerability to the various problems subsumed under the label of mental illness.

More recently it has been discovered that what is called social support—defined as the amount of help, comfort, information, and advice received from one's family and friends—is also closely related to one's state of adjustment and well-being. In other words, people who belong to a network of friends, family, neighbors, and coworkers on whom they can rely for companionship, comfort, and assistance tend to be better adjusted from a psychological point of view than people who lack a social network altogether or whose social network is not supportive (Sarason & Sarason, 1985).

Research on social support also indicates that the lack or the loss of an important close relationship or a supportive social network is associated with greater vulnerability to medical problems as well. For example, divorced men are significantly more vulnerable to cardiovascular disease than married men (Lynch, 1981); widows and widowers are at greater risk for life threatening illnesses compared to their married counterparts within a year or so of the death of the spouse regardless of their ages (Stroebe & Stroebe, 1986); and lonely persons are more likely to develop illnesses associated with latent Epstein-Barr virus such as mononucleosis (Kiecolt-Glaser, Garner, Speicher, Penn, Holliday, & Glaser, 1984).

Similarly, numerous psychologists have suggested that the interpersonal aspects of the parent–child relationship may be as important to the subsequent life of the infant as is satisfaction of the more obvious physical needs such as proper food and shelter (Bowlby, 1969). For example, being deprived of the opportunity to form a close attachment with at least one parent or parental surrogate is associated with intellectual deficits (i.e., mental retardation) and the subsequent manifestation of some of the symptoms of severe psychological disturbance. Perhaps most striking is that such deprivation also appears to lead to certain physical and medical problems, one of which is called *deprivation dwarfism* (Gardner, 1972), which refers to the tendency of deprived infants to be significantly shorter and smaller than would otherwise have been expected. Within psychology, there is, of course, considerable debate as to what exactly accounts for these findings. Even so, it is quite clear that the nature and frequency of one's involvements with significant others are an important factor in physical as well as psychological health and the development of personality.

The fourth and fifth reasons that understanding relationships is important in the study of personality will be the focus of this chapter, and they will therefore be mentioned only briefly here. The fourth reason derives from an old and very common idea in psychology that, to a significant degree, personality is formed and develops through interactions with significant others, particularly in the crucible of the family. Thus, in this view, aspects of certain close relationships are seen as determining elements in the development of personality. The fifth reason concerns evidence suggesting that one's personality characteristics (e.g., traits, motives, goals, attributional style, expectations, etc.) play major roles in the number and quality of relationships a given person will have and major roles also in the outcome of any relationship in which that person engages. Indeed, some psychologists have argued that the primary purpose of a psychology of personality is to help explain social action (Hogan, 1983), which, as we have seen, largely consists of participation in close personal relationships.

Methodological Issues in Studying Relationships

Broadly speaking, there are two types of measures of relationships; qualitative and quantitative. *Qualitative measures* refer to indications of the perceptions, feelings, or beliefs of one or both members of a relationship. Examples of qualitative measures include satisfaction with the relationship, commitment (i.e., the stated willingness of a participant to remain in the relationship), the degree of liking and love, and so on. *Quantitative measures* refer to more "objective" indices of time or frequency such as the number of friends a person has, the amount of time two friends spend together, or the duration of a relationship.

Measures of relationships also vary on the basis of *breadth of focus*. For example, one may assess feelings of satisfaction with a relationship in general versus satisfaction with a particular interaction with a relationship partner. Similarly, one may assess quantitative variables broadly (e.g., average number of daily interactions) or quite specifically (e.g., number of words spoken to the relational partner in a given interaction).

The third and perhaps most important distinction concerning the measurement of relationships concerns whose *perspective* on the relationship is being measured (Ichheiser, 1970). For example, the researcher may assess the satisfaction of one participant in a relationship by asking him or her or by asking the relational partner. Although there is generally a connection between the two, they need not be identical. For example, it is often found that men are more satisfied with their romantic and marital relationships than are their women partners (Sternberg, 1987). For this reason, one may also combine these two perspectives to create what is known as the *transactional view* of the relationship. In addition, the researcher or any other outside observer has his or her own view of the relationship, which in many instances will diverge from that of the participants. It is not uncommon, for example, for observers to hold a negative view of an emotionally tumultuous relationship, whereas the participants may express satisfaction with the same relationship. The main point here is that what a relationship appears to be will, to a large extent, depend on the perspective from which the relationship is measured and studied.

Relationship Development and Processes

Obviously, given the variety of relationships in which people participate, there is considerable diversity in the characteristics that are necessary to describe and account for them. Even so, research suggests that certain interpersonal processes and concepts are applicable across a variety of stages and types of relationships. In order to introduce these ideas and to describe the course of a "typical" relationship we next turn to the questions of how relationships are formed and how they change over time.

Initiation

Every relationship may be described as having four logically distinct stages or phases. The first of these is the *initiation* phase, during which subsequent relational participants become aware of each other, meet, interact, become acquainted, and begin to affiliate (i.e., choose to be together, spend time together, etc.). How and why the participants become acquainted will depend, of course, on a variety of factors, particularly the type of relationship involved. In fact, in some relationships such as those between parents and their children, the initiation phase is quite different from, for example, a friendship. For many relationships, the initiation phase corresponds to what is called the *acquaintanceship process*. Research indicates that many factors contribute to the determination of the one, among all other persons, with whom we become acquainted and choose to affiliate. Some of these factors involve *characteristics of the person* (i.e., the person whose relationships or affiliation we are trying to explain). Examples of relevant person characteristics are *shyness* and *sociability*. Shyness refers to the tendency to become excessively self-focused and anxious in the presence of others and sociability is defined as one's level of interest in being with and interacting with other people versus being alone. For example, research indicates that extremely shy persons often avoid interpersonal opportunities that might lead to the development of new relationships and thus they tend to have smaller social networks and fewer friends and they rely more extensively on family members as opposed to friends for social contact (Jones, Cheek, & Briggs, 1986).

Another set of factors that contribute to the extent of initial affiliation includes *characteristics of the other* (i.e., the person with whom one chooses to affiliate). One important category here is *desirable characteristics,* such as *physical attractiveness* and *social status*. For example, research shows that we prefer to affiliate with physically attractive people as compared to unattractive people (cf. Berscheid & Walster, 1969). However, it is important to note that because such characteristics are desirable for almost everyone, these effects are perhaps moderated by a tendency to select others whose physical and social characteristics match one's own.

A third set of factors that influence affiliation during the initiation phase of a relationship involves *characteristics of the situation* in which the potential relational partners find themselves. For example, *propinquity,* or physical closeness (e.g., living in close proximity), provides greater opportunities for meeting and interacting and thus may contribute to the development of a relationship (Newcomb, 1961). Also, when one is afraid or in a threatening situation there is a tendency to want to affiliate with others (Schachter, 1959) either for *social comparison* (to see how others are feeling and coping with the threat) or *fear reduction* (i.e., it is comforting to be with others when afraid).

In addition, the tendency to initiate a relationship through affiliation is often based on the interplay or combination of these factors. For example, as was suggested, there is evidence that *similarity* between two people on certain key variables such as beliefs, social standing, physical attractiveness, group identification, and so on, is conducive to initial affiliation (e.g., Byrne, 1971). Similarly, when choosing to affiliate under conditions of external threat we typically prefer to affiliate with others who are similar to us or who face similar threats (Schachter, 1959).

The examples of each category are far from complete and, as if to make matters worse, they pertain primarily to certain "voluntary" relationships (e.g., friendships, dating relationships). As noted earlier, some relationships develop as a consequence of other life involvements such as marriage and having children, and this applies to some of one's most important relationships, such as those between parents and children. On the other hand, these factors may influence how even such "given" relationships evolve. For example, characteristics of the child such as having an "easy" or "difficult" temperament may contribute to the parents' effectiveness at raising the child.

Enhancement

The second stage of a relationship may be called the *enhancement* phase. Typically, during this period the participants get to know each other better, often by self-disclosing intimate and private information about themselves. During this stage, participants may become attracted toward each other and, just as important, begin to feel the sort of emotional bond or tie toward the other discussed earlier. Also, it is during this phase that participants begin to feel and act interdependently and to identify themselves to themselves and others as a pair, a couple, friends, and so on.

Once two people begin to affiliate with each other, the extent of the enhancement phase is determined, in part, by the degree of mutual attraction between the two participants. Research indicates that many of the same factors that increase the probability of affiliation also, generally speaking, increase attraction. In addition, other factors such as *mutual liking, shared interests, common group affiliations* and, in certain relationships, *sexual intimacy* enhance feelings of closeness, satisfaction, and commitment and thus facilitate the continued development of the relationship. In addition, *self-disclosure* (the process by which participants in a relationship share information and reveal themselves to each other, including aspects of their identities, their thoughts, feelings, and their personalities) has been described as the vehicle through which close personal relationships are formed (Jourard, 1964). Research also suggests, however, that disclosures vary according to the type of relationship and what is considered to be appropriate to the situation (Derlega, Wilson, & Chaikin, 1976). Similarly, reciprocity of various kinds—exchanging favors, compliments, invitations—also contributes to relationship development, at least in the early stages. Finally, *attitude similarity,* or the degree to which participants agree on important social, political, and religious issues has been shown to be related to attraction toward others and hence the enhancement of relationships (Byrne, 1971). When people share our attitudes and values, it confirms our view of the world, which is positively reinforcing and thereby increases attraction for that person.

One approach to attraction suggested that people whose personalities are opposite on certain dimensions (particularly dominance-submissiveness and nurturance-succorance) are more likely to select each other as mates. Winch (1958) proposed that (1) people select partners from among available others based on their maximum potential for need gratification, and (2) they select others whose needs are complementary to their own. So, for example, a highly dominant person might be attracted to a very submissive person and vice versa. Although Winch produced data supportive of this view, some research has suggested that complementarity is restricted to long-term relationships (Kerckhoff & Davis, 1962) and other researchers have not been able to confirm its existence at all (Levinger, Senn, & Jorgensen, 1970).

Again, this is not all that can be said about the enhancement of a relationship. For one thing, as noted earlier, some relationships develop beyond the initial stages because of negative influences. More frequently, relationships may simply "endure" due to the circumstances outside the relationship itself (e.g., social norms regarding caring for one's children). Also, research indicates that there are limitations on these processes and that they may change over the course of a relationship. For example, Clark and Mills (1979) have demonstrated that perfectly reciprocal relationships are viewed as new or superficial and that nonreciprocal behaviors (i.e., where one partner does more for the other) are seen as evidence of genuine love and caring.

Maintenance

The third stage of a relationship, which—except by the passage of time—is often indistinguishable from enhancement, is the *maintenance* phase. The primary issue during the maintenance phase is how the relationship develops after it is more or less established. In many cases this stage will be associated with greater closeness and interdependence. Alternatively, this period in a relationship may involve a loss of interest on the part of one or both participants and a weakening of the emotional bond on which the relationship was established, either suddenly or through a slower process of disengagement. Again, many factors contribute to what happens during the maintenance phase (e.g., the development of alternative and competing relationships, physical separation) including factors external to the relationship itself.

In many ways less is known about the maintenance of relationships than about their initiation and enhancement because research has tended to focus on these earlier stages. Contrary to what one might think, some research does suggest that relationships of longer duration such as longer marriages are not necessarily more satisfying (Rollins & Cannon, 1974), but it is possible that the timing of certain life events confounds the interpretation of such data (e.g., the ages of one's children and accompanying child-rearing responsibilities, career changes, etc.). Also, it has been argued that in romantic relationships the couple must transform the basis of the relationship from one of passionate love (dominated by sexual desire) to one based on companionate concerns—hopefully with moments of passion interspersed here and there—in order for the relationship to endure (Berscheid & Walster, 1969).

One of the more common ways of describing the maintenance phase of a relationship involves theories based on analogies to economic exchange, that is, the idea that a relationship is built and maintained on the exchange of personal qualities or resources (e.g., Foa & Foa, 1976). One such model known as *exchange theory*—which is also used to explain the earlier stages of a relationship—suggests that the outcome of the maintenance phase will depend on the participants' respective levels of comparisons for alternatives (Thibaut & Kelley, 1959). Specifically, the theory predicts that a couple will remain together if the ratio of what they obtain from the relationship relative to what they have to give to it is greater than it would be for any possible alternative relationship, and relevant research supports this prediction. In any case, it is clear that once developed, relationships remain dynamic processes and, typically, must be enhanced further or they will deteriorate.

Termination

Finally, all relationships have a *termination* phase. Whether as the result of drifting apart, breaking up, running away, getting a divorce, or death, one way or another all relationships come to an end. As with the earlier stages, a variety of factors apparently contribute not only to how and when the relationship will end, but also how participants will respond given the timing and the type of termination. One of the dominant factors appears to be the length and quality of the relationship before it is terminated. Widows who report having been more satisfied with their marital partner experience more difficulties in adjusting to the loss of the spouse than those who were less satisfied. Another set of factors determining the outcome of the termination phase involves the circumstances of the termination and the behaviors it invokes. For example, widows who "rehearse" what they would do should their spouse die adjust more readily (Remondet, Hansson, Rule, & Winfrey, 1987).

Alternative models of relationship stages and development have been proposed. For example, Levinger and Snoek (1972) described a process in which partners in a relationship progress from *zero contact* (no awareness of one another) through *surface contact* (limited and largely independent interaction) to *mutality* (various degrees of inter-dependency). Perhaps the most important thing to keep in mind about relationship stages is that any attempt to describe them means imposing static concepts on what is a highly complex and dynamic series of processes. Thus, for example, in all such models stages are not fixed nor absolutely discrete; there is considerable overlap between phases with one phase fading imperceptibly into the next.

Some Conceptual Issues

Relationship Dynamics

In the development of relationships, whether or not a given relationship will develop into one providing mutual satisfaction for the participants varies as a function of many variables and also as a function of the stage of the relationship in question. What is considered attractive or even appropriate at one stage in a relationship may be highly undesirable at another. For example, although research shows that intimate self-disclosures are important to enhance ongoing rela-tionships, the same disclosures offered shortly after meeting someone may have the opposite effect. In fact, some theories of relationships hold that the factors that determine relationship enhancement or termination will depend on the extent to which the relationship has developed previously. For example, Murstein's (1972) *stimulus-value-role* theory suggests that the interpersonal qualities exchanged in the development of a relationship begin with the "superficial" stimulus factors (e.g., physical attractiveness), then move to "deeper" value qualities (e.g., attitude and belief similarity), and finally move to how the participants behave or the roles they assume within the relationship (e.g., shared expectations regarding respective roles).

Subjectivity and Imbalance in Relationships

Research on relationships naturally has tended to focus on the more objective (i.e., more easily quantifiable) aspects of relationships. Similarly, many theories of relationships emphasize structural proper-ties such as balance and reciprocity. Even so, there is considerable evidence that, to a large extent, much of what happens in a relationship is subjective (i.e., in the eye of the beholder) and that, in some cases, the existence of the relationship may exist only in the mind of one participant (cf., Sternberg, 1987). Also, although many relational phenomena are characterized by balance and reciprocity, many are not. The parent-child relationship is not balanced in any usual sense of the term and recent evidence suggests that reciprocity tends to characterize the early stages of relationships or less intimate relationships (Clark & Mills, 1979).

The reasons for this are varied. In part, it depends on the issue of measurement perspectives discussed earlier. Also, in part, it is due to the inherently subjective nature of the various processes involved in the development of relationships such as perception, communication, and memory. Finally, varying characterizations of relationships such as, for example, whether or not they are reciprocal, depend on the type and stage of a relationship being described, as suggested by Murstein (1972).

Proximal Versus Distal Explanations

Most research and theory about relationships in psychology deals with what might be called proximal causes and processes, that is, factors that immediately influence whether a given person will affiliate with a particular other person in a particular situation, or why one woman is attracted to a specific man and not to other men. In addition, however, there are distal reasons for affiliation, attraction, love, and the development of relationships. These concern questions such as why human beings as a species are so affiliative in general compared to other species of animals. Answers to such distal questions involve, in part, issues of human biology, genetics, and evolution. For example, there is evidence that human babies are born with a special receptivity to human stimuli, thereby enhancing the closeness of the parent-infant relationship. Similarly, human behavior has an evolutionary-biological history. People have always lived in groups and group living not only encourages the development of language and culture but is likely one of the main factors giving humans an evolutionary advantage. For example, anthropologists explain enhanced human intelligence as a function of the complexity of human relationships (cf. Hogan, 1983).

Another set of distal factors contributing to the development of relationships concerns the culture in which an individual is raised. Different cultures (and different time periods within a given culture) create varying rules and expectations (called *norms*) regarding how relationships should be established and progress. In the United States the current system of marital courtship emphasizing choice and love between romantic partners seems to have evolved from earlier family-influenced systems of courtship as the result of dramatic changes in American lifestyle. For example, the shift from an agrarian to a service-oriented economy and lifestyle, the advent of widely available transportation, and greater free time on the part of adolescents and young adults are believed to have shaped contemporary ideas of love and marriage (Murstein, 1986).

The main point here is that relationships do not develop in a vacuum. To some extent what a relationship is or what it can become depends upon the biological history and propensities of the organisms engaging in the relationship and the cultural history and norms of the society in which the relationship unfolds.

Personality and Relationships

As suggested earlier, there are basically two ways of thinking about the connections between personality and relationships. The first is how and why relationships influence the development of personality, particularly during the early stages of life. The second concerns how personality characteristics contribute to the development of relationships, and this issue is especially relevant from adolescence on when personality change is typically less fluid and dramatic. This distinction is an arbitrary one for the sake of clarity of discussion, however. In fact, most theories that have something to say about one will have something to say about the other. Moreover, the dominant view is one of *reciprocal influence*; that is, relationships influence personality and personality influences relationships both simultaneously and sequentially. In any case, the first set of ideas to consider is the role of relationships in the development of personality or the type of person one becomes.

Relationship Influence in the Development of Personality

Early Conceptualizations

One of the first descriptions of how personality is shaped by one's relationships is embedded in a psychoanalytic theory proposed by Freud (see chapter 5, Personality Development). Freud was interested in the problem of neurosis, a type of disturbed personality characterized by guilt, anxiety, self-defeating behaviors and, above all, a lack of insight into the origins and nature of one's problems. Through the treatment of his neurotic patients Freud developed a comprehensive theory of personality of which even a brief description is beyond the scope of this chapter. Nevertheless, it is important to describe a few key concepts because of the influence of the psychoanalytic tradition on theories of personality development.

Freud assumed that the personality of every individual developed through identifiable stages and that the manner and success of such development ultimately resulted in the adult personality. As development progresses, inevitable sources of anxiety appear (e.g., fear of bodily harm based on the anatomical differences of the opposite-sex parent, fear of abandonment, etc.) that result in unconscious attempts to reduce the anxiety. One of the ways in which this is done, according to Freud, is called *defensive identification*. In defensive identification one internalizes (i.e., literally puts inside oneself) the image of the same-sex parent and becomes like that person.

According to Freud, one's relations to adult authority are a continuation of this earlier identification; one reacts to authority with a mixture of admiration and fear—in other words, defensive identification. And this is the best possible outcome. Failures to successfully identify with the same-sex parent subsequently may result in any of a variety of neurotic personality syndromes. Also, Freud argued that excessive parental indulgence or frustration of the child's needs at a given stage of development results in specific personality problems for the child. In other words, a parent who is too threatening or so indulgent as not to represent authority may engender in the child an unsuccessful and neurotic identity. In addition, Freud argued that the inevitable internal conflict between the socialized component of the personality (the superego) and the animalistic component (the id) was a continuing source of anxiety for the rational component of the personality (the ego), frequently resulting in unconscious attempts to defend against the anxiety that undermined the ego's ability to remain rational and conscious.

Many objections to the Freudian model of relationships, as well as the theory more generally, have been raised over the years. On the other hand, Freud had an enormous impact on subsequent conceptualizations. One such development included personality theories that, although they retained much of the original psychoanalytic conceptualization, changed some of the concepts or added new ideas. Collectively these theorists are known as *neo-Freudians* and include such writers as Alfred Adler, Eric Fromm, and Karen Horney. The principal difference between these approaches and Freud's theorizing concerns the greater role attributed to social and relational experiences in the development of personality. For example, in contrast to Freud, Adler saw strivings for social superiority as the driving force in personality development, whereas Horney posited certain "neurotic needs" such as wanting to be liked by everyone as a determining factor in the development of psychological disturbances.

Perhaps the most significant benefactor of the psychoanalytic tradition and certainly the most thoroughly interpersonal is the theory proposed by Harry Stack Sullivan (1953), a New York psychiatrist. Originally an adherent of Freud's theory, Sullivan later was influenced by sociological thinking about relationships, particularly the work of Mead and Cooley, who had formulated the idea of the "looking-glass self." This means that the *self-concept* (an important dimension in the study of personality) forms as a function of the responses of others that reflect how one acts and what one is. Sullivan argued that the development of the personality passes through six stages, each involving intimacy with another individual. Furthermore, in addition to the satisfaction of physical needs, a sense of security from others is seen as the driving force behind personality development.

Three additional components of Sullivan's theory are of greatest relevance to the present discussion, however. First, he held that the view a person holds of himself or herself results from a process called *consensual validation;* that is, one's view of oneself derives from confirmations by intimate others of various features. Second, Sullivan argued that anxiety results in the *self-system;* that is, the self develops in an attempt to avoid anxiety through distortions of what one is. Third, and most important, personality is composed of experiences with others and does not exist apart from its manifestation in one's interactions with significant others. So in Sullivan's theory the influence of relationships on personality is more or less complete. Personality not only derives from one's interactions and relationships with significant others (e.g., the family, loved ones, friends, etc.); to Sullivan it makes no sense to speak of personality apart from interactions with significant others. Moreover, an individual is disturbed, according to Sullivan, to the extent that his or her interactions and relationships make it imperative that he or she act in such a disturbed manner.

It has been argued that Sullivan's view has been even more influential than that of Freud at least with respect to developments in the psychology of relationships and that his theory anticipated or contributed to many subsequent theories, particularly those involving relationships among persons with psychological disorders (Swensen, 1973). On the other hand, all of the approaches just described are limited in important ways. For one thing, they were proposed by therapists whose ideas derived from their work with disturbed individuals and may or may not be fully reflective of the relationships of nondisturbed individuals. In addition, these approaches are not particularly empirical. This means that the ideas proposed are based on clinical observations rather than controlled studies and experiments. Thus it is difficult to assess the utility of the concepts and claims of these theories.

Contemporary Approaches

More contemporary approaches to explaining the influence of relationships on personality tend to be closely tied to empirical (research) demonstrations. Despite the variety of conceptual approaches that point to family and parent-child relationships as the origins of personality and despite also the apparent "logic" of such ideas, it is amazing how difficult these propositions have been to substantiate empirically (Hartup, 1986). Part of the difficulty derives from ethical constraints on research—parents cannot be compelled to raise their children using specific techniques in order to test their influence on personality development. Despite such difficulties and continuing controversies regarding how available research should be interpreted, many observers agree that relationships have a causal influence on the development of personality.

Although there are many theories addressing some aspect of this issue, the most influential among them has been what is known as *attachment theory* (Bowlby, 1969, 1973; see also chapter 5, Personality Development). Attachment theory holds that there is a mutually instinctive pattern involved in the attachment between human infants and their caregivers, such that a given behavior on the part of a child (e.g., crying, smiling, etc.) is maintained by the responses of the caregiver and, specifically, the extent to which the child's behavior serves to keep the caregiver close. The degree or type of attachment, in turn, has consequences for individual and social development of the infant, according to the theory. For example, infants whose caregivers are responsive should become "securely" attached and, because of this, able subsequently to tolerate separations from the caregiver with confidence. Other infants, however, may be only "anxiously" attached, leading to less adaptive behaviors in the face of separation.

As an illustration, Ainsworth and Bell (1969) classified mother-infant interactions based on observations of feeding from birth until about one year of age. In one pattern the mothers were sensitive to the demands and behaviors of their infants, permitting them to play an active part in determining the timing, pacing, and termination of feeding. Another group of mothers were relatively insensitive and unresponsive to their babies during the feeding process. Subsequently, these researchers measured the strength of their attachment and exploratory behavior in a series of standardized situations involving various combinations of the presence and absence of the mother in a strange situation (e.g., observing the apparent distress, disruption of play, etc., of infants when left alone). Infants who subsequently were seen as attached but who could also use the presence of their mother as a secure base for exploration were from the feeding interaction group in which the mothers had been most sensitive to their signals. Of the infants who lacked interest in regaining or maintaining contact with their mothers, most were from the group whose mothers had been least sensitive to them in the early feeding situation. Many other linkages between the quality of the infant-caregiver relationship and subsequent personality development have been demonstrated as well (cf. Bretherton & Waters, 1985). For example, infants whose mothers were insensitive to their "signals" during the first three months of life—or whose mothers say (or act as if) they do not like physical contact with them—resist or avoid reunions following brief separations. More important, research indicates that patterns of early attachment predict subsequent emotional, cognitive, and interpersonal characteristics and behaviors. Thus, similar to the earlier psychodynamic models, attachment theory emphasizes the role of the prototypical relationship in the individual's later adaptability and relationships.

Personality Influences on the Development of Relationships

As noted earlier, the second way to approach the connections between personality and relationships is to examine the role of personality in the quality and quantity of close personal relationships. Literally dozens of personality dimensions have been investigated in this regard. Rather than attempt to survey the wide variety of studies that have assessed the predictability of personality dimensions for measures of relationships, it might be useful to focus on a particular issue, that of loneliness.

Psychology of Loneliness

Loneliness is defined as having a smaller or less satisfying network of social and intimate relationships than one desires (cf. Peplau & Perlman, 1982). As such, it is a psychological condition reflecting what one feels and thinks about one's interpersonal life and therefore is not identical to solitude or being alone (see Activity Box). Previous research suggests that it is a common and persistent experience that may contribute to a variety of individual and social problems. As is the case with most negative psychological conditions, loneliness is more common among single persons, and several studies have shown that loneliness decreases with age (Peplau & Perlman, 1982).

Much of the research on loneliness has focused on the status and quality of the lonely person's relationships. There is considerable evidence that, as one might expect, lonely persons report having fewer friends, spending less time with close friends and family members, and among unmarried persons, having fewer dates and fewer dating partners. The evidence also suggests, however, that loneliness is more strongly associated with qualitative measures of relationships such as dissatisfaction with one's friends and family than it is with quantitative measures such as number of friends and the amount of time spent with others (Jones, Carpenter, & Quintana, 1985a; Peplau & Perlman, 1982).

Loneliness is an unpleasant condition and therefore it is not surprising that its occurrence is accompanied by a variety of negative and undesirable emotions and cognitive states such as anxiety, depression, hostility, poor self-regard, and so on (Russell, Peplau & Cutrona, 1980). Beyond such negative states, however, research on loneliness has suggested that the worst part about it may be its association with particular behaviors, feelings, and perceptions that tend to interfere with the establishment or restoration of mutually satisfying relationships. In other words, once a person becomes lonely he or she may behave in a way that reduces the likelihood of establishing new friendships.

The high frequency of negative emotions and thoughts and ineffective interpersonal behaviors among lonely persons has been demonstrated in several related studies focusing on interactions among strangers (Bell, 1985; Jones, Freemon, & Goswick, 1981; Jones, Sansone, & Helm, 1983). Typically, college students who are strangers to one another are asked to participate in brief conversations in pairs or groups of students, after which they are asked to rate themselves and their partners (or fellow group members) on several relevant interper-

ACTIVITY BOX

Experience of Loneliness in Various Situations

In addition to personality factors, loneliness is influenced by various situations and experiences. Listed below are brief descriptions of several situations and events experienced by college students from time to time. Read each description and indicate on the scale below how lonely each situation would make you feel. Then you may compare your answers to those given by a large group of college students in a study reported by Jones, Cavert, Snider, and Bruce (1985b). Use the following scale in making your judgments:

1 = This would not make me feel lonely.
2 = This would make me feel slightly lonely.
3 = This would make me feel somewhat lonely.
4 = This would make me feel lonely.
5 = This would make me feel extremely lonely.

Descriptions

_____ 1. Being alone at night
_____ 2. Being away from all my friends

sonal dimensions—for example, friendliness, attraction, honesty, and so on. Also, participants' views of partners' views (called metaperceptions) are sometimes assessed.

These studies have demonstrated that high as compared to low lonely participants tend to rate themselves negatively following laboratory interactions with strangers; specifically, lonely participants are more likely to rate themselves as having been less honest, less open, less warm, and less friendly in both dyadic and group settings (Jones et al., 1981; Jones et al., 1983). Also, lonely participants expected to be rated negatively by their partners and fellow group members along the same dimensions. Similarly, Bell (1985) found that high lonely participants expected their partners to be less interested in continued interactions with them. Moreover, high lonely as contrasted with low lonely participants tended to rate their partners more negatively in some cases, indicating less interest in continued interactions with their partners, less interpersonal attraction for partners, and less interest in developing a friendship with their partner (Bell, 1985; Jones et al., 1981; Jones et al., 1983). Furthermore, lonelier participants acquired less information

---

   ——   3. Listening to a sad song
   ——   4. Being away from my family
   ——   5. When I am left out of parties or other activities
   ——   6. The first day at a new school
   ——   7. Not having any friends
   ——   8. Being "stood up" by a date or a friend
   ——   9. If my boy/girlfriend "broke up" with me
   —— 10. After arguing with my parents
   —— 11. When someone stops being my friend
   —— 12. When I am alone on weekends
   —— 13. When with others with whom I disagree
   —— 14. When I am too busy to be with others
   —— 15. When watching a sad movie

Average response given by 117 college students about the amount of loneliness experienced in various situations: 1 = 2.44; 2 = 3.20; 3 = 2.83; 4 = 2.85; 5 = 3.73; 6 = 3.08; 7 = 4.30; 8 = 3.54; 9 = 4.11; 10 = 2.66; 11 = 3.22; 12 = 3.02; 13 = 1.77; 14 = 3.21; 15 = 2.19.

about their partners (e.g., background, interests, etc.) during such interactions and one study showed that the tendency on the part of lonelier participants to rate themselves negatively and to expect negative ratings remained stable over a two-month period during which continued interactions occurred (Jones et al., 1981).

To summarize, following brief interactions with strangers, lonely persons perceive themselves and their fellow participants in a less favorable light and they expect negative ratings if not outright rejection from their fellow participants. Also, loneliness appears to be related to gaining less information from initial interactions with participants. This latter finding might be due to partners' revealing less information to lonely persons or to lonely persons paying less attention to their partners. Research on loneliness and actual interpersonal behavior favors the latter hypothesis.

On the other hand, several studies found only modest support for the expectation that the partners of lonely participants in these studies would rate them more negatively (e.g., Jones et al., 1983). In one study (Jones et al., 1981) high as compared to low lonely participants were rated lower on friendliness, interpersonal attractiveness, and leadership. Also, lonelier participants have been rated as "more difficult to get to know" (Solano, Batten, & Parish, 1982) or as "liking themselves less" (Jones et al., 1983). Even so, the evidence that lonely persons are rejected by their interaction partners is not strong.

And yet there is also evidence that loneliness is related to certain conversational behaviors emitted during interactions with strangers. For example, in such settings, high as compared to low lonely college students have been found to talk less, ask fewer questions, change the topic more frequently, and to attend less to their interaction partners (Bell, 1985; Jones, Hobbs, & Hockenbury, 1982). Putting the major findings together we may conclude that lonely persons appear to interact with strangers in an unresponsive and self-focused manner, to talk relatively more about themselves, and to ask few questions of their interaction partners. Contrary to what one might expect, such behavior does not seem to lead to extensive rejection on the part of others. Instead, lonely people themselves appear to form a very negative impression of their own behavior, a negative impression of their partners, and the expectation that their partners do not like them. Under such circumstances, it would appear that lonely persons reject and withdraw from others—perhaps, in their minds, before they can be rejected by others. Whatever the reasons, given such behavior it is not surprising that lonely people tend to remain lonely over considerable periods of time (Cutrona, 1982).

Because of the strong likelihood that these reactions and behaviors will not alleviate one's condition of loneliness and given the unpleasantness of loneliness itself, why do lonely people behave this way? Although there are undoubtedly various reasons, one potential explanation is that people who are less effective at interacting with others are more likely to develop loneliness and more likely also to behave in the manner described. In fact, research on loneliness has suggested several connections to personality dimensions reflecting generally ineffective patterns of social interaction including, for example, shyness, low empathy, low social risk taking, heterosocial anxiety, external locus of control, alienation, and low self-esteem (cf. Peplau & Perlman, 1982).

But given the variety of personality dimensions related to loneliness, two central questions remain. First, to what extent is loneliness determined by pre-existent personality factors or to what extent does the development of loneliness result in the development of certain personality characteristics such as shyness? In other words, what is the direction of the association between loneliness and personality? Second, it is reasonable to assume—and there is substantial evidence to suggest—that many of the personality correlates of loneliness are themselves correlated. Thus, the question arises as to which personality variables or combination of variables best predict loneliness. Fortunately, there are data with which to address both issues.

Regarding the issue of directionality, some evidence from longitudinal studies tentatively favors the hypothesis that the personality correlates of loneliness precede and contribute to the development of loneliness rather than vice versa (e.g., Jones, Cavert, Snider, & Bruce, 1985b; Shaver, Furman, & Buhmeister, 1985). For example, shy students going away to college appear to be more vulnerable to developing loneliness. Also, several studies have demonstrated that social skills, training procedures, and other intervention strategies designed to improve skills and reduce social anxiety, not only do so, but also result in reductions in loneliness that suggest a causal connection between social skill dimensions of personality and the experience of loneliness (e.g., Jones, Hobbs, & Hockenbury, 1982).

With respect to the second issue, Jones et al. (1985a) grouped a large number of self-reported personality variables previously found to be associated with loneliness (using a statistical procedure called factor analysis) and then compared the resultant groups with scores on a standard measure of loneliness. Two groups of scores appeared to be most strongly and more or less equally related to loneliness. One composite variable, which might be termed *initiation skills,* included high levels of such personality dimensions as masculinity and assertiveness and low levels of personality variables such as shyness. The second factor, which might be termed *enhancement skills,* contained variables such as empathy, self-esteem, self-disclosure, femininity, and trust, all at high levels. This basic pattern of results has been replicated by Wittenberg and Reis (1986).

Relational Competence

Both initiation and enhancement skills might be thought of as those aspects of personality that facilitate the development of close personal relationships and hence provide a barrier to the experience of loneliness. In this regard, some writers (e.g., Hansson, Jones, & Carpenter, 1984) have called such characteristics *relational competence,* meaning that such characteristics make the acquisition and maintenance of mutually satisfying relationships easier and more effective. In other words, the successful completion of each stage of relationship development would be facilitated by certain abilities as well as freedom from inhibitory social anxieties such as shyness. For example, the initiation phase of a relationship often requires the ability to be assertive in ambiguous social settings (e.g., parties, social gatherings, first meetings, etc.) and therefore would place a premium on personality characteristics such as high independence and low shyness. By contrast, the enhancement and maintenance phases of relationships would be facilitated by the ability to take the perspective of one's partner, by listening, openness, and empathy. Finally, once the relationship has ceased to exist in the termination phase, both types of personality dimensions would be required to acquire and establish new relationships.

Research indicates that persons high in relational competence not only report having more friends and more satisfying relationships among both family and friends, but also that they are better able to adapt to changes and stress in their relationships and in their lives generally. For example, relational competence has been found to be important in acquiring and maintaining a supportive network of friends and family (Jones, 1984), adjusting to medical conditions such as diabetes (Carpenter, Hansson, Rountree, & Jones, 1983), to old age (Hansson, 1986), and in avoiding abusive and ineffective child-rearing patterns in response to the stresses to raising children (Kugler & Hansson, 1988). Thus, research on the concept of relational competence emphasizes the role of one's personality in the development and maintenance of one's relationships.

Concluding Remarks

The concepts of relationships and personality refer to complex interpersonal and psychological processes that are fundamentally involved in the full spectrum of human behavior and experience. As a consequence, efforts to draw broad conclusions regarding their mutual influences and connections necessarily omit considerable qualifying detail and thereby risk oversimplification. Nonetheless, a few concluding and summary comments are in order. First, most relevant theories, to varying degrees, emphasize that the mutual influence of personality and relationships is dynamic; each influences the development and outcome of the other. Second, many theories and much research in personality have focused on the role of early parent-child relationships in the formation of personality; for example, the degree of attachment between an infant and his or her primary caregiver. In addition, although the effects of relationships on personality development are undoubtedly greater early in life, subsequent relationships during childhood, adolescence, adulthood, and old age also may contribute to the shaping of various aspects of personality organization and structure (e.g., identity, emotional and cognitive styles, motives, adjustment, etc.). Thus, the degree of influence may well "narrow" over the life course as personality assumes consistency, but each stage of life presents its own unique challenges. Therefore, personality change and adaptation may be influenced by available relationships and support networks at any point in life.

Third, what a person becomes plays a major role also in the quality and quantity of relationships in which he or she engages. In adolescence and adulthood the influence of personality on the individual's efforts at, for example, acquiring friends, as well as other's reactions to such efforts has been extensively documented, particularly with respect to certain dimensions such as shyness and sociability. Less obviously, the personality and behavioral tendencies of the infant may also determine, in part, the vigor and effectiveness of parental nurturance. Fourth, although a wealth of personality dimensions has been related to important relational outcomes, recent research supports the idea that personality dimensions critical to relationships are organized into a structure that resembles the major stages of relational development and change. In other words, personality dimensions that facilitate or inhibit meeting people, talking to strangers, and the like differ, to some extent, from the dimensions that facilitate or inhibit psychological and sexual intimacy, self-disclosure, and long-term commitment.

Finally, research and theorizing on the nexus of personality and relationships will, of course, continue and may result in the modification of at least some of the ideas and conclusions presented in this chapter. This is as it should be. It is unlikely, however, that future conceptions will diminish or detract from the apparent importance and centrality of personality and relationships to an understanding of human behavior and experience.

Summary

An interpersonal relationship may be defined as a state of mutual awareness in which participants feel an emotional bond toward each other. Understanding relationships is necessary for understanding personality because relationships: (1) are central and important to life; (2) form the context in which other experiences evolve; (3) play a role in adjustment and health; (4) contribute to the development of personality; and (5) are determined, in part, by one's personality. Measures of relationships may be divided into qualitative versus quantitative approaches and may also be distinguished on the basis of breadth of focus and perspective. Relationships may be described as developing through four phases: initiation, enhancement, maintenance, and termination. The factors that determine the nature and closeness of a relationship vary as a function of phase and the type of relationship and include characteristics of the person, characteristics of the other, and characteristics of the situation.

Several theories have suggested how personality is formed in conjunction with the prototypical relationship between an infant and caregiver. Prominent among such theories are the ideas of Freud, the neo-Freudians, and attachment theory. The influence on the development of relationships of a variety of personality dimensions has been investigated. For example, loneliness, defined as dissatisfaction with the relationships one has, is related to various dimensions of personality including negative emotions and ineffective interpersonal styles such as shyness. Moreover, the personality dimensions associated with loneliness appear to lead to less responsive and self-focused interpersonal behaviors that reduce the likelihood that any given acquaintanceship will result in a mutually satisfying relationship. Relational competence, consisting of initiation and enhancement skills, is related to one's vulnerability to the experience of loneliness under conditions of stress and also has been proposed as a model for describing the influence of various personality dimensions on the development, maintenance, and termination of relationships.

SUGGESTED READINGS

Bowlby, J. (1969). *Attachment and loss. Vol. 1. Attachment.* London: Hogarth. A presentation of Bowlby's view of the instinctive patterns of attachment-seeking and attachment-providing behaviors by infant and caregiver.

Jones, W. H., Cheek, J. M., & Briggs, S. R. (Eds.). (1986). *Shyness: Perspectives on research and treatment.* New York: Plenum. A comprehensive review of research and therapeutic interventions on shyness.

Jones, W. H., Hobbs, S. A., & Hockenbury, D. (1982). Loneliness and social skill deficits. *Journal of Personality and Social Psychology, 42,* 682–689. This article describes how deficits in conversational skills may contribute to loneliness.

Peplau, L. A., & Perlman, D. (Eds.). (1982). *Loneliness: A sourcebook of current theory, research and therapy.* New York: Wi-

ley-Interscience. An excellent summary of work being conducted on loneliness. It includes personality scales for measuring loneliness.

Young, J. E. (1986). A cognitive-behavioral approach to friendship disorders. In V. J. Derlega & B. A. Winstead (Eds.), *Friendship and social interaction* (pp. 247–276). New York: Springer-Verlag. A cognitive behavior therapist describes the psychological problems and solutions to loneliness.

REFERENCES

Ainsworth, M. D. S., & Bell, S. M. (1969). Some contemporary patterns of mother–infant interaction in the feeding situation. In J. A. Ambrose (Ed.), *Stimulation in early infancy* (pp. 133–170). London: Academic Press.

Bell, R. A. (1985). Conversational involvement and loneliness. *Communication Monographs, 52,* 1317–1318.

Berscheid, E., & Walster, E. (1969). *Interpersonal attraction.* Reading, MA: Addison-Wesley.

Bowlby, J. (1969). *Attachment and loss, Vol. 1. Attachment.* London: Hogarth.

Bowlby, J. (1973). *Attachment and loss. Vol. 2. Anxiety and anger.* London: Hogarth.

Bretherton, I., & Waters, E. (Eds.). (1985). *Growing points of attachment theory and research.* Chicago: Society for Research in Child Development.

Byrne, D. (1971). *The attraction paradigm.* New York: Academic Press.

Carpenter, B. N., Hansson, R. O., Rountree, R., & Jones, W. H. (1983). Relational competence and adjustment in diabetic patients. *Journal of Social and Clinical Psychology, 1,* 359–369.

Clark, M. S., & Mills, J. (1979). Interpersonal attraction in exchange and communal relationships. *Journal of Personality and Social Psychology, 37,* 12–24.

Cutrona, C. E. (1982). Transition to college: Loneliness and the process of social adjustment. In L. A. Peplau & D. Perlman (Eds.), *Loneliness: A sourcebook of current theory, research and therapy* (pp. 291–309). New York: Wiley-Interscience.

Derlega, V. J., Wilson, M., & Chaikin, A. L. (1976). Friendship and disclosure reciprocity. *Journal of Personality and Social Psychology, 34,* 578–582.

Foa, E. B., & Foa, U. G. (1976). Resource theory of social exchange. In J. W. Thibaut, J. T. Spence, & R. C. Carson (Eds.), *Contemporary topics in social psychology* (pp. 99–131). Morristown, NJ: General Learning Press.

Gardner, L. (1972). Deprivation dwarfism. *Scientific American, 227,* 76–82.

Hafner, R. J. (1986). *Marriage and mental illness.* New York: Guilford.

Hansson, R. O. (1986). Relational competence, relationships, and adjustment in old age. *Journal of Personality and Social Psychology, 50,* 1050–1058.

Hansson, R. O., Jones, W. H., & Carpenter, B. N. (1984). Relational competence and social support. In P. Shaver (Ed.), *Review of personality and social psychology, Vol 5. Emotions, relationships and health* (pp. 265–284). Beverly Hills, CA.: Sage.

Hartup, W. W. (1986). On relationships and development. In W. W. Hartup & Z. Rubin (Eds.), *Relationships and development* (pp. 1–26). Hillsdale, NJ: Erlbaum.

Hogan, R. (1983). A socioanalytic theory of personality. In M. M. Page (Ed.), *Personality, current theory & research. Nebraska symposium on motivation 1982* (pp. 55–90). Lincoln, NE: University of Nebraska Press.

Ichheiser, G. (1970). *Appearances and realities.* San Francisco: Jossey-Bass.

Jones, W. H. (1984, August). *Relational competence in loneliness and social support.* Paper presented at the annual meeting of the American Psychological Association, Toronto, Ontario, Canada.

Jones, W. H., Carpenter, B. N., & Quintana, D. (1985a). Personality and interpersonal predictors of loneliness in two cultures. *Journal of Personality and Social Psychology, 48,* 1503–1511.

Jones, W. H., Cavert, C. W., Snider, R., & Bruce, T. (1985b). Relational stress: An analysis of situations and events associated with loneliness. In S. Duck & D. Perlman (Eds.), *Understanding personal relationships* (pp. 221–242). London: Sage.

Jones, W. H., Cheek, J. M., & Briggs, S. R. (Eds.). (1986). *Shyness: Perspectives on research and treatment.* New York: Plenum.

Jones, W. H., Freemon, J. E., & Goswick, R. A. (1981). The persistence of loneliness: Self and other determinants. *Journal of Personality, 49,* 27–48.

Jones, W. H., Hobbs, S. A., & Hockenbury, D. (1982). Loneliness and social skill deficits. *Journal of Personality and Social Psychology, 42,* 682–689.

Jones, W. H., Sansone, C., & Helm, B. (1983). Loneliness and interpersonal judgments. *Personality and Social Psychology Bulletin, 9,* 437–441.

Jourard, S. M. (1964). *The transparent self.* Princeton, NJ: Van Nostrand Reinhold.

Kerckhoff, A. C., & Davis, K. E. (1962). Value consensus and need complementarity in mate selection. *American Sociological Review, 27,* 295–303.

Kiecolt-Glaser, J. K., Garner, W., Speicher, C., Penn, G. M., Holliday, J., & Glaser, R. (1984). Psychosocial modifiers of immunocompetence in medical students. *Psychosomatic Medicine, 46,* 7–14.

Kugler, K. E., & Hansson, R. O. (1988). Relational competence and social support among parents at risk of child abuse. *Family Relations, 37,* 328–332.

Larson, R., Csikszentmihalyi, M., & Graef, R. (1982). Time alone in daily experience: Loneliness or renewal? In L. A. Peplau & D. Perlman (Eds.), *Loneliness: A sourcebook of current theory, research and therapy* (pp. 40–53). New York: Wiley-Interscience.

Levinger, G., Senn, D. J., & Jorgensen, B. W. (1970). Progress toward permanence in courtship: A test of the Kerckhoff-Davis hypotheses. *Sociometry, 33,* 427–443.

Levinger, G., & Snoek, J. D. (1972). *Attraction in relationship: A new look at interpersonal attraction.* Morristown, NJ: General Learning Press.

Lynch, J. J. (1981). *The broken heart: The medical consequences of loneliness in America.* New York: Basic Books.

Miller, R. S. (1986). Embarrassment: Causes and consequences. In W. H. Jones, J. M. Cheek, & S. R. Briggs (Eds.), *Shyness: Perspectives on research and treatment* (pp. 295–311). New York: Plenum.

Murstein, B. I. (1972). Physical attraction and marital choice. *Journal of Personality and Social Psychology, 33,* 8–12.

Murstein, B. I. (1986). *Paths to marriage.* Beverly Hills, CA.: Sage.

Newcomb, T. M. (1961). *The acquaintance process.* New York: Holt, Rinehart & Winston.

Peplau, L. A., & Perlman, D. (Eds.). (1982). *Loneliness: A sourcebook of current theory, research and therapy.* New York: Wiley-Interscience.

Remondet, J. H., Hansson, R. O., Rule, B., & Winfrey, G. (1987). Rehearsal for widowhood. *Journal of Social and Clinical Psychology, 5,* 285–297.

Rollins, B., & Cannon, K. (1974). Marital satisfaction over the family life cycle: A reevaluation. *Journal of Marriage and the Family, 36,* 271–282.

Russell, D., Peplau, L. A., & Cutrona, C. E. (1980). The revised UCLA Loneliness Scale: Concurrent and discriminant validity evidence. *Journal of Personality and Social Psychology, 39,* 472–480.

Sarason, I. G., & Sarason, B. R. (Eds.). (1985). *Social support: Theory, research and applications.* Boston: Matinus Nijhoff.

Schachter, S. (1959). *The psychology of affiliation.* Stanford, CA.: Stanford University Press.

Shaver, P., Furman, W., & Buhmeister, D. (1985). Transition to college. Network changes, social skills, and loneliness. In S. Duck & D. Perlman (Eds.), *Understanding personal relationships* (pp. 193–220). London: Sage.

Solano, C. H., Batten, P. G., & Parish, E. A. (1982). Loneliness and patterns of self-disclosure. *Journal of Personality and Social Psychology, 43,* 524–531.

Sternberg, R. (1987). Explorations of love. In W. H. Jones & D. Perlman (Eds.), *Advances in personal relationships, Vol. 1* (pp. 171–196). Greenwich, CT.: JAI Press.

Stroebe, W., & Stroebe, M. S. (1986). Beyond marriage: The impact of partner loss on health. In R. Gilmour & S. Duck (Eds.), *The emerging field of personal relationships* (pp. 203–224). Hillsdale, NJ: Erlbaum.

Sullivan, H. S. (1953). *The interpersonal theory of psychiatry.* New York: Norton.

Swensen, C. H. (1973). *Introduction to interpersonal relations.* Glenview, IL: Scott, Foresman.

Thibaut, J. W., & Kelley, H. H. (1959). *The social psychology of groups.* New York: Wiley.

Winch, R. F. (1958). *Mate-selection: A study of complementary needs.* New York: Harper & Row.

Wittenberg, M. T., & Reis, H. T. (1986). Loneliness, social skills, and social perception. *Personality and Social Psychology Bulletin, 12,* 121–130.

CONTRIBUTORS

Roy Baumeister
Department of Psychology
Case Western Reserve University

Hal S. Bertilson
Office of Natural and Social
Sciences
Kearney State College

Stephen R. Briggs
Department of Psychology
University of Tulsa

Jerry M. Burger
Department of Psychology
University of Santa Clara

Jonathan M. Cheek
Department of Psychology
Wellesley College

Richard J. Davidson
Department of Psychology
University of Wisconsin—Madison

Mark H. Davis
Department of Psychology
Eckerd College

Valerian J. Derlega
Department of Psychology
Old Dominion University

Nicholas Emler
Department of Psychology
University of Dundee, Scotland

Stephen L. Franzoi
Department of Psychology
Marquette University

David C. Funder
Department of Psychology
University of California—Riverside

Clyde Hendrick
Department of Psychology
Texas Tech University

Susan S. Hendrick
Department of Psychology
Texas Tech University

Thomas Hill
Department of Psychology
University of Tulsa

Warren H. Jones
Department of Psychology
University of Tennessee

Douglas T. Kenrick
Department of Psychology
Arizona State University

Randy J. Larsen
Department of Psychological
Sciences
Purdue University

Pawel Lewicki
Department of Psychology
University of Tulsa

James E. Maddux
Department of Psychology
George Mason University

Dan P. McAdams
School of Education and Social
Policy
Northwestern University

Charles K. Prokop
Department of Psychology
University of North Carolina
at Asheville

David C. Rowe
Department of Family Studies
University of Arizona

Rhoda K. Unger
Department of Psychology
Montclair State College

Patricia L. Waters
Department of Psychology
University of Denver

Barbara A. Winstead
Department of Psychology
Old Dominion University

NAME INDEX

Abelson, R. P., 154, 165, 185, 186, 342
Abramson, L. Y., 187, 290
Aderman, D., 328, 339
Adler, A., 116, 136–39, 522
Adler, N. L., 443
Agostinelli, G., 363
Ahern, G. L., 100
Ainsworth, M. D. S., 122, 144, 524
Alexander, A. B., 484
Alexander, F., 484, 485
Alford, L. B., 98
Allen, A., 164
Allen, C. K., 291
Allen, V. L., 291
Allport, G. W., 8, 9, 21, 23, 44, 88, 167, 180
Amabile, T. M., 163
Amelang, M., 162
Anderson, S. M., 276, 296
Angleitner, A., 44
Ansbacher, H. L., 138, 289
Ansbacher, R. R., 138, 289
Archer, R. L., 450
Arend, R., 124, 128
Aristotle, 180
Arkin, R. M., 292, 307
Aronson, E., 318
Atherton, S. C., 240
Atkinson, J. W., 247
Averill, J. R., 292, 410, 471, 478

Bakan, D., 197
Bandura, A., 8, 131, 232, 235, 240,

245, 248, 472, 473, 474–75
Bar-Tal, D., 295
Bar-Zohar, Y., 295
Barefoot, J. C., 485, 491
Barnes, G. E., 439
Barnes, J., 253
Barnes, M., 170
Baron, R. A., 460, 471, 472, 473
Baron, R. M., 157
Barrett, K. C., 128
Bartone, P. T., 487, 488, 489
Baruch, R., 194
Batten, P. G., 528
Baum, A., 299, 493
Baumeister, R. F., 315, 349–80
Baumgardner, A. H., 292, 369
Baumrind, D., 134
Baur, K., 437, 443, 444
Beccaria, C., 384
Beck, A. T., 242
Beck, S., 444
Bell, A., 436, 443
Bell, R. A., 526, 527, 528
Bell, R. R., 441
Bell, S. M., 122, 524
Bem, D. J., 141–42, 145, 161, 164, 167
Bem, S. L., 272, 273, 275–78
Benassi, V. A., 296
Bennett, E. L., 92
Bentham, J., 384
Bentler, P. M., 437
Berg, J. H., 450
Berglas, S. C., 365

Bergman, A., 353
Berkowitz, L., 461 468, 469–70, 471, 475
Bernard, H. S., 373
Berscheid, E., 161, 515, 518
Bertilson, H. S., 457–78
Bigelow, B. J., 140
Billy, J. O. G., 437
Blascovich, J., 359, 360
Blehar, M. C., 122, 144
Block, J., 125, 135, 161, 165, 464, 468
Block, J. H., 125, 135, 161
Bloom, A. R., 194
Blos, P., 371, 374
Blum, J. E., 76
Blumenthal, J., 491
Bollmeier, L. N., 485
Booth-Kewley, S., 491
Borden, R. J., 475
Borkenau, P., 162
Boss, A., 226
Bouchard, T. J., Jr., 56, 70, 75
Bouffard, D. L., 167
Bourne, E., 373
Bower, G. H., 414
Bowlby, J., 122, 125, 139, 140, 144, 184, 198, 512, 524
Box, S., 389
Boyatzis, R. E., 194
Bradburn, N. M., 414
Brand, P., 200
Brecher, E. M., 435, 436
Breen, L. J., 295

Breger, L., 184
Brehm, S. S., 291
Brenner, C., 140
Bretherton, I., 525
Breuer, J., 472
Brewer, L. C., 321, 328, 339
Briggs, S. R., 15–53, 515
Brim, O. G., 353
Brody, N., 214
Brooks-Gunn, J., 352, 353
Brown, R., 291
Brownlee, E. A., 369
Bruce, T., 526, 529
Bryan, J., 163
Bryant, F. B., 199
Buchsbaum, M. S., 97, 98
Buder, J., 354
Buechler, S., 411
Buhmeister, D., 529
Bullard, N. G., 307
Bullough, V. L., 436
Burger, J. M., 287–312
Burt, C., 76
Burton, R. V., 391
Buss, A. H., 320, 321, 322, 328–
    36, 341, 342, 466, 468
Buss, D. M., 170, 330
Butcher, J. N., 485
Butterfield, E. C., 208
Byrne, D., 446, 447, 515, 516

Cadoret, R. J., 80
Cain, C. A., 80
Campbell, A., 414
Campbell, D. T., 43
Campbell, J. D., 362, 363
Campos, J. J., 128
Cannon, K., 518
Caplovitz, D., 414
Carlson, L., 192
Carpenter, B. N., 525, 529, 530
Carroll, J. L., 442
Carson, R. C., 485
Carver, C. S., 321, 327, 328, 330,
    335, 336–41, 343–44, 496, 497
Caspi, A., 141–42, 148
Cassidy, J., 124, 125, 126, 128
Castro, F., 155, 157
Cattell, R. B., 8, 69
Cavert, C. W., 526, 529
Chaikin, A. L., 516
Chaplin, W. F., 36
Chaskes, J. B., 441

Chassin, L., 363
Cheek, J. M., 113–45, 157, 162,
    164, 315, 515
Cheek, J. V. P., 439
Chesney, M. A., 490
Chester, N. L., 194
Child, P., 365
Chomsky, N., 215, 218
Christie, R., 298
Cicero, 36
Clark, L. A., 412
Clark, M. S., 517, 520
Clark, R. A., 247
Clement, U., 442
Cochrane, R., 397
Cohen, L. J., 492
Coleman, J. C., 485
Coles, M. G. H., 95
Collins, B. E., 298
Collins, D. L., 493
Colvin, C. R., 157, 161, 162
Comstock, G. W., 488
Conger, J. C., 243
Connelly, F., 295
Constantian, C. A., 198
Constantinople, A., 272
Converse, P. E., 414
Cook, E. W., 96
Cook, T. D., 170
Cook, W., 491
Cookson, D., 139
Cooley, C. H., 162, 317, 522
Cooper, H. M., 295, 300, 302, 303
Coopersmith, S., 355
Costa, P. T., Jr., 45, 46, 47, 68,
    419, 487, 489, 491
Courington, S., 488, 504
Coursey, R. D., 98
Courtney, B. E., 357
Cowles, A., 299
Crick, Francis, 61
Crider, A., 95
Crocker, J., 363
Cronbach, L. J., 40, 48, 389
Crooks, R., 437, 443, 444
Crowe, R. R., 80
Crowne, D. P., 476
Csikszentmihalyi, M., 511
Cutrona, C. E., 526, 528
Czyzewska, M., 214, 216, 226

Dahl, R. H., 168
Dahlstrom, W. G., 485, 491

Daignault, G., 295
Damasio, A. R., 214
Damon, W., 353, 372
Dantchik, A., 167
Darley, J., 386
Darwin, Charles, 178
Davidson, R. J., 87–112
Davidson, W., 269, 270
Davis, K. E., 517
Davis, M. H., 313–47
Davis, M. S., 436, 442
Deaux, K., 264, 268, 270, 280, 282
deCharms, R., 289, 299
Defour, C. L., 296
DeFries, J. C., 64, 76, 80
DeLamater, J., 441
Dembroski, T. M., 302, 491
Denenberg, V. H., 99
Dengerink, H. A., 476, 477
Derlega, V. J., 1–12, 263–86, 450,
    516
Derryberry, D., 107
DeSoto, C. B., 165
Devr, J. L., 130
Diamond, M. C., 92
DiClemente, C. C., 241
Diener, E., 102, 413, 414, 417,
    418, 419, 421, 422, 424, 427,
    428
Dimsdale, J. E., 491
Dobroth, J. M., 162, 164
Dollard, J., 7–8, 10, 472
Doob, L., 472
Dornbusch, S. M., 157
Duval, S., 321, 325
Dweck, C. S., 269, 270, 291

Eagleston, J. R., 490
Eagly, A. H., 267, 281
Edelberg, W., 161
Eisen, M., 354
Elder, G., 141–42, 145
Ellis, H. H., 435, 436
Emler, N., 381–406
Emmons, C. A., 442
Emmons, R. A., 102, 185, 186,
    413, 414, 419, 422, 427
Endler, N. S., 167
Engelse, J. A., 321
Enna, B., 269, 270
Entwisle, D. R., 193
Epstein, S., 40, 165, 166
Eriksen, C. W., 213

Erikson, E. H., 122, 192, 353
Eron, L. D., 460, 465, 468
Eysenck, H. J., 8, 36, 68–69, 89, 139, 397, 439, 465, 466, 467
Eysenck, S. B. G., 69
Ezrin, C., 485

Fancher, R. E., 57
Farber, I. E., 151, 154, 182
Farris, E., 268
Farrow, D. L., 196
Fazio R. H., 331
Feld, S., 414
Fenigstein, A., 320, 321, 322, 334
Ferrell, M. L., 442
Festinger, L., 178
Field, P., 362
Findley, M. J., 295
Fine, R. L., 325
Finner, S., 440
Fischbein, S., 77
Fishbaugh, L., 281
Fisher, R. A., 60
Fisher, W. A., 446, 447
Fiske, D. W., 34–35, 43
Fiske, S. T., 368, 473
Fleming, J. S., 357
Floderus, B., 488
Flynn, J. R., 79
Foa, E. B., 518
Foa, U. G., 518
Fodor, E. M., 195, 196, 197
Folkman, S., 296
Fonda, J., 233
Foote, F. H., 442, 434, 446
Ford, L. H., 353
Fordyce, M. W., 414
Fowles, D. C., 95
Fox, N. A., 104
Franzoi, S. L., 313–47
Frederick, S. L., 99
Freemon, J. E., 527, 528
French, T. M., 484
Freud, A., 121
Freud, S., 5–6, 9, 88, 115, 116–21, 179, 212–13, 227, 317, 385, 435, 472, 483, 484, 521–22
Frey, D., 328
Friberg, L., 56
Friedman, H. S., 491
Friedman, M., 489, 490
Froming, W. J., 335, 340, 341
Fromm, Eric, 522

Fujioka, T., 365
Fulker, D. W., 465, 466, 467
Funder, D. C., 155, 157, 158, 161, 162, 164, 165, 167, 168
Furman, W. 529

Gaines, B., 369
Gainotti, G., 99
Galanter, E., 185, 186, 336
Gale, A., 95
Galton, F., 57–60
Gangestad, S., 319, 440–41
Gardner, L., 513
Garner, W., 512
Geen, R. G., 475
Genung, V., 167
George, L., 436
Gergen, K. J., 9, 150, 154
Gerrard, M., 442
Geschwind, N., 99
Gibbons, F. X., 327, 331, 339
Gibson, H., 390
Gilligan, C., 200
Gilmore, T. M., 295
Glaser, R., 512
Glass, D. C., 296, 321
Glick, S. D., 99
Glucksberg, S., 214
Gold, M., 389, 391
Goldberg, E. L., 488
Goldberg, L. R., 36, 44, 362, 488, 151, 157
Goldman, W., 161
Goldsmith, H. H., 128
Goldstein, I. L., 318
Goldstein, K., 98
Goleman, D., 369
Gormly, J., 161
Goswick, R. A., 526, 527, 528
Gove, F. L., 124, 128
Graef, R., 511
Graham, J. W., 299
Grant, V. W., 443
Gray, J. A., 89, 421
Green, S. E., 444, 446, 447
Greenberg, M., 99
Greenberger, D. B., 291
Greene, D., 363
Greenwald, A. G., 354, 369
Gregory, R. L., 155
Griffin, J. J., 369
Griffith, W., 268
Guilford, J. P., 460

Gur, R. C., 99, 108, 316–17
Gurin, G., 414

Hackett, T. P., 491
Hadish, W. R., 170
Hafner, R. J. 512
Haier, R. J., 98
Hall, C. S., 3
Hammersmith, S., 443
Haney, T. L., 491
Hansson, R. O., 518, 530
Harlow, H. F., 122
Harrington, D., 135
Harris, V. A., 155
Hart, D., 353
Hartshorne, H., 165, 386–87, 389, 391
Hartup, W. W., 524
Hass, R. G., 321
Hastorf, A. H., 157
Hathaway, S. R., 465
Havighurst, R., 383, 389
Hay, D. A., 64
Hazan C., 126, 127, 128
Hearnshaw, L., 76
Heather, N., 390, 399
Helm, B., 526, 527, 528
Helmreich, R. L., 264, 272, 273, 275, 280
Hemans, L. T., 306
Hembree, E. A., 104
Henderson, N. D., 76
Hendrick, C., 264, 433–53
Hendrick, S. S., 433–53
Henriques, J. B., 95, 96, 100, 103
Hertzman, M., 315
Higgins, E. T., 367
Hill, T., 207–29
Hillery, J. M., 182
Hilton, I., 138
Hindelang, M., 390
Hippocrates, 180
Hiroto, D. S., 290
Hirschi, T., 390, 400
Hite, S., 436
Hobbs, S. A., 528, 529
Hochberg, J., 215, 218
Hockenbury, D., 528, 529
Hodes, R. L., 96
Hoffman, H., 214, 217
Hoffman, M. L., 184
Hogan, R., 165, 179, 198, 315, 513, 520

Hokanson, J. E., 473
Holliday, J., 512
Hollon, S. H., 242
Holmes, T. H., 486, 487, 498
Holroyd, K. A., 489
Hood, R., 331
Horner, M., 368
Horney, K., 120, 136, 140–41, 522
House, P., 363
Houts, A. C., 170
Huba, G. J., 437
Huesmann, L. R., 460, 465, 468
Hull, C. L., 181, 184
Hull, J. G., 328, 339, 503
Humphries, C., 335
Hungerbuhler, J. P., 99
Hunt, E., 77
Hunt, P. J., 182
Hunter, S., 450
Hutton, D. G., 355, 362
Hyde, J. S., 442

Ichheiser, G., 514
Ickes, W., 167, 168, 321
Izard, C. E, 104, 192, 195, 410–11

Jacklin, C. N., 266–67
Jackson, R. J., 198
Jacoby, L. L., 214
Jaffe, Y., 442
James, W., 163, 180, 317, 354
Jamner, L. D., 95
Janda, L. H., 444
Janis, I. L., 362
Jarvik, L. F., 76
Jefferson, T., 288
Jemmott, J. B., 197
Jenkins, C. D., 490
Jennings, W. S., 398–99
Jensen, 75
Jessor, R., 437
Jessor, S. L., 437
John, O. P., 36, 44
Johnson, J., 97
Johnson, V., 436
Jones, E. E., 155, 185, 365
Jones, W. H., 1–12, 509–32
Jorgensen, B. W., 517
Joseph, J. G., 442
Jourard, S. M., 516
Jung, C. G., 315
Jurich, A. P., 441
Jurich, J. A., 441

Kabat, L. G., 163
Kagan, J., 93, 96, 98, 104, 192, 353
Kahn, S., 500
Kaplan, A., 19
Kaplan, G. D., 299
Kaplan, H., 444
Kaplan, N., 124, 126, 128
Karabenick, S. A., 268
Katz, A. M., 303
Kauff, D. M., 214
Keane, S. P., 243
Keating, J. P., 291
Keel, R., 167
Keller, A., 353
Kelley, H. H., 178, 185, 518
Kelley, K., 152, 446, 447
Kelly, A., 100
Kelly, G. A., 178, 292
Kelly, K. L., 143
Kennedy, J. F., 79, 150, 160–61
Kenny, D. A., 168
Kenrick, D. T., 157, 158, 162, 164, 167, 168, 169, 170
Kerckhoff, A. C., 517
Kessler, R. C., 442
Kiecolt-Glaser, J. K., 512
Kihlstrom, J., 214
Kilkenny, R., 398–99
Kinsey, A. C., 435–36
Kirsch, I., 244
Kirshnit, C., 198
Klien, M., 392
Kline, P., 95, 118
Klinger, E., 185, 186
Knafo, D., 442
Kobak, R., 122, 127, 128
Kobasa, S. C., 488, 497, 498, 499, 500, 501–2, 504
Kock, S. W., 194
Kohlberg, L., 397–99
Kolata, G., 60
Kolers, P. A., 214, 215
Kolin, E. A., 440, 450
Kong, Y., 491
Konner, M., 184
Koropsak, E., 473
Krantz, D. S., 299
Krech, D., 92
Krull, D. S., 355
Kruse, M., 442
Kubos, K. L., 99
Kugler, K. E., 530
Kunda, Z., 363

Kunst-Wilson, W. R., 221

Lachman, J. L., 208
Lachman, R., 208
LaFrenier, P., 124
Lakey, B., 297
Lamb, M. E., 128
Lamiell, J. T., 24
Lang, P., 96
Langer, E. J., 291, 303
LaPiere, R. T., 342
Larsen, R. J., 102, 407–32
Larson, R., 511
Latane, B., 386
LaTorre, D., 292
LaVoie, L., 168
Lawler, K. A., 503
Lawroski, N., 124
Lazarus, R. S., 292, 296, 489
Le Bon, G., 385
Leary, M. R., 240, 254, 255
Lee, J. A., 451
Lee, K. L., 491
Lefcourt, H. M., 290, 294, 295, 296, 297
Lefkowitz, M. M., 460, 465, 468
Leiblum, S. R., 445
Lenney, E., 268, 277, 278
Lensky, D. B., 200
Lester, R., 200
Levenson, H., 298
Leventhal, H., 99, 473
Levine, A., 299
Levine, S., 102, 419, 422
Levinger, G., 517, 518–19
Levinson, D. J., 375
Levy, A. S., 328, 339
Lewicki, P., 207–29
Lewicki, R. J., 303
Lewin, K., 184
Lewis, H. B., 315
Lewis, J., 77
Lewis, M., 104, 352, 353
Lewis, P., 161
Licht, B. G., 291
Lichter, S. R., 195
Lincoln, Abraham, 288
Lind, E., 488
Linder, D., 318
Lindzey, G., 3
Little, B. R., 185, 186
Locke, J., 82, 179
Loehlin, J. C., 76

Lopyan, K. J., 340, 341
Lowell, E. L., 247
Luckey, E. B., 441
Lund, J., 161
Lunn, R., 95
Lunneborg, C., 77
Lykes, M. B., 264, 283
Lykken, D. T., 56, 70
Lynch, J. J., 512

Maccoby, E. E., 266–67
MacCorquodale, P., 441
MacDougall, J. M., 302, 491
Machover, K., 315
MacKinnon, D. W., 21
Maddi, S. R., 4, 487, 488, 489, 500, 501–2, 504
Maddux, J. E., 231–61
Maer, F., 109
Magnusson, D., 167
Mahler, M. S., 353
Mahone, C. H., 193
Maides, S., 299
Main, M., 124, 125, 126, 128
Malamuth, N. M., 439
Manning, M. M., 241
Maracek, J., 368
Marcia, J. E., 371, 373
Marks, G., 299
Markus, G. B., 139
Markus, H., 178, 185, 186, 366
Marlowe, D. A., 476
Martin, R. A., 297
Maruyama, G., 139
Maslow, A. H., 6, 178
Masters, William, 436
Masuda, M., 498
May, M. A., 165, 386–87, 391
May, R., 6
McAdams, D. P., 175–200
McArthur, L. Z., 157
McCallum, D. M., 501, 502, 503
McClearn, G. E., 56, 64
McClelland, D. C., 162, 187, 192, 193, 194, 195, 196, 197, 220, 247
McCloskey, M., 214
McCrae, R. R., 45, 46, 47, 68, 162, 419, 491
McDougall, W., 180
McFann, H. H., 182
McFarlin, D. B., 359, 360
McGue, M., 75

McGuire, C. V., 365
McGuire, W. J., 365
McKinley, J. C., 465
McNamara, W., 200
McWard, J., 292
Meacham, J. A., 353
Mead, G. H., 317, 522
Medley, D., 491
Meehl, P. E., 40
Meissner, P. B., 315
Mendonca, P. J., 291
Merz, J., 321
Mettee, D., 368
Meyer, A., 485
Miles, C. C., 271
Miller, G. A., 185, 186, 336
Miller, J. B., 120
Miller, L. C., 450
Miller, N., 139, 472
Miller, N. E., 7–8, 10
Miller, R. S., 296, 511
Miller, S. M., 292
Mills, J., 517, 520
Mischel, W., 8, 9, 161, 164–65, 386
Mohr, D. M., 354
Monat, A., 292
Monson, T. C., 161, 167
Montemayor, R., 354
Montgomery, S. B., 442
Monty, R. A., 291
Morash, 374
Morawski, J. G., 266, 271, 272, 275, 283
Morrison, S., 390
Morton, T. L., 450
Mosher, D. L., 444, 446, 447
Moskowitz, D. S., 389
Motti, P., 124
Mowrer, O., 472
Mueller, E., 140
Murphy, D. L., 98
Murray, H. A., 180, 187
Murstein, B. I., 519, 520
Musante, L., 302
Muzzy, R. E., 157

Nasby, W., 331
Nass, G. D., 441
Nauta, W. J. H., 100
Neale, M. C., 465, 466, 467
Nelson, S., 269, 270
Neumann, M., 445

Newcomb, M. D., 437
Newcomb, T. M., 515
Nias, D. K. B., 465, 466, 467
Nichols, R. C., 76
Nisbett, R. E., 151, 154, 214, 363
Nord, W. R., 295
Norman, W. T., 157
Norton, L. W., 253
Norton, L. W., 240, 251, 255
Nowack, K. M., 503
Nurius, P. S., 366–67
Nye, F. J., 390
Nyquist, 282

O'Brien, E. J., 165
O'Gorman, J. G., 95
O'Grady, K. E., 444
O'Leary, A., 255
Oakman, J. A., 307
Odbert, H. S., 44
Olds, J., 182
Olweus, D., 464, 468
Orlofsky, J. L., 275
Ostendorf, F., 44
Ostrow, D. G., 442
Overholser, J. C., 444
Oyserman, D., 367
Ozer, D. J., 165

Pack, S. J., 280
Palys, T. S., 185, 186
Pandey, J., 268
Parish, E. A., 528
Parke, R. D., 130
Parkes, K. R., 297
Patterson, G. R., 467, 474
Paulhus, D. L., 298
Pavlov, I. P., 88
Peale, N. V., 496
Pearson, K., 60
Pedersen, N. L., 56
Pelham, B. W., 355
Penn, G. M., 512
Penrose, G., 268
Peplau, L. A., 525, 526, 529
Perkins, D. V., 487
Perlman, D., 438, 450, 525, 529
Perlmuter, L. C., 291
Peterson, C., 131, 187, 290, 496
Peterson, M., 36
Petrie, A., 96, 97
Pfrang, H., 439
Phares, E. J., 294

Phillips, D., 475
Piaget, J., 140
Pigg, R., 475
Piliavin, J., 268
Pine, F., 353
Plato, 177, 178
Plomin, R., 56, 64, 65, 76, 80, 466
Pope, A., 177, 178
Powers, J., 198
Predmore, S. C., 369
Presson C. C., 363
Pribram, K. H., 185, 186, 336
Price, L., 440, 450
Price, R. H., 167
Price, T. R., 99
Prociuk, T. J., 295
Prokop, C. K., 481–505
Pryor, J. B., 331
Puccetti, M. C., 487, 488, 489, 501–2

Quanty, M. B., 472, 473
Quintana, D., 525, 529

Rahe, R. H., 486, 487, 488
Ransdell, H. J., 168
Rao, K., 99
Rausch, M. L., 168
Rausche, A., 439
Reber, A. S., 214
Reicher, S., 392, 397, 399, 401, 403
Reid, D. W., 295
Reis, H. T., 530
Reiss, I. L., 437, 446
Reivich, M., 108
Remondet, J. H., 518
Reznick, J. S., 93, 96, 98
Rhodewalt, F., 365
Rich, S., 56, 70
Richardson, J. L., 299
Richardson, S. A., 157
Ricks, D. F., 415–17, 428
Riggio, R. E., 321
Robinson, R. G., 99
Rock, I., 215
Rodgers, W. L., 414
Rodin, J., 291
Roediger, H. L., III, 215
Rogers, C. R., 6, 9, 116, 131, 132–33, 134, 135, 140, 178, 289, 354–55
Rogers, R. W., 250, 251, 256
Rollins, B., 518

Rosen, R. C., 445
Rosenberg, B. G., 139
Rosenberg, F., 354
Rosenberg, M., 354
Rosenfield, D., 268
Rosenheim, E., 445
Rosenman, R. H., 489, 490, 491
Rosensweig, M. R., 92
Ross, A., 392, 397, 399, 403
Ross, L., 154, 155, 363
Roth, R. S., 100
Roth, S., 492
Rothbart, M. K., 107
Rothman, S., 195
Rotter, J. B., 8, 184, 245, 293, 294, 297, 315, 499
Rountree, R., 530
Rousseau, J. J., 177
Rowe, D. C., 55–85
Rubin, I. M., 193–94
Rule, B., 518
Runyan, W. M., 24
Rushton, J. P., 170, 465, 466, 467
Russell, D., 526
Russell, J. A., 411, 412
Rutter, M., 128

Sackheim, H. A., 99, 316–17
Sadalla, E. K., 167, 170
Saleh, W. E., 297
Sandler, I. N., 297
Sansone, C., 526, 527, 528
Sarason, B. R., 512
Sarason, I. G., 512
Saron, C. D., 100, 103
Sasaki, I., 226
Sawin, 282
Scarr, S., 72–73, 79
Sceery, A., 122, 127, 128
Schachter, S., 139, 515
Schank, R. C., 154
Scheidel, D. G., 373
Scheier, M. F., 320, 321, 322, 328, 330, 335–41, 343–44, 496, 497
Schenk, J., 439
Scher, S. J., 369
Schlenker, B. R., 254, 318
Schmeid, L. A., 503
Schmidt, D. E., 291
Schmidt, G., 442
Schneider, D. J., 358
Schnerring, D. A., 304
Schork, E., 124

Schroeder, D. H., 487, 489
Schutte, N. A., 167
Schwartz, G. E., 90, 100, 109
Schwartz, I., 363
Schwartz, J. C., 389
Schwarzenegger, A., 233
Seamon, J. G., 214
Sears, R., 472
Segal, N. L., 56, 70
Seligman, M. E. P., 187, 290, 496
Selye, H., 485, 486
Senn, D. J., 517
Sentis, K., 178, 185
Senulis, J., 100, 103
Shapiro, J. J., 373
Shapiro, R. M., 99
Shaver, P., 126, 127, 128, 264, 529
Shearer, S. L., 100
Sherer, M., 250, 251
Sherk, D., 296
Sherman, S. J., 363
Shiller, V. M., 104
Shontz, E. C., 2, 460
Short, J. F., 390
Shrauger, J. S., 369, 359
Silberman, E. K., 99
Silverman, J., 97
Simmons, R., 354
Simpson, J. A., 319, 440–41
Sinatra, F., 150
Sinatra, N., 152
Singer, J. E., 296, 493
Singh, S., 194
Skelton, A., 365
Skinner, B. F., 6, 9, 130, 179, 289
Skrypnek, B. J., 282
Slapion-Foote, M. J., 434, 442, 446
Smith, L. H., 182
Smith, N., 222
Smith, N. G., 304
Smith, T., 195
Smollar, J., 140
Snider, R., 526, 529
Snidman, N., 93, 96, 98
Snoek, J. D., 518–19
Snyder, M., 161, 167, 168, 282, 315, 318, 319, 440–41
Solano, C., 165
Solano, C. H., 528
Solomon, R. L., 183
Sorenson, R., 436
Sorman, P. B., 359
Speicher, C., 512

Spence, J. T., 272, 273, 264, 275, 280, 282
Spence, K. W., 181, 182
Spielberger, C. D., 182
Spitz, R. A., 122
Spitzer, S. P., 438
Sroufe, L. A., 124, 128, 198
Stanley, M. A., 237, 241, 248, 257
Stapp, J., 272, 273
Starr, L. B., 99
Stayton, D. J., 122
Steenbarger, B. N., 328, 339
Stenberg, C., 128
Stenslie, C. E., 100
Stephan, W. G., 268
Stephens, D., 167
Stern, D. N., 197
Sternberg, R., 514, 519
Stewart, A. J., 194, 196, 264, 283
Stinus, L., 100
Stoltenberg, C. D., 251, 253
Stratton, J. R., 438
Straus A., 100, 103
Strickland, B. R., 298
Strickland, L. H., 303
Stringfield, D. O., 162, 164, 168
Stroebe, M. S., 512
Stroebe, W., 512
Sugawara, K., 321
Sullivan, H. S., 136, 139, 522, 523
Suls, J., 363
Sutton-Smith, B., 139
Swann, W. B., 355, 369
Swann, W. B., Jr., 319
Sweeney, C., 268
Sweeney, P. D., 296
Swensen, C. H., 523

Taba, H., 383, 389
Tanke, E. D., 161, 319
Tavris, C., 471
Taylor, J. A., 181
Taylor, S. E., 289, 368, 473
Taylor, S. P., 476, 461
Teasdale, J. D., 187, 290
Tellegen, A., 56, 70, 412
Terman, L. M., 271
Theophrastus, 180
Theorell, T., 488
Thibaut, J. W., 518
Thompson, S. C., 292
Tice, D. M., 354, 355, 360, 362, 373

Toch, H., 458, 459, 462, 467, 478
Tolman, E. C., 184
Tolone, W. L., 442
Tomarken, A. J., 99, 100, 103
Tomkins, S. S., 410
Tranel, D., 214
Trost, M. R., 169, 170
Tucker, D. M., 99, 100
Turkat, D., 358
Turner, R. G., 36, 321, 331
Tursky, B., 95
Tushup, R., 440
Twain, M., 288

Udry, J. R., 437
Unger, R. K., 263–86

Vaillant, G. E., 199
Van Treuren, R. R., 503
Varma, A. O., 76
Veroff, J., 193, 196 , 414
Vershure, B., 170
Virnelli, S., 503
Vleeming, R. G., 321
Volk, K. D., 442
Vreeland, R. S., 157

Wachtel, P., 167
Wagenhals, W. L., 168
Wainer, H. A., 193–94
Walbek, N., 163
Walder, L. O., 460, 465, 468
Walker, G. R., 340, 341
Wall, S., 122, 144
Wallston, B. S., 298, 299
Wallston, K. A., 298, 299
Walsh, R. H., 442
Walster, E., 515, 518
Wan, C. K., 363
Wapner, S., 315
Ware, E. E., 296
Waterman, A. S., 372
Waters, E., 122, 124, 144, 198, 525
Waters, P. L., 113–45
Watson, D., 412
Watson, J. B., 61, 115–16, 129–31
Weiler, S., 436
Weiman, A. L., 99
Weinberg, M., 436, 443
Weinberg, R. A., 79
Weinberger, D. A., 90
Weiner, H., 484
Weingartner, H., 99

Weinraub, M., 104
Weintraub, J. K., 497
Weiss, J. G., 390
Werts, C. E., 151
Wessman, A. E., 415–17, 428
West, D. J., 390
Whalen, R., 491
White, L., 268
White, L. A., 446, 447
White, R. W., 195, 244, 289, 299
Wicker, A. W., 342
Wicklund, R. A., 321, 324–28, 331, 336, 338, 339, 341
Wideman, M. V., 299
Wiebe, D. J., 501, 502, 503
Wilcox, K. J., 56, 70
Willerman, L., 36
Willers, K. R., 473
Williams, R. B., 485, 491
Wilson, E. O., 178
Wilson, J. F., 493
Wilson, M., 516
Wilson, R. S., 76
Wilson, T. D., 214
Winch, R. F., 517
Winfrey, G., 518
Winstead, B. A., 1–12, 263–86, 450
Winter, D. G., 188, 192, 195, 196
Winton, M., 390, 399
Winton, W., 365
Wippman, J., 124
Witherspoon, D., 214
Witkin, H. A., 315
Wittenberg, M. T., 530
Wong, P. T. P., 450
Wood, W., 281
Wortman, C. B., 442
Wurtele, S. K., 258
Wyler, A. R., 498
Wylie, R. C., 355

Young, R. D., 332
Youniss, J., 140
Yutzey, D. A., 99

Zajonc, R. B., 139, 182, 211, 221
Zanna, M. P., 280
Zimbardo, P., 386
Zonderman, A. B., 491
Zoob, I., 440, 450
Zuckerman, M., 97, 440, 450

SUBJECT INDEX

Academic achievement, and locus
    of control, 295–96
Achievement motivation
    individual differences in,
        191–94
    and personal efficacy, 246–47
Active genotype-environment
        correlations, 466
Adolescent delinquency, 80
Adolescents
    and identity crisis, 374–75
    moral conduct of, 391–404
Adoption study method of
        intellectual abilities and
        heredity, 58–59
Affect intensity, 421–22
    assessment and variability,
        422–27
    positive versus negative,
        429–30
    research on persons with
        high/low, 427–29
Affect Intensity Measure (AIM),
        424–25
Affective reactivity, individual
        differences in, 100–108
Agape love style, 451–52
Aggregation, principle of, 40
Aggression, 459–60
    and anger, 468–71
    as catharsis, 471–72
        behavioral, 473–74
        emotional, 472–73

definition of, 460–63
development of antisocial
        behavior, 467–68
habits in, 474–76
heritability in
        behavioral genetics, 465–66
        temperament, 466–67
hostile, 461
impulsive, 461
instrumental, 461
longitudinal stability of,
        462–65
and personality, 459–60
rational, 461, 476–77
AIM (Affect Intensity Measure),
        424–25
AIST (Attitude Interest Analysis
        Test), 271–72
American Psychiatric Association,
        79
Anal stage, of personality
        development, 118–19
Androgynous person, 272–75,
        276–77
Anger
    and aggression, 468–71
    and motivation, 195
Anonymity of society, and
        conduct visibility,
        399–401
Anterior activation asymmetry,
        individual differences in,
        100–108

Antisocial behavior, development
        of, 467–68
Approval motivation, 476–77
Aspiration level, and personal
        efficacy, 244–45
Attachment theory
    and personality development,
        524
    research on, 121–25
        and intimacy, 127–28,
            197–98
        internal working models, 125
        continuity of, 125–26
        measuring adult patterns,
            126–27
Attitude Interest Analysis Test
        (AIST), 271–72
Attitude similarity, and
        relationships, 516–17
Attribution(s)
    definition of, 185
    of intent, 477
    and motivation, 185, 187
Authoritarianism
    in children, 61
    family correlations for, 72–74
    genetic influence on, 70
    in parenting, 134–35

Baltimore Longitudinal Study of
        Aging, 45, 47
Behavior, private versus public
        standards of, 339–41

547

Behavioral catharsis, 472, 473–74
Behavioral genetics. *See also*
    Heredity
  and aggression, 465–66
  history of, 57–60
  modern
    abnormal traits, 79–80
    apportioning trait variation,
      62–65
    findings and implications,
      68–80
    foundations of, 60–68
    genetic and environmental
      effects, 66–68
    intellectual traits, 75–79
    nonintellectual personality
      traits, 68–71, 74
    shared and nonshared
      environment, 65–66
    shared versus nonshared
      heredity, 65
    single versus polygenic traits,
      61–62
Behaviorism
  operant, 179
  and social learning theory,
    129–31
Bem Sex Role Inventory (BSRI),
    273, 275, 276, 277–78
Bias
  judgmental, 155
  halo, 37–38
  leniency, 37–38
Biofeedback, 243
Biosocial/sociocultural tradition
  individual psychology, 136–39
  peer influences, 139–40
  sociocultural approach, 140–43
Brain
  anterior asymmetry and
    affective reactivity,
    100–108
  measures of electrical activity,
    96–97
BSRI (Bem Sex Role Inventory),
    273, 275, 276, 277–78
Bully, 458–59

Cardiovascular activity, measures
    of, 95–96
Catharsis
  and aggression, 471–72

behavioral, 472, 473–74
  emotional, 472–73
Catharters, and aggression, 459
Central traits, 221–22
Cerebral asymmetry, and affective
    style, 98–109
Child-rearing
  and creativity, 135–36
  and instrumental competence,
    134–35
Chumship, 139–40
Clarification of knowledge, and
    private self focus, 328, 329
Classical conditioning, 129–30
Clinical psychology, 3
Coercion model of antisocial
    behavior, 467–68
Cognitive neoassociative theory,
    474–75
Cognitive social learning theory, 8
College stresses, scale of, 494–95
Common traits, 23
Conceptualization
  definition of, 19
  measurement of, 19–21
Conduct visibility, and anonymity
    of society, 399–401
Conscientiousness, measurement
    of, 20
Consensual validation, 523
Construction, 470
Construct validity, 42–43
Content validity, 42
Continuity, and identity, 370
Control, 288–89
  differences in motivation for,
    299–302
    affective responses, 307–8
    cognitive responses, 303–4
    motivational responses,
      304–6
  perceived
    individual differences in,
      293–94
    negative aspects of, 291–93
    positive aspects of, 290–91
Control-theory model, 336–41
Convergent validity, 47
Coronary heart disease, and
    hostility, 489–92
Correlate, of personality, 91–92
Correlation coefficient, 42–43

Creativity, positive regard and,
    135–36
Criminality, theory of, 397
Criterion validity, 41
Cross-sex-typed person, 273, 277
Cumulative continuity, and
    personality development,
    141–42
Cybernetic model, 336–41

Defense mechanisms, 121, 316
Defensive identification, 522
Deoxyribose nucleic acid (DNA),
    61
Dependent variables, 90
Deprivation dwarfism, 513
Desirability of Control (DC)
    Scale, 300–8
Developmental psychology, 3
Differentiation, and identity, 370
Discriminant validity, 47
Disinhibition, 475
Displacement, 121
Dizygotic twins, 67
  IQ scores of, 75–78
DNA (deoxyribose nucleic acid),
    61
Drive theory of motivation,
    181–82

Effectance motivation, and
    personal efficacy, 244
Electrophysiologial studies,
    99–100
Electrodermal measurement, 95
Emotional arousal, and
    self-efficacy, 236–37
Emotional catharsis, 472–73
Emotional life
  content of, 410–12
    contemporaneous measures
      of, 415–16
    and happiness, 416–21
    positive and negative,
      412–13
    questionnaire measures of,
      413–15
    versus style, 409–10
  dimensions of, 410–12
  states versus traits, 408–9
  style of
    versus content, 409–10

intensity, 421–24
research on intense/
  nonintense people,
  427–29
Encoding algorithms, 213
Encoding biases, self-perpetuation
  of, 222–26
Enhancement phase, of
  relationships, 516–17
Enhancement skills, 529–30
Entrepreneurship, and motivation,
  193–94
Environment, and behavioral
  genetics, 61, 65–66
EPAQ (Extended Personality
  Attributes Questionnaire),
  273–75
Eros love style, 451–52
Eugenics, 60
Event-related potential (ERP),
  96–97
Evocative genotype-environment
  correlations, 466
Exhibitionism, 443
Expectancy-value theory, 256
  and personal efficacy, 245
  of motivation, 184–85
Exploiters, and aggression, 459
Exposure effects, and the
  unconscious, 221
Extended Personality Attributes
  Questionnaire (EPAQ),
  273–75
External person, and locus of
  control, 294
Extraversion, 438
  and sexuality, 439–40

Factor analysis, 45
False consensus, 363–64
False uniqueness, 363–64
Family study method of
  intellectual abilities and
  heredity, 58
Fear, and attachment, 198
Femininity
  psychological dimensions of
    and androgyny, 272–75
  gender schema theory,
    275–78
Freudian slip, 213
Friendship episodes, 199

Frustration-aggression hypothesis,
  468
Fundamental attribution error,
  185

Gender
  distinction between sex and,
    265–66
  and sexuality, 441–42
Gender-inappropriate behavior,
  277
  avoidance of, 278–79
Gender schema theory, 275–78
Gender schematic person, 276–77
General Adaptation Syndrome
  (GAS), 485–86
Generalized expectancies, 294
Genital stage, of personality
  development, 120
Genotype, 62
Genotype-environment
  correlations, 466
Groupthink, 196

Halo bias, 37, 38
Happiness, and emotional
  content, 416–21
Hardiness
  stress, illness and, 497–50
  and Type A Behaviour Pattern
    (TABP), 502–3
Health behavior, and self-efficacy
  theory, 255–58
Health Locus of Control Scales,
  299
Health problems, and power
  motivation, 197
Health psychology, 255
Hemisphericity, measuring, 108–9
Heredity. See also Behavioral
  genetics
  disguised in environmental
    concepts, 80–82
  influence on intellectual
    abilities, 58
  shared vs. nonshared, 65
Homosexuality, 442–43
Hostile aggression, 461
Hostility, and type A behavior
  pattern, 489–92
Humanistic psychology, 6,
  131–33
  child-rearing styles and

instrumental competence,
  134–35
fully functioning person, 133
positive regard and creativity,
  135–36

Ideal self, 325
Identity, 351–52
  and self-concept, 350–51
  structure and function of,
    370–71
Identity crises
  foreclosure status, 372
  identity achieved, 371
  identity conflict, 373, 375–76
  identity deficit, 373–75
  identity diffusion, 373–76
  moratorium status, 371–72
Illness
  definitions of, 485–89
  and stress, 482–83
    approach and avoidance,
      492–95
    and hardiness, 497–50
    history of, 483–85
    optimism and pessimism,
      495–97
    type A behavior pattern and
      hostility, 489–92
Illusion of control, 303
Impression management, 35, 318
Impulsive aggression, 461
Independent variables, 91
Individual differences, and
  motivation, 180
Individual psychology, 136–38
  contemporary research on,
    138–39
Infant
  and attachment research,
    121–28
  response of, to maternal
    separation, 105–6
Inferiority complex, causes of,
  137
Information processing
  nonconscious, 214–15
  properties of algorithms,
    218–19
  in social situations, 215–18
Information processing model,
  and the unconscious, 213

Ingratiation, 318
Inhibited sexual desire, 445
Initiation phase, of relationships, 514–16
Initiation skills, 529
Instrumental aggression, 461
Instrumental competence, and child-rearing, 134–35
Instrumental conditioning, 129, 130
Intellectual abilities, hereditary influence on, 58
Intensification of affect, and private self focus, 328–29
Intensity of emotion 421–27 research on, 427–29
Interest-excitement, and motivation, 191–92, 195
Internal consistency, 41
Internal person, and locus of control, 294
Internal working model, and attachment theory, 125 continuity of, 125–26
Interobserver agreement, 41
Interpersonal continuity, and personality development, 142
Intimacy, and attachment, 127–28
Intimacy motive, individual differences in, 188–91, 197–200
Introversion, 438 and sexuality, 439–40
IQ scores, inheritance of, 75–79

Jenkins Activity Survey (JAS), 490, 502
Joy, and attachment, 198
Judgment, and personality traits errors of, 154–57 lack of agreement between judges, 157–58

Latency stage, of personality development, 120
Leadership measurement of, in OSS Assessment Project, 26–32, 42–43 and power motivation, 195–96

Learned helplessness, 290
Learning theory, 6
Leniency bias, 37–38
Life Orientation Test, 496–97
Locus of control individual differences in, 293–94 academic achievement, 295–96 between internal and external persons, 294–95 coping with stress, 296–97 issues in research specificity, 297, 298–99 unidimensionality, 297–98 and personal efficacy, 245–46
Locus of Control Scale, 297, 299
Loneliness psychology of, 525–30 in various situations, 526–27
Looking-glass self, 317
Love, integrating with sex, 451–52
Love Attitudes Scale, 445–46
Ludus love style, 451–52

Maintenance phase, of relationships, 517–18
Mania love style, 451–52
Manifest Anxiety Scale (MAS), 181
Marital satisfaction, and power motivation, 196
Masculinity psychological dimensions of and androgyny, 272–75 early research, 271–72 gender schema theory, 275–78
MAS (Manifest Anxiety Scale), 181
Maternal separation, infants response to, 105–6
Matrix scanning procedure, and self-perpetuation mechanism, 224–26
Mediation, 243, 468
Meta-analysis, and sex differences in behavior, 267
Method variance, 43
Mind, tripartite structure of, 117
Monozygotic twins

IQ scores of, 75–78 personality traits of, 67, 69, 71, 74–80
Moral character, 382–83 and consistency of conduct, 391–93 deviance and attitudes to authority, 394–96 explanations of, 401–4 history of psychology of, 384–86 measuring experimental tests, 386–88 official records, 388–89 reputational measures, 389–90 self-reports, 390–91 theories of individual differences in, 393–97 deficient moral insight, 397–99 neurotic extraverts, 397
Moral development, theory of, 397–99
Motivation biology versus cognition in, 180 drive, reward, instinct, 181–84 effectance, and personal efficacy, 244 expectancy-value theory of, 184–85 individual differences in achievement motive, 191–94 in intimacy motive, 197–200 in power motive, 194–97 in social motives 187–91 objective self-awareness (OSA) theory, 324–28 opponent-process theory of, 183 traditions in study of, 176 diversity, 180 expectancies, schemas, attributions, 184–87 neutrality, 179–80 optimism, 177–78 pessimism, 178–79

Nature-nurture debate, 57–60
Neoassociative theory, 468–71

NEO Personality Inventory, 47
Nonconscious information
    processing, 214–15
    properties of algorithms,
        218–19
    in social situations, 215–18
Nonconscious perception,
    209–10
Norm enforcers, and aggression,
    459
Norms, 520

Objective self awareness (OSA)
    theory, 324–28
Observational learning, 129,
    130–31
Oedipus complex, 120
Office of Strategic Services (OSS)
    Assessment Project. See
    OSS Assessment Project
Operant behaviorism, 179
Operant conditioning, 129, 130
Operational definition, 26
Opponent-process theory of
    motivation, 183
Optimism, and illness, 495–97
Oral stage, of personality
    development, 118
Organ inferiority, 137
OSA (objective self awareness)
    theory, 324–28
OSS Assessment Project, 22–24,
    42–43
    procedures, 25–32
    putting pieces together, 32–33
Outcome expectancy, 233–35,
    249–54, 255, 256, 257–58
Outcome value, 235, 249,
    251–54, 256, 258
Overattribution, 155

PAQ (Personal Attributes
    Questionnaire), 273, 275
Passive genotype-environment
    correlations, 466
Peeping Tomism, 443
Perceived control
    individual differences in,
        293–94
    academic achievement,
        295–96
    between internal and

external persons, 294–95
    coping with stress, 296–97
    negative aspects of, 291–93
    positive aspects of, 290–91
Perceptual feedback, 332–35
Perceptual-motor theory, and
    aggression, 473
Performance experiences, and
    self-efficacy, 235–36
Permissiveness and
    Instrumentality, 451–52
Permissive parents, 134–35
Personal Attributes Questionnaire
    (PAQ), 273, 275
Personal efficacy. See also
    Self-efficacy, 243–44
    and achievement
        motivation/need, 246–47
    and effectance motivation, 244
    and expectancy-value theory,
        245
    and level of aspiration, 244–45
    and locus of control, 245–46
    and psychological adjustment,
        237, 240–43
    self-concept and self-esteem,
        246
Personality
    and aggression, 459–60
    biological approaches to study
        of biological measures,
            89–91
        cerebral asymmetry and
            affective style, 98–109
        correlate or substrate, 91–92
        physiological measures in,
            94–98
        psychometric considerations,
            93
        resting or task-related
            measures, 93–94
        substrates and cause, 92–93
    characteristics of, 3–4
    concept of, 21–22
    definitions of, 2–4
    and development of
        relationships psychology of
        loneliness, 525–30
    in 1990s, 9–10
    and stress and illness
        approach and avoidance,
            492–95

optimism and pessimism,
            495–97
        type A behavior pattern and
            hostility, 489–92
    theories of, 4–9
    and the unconscious, 208–12
        information processing
            model, 213
        psychoanalytic tradition,
            212–13
Personality development and
    relationships
    contemporary approaches,
        523–25
    early conceptualizations,
        521–23
    relational competence, 530
    theories of
        attachment research, 121–28
        biosocial/sociocultural
            tradition, 136–43
        humanistic psychology,
            131–33
        overview, 115–16
        psychoanalytic tradition,
            116–21
        social learning and
            behaviorism, 129–31
        transactional, 143
Personality measurement
    concept of personality, 21–22
    measuring a concept, 19–21
    measuring variables, 17–19
    methods for, 24–25
        classifying, 34–39
    OSS Assessment Project,
        16–17, 22–24
        procedures, 25–32
        putting pieces together,
            32–33
    reliability of, 39–41
    validity of, 41
        construct, 42–43
        content, 42
        criterion, 41
    variables in
        choice of, 43–48
        reason for measurement,
            48–50
Personality psychology, 3
    and the unconscious, 219–20
        exposure effects, 221

self-image bias, 221–22
Personality traits
abnormal, 79–80
apportioning variation, 62–65
critical hypotheses on existence
of, 150–53
baserate accuracy, 152,
158–60
differential settings, 152,
163–64
evidence against, 166–67
eye of beholder, 151–52,
154–58
observers in cahoots, 152,
161–63
stereotypes, 152, 160–61
weak behavioral
consistencies, 152, 164–65
environmental influences,
65–66
size of, 66–68
genetic influences, 65
size of, 66–68
intellectual, 75–79
nonintellectual, 68–71, 74
relationship between
psychosexual stages and,
119
single versus polygenic, 61–62
study of
combining personality and
social psychology, 168–69
gene-environment
interactions, 169–70
person-situation interactions,
167–68
Personality variables
choice of, 43–48
reason for measurement, 48–50
taxonomy of, 44–48
Person-situation debate on
existence of personality
traits, 150–71
Pessimism, and illness, 495–97
Phallic stage, of personality
development, 117, 119–20
Phenotype, 62
Polygenic traits, 61
Ponzo illusion, 155, 156
Positive self-regard, 132–33
Power motive, individual
differences in, 188–91,
194–97

Pragma love style, 451–52
Prejudice, and self-esteem,
362–63
Pressure removers, and
aggression, 459
Private standards of behavior,
versus public standards,
339–41
Probands, 79
Projection, 121
Protection motivation theory, 256
Psychoanalytic tradition, 5, 116
defense mechanisms, 121
psychosexual stages, 117–18
anal stage, 118–19
genital stage, 120
latency stage, 120
oral stage, 118
phallic stage, 117, 119–20
tripartite structure of the mind,
117
and the unconscious, 212–13
Psychological adjustment, and
personal efficacy, 237,
240–43
Psychological freedom, 135
Psychological safety, 135
Psychology
clinical, 2
developmental, 3
personality, 3
sensory-perceptual, 3
social, 3
Psychosexual stages
of personality development,
117–18
anal stage, 118–19
genital stage, 120
latency stage, 120
oral stage, 117, 118
phallic stage, 117, 119–20
relationship between, and
personality traits, 119
Psychosocial moratorium, 372

Qualitative/quantitative measures,
of relationships, 513

Radical behaviorists, 6–7
Rater bias, forms of, 37–38
Rational aggression, 461
Reaction formation, 121

Real self, 325
Reciprocal influence, 521
Reiss Male and Female
Premarital Sexual
Permissiveness Scale, 447
Relational competence, 530
Relationships
definition of, 510–11
development and processes
enhancement, 516–17
initiation, 514–16
maintenance, 517–18
termination, 518–19
dynamics of, 519
personality and development of
psychology of loneliness,
525–30
relational competence, 530
and personality development
contemporary approaches,
523–25
early conceptualizations,
521–23
proximal versus distal, 520–21
studying
importance of, 511–13
methodological issues in,
513–14
subjectivity and imbalance in,
519–20
Relaxation training, 243
Reliability
of personality measurement,
39–41
types of, 41
Rep-defenders, and aggression,
459
Repression, 121
Reputation, and self-concept,
394–96
Revised Mosher Guilt Inventory,
446, 447

Sadness, and attachment, 198
Sadomasochism, 443–44
Schemata, 473
Schizophrenia, inheritance of, 80
Selective placement, 68
Self-awareness
private, 315, 316–17, 320
public, 315, 317, 320
and self-consciousness, 314–16

and self-consciousness theories
  control-theory model,
    336–41
  objective self-awareness,
    324–28
  self awareness versus
    self-consciousness, 319–20
  Self-Consciousness Scale (SCS),
    320–21
  self-consciousness theory,
    328–36
  University of Texas research,
    321
Self-concept, 351, 523
  formation of, 352–54
  and identity, 350–51
  maintaining, and self-esteem,
    368–69
  and personal efficacy, 246
  possible selves, 366–68
  and reputation, 394–96
  and self-esteem, 354–56
    measuring, 356–57
    research on, 357–64
  self-schemas, 366
  spontaneous, 364–66
Self-consciousness
  private, 320
  public, 320
  and self-awareness, 314–16
  Self-Consciousness Scale (SCS),
    320–21 322–23, 330, 333
Self-consciousness theories
  Buss's theory, 328–36
  control-theory model, 336–41
  objective self-awareness,
    324–28
  self awareness versus
    self-consciousness, 319–20
  Self-Consciousness Scale (SCS),
    320–21
  University of Texas research,
    321
Self-consciousness theory
  private self-aspects, 328–32
  public self-aspects, 332–36
Self-deception, 35, 316, 317
Self-defenders, and aggression,
    459
Self-disclosure, and relationships,
    516
Self-efficacy. See also Personal
    efficacy

expectancy, 129, 131, 233–35,
    249–54, 255, 256, 257
  perceived, 131
Self-efficacy theory
  cognitive processes, 233–35
  increasing self-efficacy, 238–41
  research on, 247–49
    models of health behavior,
      255–58
    relationship between
      components, 249–54
    and social anxiety, 254–55
  sources of self-efficacy, 235–37
Self-esteem, 351, 354–56
  maintaining self-concept and,
    368–69
  measuring, 356–57
  and personal efficacy, 246
  research on, 357–58
    false consensus, false
      uniqueness, 363–64
    measuring, 357–58
    performance and persistence,
      358–62
    prejudice, 362–63
    situationality and influence,
      362
  and sexuality, 438–39
Self-handicapping behavior, 292
Self-image bias, and the
    unconscious, 221–22
Self-image defenders, and
    aggression 459
Self-image promoter, and
    aggression, 458
Self-indulgers, and aggression,
    459
Self-monitoring, 319
Self-presentational model, 254,
    318
Self-report questionnaire, 35
Sensory-perceptual psychology, 3
Seriousness of Illness Rating
    Scale, 498
Sex
  antecedents of differences,
    269–70
  distinction between, and
    gender, 265–66
  as social category, 279–82
  as subject variable, 266–69
    limitations to use, 270
Sex researchers, 435–36

Sex-typed person, 273, 276–77
Sexual Attitudes Scale, 446–47,
    448–49, 451
Sexuality, 434–35
  attitudes toward
    gender differences, 451
    integrating sex with love,
      451–52
    measurement of, 445–47
    personality variables, 450–51
    sociocultural variables, 447,
      450
  dysfunction, 444–45
  and gender, 441–42
  and personality variables
    introversion-extraversion,
      439–40
    self-esteem, 438–39
    self-monitoring, 440–41
    sensation seeking, 440
  preference, 442–43
  researchers on, 435–36
  research on personality and
    interpersonal influences,
      437
  sociocultural influences,
    436–37
  variants, 443–44
Sexual Opinion Survey, 446, 447
Sexual Practices and Communion,
    451–52
Skin conductance level (SCL), 95
Skin conductance response (SCR),
    95
Social anxiety, 320–21, 476
  and self-efficacy theory,
    254–55
Social facilitation, and motivation,
    182
Social learning theory, 474–75
  and aggression, 472
  and behaviorism, 129–31
Social psychology, 3
Social Readjustment Rating Scale
    (SRRS), 487, 498
Sociocultural theory, 140–41
  contemporary research on,
    141–43
Specificity, and locus of control,
    297, 298–99
Spontaneous skin conductance
    responses (SSCR), 95
SRRS (Social Readjustment

Rating Scale), 487

State experience report, comparison with trait tendency report, 35–36

Stimulus-value-role theory, 519

Storge love style, 451–52

Stress
coping with, 296–97
definitions of, 485–89
and illness, 482–83
approach and avoidance, 492–95
and hardiness, 497–50
history of, 483–85
optimism and pessimism, 495–97
type A behavior pattern and hostility, 489–92

Structural equation modeling, 66

Structured Interview (SI), 490–91

Subliminal stimuli, 221

Substrate, of personality, 91–92, 96

Symbolic interactionism, theory of, 317–18

Tabula rasa, 179

TAT (Thematic Apperception Test), 187–200

Taxonomy, of personality variables, 44–48

Tay-Sachs syndrome, 62

Temperament, and aggression, 466–67

Termination phase, of relationships, 518–19

Test-Operate-Test-Exit (TOTE), 336–39

Test-retest reliability, 41

Thematic Apperception Test (TAT), 187–200

TOTE (Test-Operate-Test-Exit), 336–39

Trait tendency report, comparison with state experience report, 35–36

Trait theories of personality, 8–9

Triangulation principle, of measurement, 24

Twin study method of heredity and intellectual abilities, 59–60

Type A behavior pattern
and hardiness, 502–3
and hostility, 489–92

Unconsciousness
and personality, 208–12
information processing model, 213
nonconscious information processing, 214–19
psychoanalytic tradition, 212–13

and personality psychology, 219–20
exposure effects, 221
self-image bias, 221–22
and self-perpetuation of encoding biases, 222–24
mechanism of, 224–26

Undifferentiated person, and sex, 273

Unidimensionality, and locus of control, 297–98

University of Texas, research at, 321

Validity
convergent, 47
discriminant, 47
of personality measurement, 41

Value, 18–19

Variables
definition of, 17
dependent, 90
independent, 91

Verbal persuasion, and self-efficacy, 236

Vicarious experiences, and self-efficacy, 236

Vicarious reinforcement, 131

Violent men, categories of, 458–59